Past-it Notes

Scrambled Oeuvres by Maureen Lipman

How Was It For You?

Something To Fall Back On

You Got an 'Ology

Thank You For Having Me

When's It Coming Out?

You Can Read Me Like A Book

Lip Reading

By Jack Rosenthal: An Autobiography In Six Acts

The Gibbon's In Decline, But The Horse Is Stable

Past-it Notes

Maureen Lipman

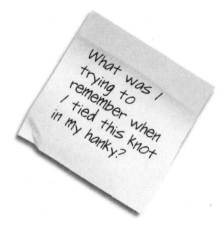

JR
BOOKS

First published in Great Britain in 2008 by
JR Books, 10 Greenland Street, London NW1 0ND
www.jrbooks.com

A catalogue record for this book is available from the British Library.

ISBN 978-1-906217-75-4

3 5 7 9 10 8 6 4

Typeset by SX Composing DTP, Rayleigh, Essex
Printed by MPG Books, Bodmin, Cornwall

Many thanks to Robson Books/Anova for permission to reproduce text from *Lip Reading* and *Jack Rosenthal: An Autobiography in Six Acts*.

Contents

Contents

Foreword

It has been nine years since publisher Jeremy Robson and I have brought out a book. Before that I tended to write one every three or four years by combining my regular back page articles from *Good Housekeeping* with a retrospective flip through the intervening work/family/general whinge. A few snaps from the shows, rather too many painful puns, a tortuous title, a sleepless last-minute choice of cover photo and, to the accompaniment of the pop of a few bottles of pop, we'd be on the rocky road to retail. *Lip Reading* was the sixth book of this kind and a quick glance at the cover tells me it was billed in paperback as 'The number one best seller' and who am I to argue with a printed brag?

Blithely, I would then survive the cheerful indifference of Terry Wogan – or the current expletive-strewn model of Sir Tel – and several mud-locked literary festivals later, after signing and smiling fixedly at the 90th person to say 'I bet your wrist gets tired, doesn't it?' I would sign off, go back to the day job, and forget about the whole pantomime until Jeremy rang to say: 'It's number eleven in *The Bookmaker* top ten' or 'There's a lot of competition out there but you're holding your own' or 'Nice weather, isn't it . . . how are the kids?'.

Six years ago, though, something happened which stopped me writing my wry 'everything happens to me' columns. Quite suddenly everything *did* happen to me. And although we laughed through the crisis, sometimes fit to bust, to be honest it wasn't always funny. Between 2004 and 2007 I lost my mother, Zelma, my muse, in a morning, and nursed my husband, my rock of ages, from sickness through remission to the end.

Then came numbness. To relieve it, I finished a book of comic verse called *The Gibbon's in Decline but the Horse is Stable* to raise money for Myeloma UK, completed Jack's autobiography, *By Jack Rosenthal*, and was hypnotised by Paul McKenna not to cry in public whilst talking about them. It worked a treat until on Breakfast TV Fern Britton threw me a googly in the form of 'Do you still hear Jack's voice around the house?', and my subconscious crumpled and took me with it.

In the next three years, I returned to work in children's TV, ventured into pantomime at the Old Vic, did six months in a West End play, took my first holiday alone to a Greek island, wrote a weekly column for the *Guardian* newspaper, saw my son Adam marry his childhood sweetheart

ix

in Mayfair, moved, after thirty years, from a house on a hill in north London to a lower ground flat in the Paddington Basin, and fell in and out of a troubling and somewhat public love affair. Who had time to write? Who knew where there was any paper which wasn't damp?

I'd always been able to make mountains out of molehills. Now the Himalayas had sprung up outside my picket fence and I didn't have the right boots. I knew grief from the inside. I knew what widow stood for and how it made one feel – it even gave me a fresh perspective on Widow Twanky. I wasn't lonely. Lord knows, I could sometimes use a drop of being alone – this apartment teems with Maureen's little female helpers, including the bitch in my life, Diva the beauteous Basenji. The only male about the house is Warren, the apricot velvet rabbit who inhabits the central courtyard of the flat, and inhibited two and a half grand's worth of plants and greets me each morning from a standing position, leaning one elbow on the French windows like Road Runner, pointedly tapping his watch.

I was a bit confused about the rest of my life. Les the Shaman, who came to see me at the behest of Rosie, my secretary, said I must just be patient . . . oh, and I should invoke the spirit of Frog when I bathe at night. I think that was his pagan way of telling me that a girl has to kiss a lot of frogs before her second prince comes along. Apparently this is the year when I'll normalise. I hope he's right. The work is coming in – a Chekhov play, a sit-com, an exciting documentary – taking a piano to as near as I can get to Burma and Aung San Suu Kyi – if it happens. Soon folk will maybe stop saying 'Are you still doing it?' as I walk track-suited and pinched-faced round the park with pockets full of pooh bags and corned beef, occasionally – which is not a good thing – getting the two confused.

This saturated ('still, it's good for the gardens') summer Adam and I travelled to Preston, Lancashire, to give the first Jack Rosenthal Award for screenwriting to a young graduate. These ceremonies always move me by the sheer overwhelming presence of so many hope-filled lads and lasses. I love the way you can tell a student's character from the way they traverse the six yards between mounting the stage and shaking the hand of the Chancellor. The cries of 'Yeah, go Louise/Tom!' for the popular ones and the filled silences for the ones who follow the popular ones. The trademark rebellion shoes and the graceless trudge they enforce. The open-faced, uncool choir and the hot fanfare of trumpets. Frankly, I'm in need of a hypnosis top-up before I step up onto the dais. On this occasion the eulogy about Jack's work was eloquent and I could feel the lump rising in my throat and the tell-tale signs of wobble attending my lips. I spoke sternly to myself in a low, internal growl – 'Stop it! *Stoppit!*' – but my self wasn't listening and as I heard my name announced, my eyes were a blur and I hadn't got a thought in my head other than 'Please don't let me blub in front of several hundred graduates and their Mums and Dads and Aunties.'

I stood blinking and breathing for just long enough to be a worry, then, taking the lectern stand I said in tremulous but trumpet-like tones: 'We all of us, in this room, have one thing in common.' I paused again. 'We none of us have the slightest idea what I'm going to say next.'

There was a delayed laugh which I used to steady myself, then I proceeded loudly and dramatically (mostly in order to harness the emotions coursing through me) to give the most rousing address I've ever given – maybe *anyone's* ever given, including Henry IV, both parts. Afterwards, when I took my seat, my face was scarlet – as I might add was the face of the 'signing for the deaf' presenter. My ceremonial robes were sliding off me and the blood was pounding so hard in my veins that I could hear it.

In short, it's not over yet. I'm still the same woman who was shaped by my life alongside Jack Rosenthal, and I'm still being influenced by his memory four years after his death. He peppers my thoughts and my conversation and it is not easy, nor will it ever be, to have a relationship with another man which doesn't somehow include him. I'm trying though, and slowly and softly, with the help of a real gentleman, I might just be getting there.

This book is therefore a compilation of the best of the old Maureen and some of the current working model. There's nothing in it that hasn't actually happened, although people often tell me they laughed like a canned audience when reading one of my books but didn't believe a word of it. When someone asked me if I would give my permission for them to write a biography I hooted and told them there was absolutely nothing that had happened to me which hadn't already been milked to a peaceful death. Of course there is, but that's between me and my diary and I haven't kept one of those since I got *Bunty* on a Thursday and was waiting for my braces to come off and my breasts to come up.

Talking of which, it goes without saying that Jordan, aka Katie Price, *actually* wrote this book and Lynne Truss checked the punctuation. I've left out, after some consideration, the magical realism, the abused childhood – especially the part where I was kept in a tin of Tuxon shoe polish (oxtail hue) for a week – and my great-grandmother's recipe for tempura schmaltz-herring in a lokshen velouté.

I trust most of my readers are old enough to have forgotten they have read some chapters before, in another life, whilst waiting for the podiatrist to remove the hard skin from their fallen arches. I trust, too, that they will find the new material controversial enough to alert their fellow residents to picket individual branches of Waterstone's to remove this book immediately from its position in 'Obscure Jewish Humour' and place it in the front window under a banner saying 'Buy *Past-it Notes* and get all you can eat, FREE, at any Turks and Caicos bistrasserie of your choice!'

I owe this comp-elation to my friend Jeremy Robson of JR Books. It has been a long and lovely journey. PS You were right not to let me have one past-it note which read: 'After fifty, only wear plum lipstick if you actually *want* your lips to resemble an anus.'

My thanks go to *Good Housekeeping* and *The Guardian* for the sneak previews. To my editor Liz Rose for patient optimism in the face of impatient procrastination and Lesley Wilson for being both efficient and cheerful.

Thanks to Rosie Heaphy, my secretary, and Natalie Percy in to whom the words 'Has anybody seen my . . .?' strike mortal terror; and to Adam, Taina and Amy for the unconditional love.

Band Box

I awoke to the sound of the *Today* programme where an elderly brass band player from Derby was telling Sarah Montague that his beloved band, which he had joined in 1947, was about to be . . . disbanded. In desperation he'd appealed for help from the local paper, which ran the story. It was taken up by local television and soon the band, which had been whittled down by time and circumstance to two instrumentalists, received eleven young applicants. Thirteen players to date, then. Lucky for some.

By now, it was two minutes to nine, so Sarah rapidly announced the names of *Today*'s editors and told listeners that the re-formed band would play us out. I expected them to sound like a braking milk float. Instead, the first notes of those bright, yearning horns made tears hurtle from my eyes to the pillow. I phoned my daughter, who is too young to be a Radio 4 listener but does it to keep me company, fully expecting her, too, to be in mid-blub.

Hearing my adenoidal tones she said, worriedly, 'Are you alright, Mod?'

I asked her if she'd been listening to the brass band. She hadn't and, what's more, she wasn't too sure that she believed my rationale of my early morning lachrimosity.

'Are you really alright?' she enquired. 'Honestly?'

'Yes, I'm fine, it was just that sound,' I warbled snottily.

'No, but are you OK though, *really*?' she persisted. 'You're not depressed are you? Because I had this really *awful* dream about you.'

'Oh, darling, I'm so sorry. What was it?'

'Well, I dreamt you were really unhappy. I mean really *really* unhappy.'

'Oh, darling. Well, I'm not, it was just the brass b . . .'

'No, but you *were* in the dream,' she insisted. 'I mean, you were *soooo* unhappy – and I was so unbelievably worried that I turned turquoise.'

There are many stories in *The Naked City*. This has been one of them. And if you're old enough to remember that reference then you're probably wearing half-glasses to read this and take half an aspirin a day to keep everything thinned out. I am being enigmatic in order to raise several queries:

    a)   Is it a fact that all first-born children are worriers and is it because we don't have a clue how to cope with them when we bring them home from the hospital? So that what they read on our faces is

1

worry, which makes them feel there is something *worrying* about them?

b) Isn't it true that journalists get a very bad press in spite of the fact that, just occasionally, they change people's lives for the better?

c) Isn't it true that music has power to move us in a way that cuts through reason and by-passes joined-up thought?

I'll deal with the answers to my questions in order, shall I?

a) Am I concerned about the state of mind of my anxious first-born? Not really. She's pure gold to me and in fairness, with a following wind and the right accessories, turquoise can be a stunning summer colour, though not necessarily for the skin.

b) Journalists, with the highest insurance risk – just below actors – are probably in the bottom league of global popularity stakes, but though I loathe their muck-raking as much as other members of my profession and the good citizens of Tunbridge Wells, I've seldom met one face to face whose company around a clinking table I haven't thoroughly enjoyed.

Which brings me to c):

When I set out for the Barbican and a jazz concert I knew little about except it was in celebration of the 80th birthdays of Cleo Laine and Johnny Dankworth, it was with a heavy heart and a heavier cold. I was expecting traffic, confusion and a late-comer's seat behind a pillar. Instead, the journey was a doddle, the parking and venue-finding likewise, and the concert – well, as I suggested, sometimes music is the only language where you can truly trust the words. The audience became one joyous body and I was the snapping finger on its right hand. Johnny might have looked his years when he came on stage but when he lifted his baton to conduct the London Symphony Orchestra and the jazz combo which included his son Alex on double bass, he became a lithe and springy adolescent.

I like to look at musicians. They seem to fill their skins. Their concentration and their lack of self-consciousness dazzle me, and of course I never get that 'I could have done it better' feeling. As for the Dame herself, splendid in a vibrant gown of – yes – turquoise, she moved me to a quiver with a song, new to me, called 'He was the one', and she and her velour vocals seem to improve like fine Muscat.

With Ken Wheeler skulking on with magic trumpet held in defence of his shyness, two feisty women on trombones, dynamic and dangerous horn players, and the LSO proving that with that kind of keenness 'crossing over' really can work, it brought me back to where I started. Top Brass.

Flat Spin

I suddenly live in Paddington. You might call it Bayswater or even Kensington Gardens if you really wanted to push your luck. After twenty-nine years of North London-living in Muswell Hill and a couple of childless years before that in leafy and liberal Hampstead, when the R word – as in responsibility – was not in our lexicon, I have crossed the house. I've become a West London resident. It feels like a divorce. But an amicable one.

Jack and I talked of moving into town for years and often scoured the Sunday papers for flats in Belsize Park and Maida Vale. Still North – after all, once a professional Northerner, always a professional Northerner – and once or twice we even checked one of them out before scurrying back contentedly to our roomy Edwardian house with its own roomy Edwardian garden. After his death it seemed important to stay where I was, to maintain some sort of security. Sometimes, as I turned into the drive after a spell away or even a night out I would fancy that he'd be there to open the door to shed light on me as I parked the car. One time I came back from a short trip and there were two welcoming sentinels on either side of the steps. They were pink hollyhocks, five foot high, which had forced their way through tiny cracks in the concrete. Such strength of purpose, such tenacity, made me smile and, feel oddly safe.

After eight months of dealing with the practicalities of bereavement, I took a job. It was a kids' series, called *The Fugitive*, well written, to be shot at Three Mile Studios in the East End of London, and my part was an old eco-warrior/former scientist, holed up for years in the woods, who befriends the young hero and helps him save the world from untold horror. To be honest, I think I did the whole thing in a daze. I was often tearful and occasionally in the world of the blurred and bewildered, but I got through the six-week shoot with my dignity intact and with a new colleague who would shape the next phase of my life.

Natalie (Nats) Percy was a spiky-haired kid – or so I thought, although she's actually Adam's age – who seemed to be in charge of props. She was short and square with a pretty, gamine face, bright green eyes and jeans cut well below the builder's plumb line. Occasionally she would bring a bag or a torch or a dog to my trailer, always cheerful and with a kind word or a cuppa. One day she, or someone on the set, told me that she was living and sleeping in her van because the commute to her home in Rye was impossible. Later I found out that the home in Rye was upstairs in a pub and that she had been living off her wits since she was twelve. Without forward thinking of any kind, entirely on an instinct, one day I asked her if she wanted to take Amy's old room up in the attic for the duration of the film. She thought about it for a day and said, 'Yeah, that would be great.'

It was a daring proposition, but almost three years later she is still with me and both she and her business cards convey that she is The Angel in the Attic. She became an invaluable assistant. I gave her a home and a family – her parents had six marriages between them and none of them seemed to include her – and she gave me a pair of capable hands, care, foresight and practical assistance. She had her own drill, for heaven's sake! She could mend a computer, paint a wall, cook a Guinness and beef pie, get under a car with a bag of chisels and some Swarfega and make it go vroom-vroom.

She also found the flat I'm now living in, after months of trawling through property sites on the Internet.

'It's in Paddington,' she told me guardedly one evening as I came home from a long day of being a mouse in a voice-over studio. 'I know – I *know*, but you ought to see it . . . It's *well*-nice.'

'*Well*-nice?' I repeated. 'Paddington?' I repeated. 'Jack would turn in his grave. No way.'

'Alright, but it's massive and it's been all done up inside and it's in your price range . . . I've got it up on the screen, just have a look.'

'Pointless', I said. 'Thanks anyway, but I used to stay in Paddington years ago and it was an absolute dump . . . Where exactly is it?' She told me. 'That's where Annabel had her flat – top of an old building – good views – dodgy area . . . no, no, no . . . Is it a top floor?'

'Er, no, it's a lower ground.'

'That clinches it! Never!' I hooted. 'Dark and damp and dangerous when you go home late and it's raining and the steps are' – she slid some photos hot off the copier onto the table – 'always slippery. Besides,' I added, 'didn't that psychic in Birmingham tell me I should always live in a high place because my moods will . . .' I looked. 'My moods . . .' I looked again. The pictures showed light, airy, high-ceilinged room after room, arched dining area/kitchen, two walled courtyards, six French windows, guest suite, granny flat, fireplace, steam shower, entry-phone, wooden floors, marble floors, fancy kitchen – even an *ice dispenser*, for heaven's sake.

'Phone up,' I breathed. 'Get me a viewing.'

Forty-three years of living in London and I didn't actually know how to drive to Paddington. With Sat Nav's help I found the flat – took one look at the glass shelves, underlit between hall and living room, and knew they were exactly the spot for Jack's sculptures. I put in my offer that evening. Paddington it was.

I had recently been to a painting evening at the Westbourne Studios so it had to be somewhere near there. The class was in a nightclub setting but one room off was reserved for Fig 108, a club for closet painters where acrylics and canvases were provided and you could paint till all hours of the night if you liked, with a glass of wine and a bowl of French fries by your easel. My paintings were a shocking revelation. I'd hung up my brush in 1965 after getting an E for 'A' level Art. Suddenly I was painting in authoritative fashion, throwing orange paint at the canvas for all the world like someone who knew what she was doing. Sponge and comb in hand I then started raking through the applied paint and to my delight seemed to uncover on the canvas things that were already under the paint. Sea creatures emerged, crocodiles crept out, weird and winding crustaceans crawled up from the depths. It was consuming.

Young people strolled by, taking respite from the raving outside in the club, and double-took.

'What's it meant to be?' they asked.

'F— knows,' I replied, brush and bit between teeth. They hurried on.

Finally the friend who had taken me to Fig 108 came over. 'Do you want to go on?' she asked, looking sideways in startled fashion at the Hieronymus Bosch landscape seeping out of my hand.

'Why? What's the time?'

'Er, two-thirty in the morning.'

It was a meditation and when I looked at it the next day, my hair stood up on end. I couldn't wait to get back and do another. Strangely, it never occurred to me to set up an easel at home. So back I went the following week and this time a labyrinthine jungle appeared in shades of dark green and violet. 'Annihilating all that's made/to a green thought in a green shade . . .' Why did that quote remind me of Jack? Next time, some months later, a lime-coloured landscape suddenly after four hours and ten minutes transmogrified itself into Burma and the Lady herself hovering over it. I was gobsmacked by it all. Clearly this was cheaper than a psychiatrist and did the same job.

Synchronistically, I was approached by a TV company to contribute a painting, along with six other amateurs, to the Summer Exhibition at the Royal Academy. They would pitch up on various dates of my theatre tour and film my fulminations. Armed with Diva, a dog-bed, a script, a suitcase, a painting kit and easel, I set off for Oxford. The weather was fine and the delightful Parsonage Hotel welcomed us, crew, canine and all, with gentle goodwill. Sadly, I couldn't paint when being watched. It came out all wrong – self-conscious and lacking in the spontaneity which had so excited me. But my 'Four Seasons' painting was on celluloid now, and so I kept going at it, murdering it more and more after each show and sleeping fitfully amidst the smell of acrylic paint and dog.

By the time the day arrived when the crew came to film me loading the complete works into a cab and heading for the RA, 'The Four Seasons' was a disaster. Two of the sections, 'Summer' and 'Winter' were OK if you like hell horses with burning eyes and strange, shrouded, golden monk-like figures, but the other two were overlaid with bits of collage and spattered with paint, card and even bunched Kleenex. When I took the four paintings into Eastbourne Terrace to hail a cab, the driver leaned out and scratched his head like Sid James in *Taxi*.

'I want to take these to the Royal Academy,' I said.

He looked from me to the camera crew and back to the paintings and said, 'Are you *sure*?'

The Academy rejected my offerings, but was I down-hearted? No – not at all. I've auctioned the jungle for £250 to fund a new roof at the King's Head – yes, alright, it was bought by my friend Valerie Grove, and no, I don't see it on her wall, but still it's a sale! And I've made three new painting friends through the programme and been told by total strangers that I wuz robbed, so I should be (and am) grateful. And I have a new painting case standing unused in my dazzling vaulted kitchen/diner and, although I no longer take a newspaper or watch TV, I don't have a single moment, do I, to do the one thing which makes me the happiest.

As Christmas approached I was offered a pantomime at the Old Vic. I was in no state for pantomime, which is three shows a day of high octane energy and audience participation, and actors only do it for the sensational wages (except for Christopher Biggins and Lesley Joseph who *love* it and would do it for a year's supply of knicker elastic and a frozen fisherman's pie). Along with commercials, it is one of the few ways that an actor can earn a decent living. Bobby Davro and the big boys can get over £100,000. I was tempted.

This was slightly different, said my agent. This was *classical* pantomime, with a script written by a RSC writer and directed by Sean Mathias, with proper actors in key roles and Sir Ian McKellen playing Widow Twanky, and not nearly so many jokes about Simon Cowell, and fewer performances in Xmas week.

'What's the part?'

'Well, it's Wishee Washee, but –'

'Oh, Twanky's sidekick. Good.'

'But in the adaptation he's called Dim Sum.'

'That's not incredibly funny.'

'It made *me* laugh.'

'Exactly.'

'They'll write it around you if you say yes, and you'll have input into the scenes.' He was winning.

'Right . . . sounds interesting enough. What's the catch?'

'All the cast are on the same whack.'

'And the whack would be?

Silence.

'Is it a Bobby Davro whack?' I knew the answer even as I asked the question.

The sum he mentioned was £500 per week for rehearsals and two thousand for ten or twelve and in Xmas week fourteen performances a week. Bit of a Gwyneth, really – as in 'paltry'.

Every bone in my body screamed 'No!' I was a widow myself of only ten months' standing. Wouldn't it look a bit undignified? Apparently Dim Sum wore tweed plus fours and a moustache. Would I cope? I was a bit frail, trying to finish the autobiography that Jack had started, prone to night frets and sudden unstoppable tears. Widow Hanky.

'Don't read it, don't read it, don't read it,' drummed the mantra in my head.

'Sorry,' I sighed. 'Tell them . . . I . . . I . . . I'll have a look at the script.' I was beaten already.

Now, I'm a girl who likes a spot of improvisation. This time, though, we had three weeks to mount an unfinished script and I was in no mood to stand in a circle every morning with other actors throwing a ball to one another. My nerves were taut and I wanted to run miles away. After rehearsing each scene we then sat around a table with the writer, Billie Brown, and picked the scene apart and put it back together with more jokes. Since my idea of heaven is being in the room on the twenty-third floor where Larry Gelbiert, Woody Allen, the Simon brothers and others wrote *The Sid Caesar Show*, this should have appealed. It didn't. The show was limping and Ian was worrying away at the thin material like a Staffordshire bull terrier with a venison ear.

'But Shawnie,' he would moan, 'I can't understand Twanky's reasoning here.'

Sean, a loving ex-partner of Ian's, would roll his eyes to the ceiling.

'Reasoning? Reasoning? Ian dear, it's *panto*, for Christ's sake! Reason doesn't come into it.'

'Yes, but darling boy, if I was a mother and my son came home pursued by the police, I wouldn't hide him by hanging him on the washing line!'

Sean would trawl his hands through his hair and, becoming increasingly Welsh by the second, would bleat, 'You're a man, Ian! Your breasts are balloons, for God's sake! The fucking policemen are wearing striped socks and running on the spot in unison! *King Lear* it's not!'

'Yes, I know that, Shawnie, but wouldn't it be better if I shopped him for not telling the truth?'

'No, it fucking wouldn't because that would be the end of the show and the kids haven't even shouted "It's behind you!" yet!'

During the technical rehearsal, the princess, several chorus girls and I stand in line to kow-tow to Sam Kelly's dozy Emperor. 'Go in the middle,' calls Sean from the darkened stalls. I do, and feel a sharp pain in my hip at the same moment as everyone else emits shrill cries. A nine-foot plank, not nailed in properly, had fallen on four of us, hitting my hip, Julia's ear, Cat's foot and Leah's back. Arnica and ice packs appeared but since we'd dispersed the weight of the blow between us we were all OK and limped on. Later Ian sweetly joined me in turning on the Christmas lights in The Cut in Waterloo and we returned to the rehearsals bearing flowers which I donated to Roger Allam, our Abbanazar, on the grounds that so far he was Best in Show.

At one low point in the rehearsals I quit the show twice in the same day. The second time, in the middle of some weird choreography involving a different hand gesture for every word of the song, I murmured 'I'm out of here' and jumped into my car. I got as far as the Aldwych Theatre and phoned Sean to tell him I'd left and he should replace me.

'Oh, turn the car round and get back here, you daft tart,' he said. I did.

The company were very dubious about the show. Nobody thought it would work. Before we opened I asked Sean if he thought Ian was going to be funny. I really wasn't sure. He looked at me and smiled. 'Oh, ye of little faith. He'll take one look at that audience and you won't know what's hit you.'

And he did. Costumed and wigged he burst out of his dressing-room and onto that stage like Les Dawson on amphetamines. It was quite extraordinary. I've never seen such a transformation. The rest of the company stood back in awe and the reviews said it all. They raved about Ian's Twanky, Roger Allam's fruity and dastardly Abbanazar, and the wit of the production. As for me and my moustachioed Dim, I seemed to puzzle the critics. What was I doing in it? *Underused*, was the phrase I most remember seeing. Funnily enough though, as the kids poured in, I began to enjoy myself, and that, of course, was the secret. For the next six weeks I was contentedly in the hottest ticket in town. A year later, they repeated the whole exercise, but by then I was rehearsing another play and threw over my plus fours to Frances Barber with some regret and some relief.

By now, I had put in my bid for the flat, but only two couples had looked around my house and no one had made an offer. My bid was accepted. I stayed calm. My accountant, Raymond, came round and we were sitting in the dining-room talking about the heinous nature of bridging loans when the phone rang. The second couple wanted my house for the asking price. It was, as my late father would have said, *beshert* – destiny.

About this time, I had 'destined' myself into a new and rather public relationship with lets call him Mr Energy, a Glasgow businessman. The period just before I moved house, was when our flurry of fascination with one another was at its height. I was wild again. Beguiled again. And unaware that the whimpering, simpering child again element was much more in the foreground than I realised. I was rehearsing in the American Church in Tottenham Court Road. It was a comedy revival – *Martha, Josie and the Chinese Elvis* by Charlotte Jones – for a pre-West End tour. It was 23rd January, the day before the move. Nats had taken twenty car loads of ephemera to the local tip, the house was stripped of *chatchkas* (knick-knacks). I had been given one day off to leave 30 years behind me.

Waiting to enter the scene, I got a goalpost moving text from Mr E: 'I'm coming through from a meeting in the City. Meet me.'

'You're in London?'

'I am. Can you meet me?'

'I'm in rehearsal.'

'Can you not get out for a minute?'

'No. You don't do things like that – it's not –'

'Five minutes. Just tell them you –'

'It doesn't work that way, you can't just –'

'You can't? I bet you can.'

'Er – I – I'll –'

'I'll walk up, you walk down. Five minutes . . .'

In a trance I tapped Rachel, my director, on the arm and said, 'Sorry, I – er – have to go now . . .'

'Go?' She looked at me askance. 'Go where?'

'Er . . . out.'

I gave her a watery smile and left her staring at my back. Once outside I charged like a Cadbury's Milk Flake advert, past all the homogenised displays of WPCs and Laptops and Printers and DVDs and Mobile Phone Chargers and into the arms of my businessman. In the absence of a station buffet and Rachmaninov, we evaporated into Starbucks and talked and gazed and the rest of it. Twenty-three minutes later than I'd promised to return to my place of work, I stood up to leave, looked for my bag and realised immediately that it, and everything I needed for the next day's move – let alone for the rest of my life – had been stolen.

The next day was moving day. I drove off at the same time as the removal vans with £4.50 in my pocket and a puppy in a sheepskin bed on the passenger seat. I waved goodbye to the house, my home for twenty-seven years. Goodbye to the telephone box, which had been wheeled two hundred and fifty yards on tracks through the garage by BT, the pillar box which I'd prized out of the post office. Goodbye to the observatory with the electric roof and the eight-inch Newtonian reflector given to me by BT's advertising company, goodbye to the massive wrought iron swinging seat I'd bought in Chalk Farm in lieu of a flat for Amy, painted garden green to match the Victorian garden shed I'd always planned to write in. Goodbye to the twenty-eight flowering yucca plants, Pushkin's grave (marked by a stone cat), the purple clematis, the vine over the front door, the passion flower, the two sentinel hollyhocks, the much-photographed Smallbone kitchen, scene of so many brunches and parties and late night cups of hot milk and cinnamon . . . The wing chair where Jack sat so contentedly, Draft Three on his lap, watching the garden grow or waiting for Zelma to disturb him with a rhetorical question. Goodbye to the past, the oh-so-recent past.

Gentleman's Residence, the advert had said when we first went to view the house in 1980. We were shown around by a charming elderly couple, Mr and Mrs Webb, whose family had grown and flown. Immediately we knew it was a happy house. Almost three decades later, it would be renovated and a nursery added for the young couple who'd bought it from me. Still, it was just a house I was leaving. Not my life with Jack. I wasn't leaving him behind. He was in my heart, my blood, my memory and every look and sound that came out of our kids. So off I went, with not too many backward glances. Moving moment, though, moving out. Moving on.

When I reached the new flat, two over-coated figures stood outside. One was Mr E and the other his financial adviser. Mr E was holding an envelope filled with notes to the tune of a thousand pounds, and the keys to my flat.

'You'll need this,' he said, handing me the envelope. 'The estate agent came by and asked me if I was waiting for Maureen Lipman. I said I was and he gave me the keys.'

We walked into the flat together and he loved it. It was light, clean and funky and a fifteen-minute fast train ride from Heathrow. The future beckoned, but unbeknown to me, with a slightly bent finger. The past was an infinitely easier place to live in. How was it for me?

Au Pairfect

My husband Jack and I recently decided that we both need a wife. An old-fashioned, domesticated, dedicated wifely sort of wife – probably gingham-clad and apple-cheeked. She would be required to cook, clean, shop, organise the children, love us all indiscriminately and, most important, bake real cakes which rise and stand upside down on a rack smelling of childhood. She would, of course, leave enough mixture in the bowl for us to lick out whilst she began the pies. Pies with real crusts which overlap the edges and curl up with disdain at the very mention of the words 'Jus-rol'.

Like most wives, her salary would be ludicrously low and her job satisfaction totally dependent on her delight in her creatures' comfort. Unlike most wives, her conjugal duties would be less than minimal – the odd hug when the accountant has delivered a body-blow, or a floury pat on the arm after a hard day at the rehearsal rooms.

At this point reality intrudes. The likelihood of finding Mrs Right is pretty scant. So, in the interim, I've had various Miss Wrongs, a few near Mrs, and the odd obscure object of desire. Au pairs, demi pairs, mother's helps and cleaners have passed through the last nine years of our lives like so many viruses or bonuses.

We started well. Gillian was from the North-East – jolly sensible she was, too. Lived in the boxroom and calmly accepted that the sink was in the living-room, the fridge was in the bathroom and the builders in Majorca. After a year she went off to become a nurse, presumably benefiting enormously from a year's national service with a batch of fruitcakes in North London.

I soon discovered that I was totally miscast in the role of employer. I could be friend, mother confessor, or Rent-A-Dress, but I couldn't be boss. Can't. I still find it impossible to complain about a job undone or wrongly done without apologising profusely throughout and leaving the room half-way through as though the words sound *nicer* coming from another place. For years 'Will you be in tonight, Maria?' was synonymous with 'It's all right, Jack, we can go out for dinner after all'.

Of course, if they're beautiful you've every right to feel humble. My friend, Louie, tells of a stunning Austrian au pair who came downstairs one night and discreetly asked, 'Would it be all right if I watch BBC2

11

tonight? One of my films is on.' They were just nicely over the shock of having the toast of Austria doing their morning toast, when she ran off with the husband of their closest friend. Or he ran off with her. Anyway, they both ran. Presumably to the nearest schloss to shloff it all off.

Terumi was our first Oriental au pair. She bowled into Heathrow, after a 22-hour flight from Tokyo, five feet eleven inches tall and so embarrassed by her height that she hid her beautiful face in a Princess Diana-like stoop. She had never slept on a bed and always took her food to her room. She would make a careful salad. Then fry an egg. Then wash up. *Then* place the egg on the salad and carry the warmish clump up to her room.

The children loved her because she said nothing, but said it kneeling at their level. She never went out, except to school, and wore a uniform of jeans and shirts.

When summer came, we took her to Cyprus, where she donned a tiny red bikini and drove the local men insane. The waiters, who seemed unused to pretty, six-foot Japanese girls in bikinis, went wild and began swarming up the side of the hotel at midnight, and following her about the island in an eager, red-coated phalanx. She appeared highly puzzled.

Just before her year was up, she fell in love with a sweet Irish bus driver, and he with her. Her last six weeks were spent at a Kentish Town Irish dance hall, whirling madly to the music of Philomena Begley and the Allstars.

When she left, she cried. And so did I. 'I have been very bad au pair,' she sobbed, in the longest sentence I'd ever heard her say. I joined in her tears, and insisted she was the best six-foot Japanese au pair I'd ever had. She protested vehemently, and, castigating herself all the way to Heathrow, she flew out of our lives.

Providing the right environment for a young girl from a different country is as much a matter of chance as finding the right person to marry. A friend of mine, finding herself without help at a crucial time of work, hired a sweet Yugoslavian girl from an agency at five o'clock one afternoon. She was plump and amiable in her Laura Ashley smock and seemed keen to please, and glad to have found a home after being inexplicably fired from her previous one. At two-thirty the following morning, one of the children appeared at my friend's bedroom door – 'Mummy, Gerda's making funny noises.' En famille, they stood outside Gerda's room and listened to the low moaning and groaning, issuing from within. My friend went in, to be greeted by a stoical silence punctuated only by groans. 'If-you-don't-tell-me-what-hurts-how-can-I-help-you?' she shouted, her Serbo-Croat being less than perfect. Finally, they called an ambulance. After a brief examination, the ambulance man said, 'Would you mind getting the manual from the driver's seat, and turn to the chapter on Home Deliveries?' 'But I don't know the girl,' spluttered Gerda's employer of nine and a half hours. 'Take her to a hospital!' 'Too late for that, luv, she's three fingers dilated. Hot water – and be quick about it.' The next hour became a 1950s B movie, while she and her husband paced the foot of the stairs waiting for the prescribed yowl. Years later we used the idea for an episode of *Agony* – and everyone said it was far-fetched and couldn't happen . . .

There comes a time in every au pair employer's life when another three weeks of saying 'Zis is ze washing machine' and 'No, when you pick up the phone it isn't enough to say "Ya, Rosenballs?"' is anathema. At such moments, the urge to buy British is very strong. You then put a carefully worded advert in *The Lady*. After which, if you're lucky, you get two or even three replies. You then meet the prospective applicants at Paddington, drive them home, show them the animals, and drive them back again.

One such applicant was Sharon from Southampton. She seemed painfully shy, but her erstwhile employer – who arrived with her – assured us of her efficiency, humour and love of children. She arrived a week later, looking cross-eyed with the effort not to cry. She unpacked her case, came downstairs, had dinner, ignored the children – and the dishes – and silently cried. A lot. We comforted her and assured her she'd feel better tomorrow. And, sure enough, the next day she got up about 9.30, came down, ate a hearty breakfast and burst into tears. After two days of this, to cheer her up I asked her what she'd like to do now that she was in London. 'Oi wanna Starsky and 'Utch T-shirt,' she muttered darkly. We got her one, and that night she didn't cry before dinner. *After* dinner she howled like a coyote – whilst I did the dishes. I asked her what was so terrible about the job, didn't she like us? 'Oh, yes,' she hiccupped. 'It's just Oi miss my owld boss – she used to lark about so.' 'Lark about?' I muttered even darkly-er. 'Well, we'd throw soap suds at each other and larf, and then we'd roll about on the floor together, you know, larkin' about. Oo, we did larf!' Next day, she was larfin' when we took her to Paddington – and we were rollin' around when we waved her goodbye.

Of course, in between the disasters, there are girls without whom you don't believe you can go on living. For two years we had Ruth, who was Swiss with an English sense of humour. After surviving the baptism of fire that my kids invariably impose on newcomers, like screaming tantrums in the Post Office and accusations of cruelty on being denied a £10 box of Terry's of York, Ruth went from au pair to elder daughter. Finally, Jack and I gave her away to her delightful English boyfriend in a marriage ceremony on our lawn. She wore a Victorian dress I'd bought in an auction; and the ceremony was characterised by the delivery of a new carpet for us from John Lewis, causing all the wedding guests to troop into the front room and express their disappointment, after which it was rolled up and returned. The couple continued to live with us for another year, and, in a kibbutz-like way, it was a perfect arrangement.

I'll skip over the one who, for a wedding, 'borrowed' my best silk suit (bought in a moment of madness for the *Parkinson Show*) and came back with it scrunched up in a bag between mud-covered boots and a Braun Ladyshave. It was generously spattered with HP Sauce. All I could think was it must have been some wedding!

For the past couple of years, and at the risk of sounding like an enthusiastic Percy Thrower, we've been having a lovely run of Swedes. Mostly their English is better than mine, and I can't think what they're doing here. But they're loving, intelligent, merry and good-tempered, fond of a good rock concert or two and the odd evening at The Bull and Bush – which suits me fine. The first, the patient and sensible Lisa, we hear is now a balloon-dancer back in Sweden . . . which leads me to ask, 'Is working for the Rosenthals a high-risk profession?'

I can't help thinking what a dreadful au pair I would have made. At 19 my housework would have been even more risible than it is now, my organisation more hopeless, and my only advantage the ability to amuse the kids with vivid impersonations of their parents. Also, my mother would have phoned nightly. And sent fishballs by overseas mail.

When my brother and I were small, a local girl called Sheila lived with us for about twelve years. I console myself in times of crisis with the thought that, if permanence of that nature and mother at home to boot can breed a mass of insecurities like me, then perhaps – with my yearly change of nationalities and natures – I could be doing something right.

Of course, it's always worse when my mother is staying and doing her 'groping around the skirting board looking for and finding evidence of domestic negligence' act. She has a way with a glance (i.e. a five-minute stare) or a whisper (i.e. you could hear it in Hastings) which can turn the atmosphere in the house from *Little Women* into *Rocky III*. 'It's nothing to do with me but – she's on the phone AGAIN, don't you mind?' or 'Would you like me to put out Adam's clothes for the morning, as no one seems to have done it . . .?' I reckon if they survive the grandma, they'll probably survive the kids.

My latest and greatest au pair story, however, began when I placed an advertisement in an Australian newspaper. This was in the belief that we spoke the same language. I might as well have placed an ad in the *Salonica Gleaner*. Out of sixty replies I picked on the girl who wrote from the Arboglen Nursery. She drove, seemed very mature and came well-recommended.

I was rather surprised to hear a male voice on the stairs the following morning answering Jack's query about how she had slept. It seemed that the Quantas pilot had been left stranded and spent the night – still, at least she'd be fun with the kids. She wasn't. She treated them like aliens.

'Tell me, Sandi,' I chirped during the washing up, 'how many children were in your care at the nursery?' Her face registered pure misunderstanding. 'How do you mean?'

'I mean, how many of the children in the Arboglen Nursery did you actually look after?' Apart from speaking Swedish, I had no other way of phrasing it.

'Oh, no,' the penny dropped. 'Oh, no, you've got it wrong. No. They weren't children. They were pot plants.'

Bring out the Baby Bio, Mother needs some help.

Zuckerman: A Life

A tortoise is, I suppose, a Jewish pet. It knows its place. Outside on the lawn. It doesn't bark. It doesn't tear the Dralon. And it never raises the question of kosher dogfood. It's also not unlucky, like birds, unluckily enough. To this day I can't even buy a tea-towel with a bird on it. For fear. Of what? I hear you, not unreasonably, ask. Well, historically, mythically and somewhat obviously the bird is a symbol of flight; and a symbol of flight is the last thing you want to look at when you've just unpacked your bags after the last pogrom and said, 'Never again!'

Be that as it may, and it may be or not, depending on how much you believe my Auntie Bella, the entreaties of my brother and myself thirty years ago for a fluffy friend to take on walks to the car and back, fell on house-proud ears. Finally, after one particularly protracted 'last of the summer whines', we were allowed a four-legged friend: a tortoise. Ecstatic with joy, we gazed at its four legs, waited three days for its head to appear, saw the marked similarity between the expression on its face and that on its leg, and lost all interest.

How little we knew. And how empty of reptile lore, therefore, have been the next thirty years. Accompany me, if you will, to the Muswell Hill pet-shop, on the occasion of my daughter's sixth birthday and a lip-biting dilemma. Stand with me, before a shelf of tortoises, all slightly variable in size, all identical in expression. Or lack of it. See the hope on my face, as I pray that the right reptile for the Family Rosenthal will show, by some small but meaningful gesture, that my choice is inevitable. Nothing much – just a minor shell adjustment, an imperceptible 'Hi, there, Mother!', even a lewd wink. Nothing. I shut my eyes and chose Zuckerman. For it was he.

I took him home in a Winalot box, with a nice Webb's lettuce and no idea what to do with him. I showed him the garden, newly terraced, and put him in a sunny spot with the nice Webb's. Headless, he retained all the appeal of a piece of crazy paving, and showed no interest whatsoever in his dinner. 'He's probably getting his bearings,' said Jack. 'I'll take the outside leaves off the lettuce for him. He'll soon settle.' Thus began the first hint of the relationship that was to form between my husband and a thirty-nine-year-old Greek female of dubious background and highly eccentric character. But more of that later.

The kids showed nominally more interest in their tortoise than my brother and I had in ours. They offered some birthday cake to what turned out to be his tail, and that was more or less that. (They named him Zuckerman after a naughty schoolboy in Jack's play, *The Evacuees* – all snotty-nosed, trailing shoelaces and wily wit. The kids would watch the play over and over, on the video, on wet afternoons.) By and large, he was mostly ignored. And the feeling was mutual.

The turning-point came when Zucky began to sprint. It was an astonishing sight. We were sitting at the living-room table, when a flash went past the window. Was it a bird? (Unlucky for some.) Was it a plane? No, it was old Supershell, actually legging it across the lawn towards the wire fence separating us from next door, if not at the rate of knots then certainly not at a bad rate. You could've knocked me down with a week-old Webb's.

Was this rare streak of tortoise athleticism a flash in the pan? Or was it time for a fast call to one of the Mr McWhirters. Or perhaps the *Sun* newspaper – 'Phew! What a Tortoise!' Breath bated, we waited. Place him back at the other end of the lawn and – whoosh! – all four legs akimbo, head and tail erect, he went for that gold like a prehensile Seb Coe.

But what exactly was the nature of the gold? What luscious scent could make a taciturn tortoise turn his back on today's Cos and hare off towards next door's fence? (Yes, in this story, Zuckerman plays both the Tortoise *and* the Hare.) The following day we found out. Enter the man next door. Jim. Short of temper and red of face. (I'm sorry this sounds like a Worzel Gummidge story, played out in North London, but it is, and was.) In his hand, one tortoise, legs waving sheepishly – if that's not too tautological for you.

'It was at my lettuces!' by way of explanation.

'My goodness, Jim,' I grovelled, 'I *am* sorry. I can't understand it. It must have dug a hole under the fence. I'll check it and nail it down. The fence I mean.'

'Garrumph!' Yes, he actually said it. And left.

We checked the fence. It was secure. Two days later it happened again. Jim's face was even redder. 'I'll have to put it over t'back fence if it does it again.'

Over t'back fence. The death-knell for small, slow creatures of ill-heated brain. Into the British Rail Experimental Paint Yard section of Ally Pally Park. Surely Zucky wouldn't end his days tethered to a stake through the shell painted Buffet Car beige? We checked the fence again. The next day we watched in shifts. During one of mine, I glanced through the window and did a triple-take worthy of Harpo Marx. Zuckerman was not on the lawn. Zuckerman was not in the flower-bed. I rushed upstairs to spy on

17

next door's lettuce. Zuckermanless. And then I saw him. It was a sight that filled me with awe. Zuckerman was halfway up the garden fence. He had climbed roughly two feet up the wire netting, and now hung on with three legs while exploring with the fourth for the next crampon or whatever the word is if you're a tortoise. Tampon, I suppose. Yes, Zucky was now going for the Decathlon. By the autumn, the family was treating him with a new respect: he was growing as eccentric as the rest of us. Occasionally he would fall off the fence and lie in an undignified position on his shell, revealing what a ratty little reptile he'd be without it. His legs and toes would wave wildly until someone came to turn him the right way up again, at which point he would attempt to look as though it had never happened – and certainly not to him – and saunter casually away from the fence. Almost whistling.

Then came the winter of our discontent. As the book says, in the winter tortoises stop walking, stop eating and finally – just stop. It soon became clear, however, that although Zuckerman might be Olympic standard in night-time pole-vaulting he was somewhat ignorant of one of the three instincts with which the Lord endowed his species. Hibernation. He tried. His idea of a *good* try was to bury his head and front paws, then knock off work for a week, and sit there like a rejected meat pie. In vain, we tried boxes filled with straw, warm cellars, garden sheds, etc. At one point Jack had him in his study where he worked, cementing the strong bond between them. One would type and the other would potter. One would occasionally excrete but the other didn't seem to mind. Greater love . . .

Finally, and well into December – like an overtired and recalcitrant child – he fell into a deep and presumably dreamless sleep, and was put in the garden shed for the duration. For the next couple of months it was as if he'd never been. And had it not been that with that first rustle of a warmish spring came the first rustle of a friendly gardener popping round to do the 'few bits and pieces that can be done', which obviously included a trip to the shed, we might never have known that Zuckerman was out of his straw. Jack raced to the bedside. The patient, who was alive (but as Dorothy Parker said after Calvin Coolidge's death, 'How could they tell?'), wouldn't eat, move, or bring his head out. Was it 'Hang up your climbing boots' time for Zucky.

Jack said no. He took Zucky to the vet, filled in all the forms – 'Zuckerman Rosenthal' (ethnic enough, do you think?), Age – nine months since bought, Past Medical History – none, Complaint – inability on owners' part to know whether animal is dead or not.

'Oh yes,' said Mr Hill, 'common enough.' Jack and Ruth (our then au pair girl, whom he'd brought along – presumably expecting Zucky to throw a tantrum) listened, rapt, while the expert gave Zucky his first life-saving injection. He explained that people shipped these poor creatures over from the Continent, in their hundreds, thrown into the hold like a batch of live lasagna. Then other people bought them, with no knowledge of how to keep them (I needed Tortoise Guilt to add to Working Mother and Loving Daughter Guilt).

It seemed that Zucky had woken up too soon due to a combination of not having eaten enough to feed him during the full hibernation, and the warmish spring. His brain was now too frozen for him to know that he was alive. Jack's glasses, I expect, gleamed with attentiveness.

'He'll have to be made to eat,' said Mr Hill briskly, as though it was the easiest task in the world. 'Lucky you spotted him. Lots don't, and then, come the summer, they look for their pets, and what do they find? Liquid tortoise.'

When I arrived home, it was to find Jack, Ruth and the kids and the corpse (?) of Zuckerman, standing contemplating the pantry. Jack had a small syringe in one hand and two cotton buds in the other, and was engaged in the mind-boggling decision of whether to give the patient warmed-up chicken soup or tomato soup. For obvious reasons, that night Zucky ate Kosher.

But first, Jack gently swabbed his crusted eyes, placed him in a bath of lukewarm water – elbow in water, just like the old days – up to his haunches . . . fetters . . . plimsoll line . . . whatever, then he forced his jammed-up mouth open with tweezers, revealing a sight which made Jaba in *Return of the Jedi* look attractive. Finally the warmed-up chicken soup (minus matzo balls) was syringed in. If Zuckerman felt any surprise at a regime which would cost £150 at a good health farm, he certainly didn't show it. The main problem was keeping his head out once they'd got it out, which required a merciless grip where his ears would have been had he had any.

Sweating with triumph at the amount accomplished so far, Jack gazed up through soup-misted glasses and said, 'I've got to get him some herring. It's full of iron.' My nose twitched, and it wasn't just the mention of herrings. What was occurring was more than paternal duty. It was undoubtedly love.

Each day, Zuckerman's smorgasbord grew more varied, until at last the day came when, confronted by Iceberg lettuce and wild strawberries, he gave in; opened one eye, raised his upper jaw and clamped it firmly on the lettuce. He didn't eat it, you understand. But it was a start. The old, evolutionary instincts came surging back, and within a few weeks it was midnight feasts for the two of them in the study . . . Jack eating his herring chopped, and Zucky raw. Neil Simon could write a play about it. Jack Rosenthal could write a play about it. Who needs me? (Years later Jack wrote the play. It was called *Tortoise* and was part of a series of plays for television called *Articles for Sale* which, finally, was never made.)

Anyway, a life had been saved and a bond strengthened, and the spring and summer passed in a now-familiar manner, tortoise-wise. Zucky, once more, climbed, ran and stole next-door's lettuce. The boy was a hooligan. Disturbed certainly. The signs were that Jim would shortly take out a contract for his life. British Experimental Tortoise. Each night, Jack battened down the fences and put his little friend to sleep on the patio. And came the autumn. This time Zucky obliged us by hibernating at the right time in the right way. You know, like he was a tortoise. Then the dumb cluck went and woke up in February.

This time Mr Hill sent Jack to a Reptile Expert. His receptionist was sympathetic. 'Oh poor thing,' she crooned, 'I've had just the same thing with my python.' The Expert himself was alarmed by Zucky's appearance. In the course of his examination, he weighed him, took his temperature and revealed, almost en passant that Zuckerman was Greek, probably about thirty-nine years old, and not surprisingly when you think about it – a female!

Without allowing a second for this extraordinary revelation to sink in, he added 'And she's dying.' Zuckerwoman had one week to live. During that time she had to be bathed as before and kept under a 300-watt infra-red lamp, placed exactly eighteen inches above her head. If she lost more bodyweight then presumably – liquid tortoise! And she couldn't eat until her body temperature reached a certain heat.

As I left for work, Jack was tearing off in the direction of the North Circular, heading for every hairdresser's suppliers in North London, or if need be the world. Six hours later, he returned triumphant. He'd managed to borrow one until Friday. He measured eighteen inches above Zucky's shell and with trembling hands and many a glance at the clock, he began the tortuous(!) business of fixing the heavy lamp by means of double-sided tape, piles of books and much amateur Heath-Robinsonry into its exact position. Ten minutes later it blew, and so did Jack. This time he headed for the West End.

In due course, another infra-red lamp was installed in the study and yet another was returned to the wholesalers off the North Circular at a cost of – but what cost love? It stood on a piece of hardboard, which was liberally strew with out-of-season Iceberg lettuce (from Harrods, yet, special delivery), two or three herrings and the odd apricot, another great favourite of tortoise according to a lady on a tortoise phone-in on LBC. (You understand my meaning when I say tortoise phone-in. Of course I mean tortoise-*owners* phone in; although sometimes I'm convinced these programmes would be a hell of a lot more articulate if it were the tortoises who phoned.) Impassive and headless as ever, Zuckerman sat, and no doubt somewhere in those semi-frozen brains she awaited the next set of inexplicable indignities.

Meanwhile Jack's behaviour grew more and more suspicious. As the hours and then the days passed, he would often come out of his study, looking green and complaining of dizziness. 'Could it be the infra-red herring cocktail giving you radiation sickness?' I suggested. 'Why not move her to the cellar?'

'No, she should be where I can keep my eye on her,' he said stoutly.

Every day the ritual continued . . . the twice-daily bath in a deep tray, the deep all-over tanning. The syringing had stopped, thank goodness, as I was down to my last can of Bean and Barley, and the apricots lay rotting on the hardboard. As did Zuckerman. See what I mean about a Jewish pet? You work, you slave, fingers to the bone, you bathe, you syringe, you work in a dangerously hot room – and what thanks do you get? Nothing. Not a thank you, not a gesture, not a nice box of Black Magic. Nothing. And the times he'd told her to keep warm!

Do you know, I even caught him playing thirty-nine-year-old band tunes to that tortoise on his violin one day. Actually thumbing through *Favourites From the War Years*, looking for a jolly, rejuvenating, hopefully Greek ditty, no doubt. The nearest he came was 'Kiss Me Goodnight, Sergeant Major' – I tell you I was shocked. I thought of writing to Anna Raeburn, but I feared she'd say she was going through the same thing herself.

Matters came to a head, as matters and pimples always do, on the Friday when Jack was *still* working on *Yentl* with Barbra Streisand. With only one day left of Zuckerman's life expectancy, he was called in urgently to discuss Draft Eleven with herself and the Heads of United Artists (which sit on the wafer-thin, silk-shirted bodies of United Artists). I wasn't working that day, so I was asked to reptile-sit. With some reluctance, but already thinking no doubt of dining out, one day, on this Magnificent Obsession, I agreed. He left the phone number of the hotel, where they were 'taking a meeting', and clear instructions to check on Zucky's condition every half hour.

The kids were at school. I began listlessly to do some housework. Perhaps if I *had* a list I'd be a better housewife. However . . .

Suddenly distracted by the need to chat to my friend, Lizzy, I sat down by the phone in Jack's study. The smell was rich and the vegetation on the floor somewhat noxious. The Melina Mercouri of the tortoise world (equally without her marbles) sat giving her street furniture impersonation. I placed her under the lamp and put a fresh apricot (again out of season, of course) by her nose. And rang Lizzy. We'd been chatting for some time, a long time when I come to think about it, about Life and Art and the price of rawlplugs, when my attention was caught and the words dried up in my throat. Zuckerman's head was out.

'Zuckerman's head's out, Lizzy!' . . . presumably she thought this was a coded message. I put the phone down, crept towards the floodlit animal, pushed an apricot near her nose, and picked up the phone again. 'It's the tortoise,' I began to whisper, 'she's – arrrgh!!' Even as I spoke, her snake-like head came forward another inch revealing much-gnarled neck. Then, as if by divine command, her head twisted on its axis, her jaws parted and she sank her teeth into half an apricot. I began to cry.

Typical, wasn't it? The bloody animal wakes up for me, whilst Jack, who'd nursed her back from near-liquidization, gets a faceful of Megastar. I put the phone down on a confused Lizzy and phoned the Berkeley Hotel. I'd give Jack a real coded message this time.

'Miss Streisand's suite,' I tried to sound authoritative. 'Who are you calling?' came back the regulation bark. 'Mr Jack Rosenthal . . . it's his wife . . . it's important . . .' I petered out. Relieved, I heard Jack's voice, 'Yes, love?'

'OK,' I whispered, 'show no reaction. I'm sorry to disturb you . . . it's just that Zuckerman's eaten half an apricot and I thought you'd –'

Show no reaction! The man was beside himself . . . 'She ate an apri – a half?? Will she eat the other half? Look . . . Oh, God, that's wonderful! Oh, thank God! Look, try her on the herring! Oh, love, that's fantastic . . . Oh, well done! Listen, I'll be home in an hour – just keep her . . .' He faded out a bit and his voice took on a slightly more formal note. I knew what had happened.

In his ecstasy, he'd glanced up at a sea of Californian faces, gold pens airborne, glossed lips open, gazing at their deeply deranged screenwriter with a mixture of pity and despair.

'Everything okay, Jack?' Finally the Megastar spoke. 'Oh, yes, thanks,' he wiped his brow and grinned. And for one minute made the fatal error of crediting Hollywood film executives with a sense of humour. 'It was the tortoise . . . er, Zuckerman . . . she was dying . . . today was her deadline . . . and that was Maureen telling me she's just had a bit of . . . er . . . soft fruit . . . and . . . er.' The room was rife with lack of interest.

'A tortoise?' said the head of the bottom-line. 'You mean like a turtle or something?'

'Yes!' said Jack, willing and able to launch into his favourite topic. 'You see, she was too cold to know she was alive and I've been bathing her and . . .' The silence was cavernous. The ground failed to open for him, but the mouth of the head of scripts did. 'Great, OK, fine, well now . . . page 43, Draft Eleven, you know when Yentl says to Avigdor . . .' So ended

United Artists' part in Zuckerman's life, another example, as Jack so rightly put it, of Hollywood getting its priorities wrong.

Meanwhile, back in Muswell Hill we were a merry throng. Zucky regained her strength, and, after a long convalescence, much helped by songs from *Zorba the Greek* and the *Best of Nana Mouskouri*, played by her loving benefactor, she grew strong enough to venture outside for increasingly long spells, and ultimately to play her old part of the Lettuce Kleptomaniac again.

Impossible though it may sound, the story isn't over yet. One day, well into the summer, when we'd stopped watching her and stopped apologising for her lack of social graces and due regard for property, she disappeared.

In vain we questioned Jim as to whether he'd been practising discus throwing with a four-legged discus. His answer was no, but his face read 'But give me half a chance . . .' En famille, we scoured Ally Pally Park, all six of us, including au pair and cat, shouting 'Zuckerman!' at the tops of our voices. We somehow hoped our cries would penetrate the sides of her head where her ears might've been. Tearfully we told the Park Keeper of our loss. He promised to keep his eyes open. We thanked him and headed back home – Jack lingering behind the rest of us hopefully whistling 'Take the Water or the Wine'. Believe it or not, on our second search we found her. Plodding her way across the park in search of sex with a perfect stranger, Ally Pally Park being her idea of a singles bar, I presume. It was hard to tell whether she was pleased to see us or not. She gave a low hiss when we picked her up which seemed to me remarkably low in gratitude.

Back on the lawn she seemed to be back in her anorexic phase and turned up her nose, indeed turned up her whole head at whatever we offered. The summer was ending and we reckoned it was probably hibernation time again.

Two days later she was gone. You know, when a kid leaves home enough times you finally gotta get the message. We searched again but with no luck. We informed the Park Keepers to start looking for her again, having first informed them to stop, and this time they fixed us with a baleful look not entirely unlike one of Zuckerman's, who could be full of bale like you wouldn't believe!

The days turned into weeks and we finally had to admit that Zucky was probably headed for the Greek mainland now. Sadly we resigned ourselves to her loss – some of us with greater difficulty than others. Her final joke at our expense came, as usual, whilst Jack was out. It came in the form of a Park Keeper – he stood on the step, brown-suited with a carrier bag. Which moved.

'Who's a lucky lady, then?' I wasn't sure whether he meant me or the contents of the bag, but was too happy to care. I flung my arms around his neck, got out the fatted lettuce from the fridge and with many a pat, stroke and admonishment, I put her back once again in her verdant prison.

I couldn't wait for her 'father', the fiddle-playing maniac last remembered giving her the kiss of life, to come home. I actually kept running to the front-room window whenever I heard a car. The kids were all excited, too, and kept checking on her progress on the lawn. She seemed pretty well fixed in one position – maybe her Houdini days were over.

'Hello, love.' The front door banged. It was he.

'All together now [to the tune of "Hello Dolly"] – Hello Zucky, well hello, Zucky, it's so nice to have you back where you belong. You're looking swell, Zucky, I can tell, Zucky . . .' etc.

He was stunned with disbelief and delight. We dragged him on to the lawn and looked at the expression on his face. He took off his glasses, bent down to greet his little taramasalata. He stood up again and blinked.

'It's not Zuckerman,' he said.

'What's not Zuckerman?' The thought had never crossed my mind.

'That. It's someone else. Different markings. Not Zucky. It's just a tortoise.'

It's difficult to describe our feelings really. How can you start again at the same point of love and exasperation and dependency and history for Godsake, with a totally new tortoise? With different markings? We tried. But two days later when she disappeared off the face of the lawn, I can't say we were anything but relieved. Presumably Zucky's understudy was a forty-year-old Turkish tortoise looking for exactly what Zuck was looking for, regardless of race, colour and markings. Presumably he was mad as hell when, just having got within sniffing distance of the tortoise equivalent of casual sex, he was picked up, placed in a Sainsbury's bag, and thrust into the smothering world of North London Family Life. Presumably before the winter set in they found each other – please God. Let's just hope, for all our sakes, that the sodding earth moved! Particularly the earth around the British Rail Experimental Paint Yard.

We're just a one-animal family now. Same old cat – Pushkin Rosenthal. Her eccentricities are confined to Grievous Bodily Harm to Wilton carpets and chintz-covered furniture. The kids want a gerbil but they've no chance. No chance at all. I know who'd end up cleaning out its cage, mincing its morsels and supplying it with old scripts to tear. And he's not doing it. Honestly, wouldn't you give anything to get under the duvet in October and wake up in May to a warm bath, a mouthful of chicken soup – and to a face full of love ready to tend your slightest whim?

We now have a large yellow tortoise made of stone, every bit as responsive as her predecessor. We bought it in a Cuffley garden centre out of sentiment and a deep desire to avoid buying patio paving stones. Some weeks later, sitting in the garden, Sara, my agent, mused, 'That tortoise hasn't moved an inch in three hours.' Adam sprang to Zuckerman II's defence – 'Neither have *you*,' he countered.

Amy now wants a duck. You'll be surprised to hear that I said 'No.' The following day, I kid you not, at a recording session in Bushey, someone offered me one. I looked upon it as an omen. And said 'No' again. Recently, a gentleman in the wholesale publishing world told me that ducks make the loveliest pets. He had fourteen. Indian Runners, they're called. 'They don't need much water,' he said in reply to my doubts about bringing home a pond from the garden centre. 'They only go in when it rains. And they'll eat anything. If you haven't got any corn, they love a bit of lettuce or mashed-up veg. Ours poke their heads through the cat flap at feeding time.'

I could feel myself falling in love, so I spoke to myself severely about piles of duck-poo and constant quacking. Then, just as I was beating my better nature into a fluffy pulp, he said it. The sentence which is surely going to change my life for the duckier. Are you sitting comfortably? Then I'll begin:

'In the summer,' he smiled, 'when it's a lovely day and all the windows are open, I love to sit in the lounge and watch the cricket. One day, I heard a quack which sounded quite near – but I didn't pay much attention till a flash of white caught the corner of my eye. I looked down and there were three of my ducks, Big Daffy, Daphne and Doris, sitting in a line, glued to the telly, following Botham with either side of their heads. They watched solidly till my wife came home and I had to shoo them out of the lounge. Now they invariably come in for *Sportsview* to check if there's any cricket. If not, they don't bother.'

And you thought 'out for a duck' was an allegory, didn't you? The family argument at the moment is whether to call them Aqua and Via Duck or Duck Whittington and Duck Turpin. Watch this space.

In fact, we never got them. We ducked out of it. After Pushkin went to that great upholsteria in the sky, we talked long and hard about a dog and even decided on the breed.

'When we've moved,' said Jack, 'we'll go to Battersea and we'll just know. When the time's right.'

Of course it never was right and it was two years after Jack died that the kids gave me a piece of paper on my birthday. It said: 'Your Basenji puppy will be born in August', and showed me a photo of a tiny brown and white piglet-y sphere. 'We're buying him for you,' they said, and my eyes misted over.

I had seen a Basenji – the barkless dog of the Congo, since you ask – on a lead with his mistress whilst I was filming a programme about Art Deco in Soho. He walked elegantly up to me, leaned solidly against my leg, looked up – five worried furrows on his brown brow – and I tumbled into love. His name was Alfie and he went to work every day with Vivienne Clore, agent to Jo Brand and other famed comics. She told me he was adorable, couldn't be let off the lead, and was more cat than dog.

The time was right, and I knew.

As it turned out, my Basenji puppy came from a different source. My barkless dog of the Congo hailed from Ealing. I went to meet the breeder, Tom Rabitte. The puppy's mother-to-be, Linnie, and her grandmother leaned on me and put their beautiful foxy heads on my chest. When the puppies were whelped I went back to Ealing and bonded with the one he'd designated as mine. She was indistinguishable from the other six but for the white markings on her neck and I was scared I might be missing something. I thought I'd call her Florence after the unlikely soprano Florence Foster Jenkins, whom I was playing in the West End play, *Glorious*, but by the time I'd carried her home to Muswell Hill she was Diva.

It was a dangerous name to choose and she's lived up to it. Smart? How long have you got? She has me wrapped around her dew claw and I wish to hell I'd called her Placido. She has ten tricks, eats only cooked mince or chicken, opens doors by the handle, runs off the lead like a tornado with greyhounds, bull mastiffs or any dog of any size, and has never, at two years old, been left on her own without eating my knickers or chewing the computer leads. How Jack would have loved and waited on her.

Meanwhile *Tortoise*, Jack's play for TV which was never made, was adapted for radio by Amy and aired on New Year's Day, 2008, on Radio 4, starring Stephen Mangan as a man so obsessed with saving the life of his tortoise that he fails to notice that his wife (Felicity Montague) is having an affair with another man. In the end, both man and tortoise are brought out of their shell by the love of a good woman. I directed it with Dirk Maggs for Above the Title Productions, and the circle was completed.

Watching David Attenborough's staggering television programme about cold-blooded creatures, I was mesmerised by the sight and plight of Lonesome George, the seventy-six-year-old Pinto tortoise, the last survivor of his species. Giraffe-necked, beady-eyed and loose-skinned, he remembers how to eat but not how to have sex. I have no idea why I felt such a strong sense of identification with him.

In My Natural Habit 'at

It is a habit of mine to observe the habits of my fellow eccentrics. (Yesterday I saw a man at the Archway Road crossing, wearing a yellow hat, a khaki jumpsuit, brown boots and a tortoiseshell cat on his shoulder. He looked like a poster for a panto. I wondered if the cat always went for a walk, well, a sit, with him; and, if so, how the habit started. Were the matching outfits an afterthought or was the cat perhaps velcro'd to his shoulder pads?)

I myself have no habits worth mentioning, unless you count falling over my own ankles a lot (but only when walking – never when sitting, lying or crossing the Archway Road). Oh, and I don't like whistling. It makes my teeth itch. A visit from the window cleaner can virtually turn my mouth inside out. Oh, and when I was a child, I couldn't stand anyone touching me – unless I touched them back. This was irritating at the age of nine, but positively lethal by the time I reached sixteen, and could be said to answer for a lot.

My husband has a lot of habits. Indeed, one of the bonds between us during our early courtship was his ability to catch me just before I fell over, and his apparent appreciation of my touching him back every time he touched me. One of his strangest is his 'cigarette routine'. Years ago, he was working with a writer who was paralysed and worked in a wheelchair. During a long, dour session over a comedy half-hour which wouldn't have made a tortoiseshell cat laugh, Jack reached for his customary cigarette. 'Don't do it! Don't do it!' shrieked his co-writer. 'I was just going to light a fag,' murmured Jack, somewhat taken aback. 'I know you bloody were!' said Harry. 'Do you have any idea what *happens* every time *you* light a cigarette? Every single time?' 'Yes, I lessen my life by twenty-five minutes, now do you mind if I –' 'No, you soft sod, what you actually do – what I have to *watch* you do, thirty times a day, six days a week!'

Jack blinked in puzzlement.

'You take a cigarette from the packet, then you tap it on the packet, filter side down. Twice. Then you tap your chin. Twice. Then you take a match, tap it on the box, twice, and light the cigarette.' By this time, Jack's jaw had tapped the ground. Twice. 'Then,' continued Harry (his calm was deadly), 'you take the cigarette out of your mouth, tap your nose twice and your chin twice and carry on as though all you'd done was light a cigarette.'

27

This story has two morals. One, which has nothing at all to do with the subject, is that a guy in a wheelchair can't walk away from other people's lunacy. The other is my dear old man's total ignorance of his own ornate ritual, the like of which could create a new school of advanced anthropology. Actually, he went to a hypnotherapist last week to give up the habit altogether – the smoking, not the tapping. Once there, he was played a tape, the gist of which seemed to be that if you never pick up a cigarette again – you won't smoke. Logic, innit? Habits are every bit as addictive as addictives, but it's the first time I've seen him in fourteen years when he hasn't been on fire. We shall see.

Our secretary, Christine, popped by the other day having terrible trouble with the car she's been driving for the last six years. It refused to reverse. It would do everything else it had done before – like start, stall and attack old ladies at pelican crossings. But it just wouldn't retreat. She said it was out of spite because she'd driven her father's car for three days while her own car was being serviced. She had to drive miles out of her way, in ever-increasing circles and bounce it out of parking spaces by hand. Finally she went storming back to the garage and was faced with the irrefutable evidence that her car would indeed. But only if put into reverse gear. As opposed to the position used for reversing her *father's car*. It seems incredible that six *years* of habit could be broken in just three days. A marvellous argument for brainwashing or even carwashing. Christine took it well. Her face just reversed from red to white and back to red again and she was forced to back down.

Her little girl has a lovely habit. She licks her fingers in a precise curving movement, little finger first, over and over again. When asked why she's doing it, she says, 'I'm just keeping my fingers ready.' For *what*? A lifetime with the Post Office? A page-turner for the LSO? A short-order cook for cannibals?

Adam recently completely what we lovingly called his 'Burgess and Maclean Habit'. The one where he continually glanced over his shoulders (or up in the air) or out of the corner of his eye as though trying to see who was following him. In vain we asked him what he was afraid of. Monsters? Kidnappers? Norman Tebbit? Where had we gone wrong with our child? His eyes flickered in his sleep and he began to resemble one of Ken Livingstone's salamanders. Then, one day, he stopped doing it, and we stopped asking why, so he told us. Apparently, he'd been told by some passing mystic – probably his grandfather – that God was everywhere, so he was trying to catch a glimpse of Him before He dematerialised; an attempt to outwit the Almighty at his own game, I suppose. It's as well to give up on that one as early as possible.

Amy's forte as a baby was 'gurning'. You've seen those octogenarian toothless wonders who win a yard of Real Ale by wrapping their gums round the back of their left ear while squinting up their own nostril. Well, Amy, who, in retrospect must have been teething at the time, was a brilliant face-puller. She could twist her tiny features into two terrible expressions. One like a well-weathered gargoyle. The other like Marlon Brando in *On The Waterfront*. Passers-by, when I wheeled her out for a walk, would peer over the coverlet and coo 'Aaah, what a lovely . . . er . . . *pram!*' She could also pretend to be non-verbal, thereby encouraging folk to 'Goo-goo', 'Ga-ga', 'Who's a booty?', 'Who's a dinky-winky?' etc. She'd let them finish, then turn to me and say, '*She's* stupid, isn't she?' It never failed.

My mother counts. Well, all mothers count, of course, for a great deal, but mine counts under her breath. Stairs, as she goes up them. Socks, as she rolls them. Fishballs, as she packs them in Tupperware containers. Sometimes she takes on a resemblance to those old Greek ladies counting their rosaries. Mostly I think she's muttering under her breath how sharper than a serpent's tooth it is to have a thankless child, but no, it's just another dumpling having its number taken before it hits the boiling salted water. She also hums in the middle of sentences:

HER: Do you think I should go back to the Dental Hospital with this crown? *The hills fill my heart hmmm, hm, hm . . .*
ME: Well, yes, if it's still hurting. Is it still hurting?
HER: Well, no, not really – *My heart wants to hmmm, hmmm, hm, hmm.* Well, it did this morning – *hmmmm, mmm, hmm – once more.*
ME: Well, go back there and tell them.
HER: (*adamantly*) Nooo! It's perfectly all right! *Hmm, hm, hm, hm, like a lamb when it, hm, hm.* Except when I eat. But I'm going *back. Hmm, mm,* would you?

My mother's habits have always been legendary amongst my immediate friends. Since I was interviewed by Bel Mooney on Channel 4's *Mothers By Daughters*, they've reached a larger audience. I was terribly worried about how she would view the programme, since when I accepted the job I had honestly thought it was all going to be all sweetness and light and a few gentle anecdotes. It turned out to be a rather harrowing analysis of the mother-daughter relationship, with said daughter in a pretty tearful state.

I persuaded Mum and Dad to come down before the programme was broadcast so I could show them the video. I couldn't watch. I paced up and down outside like a pre-natal parent. Afterwards I went in. The subject was wreathed in smiles.

'*That* was the *best* television programme I've ever *seen!*' she said in her special over-emphatic delivery. '*Fancy* them being able to make a *whole* programme all about *me*! And so *long*! Wasn't it *marvell*ous!' Etc., etc., etc. It was only a few hours later over the dishes that she turned to me and said: 'One thing I didn't understand. What were you crying for?'

Is it true you only see what you want to see? I felt light-headed and exonerated. The question which had precipitated my downpour was 'Do you love her?' The answer of course was 'yes'. Who could fail to love someone with such aberrations? Once, we lived in a flat where the gates were flanked by two concrete balls. Inevitably she would tell the cab driver: 'It's the one with the two round white things on the gate.' If we entered a garage she would wind down the car window and ask 'Do you happen to have such a thing as a mechanic on the job?' She would then look round in wonderment when we all snorted. After the SWET Awards, when I had missed out on the Best Actress Award for *Messiah*, she phoned me and said:

'I watched the "do", on television. Did you enjoy the evening?'

'Well, it was OK. You know . . . a bit disappointing.'

'Why? Wasn't the food any good?'

She also has an unerring need to clean behind my fitted furniture, use vats of Vim on my cookware, re-arrange all my clothes in my wardrobe and dictate to me the words I should use when phoning a complaint: 'Just phone them. *I* would. Say "*Hello*, are you *there*? *My* name is Mrs Rosenthal and I'm phoning to *complain* about the *flood* on the floor of my *utility* room. My husband and I have been *unable* to go to *Marbella* and I have had to *wait* in . . ." Then, if he says . . .' and so on and so on, until I hand over the phone and suggest she does it for me. A suggestion greeted by a loud 'NO O-O-O-O! I wouldn't know what to *say*!'.

My father has one major habit, and that is his forgetfulness. It's a familial complaint. Once, my brother and I, after weeks of long-distance intrigue and laborious Geneva/Hull/London arrangements, bought him a car. It was to be delivered, with a huge ribbon round it, on the morning of his birthday. At about noon I rang through and sang two choruses of Happy Birthday To You, before he replied: 'Thank you, sweetheart, that's very nice of you, very nice indeed. How are you?'

'Fine. Have you had a nice day so far?'

'Very, very nice indeed, love. How's Jack?'

'Oh, he's OK, thanks . . . Get any nice . . . er . . . cards?'

'Oh, yes, thank you very much. How are the kids?'

At this point I heard my mother bansheeing from the kitchen –

'The *car*, Maurice! The *car*! Have you gone stark raving *mad*! Say something about the *car*!'

At which point, and thus prompted, he remembered his two-ton present and waxed more fulsome than Sir Richard Attenborough being given an award. And you know how fulsome that is. I often wonder what would happen if you gave him a biscuit and a cup of Typhoo.

I suppose my most infuriating habit over the years has been my ability to shake my head and say 'Yes'. I've done it with jobs, I've done it with charities. Where it gets dangerous, of course, is when you do it with men. Years ago I was inveigled into a London hotel by an American who had phoned me out of the blue having seen me in a film on the plane over. It was his masterful technique which lured me:

'Be at the Langham Hotel in one hour. Do not wear black velvet trousers.'

The latter was a relief as I didn't possess any. I shook my head, but over the phone it didn't register. I shared a flat with three girls in those days, so without telling them I was going on a blind date with an actor whose only confessed film appearance was in *The Boston Strangler*, I took a taxi into town.

Striding towards me was a cowboy who was very handsome, six foot four at least, and wearing fringed boots, leather jacket and ten gallon hat. I was, of course, 'dressed up', since I assumed trousers were not *comme il faut*, in long black skirt, white organza blouse and with some kind of dead animal around me. This was 1969 and I'd never seen anything like him and he'd never seen anything like me. Particularly since the film he'd seen me in was *Up The Junction* where I was dressed like a tart. I thought of walking straight past him but it was too late.

'Marine?' he drawled. (They always call me that.)

'Er, yes, hello.'

'Hi.' He gazed deep into my mascara. 'I thought we could have a bite in my suite, so we can really talk.'

I shook my head again. And said yes. I was doomed.

We had cold beef and salad, and I was dessert. But, worry not, this is after all not the habits of Joan Collins and if the story ended any other way than how it did I wouldn't be telling it to you. Not at this price, anyway.

I saved my skin and several other bits of me by going into such a comedy routine that the gentleman concerned was first astonished, then amused, then hysterical, then incapable. I don't know where the jokes came from – That Great Comedy Store in the Sky, maybe – but were they thick and were they fast! Finally, I picked my way across his body, hitched up my skirt and went back to the Finchley Road Tube Station. All the way home I kept repeating, 'Aren't you a lucky girl then?' And shaking my head in reply.

Another man I never got to grips with was Mr Habit himself, a writer friend whose peculiarity was to do everything by the clock. And I do mean *everything*. (His life was so ordered that he actually had a chart in the kitchen listing the favourite beverages of all his friends. So it would say 'Jack – coffee – no sugar; Maureen – tea – one sugar; Denis – coffee – two saccharines'. Thus the appropriate drink would be placed on the occasional table directly your wellies hit the welcome mat.)

Morning ablutions were scheduled from 7.32 to 7.45. Press-ups from 7.46 to 7.59. Writing was from 8 till 12 and 1 till 6 . . . then came the evening! He would ring a girlfriend's number from a chart Buddied to the phone, and invite her round at roughly 7.24 precisely. At 7.24 precisely, the doorbell rang and the exquisitely trained woman arrived. Seductive music played for exactly half an hour. After that, the bedroom door closed and, I am reliably informed, the real split-second timing began. Foreplay, 4 minutes. Earlobes, 3 minutes and 28 seconds. Left breast, 6 minutes; right breast, 8. It would make an interesting Olympic sport, wouldn't it? Synchronised sex. Particularly if you did it underwater. With a peg on your nose. Smiling.

Finally, I want all Ye of Little Habits to step forward and confess. Raise your right hand – we won't look at your chewed nails – if going into a bookshop makes you want to go to the loo. Yes, I thought so. Too many to count. All of you sinners – all of you used to read your comic in the only private place in the house, didn't you? Well, the damage is irrevocable, I'm afraid. From now on the mere sight of a W. H. Smith bag will act on you like a bowl of prunes in a seaside hotel. I'd like to extemporise on the subject but – if you'll excuse me – I have to run.

Stories out of School

The deadline was up last week. Number One Daughter's next school. The decision, when made, was split-second. The build-up to the decision was just the ten years. It accelerated, of course, during the last few months. We began to bore for London and the Home Counties last February and have been emptying rooms at parties with unerring regularity ever since. Rather in the way I used to delve into people's kitchens to compare their fitted towel and tea-cloth-recess with mine, I began delving into people's educational experiences or what I larkily called 'Keith Joseph and his Quota Many Scholars'. Now this not only bores the bum off you, but it bores the bum off me. Until this present crisis, that is.

Now I'm hungry for details of Emily's mastering of the Common Entrance and Joshua's being offered the Chair of Divinity at Westminster aged eight. I crave the ratio of children to computers at one comprehensive, the number of cornets per orchestra at another, gasp with awe at tales of Remedial Maths and Social Studies.

What do I mean? In my day the only remedy for lousy maths was a lousy detention. The only social we studied was the Maccabi Club on a Sunday night. Wasn't life easier when you just accelerated to the Scholarship, put down your choice, sat the exam, failed it and went into the family business? None of this 'Open Evening' business then. Four hundred school-phobic parents on hard wooden chairs. As browbeaten now as the last time they occupied them a quarter of a century ago. The air thick with the smell of massed anxiety. Like tarts displaying their wares in the Reeperbahn – 'Hey, stranger, looking for a lovely time?' 'Hey, teacher, looking for a gifted child?'

Sometimes you have a guided tour of the schools in your area to select your *first* choice. By which I mean your *only* choice. The schools regretfully make it clear that there's such a bunfight to get in, you'd better not shop elsewhere or you don't even stand to get a bun.

And this, mind, is your State education. Once you enter the private sector, the competition is so ferocious that ten-year-olds attend crammer courses in 'Exam Technique'! Presumably this means simulating exam conditions. You know – the clock-ticking silence, the palm-sweating sickness, the pressure and sheer, bloody, blind panic. As my father would say, 'Listen . . . As long as the kids are happy   '

33

One Open Evening was due to begin at 8.30. I duly arrived at 8.25 to find that the headmistress had been in full throttle for several minutes. How's that for up Lipman-ship? The hall was jammed with eager parents, fresh from the strain of exchanging contracts to move into the catchment area. There were no seats vacant and the only way to catch any of the Head's heavily cultured pearls was to mount the stage behind her and sit on the late-comers' benches. 'What a grand idea for a first night,' I thought, as I Marcel Marceau'd my way past the other sinners. 'Excuse me,' whispered one of them, 'could I have your autograph?'

Now, I could tell from the Head's back that I wouldn't like her front. Her patter contained such winning phrases as 'I'm afraid I'm unable to invite prospective parents to look around my school' . . . 'No child who excels at English will be considered if her Maths is weak' . . . and my all-time favourite . . . 'One might say you need us rather more than we need you'. Later, she exonerated herself totally by announcing that 'there is a strong emphasis on oral work in all French letters'. By the time she'd corrected herself, four hundred sharp intakes of breath had been quelled by four hundred sharp elbows in ribs, and the only sound in the hall was that of M Lipman laughing in a matter first patented by one Sybil Fawlty.

So there we are. The decision is made. Needless to say we chose the school that means a sixty-minute round trip twice a day as opposed to the five-minute walk round the corner with friends. I keep waking up to the smell of burning boats. Alan Bennett in his play *Forty Years On* (and here I misquote) 'Education is what we remember when we've forgotten everything we've been taught.' Primary-ly the smell of the Headmaster, nicotine and sulphur from every pore and orifice. Tiny toilets and miniature milk bottles. Interminable afternoon rests that now I'd kill for. The mysterious 'fold your hands' dictum. What did they think we were doing with them in front of forty-nine other kids? Or did it just look tidier?

Secondary-ly, I remember the bike ride to school and the bus ride home. No, it makes no sense to me either, but that's what I remember. School dinners. Each day I swapped my main course for my friend's puddings. I lived on treacle sponge, tapioca, sago and Fly Cemetery for eight years. Even today the skin on a baked rice pudding can fill me with lust.

Wheeling my bike tyres over yet another appalling report to try and make it illegible: ' aureen is a t lly disr ptive fluence', and fooling no one. Smoking on the train to Wembley with the school Games Captain and others. Two puffs, seven coughs and they had us brown-handed. The interminable queue outside the Head's office and the Games Captain's brilliant alibi: 'Smoking is my only cure for period pains'. Brilliant because the mention of the word 'period' in any context other than 'Double' or 'Free' rendered the Headmistress comatose with embarrassment and we found ourselves dismissed in a puff of smoke.

The dear Geography teacher whose severe speech defect coupled with my natural indolence ensured that at the age of twenty six I still thought China was an island. The eccentric seventy-eight-year-old gym teacher with a shock of white hair, navy knee-length divided shorts, beige floor-length divided legs and a skeleton in the cupboard.

The skeleton's name was Jimmy, and with his unanimated assistance she taught us Hygiene. And you know what that meant: s-x, pr-cr-ation and p-r—ds, on which subjects most of my gang could have given the Reith Lecture with illustrated slides. In fact, it's the 'gang' I remember most. Marilyn the artist, Ann the voice, Jenny the enigma, Paddy the innocent, Kay the experience, and me, the court jester. By the time we were of an age to be revered by the Third Years, we'd already established an end-of-term routine. The school would 'surge' us on to the playing fields, make a huge circle, sit down and wait for the show. It was like Woodstock without the sex.

Once seated, they set up a chant – '*The* Horse! *The* Horse! *The* Horse!' And they were never disappointed. 'The Horse' was a poem my brother learnt in California. A very young child (me) is bullied by its pushy mother (Ann) to recite. She reluctantly comes on (i.e. is thrown) and proceeds with much lisping, stammering and hitching of knickers, to recite 'The Horse, by Maureen Lipman' – except it never gets further than the fourth line because she constantly gets the details wrong:

> 'Ve horth is ananimal wot lives in a field
> And eatsth grath all day,
> It has two ears, two eyes, two legth,
> And a coat of pearly gr . . .

Oh, no. Two legth? Ve horth?' (huge raspberry, followed by much squirming and looking through legs upside down). Then . . . 'The Horth, by Maureen Lipman . . . Ve hrth is ananimal etc. etc.' The audience-hysteria would build as the child repeatedly cocks up the poem, and it reached its peak as she begins to need the loo. Badly. Since the mother won't hear of letting her leave till she's finished reciting, the poem gets faster and more garbled than ever and is accompanied by violent squirming, knee and eye crossing and attempts at escapology. Finally, poem and contortions reach a grand climax and, midstream as it were, she quietly pees on the stage and watches its trail with silent fascination. Then, on a tremulously rising inflection – 'And that is the end of The Horth, by

35

Maureen Lipman', she does unspeakable mime to indicate the state of her underwear, socks, and shoes.

It's not easy to describe (as if you hadn't noticed), but it was the crowd-pleaser to end them all. We added a few vicious impersonations of the staff, including the Headmistress' habit of fiddling with the buttons of her blouse nearest to her . . . chests . . . (arf! arf!), topical jokes re Semolina v. Fly Cemetery school dinners and suggestions of where to put them, and ended with a song spoof based on current TV, *Double Your Money* or *Dr Kildare*. Then, amidst stamping and cheering, we ran off leaving them wanting more. Afterwards mob scenes took place in the bike sheds, where we signed hundreds of tattered autograph books . . . 'If in life you want to make all/Deal the cards and shut your cake-hole'. Up school! Up school! Right up school! Howdy and Goodbye [signature p.58], Lower VI and other major witticisms.

It all seems very innocent now when you consider we were about sixteen years old. I went to my daughter's last-day party at primary school and it was very different. Many of the girls, at eleven years of age, looked like certifiable jailbait . . . Ear-rings, swinging mini-dresses and wild, fuzzy hair flying to the thud of the disco beat. All very well, I hear you retort, times change and you're a dreary reactionary. Except these huge, pubescent girls and some of their giant counterparts amongst the boys had spent almost the entire year bullying my child to the extent we couldn't get her out of the house in the morning.

It got so bad that Jack spent one whole lunch hour crouched behind the railings watching two of these girls, described by him as resembling two nineteen-year-old hookers, tripping up littler kids and roaring their victories to imaginary crowds. He reckoned they just didn't know what to do with their physicality. I knew what to do with mine though. But I wasn't allowed near the place since it was assumed I would bang their mean heads together as soon as look at them. I would have.

'The happiest days of your lives'. Whoever said that was either contorted by hindsight or hadn't had an afternoon rest since 1945. But, rest assured, that's what I'll be telling my daughter from now till next September. 'Don't let school interfere with your education,' said George Bernard Shaw. When will we ever learn?

Pumping Irony

I've been thinking lately about 'working my body'. Feeling that 'burn', perhaps even releasing the odd modicum of oxygen to my brain. It's mostly because when I go out people keep asking me what's wrong. I can't face my face first thing in the morning – so in order to avoid the confrontation I stagger out of the house looking like the Ghost of Christmas Past, and spend all day answering thoughtful queries from members of the public about how long I've got to live.

However, a change of rhythm is definitely needed, and I've nothing but praise for the power of physical exertion. At present my idea of a good work-out is a two-hour worry about the bags under my eyes, but in the past I have dabbled in legwarmer-land, in fact, many's the morning you may have glimpsed me on the way out of my Lotte Berk muscle-tightening class, blithely attempting to walk unaided to my car, both legs shaking so violently that I am forced to seek support from passing wing mirrors.

Before jogging gave you anorexia, I was out there on the Heath breaking in my track suit and hoping I looked as though I'd been doing it since the days it was called 'running'. I started out as the book suggested, at 15 minutes – worked my way up to 17, back down to 10, and packed it in.

For a short spell I jogged around the park, with the kids, *before school*. One morning we jogged down to the animal enclosure, where one of the llamas entertained us with the world's largest, loudest and most vituperative fart. It convulsed all three of us so much, that every other morning was an anti-climax, and we packed that in too. (I like to think that the llama was somehow expressing her subtle comment on the whole exercise boom.)

Then it was swimming. Just back from holiday with the right number of white stripes, I made the decision to keep up the swimming, ignoring the fact that it was not quite the same without iced coke, bougainvillaea and a language barrier. The swim itself was fine – it's the software which depressed me. The fight for supremacy between myself, a 5p piece, and an old tin locker. The 'OH, YES, YOU WILL GO IN.' 'OH, NO, I WON'T.' 'OH, YES, YOU WILL.' – Kick – OW! syndrome.

The changing cubicle with the curtain which just covers your thighs so you are forced to undress hunched into a figure of eight by shyness and cold. The journey to the aforementioned locker, re-arranging your pile of clothes into the order required for putting them back on again. The fight to open the locker. The fight to lock it. The right to re-open it when you discover you've still got your glasses on. The shamefaced dodge through the obligatory shower. The chill of real fear when you discover the pool to be full of seven hundred post-examination sixth-formers who've been sent there to work off excess energy.

All this and nothing to look forward to but the return journey. An action replay with hypothermia. Finding the number of the locker without your glasses. Attempting to wrench the elastic band and key off your damp and deeply grooved wrist. And finally – the unkindest cut of all – apart from the one on your wrist – the inevitable fall of your knickers on to the sodden floor as you balance upside down on the cubicle bench, trying to put your socks on in private. Then it's a wet head hitting the outside air, and soggy cellulite all the way home. Uphill.

There must be an easier way of dealing with fatty deposits. I like yoga. The people are nice, the pace is civilised, and nobody dresses like a shiny barber's pole, or yells, 'Listen up! – stretch that tendon!' And karate was great. Once I'd got over the embarrassment. There's a good deal of bowing and saying 'oos' involved, you see, and my cousin Maurice's judo suit did tend to stay the same rigid shape with or without me in it. But nobody laughed at me. Nobody laughed at anything. The discipline is everything, and when thirty-five people all make the same movement and shout 'Ki-ay!' at the same time, it's as beautiful as any ballet. Of course, the first time I heard it I thought I'd been shot and fell over!

Why did I give up? I suppose lack of dedication and competitiveness, really. I felt the same way about ski-ing. Something to do with dressing up in funny clothes, dragging yourself and twelve pounds of equipment half way up a mountain, frightened to death and maroon-nosed, just to come down again. Too much like show-business for my money.

The best part of a 'long-run' in the world of exercise, is the weekly camaraderie. That brave bunch of faces, thighs and accents who give up their every Wednesday in pursuit of keeping, catching or betraying their man. How I loved the sessions of ruthless self-punishment, all done on automatic pilot, whilst the stories of sex in the suburbs poured breathlessly out. I always wanted to write a play about it: 'And stretch-two-three – *he didn't!* – Lift those buttocks – *so what did you say? – You didn't!!* And heels back over your head – *You know, if I were you, I'd write to Claire Rayner about that* – And relax those legs-two-three – *I mean, it's not natural!*'

Still I can't help feeling that the bottom is about to fall out of the exercise boom, if you'll pardon the pun. It may be good for our self-esteem to have a body beautiful – but when you look around at some of the high priestesses, I doubt it. 'Britt Ekland's Sensual Fitness Programme' screamed a tabloid hoarding. I know – I shouldn't have read on – but once you've dirtied your hands and dressing-gown on a Sunday paper, you might as well dirty your mind. One of the pearls dropped by our comely Swede is that an all-over massage with warm oil is the perfect prelude for a night of love-making. I must remember that next time I'm cleaning out the chip pan. There are also exercises to firm and trim the 'muscles you need for love'. Like your brain, presumably. And others to raise the bottom. Alternatively you could just read articles like Britt's and have the bum *bored* off you.

In other words, it's just another psychological soft-sell. A part of the 'I'm OK, you're OK – I love my body i.e. I love myself, therefore I can give you L.O.V.E.' and other such self-congratulatory clap-trap. I mean, are we entirely what we look as well as what we eat? Sure it would be nice to look like Joan Collins at fifty – it would also be nice if it didn't matter if we looked like Sandy Gall! Look at Mrs Thatcher (it's all right, it's only for a minute, I promise). Look at that careful, combed, co-ordinated image. A calculated look for a calculating woman. And of course the public loves it! Because she's made the best of herself? Or because the Saatchi Brothers have made the best of Herself.

Equally, they revile Mrs Shirley Williams on the grounds that she has flyaway hair and dresses for comfort – i.e. she *is* herself. All I'm saying is – doesn't 'Body Consciousness' finally negate all the insecurities, eccentricities, charm and therefore humour which grow alongside dumpy defects? May I produce the evidence here, me Lud, in order to pour vitriol from a great height on to legwarmer-land and Fondaerobics. I took part in a radio interview not long ago together with an apostle of weight-training for women. She was gorgeous. She was glowing. She was fulfilled. (I know all this because she told us so.) She was also wearing a leotard. On radio? I heard myself getting cross and so did several thousand listeners. If only some fully flexed, flawless, fatless proselyte would admit that the chief reason for their love of leaping into print on the joys of exercise was MONEY.

There's a bandwagon going round. It went around turning dance halls into bingo halls and bowling alleys. It forced us all into wearing a hula-hoop instead of a waspie, it put us on skateboards, it fastened a yo-yo to our fingers and it forced the same fingers round a Rubik cube. It's very, very clever and a lot of people are getting very, very rich from it, and bloody good luck to them. I just don't happen to subscribe to a programme which is never going to turn me into Victoria Principal. If it helps while away the hours, terrific! If it keeps a few kids by the barre instead of by the bar, even better. If it brings a sense of companionship and well-being to both housewives and sweat-band manufacturers – Hallelujah! Just so long as that's all, just so long as it ain't a new Messiah. Oh, please, not that. Don't let him come in footless tights and wristbands with an Adidas bag. That's all I ask – I never could stand organised worship.

However. Before some kindly soul points out that she saw me there, I wish to confess. I joined a health club last year. I did it partly because of the swimming pool, partly because in my new role as lack-of-exercise-pundit, I was hoping for a discount. Unfortunately, my punditry didn't reach as far as North London, and I jolly well paid what everyone else paid and lumped it. (Whatever does that mean? 'If you don't like it, *lump it*' – I've wondered for decades!)

My membership allowed me to swim, jacuzzi or sauna till 6 o'clock weekdays, and from 6 pm at weekends. This made me an off-peak member – which could hardly describe me better. The kids were extra every time. They loved it, pin-ball machines, video, food bar and all – and wanted to go every day. There was, however, a preponderance of women who swam in pairs in gold eye-shadow, who shouted at the kids for being there. Their entire reason for being there was to get away from *theirs*. Once, in mid-breast stroke, an elderly man swam up and said, 'I hope you don't mind my asking but I wonder if you could define the nature of good comedy?' I almost drowned. Then, treading water, I gave him a considered and rather erudite analysis of the whole business – which you'll find dried out in a later chapter. At the end of my diatribe he said, 'Because I'm the treasurer of the East Ambleside Amateur Players group and I wondered if your husband could write a play for us?'

I think I really blew it with the 'Born Again Bounce Brigade' on *The Gloria Hunniford Show* last year. I was the first guest, followed by Frank Carson, the mad Irish comic, and a certain American movie star, Miss Raquel Welch, flogging her fitness philosophy and, incidentally, her book. We didn't meet before the show as she was late arriving from Manchester, but rumours filtered through that she had already astonished the researcher by demanding a hard-boiled egg. Then, it seems, they got her into the make-up room and Frank Carson accosted her with his own special brand of blarney.

'Oh, Miss Welch,' he crowed, kissing her hand and arm, 'I've loved you since I was a boy.' You can imagine how well *that* went down – I mean, you don't even talk to these people except through their entourage, let alone insult them and handle their limbs. 'I want you to be in my latest fillum,' he went on, 'it's called *The Wreck of the Hesperus*.' Well. Suffice to say she ran from the make-up room and hid in the toilets. Presumably they lured her back with fresh hard-boiled eggs because it was in the make-up room monitor that she saw ME.

'You keep very slim, Maureen. Do you have a fitness routine yourself?' said a well-primed Gloria.

'Oh, absolutely. I couldn't function without it,' I bare faced. 'It's very arduous but I stick to it rigidly. What do I do? Well – first thing I do as soon as I wake up is have a total stretch. I stretch out my arm, like this, and wrap the fingers round a huge mug of tea – like this – bringing the mug up to the mouth, rather like this. Here I exercise all the muscles up this arm and in the mouth, neck and throat. After this, I lie back in the bed in a curled-up position – like this – and represent a sleeping cat. Thirty minutes later I wake up again, fall to the carpet and crawl into the bathroom, making low groaning noises, which exercise the vocal chords. Once in the bathroom I look in the mirror and go "Yaaarghhhh!" which, again works wonders in the chest cavity and waters the eyes. After this, I jog downstairs to the kitchen, stretch all the way up to the cupboard for a packet of salt and vinegar crisps and head for the front door. Then I close the door behind me, breathe and just walk . . . to the car, where I exercise the jaw and tongue muscles by screaming at passing drivers who try to carve me up . . .'

The audience were laughing and identifying away, as was Gloria, and a good time was had by all. Save one. Miss Welch was apparently apoplectic in the make-up room.

'Who is that woman? How dare they invite me on this show and make me follow that dreadful woman? I did NOT come here to be insulted, etc . . .' and out she stalked with her multi-coloured entourage in tow.

News travels fast in TV and within seconds the director, producer, researcher and probably a couple of hens were pleading with her in corridors, assuring her that I was absolutely nobody, that they had no idea I was going to say those terrible things, and certainly she could have a transcript of Gloria's questions and my answers.

Meanwhile, safe in my innocence of all this, I finished my shtick, and sat with Frank and Sandra Dickinson off stage in a little hospitality section. As Miss Welch tottered by, clad in a brown jersey dress that appeared to be on the *inside* of her skin, I patted the empty chair and said, 'Would you like to sit down?' Well, if looks could kill, I'd be writing this chapter sitting on a celestial cloud with a harp on my knee and wings on my glasses. Still in my ignorance, I thought that was just nerves. She did her bit and tottered off. Whereupon I said 'Well done' or 'Jolly good' or some equally fatuous remark. 'Thayank you,' she spat, and departed for ever.

Why am I telling you? To illustrate, as if you didn't already know, that if you look like Raquel Welch the last thing you need to develop is a sense of humour. I mean, can you imagine the average man in a hotel room with Raquel Welch saying, 'So what's new? You heard any good jokes lately?' No, of course you can't. Happens to me all the time.

I wonder if Golda Meir's life would have been more fulfilling if she'd read the chapter in Fonda's book on 'Beginners' Buttocks'? She might have lost her 'saddle-bags and falling butt' (sic) but would she have increased her charisma? She had more lovers than most of us have even fantasised over . . . and she looked like Lyndon Johnson's body double! I rest my face.

Travels With Me Aren't ...

Our friend Willis can't wait for us to go on holiday. That is, he can't wait for us to come back. I can hear his little long-distance voice (live from Keighley): 'Well, go on then – what went wrong?' And of course, the more gruesome the tale, the more helpless the glee. And we never disappoint him. From the moment the post-Christmas palms and oil-skinned nymphettes start swaying across the corner of my living-room, and the voices of the richest actors in the land seduce me to foreign climes, I shut my eyes and think of Willis. Somehow this keeps me well clear of my local Travelorama. Like good wine, our family does not travel well.

It started long before I ever had one. A family of my own, I mean. As a Yorkshire child we invariably took our fortnight's jaunt in Bridlington, Hornsey or Scarborough – occasionally venturing down south as far as Tankerton or Margate. The familiar photographs of my brother and me in one-piece bathing suits – one piece each, of course – and wind-swept hair, brandishing spades and teeth, cover the fountain at Butlins as well as the Esplanade at Eastbourne. I don't remember much about these holidays except that the countryside never entered into them. There was sand, sea, ice cream, small hotels and amusement arcades in the rain. 'Give the kids five bob's worth of change, Maurice. We'll be having a cup of tea in the Palm Court lounge – all right? Just there, this side of the road, so don't cross. The Palm Court. Don't forget. Tuck your vest in, Geoffrey. Pinch your cheeks, Maureen. And don't talk to any strange men!' Geoffrey leaping off to get away from the child who'd foiled his life by being born. Me spending two shillings on the 'lucky dip' – a prize every time, and the rest on the Laughing Clown, loving the crowd which gathered round.

No camping, though; or climbing; or walking; or cycling. Not for a nice Jewish family. It was just an extension of home really, where Mother didn't have to cook – and boy, could we taste the difference. Or even oy, could we taste the difference. 'Do you know that's the whole pleasure of a holiday to me, not having to cook, just having it put in front of you and just getting up and leaving all the mess behind you.' Only thirty years later do I understand what she meant.

My strongest memory is of a Blackpool guest-house where our two holidaying families were served cracked cups of tea in the cramped and mangy lounge by a disreputable, greasy-jacketed waiter. It was on Day

Two it became highly obvious that we'd made a bad choice. My mother, returning from the loo, stage-whispered: 'Those toilets are absolutely filthy.' The waiter, who actually had his thumb in the teacup when he filled it, looked up sharply. 'Oh, sorry about that, love, I'll go and see to that right away.' Putting down the cup, he left the lounge, returning minutes later to continue his pouring. 'Did you tell someone?' said my mother as he handed her a plate of sandwiches. 'Nah, there wuz no one about, so I just give it a quick lick over meself while I were at it. Do you want sugar with this, love?'

By the time I was a teenager, holidays meant gaggles of girls and 'Abroad'. By the age of fourteen my brother, as president of the B'nai Brith youth club, had been chosen to represent England at an American summer camp. He'd set off a callow boy and returned a Callowfornian. I was hoping for the same glint two years later, when I was elected to go to the same camp. I was jubilant when I phoned home the news, and positively distraught when they refused point-blank to let me go. One law for the son, another for the daughter. Sexism would never hit me so hard again. I was devastated, and still mourn the woman I might have been had I gone. Instead I stayed tied to those pinny strings and my teenage years were shambolic because of it. The rebellion which hovered did not emerge for another twenty years. But that's another story. And another book.

In 1966 I travelled with a party of young things to Israel. I was sixteen years old, not particularly sweet, and as green as baize. None of which prevented me from becoming shipbound confidante for the sexual goings-on of the entire party. How wisely and with how much nodding of sage head did I advise one particularly enthusiastic participant of Deck Coitus to give her sailor the elbow, and how round were my eyes when she informed me she'd given him a good deal more than her elbow – 'twice' – on the maindeck – standing up! I learned a lot on that journey.

Once there and confined to a sort of kosher Butlins, I fell madly in love with a visiting actor chappy who didn't know I existed. The one overwhelmingly important conversation I had with him, seated under the high stilts which supported the building, was somewhat interrupted by the nightly camp ritual – when the entire area was sprayed with fertiliser – a rare case of the shit actually hitting the fan.

The return journey was by train and was dampened by Arthur, the organiser, a bizarre, red-faced little Scotsman who spent the entire three weeks trying (and failing) to get laid. In his pursuit of a spot of earth-moving he had omitted to purchase 'return tickets for his party', who, therefore, were forced to stand all the way from Athens to Calais. This would have been just about bearable had not my presents included a

4' × 3' representation of the Ancient City of Jerusalem (executed in fluorescent paint on black felt) with which I scarred the moving parts of every passenger who had the temerity to seek a way past me in search of the non-existent buffet car.

Rimini, Ibiza, Majorca – my album reveals the same shots of the same giggle of girls on identical beaches, in identical two-piece costumes, squinting into the sun, coke bottles held high and flanked by boys never seen before or since the photograph was taken. You'd think your whole life was spent on a beach, wouldn't you? Or blowing out candles.

It wasn't till I met Jack though, that I became a really seasoned traveller. Take our trip to the Dordogne – we borrowed a tiny cottage in Riberac and motored down there, stocking up on cheese and wine just as the colour supplements tell you to. The sun blazed down, the cottage was divine and I developed a sun rash which turned my skin piebald. I cut out the wine and cut out the cheese and finally, cut out of the area – but not before we'd indulged ourselves in one really fine French meal in a four-star hotel picked from the *Guide Michelin*. The outside of the Hotel d'gastro-itis was covered in badges, crests, stars, awards, and the inside won First Prize for gloom. We whispered our order to the maitre d' who appeared not to hear in French. We accepted with alacrity (which means 10 per cent) his suggestion, no, his command, that we start with the famous spécialité de la region, a home-made 'rillette'. In time (and by that I mean about a week and a half), a plate of axle grease was placed in front of us – I had an unshakable desire to be in the Golden Egg in Hounslow.

ME (*sotto voice*): 'Jack – we'll have to go.'
JACK: 'We can't. We've ordered.'
ME: 'It's alright, I'll be very ill.'

I stood up, swayed and reeled about in an over-the-top fashion and clutched the air saying, 'De l'eau, de l'eau.' Jack leapt to his feet, sending the priceless goose-grease flying in an arc de triomphe, and with a wave of traveller's cheques, and a flurry of 'pas necessaire', we found ourselves back outside the badges, the crests and the stars. By this time I was green in the face with the effort to be convincingly ill. 'Are you all right?' whispered Jack, half in character. 'You look terrible.' 'I know. Good, wasn't it?' I grinned and promptly threw up sur l'herbe.

Some months after the birth of our firstborn, we decided to take a ten-day break in the sun. It being February (I find it's usually February when there's a gap in our proceedings), we settled on the island of Tenerife as being the shortest flight to the warmest place. We packed the burn cream and the boiled sweets, left Amy with doting grandparents, and flew off misty-eyed at the thought of seeing her again.

We landed on the said rock through a set of cumulus and nimbus that could maybe be described as Mancunian. Grey was the day, wet was the weather, and on its merry way to Colombo was the luggage. After a desperate search and the subsequent filling in of many forms, we got on a bus filled with irate holidaymakers who tut-tutted us all the way down the aisle, and slowly bumped and ground our way to the hotel, which was full of small green bananas and one or two of Jack's relatives sheltering from the rain. (Apparently when the weather was going to be fine you could see the top of the mountain opposite. We never did.) Once there we discovered that the gourmet menu meant gourmet fish (unknown variety) and chips, gourmet chicken in a basket, and gourmet pizza followed by a small green gourmet banana. Beware of small green bananas, readers – they mean unjust desserts. We also had them for breakfast. After the third such breakfast of small green bananas, I noticed an alarming desire to hurl them at the wall. Which I gave vent to. The feeling was so satisfying, that I gave vent to it every morning of our stay. The weather only perked up for the last few days, and our phone bill was the price of a week in the Seychelles.

Portugal – in the Algarve – was pure pleasure. Willis was mortified, but we healed the rift with Florida – oh boy, and how! It started with the flight. Two kids under six, one au pair and a typhoon over Miami. The weather report said it was the worst February since 1946. The orange crop had been virtually annihilated. Fourteen hours and two identical styrofoam dinners later, we arrived at Miami airport having been re-routed via Boston. It was four o'clock in the morning, and oh wow, what a welcome! We stood for almost two hours in a slowly shuffling queue of Cuban immigrants and holiday-makers, whilst the Mafia-faced customs men barked 'Any plants, fruits or seeds?' into our fatigued faces. Once having convinced them that our last intention on earth was to smuggle aspidistras into their bloody country, we limped through the X-ray arch and all hell broke loose.

After our release and the confiscation of Adam's toy pistol, we drove through driving rain and actual hailstones to the hotel, and somehow got through the remaining fortnight. My most cherished memories are of schlepping the family around Disneyland with Joyce Grenfell-like enthusiasm, trying desperately to ignore the feeling that I'd somehow wandered on to the set of *The Prisoner*. (You know the sort of thing – a soft voice over the tannoy as you leave your car, 'You have parked your car in Dopey 412. Please remember that you have parked your car in Dopey 412. There are over 60,000 cars parked here every day . . . so if you forget that you've parked in Dopey 412 . . . we will be forced to set fire to your leg.')

My two eccentric children found a plot of concrete with a flower bed in which to continue their imaginary game, and ignored their surroundings. 'But darlings *look* – there's Mickey Mouse' – the real thing was actually standing there, human-sized and waiting to be patted.

'Oh, Mod – don't spoil our ga-ame, I'm being the mean school teacher and Adam is being Heidi.'

Exit Mickey stage left. Piqued.

Then there was that last-minute hol in Ibiza. Ever slept on a foam mattress in 85°F? I had to hang them out each morning for fear the chambermaid would think we were incontinent! Ever slept on a foam mattress with the hotel disco playing inside the bedroom? It wasn't till I got home and was lying in hospital with pneumonia that I realised the never-ending tune was 'Last Night a DJ Saved My Life', not 'Last Night a Bidet Saved My Life'. My version would've sold more copies!

Once we went to Menorca for two weeks, after a hectic stint in a West End farce. We traded one farce for another. As the plane touched down, with me hysterically chewing gum (for my ears) and praying (for my life), the pilot announced the weather conditions to be cloudy, drizzly and more or less beyond hope. At the airport we were met by the representative of the travel firm. No name, but it should be written in neon. She gave car keys to the rest of the party and sent them on their way. Not so with us. 'I'll drive, you follow,' she said, gamely adjusting her sou' wester. 'Why?' I ventured. 'Oh, you'd *never* find it on your own,' she tossed back over a wet shoulder. We drove in noisy silence till she suddenly took a vicious left off the road and up a dirt-track of red earth, strewn with unfinished concrete newel-posts. 'No!' I whimpered aggressively. 'Turn back, it's no good, I'm not staying!' Jack was calmer. (What do I mean was? *Is*.) 'Wait,' he screamed soothingly, 'it may be a short cut.' It was. To *another* dirt-track. At the end of which was a villa and nothing else. I was out of that car so fast the rain missed me completely. 'No good, can't stay, too desolate, too far from beach.' In vain she extolled the virtues of the villa, dishwasher and all. But one look at the swimming pool, set neatly in a pile of red rubble and open drainage was enough to propel me straight into the car and back across the island to the only other available villa. No pool, but on the beach. We took it. Damp, cold and uninhabited as it was. We unpacked everything, wrung out the sheets and were attempting to ask the Spanish housekeeper, in flawless pidgin, how to l-l-light the c-c-calor gas s-s-stove, when the front door opened and two suitcases came in. They were followed by the owner of the villa, who'd arrived unannounced for his annual two weeks' hols.

Suffice to say, we decided to move again, the moment he threw us out. This time to an even damper and more pool-less and beach-less villa. The rest of the meteorological disaster was spent drying socks and knickers over the stove and rubbing butter on a stray dog's ticks. That made you prick up your ears, didn't it? It had much the same effect on the dog. It's an old Swedish custom, apparently, and one that seems to work. The tick, not being Swedish, is obviously shocked to the core when buttered, so that the mere flick of a forefinger sends it leaping on its way like greased lightning. A bit like us, on our way home. No more. No more holidays abroad. 'Jack,' I swore, 'if I ever mention going abroad again I want you to hit me on the head with a rolled up travel agent.'

Best hols I ever had was one week in St Tropez out of season. There was a gang of us. One couple had a flat there they'd rented each autumn for twenty-four years, they knew the place backwards. Every day we'd drive to a beautiful empty beach and bask there. At lunchtime we ate French fries, and I can still taste them. In the evening we strolled around the bars and shops, dined like kings and laughed till two. We almost managed the language, too, after a shaky start. My friends Julia and Jerry, Jack and I sat in a café debating who had the courage to ask for something to munch on before dinner arrived. Finally I called the waiter and said, 'We are hungry', in well-rehearsed French. He raised an eyebrow and left. 'Nous avons faim, s'il vous plait' had come out 'Avez-vous femme?' And even in France they balk at asking for a woman before dinner.

I must add a postscript to the tale of St Tropez. It was September when we were there, and the following February, Bobby and her husband, Derek, the ringleader of the expedition, asked us all round for a 'Paella Reunion'. We hadn't seen the old crowd since the holiday and, in a flash of foolishness, I suggested to Jack that we should turn up exactly as they'd last seen us. Now, it would have been a quaint idea in, say, early May, or even late December, but this was not only February, it was the coldest February since the Punic Wars, and the ground was frozen to a sheet of ice. Everyone walked miles to the tube station rather than taking their cars up the glaciers, and I remember with pleasure Jack walking me to Highgate Tube to record an episode of *Agony* at Waterloo. The reason I remember it so vividly is that it was our first chance to talk to each other alone and unexhausted for seven years.

But I digress, which at this stage of the book will not surprise you. I wore a blue and white bikini, a large sun-hat with cherries on, plastic beach shoes, sunglasses and a nose-guard. Jack wore trunks, flippers, a sun-visor, a beach bag and a large out-of-season water melon from Fortnums (which cost more than the holiday!). We applied sun-tan cream in zig-zag lines ready for smearing. We wore coats over this but we were less than comfortable and stopping at the off-licence for a bottle of Pouilly-Fuissé beggars description.

The car slowly crawled the distance to Hampstead and painfully slid up

Parliament Hill. Then Jack uttered the fateful sentence: 'What number do Bobby and Derek live at?' It would take a whole other book to describe our knocking at all the basement-flat doors in Parliament Hill, and the numbers which slammed in our sun-creamed faces. We began by asking for Bobby's number, but after a while, we asked only for shelter from the blinding, freezing cold. When we reached their flat, we were speechless, blue and totally numb.

And the hosts? They were too hysterical to ask us in! We stood at the door like two stalactites on vacation, whilst they hooted and pointed and wept and rolled on the floor clutching their innards. Of course, we'd forgotten to bring clothes and had to be kitted up in sweaters and pyjama bottoms, but it was actually worth it. As the dinner progressed, there was always someone who would look at us in mid-conversation, and explode all over again, till we all lay exhausted over the paella. It was a bit like a holiday, really.

There is a joke which goes: 'What's the difference between Los Angeles and yoghurt?' The answer is: 'Yoghurt has a live culture.' Los Angeles is the place Jack goes to have his hair greyed, his lines delineated and his cranium numbed. It's the place where the sky is always blue and so are the screenwriters. Where the storyline is accepted on Monday by the twenty-four-year-old head of a studio, and rejected on the Thursday by his sixteen-year-old replacement. It is the place where eye-bags are called 'allergy sacks', and A *Bridge Too Far* is the only person in town who hasn't had his nose fixed.

'In *Movie of the Week*,' said one pubescent studio executive, 'we work on three kinds of scenario – Heart, Stomach and Groin.' He paused for effect. 'Heart means love, Stomach means horror and Groin means sexploitation.'

'Really?' mused Jack, 'I'm afraid I only do elbow.'

Don't laugh. The next day the guy phoned Jack's agent and said, 'We have to work with this Britisher who only does elbow – sounds really interesting.'

Another time he went into an office and heard the producer speaking to his girlfriend on the phone. 'Come over and pick me up, honey,' he yawned, 'I'll be through in fifteen minutes. I just gotta see this schmuck from England.'

By the time she arrived, he'd discovered that Jack had written the Streisand film *Yentl*. 'Come in, sweetheart, I want you to meet one of England's greatest writers. This man is dynamite, he is responsible for some of the finest screenwriting . . .'

'Hello,' said Jack, 'I'm the schmuck from England.'

This trip I went with him. No one was going to treat my man mean without getting a couple of my fingers in the eyes by way of explanation. I determined to hate the place. I wasn't going to work there – not that I'd been asked to. No one knew me from Eve. Still, I thought, I might perhaps see a few agents whilst I was there, so before I left I phoned my agent and said, 'Whilst I'm there, should I, er, you know, should I do anything?'

'Oh, yes, darling,' she said, brightly, 'Could you bring me some Georgio perfume?'

I had a ball. We reached the airport to find that Jack's first-class seat had not been cashed in for two in club class as promised, but that *he* was in club and I appeared to be in a locker on flight-deck. Mind you, I was travelling as 'wife', which is Californian for hand luggage! That was easily solved – you just put your hand in your pocket and pay out more money than you have earned in six weeks, and the problem disappears like magic.

The flight itself was a lark owing to the fact that most of the stewards were fans of *Agony*, it was our twelfth wedding anniversary – the polystyrene one, isn't it? – and they bombarded us with enough champagne and British Airways toilet bags to bath Cleopatra. We watched Ryan O'Neal in *Irreconcilable Differences*, which should have won an award – for us, I mean, for sitting through it – and arrived in LA ready to do the town. At four o'clock in the morning, English time, we sat down to our evening meal, then strolled back to our hotel, which was swarming with large black bodyguards with walkie-talkie machines and large black transit vans, who were on guard for small black superstar, Prince, who was staying there.

Each day I met old friends and shopped. Since the dollar was almost at parity with the pound, a pair of dungarees for Amy cost £40. Still, when the guilt sets in because you're here and they're there, £40 is very, very cheap, especially when you get them home and they reach her knees – leading to more guilt because how could you forget the length of your own firstborn?

I also encountered some unknown Californian relatives who were so thrilled to see us, it was both touching and embarrassing. For example, whilst shopping for a jacket in one of the big stores, my Auntie Gladys, a Californian for forty years, said to the salesperson, 'My niece from England wants to try on the blue jacket. She's just won the Laurence Olivier Award.' Can you imagine my face?

My incredible discovery was that my grandfather's brothers and sisters had been a famous Russian dance troupe called the Boris Fridkin Troupe, who had worked for George M Cohan. The sepia-coloured pictures of my fabulous ancestors were a revelation to me, more so since I'd had no inkling that anyone in my family had ever been in the professional theatre. 'I don't know where she gets it from' had been the frequent lament in our house. Apparently, my great-uncle Sid had been on the stage at the age of two and a half, billed as the 'pocket George Landrush'. No, neither have I – but I bet someone reading this has . . . all contributions deliriously awaited.

I did go to see an agent whilst I was there. Jack typed out a résumé which was so impressive that even I wanted to take me on as a client. He carefully put all the awards nominations up front, followed by the most prestigious names I'd worked with, then a list of credits. I was embarrassed. He said, 'I promise you it's the only way – the slightest suggestion of British reserve, of self-deprecation and you're billed a *loser*.' I must say, the agent was apologetic for not knowing me, and really k-o'd by the résumé. He was also pleasant company and we had a really good laugh. But he hadn't the vaguest idea what he would *do* with me. I didn't fit into any known category. I had to agree.

I met up with another agent from England, my ex-agent in fact, Barry Krost. He's now involved in both music and film production, and heavily involved in running several gay banks. Yes, really. He and some associates realised that the ideal bank client was no longer a middle-aged, upwardly mobile family man with 2.2 children and a hefty mortgage. That same client now had 2.2 ex-wives, 4.4 children, hefty alimony and a pacemaker. Your average single parent or gay couple, on the other hand, had few dependants, a well-paid job and could not get a mortgage for money let alone love. The rest is future history. They now have six branches and are growing gaily. Only in California? I shouldn't bank on it!

Everyone went to bed very early. As soon as the decaff hit the table, everyone stood up to leave. At first I was convinced it was my jokes, but I was reassured to the contrary. They all have to be in the gym by 6am in order to be showered and taking a business meeting by 7.30am. Let's face it, they're all bloody mad. At any rate I enjoyed my week, miserable weather and all, and came back, for me, surprisingly refreshed. What does a Californian make for dinner? Reservations.

Eating the Hand that Bites You

Now let's talk about oral gratification. There. That made you sit up, didn't it? I'm referring, of course, to food.

Many hundreds of years ago when Jack and I first met in Manchester, we decided to discuss our common grounds over Jewish food. The large restaurant was deserted, save for one man and one waiter. They were screaming abuse at one another. As we walked in, the customer rose to his feet, and purple in the face, and arms at right angles to his body, he shrieked in our direction: 'Tell me – if you order braised steak, does it *necessarily* mean you've got to have *gravy*?' We stammered in unison: 'Er – er – *yes*', thus proving that one of the things we had in common was the knowledge that in Jewish restaurants the waiter is always right.

It's not as though I'm argumentative by nature. *Oh, no, I'm not!* Take the little Chinese restaurant in Hampstead we used to frequent. The proprietor was warm and welcoming, the ambience amicable and the food piquant – well, Peking to be perfectly accurate. One night the service was unbearably slow. We didn't complain to the owner, however, as his utterly inscrutable expression revealed he was as worried as we by the ominous crashings and hissings emanating from his kitchen. Finally our food arrived. We leapt at it. Three minutes later, two Chinese chefs leapt at us. Screaming Oriental expletives at one another, they circled the tables brandishing matching meat-cleavers and emptying the restaurant in two shakes of a bottle of soy sauce. Only Jack and I continued eating, more concerned with losing our spring rolls than the sides of our ears. We paid our bill as the police removed the battling bantam-weights, and we assured our shaken host that our enjoyment of numbers 43, 17 and 91 had in no way been diminished by the novel floor show, and we would be back to see him very soon. We never returned and I feel a cleaver-like stab of guilt every time I pass.

After all, it can't be easy providing the perfect ambience for a diverse and disparate group of diners every night. I've been totally defeated by fish fingers for five. In the Sixties, when there was only one of me, I used to frequent a fashionable 'tranny' café in Battersea, where the colourful and largely rectangular Polish owner would serve up the nectar of the gods for the price of a tin of creamed rice. Here, long-distance lorry drivers would nestle up against Chelsea 'lardies' for the chance to sample Stanley's duck in orange sauce – price 7s 6d, served by his wispy and drily sexy Irish wife, Vera. Believe it or not I used to do a cabaret after dinner consisting of a pantomime striptease, and a long-winded joke about a lady with an over-developed right breast. The high point of the evening was when Stan reeled, vodka-strewn, from his tiny, torrid kitchen, placed a heavily tattooed arm around your shoulder and launched into show-business: 'Dere's dis Eskimo – he got a penis this big . . .' Mid-demonstration, Vera would flit effortlessly past, balancing twenty plates and breathe: 'Will ye cover up yer sinful mouth this instant, Stanley.' Every meal was an experience, every night a party. Like the Sixties, it expanded into twice its importance and suddenly disappeared. I've missed it and them ever since. (Since writing this a plump little bird has assured me that Vera is back in business – must dash . . .)

Mind you, I don't have to *sit down* in a café to incite aggro. Rehearsing in a draughty barracks in Camberwell, five of us decided on a hot Indian take-away. We waited the obligatory four hours and Took It Away. It was Liza Goddard, a genuine animal-lover, who discovered the first creepy which crawleth on its belly on the face of her lettuce. 'Oh, dear, livestock,' she said cheerily. Then, 'Oh, another. Different colour.' By now all five of us were spitting, yucking and generally over-acting to a degree. I spent the following hour combing through every leaf with David Bellamy-like intensity until I'd discovered an entomologist's paradise. What to do? Should I phone Channel 4 and suggest a small documentary for *Wildlife on 4*, or should I arm myself with fellow actor, Christopher Timothy, and take all the creatures great and small back to the take-away? We chose the latter.

The man behind the counter gave a performance worthy of Ben Kingsley's Oscar – he would lose family, friends and job if the manager found out. Mortified, we offered to accept half the refund and handed over the bugs – at which point he foolishly admitted he *was* the manager, and offered us a free meal instead. With the grace of a grasshopper I leapt over the counter, retrieved the evidence and fled in search of the telephone number of the nearest Health Department.

After twenty minutes and numerous wrong offices, I spent a full half hour explaining the event to a sympathetic lady at the other end of the line. 'Ugh, there wasn't! . . . Urrgh, how awful!' she exclaimed. 'Well, where do we go from here?' I asked her. 'I don't know,' she confessed. 'This is the casualty department at King's College Hospital.'

Then there are the places which specialise in gimmicks but no food. 'Hi, there, I'm Martha, your waitress for tonight,' said a mouthful of orthodentistry in a downtown Florida café modestly called 'Old Possum's Famous Fabulous Olde Worlde Eatery'. (It's my favourite name – along with 'fishtique' and 'Shish and Donerama'!) As the iced water hit our root-canals, Martha hit the table with either the complete works of Dickens or an 84-page leather-bound menu. It was the latter, and contained prose as purple as the face of the man who didn't want gravy with his braised steak. 'Succulent, sizzling super scrumpy burger, nestling on a savoury sea of crispy frozen-berg lettuce with breath-bating blue cheese and Possum's famous boysenberry dressing . . .' We ordered an omelette and agreed to sample a plate of their Famous French Fries. They came in a basket. Hot potato crisps accompanied by two dips. One maple syrup and the other sour cream. Being British and loath to be 'Uncle Dick' in a famous Eatery, we left. 'Have a nice day now,' cooed a bewildered Martha.

One night in downtown Key Biscayne we went to a kosher restaurant. There was a marvellously laid-back waitress, the sort played by Patricia Neal in movies of the early Seventies. Very thin and dry, her chest caved backwards and her pelvis forward like an out-of-condition mannequin. She scarcely looked up as we placed our order. 'Uh-hu . . . uh-hu . . . uh-hu.' As a postscript, she murmured, 'Ya want soda water with this?'

'No, thank you,' Jack replied. There was a pause. She looked up. She regarded us blankly. Then she said, 'You Jewish?'

'Er . . . yes?' We were pretty sure on that score, but failed to see the connection. *Now* we had her interest. 'You Jewish and you don't want soda water?' 'Er . . . yes. No. We don't. Why, for heaven's sake?' She let her pad drop, sat down at the table and regarded us with the mixture of sorrow and pity usually reserved for cannibals by a missionary.

'Well, howya gonna eat it all? Ah mean, if yu Jewish yu come in heah, yu drink the soup, y' eat the liver, y' eat the kishkes, you swaller some soda water, yu burp, yu eat some more, yu drink some more, yu burp some more so's yu can eat some more. Now. Are y' absolutely sure yu don't want soda?'

She was wonderful. A complete character. Throughout the dinner I absorbed her like a Vitamin C capsule, and she's still in there, waiting to be unleashed on the right part.

Of course, working in a kitchen is hell. No one knows that better than me – except maybe Arnold Wesker. After a childhood spent reading in the loo every time there was table laying or washing up to do, I spent one summer holiday begging my parents to allow me to join my schoolfriends who were working in a Bridlington café. They finally acquiesced, a wise move on their part. I packed a huge trunk, waved a tearful farewell, travelled the fourteen-mile journey snivelling, and was back home within one week. Fired. For total inefficiency. I'd soon learned to belt out the vernacular 'One Sos Tom Streaky Without', but so clumsy, disorganised and exhausted was I after two days, that the boss demoted me to the toffee apple stand outside. There I cocked up the money, jammed up the toffee machine and was sent home, lugging six weeks' luggage by taxi. Later, my friends told me the boss had said if they ever brought that bloody disaster with them again, he'd fire the lot of them.

Nowadays my food tract describes raised voices, but these are mostly at home. '*Will* you take that knife out of your mouth!' 'Cut it, don't *tear* it – God, it's like eating with animals!' 'Yes I know Daddy's elbows are on the table but . . . he's tired!' And, 'There will be no pudding unless you at least *try* the mangetouts . . .' And 'Yes of course they make you see in the sodding dark!'

Of course it was never like that in my day. Mealtimes at home in Hull meant a very hot dinner on a very cold plate. None of this helping yourselves to vegetables from a casserole business – it all came in a delicious, but compact mass, followed somewhat later by my mother, who threw down her food fast enough to be up to serve dessert the second her last potato disappeared. 'Why don't you sit down, love?' was the constant enquiry, though it never occurred to the enquirers to stand up and give her a hand.

Incidentally, and here I lower my voice, what do you reckon to this 'barbecue' business? No, go on, I won't say anything. Everyone keeps saying 'Have you got a barbecue?' Rather in the way they used to say 'Have you got a wok?' or even 'Have you got herpes?' And lately I've taken to dropping large barbecue-shaped hints in the direction of my husband, who hates them – the barbecues and the hints. His claim is that every barbecued meal he's ever had has been cold and black and tasted of worsted. I'm sure he's wrong but there is a morsel of truth in his barb. *Do* we really like standing on a chilly patio with a plate full of coleslaw and a rapidly cooling baked potato, waiting for the next batch of lamb chops to be singed, whilst making devastating small talk to the man from next door who's only been invited because of the wind direction. 'Oh, mercantile shipping? Gosh, how unusual! Do you see many of them? Ships, I mean.'

There's a lot to be said for beans on toast and a fried egg, whilst watching *Film Night*. I'm sorry to 'producer-and-saviour-drop', but we once cooked dinner for David and Patsy Puttnam – it was fish and chips and rice pudding with a skin on. It really went down better than three weeks with Anton Mosiman. Actually, my best-ever dinner party conversation went like this:

ME (*after an animated twenty minutes to the man on my left, to the man on my right*): 'And what sort of work do you do, er – (*glance at place card*) – Jeremy?

HE (*after gazing morosely into my face*): 'I study the corneas of chickens' eyes.'
ME: 'Oh super! A little more coq au vin?'

I've just read Jack the last page, and he said that's all right, but everyone who's ever given us a barbecue will be insulted. I then counted them up on two hands and agreed to cut out the paragraph. He then said, 'Well, I suppose it's OK. I've nothing against barbecues really, it's just that ovens are so clever, aren't they? I mean, you don't drip it all down your trouser-leg when you're trying to talk. If I want my dinner burnt on the outside and raw on the inside, I can have it in the comfort of my own home.'

As far as being a good hostess myself, I can honestly say that I am unique. I owe half of London dinner, and large chunks of the Home Counties, too. In my defence I must point out that I am an excellent guest. Witty as all get out, wildly appreciative of décor and cuisine, abstemious yet high as a kite on other people's lack of sobriety. I also give myself total nervous exhaustion when I do have what my mother calls 'an evening', by over-shopping, over-cooking and overdoing it all to a ridiculous degree, so that by the time the guests arrive, I'm hyperactive and bloated with testing, tasting and sampling. And, like an opening night, it almost always goes well and I'm smug enough to plan the next one whilst stacking the plates from the current one into the dishwasher.

My most enduring restaurant memory is of a stony-faced American couple who ate a three-course meal in total silence in a West End bistro. Very occasionally she would sigh heavily. He would glance up, then quickly avert his eyes. Too quickly. Once or twice she, too, pointedly shifted her position between courses or studiously adjusted her make-up in a small gold hand-mirror. Once he put down his wine glass with unnecessary vigour and ground his crowns. The silence was more highly charged than the customers. Finally, it broke. Leaning tentatively across, he made some inaudible enquiry. She straightened her spine, placed her fork on her plate, fixed him with her astigmatism and growled with great deliberation, 'It's not the boeuf bourguignon, Henry – it's the last twenty-three years!'

Hair Today

Last week Jack went for a haircut. He came back looking as though he'd had his head sharpened.

'It'll settle down,' he said, gamely, plucking frantically at his empty head in an attempt to lengthen the remaining hairs.

'It's nice,' I lied, as we headed towards the kettle in search of comfort. Later, over a two-day-old custard tart, he confessed rather wanly that he'd been waiting forty-five years for a haircut like the one he had in his mind. He added that he remained optimistic up to and including this very day. I don't.

Every time I enter a hairdressing salon, be it Mr Damien of Dalston or Lord Sassoon of Sloane, I get the same feeling. It's not exactly 'sinking' like 3.30pm when the dentist will see you at four, nor 'elated' like the sight of a loved one at Euston, but with its mixture of fear, hope and blind faith, it bears more than a passing resemblance to the feeling you get when your waters break.

It's a very emotive subject, hair. If you saw the television documentary *Mothers By Daughters* you'll know that it was the single strand that bound together the likes of Elisabeth Lutyens, Barbara Windsor, Bernadette Devlin, and – me. Though our backgrounds were as different as our mothers, and though we all were interviewed quite separately, it seemed there came a point in each programme when the inevitable happened: 'My mother was always messing about with my hair' – 'Whenever I see my mother, I always have to make sure my hair is perfect . . .' – 'She wasn't just forever brushing it – she was forever worrying it!' We collectively remembered the aggravation of being perpetually primped and permed and plaited, as though the tops of our heads were symbols of their dissatisfaction with the rest of us.

At least now, when I tell my daughter that she looks like a drowned rat, I have the advantage of knowing that the primaeval echo is a primaeval echo and not just nagging.

I wonder, does the colour lilac have a strong effect on you? Does it remind you of Elizabeth Taylor's corneas, or like me, does it transport you back to the salon where you had your first perm? After years of rags, pincurls and the fearsome wave clips which attacked plump little fingers at the drop of an elder brother (and all this before I was on solids), I emerged in photographs a button-eyed child on a Bridlington beach with one startled curl in the middle of her head.

Bathnights were followed by a ritual head-toasting in front of the electric fire – and a night's sleep rendered impossible by virtue of my scalp being quietly acupunctured by its surrounding hardware. Which could account for a lot.

But back to that salon. Along with the lilac claustrophobia came the lilac smell. Thick, sticky, heady, hot and sweet like the tropical house at Kew. It hit you in waves as you went in. Hours later it was superseded by enough ammonia to bleach tar. And finally the nice natural smell of lacquer sprayed on – straight into the eyes. Which at least prevented you from seeing what two mirrors would have you believe. Then you prayed. Shut your eyes and prayed – it was all an optical illusion. 'Thank you. It's great. Really. Great.' (This to a murderer.) Then you paid your money and cried for a week with your school scarf wrapped round your head.

Every perm I ever had turned out the same. Flat on top like 'Her Majesty', then erupting around the ear region into a mass of chipolatas, bearing scant resemblance to either the hair I had before or the hair of any living creature save an Irish Water Spaniel. Back home in the bedroom, I'd pull it, stretch it, bend it in a reverse direction and occasionally iron it in brown paper. But in vain. Nothing, but nothing, has the resilience of a recently permed head of hair.

'It'll soon drop,' my mother would helpfully remark.

'I wish it *would* – out,' I wailed. 'Look at it, it's like a woolly hat – and it stinks.'

'It's nice.' The final insult – 'It makes your face look fuller.' This was the one which engineered the head into a basin full of water – a kamikaze gesture if ever there was one. For it was only then that the full extent of the damage could be seen.

Still, it only lasted six months. And somewhere in the sixth month it suddenly looked good. Bouncy, loose, soft – you know, like – hair. That stage lasted a week and during that time you relented entirely on your campaign against the permanent wave industry and started wearing your lilac waspie again. Six hours later you were the possessor of the same lank, lustreless disaster area that drove you salon-wards in the first place. Plus split ends and rust.

All of which brings me to my text for the day. Hairdressers and why I wish I could dress my own. I'm forever changing my crimper and wishing I hadn't. I've been head-hunted off the street by an ex-stylist, actually, while perfectly happy with the one I've had. Once in there he lifted the odd colpoon of my hair as though retrieving a diamond from a dog-turd and said 'My dear – who did this to you?' Immediately I became a supergrass and quite rightly got tarred and feathered for it. With the new haircut I was too embarrassed to return to the old hairdresser and too cross to remain with the new one.

I wonder if it all dates back to the lilac salon, and the occasion of the nits. It's one of those moments which are emblazoned on my heart like a suburban version of 'Calais' on Mary Tudor's. I remember sitting in the leatherette swivel, a bri-nylon cape swathed around my pounding heart and a copy of *Modern Screen* on my lap. 'Is Liz infanticipating? Only Eddie knows and he ain't tellin',' screamed Louella. A pretty stylist, with freckles I'd have killed for, was combing out my wet hair when she suddenly and inexplicably left. Never to return. The minutes passed. I'd said nothing to upset her, my conscience was clear, and I'd never felt guiltier in my life. Several more minutes of stage whispers later, the owner of the shop, a lady well known to my mother and her circle, came over and without a word of explanation took over my head. If ever I knew I was lousy, it was then.

I must be honest, if only for a paragraph. I've been very pleased with my hair on occasions. At least it doesn't usually give me cause for abject despair as the rest of me often does. Possibly because by the time it's grown, it's dead.

I have a photograph of myself back in the heady Sixties where my hair is shoulder length, copper red and cut in the 'new' shaggy, layered long back and sides look. I think at that moment I peaked – coiffure-wise. It's too late to recapture the hairstyle – no offence to Sarah Ferguson intended – and the glow was as much to do with youth as it was to do with being a redhead. At the time, it gave me a certain glamour, enhanced the wardrobe and made the wisecracks seem wiser and more cracked. Too much autumnal hue, however, can make one head for a Fall! And all that bleach every six weeks! By the time I'd had Amy I'd come to a crossroads of decision – Red Hair or Disposal Nappies. Heads you lose – tails you win.

As for blondes having more fun, well, let me dispel that rumour forever. They do. On the occasions when I've been blonde in TV plays, the difference in the amount of fun I had was so marked that I'd gladly trade in my Moulinex to be permanently platinum of hair, eyebrows and other pertinent bits.

These days I've taken to sending Jack to Sheila down the road. He comes back a very happy man. I presume it was because of the haircut. Then I sent along my brother, who had flown in with a thatched head from Geneva where he lives, and flew out again as svelte as a sea-lion. Now I go along too. It's great to have your hair washed in the kitchen sink and cut in the conservatory, then to have a really good moan about almost everything. Cheaper than an analyst and you come out looking less streaky.

There was, in the Seventies, the real epoch of the hairdresser as self-styled psychoanalyst. This peaked with Warren Beatty's film *Shampoo* which, although well 'over the crown', was often very accurate. Certainly my then hairdresser Ricci Burns would give me wonderful advice whilst teasing my roots: 'Don't make a daughter out of Amy – make a friend.' This when I was having troubles with Number One Daughter. 'Take your old man on holiday – tomorrow!' when I was bleary-eyed and weepy. And 'Don't do a thing to your nose, you'll ruin yourself!' This from a man who sees more of his plastic surgeon than he sees of his milkman. Bless him, he's always right, damn him! Or maybe I'm just so grateful for a chance to sit down and a captive ear that I just blurt till I feel better.

Even Adam, when forced into the Cypriot barber's on the Broadway, behaves accordingly. It's a real *man*'s barber's, you know, with a pole and Durex and copies of *What Car?*. He sits on a wooden plank over a maroon leatherette swivel chair and honestly, no sooner has his bum hit the plank than squeaky voiced he starts with the man's talk. 'So how's your team doing, then? You still supporting Tottenham, are you? Why don't you try a decent team like Manchester United? I mean, who have they got apart from Hoddle? No, but did you see us murder Videoton and with only ten men – Oh, what a referee . . .' Etc., etc. The barber adores him.

Actually, I have noticed the appearance of some strange, wiry, irregular-shaped hairs – in my head, I hasten to add – leading to the purchase of a home henna kit. I now have strange, wiry, irregular-shaped yellow hairs, a magenta-coloured sink and slimey green bits on my dressing-gown. Hair today . . . none tomorrow . . .

It's fourteen year or so since I wrote this and Ricci Burns has long given up hairdressing and gives out marital advice instead from his exclusive gown shop. My style hasn't changed much except for a daring bit of spikiness here and there which I took up a couple of months after Zoë Wanamaker and Ruby Wax had given it up. It never changes does it, the hair thing? Years and years and bottles of bleach and vats of 'product' later and I'm still reluctant to make an appointment, anxious to get out the minute I'm in and always on the search for some kind of 'solution' which sorts me out, without chemicals – naturally. When I'm on tour, I can walk into any salon in any pedestrianised street – for aren't they all, these days, and how heinous is that? (Gap/Monsoon/Next/Clinton's Cards/Primark/Gap/Monsoon – don't get me started, where was I?) Yes, any salon and get a decent cut first time round. Why is that? Because they see your face for the first time and cut round it observantly? Try going for a second cut in the same place – yup, it's a tonsure.

Even if I do have a good cut it needs redoing after two weeks and those two weeks are in the middle of the colour cycle and wild stallions won't make me go to a salon twice in the same month, so what do I do? I Hold my head over the waste bin and, with a pair of nail scissors, I snip into it until the bathroom is furry and I can manage the hair without resource to 'Mud', 'Fudge', 'Clay', 'Gel' or any other kind of salon cement. At least when they say, 'Who cut this?' I can just grin and say, 'I did.'

It will never change I wrote later in the *Guardian*:

Well, on my own head be it. I brought it on myself and I've no one else to blame. Some people, actually, say they like it. Others say, 'Stop moaning, it'll grow.'

Here's the thing, as my American cousins might say. I was driving to Harrow and Weald, one Saturday night – I know, you had no idea my life was so glamorous – to see a chum's new house, and being too lazy and/or arrogant to consult the *A to Z* and knowing that the Tom-Tom woman will be a know-it-all, I turned the radio to LBC (London Broadcasting Company) to check the traffic reports. I almost never listen to talk show radio on the grounds that anyone who calls up a radio station with an opinion is either sad, barking or a paid-up member of the BNP, but my attention was caught immediately. The presenter, Jo Parkinson, was having her hair cut. On radio. This appealed. I was once on *Loose Ends* with an escapologist who freed himself from a sack bound with chains during the time it took to titter at Ned Sherrin's scriptwriters' idea of a topical gag. I pricked up my ears.

The hairdresser explained that he was using a piece of glass, so sharp that you could slice the hairs off a kipper hurled at a rotary fan on a hot St Agnes Eve. Well, he didn't exactly say that, but it was of the order that it had been custom-designed by a famous glass laboratory and was deadly sharp. It was good-bye forever to split ends, you would wake up in the morning with your hair in the same shape as you took it to bed and shake it into shape after swimming the Channel. No product necessary. And quick? From feeling your phrenology to sweeping your remnants up from the Amtico would be only seven minutes and would set you back a mere £300. Whey hey! A snip! Hang on – *how much*? I was laughing all the way through Harrow and well-nigh hysterical by the time I reached Weald.

Something about the item stuck, though and I had to find out more. So later that week I rang the programme in my perky assistant-sounding tone and the upshot was that he was coming to London that week and would be delighted to come to Casa Rosenthal and give me a free demo. This was extremely over-exciting. I have this unshakeable belief that at the first signs of synchronicity of any kind, I'm meant to go with the flow.

'You sure you want to do this the day before your party, Mod?' said the daughter.

'Yeah, sure, why not? I'll be wearing a *het* anyway and my hair grows like cress in compost,' was my defiant retort. 'I mean, why did I suddenly turn the radio on to LBC if I wasn't *meant* to hear about him?'

You might think the Third Age would have removed something of the New Age, at my age, but you'd be wrong.

It was truly kind of the hairdresser to come to my house with his bonny male assistant, and the cut took an hour, not seven minutes, during which time he talked non-stop about how his life was devoted to cutting hair for Jesus. I grew weary as I always do when I'm talked at and declined his thoughtful offer to pray with me before leaving. I agreed he could style it how he liked and made only one stipulation: that I wasn't wild about my long neck and needed hair around it to bring my head closer to the rest of my body. He agreed.

I could feel that he was drying my hair forward onto my face. I don't really have much of a face so I usually keep the hair off it. When I looked in the mirror I swallowed, then, with a deadly quietness that my kids always knew meant 'Head for the hills, she's on simmer', I said, 'Thank you. It was an experiment. My own fault. I have a party tomorrow. I look like Arthur Scargill. Please cut off those long straggly tendrils, I am not a shop girl of 17, and give me the blow dryer. *Thank* you.'

'It's taken ten years off you,' he said defiantly. 'You wait until your friends see it. You don't look like a housewife.'

I ran up the stairs, washed it, dried it and pulled it practically out of my head, which gave me an excuse to shed a few vain (in both senses) tears. Meanwhile the two men soberly packed up their bags, sprays, curved combs, changeable glass heads and left for the station. Nobody prayed except me. For a wig.

I've been waiting for the compliments ever since. Una Stubbs told me the shape at the back was fabulous. Pedro, another great crimper, expressed astonishment that I'd done such a thing but thought I was lucky it had turned out OK. It is a *very* short, low maintenance haircut. On anyone but me.

August 2008. I've just had the pleasure of watching my topiary expert cut down to a twig by the panel of Dragon's Den. Ah sweet mystery of life. Let's face it, dead or not, your hair has a life of its own. It's forever scheming how it can droop on you once a month just when you need its help. How it can send out scouts to spring out of what you thought was a beauty spot – how it can alarm you by turning grey or standing on end, given the right set of circumstances. How it can stand the combined onslaught of rain, chlorine, ultra violet rays, leather Fedoras and even those rubber caps through which strands are pulled in order to be high-lit

– giving the wearer a strong resemblance to those stalks of cress you grew on blotting paper.

I imagine it will continue growing long after I am underground or in the kidney repository – so perhaps it's time I awarded it the respect it deserves. Say kids – we could even do a musical about it – *Hair?*   no, wouldn't work. Perhaps I'll just clean out my hairbrush.

Dressing Down

I bought this leather suit for a TV charades game called *Give Us A Clue*. It was five to six on the evening before the recording when I discovered my wardrobe was full of nothing to wear. Now, I don't like leather *per se*, except on a cow or the sole of my shoe – it's too prone to Ribena stains and squeaking – but charades players can't be choosers and even downtown Muswell Hill is closed by six o'clock.

So I bought it. The jacket was cornflower blue with padded shoulders, voluminous pouches and an odd aertexy-texture here and there. The skirt was straight and dangerously split. The shop girls pronounced it 'reelynice' and I happily paid up more money than I would earn for three editions of *Give Us A Clue* and lugged it home in a plastic portmanteau.

Later that night, I had a 'try-on'. Jack and the au pair looked horrified, and Amy pronounced it 'fat'. Fat was right. It was huge on top and sort of tapered from the hips. It was also very blue. All in all I looked like a burning gas-jet. Glumly, I packed it back in its plastic, wore a well-worn favourite on the show and collected the biggest credit note I've ever possessed.

This meant, over the next few weeks, I could buy *free* clothes. At least that's what it felt like. The piece of paper made me feel quite light-headed. 'I'll have one of those, two of these, a pair of those, now, how much have I got left?'

It's always a mistake to spend a lot on clothes. I remember buying a silk gypsy dress trimmed with antique lace for the premiere of the ill-fated musical version of Jack's TV play *Bar Mitzvah Boy*. Someone sprayed a little champagne on it, so I took it to a high-class cleaner's who turned three spots into a Rorschach test. The dress lasted slightly longer than the show – about ten weeks. And neither of them will ever be revived.

Most of the parts I play on stage or TV require either appalling taste or a trip to the Oxfam shop, and the only time I've ever worn designer-clothes was for the series *Agony*. The costume lady and I would wander down South Molton Street saying 'We'll take these shoes in the blue, the brown and the yellow, with matching tights, the mustard-checked trousers with the Missoni cardigan and throw in two silk shirts, one burgundy and one cerise.' All the clothes were slightly dotty (slightly? Most of the time I looked like Pass the Parcel). But I loved them, and they never dated or fell apart, unlike their wearer, who, throughout three series, did both.

As teenagers, my friends and I used to dress like forty-five-year-olds. I have pictures of myself, back in Hull, wearing a navy two-piece suit (with pleated skirt and lacy collar), a dog's dinner hat, white gloves and clutching a clutch bag. I looked like something on its way out of the Conservative Party Conference. In this erotic ensemble we would visit the synagogue on a Saturday morning, where we'd giggle disgracefully, ogle the talent below, then repair to the local expresso bar for a – wait for it – frothy coffee. Well tanked up we'd march round the two department stores buying American Tan stockings and a 33⅓ rpm Cliff Richard, then straight to the Fourth Floor for – AFTERNOON TEA! WITH CAKES! Am I shocking you? I also possessed a pink puff-ball evening dress with a boned top and a skirt of increasing hoops, ending with a tiny one which just circled the knees. It was fine till I sat down, whereupon the whole skirt rose up and covered my head, exposing American Tan-covered knock-knees.

By the time I hit Drama School, I dressed entirely in mix 'n' match. For my first day I wore a green woolly dress, emerald-green tights, dark green boots (painted), a grey-green hat with a pom-pom and lurid green eye-shadow to the brow. My fellow-student, Philip Sayer, told me later that I looked like a big blade of grass. As the term progressed, my gear got more and more way-out, venturing into floor-length coats, old theatrical costumes and floppy Fedoras. It got so bad that, at holiday times, my mother used to wear dark glasses and a beard to meet me off the train.

I still adore dressing up. A couple of years ago, our friend Astrid had her American parents to stay and wanted to introduce them to her nice English friends. I suggested to Jack we dressed as Beefeaters. As always, and to my amazement, he agreed. I hired the outfits from Bermans, and they threw in a free pike. The costumes were glorious. That scarlet suit really suited me, and you should have felt the quality! I don't think I shall ever see a sight to equal that of Jack struggling into a pair of red tights. 'How do you *do* it??' he implored, heels over metatarsals and crutch by knees. 'Shut up and keep still while I put your rosettes on,' was my wifely response. 'Do you realise,' I added, 'that somewhere in London, right now, a real Beefeater is stepping into this garb, and saying to his kids – "Goodbye Darren, goodbye Wayne, Daddy's off to guard the Tower. Be good boys for Mummy."'

Sandi, our Australian au pair, took a photo of us. Previously we had taken one of her in the outfit. She sent it to Sydney with a one-line message: 'Dear Mum and Dad, I have changed my job. Love Sandi'.

After popping next door to borrow a cup of sugar, which left them hysterical, we drove to Hampstead. I won't try to describe the faces of the other motorists, nor the struggle to get an eight-foot pike into a Ford Escort. Suffice to say that when we arrived, Astrid was watering the window-boxes and she almost broke the World Free-Falling record. 'I don't believe what I'm seeing! Honey, there are two Beefeaters parking outside our – Oh, my Gaaaad!!' I don't want you to think we do this sort of thing a lot – just because we do – but it was truly worth it. If only for the length of time we all spent with our knees crossed. Crying.

More recently, we went (normally dressed) to a friend's barbecue, where the lady making the salads turned out to be a part-time prostitute. I might tell you the subject only came up during a discussion about the televising of the House of Lords. You may draw your own conclusion as to how one topic led to the other.

Now this lady was plump, bonny, well-balanced, witty, down-to-earth. Like your husband's sister or the lady on the cashpoint in Fenwick's. 'I can't take my clothes off in front of anyone – not even another woman,' she said. 'I get there in my jeans and T-shirt as average as a Persil mum, but from the moment I put on my two layers of make-up, my six-inch heels and my leopard-skin top, I *am* the part. And when the door bell rings and I hear the clip-clop of my stilettos on the wooden floor, well, dears, I'm anything they want me to be.'

I expect that's what they mean by Clothes Maketh the Man.

I've just remembered, I once had another leather suit. It was a trouser suit and it was made by some mad Mexicans I'd encountered in the Kings Road. They 'sculpted skin to match your soul'. I almost died when I saw their interpretation of my soul. The flared leather trousers were bottle-green and had a luminous orange panel starting at the stomach and tapering into the crutch. The top was cut under the bust and fastened with a silver brooch. When I asked Miguel what I should wear underneath it, he grinned and said, 'Honly ze breasts!' 'Not *zese* breasts, Chutney,' I replied and set off in search of a polo neck.

In an ideal world, I'd have only one style of dress. But I'd have it in scores of different materials. Silk, denim, taffeta, tweed. I know the style of the dress. It's the Fifties Look, with a cinched waist, raglan sleeves and crisp white cuffs. It's the sort of dress that was worn in the movies by the wise-cracking girl in the office who never got the man. In fact, this wise-cracking girl wore it for *Give Us A Clue* instead of the blue cow. Tune in and let me know if I should proceed further with The Look or whether you prefer me bovine.

Ladies, Excuse Me . . .

Is dancing the true expression of happiness and, if so, when did you last get happy? Now I am a genius on the floor – but only the floor of my head. My dearly beloved partner is one of the 'shifting-his-weight-from-left-to-right-while-moving-in-a-southerly-direction-back-to-the-chair-whence-he-came' brigade. This necessitates a choice. I can either shift with him, my hands draped lovingly around his neck, talking animatedly away as if to suggest we have more important things to do than *dance*! Or, I can prance and strut alone, my outstretched palms climbing imaginary walls and my hips rotating relentlessly whilst he continues his aimless shift work. Only this time, with a radish-coloured face which he tries to hide in his breast pocket.

My first memory of dancing in public was on my father's feet. It was no doubt a family wedding or a bar mitzvah, because I dimly recall a lot of beaded dresses and painful cheek-pinching from on high. I was at my most stunning, in smocked Viyella with just a hint of protruding teeth peeping alluringly through a protruding lip. The music was probably 'I'd like to get you on a slow boat to China', my father's shoes were black and shiny, and throughout it, I trod, slid off and generally massacred them while clinging tenaciously to his thumbs, until I fell asleep and was carried home.

Every Saturday, my friend Bernice and I would attend the Muriel Riley School of Ballroom Dancing of Anlaby Road, Hull. Once there we paid our half-crown and changed into our silver-strapped dancing shoes. The floor was a sea of sliding, skidding, shrieking children until such moment as Miss Riley Herself – ''Er indoors' if ever there was one – 'she who must be displayed', even, and her partner came on the floor to dazzle our ten-year-old eyes with their virtuosity. Quickstep, Foxtrot, Waltz and Samba – Bernice and I taking it in turns to be the man. No wonder, twenty-eight years later, I keep putting my arms round men's waists as soon as the band strikes up. Not to mention standing on their feet, grasping their thumbs and falling asleep on them.

Anyway, after the interval and its obligatory vat of Vimto (never try to recapture the flavour of Vimto. Either it's changed, I've changed, or it always tasted like scented Harpic), we resumed the floor for the Palais-Glide, the Gay Gordons, the Polka and la pièce de résidance – the Cha Cha. This latter was regarded as slightly naughty, with its Latin rhythms and its suggestive hip movements. Bernice and I managed to keep our animal instincts under control though; an unremarkable task since there were at least twelve women to every man present.

'Anything funny happen to you on the dance floor?' I asked the butcher in Market Place today, by way of a change from 'How's the liver looking?' and 'Can you pluck its legs, please?' The reply was instantaneous. 'Never use one, love, not since I tore me two-tone Tiger Mohair trousers doing the Twist.' 'Left standing in me Bum Freezer for all the world to see.' The Twist! Have you ever looked at all that footage of the beehived, miniskirted, stovepipe-trousered aliens that we were, screwing our right legs into the parquet whilst ferrying our upper bodies in an opposing direction and our elbows into each other's navels? It's as archaic as the Minuet.

Mind you, it takes a lot to topple the 'Birdie Dance' for sheer inanity. I once watched Jack being dragged on to the floor by an overbearing Entertainments Officer in a holiday hotel. She was a big girl, from Amsterdam, known to the residents as 'Dutch Gilda'; and when she shouted 'I need volunteers!' you knew to get the hell out. At least I knew. Jacko just thought he was having a quiet coke by the bar. Next thing he knew he was being yanked through the air by the scruff of his windjammer and was frenziedly flapping his fingers, revolving his torso and sinking to his knees to the most tuneless tune ever known to man or bird, while the audience bellowed their approval and his wife hooted so loudly she wet herself. 'Anglaterra huit points,' howled our dear old Dutch, and presented him with an Ibizan Biro for effort.

Can you imagine the terror and sheer ignominy of the time when a girl went to a ball dressed like a box of Quality Street and had to get her card filled up with prospective partners for every dance? I know exactly where I would have been. Up in the powder-room with 'the vapours', forging the names of every man I knew who couldn't make it that night.

Jack says his trick at the Palais de Danse was always to unbutton his jacket before embarking on the three-mile walk across the floor to ask a girl to dance. That way you had something macho to do with your hands on the way over, i.e. button it up again. And by the time you reached her and were told 'Ask me friend, I'm sweatin'' you could suavely unbutton it again on the way back. It worked for Victor Mature, he claimed. The funniest pick-up line I ever heard was ''Ere, my mate thinks your mate's f—-ing excellent!'

We once went to a famous Palais to research a play about ballrooms, and it was one of the saddest evenings I can recall. There were all the fellas, dressed to the eights, standing round the bar in faceless clumps as though their one interest was to gerra few in. There were the women at the tables, smoking Bette Davis-ly and gazing resolutely anywhere but at the men. It was all a bit too late – it was the scene of my youth with the same cast twenty years later. Same suits, same faces – just older and shinier and more hopeless. Perhaps we just picked a bad night. Perhaps they did.

As for discos, well, frankly, my dears, I've had them up to here (gestures to ear level). The invention of strobe lighting finally finished all hitherto-unfulfilled aspirations to be a jet-setting go-go dancer. Physical symptoms seem to set in and my tendency to attempt *speech* above the tremolo can result in unattractive vomiting. Two experiences stand out. One was the opening of the new Hippodrome when I was squired by hat designer David Shilling. He decided to dress as Bonnie Prince Charlie that night. It was not a fancy dress ball. I was wearing a couple of very expensive handkerchiefs, and in order to avoid seeing each other, we danced like demons possessed for hundreds of hours and came out feeling purged. The following day most of the skin fell off my feet. It was, I think, nature's way of telling me never to startle the ends of my legs without prior consultation.

The second occasion was with the hairdresser Ricci Burns in a now defunct club called Del Aretusa, when the music changed, unannounced, from Rolling Stones to Richard Strauss. Hypnotised by its power and no doubt stoned out of our tiny trees – we began to whirl. And spin. And whirl. And spin. The last thing I remember is the sound my head made against the wall, and as I lost consciousness, I was vaguely aware of the Blue Danube closing over me. At least Disco has got rid of the wallflower. Except in the garden. By the wall. Actually it was probably wartime which did that, women dancing together in armies, whilst the men did it for real. But your partner was basically a substitute for a man. Nowadays, anyone can dance with anything, since everyone is actually dancing alone. And it's men who've been released. Free now to preen and prance and strut and astonish us with their breakdancing and body-popping routines – surely the most exciting dance advance for years.

When Jazz Dancing first hit town, I went to the Dance Centre in Covent Garden. It felt a bit like walking into an all-Black, anti-Semitic, gay club. In Argentina. I was hopelessly conspicuous, as though my legs had 'Muscle-free Zone' printed on them, and my feet, 'Les Grands Bateaux'. I intended to attend a class held by the legendary Matt Mattox – affectionately known to those who stood behind him in class as Butt Buttox. I managed to make it to the changing-rooms quite uneventfully by keeping my eyes crossed every time some pale-faced, huge-eyed, leotarded nymph pattered past me on points, and was just about to unravel a pair of support tights when I saw a dancer, standing in front of the floor-to-ceiling mirror. I could tell she was a dancer because she was stark naked but for one pink ballet shoe. She was crying large, silent tears which made her meticulous mascara run in rivulets down her beautifully ravaged face. She watched herself in the mirror as she cried. It was a poignant scene which not only summed up the Dance Centre, but drove me out into the street that you couldn't see my toes for twinkling.

We have the most wonderful Greek family living next door and I tell you, when those fellas feel the spirit moving and they get up and dance, you really know where music touches you the most. It all seems based on some kind of endurance as they stoop down to the ground balancing on one leg, then spring over the leg on which they're balanced. Often it's very slow too, which makes it even sexier, if you follow my drift. And it's nothing to do with age – in fact, the older they are, the more meaningful the dance.

As for the ballet, well, I'm told by them that know, naming no names but follow my glance, that they're all at it like rabbits or knives or whatever, and that for most dancers sex is something to be taken like food or breath or vitamin pills. I expect if you are physically as perfectly tuned as is your average common or garden sylphide, one's senses are equally heightened, or am I talking through my tutu?

I remember a friend of mine who was 'courting' a ballerina being so overwhelmed by the sight of her body falling into the most incredible poses and attitudes whilst they were making love, that it completely and humiliatingly put him off his stroke. 'It's all right, love,' she purred, stretching herself languorously, 'it happens all the time, don't let it worry you.' It took him months to, as it were, get his confidence up.

My overwhelming ballet memory is of a moonlit amphitheatre in Haifa, Israel, with a backdrop of the star-studded Mediterranean, and the tiny figures of Margot Fonteyn and Rudolph Nureyev spinning in space below my seventeen-year-old eyes. Throughout my childhood, whenever a male dancer leaped across our Bush 18-inch telly (usually during *Sunday Night at the London Palladium*), my mother would groan, 'Ugh! I can't bear to look at them in those tights. Ugh! I think it's *revolting*. Ugh!' until the sheer obscenity of it drove her out into the kitchenette, where she would bang about until Bruce Forsyth came back on.

This rarefied atmosphere, you'll be surprised to hear, produced few balletomanes. But in Israel that night, one was born.

Quite the best memory I have of dancing was a couple of weeks ago, whilst driving past Great Portland Street tube station. There on the pavement was a scruffy old man, bald, toothless and extremely plastered. To the music of the spheres (one supposes) he was breakdancing and body-popping with great concentration and even greater joie-de-vivre. I stopped the car, contemplated giving him Arlene Phillips's phone number, gave him a quid instead and sashayed merrily home.

Abscess Makes the Heart . . .

From an early age, well, roughly from the moment the placenta hit the pedal-bin and my mother found there was no way she could return me for a credit note, I realised I needed help with my looks. It was 1946, and the Korean War was news. I had a sallow skin, dark little currant eyes, straight black hair and the refugee jokes flew thick and fast.

My brother, who was described at birth as a 'nose on a pillow' had developed into an infant prodigy with golden curls, courtesy of the 'Twinky' lotion and his mother's rotating finger, and a nose which was normal but pink – with being pushed up into a retroussé by the same finger.

Old Chu Chin Chow's hair resisted everything but gravity and my skin grew used to the ritual torture involved in entering anyone else's home. 'Pinch your cheeks, Maureen,' came the hissed command.

'Why?'

'You look blech' (Yiddish for pasty).

I was eighteen before I dared enter a room without thumbprints on my face.

The second teeth, of course, came out horizontal, and by the age of twelve I'd broken my nose falling down a disused ornamental well, and my front tooth falling off my bike. I confess to being a dentist's dilemma. They dread seeing me, and the feeling is entirely mutual. The minute I enter the room with the horizontal chair and the red water, I take on a marked resemblance to an Edvard Munch painting, and have been known to scream in an insane fashion when asked to fill in a form. This dates back, like most things in life, to early childhood. For some unaccountable reason, I have always disliked having a big, hairy hand in my mouth, hurting me like hell. I know it's foolish, but there you are. It's not for want of trying. I've endeavoured to come to terms with this prejudiced view of dentistry since I gave up having Bonjela rubbed on my gums.

Teeth are a pain in the neck from cradle to coffin. (That could have come straight out of *The Penguin Dictionary of Quotations*. And probably did.) Dentistry is a very high-risk occupation. To me especially. I left my last dentist because he believed that Mahler played very loud was an excellent anaesthetic. It obviously was. For him. Towards the end I began fainting as a means of drowning out all three of us.

71

I blame Him upstairs. How can thirty or so distorted pieces of enamelled ivory thrust their way through the nerve-ends of your skin in a pleasant way? Think how they would feel coming through your feet. Mind you, they'd get about the same wear and tear, but marginally less sugar, I suppose.

I don't remember much about my first teeth, but I vividly recall the permanent ones. One day I just looked down and saw two flat, white surfaces looking back. Close scrutiny showed them to be my front incisors which had chosen to grow at an angle of forty-five degrees from their more retiring relatives. To these offending tusks I now realise I owe a debt of gratitude. They taught me to be funny. Ever noticed how many comics have an overbite problem? Make 'em laugh before they punch your teeth in.

For the next ten years it was a question of bracing myself against the world. My mouth looked like the inside of a Moulimix. The teeth retreated, paused, fortified themselves and lunged out again, like the Charge of the White Brigade. I even sported a brace when my first boyfriend came home from university. He was awfully understanding, but I only hung on to him by the skin of my teeth.

Nowadays dentists believe in gentle pressure, particularly on the parents' bank account. One of my children models a night-time appliance which goes round the head, looks like a cross between a chastity belt and a BMX biker and appears to work by means of two rubber bands. In the era of the silicon chip, that's progress?

At the age of twelve, demonstrating the non-existent six speeds on my bicycle (Arbonate by name – Bike-Arbonate, geddit?), I jammed on the brakes, transcended the handlebars, and landed on one tooth. I counted to ten and then got up, but the tooth stayed down. And out. Since then my mouth has remained a mystery to me.

My first dentist had halitosis. Now, as my mother was always saying, 'Breathe on me' before we left the house, in case there was a use for the Milk of Magnesia she kept in her clutch bag, I naturally assumed it was *my* breath that smelled, and consequently tried to hold it for as long as his face was near mine. This led to regular bouts of hyperventilation which were explained away by my being 'highly strung'.

Another one gave me gas for an extraction. The next thing I remember was the ghastly hissing sound followed by a blood-curdling shriek as the dentist leapt about the surgery, clutching his bleeding hand and screaming 'She bit me, the little shit bit me!'

There's a certain time of day inexorably associated with dentistry. It's about 3.15 in the afternoon. It stems from the middle of Double Geography, when you remembered you were leaving early for 'just a check up' i.e. four hundred fillings and a twenty-minute wince. The feeling was as if a piece of dry cardboard had been inserted in your diaphragm, and it stayed there until you reached the smell of the surgery, where it began to thud. Once in the waiting-room, you placed a nine-year-old copy of *Dandy* over your whole face and tried very hard to transmogrify yourself into a rubber plant.

Coronation Day came twice on the days I had my front teeth crowned. My front teeth have been crowned more often than the Habsburgs. The first time was after seeing myself in the film *Up The Junction*. I decided I looked a dead ringer for Arkle, and fled the cinema in search of a tooth-carpenter. The bit I like best in what follows such a decision is the 'shade card'. (This is where your particular shade of tooth is matched up against a chart to avoid the mix 'n' match look). The expert flicks past all the whites and creams and settles on mayonnaise yellow as your best blend. Smile, please, you're on yellowvision.

Some years later, I noticed the precious porcelain was on the advance again. Several hundred pounds later, I re-emerged as snow-capped as an Alp and ready to out-dazzle the cast of *Dynasty*. My next offer of work was to play Rachel in a masterpiece of a play called *Messiah*. Rachel possessed the most protruding teeth in Poland. Believe it or not, I had to go back to the dentist's and ask him to fix false buck-teeth over the top of my straight new crowns. My greatest fear was that during the most emotional scenes of the play I would spit the teeth out into the eye of *The Times* critic, who no doubt would've given his eye-teeth for such a happening.

I recently worked with Michael Gambon who, occasionally, over-enunciated certain words. He would say, 'She was stretching out for the crisps' (pronounced 'Krrisspps'). We roared with laughter at his characterisation. He protested it was the fault of his dodgy teeth. After the show finished he confessed he was going to a Harley Street dentist to have them all crowned. Wickedly, I found out his dentist's name and placed a discreet phone call. Oh, to have been a fly on that spittoon when he emerged from the anaesthetic and heard the dentist say, 'Could you just try to say "She was stretching out for the crisps"?'

When Jack and I first met we were immediately drawn to each other's overbite. Apparently he used to box at school, and since his long left ensured he was never hit in the face, he couldn't understand why he always left the ring with his face covered in blood. Until he realised his defensive right glove was constantly beating a tattoo on his buck-teeth and buck-lip. The only boxer disqualified for punching himself to a pulp.

Even now, the merest kiss en passant often results in such a clash of glasses, noses and teeth that it's really safer just to blow one. Kiss, that is. During a memorable period, when we were both visiting a dental hospital for gum treatment, the nightly flossing, single-head and double-head brushing, plaque-disclosing and mouthwashing took so long it became a whole new form of contraception. University College Hospital should have a plaque for it.

One of my dentists spends his mornings in the surgery, his afternoons in the House of Lords, where he is an hereditary peer, and his evenings playing in a jazz band. Another, in Chelsea, was recommended to me by an actor friend who was equally dento-phobic. Apparently this gentle practitioner put you to sleep with a nice, calming injection in the arm and you woke up healed, sprightly and well rested. Unfortunately, I enjoyed this experience so much that I began having it for a scale and polish. On one occasion the dentist told me he'd got an antidote to the injection which brought the sleeper round immediately so that you were in a fit state to drive home. He gave me it, but I was so programmed to fit in a good night's sleep that I lay on his sofa snoring for a further two hours until he panicked and started slapping me round the gills. I finally found a nice, chatty, hi-tech South African dentist in Totteridge, who is genetically incapable of causing me pain, and have been happily under his aegis for some years now. It was a short but vital schlepp from where I used to live in North London, but from Paddington I need a full tank and satellite navigation.

Do you wonder why the Tooth Fairy continues to be the only growth industry in Britain? Fifty pence a tooth and double if you forget to let her in. I'm thinking of asking ACAS for a meeting with her. To discuss role-reversal . . . if I leave a new pound piece under my pillow, will she leave me a new tooth?

I saw my dentist only this week. He stuck back part of a crown with superglue. It had come out whilst I was eating a natural sea sponge at a dinner party. It was Annie's idea of a joke. All the other guests had a baked cheese thing covered in a tomato sauce. Knowing I don't eat cheese she'd thoughtfully prepared me an alternative. After trying to cut it, I put the whole thing in my mouth, and chewed away, laughing, till my crown fell out.

I've asked the dentist to cook the bill and send it to her.

They Also Serve Who Only Wait and Stand-in . . .

The actor's nightmare is entering a theatre to be told by a departing back 'Good luck tonight.' No one listens to his protestations that he knows neither the part nor even the play and the nightmare continues until he is dressed in a period costume and pushed centre stage to face a faceless audience of thousands with his mouth open and nothing coming out. At that moment you wake up, change your pyjamas and, if you're sensible, your career.

I once dreamed I was playing a principal boy in a Victorian-type pantomime with raked (sloping) stage and footlights. In mid thigh-slap and just about to launch into a spirited rendition of 'On a wonderful day like today', I felt an insistent tugging at my tabard. Glancing down briefly, I saw my son's upturned face and heard the words, 'Mod – I want to wee-wee.' Momentary pause, then 'I defy any cloud to appear in the sky (psst – go to Daddy) – defy any rainbow——'

'But I need to wee-wee.'

'Geroff!'

Finally, of course, as I sang, he peed. It ran straight down the stage and fused the footlights.

Classic anxiety, of course – I've read my Kitchen Shrink – but in real life the role of understudy can be just as alarming. I once 'covered' Diana Rigg in Stoppard's *Jumpers* at the Old Vic. Mostly, I just slunk around the rehearsal room, admiring the verve of her performance and convinced that she would never be 'off'. Once the play had opened I had the happiest few months of my life in the understudies' dressing-room, giggling myself stupid and learning to crochet. What we found to glue us helplessly to our chairs long after the curtain had come down I'll never know, and, since I never learned to cast off, what started out as a cushion cover was soon big enough to carpet Versailles and so heavy it had to be transported to and from the theatre by taxi. It's been slowly unwinding itself ever since (well, who hasn't?) and will quietly become an egg cosy quite soon, but God, I wish I could encapsulate the amounts of laughter crocheted into its woolly being.

Before I become hooked on the subject, I must tell you that the dreaded night arrived. Diana hurt her back. I tried to hurt mine and failed. Still, I was cool (at twenty-four, who isn't?). I knew the lines and had actually had a couple of rehearsals. The dress was taken in and let out in the relevant places, I had a new blonde wig in which I intended to have a lot more fun, and I sat making up my face in Diana's dressing-room mirror surrounded by Interflora. My heart appeared to be beating *outside* my body – but I was cool. Then, over the tannoy, I heard the announcement to the audience – 'Owing to the indisposition of Miss Diana Rigg –' there followed the loudest and most concerted groan I've ever heard. The Manager strove to continue. So did I. 'So – so in tonight's performance the part of Dottie will be played by Maureen Lipman.' Maybe they didn't all say 'WHO? WHO?' but that's what I heard. Maybe it was just an owl!

The next thing I remember was my first entrance. Seated on a crescent moon Dottie glides in, mike in hand, and sings 'By the light of the silvery . . .' She then forgets the next word. Then 'Shine on, shine on harvest . . .' she forgets again. Naturally the audience thought it was the understudy who had 'dried', not the character, and for a minute the place felt as dangerous as a bullring. Very Good Theatre, I suppose, but not so good for the rapid ageing process. That night I grew up fast. I have a letter from Kenneth Tynan, sent to me after I'd played the part for a week, in which he said: 'Dottie is a woman who uses her body to humiliate men. If you hadn't stripped, you wouldn't have been playing all of the part. One day we must have a chat about the other implications of nudity. We are wrongly taught to say, "I have a body". The correct statement is "I am a body".' I didn't realise at the time the double edge to his correction.

More recently, in Philip King's vintage farce called *See How They Run* in which I was appearing, the leading lady lost her voice three days before the show opened. We were playing to preview audiences of over a thousand people, and without a single rehearsal, in a huge and complex part, the understudy, Diana de Nimes, got through the whole show without a prompt. Afterwards, she confessed that every time a bell rang, a door opened or a set of French windows parted, she had absolutely no idea who was coming through them. As a diet, an experience like that has no parallel. She dropped half a stone in forty-eight hours and gained, I like to think, a foot and a half in stature. In the same show, the part of Mr Humphrey – the timid vicar who arrives in Act III, witnesses a scene of four vicars in various stages of undress, and quietly steals the show – was played by Derek Nimmo. Now Derek is a well-known social butterfly, entrepreneur, dilettante and general good liver who likes to put in a full day about twice as many appointments as you or I might have in a Boots year-ahead-planner. The night we opened the curtain went up at seven o'clock. No sign of Derek. By five to eight his understudy had a lime-green skin and was vibrating like a cricket. At eight Derek arrived, leaving himself hardly more than a few minutes to slip out of his dinner suit into his dog collar and saunter into Act III as the doorbell rang and his fellow actors said, 'Who can that be?' It transpired he'd been doing two episodes of *Just a Minute* at BBC Radio: one just as our curtain was rising in Shaftesbury Avenue, and the second as we were having our interval cuppa.

The point of this story is that Derek's sang-froid was everybody's else sang-chaude. Now me, personally, I have to be inside the theatre an hour and a half before curtain up or my eyes start to twitch. Once in the sanctity of my dressing-room, I don a dressing-gown, take my make-up off, read my mail, arrange flowers, lie down, do deep-breathing, sing a little, warm up my voice a little, finally, stand on my head against the door in the belief that the rush of blood will make my brain agile. It is at this point that somebody like the wardrobe mistress comes in and I fall to the ground and play the performance with my head on my shoulder like a budgie.

Quite seriously, I can't bear my routine to be altered even by a visitor an hour before the show. Liza Goddard, with whom I shared adjoining dressing-rooms in *See How They Run*, is totally imperturbable and entertained her mother, her eight-year-old son and her Golden Retriever in the dressing-room till ten minutes before curtain up on the first night. I was a vicarious nervous wreck, stuffing 'Quiet Life' tablets into my mouth and deep-breathing into a state of hyperventilation. Meanwhile, back at the Beeb, Lord Derek of Nimmo was doing battle with Nicholas Parsons and his understudy was doing battle with the kaolin and morphine.

Julia McKenzie tells a story of touring with *Rose-Marie* with David Whitfield. The leading lady was taken ill, and the understudy didn't know the words, and Julia swears she heard this voice say 'I'll do it', looked round to see who said it, and found it was her. She was nineteen, full of confidence, not a nerve in her body and with a voice that could shatter a chandelier. She went on that night and played the romantic fur-trapper's daughter with every fibre of her being. After a week she was cooing the 'Indian Love Song' with such passionate abandon, that she knew that her future was inexorably tied to romantic operetta. When the show was over, in a rosy afterglow she received the producer in her dressing-room, eyelashes fluttering in expectation. 'Julia,' he said, looking deep into her eyes, 'you've got a great future. In comedy.'

Even in real life I've occasionally found myself playing the understudy part when billed as myself. I once opened a charity bazaar in a London synagogue somewhere. After the speech and in order to appear ordinary and approachable, I walked about the stalls. I was eyeing some macaroons when the stallholder eyed me with that by-now-familiar look: 'Haven't I seen you somewhere before?'

I laughed painfully. 'Er, yes, I expect so – I just opened the . . .'

'You look so familiar!' she persisted. 'Where do I know you from?'

Before I had a chance to cast her mind back, she'd grabbed her fellow salesperson by the angora, yanked her round and, 'Millie, look at this girl – who does she remind you of?'

Millie looked superior and aghast at the same time. 'Have you gone *mad*, Sissy?' she expostulated. '*She's* just opened the bazaar for us. *She's* just made the speech. *This* is Miriam Karlin.' I didn't contradict. I just lowered my voice an octave and bought a madeira cake.

Recently, at a London Club, I met the Bogus Prince Charles. He makes a very decent living, thank you, with one hand behind his back, his teeth clenched behind his vowel sounds and his ears, believe it or not, plugged from behind to make them stick out like his Royal Counterpart's. I still felt slightly overawed meeting him which says a lot about the times we live in when the notoriety value of a good fake is almost as powerful as the real thing.

Probably the world's greatest understudy was Old Mother Riley's. Arthur Lucan, who played the old washerwoman for most of his life, was fond of a drop or two of gin to drown his sorrows. He'd have done better to drown his wife Kitty, the cause of most of them. If Arthur was too 'tired and emotional' to appear on stage, then Roy Rollande would go on, unannounced, to play the part. And no one ever knew the difference. So perfect was the impersonation in every detail that thousands of people who remember seeing Mother Riley live on stage, will never know whether what they roared with laughter at was in fact the perfect double. Last year I played Kitty McShane, the wife of Arthur Lucan, in a stage and ultimately a TV play, called *On Your Way, Riley*. In the act, Kitty played Old Mother Riley's wayward daughter, but in life she ruled him with a rod of iron. She kept the money, dealt with the contracts, made the bookings and gave him his bus fare, whilst swanning around with a fur coat on one arm, and her lover on the other. It was almost impossible to find anyone who'd known the couple who had a good word to say about Kitty.

But I liked her. If you're playing a villain you have to. Often when I drove to rehearsals and someone carved me up in the traffic, I would scream at them in a brogue as ' tick as treacle'. The play was a great success for Brian Murphy, who played Arthur, for the production and for the play. Oh, and me. She was so different from anyone else I'd ever done – so big and so vulgar – and finding the reasons for her awful, bullying behaviour was intriguing. She had been one of a family of eighteen children and married Arthur at the age of fifteen. It seemed apparent that the hardness was a cover-up for the ensuing disappointment and the anger was misplaced frustration.

On the last night of the show, Jack and I were wanly clearing the eight weeks' worth of life that had been stored in my cupboard-sized dressing-room, when there was a knock at the door. It was two of Arthur Lucan's great-grandchildren, who were avid followers of the show, and we welcomed them in for a drink. There was another knock. It was the ex-Rabbi's daughter from Hull and her Iranian boyfriend. We cleaned out more glasses and tried to ally the two worlds, whilst still packing the bags. At the third knock we were pleased to see two gay friends who were still mopping up tears from the death of Arthur. By now, we were raising our elbows in turns, and as the next knock came, we all swayed to the right in order to prise the door open.

The couple were strangers. He was very tall. A big man. She was small and distraught. They were both Irish. 'We're relatives of Kitty's,' she blinked, 'and I've just come to say she wasn't like that at all. She wasn't vulgar at all, and she didn't use that kind of language, and you've no roight . . .' At this, the tall man leant over, slowly jabbed his finger into my chest. 'Your actin' was great, but your accent was f—-in' doiabolical!'

'Oh, thank you, will you have a drink?' Suddenly I was Brian Sewell. 'Have you met er, Arthur Lucan's great-granddaughters? This is . . .'

No sooner were de words out of me mooth, than the wailin' started. 'Oh, will you look at this one, sure, isn't she just like me mother's sister, and how old would you be? So your father was Donald's . . .'

A twenty-year-old family feud was being healed in my eight-by-six-foot dressing-room on a Saturday night, after two shows.

'Has anybody not got a dr –' There was a knock at the door.

'Yes?' I screamed.

'Hello, Maureen? It's Sir Bernard and Lady Miles – can we come in and say hello?'

Well, it was as motley a string of introductions as ever I'd had the pleasure to make. Somehow we all oozed out of the dressing-room and into the green room, and somehow we all stayed friends.

Meanwhile, back in the eight-by-six, Jack packed up the remnants, pulled down the telegrams and loaded up the car. They also serve . . .

After the transmission of the television *On Your Way, Riley*, Roy Rollande phoned me up. He was very moved, and said repeatedly, 'It was her. It was her. I lived, worked and slept with this person, and it was her. I'm ringing up with sincerity, and there's not much of that in this business. Wonderful.'

To all intents and purposes, Roy Rollande and Arthur Lucan were the same person; it had to be the highest compliment an understudy ever paid to a 'stand-in', and I was banjaxed with it all.

Occasionally I have 'stood-in' as that other great British villainess,

Margaret Hilda Thatcher, a task which gives me even more malicious pleasure. I have my own navy suit, tie-neck blouse, court shoes, brooch, pearls, bag and wig, and am available for weddings, bar mitzvahs and hooplas. No, seriously, the surprising element is that I'm nearly always booed as I enter, and on one occasion, at Stratford Theatre East, had a boot thrown at me. With only moderately quick-wittedness I boomed: 'This is typical left-wing hooliganism, when in doubt, put the boot in.' That shut them up. Once a sense of humour was revealed, they knew I wasn't she.

I start the act by saying graciously: 'No, don't get up. Stay kneeling exactly where you are,' and continue, 'No times are hard. I've seen to that. But it's no use tummy-aching about unemployment. As I said at the start of my reign . . . (*roars of approval*) . . . it's never too late to start your own family business. All you need is drive, initiative and bloody rich parents.' More roars. Soft, feminine voice and deep, searching look into camera, noting where the key light is . . . 'I was asked recently if I would care to patronise the Arts. And I said, "Why, I'll patronise anybody . . ."'

Another masquerade happened after 'doing the lady' for an OAP Labour Rally at the Festival Hall. Neil Kinnock was there. Originally he was going to do a bit of a skit with me on the platform, but I think he was still struggling with his image at the time and decided against it. Afterwards I packed up the wig and clothes in a large bag and sped off to King's Cross to catch a train to Hull where I was due to meet my folks for some kind of family 'do'. I was being met in Hull by my Uncle Louis, who's a Labour Councillor, and it occurred to me that it might amuse him to see Margaret Thatcher step off the train to greet him. So, round about Brough or Goole, I nipped into the Ladies, put on all the gear again, jammed on the wig with a little soap round the hairline to keep the dark hair back and painted in the droop-lines round the eyes. I stayed secreted in the loo for as long as I dared, then hovered in the corridor, ignoring the suspicious looks of fellow-travellers till Paragon Station.

First off the train, I walked briskly and purposefully towards the ticket-barrier hardly able to keep my face straight for thinking of his. Being myopic, I couldn't actually see him, but about fifty yards from where I thought he might be, I started with the "ere's-me-'ead-me-arse-is-followin' walk, the sick-as-a-parrot smile and the 'Sincerity-is-my-middle-name' angle of head.

I need hardly tell you he wasn't there. Sheepishly I handed in my ticket and bravely hung around the news-stand for all of twenty seconds before making a bolt for the telephone kiosk, where I kept a hunched vigil while phoning his home. Naturally enough, the times of the trains had been confused and it was a sadly chastened leaderene-clone who ultimately crab-walked to the taxi-rank. Once within the bosom of my family, the joke went down very well when I told how it was but, quite honestly, you really had to be there.

The ultimate stand-in story, which may be apocryphal, stars that veteran actor and imbiber Wilfred Lawson, getting steadily stewed with a stranger one lunchtime in a Shaftesbury Avenue pub. After closing time he insisted his new friend accompany him to a matinée in a nearby theatre. They crept noisily to their seats whilst the first act was in progress, and after a few moments elapsed, Lawson tapped his friend on the arm. 'You see the fellow in the armchair?' He did. 'Well, in a minute there'll be a knock at the door and he goes to answer it, see?' He did. 'And do you know what happens?' He didn't. 'The door opens and I come on.'

I like to think of that story purely from the point of view of his understudy.

A Potted Life

Nothing chills the soul like the front-of-house manager visiting your dressing-room before a show to say: 'Do you want to know who's in tonight?' No, of course I bloody don't! Who? For the rest of the evening your erstwhile naturalistic performance becomes a parody of itself as you strive to re-create your notices for the benefit of an onlooker.

Once, after a performance of *The Front Page* at the Old Vic in 1973, in which I played Molly Molloy, the first of many 'tarts with hearts', a backstage visitor enthused, 'I just loved the things you did with your feet!'

'What things?' I demanded. Tartly.

'Oh, come on, you know what I mean – the foot business!'

I was baffled, frankly, and spent the following twelve performances bent double, playing the part of a tart with a bunion, as I gazed unceasingly down at my own feet trying to catch a glimpse of what they were doing in front of my back, and without my prior knowledge.

Acting requires absorption, but not self-absorption and, in the actor's mind, the question must always be 'Why am I doing this?', not 'How am I doing it?' That road leads to self-indulgence, and we've all seen enough of that from the West End to the local 'art-dram soc' to want our ten quid back and a lift straight back to the video shop.

'How did you start to be an actress?' A voice from the hall. Thank you, dear, you've just saved me from pontificating.

It was very easy. I think I started acting in my romper suit. I was performing from the age of four, by the simple virtue of being nailed to the sideboard by my mother, an actress manqué if ever there was one, and encouraged or coerced to do Alma Cogan impersonations. 'You dree-e-eamboat, you lovable dree-e-eamboat. The kisses you gave me . . .'

'Roll your eyes, Maureen,' beamed my mother. 'Do the laugh in your voice!' and mock and roll I did – right around the clock. And thus was born a minor local celebrity, the sort of precocious infant I would loathe nowadays, if I didn't know from first-hand experience how hard it was not to 'perform'. When the act, once encouraged, just bubbled out of you; when the people laughed and clapped for more. No doubt I felt for the first time bigger and brighter than my bigger and brighter elder brother.

There was never any doubts about my vocation. Nun-like, with some prodigiously bad habits, I soon increased my repertoire of songs and impersonations and, by incorporating most of the neighbourhood children into a sort of backing group, I was soon staging regular shows in the back garage. Sketches, poems and parodies were added, and the show usually ended emotionally with the cast singing the National Anthem, whilst standing to attention, and saluting. A salutary experience for all ten members of the audience.

Once at secondary school, I was clearly the lucky one. Unremarkable in appearance, being undersized, sallow-skinned and with a bit too much ratio of nose to face, I was equally average in all academic subjects barring English (at which I occasionally shone) and Maths (at which I was so appalling I was forced to cheat in my mock 'O' levels and still got 18%). I was lucky because I knew what I was going to be. So when the dreaded Careers Officer came to call, I was in and out in a flash. 'An actress?' she smirked, looking me up and down. 'Well, it's a very hard profession, you'll need something to fall back on, you know.' I know . . . I know. I'd heard nothing but 'falling backwards' ever since I first mentioned my ambition. It was always delivered with a faint look of pity and disparagement. 'I'll just have to fall back on the casting couch,' said the sassy thirteen-year-old with the glasses and the brace. (I've been awaiting that casting couch ever since! Mostly I sit on it while they tell me their casting problems.) Still, many of my friends ended up in banks or offices simply because their ambition hadn't peaked by the time the C.O. chose to call.

My big moment came whilst playing Dr Faustus in the school play. Yes, it was an all-girls' school. At fourteen, I was a committed, if not entirely convincing mediaeval scholar and, save the somewhat giggly moment when I had to kiss Helen of Troy (Susan Downing, a natural blonde) and say, 'Is this the face that launched a thousand ships?', I was a credit to Miss Nicholson's direction. For this performance I received my first and best-ever review in the *Hull Daily Mail*: 'Maureen Lipman. Remember that name, for one day you will see it alongside that of Tom Courtenay and other well-known Hull stars.' It's the only good review I've ever remembered, although all the rude ones are engraved on my bile duct.

What I chiefly remember, though, is the feeling the morning after the last night of the school play. Plays usually had a three-night run, and going back to being 'ordinary' again was dire. All lessons; no rehearsals; no coming in late the next morning; no sick feeling in the pit of the stomach at tea-time. All this coupled with the feeling that somewhere, someone was determined to put me back in my place for fear 'it' had all gone to my head. Which, of course, it had!

[Years later, back in the school hall with Joan Nicholson, filming a programme called *Map of Comedy* for Granada, I asked her why she had chosen such a difficult and cerebral play for fourteen-year-old girls to perform. She looked askance, as well she might.

'Well, why ever not? It was a good play and if I had someone who could play the part I saw no reason why we shouldn't do it just because of our gender.'

You wouldn't describe Miss Nicholson as a prototype feminist but that's in principle what she was.

'So tell me,' I led on, 'if I was so good in *Faustus*, why, when you did *Much Ado About Nothing* the following year, didn't you give me the part of Beatrice? I was born to play that role.'

She smiled. 'Why do you think?'

I knew the answer before I asked the question. 'I got big-headed, didn't I?'

She smiled again. 'Let's just say I thought it might do you good to play the important role of Margaret, the serving woman.'

So the only Beatrice the world will ever see me play is the one at the end of a phone saying, 'Anthony, people will always need plates!']

Nowadays when a long run of a play has ended, I feel only relief. That first evening at home, feet up and mindless telly on by 6.30, is the show-business equivalent of sitting in a Radox bath with a piece of water melon.

When the time came to apply to university, I filled in all the appropriate forms – including the question 'Which career do you wish to pursue?' and the relevant answer 'Actress'. In spite of my three decent 'A' levels, none of them would even interview me. Turning out thespians was not part of their brief. Undaunted, I applied to a couple of drama schools. The Rose Bruford School kept me there all day. I'd travelled down with my mother, of course. The prospect of her seventeen-year-old daughter getting on a train all alone filled her with a dread that could only be assuaged by her company. Somehow, at the time, it didn't bother me. I think I was secretly relieved – large drip that I was.

We arrived, along with two hundred other hopefuls, to spend a fraught six hours singing for our supper to the grand matriarchal shape of Miss Bruford herself. At one point, I seem to remember being asked to be a cup and saucer. Using every trace of imagination, I placed one hand on my waist and rocked about a bit. Later, all two hundred of us were told to be slaves begging for our freedom – from guess who? Miss Bruford herself! She sat on a rostrum at one end of the hall – the slaves set off from the other. We implored, we begged, we crawled on our bellies on the face of the earth. In short, we humiliated ourselves, shamelessly, for the chance of a place in the academy. At the time I was furious – in retrospect, it was a fair example of the life to come.

At LAMDA, life was granda. A team of human beings including the actress, Andrée Melly, heard my 'Lady Percy', laughed at my 'Sabina' from *The Skin of Our Teeth* (complete with imaginary flying props) and, without further ado, I was 'in'. I met Andrée recently and she told me she had never forgotten my audition. I was thrilled as she went on to describe to someone how I had done Titania from *A Midsummer Night's Dream*! I hadn't the heart to tell her I was the one who had done Lady Percy! LAMDA was two and a half years of spade work, some of which has remained forever. On the whole, it accomplished what all colleges of further education *must* accomplish – in that it taught me how to live away from my parents.

Not, I hasten to add, for fear you should detect signs of fast-approaching maturity, away from chaperones. Far from it. Through the *Jewish Chronicle*, I had found digs with two sisters in Barons Court. Still living in the flat of their childhood, they were now well into their middle years. One went to market, one stayed home. It didn't take them too long to disapprove of me. As I learned to stay out late in the Earls Court Road, picking wax off candles and discussing the vagaries of tongue and jaw relaxation, so the sisters learned to put the dinner back in the oven and purse their lips. Every time I arrived home I felt more and more like a drunk in a Donald McGill postcard, and I quickly began scouring the *Evening Standard* for flat-shares.

In pursuit of one such flat, I entered one of a row of telephone kiosks in Earls Court Tube Station one Saturday morning. The phone immediately began to ring. Being young and very green I picked it up. 'Er – Hello – Earls Court. This is the Earls Court –'

'Hello,' came a voice. 'Can I speak to Mr MacNamara please?'

'Er, I'm awfully sorry, but this is Earls Court Tube Station.'

'Oh, well, in that case, would you like to hold the end of my penis?'

Quick as a flash (so to speak) I replied, 'No thanks, I've just put one out,' slammed down the phone and left. As I closed the kiosk door, I saw a grinning face, and what's more, saw a lot of what the grinning face had in its hand.

I fled back to the LAMDA green-room and ordered a coffee from Joe, the Polish caretaker. 'Sugar, honey?' he said, as he would continue to say for two and a half years, in spite of my negative reply.

Nobody seemed remotely impressed with my story – just an everyday happening in SW1. Soon afterwards I moved, with fellow student, Lesley Joseph, into one half of a grim conversion off the Earls Court Road. We shared it with a student eye doctor called Rabinowitz, who had the endearing habit of taking out his eye and resting it on his cheek. When Issy said, 'I'll keep an eye out for you', he meant it. His scoring rate with the ladies was something phenomenal – particularly considering his huge girth, pallid complexion and eye-catching habits. How did he do it? One day he confided to Lesley that he only had three months to live. Soon afterwards we moved out rather than clean the oven, so we will never know whether his terminal condition was a terminal condition or simply one of the wickedest pulling acts in the business – a trompe l'oeil even.

We were an interesting mix that year at LAMDA. Annabel Leventon had been to Oxford, worked in OUDS, had a boyfriend, and a sophistication that I revered. She even had a flat of her own in which she gave Dinner Parties – divine decadence indeed. Anna Calder-Marshall had the face of an Hellenic goddess, unique talent and the instant adoration of every member of the staff. Philip Sayer from Swansea was my love and my brother from the day we met. He too had a veneer (thin) of sophistication culled from a season working at Swansea rep, and his repertoire of camp phraseology was music to my suburban ears. 'Get you, dear!' and 'Vada the bona bats, love', seemed to me the language of a very select club, and I soon learned to shriek and grimace along with the best of them. Of course, by the time I'd mastered 'the polari', as it was called, it had become, or maybe always was, the language of wardrobe assistants and wig-makers. I told you about the 'tarts with hearts' – well, alongside them I played mothers, grandmothers, nosey neighbours and best friends who never got the man. It was difficult to find an agent on the basis of these parts and, as the end of the last term came near, the atmosphere grew tense with massed neuroses. Annabel was seeing Peter Watkins about his film *Prejudice* and Anna Calder-Marshall, Franco Zeffirelli about *Romeo and Juliet*. I'll never forget her entrance into the common-room after seeing him. Everyone wanted to know how she got on. No one could bring themselves to ask. Finally, someone did. Me. In her beautiful, husky voice, lovely face all aglow, she enthused, 'Oh, Mo, he was *so* kind, really. He took one's face in his hands and told one, one had a special quality and one felt so –' 'Anna darling did one get the f—-ing part!?' This with all the fervour of the best friend who never got the man.

The week before leaving, I had a brainwave. Armed with a bag of sixpences for the phone, and a list of every casting director who'd seen the end-of-term shows, I went down to the basement phone, rang each one of them direct, and lied, appallingly. 'Hello, I do hope you don't mind my ringing you, but I'm in a bit of a dilemma. My name is Maureen Lipman and you may have seen me playing the aged mother in Tyrone Guthrie's *The Top of the Ladder*.' (Pause for comment, none came.) 'Er, what it is, you see, is that I've been approached by a documentary film company which is making a film about a young actress leaving drama school to go to her first job. Now I've got the part but' – pause for effect – 'only if I have a job to go to – if you see what I mean.' (Shorter pause.) 'Er – so, if you could see your way to giving me one, a job, I mean, in any shape or form, well then, it would be great for me and also – er – very good publicity for your theatre . . .' Mostly what I then got was a sharp click and the dialling tone; but a couple of intrepid (or gullible) directors did see fit to interview me, and to my amazement, Giles Havergal (showing early signs of the ability to step in where angels fear to tread which has put Glasgow Citizens so firmly on the theatrical map) agreed to cast me in the part of Nancy in Ann Jellicoe's play, *The Knack*, at the Watford Palace Theatre. I was in business, and you know what they say, there's no business like it – I was employed. In a play! Three men and me, and an Equity card at the end of it all. Life was rosy.

With the exception of one thing. Where was I to find a fake documentary film crew, plus equipment in time for Monday's rehearsal? The problem was a weighty one. I mulled it over for three sleepless nights and four sleepy days. Finally, I came up with the solution. When asked, I would reply, with a blankly challenging look, '*What* documentary film crew?'

Strangely enough, Giles never asked the question. Each day I braced myself for it. Each day we just rehearsed. One day the play opened, one day it closed and the question just never arose. Much later, when I was a veteran of three plays at the Palace (including a panto in which I played the Fairy of the Ring, balanced on a pogo stick, in blue hair and tinted specs), I finally put it to him. 'Giles, did you ever wonder what happened to my documentary film-makers?' 'No, dear,' he replied, sagely. 'It was perfectly apparent from the day we met that the whole concoction was a tissue of lies, but I decided to give you the part for chutzpah.' 'Chutzpah' is best defined as a small boy peeing through someone's letter box, then ringing the doorbell to ask how far it went.

Whilst finishing off at LAMDA I had been approached by the agent, Al Parker, who had seen me playing the classic role of a nine-months-pregnant French whore in *Mandrake*, a musical version of *Mandragola*. I turned up in his impressively panelled office wearing matching hat, dress, coat and boots in shades of toning beige. I looked like a buff envelope. He sat by the window, a Hitchcock-like figure, and, glancing up from his typewritten notes (red and green 2 ply), 'Well, Miss [glance at notes] Liprian, I caught your performance last night, I think you're very talented – take off your coat and show me your figure.' I took off one layer of beige and showed him another. 'Okay, you could lose a pound or two.' (In those halcyon days I weighed 10½ stone and was a big girl in the chest department. In fact, in Restoration plays which required corsets I was well known for being able to paint a coach and four disappearing into the horizon of my cleavage. Alas, two children and a decade of working in comedy have whittled it all down to a sort of scrag end.) 'Now,' he continued, 'let's talk nose jobs.' As you can imagine, I balked. Bridled visibly, even. To the extent that exactly fifteen minutes later I was seated in the Harley Street room of Dr Percy Jayes with a compass on my nose, bandying words like rhinoplasty (which presumably means having your horn remodelled), and post-surgical bruising. It was only after arranging an appointment and leafing through a sort of 'Which Nose?' that the thought struck me that it might be less painful to change my agent than to change my nose. I left Harley Street, and Cyrano-like I've remained ever since, for better or worse.

One good turn Al did for me was to send me to an interview for the film *Up The Junction*. This gritty, highly controversial documentary-drama had caused a sensation when it was shown on television and, although the film version would opt for tinsel rather than grit, it had to be a highly commercial proposition. The director was Peter Collinson. According to Mrs Al Parker (the actress Margaret Johnstone, who like every English actress of the Fifties spoke the language 'as it h(y)ed to be sp(y)oken'), he would only interview genuine cockneys, so that was how I must present myself.

Having never met one, this posed a problem. Had she said Australian, South African, Portuguese or Polish, I could have hared straight back to the Earls Court Road and called in any café or dental surgery. But a real cockney! In London? Now that was tricky; know what I mean?

I was lucky to find one in the LAMDA common-room. Her name was Celia Quicke and she put me strite roit away with a few basic vowel sounds and a diffident, slightly aggressive manner. I've always been able to absorb people's mannerisms – it's more of a trick than a talent – and it got me through the interview with the casting director and Peter Collinson, a man very much in the Swinging Sixties mould. He was tall and lean with a craggy face, open floral shirt and the manner of a well-to-do cockney barrow-boy made good. Which indeed he was.

Somehow he bought my act, and with it, the Professor Higgins appeal of showing the film-making ropes to this gawky innocent. The part was mine. Adrienne Posta and I were to play sisters, Liz Frazer our mother, and it was a thirteen-week shoot. My cup runneth bleedin' over. I moved into Battersea, a flat beneath a dentist's surgery, and would leave at six o'clock every morning for the glamorous locations of Lavender Hill and Wandsworth Bridge. Filming, I was relieved to discover, was just like acting, only the food was better. Scrambled egg butties at 6.15 in the morning were as good a substitute for sleep as any I've found, and the more waiting around the better.

I loved the endless chat – in caravans, by tea-runs, perched on rigging equipment. I still do. More than the work, actually. And I was learning.

Not a lot, but enough to get me by with some seasoned competition. There was a family feeling and I was the new baby. At weekends, Peter Collinson and his agent, Barry Krost, would show me round the King's Road, the Club del Aretusa and the Antique Hypermarket. It was very much the era of beads, bells, bell bottoms and hashish. Reelly far out, man!

I managed to conceal that I already knew these places because of my friendship with Ricci Burns, and gooped and gawped like Shirley Temple – cockney style. Because, believe it or not, after seven weeks' filming, I was still doing the act both on set and off, for fear they'd replace me if they found out. I knew about as much of the financial set-up of the film world then as I do now.

One day Peter asked me if I'd like to see the daily rushes. Now I'd never seen myself in a film since I was toddling naked in the back garden holding a snail. I was twenty-four at the time. No but truthfully, I was unprepared for the shock. There I was, huge in celluloid, with every fault magnified. Seventeen-year-old Susan George had a tiny part in the film. When she came on, the producer, Harry Fine, said, 'That girl has something. I just love that girl.' Just like in the movies! As for me, on seeing my face on film I did the only thing possible. I ran out, locked myself in the toilet and sobbed hysterically.

There was a knock at the door. 'Let me in. It's Peter.' I let him in. 'What is it? What's a matter? You're terrific . . .' 'I know. It's not that,' I hiccoughed (still in character). 'It's me . . . I look . . . I look . . . so . . . sob, sob, whinge, whinge etc.' Gently, he reassured me that the film was hard in its feel and look . . . none of us looked glamorous . . . 'You look perfect for the part . . . you *are* perfect for the part . . .' In my gratitude, I heard myself say, 'It's just that I'm . . . er . . . I'm not . . . er . . . I've got to tell you somefink, Peter . . . it's just I'm not what you fink . . . I'm not a . . . cockney. I'm – I'm from 'Ull.'

He studied me for a long moment, then said, 'That's interesting. I'm from Grimsby.'

'But I thought you were an ex-barrow-boy from the East End,' I gasped.

'How do you think I got the rights to the film for £200?' was his twinkling answer. Game, set and perfect match.

Somehow after that, though, things were never quite the same. Both of us had had our covers blown and a slight wariness between us replaced the nice, comfortable Eliza/Higgins rapport of erstwhile.

The film was premièred at the Clapham Odeon, for obvious reasons, and, for equally obvious reasons, I decided on a change of image. I borrowed an amazing dress from Clive, the couturier who had dressed me as a nine-months-pregnant French whore in *Mandrake* and had remained, and still remains, a buddy. I had a false tan put on which gradually deepened into a sort of olive-drab as the evening progressed, and Ricci cut my hair into a sort of helmet. The dress was peacock-blue, floral, halter-necked and swelled into balloon trousers with built-in feet. I looked like a frozen daiquiri.

When Adrienne Posta and I walked into the spotlight, they asked me to kindly step to one side while they photographed her, and that set the keynote for the evening. Even the people who recognised me didn't recognise me. Of those who did, three screamed with fright and one, Suzy Kendal, just kept patting my arm in pity. In no way could it be said that a star was born, and I was more than relieved when Watford asked me to return in triumph to play the Fairy of the Ring in *Aladdin*. Of such stuff are dreams made . . .

In 1970 I joined the Stables Theatre Club (a tiny, experimental theatre built by Granada Television in the late Sixties for the purpose of 'trying-out' small scale theatre productions which could later be transferred to television), there were three changing-rooms and a bar, the latter being a good deal more popular than the theatre with the staff of Granada, for Granada is a 'dry' station – Jewish television some call it – and certainly in the days of Bill Grundy, Michael Parkinson and the late beloved and wonderful Peter Eckersley, the staff was a distinctly 'liquid' one. What the theatre didn't have was a 'green-room' and in vain the actors' committee would request such an addition every time we had a meeting with the management. Finally they capitulated. A notice went up saying 'Stables Theatre Company: your new green-room is on Floor 8 of the main Granada building'. Well, it was three hundred yards from the theatre, but it was a start. We all charged across to survey our new property – past the commissionaire – flashing our identity cards, up the lift, along the corridor and through the door of Room 808. There we stood in amazement – confronted by the sight of a *green* room! Totally green. Green carpet, green curtains, green walls and chairs of a subtly clashing biliousness. Ask and it shall be given. Literally.

There was a time when I returned to Hull after my first term at drama school, fired with the thrill of improvisational theatre. (Sometimes my fellow students and I would get on the tube in different compartments and in the course of the journey, would come together and stage a 'happening'. One of us would walk up to another and slap him across the face, or unleash a torrent of abuse in a 'foreign' language. Occasionally, we would fire out a line at top voice like 'Do you know you are the father of my unborn child?' or simply 'Did you get rid of the body?' It was enough to see the faces of the passengers as we built each conflict into a full-scale confrontation.) During a visit to the New Theatre in Hull, I met the manager whilst having drinks in the enormous stalls bar. 'This place should be used more experimentally,' I chirped from the dizzy heights of six weeks at a drama school. 'Have you ever thought of using it for improvisations?'

'Oh, aye,' he replied proudly. 'We are improving it, bit by bit.'

It was at 'The Stables' that I met Jack. We met as the result of some kind of bet, which I can only assume he won. Oh, coy maiden   shut yer face. At first meeting he reminded me of Yves Montand, although I knew Yves Montand would never have aspired to the Marks and Spencer grey V-necked pullover with black inset dickey, which he sported on the day of our first date. He told me he was learning Hebrew (it was post Six-Day War and he, like many others, was inspired to do something for the boys), and made me laugh telling me about the middle-aged Manchester mommas in the class who regarded him with the curiosity and interest due to a personable Jewish man who seemed, startlingly enough, to be single. The following day I phoned his office and in heavy, Mittel-European Mancunian announced myself as Mrs Esther Schwarzkopf.

'I want to speak to Mr Rosenthal hisself,' I demanded of Margaret, his sanguine secretary. After a hissed exchange, Hisself came on the line.

'Hello, it's Mrs Schwarzkopf from your Hebrew class, how are you, are you busy Friday night?'

'Erm, I'm sorry – who did you . . .? Pardon? Er, I can't seem –'

'Mrs Schwarzkopf! From the class. I sit in front of you every Wednesday. What's the matter with you, you don't see so good?'

'Er, no, yes! It's just that – which one . . . er . . . are . . . er, you?'

'Mrs Schwarzkopf! Esther!' I grew excited. 'The one with grapes on my hat.'

'Er, the grapes in your, er – I'm ever so sorry, I don't seem to remem . . .'

'So how many women in the class have got hats with grapes on? I sit in *front* of you.'

'Yes. I'm sure if I were to see you I'd . . .'

'Will you listen already, I haven't got all day. I want you should come to dinner on Friday night. You got a pencil?'

'Er, Mrs er, Schwarzkopf, it's very nice of you to ask me, but I, er, I always visit my mother in Blackpool on a Fri –'

'Every Friday? You can't miss it one Friday? Listen, I've got a lovely daughter at home, very intelligent with the loveliest skin you've ever seen, like a . . .'

'No, I mean, I'd love to come some –'

'Listen, don't do me any favours, you don't want dinner – don't have. I'm sorry I asked.'

'No, honestly, I mean, it's extremely kind.'

'For my part I thought – a single man on his own in Manchester at the weekend . . .'

'Yes, but . . .'

'No, forget it, don't even think from it. I'll put the Helzel back in the freezer and "fartic" – it's done.'

'But, Mrs Schwar –'

'Goodbye. I'm only sorry I intruded on your time and goodbye.' SLAM.

This little jape set the seal on our future life. Even after sixteen years together I can still steal his chips by dint of a sudden glance over his shoulder and a shocked expression, indicating 'WHO'S THAT?' It was several hours later in the Stables' bar when he related the episode to me, and it was only the flaring of my give-away nostrils that he caught on. 'Mrs Schwarzkopf!' he choked into his lager. 'Of course! Who else? And I've been torturing myself with guilt ever since! I was only looking up her bloody name in the phone book to send flowers, wasn't I?'

It was at the Stables Theatre that I gave of my black serving maid, Zanche, in the Jacobean tragedy of *The White Devil*. For this remarkable ethnic feat I wore two coats of black and copper greasepaint – polishing each coat – a frizzed wig, time-saving black gloves, white neck ruff and more gold eyeshadow than you see at a fork supper at the Marbella Club. One night when I was merrily involved in a game of dressing-room Scrabble, I heard the unthinkable over the Tannoy: 'Miss Lipman, you're off!' (Theatrical terminology for 'Get ON you berk!') Like a cartoon cat I leapt down the corridor and screeched to a casual halt on stage. The cast regarded me with strange expressions. I regarded them back with the expression of one who'd never actually *seen* an actor's expression before.

My usually myopic gaze spread to the audience. It was a studio theatre and they were close, but instead of the usual comforting blur, I saw eyes, nostrils, hairs in nostrils and liquorice in dentures. It didn't take a giant intellect, which was fortunate, for I was not the possessor of one, to realise that this particular sixteenth-century black maidservant was still wearing blue-tinted, steel-rimmed, hippy-style spectacles.

I raised my hands to remove the anachronisms and couldn't help but notice that they were as white as – well, ungloved snow! My exit was as inelegant as had been my entrance, and there must be many people who, even today, remain puzzled by the unexplained symbolism of the bespectacled penguin in Act III of Webster's play. Tragic really.

After this triumph, I returned to London for a comedy series called *Don't Ask Us We're New Here*. It starred five fresh new faces (including my own), and was utterly forgettable. Jack used to visit me in London, but he was a Manchester lad, and London, to him, was a place to visit, deposit a script or an idea, and catch a train out. Somehow we commuted our relationship until with gentle pressure (like throwing myself on to the tracks at Piccadilly Central) I persuaded him to come down South. He claims it took twenty minutes to feel at home. We lived in Hampstead in a friend's vacant flat, and I used to cycle to work at the Old Vic in Waterloo. It must be about eight miles and coming home, all uphill, would render me comatose and wheezing each night. We rehearsed all day for one play and played or understudied one another at night. I was very, very happy.

We got married in '73 and I went back on stage after our two-day honeymoon. We went to a baronial castle somewhere in Norfolk, with suits of armour, four-poster beds and several stars for sumptuousness. It was as jolly as Juliet's crypt, and we fled to Bognor Regis and wet walks by the sea. It was perfect. The wedding itself was amusing. I wore a petrol-blue Gina Fratini dress, slightly period in feel, and a large cream hat. Jack wore a dark brown suit, and his only tie. My parents arrived from Hull, Mother looking lovely in a pale green coat and dress, and a pink flowered hat, and carrying five hundred fishballs in a plastic bag – for fear there wouldn't be enough food. She was right, as it happened. Jack's mother arrived from Blackpool doing the same.

All sides were relieved that we were finally legalising our relationship. The first time I had taken Jack home was the first time I'd ever been able to take anyone home, since my earlier affairs would all have been deemed unsuitable for one reason or another. I was supposed to be living in digs in Manchester in Fog Lane, would you believe? – though since Jack had a nearby flat, I wasn't spending a great deal of time there. At home, of course, I was placed in my own bedroom, with the teddies, and Jack got the boxroom. Naturally enough I found it hard to sleep and was pacing about when my mother, as always majoring in the rhetorical, called 'Can't you sleep?' On hearing the negative reply she suggested I came in for a chat – which I did. My father grew more and more annoyed at this intrusion into his shut-eye and finally, after dark mutterings and much thrashing about of limbs, he got up and stalked into my room, where he re-instated himself in the snooker hall of his dreams. I ultimately settled down with mother and the night passed normally away.

Except for Jack. Unaware of this game of musical beds, he awoke at 5.30, and remembered where he was. Then he remembered where I was, crept out on to the landing, creaked his way past my parents' room, silently negotiated the door into my room and gratefully got into the single bed with my father. It was only after he'd kissed the short hairs at the back of his neck, and my father had whirled around saying 'What the bloody hell do you think you're doing?' that he realised his mistake.

'I – I – wondered if you'd like a cup of tea . . . ?' he stammered.

It took a long while for Maurice to totally trust the man who was to marry his daughter.

Of course, after four years my parents wouldn't wait. People were beginning to *talk*. There is a photo in their lounge which says it all. It shows the whole family at their silver wedding. My brother and his wife, my parents, myself, all beaming and resplendent in evening dress, and slightly away from the party to the left, my beloved, looking suspiciously like a BO advert. This was unceremoniously arranged by my mother. For fear again. This time the fear was that in the event of 'nothing coming of it' (i.e. our relationship), she could always cut him off the edge of the picture!

So, back to the wedding. Looking back, we should have been married in Hull with everyone who'd known me since cheek-pinching days, Mum and Dad in full regalia surrounded by their friends. That's what your wedding's all about, isn't it? At the time, and in my euphoria at being in the National Theatre Company, I didn't want to know that. I assumed that the people who were with me *now* would be with me *always*. Jack had rallied a colourful Manchester rabbi and we were to be wed in the West London Reform Synagogue, of which we are now members. I didn't even think to hire a limo – just a dirty old mini-cab – and I dropped in at Ricci Burns's flat on the way for a crimp and a glass of bubbly, then off we all went.

Outside the synagogue I was left alone with my Dad. Always a sentimental, emotional and highly forgetful man, he held my hand, kissed me and said, 'Mammele, I wish you every happiness in the world, you look lovely and you should only have a wonderful life together. I'll see you in there.' So saying, to my amazement, he left me outside the shule, with the organ playing the Wedding March and no one to accompany me down the aisle. To those who know my father this will come as no surprise. He once took my mother to the pictures and, hating the film, arranged to nip into the Station Hotel for a game of snooker and pick her up after the film. After waiting twenty minutes she went home. Where was her husband? He'd completely forgotten he was married and gone home to his mother's.

So there I was, pulling open the big double doors – jamming my foot in them and hissing at his departing back, 'Dad – psst! DAD! Have you gone *mad*? Come *back* – you've got to walk me down the BLOOMIN' AISLE!! You're my father!' Back he came, blustering very slightly, and embarked on the moment he'd spent his fatherhood waiting for.

I seem to remember, with horror, that the rabbi gave a list of both our credits under the canopy. 'Er, Jack, of course, has written *Coronation Street* and, er, *Dustbinmen* and, oh, *The Lovers* – very, very good stuff; and his lovely bride, also, in her own right, a member of the, er, National

Theatre Company, and between them they should have many years of success and happiness . . .' I remember shifting uneasily in my fear that with such a distinguished audience he might be tempted into a few choruses of 'Is this the little girl I carried, is this the little girl who played?' and perhaps a story, a hymn and a prayer.

Louie Ramsey was my 'best woman' and sang 'Happiness is just a thing called Mo', at the reception, which broke me right up, and it all went off like a wedding.

My Husbandry and I

I'm about to be profound for posterity and I expect you to have at hand a sheet of 2-ply, a square of card, a pair of pinking shears and an adhesive of your choice. For herewith I give you 'The Lipman guide to domestic tips, folklore superstitions and husbandry' – possibly the thinnest and most useless tract in the non-Esperanto speaking world.

I'll start with tips – since I only know five it won't take long. The first two concern the cooking of a duck, which I personally do once or twice a summer solstice, if at all, as anyone knows one large duck feeds roughly two under-fives and one member of the corps de ballet before it's reduced to soup bones. Nevertheless, if you *are* roasting one, do it over a shallow pan of water to draw off the fat, thus making it crispy. If you wish your duck to be wind-dried, then use the method favoured by Julia McKenzie, who hangs it over the shower head whilst blow drying it with a fan heater on an upturned wastepaper bin. Yes – you knew she was talented but you never knew she was mad as a snake! Stick with me, kids, I promise you revelations that would drive a *Sun* reader to Jane Austen.

Now. If you want a flesh-coloured bra, soak a white one in cold tea. Alternatively if you go bra-less you could soak your breasts in cold tea. PG Tits, I suppose. And for really shiny brass knobs, soak 'em in Brown Sauce. This is a little known fact which actually works. I don't know why they don't brag about it in their advertising. 'If our product can bring a shine to your knobs, just think what it can do to your stomach!'

Then there's carnations. I'm not going too fast for you, am I? Carnations, and how to keep them fresh in a vase for up to four weeks. You've heard of Carnation Milk, haven't you? Well, get ready for Carnation Lemonade. Yes, you stand your blooms in a vaseful of 7-Up and 'up' they'll stay, as fresh as a bloomin' daisy for a whole month. No, I *don't* know if it will have the same effect on other limp things. And no postal queries, please, as to whether Diet Pepsi or Root Beer will work as well – just take Derek the wig-dresser's word for it, as I did, and your pinks will be in the pink. He also recommends a drop of bleach in the chrysanths, but I draw the line at bullying. I could happily peroxide a germ, a shirt collar or an unwanted facial hair, but not something that's fought its way through fertiliser and lived.

On the medical front I cannot advise you too strongly to try the Bach

96

Flower Rescue Remedy. It comes in a small bottle from most homeopathic chemists, and I find it cures me of whatever I think I've got, i.e. everything in the *Pears Medical Encyclopaedia*. In the odd moments of stress, shock and general hysteria which make up 93% of my life, I find it invaluably calming. (During the run of *Wonderful Town*, the stage musical, my little bottle ministered to a migrainous musical director, a fainting co-star and any number of cases of chorus throat and hoofer's ligament.) I *used* also to have a bottle of homeopathic pills which were labelled 'For Fear of Oncoming Events'. I carried them everywhere but never used them since my fear of not having enough left for tomorrow was greater than my fear of any event that might 'come on'.

Much unorthodox medical advice came from a sturdy Irish lady who once 'did for me', in more ways than one. Amongst her 'pearls' was a sure-fire cure for removing verrucas which involved the burying of a piece of raw meat at a crossroads. Presumably this folklore stemmed from the days before tarmac. I have this picture of myself in the dead of night limping through N10 with a plateful of steak tartare and a pneumatic drill . . .

Her other gem concerned nits and went somethin' like this: 'Der was eleven of us at home, and at noight me mother used to make us all rinse our heads in a bottle of our wee-wee. And I tell you dis, Mareeen, not one of us was *ever lousy*!' Nor popular, I fear.

As far as superstitions go, I don't believe in *one* of them! Touch wood. God, I wish I had a Beauty Flash ampoule for every time my mother made me sit down and count to ten because I'd left my plimsolls under the bed and had to come back for them. ('Mother, I'm ten minutes late' – 'It won't take a second' – 'It'll take ten' – 'It's bad luck' – 'Oh, for heaven's sake! Onetwothffssnenten! There!' The resulting good luck earned you trapped fingers and a detention for unpunctuality.) Not to mention the mounds of salt I've thrown over my left shoulder into the eyes of passing au pairs, who think their employer is a pervert, nor the screams that ensue when shoes go on the table, knives get crossed or you happen unavoidably to cross on the stairs. Arguments and bad luck will follow – particularly if the stairwell is narrow and there's a black cat approaching from the left. Sally, my dresser at the theatre, got the shock of her life when she tried to sew up the hem of my dress just as I was going on. 'Bite me! Bite me!' I yelled. 'Why?' she asked, justifiably enough. 'I don't bloody know – just bite me, or I'll forget my lines!' Bless her, she did it – rather heartily, I thought.

If I were to tell you the elaborate ritual I go through before going on stage, to ensure I never 'dry' – you'd smirk. Suffice to say it takes me at least three quarters of an hour and involves standing on my head, deep breathing, repetitions of mindless phrases and the putting on of clothes, make-up and jewellery in a precise order – left ear-ring before right, etc., muttering all the while.

The other day a pleasantly shy young man from Hospital Radio came to interview me in my dressing-room, bearing tape recorder and carefully researched questions. He began nervously, 'Miss Lipman, you have played many varied roles in your career, from Lucy in *Dracula* to the Third Witch in *Macbeth* . . .'

'Stop right there, please!' came my peremptory voice. 'And go out of the room – close the door – go *on* – I'll explain later – turn round three times, knock on the door and ask to come in – off you go!'

Poor soul, I thought he was going to be sick, but how else could I avoid the appalling curse which descends as sure as a politician on a baby, on him who utters the name of the Scottish play within theatre walls.

And gloves. How many times have I dropped one in the street and had to wait till a complete stranger walks past to say, 'Excuse me, but would you mind picking up my glove for me? Er – no, I'm not paralysed, I'm superstitious. Oh – and I'm afraid I won't be able to say "thank you" afterwards – it's unlucky – but I will be very grateful – oh, thank you – oh shit! I've said it! Oh, I'm sorry I said shit . . .' etc?

Who was it, I want to know, who first decreed that neither lilac nor hawthorn should be brought into the house until the geese's eggs have hatched? And will I have to buy a bloody goose to find out? Will a dropped spoon forever mean a disappointment rather than dented lino, and does it bother me that if I dry my hands on the towel at the same time as someone else we'll never speak again? Must I forever wait for a second magpie, be delighted when I step in a 'lucky' dog poo (for whom?) and say 'Kenen Ahorah' every time I mention something is going *well* in the company of elderly Jewish relatives, for fear of the evil eye?

In Mel Brookes' and Carl Reiner's record *The 2000 Year Old Man*, Reiner asks the 2000-year-old man what is the secret of his amazing longevity. Brookes replies: 'I never run for a bus. There'll always be another. I never touch fried food. I stay out of any small Italian car and I eat a nectarine a day. I love that fruit! Half a peach, half a plum. Even a rotten one is good. I'd rather have a rotten nectarine than a fine plum.'

You think he's wrong? I suppose you think you're safe if you avoid ladders and cholesterol and keep a stone with a hole through it under your bed to ward off arthritis? You should be so lucky!

The Jewel and the Clown

Now take my jewellery collection – please! Listen, if you can find it, you can have it. Over the years, my heirlooms have been moved from a wooden tool-box to a cardboard egg box and finally, for increased security, into an elderly plant pot under the dressing-table. Here they rest in a curious system known only to me and best described as a 'wodge', which would drive any self-respecting burglar to phone 999 for assistance.

The system works perfectly well for me. Should I require a second ear-ring to go with the one I've dug out of the pocket of my jacket, I merely turn the wodge upside down on the carpet, scrabble around for eight to ten minutes, find the missing link and scoop everything back into the pot. Then all that's required is a couple of butterflies to hold the ear-rings in place. This necessitates tipping the whole shebang on to the carpet again, and extracting the little bleeders by the use of a plastic straw and a fair amount of suction.

Once found, the tiny gilt stick at the back of the ear-ring is forced through the hole in the butterfly which is deliberately made smaller than the stick in order to propel the butterfly, frisking through the air, into the clothes basket, giving it its pretty name and the washing machine a breakdown in its filter pipe. This is no problem either, as your repair man will be glad to pop round Wednesday morning or afternoon (can't say which) four months hence for a coming-out and going-home fee, *if* you have a set of wheels, a jack and long-nosed pliers.

Where was I? Jewellery. Yes, I used to have a wedding ring. Well, five, actually. A very classy Wendy Ramshaw set, purchased by me in the absence of my then fiancé, from the Electrum Gallery. Two flat gold bands and three silver, with moonstones of various shapes set at angles to make a sculpted whole. Very modern, very chic. 'Ooooh,' said my mother as I flashed a very un-Fergie-like finger at her. 'Isn't it . . . unusual?' Many bliss-filled years later, I was down to two moonstones and no wedding ring. I last saw it at the TV Centre during a play in which I decided it was too upmarket for the down-trodden character I was playing. After wrenching it off by dogged and persistent use of an entire bar of Palmolive, I swapped it for a conventional band of gilt-veneered brass and spent the next few hours twisting it round my finger to indicate some emotion since forgotten.

Fellow sentimentalists, I never saw my wedding ring again. Went home in the fake and by the time I'd rung up in hysterics, it had disappeared into the 7000 shoeboxes of the Prop Jewellery department with a polite but firm 'This company disclaims any responsibility for articles lost within its radii, so yah, boo, sucks, tough titty, get a new one!'

For a few weeks, I wandered around single again, hoping that Jack would notice (he didn't). Then, one day, my attention was caught by one of those Russian wedding rings which twist round each other in tastefully differing hues. My finger was measured through a card with a hole in it, and the ring slipped on – well, shoved, 'cos I've these largish knuckles to my fingers; knuck-fingered as well as knock-kneed – and, to my embarrassment, once on, it refused to come off. After several minutes of jocular twisting and wrenching, you will not be surprised to hear that the jeweller and I decided unanimously that the Bolshevik band was absolutely perfect, and I duly paid up and wore it until I played my next single girl and out came the Palmolive. However, this time, the finger that does dishes just grew as raw as my face and the day before opening night I had it sawn off. The ring, not the finger. So next time you see me, don't say 'I'll give you a ring', 'cos I'm likely to give you a knuckle sandwich.

One wedding anniversary – I think it was our eleventh; the tin foil one, isn't it? – Jack bought me a truly sensational present. Normally, a few weeks before a birthday or a Christmas, he starts wearing the look of a beagle who can't remember where he's buried his bone and starts sniffing around for clues with overwhelming subtlety. None of that happened, however, that February. Just Piers Brosnan smoothness, the occasional smirk, and even one or two 'Everything's perfectly under control, m'dear'. Having nothing brilliant lined up myself, I panicked and ordered him a stained glass window for his birthday.

I was presented with a silver ring in the shape of a dressing-room door (featuring my name, a gold star and a tiny door knob) which opened. Inside was a room with a tiny gold chair in front of a mirror circled by light bulbs, shoes on the floor, dressing-gown on the back of the door, flowers on the shelf. I can't tell you how beautiful it was. Is. I've actually hung on to it; I still have it. Mind you, I had to have it changed into a pendant as the door kept opening every time I changed gear and while wearing it under a glove, it looked as if I had a ganglion. (For those of you without a medical bent, a ganglion is a lump of tissue which suddenly appears on hand, foot or head, or in a tendon sheath. When my mother gets one, she asks me to hit it with a copy of *Chambers Twentieth Century Dictionary*, after which it apparently sulks and goes away. Who wouldn't?)

Bobby Cartlidge, who'd made the ring, carefully donned her eyeglass and smelting kit and adapted it for the neck. She's a gem of a jeweller, a

Freeman of the City of London. Her own ring is a Victorian parlour which opens to reveal a roaring fire, a cat asleep on the mat, a rocking chair and a round table with long fringed cloth. Unique and marvellous.

En passant, she told me a wonderful story about when she and her husband Derek were young and struggling to make a crust. It was in the days before the invention of tape. The only way of recording sound was on a 78 rpm disc, four minutes each side – a bit like breast feeding. Derek had his own disc cutters and HMV gave out his number for special recordings. One day someone rang and said, 'Can you get down to Ramsgate today to record a talking dog?' 'Can I ever!' said Derek, one foot out of the door and his ball and biscuit in his hand. (Now steady on, 'ball and biscuit' was the vernacular for disc and microphone.)

It was, he says, the oldest dog he'd ever seen, and it refused to bark a single syllable. The disc only lasted four minutes, and since the disc and the petrol were just about all his worldly goods, the situation grew desperate.

Finally the owner said, 'Come along, Fido, what's 19/11d from a pound?' To which the dog said wearily, 'Woof.' And the dog and its owner practically expired with excitement.

Bobby and Derek returned to London with a short but meaningful dog recording. Over the next few weeks they recorded a talking parrot, a Siamese cat that made baby noises, and they were feeling pretty well pleased with their new little niche.

One day the phone rang and a voice said, 'Do you do Barmitzvahs?' 'All the time, madam,' said Derek, who'd never heard the words. This was, after all, *years* before Mr Rosenthal's play *Bar Mitzvah Boy*. He took down the details and agreed to be there on the day. Then he put down the phone and said to Bobby, 'What kind of dog is a Barmitzvah?'

Bobby came originally from Germany and had never heard of the species. They tried to look it up in the Ganglion Basher. Curiously enough, it wasn't there.

'Perhaps it's not a dog,' said Bobby. 'It could be some other sort of animal.'

Derek nodded. 'Well, she said we've to be at the Porchester Hall on Saturday morning. That's where the baths are, isn't it? Maybe it's a reptile . . .'

In desperation they rang London Zoo. (Honestly, I promise you this is true.) They spoke to the admin office and asked if they had such a thing as a Barmitzvah in their Zoo.

'What kind of animal is that?' asked the administrator. On being told it might possibly be amphibious he added. 'Right, I'll put you through to the Reptile House.'

101

'Do you happen to have such a thing as a Barmitzvah amongst your inhabitants?' enquired Derek. 'Er, I'm not sure what species of reptile it is. We're going to record it in the Porchester Baths so it could be some sort of porpoise or – oh, you haven't – no, well, we've not heard of it either. I just thought with your knowledge of – yes, I see. Well, thank you, anyway.'

The following Saturday Bobby and Derek, wearing sou'westers, waterproof capes and wellington boots, with their recording equipment encased in plastic, arrived at the Porchester Hall to see five hundred elegantly dressed Jewish people milling round the thirteen-year-old boy in whose honour the celebration was. The only fish worth recording had been dead for some time and was sitting nicely fried on five hundred plates.

An elderly Jewish lady sits in a park, polishing her rings. A man in a raincoat runs up to her opens his coat, flashes her and runs away. She calmly continues polishing her rings. He approaches her again and this time flashes for longer. Again, she doesn't bat an eyelid, but carries on polishing – finally, he returns, stands bodly in front of her, opens his Mac and stands there fully exposed, daring her to scream. She looks up from her hands – looks at him fair and square and says: 'You call that a lining!'

Whoops Apocryphal

They always start 'This friend of mine was telling me about his wife's sister-in-law, Debbie, and her car . . .' The story which follows is so far-fetched and improbable that it has to be grounded in relatively familiar territory to preclude an immediate response of 'Oh, get off! I don't believe it – pull the other one, it's gone to gangrene. No, it's really a joke, though. Isn't it?'

Debbie's car, it would seem, kept breaking down and one Saturday morning finally found her husband in his old blue denims working, somewhat reluctantly, under the chassis. Well pleased to have laid him so low, she goes off shopping with a cheery 'Goodbyee.' On returning an hour or so later, she sees him in the same supine position. Feeling rather touched, she decides he should be, too, and creeping up, in one deft movement unzips his fly and gives him a grateful pat on what could be described as his 'wedding tackle'.

One can only assume these were the heady, early days of their marriage. Given another eight or nine years, there's many a husband of my acquaintance who might have tersely responded with 'Oh, hello, love – I've put the carrots on a low light and did you remember the hosepipe extension?'

Where was I? Oh, yes, Debbie. Well. Off she toddles into the house, delighted by the diligence, not to mention the responsiveness of her husband, who she's now somewhat surprised to see making two cups of Typhoo in the kitchen. One for him and the other for the mechanic he'd called in who was now outside working under the car. Wearing good old reliable blue denims, presumably unzipped.

Debbie's embarrassed. She and her husband shuffle outside to explain and apologise, only to find the abused mechanic lying in a pool of blood. His own. Obviously when the assault on his lower half took place, his upper half had jerked into direct contact with acres of hefty car-part and he's been knocked unconscious.

Believe it or not, the story continues. The couple phone 999 for an ambulance. The ambulance men drag out mechanic, put him on stretcher and start to leave, stopping to ask how the accident occurred. On hearing couple's honest account, they start to laugh, try to stop, become hysterical and finally drop stretcher and mechanic, breaking arms of both. True or false? Only Debbie can tell us and she's probably still in hiding.

Then there's the dinner party. Let's call her Deirdre. Inter-course, as it were, conversation flowing well between high-profile guests, she goes into the kitchen to garni the whole poached salmon. Unfortunately, she's been pre-empted in this en-devour by her cat, Nelly, who is garni-ing the fish in the only way it knows how. Desperate, Deirdre wrestles with her scruples for a whole thirty seconds before kicking the cat out, rearranging the chewed bits, covering the whole with a cucumber, six lemons and a parsley bush, and making a flushed re-entry into the dining-room. The dinner party's a wow. Everyone especially loves the salmon. Back in the kitchen to make coffee, Deirdre opens the door to let in Nelly only to find the cat stone dead on the stone steps, feet and legs rigid with mortis.

Collapse of Deirdre into roughly the same position. Husband and she decide that possible salmoNelly of high-profiles is unthinkable; they confess crime. Whereupon twelve of them go to local hospital and are unceremoniously stomach-pumped. Odd cries of 'Thanks for an unforgettable evening!' ringing in her ears, Deirdre and husband return home, lift cat from doorstep – to find note underneath, as follows: 'In haste – I apologise most dreadfully but your cat leapt out in front of my car. Nothing I could do. Saw you were entertaining and didn't want to disturb the party.' Signed by A Neighbour.

Even more silly women people the mother/child story circuit. (And why not? We are never more certifiable than when attacking or protecting our young.) The woman on the bus whose child is wiping her lolly back and forth on the fur collar of the lady in front: 'Don't do that, Tracey! You'll get hairs on your lolly!' Or the woman on the country bus whose sixth and final child has just started school. She breathes the sigh of the long-last rid and finds herself grabbing the sleeve of the elderly man beside her, pointing wildly out of the window and shouting 'Look, darling! MOO-COWS!' She's the self-same 'friend of mine', no doubt, who was so anxious to impress her husband's new boss as being an active and supportive wife in spite of the six appendages, that she sent them all to her mother's on the night the boss was due for dinner. The house was spotless, the food divine, the conversation stimulating. It was only after the boss had left and she was congratulating herself on being a perfect hostess, that her husband asked her what the hell she'd thought she'd been doing – leaning over and cutting up the boss's meat into tiny pieces while holding a conversation with his wife on the Post-Impressionists?

In fact the only male protagonist in the world of the Apocryphal crops up in a story about a famous actor-chappie (could've been Ralph Richardson – he's at the centre of most actor-chappie stories) who was invited to the legendary country mansion of two moneyed theatregoers of limp-wristed but impeccable taste. Let's call it 'Smacked Bottom Villa'. He is housed for the night in the Peacock Room – so called because of its hand-printed silk murals of peacock motif, each panel being of custom-design and exquisite delicacy. During the night and needing the bathroom, he gropes his way towards the light switch, knocking over what he takes to be a vase of water. He continues groping along the walls till he finds the switch. In the glaring light he looks down at his blackened hands and realises it was not a vase he'd tipped up but an ink-well. And there all over the silk mural are his fingerprints to prove it. Without pausing for breath, he dresses, packs, and under night's cover he leaves the house and thumbs his way back to London.

He lives with this on his conscience for many months till, at last, he writes an explanatory letter to his hosts' London home with an invitation to his approaching first night. A letter arrives inviting him to tea the day after and mentioning neither peacocks nor ink. He arrives at the portals of the Eaton Square house, is ushered by the butler into the satin drawing-room and sits heavily in a large wing chair to await his hosts. After a while he rises to adjust what he takes to be an intrusive cushion and finds he has totally suffocated the couple's pet chihuahua.

Legend also has it that a family drove their estate car across to the continent. In the car were mother, father, three children and paternal grandmother. They reached the South of France and for a few days all was sun, sea and beaucoup de plage, when after a particularly full bowl of moules marinière, the elderly grandmother collapsed. They got her to the nearest hospital, but it was, alas, too late. Grandma had passed on.

To bury her on French soil was out of the question. There was nothing for it but to drive her body back to – well – to English soil. But how? The car was full of kids and it would be too unsettling and, let's face it, too pungent to sit her in her normal seat next to the baby. In the end they hardened their hearts, wrapped her up in a groundsheet and tied her on to the roof-rack. Then off they went at a somewhat sedate pace. After several hundred miles, they drove into a motorway café, to fill up both family and car. They ate well, washed and freshened up and returned to where their car was parked. Except it wasn't. It was of course disparu, vanished, kaput, stolen, filched, GONE. With a roof-rack full of late Grandma.

It has to be said that this macabre story is only funny from the villains' point of view. They see the bulky roof-rack, spend furtive minutes breaking into the vehicle, drive off like madmen, and finally stop at a safe hideout to unpack the booty. Except the booty is one very dead old lady in a groundsheet. Then, how does the family explain the theft to le gendarme? Franglais gone frantic: 'D'accord, Monsieur, est-ce que vous me dites que votre grand'mere 'as been, 'ow you say, remové de votre roof-rack? Encore une fois, s'il vous plaît?'

Sometimes a shaggy dog story can be told with such dead pan that you believe all the way that it's factual. There's a hair's breadth between shaggy and apocryphal. Which reminds me – only the other day, driving back from the country, I hit something large which felt like a dog. I stopped and got out, only to find a large hare lying by the front wheels. It was a pitiful sight, shocked into a quivering, twitching paralysis. I was luckily able to flag down a police car and a vet was called. I felt sure the hare would die before he arrived but somehow, the creature lived. I explained the accident to the vet in trembling tones. 'Don't worry, madam,' soothed the vet, bringing out from his medicine bag an aerosol can with which he sprayed the surprised animal. A moment later, and to all our amazement, the hare jumped to its feet, shook itself, hopped blithely over the fence into a field of buttercups, and, waving his right paw in the air as if to say 'Cheerio', disappeared from sight.

I was stunned, and, turning to the vet, said, 'What on earth was in that spray?' 'Oh, that,' he replied nonchalantly, 'was a new kind of hare restorer.' 'But,' I wanted to know, 'why was it waving its right paw at us like that?' 'Oh, well, you see, it's the hare restorer with the permanent wave!'

Yes, I know it's awful. But in its defence – it was told on *The Des O'Connor Show*. Les, my fireman friend, told it to me as though it had happened to him. I was practically weeping at the plight of that poor hare. He gets me every time, too! Only last week I was ga-ga over the saga of one of his mates at the station who'd been taken seriously ill with food poisoning after a meal in an Indian restaurant. Apparently, the only dish the guy had eaten which his friends hadn't was an onion bhaji. So when the Health Inspector visited the restaurant he checked the ingredients the chef was using. To his horror, instead of using onions, they'd been using daffodil bulbs, which were cheaper and tasted similar.

My jaw hit the lino. 'My God,' I whispered. 'What happened to the man who'd eaten them?'

'Well,' said Les gravely, 'he's still in hospital.'

'But is he going to be okay?' I persisted.

'Ye-es,' grinned Les. 'He's a bit yellow, but he's coming out in the Spring.'

Total collapse of silly little woman in kitchen.

Finally, the one I hope is true. A reporter asks Mikhail Gorbachev, 'What do you think would have happened, sir, if Mr Krushchev had been assassinated instead of President Kennedy?' Comrade G thinks for a moment before replying, 'I do not think that Mr Onassis would have married Mrs Kruschev.' If it's true then he has a real sense of humour. And, if *that's* true, what in hell did he find to talk about for nine hours to Margaret Hilda Thatcher? Surely not silly, defenceless women stories?

Getting to the Beetroot of the Problem

I was inhaling a cup of warm beetroot juice through my right nostril last night, when I suddenly thought of my readers. Would they believe it if I told them? They've accepted my eccentricities in the past, I mused. They've accepted my force-feeding a sex-starved tortoise – why should this new hobby be anything but normal? But beetroot? Up the nose? And warm? Is this gag a long-running one?

It was all down to the osteopath. I'd returned from having my crick clicked bearing 'a couple of daily exercises' to reduce the puffiness under my eyes. Now, we all know that as you approach 40 the bag under your eyes starts to feel like the one over your shoulder, but when I'm at the studio at 7.30am and I look like a cross between Willie Whitelaw and Rocky Racoon, I have been known to utter the odd expletive. I've tried sliced cucumbers (though they can dry up into little, hard courgettes), tea bags (they dye your skin ochre, which is hell to match), egg white (reputed to be what the women of *Dynasty* wear under their make-up, which probably explains why their acting is such a yolk), and every eye gel, most of which cost more per pot than a session with a good plastic surgeon.

Talking of which, I met an American plastic surgeon at a party the other night. He held court on the stairs, sporting a hair transplant which looked like one of those experiments where you grow mustard and cress on blotting paper, and always referring to himself in the third person. As in, 'So they wanted the best in the world, so they called Fritz, and Fritz said, "Sure, send her over", and twenty minutes later, Fritz had pinned back her ears and repositioned her nipples.'

His wife, who was blonde and luminous, hung on his every word as he explained that when they'd married Fritz thought her 'a boodiful woman, who needed nothing doing but her upper eyelids'. So he did them. He then did the lower ones, gave her bigger cheekbones and a tighter chin. Then he remodelled her nose. So much for above the neck.

'Don't you ever worry about all those operations?' I ventured.

'Are you kidding?' she grinned, showing a couple of hundred perfect teeth. 'It's better than a vacation. You just close your eyes and, before you know it, wake up looking like someone else.' And I don't think she meant Willie Whitelaw.

Obviously, the lady had anaesthesia addiction, and pretty soon she must have shouted, 'Come on down!' because then he reupholstered the rest of her. He enlarged her breasts. Then he made them smaller again. Or they deflated. I like to think he did it twice because the first set wouldn't fit her last year's Calvin Klein. Then he sucked the fat from her stomach and buttocks. I asked him why he didn't refrigerate her so that the fat would rise to the surface and he could just skim it off like I do with chicken soup. He looked at me with suspicion, but didn't entirely dismiss the idea out of hand.

Finally, the pièce de non-résistance. So that she would wake up in the morning looking as perfect as she did at night, he tattooed eyeliner on to her lids. 'How did she look?' 'Ordinary' is the answer. Like an attractive saleslady. She admired my socks and when I raised my skirt to show her they were tights, she moaned. 'Oh, but you have great legs; I have these tree trunks!'

Fritz shook his head miserably. 'Yup,' he volunteered, 'and there's not a damned thing even Fritz can do about *them*!'

Later, at dinner, he stopped with the hard sell and seemed genuinely convinced that he was doing a real public service by giving people the feature they long for. A sort of Louis B Mayer of Silicone Valley. Sometimes, he told me, at a party, while chatting to someone's neck wrinkles, he'd drive downtown, open up shop and do a quick carve-up as a favour. Like you and I might give a lift home, he'd give a home lift.

The most intriguing aspect of all this was how easily – in spite of the demeanour, the dead stoat on his head, the encyclopaedia sell, the wife and the mildly deranged air – he could have persuaded any woman in that room, however attractive or intelligent, to go in for an alteration. We are deeply insecure when confronted by anything that was once a medical student. I always cry at the doctor's. Even when I just take the children for their ears or Belgian measles I'm near to tears.

When my gynaecologist told me he'd have to induce my first baby because he was going on holiday the day she was due, I said, 'Oh, thank you, yes, that'll be fine.' Which, roughly translated meant, 'Why, you pin-striped prick, didn't you tell me that during the last nine months? Will it hurt? Will it affect the baby? Where are you going for your holidays? And I hope there's a sodding earthquake.'

One avuncular naturopath with a scarlet flowing beard brushed in opposite directions at the bottom, asked me copious questions about my preference for light and shade, warmth and cold, mountains and valleys, then, without further ado, filled me full of pins. Or, rather, I allowed myself to be filled with pins. He placed his little needles in my head, in my hands and in my feet. A week later I had pneumonia. I'm not saying it was his fault. Intellectually, I know I didn't get it from wind whistling through my pinholes, but in my heart I blame him.

Another memorable medic was the allergy specialist who accused my body of being allergic to wheat. Every complaint is food related, he proclaimed, producing a myriad of home-made charts with spirals, arrows and circles. He, too, asked lots of questions. Which food did I like to eat? When? And how? I was intrigued throughout by the number of big, white pills he kept popping in his mouth. Finally, I asked him what they were.

'Bisodol,' he replied. 'I suffer from appalling indigestion.'

'But surely your allergy diet would stop that, wouldn't it?'

'Oh, no,' he replied, burping, 'No, it doesn't do a damn thing for it. No, Bisodol's the only thing.'

As my confidence in him began to dwindle, I paid my £40 and rushed out for a wheatgerm sandwich.

The vital thing to remember about alternative medicine (which I'm extremely 'pro') is to keep an open mind and a straightish face. I mean, it wouldn't do to say 'I'll believe that when Nelson gets his eye back!' when told to rub aboriginal mud on your top four vertebrae for arthritis, or masturbate for migraine. Oh, wouldn't you like to know?)

Another treatment I tried on myself was cupping. It was done by Minoru, a Japanese friend of mine who is an Aikido Dan and Shiatsu masseur. It centres round a mysterious black box with tubes attached to a series of sort of wine glasses, which are placed at strategic aqua pressure points along your back, buttocks and legs. A current is then switched on which somehow sucks the flesh into the wine glass, or in my case whine-glass, turning the blobs of flesh a lurid magenta colour.

Is the question 'Why?' springing to your lips? Well, I'll tell you. It is a fast way of encouraging the toxins to leave your body. More than that I cannot say because I do not know and I'm obviously fair game for anyone who fancies the sight of quivering Beaujolais-coloured flesh in a goblet. Does it work? Well, yes, it made me feel more energetic and look considerably more patterned. It also made my husband lose several years when he walked into the bedroom to find me lying naked on the floor with blobbing glassware all over my torso and a robed Japanese gentleman squatting beside me, twiddling his big black box.

'Oh, hello, love,' he said after a momentary pause. 'It's the *Give Us a Clue* office on the phone – shall I tell them you're tied up?' In my cups was probably more to the point.

Actually he's fairly blasé about Minoru and me. Once I cut my thumb rather badly on a tin of corned beef (Orthodox Jews please don't write in) whilst he was here. I was all for the killer Casualty Department and some stitches but immediately Minoru took hold of the bleeding digit, pressed the cut together extremely hard and began shaking it above my head. He did this for at least forty minutes, which was an interesting experience in itself, since I lost all sense that the hand or arm was any part of me, and felt only this hefty lump of dough being kneaded over my head. After a while Minoru said, 'I go to car now, fetch black seaweed toothpaste.' He actually said 'brack seaweed toothpaste,' which was even more confusing, but we'll have no racial stereotypes in these pages and I'm very fond of him. 'Jack – you hold thumb and shake it while I go,' added Minoru over his shoulder. Jack rather warily took the shocked thumb and proceeded to shake it rather forlornly about. As he went through the door Minoru popped his head back and said, 'Bend the knees, Jack – bend knees.' Jack bobbed smartly into a half bend and carried on shaking from this rather uncomfortable position.

'Why do I have to bend my knees?' he asked me.

'It's probably to do with the energies coming from the lower part of the spine – it probably gives you more manoeuvring power,' I said knowledgeably.

Minoru returned with the toothpaste. 'Very good Jack,' he smiled, unscrewing the cap.

'Tell me,' said Jack, 'why do I have to do this shaking with bent knees?

Minoru looked blank. ''Cos you too tall,' he answered with Eastern logic. He then smeared brack toothpaste on my cut and I disappeared through the fixtures and fittings with the pain. Something to do with the salt? And the healing, of course. The thumb did repair but it has retained a curiously flat look like a depressed whoopee cushion and is a bit slow to spring back to life when pressed, which rather goes with the rest of me these days.

I recently spent a weekend at a Natural Healing Centre in Dorset. I was full of cynicism when I arrived, particularly when of four guests, three were journalists and one was a theatre masseuse. However, I thoroughly enjoyed my two-hour aromatherapy. They dowse to discover which are the best ones for each individual. Two of mine were majoram and rosemary. I came out smelling like a leg of lamb. In fact, they dowse for a lot of their diagnoses, using a small crystal on a chain and contact between the dowser and patient. My eyebrows were well-arched when I saw this thing start circling then suddenly reverse directions, but it turned out to be very accurate about foods which I can't tolerate, and in prescribing remedies. I knew chocolate, cheese, red wine and some dairy and wheat products were not good for me but you should have seen the pendulum when confronted with me and peanuts. It went bananas! Oddly enough, it went bananas on bananas too!

The remedies prescribed for my general health were the Bach Flower

Remedies. And I must say I have a lot of time for these plant- and herb-based cures. Whatever you do, though, don't read the book on how Professor Bach discovered them or you'll never take another. It seemed as though my big problem was 'Over-enthusiasm and enforced jollity, and taking on other people's problems!' This will come as no surprise to those who've ever encountered me on a bus or in print, and indeed I spent most of the healing weekend listening to the problems of almost everyone there. I am after all the woman who told an entire risqué joke under intra-valium anaesthetic. I have no memory of doing so but I vaguely remember hearing roaring medics and much dropping of sterilised instruments.

The best form of relaxation I know is reflexology. Amazing to think that points on your feet can directly affect the rest of your body. So, if they press a certain spot under the sole, your stomach starts rumbling. Its curative and diagnostic powers are almost a certainty, but what you don't anticipate is the sheer sensual delight of having your feet rubbed. Parts of your inner toes which have never felt the pressure of anything other than a winkle-picker or a corn plaster, start positively beaming with pediatric pleasure, and you walk out with a Spring in your step and a Fall in your arches.

Anyway, for the moment it's beetroot juice. The leaflet says you retain it in the nose, then expel it, repeating several times, and this will facilitate the elimination of large quantities of mucus. It certainly did. It also eliminated the sangfroid of my husband who entered the bathroom just as a quarter of a pint of red liquid was coursing down my nose, mouth, chin and nightie. He thought I'd cut my throat and was all for calling Casualty until I explained the root cause of my appearance. Whereupon, he was all for calling a psychiatrist.

At the end of the day, as David Coleman might say, the best tonic you can have is a good laugh. Maybe there's a small business for me – a 'chuckle clinic'. I can see it now: the front door revolves on itself so you walk inside and find yourself outside again. You finally get in, and it's decorated to look exactly like the outside did. The receptionist says, 'Good morning, can I interest you in a mother-in-law joke?' The doctor has an array of custard pies and invites you to throw one in his face after you've disagreed with his diagnoses. The in-house shop stocks tickling sticks, whoopee cushions, Mucky Pups and banana skins – all in constant demonstration. Non-stop videos show the best of Lenny Bruce, George Burns and Gracie Allen, Lucille Ball, Les Dawson, Billy Connolly, Woody Allen and the Marx Brothers, episodes of *Soap*, the original film of *La Cage aux Folles*, and *Monsieur Hulot's Holiday*. Oh – and early Australian afternoon TV runs concurrently, and such classics as Ian Nairn walking backwards towards the camera and John Cleese walking anywhere are on request buttons. In fact, you can dine at Fawlty Towers and even have your head slapped by a Basil clone.

There will also be places where you, the patient, have to keep a straight face: simulated models of church when someone has just farted during the vicar's sermon, and the headmistress's study when her bra strap has just snapped, sending one breast hurtling south at an alarming rate in the middle of her lecture on personal hygiene.

And if all else fails, there's always jokes: non-stop, we-never-close, stop-me-if-you've-'eard-it jokes. 'A man runs into a pub clutching his hand between his legs. "Oh my God, oh my God, h hell, oh – oh – aaaargh – etc," he writhes and twists in agony. "What on earth is it, Fred?" asks the barmaid. "What have you done?" He groans and twists, doubled over in pain. "I've been hit by a bleedin' cricket ball," he manages to gasp out. "Oh dear me," says the barmaid. "Have a whisky – there, now how does it feel?" "Oh – grrr – oh God – it's still terrible – aargh." The barmaid looks at him, then says, "Oh, come on, lad – I've known you long enough. Come into the back room and I'll give it a rub." Off they go into the back room, where she proceeds to undo his trousers and give him a rub better. "There now," she says, surveying him. "How do you feel now?"

'He smiles wateringly. "Well, I feel a better in myself," he gasps out, then, holding up his thumb, he adds, "but I still think the nail is going to go black."'

To apply for membership of this élite organization, please send a ticket stubs from any Ray Cooney farce in which the hero never loses his trousers. No, seriously!

In the meantime, if there's anyone out there who's had puffy eyes which suddenly went away without recourse to vegetables, needles, or Fritz and his Swiss Army knife, please send me details in a buff-coloured envelope, and I promise to make us both a very rich man.

As I write this – some years later, admittedly – I am watching the lovely, gifted Tamsin Greig, fighting High Definition lighting in a programme called *Love Soup*. These days, studio make-up is sprayed on our faces with some kind of air-pump which gets into the places no sea sponge can reach and lays down a fresh layer of epidermis for the duration. Consequently, the only way to look good on television is to have a plastic surgeon on stand-by in the wings or be fifteen years old. It may not be too many months therefore, before Harry Potter's young friend Hermione will be the next auditionee for Miss Marple. It's someone up there's idea of what the viewers want, whereas the truth is the viewers showed up in their droves to watch Judy Dench, Eileen Atkins and Julia McKenzie letting it all droop out of their bonnets in *Cranford*.

Wanted; girl presenter for peak-time TV slot. Applicant must have croaky voice, impertinent tits and an unlikely amount of hair. At the Oscars this year, Sky TV had a girl interviewing the stars who defied the job-seekers description of a TV host in any day and age but our own. She was blonde, bulk-cleavaged, unsuitably clad for one so heavily pregnant, and so vapid as to make even the intellectually challenged of Hollywood widen their surgically widened eyes in disbelief. From Anna Ford to Mariella Frostrup to this Cat, Keely, Kelly person in one high definition swipe. Not one intelligent question came near to her mouth, nor any knowledge of the films up for honours.

'Hars yors goin love?' she asked an equally pregnant Reese Witherspoon. 'Iss the standin that gets you, innit?'

Tom Wilkinson gave her a courteously long interview considering she didn't seem to know which film he was nominated for, Jodie Foster tried manfully and failed to climb down to her level, and George Clooney's iconic blend of self-deprecating wit and un-American irony whizzed straight over her plaster-haired head. Like many others in the nation, I imagine, I turned down the sound and watched the frocks and the rental work. This year's films were so macho/murder and misogyny based that *Juno*, a sweet little low budget comedy scripted by an ex-lap dancer turned lap-top chancer, was the one film which united everyone in a sigh of relief. Screwball comedy lives! Women can lead a film to box office bravura – and not a star credit in sight.

I saw Michael Parkinson recently, interviewing Joan Rivers, Sharon Osbourne and Sophie Dahl. Joan now sports a papier mâché head and can scarcely move any part of it, Sharon confessed to being Botoxed on the day of the show and Sophie, naturally lovely at thirty, had a nose-length fringe. All three stars flirted throughout with their unembellished, unreconstructed, still baggy after all these years, Shar-pei dog of a host, Parky.

Hear PJ O'Rourke, American humorist and Republican, explain to the *Today* programme why Hillary can't win the Democratic ticket. 'Not because she's a woman, we'd every man of us vote Mrs Thatcher in even though we know she's a bit dotty. No, it's because Hillary is the first wife we all got away from.' Oh, right, PJ – not because she's a Democrat and a woman and smarter, more committed and yes, more ambitious for herself and her country than commentator O'Rourke, funny though he is at our expense. Girls, girls girls! For this level of equality and self-esteem we struggled through Naomi Wolfe? I realise we've reduced male confidence in one fell swoop by calling their bluff and maybe a few of the shots, but something's not working and it looks to me both sexes are looking for an Alternative.

A Shortage of Screws

When I was asked to write a foreword to a *Punch* book on sex and marriage, I decided to mis-hear the brief and wrote a short but emotive piece on Saxon Marriage, which was easy to research if one had access to my son's last history project.

Traditionally, sex was not a big subject in my family home. If *really* pressed my mother would admit to 'only having done it twice' and her look implied this was three times too many. This grossly permissive attitude ensured her daughter would be something of a late starter. (Not for nothing was I placed somewhere between Janet Street-Porter and Margaret Thatcher in a 'sex appeal' list. I blame our dentists.) Whilst my schoolmates squirmed over Cliff's top lip, James Bond's rigid weapon and a few Humberside acne cases, I worked on a veneer of carnal sophistication as underdeveloped as my chest. The worst moment of my 16-year-old life was when my best friend and fellow wallflower found passion at the Polytechnic. There's only so long you can endure being part of a threesome, two of whom keep swapping tongues.

I must have grown up during the Sixties, because my memory positively ripples with tales of bedding strange-fellows. This one did because *Cosmopolitan* magazine told one to. Or at least told one everyone else was. It was the sexual equivalent of the whole class wearing their school berets inside-out in order to be different. There was Helen Gurley Brown telling us the world was at it like cutlery. There was Germaine Greer using rallying phrases like multiple orgasm and erogenous zones, and there were Masters and Johnson doing a David Attenborough on our intimate moments in 3D, full colour and marks out of 10.

And there were we. In satin bell-bottoms, cowbells and enough Indian cotton to empty Madras, sitting cross-legged on the parquet, rolling unpleasant substances and gazing meaningfully into each other's tinted granny glasses to the sounds of Leonard Cohen who, in retrospect, should have kept to the family tailoring business.

And you know who benefited most from the sexual revolution? *Really* unattractive men, that's who. Fellas who'd never got so much as a snog or a fondle of a Maidenform at the Hammersmith Palais half a decade before were rolling in clover. Fellas with huge T-shirted beer bellies ballooning over obscenely buckled cowboy belts. Fellas with bald pates, meandering jowls and long wisps of facial hair, who donned owlish specs and an all-seeing expression, grabbed a cheap copy of *I-Ching* and a phial of frangipani, and suddenly became 'Desirable'. The bigger the nose, the more gravy in the droopy moustache, the more the frizzy-haired, bandeaued, loose-breasted maidens hung on to their every 'Peace, man'. Every A-string they plucked was a heartstring.

Where are they now, those profits of mood? All living peacefully in Surrey, having sold the record business to finance the water beds and moved fluidly into jacuzzis at the drop of a trend.

This is the sadness, of course. By the time permissiveness had filtered through from the Big Apple to the Small Seedless, say Keighley or Cockermouth, the Germaines, the *Tatlers* and the *Cosmos* were all into celibacy – just as the car keys were about to hit the Casa Pupo shagpile rug.

I got sidetracked, as usual, by the Sixties. I meant to tell you the story of Jack's stay at the Algonquin in New York where, as he puts it, the walls were made paper-thin so that everyone could hear what Dorothy Parker kept saying. He arrived at the same time as a large, pneumatic Nordic beauty who checked into the next room. In the night he was aroused from his crossword by a piercing shriek. 'This is New York,' he reasoned, 'and the woman in the next room is being mugged and raped!'

Without further thought, he cleared his throat and rapped out Britishly, 'Are you all right, madam? Can I help you at all?' There was a silence, broken only by a girlish giggle, a man's murmur and the sound of flesh on flesh. Then they resumed what they were doing and Jack withdrew beneath the duvet. He spent the following three days skulking round the hotel to avoid meeting her, and took all his meals alone in his room.

God knows, sex is no joking matter, so here's the latest which neatly combines sex and hotels. A man checks into a brand new multi-storey hotel in New York. The bellboy says, 'Anything you want, sir, just ring.' Then – nudge, wink – 'And I mean anything. Service is our motto.' The man sits on his sumptuous hotel bed, thinks, and phones down . . . 'I'd like two brunettes, two blondes, two redheads. I'd like an assortment of whips, a leather collar, a bag of chains and a cactus.' 'A cactus?' says the bellboy doubtfully. 'Now that may be difficult at this time of night . . .' 'Well, in that case,' says our hero, 'I'll have a coffee and a prune Danish.'

Talking of service, only last week I had the kitchen specialist service department in my basement, examining their faulty extractor fan. (The only way I got them round after three months of 'All parts required for your machine are in West Germany' was to send a letter in fluent German saying, 'Where are the sodding parts for Maureen Lipman's lousy extractor fan?') While the mechanic was down there, I was in the kitchen being interviewed by a publishing gentleman about women. (No, really. Feel free to yawn – I did.) It was exactly at the point of his asking me about women's sexuality that 'the dialogue exchange I will never forget' occurred . . .

ME: 'I simply don't understand why so many of the interesting, bright, caring and beautiful women I know are hooked on the most dismal, selfish, boorish, philandering, egocentric, unattractive men . . .'

MECHANIC'S VOICE FROM BASEMENT: 'Mrs Rosenthal, I think you'll find a shortage of screws here. That's your problem.'

So there you have it. Or not, as the case may be. Just remember, every four hours a woman is being sexually harassed on the streets of this great city – and she's getting damn fed up with it.

Diary of a Showbody

Doing your first musical is like having your first baby. There's a conspiracy of silence. Oh, people will tell you how fulfilling it is to hold this glistening prize in your arms, to feel the waves of love and admiration, to know that you've accomplished the most natural and most unnatural of openings. But no one will tell you how it hurts. Or when to breathe, or how not to push when there's no one in the theatre but your husband and twenty-five Japanese medical students.

Nor will they tell you what an excellent contraceptive it is. Just about the only thing that could have lured me into bed in those days was a large tube of Algipan and a heated pad. In fact I reckon you could solve the problem of world population explosion in one season, if you put the Third World into a musical. And don't imagine Andrew Lloyd Webber hasn't thought of it.

Dan Crawford sent me the script of *Wonderful Town* saying, 'This is the Cleopatra of women's parts in musicals.' I wrote back saying, 'You bet your asp', and booked a crash course of singing lessons with Ian (The Larynx) Adam. David Toguri of *Guys and Dolls* fame was asked to choreograph. We spoke on the phone. 'I'll do it if you do it' was our mutual promise. Martin Connor was to direct, having done a production already at the Guildhall School of Music. We met and immediately established a rapport which was to continue throughout the wonderful, gruelling, whirlwind days to come. The story of two 'girls' (since the part had been created for Rosalind Russell in her heyday – i.e. in her 40s, and since Lauren Bacall played it only nine years ago in Boston, I felt suitably qualified for girlishness) who leave Ohio to find fame and fortune in New York's Greenwich Village, was a familiar one. One sister was blonde, dumb in a knowing kinda way, and gorgeous. The other was me. Smart, wise-cracking, plain and funny. It was a part for which I'd been auditioning for forty years.

Prior to rehearsals I met the lyricist Adolph Green's wife, Phyllis Newman, and her friend Jean Kennedy Smith, the youngest of the Kennedy dynasty, for dinner at the Savoy. They were to invest in the show, and along with producers Dan Crawford and Bob Fabian, we all discussed the project with barely suppressed excitement. We were to open at Watford, the scene of my first-ever professional performance (good omen), after only four weeks of rehearsals. As with every new show, I felt both pleased and apprehensive, mostly the latter. I voiced my growing feelings of inadequacy to our director. 'I'd like to sing the songs with a pianist to see if they're really in my range' – my range being about as wide as my knowledge of rugby players between the two world wars.

The great thing about singing is that it gives you an enormous buzz. Just opening your lungs wide and making a loud noise is enough to make you feel quite high with joy, even if the ensuing sound is like the cry of a baby otter in search of its mother. After singing through the score in front of another human being I felt relieved enough to sing in front of the cast and ultimately in front of thousands. Funny thing, confidence, you know. It's so fragile that one discouraging word can silence a voice for ever, just as an encouraging one can give you Ethel Merman-itis. Potential critics, take note.

Just a few weeks before we were to begin, tragedy hit the project. Bob Fabian, the delightful, urbane, silver-haired New Yorker who was co-producing, died of a heart attack. I hadn't known him long, but had liked and trusted him instinctively, and felt an ominous sadness at his untimely death. Indeed, financially the show lost some of its investors and Dan had to fight tooth and nail to find the necessary money to fund the out-of-town try-out. There was still no promise of a London theatre, but throughout the days of rehearsals we pushed this firmly to the backs of our minds.

The fronts of our minds were taken up with learning the dancing. David Toguri is the kind of man who asks as much of you as he would ask of himself. He particularly excels with actors who are untrained for dance because he somehow works around their personal eccentricities of movement. He watches what you can do and uses and improves upon it rather than asking the impossible. I claimed in *The Stage* that he could make a Volvo Estate look graceful. He certainly had me doing stuff my 40-year-old body had only had nightmares about.

In the Brazilian Conga number, where Ruth (my character) attempts to interview some Brazilian sailors whose only word of English is 'Conga', he calmly suggested that I leap sideways into the arms of three of them, who then pushed me upwards into a standing position on their hands and thus slowly over the top to land in the waiting arms of the other three. This overhead pendulum approach was a triumph – except that it threw my tensed body into a state of bone-rattled trauma from which I've yet to emerge. It was fine, once I'd got used to it, and if and when all the sailors were 'on'. If, however, one of them was off with a strained back or a bad throat (one boy in particular suffered badly with a strained throat which we later found was a result of days spent busking in Covent Garden), the replacement for all of them (known as 'the swinger' for reasons, I suppose, that he'd go on and do it for anyone) was a man at least seven inches taller than any of the others. This, coupled with his understandable panic at dancing in six different places at once if necessary, made the line-up a rather irregular shape. At the end of the number they held me up high in the air at arm's length. This meant that wherever he was replacing someone, that particular part of my anatomy was seven inches higher than anywhere else. This was all right if it was my feet, odd but acceptable if it was my head, and downright daft if it was my bottom. My body, I found, is extremely flexible, but it drew the line at being 'humped' – in the engineering sense of the word.

There were several other sky-dives in this number as well as some extremely wild and wonderful earthbound stuff. The number lasted about seven minutes and was immediately followed by the Conga *chase*, which involved running round the back of the set to the opposite side, up a flight of iron steps, along a grid and down another set of steps, whilst the set of our apartment slid on. Then followed a short but noisy scene leading into a reprise of the Conga, another lift, and the end of Act I. For the first few weeks I was clinging to the scenery, gasping for breath, sweat dripping down my face, and chest thumping so hard it fought with the timpani.

Then somehow, miraculously, you get fitter and tighter and the breath comes from somewhere and you do it. This has to be an argument in favour of hard exercise, in spite of all you've heard me say before. Sally, my dresser, used to peel my dress off me and drop it in a wringing heap on the floor, whilst I sponged myself off all over, there being no such convenience as a shower in the dressing-room. *Shower?* There was scarcely room for a flannel, but knowing the old Watford Palace well, one can't really complain. It's not the first time a theatre's exterior and auditorium have been gloriously refurbished at great expense, with the money suddenly running out before it can reach the actors' dressing-rooms. My room adjoined the boys' room. (Are you kidding? After all that running and dancing?) So I could hear the lowering of voices that indicated a particular filthy joke or the lowering of bums into whoopee cushions or whatever they'd decided to do for intellectual stimulation, whilst I was dripping into a washing-up bowl. Strangely enough, I only had one major migraine in the whole year of doing *Wonderful Town*. It was matinée day, after we'd moved into the West End, and it was bad enough to make me miss two shows. Apart from that I was trouble-free – which has to say something about the relationship of exercise to migraine. Certainly during the seven weeks between Watford and the West End, working on a television series, *The Little Princess*, I was back to my normal one a month, and since the end of the show, it's been the same story.

Has this discovery galvanised me into a life of aerobics, jogging, long-distance hula hooping and Kendo? Has it buggery! Same good intentions – one day's jogging, next day rain stops jog, next day imminent delivery of school blazer stops jog, next day slow walk down to Lark Pet Stores reveals twisted bit in foot, and jogging ceases for ever. Still, if it really seems, as I'm told, that exercise is good for the liver, which is the sluggish organ that causes migraine in the first place, then you'd think I'd be up to my ears in leotards, like a veritable Green Goddess on steroids, instead of hunched over this page with a throbbing pate and a green skin.

I'd sat in on some of the auditions for chorus and featured roles, and I found it unbearable. There is something heart-breaking about the sight of young kids on their best behaviour, desperately wanting their talent to show in its best light, in a five-minute spot. Everyone was very kind, the lights were on in the theatre and there was no suggestion of the barking voice from the stalls shouting 'Next!' but even so, there was still the strong feeling of slave begging for freedom or groupie currying favour. The worst part was when David Toguri would say, 'Do you dance?' Always the same response – a giggle, a shrug, then, 'Well, yes, I mean, I can move a bit.' The next few minutes are then torture as the flustered individual attempts to pick up simple steps and rhythms with his brain in command and his feet in total mutiny.

Jack told a story of the auditions for *Bar Mitzvah Boy*, the musical version. After a back-breaking afternoon watching acres of ethnic women singing 'Sunrise, Sunset' in headscarfs and pained expressions, a little lady came on in a purple cocktail dress. She had a red face and very shiny black hair piled into tortuous coils almost as high as she was. She was very definitely not Jewish, but she'd *heard* that this was a Jewish show, and amended her lyrics accordingly: 'Love is where you find it (I should be so lucky), Don't be blind it's all around you (oy veh) everywhere (Have I got a daughter for you!), Love is where you find it – (already) –' etc. All this delivered through a fiendishly animated face and accompanied by wild shrugging and bartering gestures.

Gradually the assembled team, director and producer crept out of the darkened theatre leaving only Jack directly in her line of vision. With his hand clamped round his mouth he nodded and smiled and finally thanked her in a clenched voice for coming in and for her song, and all the research she'd put into it. Then he laughed till he was sick.

My friend Lesley Joseph was on the receiving end of such an encounter. She turned up at the tail-end of a day of auditions for a West End musical, walked on stage to a wall of apathy, and heard a voice call out, 'Well, Miss Joseph? What have you got for us?' to which she replied, '"I've got rhythm" and "You can't take that away from me".' Wearily the voice drawled, 'Nobody's trying to, Miss Joseph, nobody's trying to.'

Pity the poor actor, for we know precisely what we do. The story goes that three men went up to Heaven and were greeted at the gates by St Peter. 'How much do you make a year?' he said, naturally enough, to the first one. To which the man replied, £300,000.' 'Go and stand over there with the surgeons and lawyers.' Then, to the second man, 'And how much do you make a year?' 'About £50,000,' replied the man, and was promptly told 'OK. Go and stand over there with the accountants.' St Peter then turned to the third man. 'How much do you earn a year?' he said. 'About £3,000,' admitted the man. St Peter stopped in his tracks, looked at him keenly and said, 'Would I have seen you in anything?'

Or in the same vein, there's the story of the director, Peter Hall, who goes to Heaven and is met by – you guessed it – St Peter at the gates. 'Before I go in,' says the director, 'just tell me something. Trevor Nunn's not in here, is he?' 'No, of course he isn't,' soothes the saint. 'Now just pop in there.' 'You're quite sure?' 'I'm quite sure.' In he goes and immediately sees before him on the walls every poster ever printed of Nunn's productions – *Macbeth, Nicholas Nickleby, Chess, Les Misérables* – his mouth falls open in disbelief, he turns to protest, then sees through the window a huge triple limousine draw up. A chauffeur leaps out and opens the door for a small neat man with a dark goatee beard, black floppy hair and beady little eyes. The director swings round in fury and yells at St Peter, 'That's unfair, you promised me faithfully that Trevor Nunn wasn't here.' St Peter smiled. 'No. No,' he says firmly. 'That's not Trevor Nunn. It's God – He just *thinks* he's Trevor Nunn.'

Meanwhile back Watford way the show was finally cast – the full quota. Cast, orchestra, musical director, stage management and all. At the time I wrote the following:

'I am a bit pushed for time this week, as I'm doing a musical. We open next Saturday and I'm not a bit worried. The other night I had this dream. We'd moved house and the new one was a converted optician's. There was a large shop front window and situated in the middle of it was a toilet. I kept pointing out that there were no curtains, but no one seemed concerned except me. Also, I had told my son Adam the new address before he went to school and he hadn't returned. It was now one o'clock in the morning. Oh, yes, and I had syphilis. The doctor told me what to do, but I'd forgotten on the way home. It had something to do with the toilet, I think.

'I woke up in a muck-sweat and told Jack about it. "It's all right, love," he said sagely. "Everyone has that dream when they're doing a musical. It's what we in show business call 'The Doing A Musical Dream'." I felt much better after that.

'Last night's dream was an improvement. I was merely an undercover spy in the home of Ferdinand and Imelda Marcos – only everyone knew. It was while wandering through Imelda's bra cupboard that I discovered a cache of children tied to their beds in conditions of horrible neglect. Well, you hardly need a coat of many colours to interpret this, do you? Give me a few ears of corn in alien bleedin' fields and I'll give you a decent night's sleep.

'Anyway, this musical – I'm not going to go on about it because by the time you read this it'll probably be a pile of old spangled tights, a maribou waist-clincher and fifteen empty wage packets in a dusty skip in Bushey. Suffice to say that your lumbering and graceless correspondent spends eight hours a day *dancing* and, at the time of going to press, my feet look as though they've been eaten. By a Dobermann pinscher. With a Cruft's medal for savagery.

'We start each day with a fifteen-minute warm-up, by the end of which I'm so knackered I want to lie down for a year. Then we have a vocal warm-up, which is a hell of a shock to the system as I'm not used to speaking before 10am – and then only to say, "Did the kids get off all right?" or "Where are my eyes?" Then we rehearse until 7.30 or 8 at night.

'The show is *Wonderful Town*. We open in Watford. I'm very fond of Watford. Twenty years ago, the Palace Theatre gave me my first job. I played the Genie of the Ring in *Aladdin* with a blue Afro, a Liverpool accent and a pogo stick. The height of understatement. Of course, in those days, Watford didn't have a traffic-free town centre and a ring road, and so I didn't spend a fortnight driving round and round the town's perimeter in search of a car park without a "full" sign until my petrol tank started whimpering for Bob Geldof's phone number. Nor did I have all four tyres slashed in the car park I finally found. Of course, twenty years ago I couldn't afford the convenience of a car.

'Mind you, I knew this musical was coming up last October. I started running again to get fit for it. Straight out of the house at 8.15am. Round the block past John the greengrocer, who dropped a box of "ten for the price of two" courgettes at the sight of me moving at something other than a meander.

'Then, as *Time* lurched by, and Christmas and three weeks' filming added volume and density to the craters on my hips, I decided to book a few days at a health farm. Peace and pampering were all that I required, and [the now defunct health farm] Inglewood, in leafy Kintbury, was happy to fit me in for a few days. I chose Inglewood because it's quite proletarian as health farms go. By which I mean not too many Sloanes quaffing pink champers in the jacuzzi or Eastern potentates being Shiatsu'd by the pool. It's warm and accessible and rather middle class . . . not unlike myself, I suppose.

'Health farms can bore the bum off you if you're not rapt by calorie counts. Actually, I ate rather well, by dint of regular circumvention of the buffet table, and thus managed to stay pleasantly pear-shaped. Not so a lady from Michigan who had lost nine stone! Not in a fortnight, mind you, but in a year at Weight Watchers. The health farm was a sort of golden handshake. Ever the opportunist, I had her correcting my Mid-West accent for the musical in the evening, whilst a plump, kindly lady from Bristol taught me how to meditate during tea break. I stuck her address label in my slipper, for future reference, and sped off, free from toxins, for my next engagement.

'Now this was the *real* treat. Two days at The Miller Howe, by Lake Windermere, with Denis and Astrid. Oh, and Jack. A visual and gastronomic paradise which I can scarcely describe without dribbling on my foolscap. "Breast of chicken with apricot and hazelnut stuffing and coffee-cream sauce," said the menu. "Eat your heart out," it should have said. I think I'd rather be there than anywhere on earth.'

Wonderful Town at Watford was wonderful. Everyone – audience and critics – loved it, and we seemed set to transfer to London. As the four weeks came to an end, however, there was still no producer prepared to put his money into a revival with an untried (in a musical) star in the lead. The papers complained daily about the number of revivals in the West End. A funny kind of snobbery about American classics grips theatre critics from time to time. In terms of the musical theatre, shows like *Annie Get Your Gun*, *Cabaret*, *West Side Story* and *Wonderful Town* represent the cream of the most productive and prestigious period of the art form. Of course such shows should be revived. To my kids they are as fresh as a new pea and, what's more, unlike today's megabuck musicals, they have a book. A play. With words. Often very witty and well-constructed words. Why do I never hear, 'I see the National are doing *another* revival of *The Orestoeia*' or 'Looks like Triumph Theatres are reviving *King Lear*'? Oh no – quite the contrary. They can't *wait* to pit Hopkins's Lear against their memory of Wolfit's Lear and Sher's Richard III against Olivier's version, and thus show off their erudition. When does a vehicle cease to be an 'old banger' and become 'vintage'? How old must it be to achieve classic status?

Kiss Me Kate is playing to packed London houses and has done so in theatres throughout the land. Possibly this is because it is under the auspices of the Royal Shakespeare Company, which gives it a certain air of legitimacy. Everyone knows that when the RSC does a comedy other than a Shakespearian one, the critics suspend disbelief, so bowled over are they by the fact that actors they've seen in the classics can actually say funny lines – out of tights! It's like watching the end-of-term show – *everything* is hilarious, and the laughter has that same quality of exaggeration.

At this period in our West End history, what the critics and the people wanted was *Chess*, *Les Misérables*, *Cats* and *Starlight Express*, all in their ways operetta. Shows without books – with, of course, the glorious exception of *Me and My Girl* which is Cinderella in Lambeth-land, and you can't argue with that! Meanwhile, we played to packed and rapturous houses in Watford and prayed for the right sugar daddy to come along before the four weeks were over and set us up in a place of our own.

One night, as the curtain came down on a wall of delight from the audience, Ray Lonnen, my co-star, said, 'I hope Lenny liked it.' 'Is Lenny Henry in, then?' I asked, pleased that the cast had kept it from me. Even the knowledge that my next-door neighbours are in makes me self-conscious. Ray smiled and said, 'Er, no – Lenny Bernstein, actually.'

Once they'd resuscitated me, I was fine. We all lined up around the stage, as in the Royal Variety show, and awaited the maestro. He came with his daughter and an entourage. He wore brown leather trousers and a peacock blue sweater. He gave me a king-sized hug, said two or three unrepeatably flattering things, and introduced me to his daughter, to pay for whose birth he had written the score of *Wonderful Town*. In three weeks. I carried away an image of a man more leonine, more dynamic, less American, more zoftig, more showbiz, and more or less the maestro.

On the same bill came Adolph Green, half of the legendary Comden and Green, book and lyric writers, whom I'm now honoured to call my friend. One day at lunch he filled me in on the days when Betty Comden, Judy Holliday and he were a singing act in Greenwich Village. I sat there like a kid at the pantomime whilst he 'did' their first visit to Hollywood, when Judy had the contract and said, 'Not unless my friends come too.' It was great hearing it from the source's mouth. In his exquisite and truly 'lived-in' apartment in New York there are memorabilia to make Barry Norman's mouth water – silver pillboxes engraved 'Frank and Mia', Eleanor Roosevelt, Noël, etc. What's more, the man doesn't seem to have an egocentric bone in his body.

The original author of *My Sister Eileen*, the play on which *Wonderful Town* was based, Jerome Chedorov, I would meet at a later date. He's a dear, gentle man, but his reaction to my costume for a routine called 'Swing' was classic. It was a black and white tango frock, covered in musical notes, which was wired to light up when I pressed a switch. 'Marine,' he said kindly, 'you look *obnoxious* in that outfit.' 'That's not really very constructive. We open tomorrow,' said the designer. 'That's OK,' said Mrs Chedorov. 'She's a pro. She can take it.'

Producer Dan Crawford is as straight as the day is long, but he does have some eccentric habits. I think he learned all he knows at the Zero Mostel school for would-be producers. One night after hoofing our combined socks off, I was scraping away a few layers of old skin in my dressing-room, when some friends came by. They had loved the show, they said, and were amazed that we couldn't get enough money to take it into the West End. 'How did you know that?' I asked, then fell backwards out of my chair on being shown a strip of paper in the programme saying, 'If you have enjoyed this show and would like to invest money in its future, then please ring the following number.' It then listed Dan's number. I was mortified. I'd thought the applause was out of genuine appreciation. I hadn't realised it was tinged with pity.

Two days later a friend rang to ask me if I'd seen the *Financial Times*. Being as how I still keep my weekly wages in the brown envelope in which they come, at the bottom of my bag, in the belief that I then know I've been *paid* and that anything else – cheques, banker's orders, giro, etc, does not count as real money (can they buy you a savoy cabbage and a pound of fig Newtons? Exactly. Not real money) – I told him, 'No, it's not part of my set reading.' He then read me an advert headed 'Lipman and Bernstein – do you believe in this combination?' Initially I had to ask myself if Leonard and I had agreed to open a firm of solicitors – however, the advert went on to ask for investment in a future West End production. That night on stage was the closest I've ever come to empathy with Cynthia Payne. 'What the hell,' I thought, 'why don't I just take the straw boater off my head and pass it round the audience?'

In the last ten days of the show, rumours grew like so many Next boutiques. The last Saturday of *Wonderful Town* was my fortieth birthday. I spent it doing two shows, with half an hour and a lot of cake in between. I can recommend it strongly as a way of ignoring the sudden onset of middle age and should you chance upon six young chorus boys, a revolving iron staircase and a thirteen-piece orchestra, it could be the same for you.

Re. the orchestra, a small detail that had escaped the notice of this novice chanteuse. I had foolishly imagined that, like actors, once a musician was employed it was for the run of the show, excluding serious catastrophes such as sudden amputation or loss of instrument. However, with musicians it's more a case of 'Yes, I'll be there for the first three nights and after that I'll be there if nothing better turns up. In which case I'll send along a dep', as in deputy, who'll busk it for the first half and learn it in the interval. Admittedly, it's a dreary job sitting in a deep black hole unable to see what's going on around you for two and a half hours a night, which is why they're mostly reading *Trout & Angler* in the arc of their anglepoises, and in some lamentable situations, chucking orange peel at Wayne Sleep. In our first week in the West End we had seven deputies and I tell you now that a complex and sustained trumpet solo in a Bernstein score, as played by someone who's just rushed in from having a quiet herring supper in Sydenham, is something I hope you never hear. There's a strong argument for having the band on stage where they can feel like part of the show, or at least join in the jokes. At Watford we all felt part of a big snappy family; ever after it was downhill.

Meanwhile the race to Shaftesbury Avenue was still on. We had a West End producer, Bill Kenwright. I finally heard that we were going to open at the glorious Queen's Theatre. (I heard this through the usual showbiz channels – Julian Holloway's barber told Julian, who told Denis King, who told me.) It was a touristless summer and our box-office advance was so small the Manager could carry it home in his Filofax.

As openings go it was just fine. The right mixture of adrenalin, joie de vivre and terminal terror. Actually a dentist I once frequented told me, after I fainted during an injection, that I was allergic to adrenalin. You could have heard my laughter from here to Sydney Harbour. Allergic to what I spend my entire life summoning up! We partied at Stringfellows where several members of the press hung round until I opened my mouth wide enough to swallow an ibis, crossed my eyes and showed my bra-straps – then snapped away merrily. The result hit the supplements on Sunday. The reviews were a smashing mixture of rave and resist. 'There are musicals around that are more glamorous, more pretentious or more bizarre,' declared the *Sunday Times*; 'this one wins by telling its story well, knowing its business, and not least by having captivating music.' 'Maureen Lipman stars, and I mean stars' said the *Sunday Times* 'like a likeable predatory bird ... half urchin and half vamp!' and in the *Express*: 'Maureen Lipman is no great shakes as a singer but her special brand of comedy is reminiscent of the immortal Fanny Brice'. The *Listener* – 'This isn't escapism – it's a life affirming treat'. My favourite came from the *International Gay Times* which said 'Emily Morgan plays the Beauty, while Maureen Lipman plays the *Brians*'.

Gradually, through the clout of Lucille Wagner, of the Bill Kenwright organisation, and through word of mouth (mostly mine) and some more great reviews, we built up to the stage where we had to buy our own 'House Full' sign for Saturday nights instead of sharing one with the NCP car park. We needed, but couldn't afford, many more actors to fill out the bigger stage – in the Broadway version they had scores of chorus – but somehow by dint of lighting, changes of persona and hats, the actors we had managed to give the impression there were three of each of them.

I flogged my number, 'One Hundred Easy Ways to Lose a Man', across the *Wogan Show*, Breakfast TV, and anywhere else they'd have it. Radio and newspaper interviewers filed in and out of the dressing-room like so many emery-boards. *Shiftwork*, Lesley Bruce's tautly written comedy thriller about a woman mini cab driver, was broadcast to excellent notices. *The Little Princess*, too, and the paperback of *How Was It For You?* It was all publicity for our homespun extravaganza. Still, we weren't an unqualified hit in the Lloyd Webber vein, and the production company were not sure enough of our staying power to risk doing the cast album, although their loyalty towards and love of the show was unquestionable. The word of mouth was still terrific, and compared to much of the rest of Shaftesbury Avenue, we were doing fine. After five months we were nominated for two Olivier Awards, audiences were up, and I said to Bill Kenwright one night after the show, 'How about doing the cast album, then?' He looked at me as though I'd just had the most original and weird idea on earth and said, 'You want to do a record? OK, we'll do one. Next week all right?' So we did. In two afternoons and more often than not, one take.

By now there was a British Rail strike, appalling weather and rampant 'flu working against us. In one week we had ice, a thaw, floods and a drought. (It's extraordinary in this country, isn't it, how the weather is a constant source of amazement to us. Cries of 'Isn't it terrible?' when the Siberian wind blows in February – or winter, as I like to think of it. 'Nationwide shortage of thermal underwear,' scream tabloids. 'Crocuses and old people hit by worst frost since *last* year.' Same with summer: 'Phew, wot a scorcher! See how shapely Tracey 39, 21, 36 gives a wet string vest a-peel!' 'What's that you want, a fan!? You must be joking, missus! I got less fans than Des O'Connor. There's a world shortage, dontcha know?')

On three successive nights I played the same scene with three totally different members of the cast. Everyone was moving around to fill in for the missing few. Also, because (in a long run) furniture has feelings too, the set representing our apartment had begun to misbehave. It slid ingeniously on its castors, but occasionally it stopped, put its little feet down and said 'That's it – no oil, no performance.' This meant that half the playing area was still in the wings and there were no doors to go through to say 'The bathroom's a little small and the kitchen . . .' Of course, once the audience know what's wrong there's nothing they like more than seeing you get out of it. On one occasion after it had stopped in mid-move, Emily Morgan (who played my dumb-blonde sister) and Ben Stevens decided to carry on acting the scene regardless of the fact that they were playing in a quarter of a doorless apartment. Suddenly the whole set juddered into action and slid on to its prescribed marks. With miraculous presence of mind Ben said, 'Gee, I see you girls are still moving in.' It got a roar of laughter and the best applause of the night.

The following day the tracks were oiled but someone omitted to clean up the oil from the stage. When Emily and I walked into our apartment we could well have been mistaken for Torville and Dean on an off-night, as we slid about the set clinging to the door posts for the sake of our equilibrium. Emily was fortunate; she got to sit on the bed looking pretty and confused. Muggins, on the other hand, had to unpack two cases, swan backwards and forwards from the bathroom, and dance and sing a number. Many people may have pondered that night whether my apparent Max Wall impression was absolutely in character, or, indeed, necessary.

Chest microphones hate me. At Watford I wore two because the first one broke down so frequently. This meant two large battery packs on my backside, which complemented the bias-cut Forties dress line not at all. So I wore a tight pantie girdle to flatten them down over support tights (for support), and stockings and suspenders for authenticity. On top of all this went French knickers for the purists in the lower stalls. I must have lost a stone in four weeks – the Maureen Lipman sweat-your-way to slimness method. Still the mikes played up – I think my magnetic field must have an irregularity. Of course, in Watford I blamed the unsophisticated system, but when, during a 'Tribute to Leonard Bernstein' evening at the Barbican, the same thing happened, I had to admit the responsibility was all mine. Four minutes before I was due on stage to sing 'One Hundred Easy Ways', two strange young men came rushing backstage and without so much as a by-your-leave, yanked my dress above my head, unpacked my battery pack, plugged a new one in, and pushed me on stage as the announcer's voice said 'And now from the Watford Palace Theatre . . .' I was a wreck. But audible.

The great mike problem has apparently been solved in *Les Misérables*, where they wear tiny throat mikes on their heads, just under their wigs. The resonance is said to be marvellous, but it was ruled out for me on the grounds that I might have looked unusual in a Forties strapless evening gown and a powdered periwig.

Prior to Christmas, business went steeply downhill, with theatregoers presumably, to a man, either in Selfridge's basement or with both hands wedged firmly up a turkey's bottom. The excuses for small houses ranged through too hot, too cold, too wet, too icy, too near the Budget, a leaked death in *EastEnders* or a Royal circumcision, no tourists (care of Colonel Gadafi Ltd), children off school, back to school, the January sales, the February and March sales, you name it – audiences are affected by it. Our advance sales were still some of the best on the Avenue, but theatre managers want to hear the thud of cash in the till, not the promise of distant Access cards.

I remember hurrying through the back of Covent Garden in between a Wednesday matinée and evening show, in cold icy weather. My mind was miles away, somewhere in the second act, and I was mumbling the lines that used to get a laugh and suddenly didn't. There's a story about the legendary Lunts going through a similar trough. Alfred Lunt just couldn't understand why he'd ceased to get a laugh on the line 'Could I have a cup of tea?' He'd tried it fast, he'd tried it slow, he'd changed the inflection, he'd emphasised different words, he'd said it fortissimo and barely audibly, and still it failed to make the audience laugh. 'What am I doing wrong?' he demanded of his wife and co-star, Lynn Fontanne. She looked him firmly in the eyes and said, 'Darling, have you thought of asking for a cup of tea, instead of asking for a laugh?'

Suddenly the sound of running footsteps interrupted my reverie. The narrow street was badly lit, and as the footsteps got nearer I turned to see a young man in a long raincoat running towards me. I froze, then turned back and started to walk more urgently. Still he ran towards me, his arm outstretched until I felt him touch my shoulder. I'll never know why, but I spun on my heels, assumed a vague karate stance recalled from one or two distant lessons and a deal of exposure to the *Karate Kid* video, and let out the longest, loudest, rawest cry you've ever heard this side of Berwick Street fruit market. 'Kiayeeee!' I roared from deep in the gut. Even *I* was shocked. As for the young man, he was paralysed. He went quite green in the gloomy light and stammered, 'I'm ssssorry – I didn't mmm-m-ean to fffrighten you. I'm a ffan of yours and I wwork in that hairdressing salon over there. I thought if you ever wanted a haircut I'dd-I'd do it for frfr-free . . .' He petered out and I thought for a minute he was going to be sick.

My turn to apologise – I tried to laugh it off, but I felt such an idiot. On the other hand I was pleased I'd made a sound at all. Women generally don't, can't. We're taught from the cradle that anger is amusing in boys and unattractive in girls. Better to whine and whinge than to have a tantrum. More girlish. We fear the reaction we'll get if our rage breaks forth. A friend of mine's life was saved in a Glasgow park by the power of her lungs. She was attacked from behind, in broad daylight, and thrown to the ground. Her first instinct was to scream (many women open their mouths to do so but nothing comes out). In her case, having been trained as a singer, she made quite the loudest noise either she or her attacker had ever heard, and in an instant he reeled back and fled.

As for me, when I reached the theatre I was quite hoarse and had to breathe steam and go heavy on the Lockets. Somewhere in Covent

Garden that young lad is probably leading a very restrained existence, avoiding all Thespians, particularly tall, dark ones with glasses and minds full of martial arts. Shame really – I could use a good haircut.

Not on Your Wellie

I've got to get away from it all. Afterwards, on the way home, I thought, 'The Country, eh?' I'd heard of it, of course. I'd even seen bits of it from the train window. Novelists always started chapters by describing it for a paragraph or two. Those were the paragraphs I skipped. In Bertolucci films it looked ever so lush, and once, in the Dordogne, we wandered into it by mistake and had a really good steak au poivre.

Oh – and health farms tend to be in it. You can tell this because they ask you on the brochure to take a taxi from the little leafy country station, and the eggs are bigger. But of course once you're *in* a health farm you could be slap-bang in the middle of Leicester Square or Limoges for all you know. They all look like stately homes with long curving drives, but then, so do most of the houses in The Bishops Avenue, Hampstead. And once you've located the light diet room, the swimming pool, the torture chamber and the TV, then the next whiff of air you'll be having is the one you'll draw at the front door with your head between your legs, after you've seen the bill.

As a child, the words 'a ride out' were synonymous with the words 'family row'. Mother suffered from car sickness and had to travel sitting on a folded copy of *The Daily Mirror* (an *incentive* to throwing up, if you ask me), and the shooting brake had to have a chain dangling from the back. To *earth* it. Not being of a scientific bent I didn't understand it then and I don't understand it now. Dad never quite knew his way outside a radius of three miles from Hull, which was apparently my mother's fault. (I thought map-reading was anti-Semitic till I was twenty-four.) Meanwhile my brother and I began fighting over who travelled in the boot and got to wave at other shooting brakes. I usually won by dint of being eighteen months younger, which led him to whistle tunefully 'on purpose' till I bit him. On such occasions we would usually end up eight miles away in the market town of Beverley, where we would buy home-made ice cream from Burgess's – I can still taste it – and retired to the Westwood to eat them, by the car. It's a fact that I swore my stage name, if ever I was famous, would be Beverley Westwood.

Trying to recapture those heady days is a daunting task, but years later Jack, myself and Sara, my agent, went up to Hull for a weekend. On which occurred the now legendary 'Jewish Picnic'. Read on if you haven't just had stitches or a baby.

It was a pleasant enough day and we all declared our eagerness for a 'ride out' to show Sara the surrounding countryside. We wanted an early start and a picnic lunch, but since it was Passover, i.e. no bread, the make-up of the picnic took a deal of discussion. Finally we buttered piles of matzos (unleavened bread) which, if you've ever buttered crackers you'll appreciate break up into flying shrapnel when approached by a knife and go damp and soggy at the mere mention of dairy produce. We added almost-hard boiled eggs ('Aw, yours has cracked, Maurice') and salad stuff and special Passover crisps (same as ordinary crisps but with Hebrew printing and a raised price), and the five of us, some rather on the largish side, wedged ourselves into the Vauxhall Chevette – 'No, honestly, I'm fine – I'll just sit forward a bit, on the edge here. Close the window? Oh, of course, sorry, I didn't realise it was blowing your hair – I just thought a bit of air might – no, no, I'm *perfectly* all right – you stay in the front and direct Maurice.'

Directing Maurice, as I'd forewarned Sara, meant Mother turning round and chatting to us, whilst Maurice drove totally erratically and without any discernible knowledge of where he was going, until such time as he'd passed the turn off, then: 'Maurice, you've missed it! I told you to go right after Ferriby Foreshore.' 'If I'd turned right after Ferriby Foreshore, we'd be in the bloody river, yer barmy bugg . . .' 'All right, Maurice, well, left then, I meant left – turn around, then. NO NOT YET!' This as he U-turned on a dual carriageway in the face of a Pickfords van and two mounted policemen. Some time later, we shuddered in anticipation in the car as he explained his predicament – and then watched navy blue arms go amicably round his shoulders, a lot of back-slapping take place, and we knew he was about to measure them both up for a suit. All was well. Just.

Back on the road we passed Burton Constable (small world, isn't it) and I foolishly remarked that I'd never seen the 'Hall'. Action Man at the wheel swung the car off the road and down the long drive and parked on the forecourt. But it was not to be. 'Maurice, what are you doing? Sara won't want to look round an 'All – it's a lovely day, we'll miss all the weather – you don't, do you, Sara? Tell him,' urged my mother. Sara, who by now would have sold her kaftan for a chance to get out of the Chevette – agreed that no, she certainly didn't need to see the Hall this visit, perhaps on another occasion . . .

Teeth and car in mid-grit, Maurice eight-point-turned back on to the road and drove doggedly off in some direction or other in search of Hornsea. Almost under his breath I heard him chunter, 'All my life I've wanted to see Burton Constable Hall . . .' It might have been the Great Wall of China he was wistfully regretting, not a small manor less than fourteen miles from where he'd lived for sixty-odd years.

Finally, and under darkening skies, we approached the Hornsea road. Various places were mentioned for the picnic but none was quite right. Too steep, too flat, too crowded, too deserted. A grassy traffic island with an integral bollard was suggested – then a lay-by with vehicles thundering past, not unlike a pantechnical Le Mans. At last we approached a leafy opening with white gates, a large expanse of greenery beyond, and a sign saying Private Golf Course Club. Aggravated, deprived and hungry, Dad veered recklessly through the gates and hurtled towards the Clubhouse – parked, got out, grabbed the picnic bag and strode off in search of a suitable watering hole, be it the 3rd or the 18th.

Mother rolled down the window and screamed at his retreating spine, 'Maurice, come back! It's a golf course! Come back! Maurice, can you hear me? Maurice! You can't take *matzos* on a golf course!'

With a face like a handicap and a dripping carrier bag Maurice came back, slammed the car door shut and reversed all the way down the gravel drive and on to the main road like a scene from *The French Connection*, or indeed any major American film of the last decade.

We did eat the picnic, finally. In Hornsea. No, not by the sea. Nor on the beach nor in a leafy park nor even on a cliff head. We ate it in the car park, still sitting in the car, only with the windows down. Silently. Then we rolled the windows up and set off again for more countryside, and finished off the fruit and crisps by the roadside. At which point Dad decided he needed a toilet. We urged him to use the hedge but he got back into the car and vanished in search of sanitation. After at least twenty minutes we watched him drive back towards us. Then we watched him drive straight past us and disappear in the other direction. Fifteen minutes later he reappeared, again driving towards us. This time we waved. Again he drove straight past us, and out of sight. This happened five more times until in the end we all formed a human chain and leaped up and down in unison, shouting his name and waving heads, arms, eyes, feet and crumbling sheets of matzos.

Clapped-out and crumb-strewn we somehow made it back home by nightfall. In eight hours we'd driven a 28-mile journey – only the clock showed an increase of nearly a hundred miles.

So don't talk to me about making hay while the piggin' sun shines and green hills far away. Not far enough, if you ask me. I've been there, mate. I've seen it. And I'm sticking to a deck chair in the Balls Pond Road and a take-away Indonesian. All right, as a concession I'll listen to the omnibus edition of *The Archers* once a week and grow my own basil.

Jack, too, could tell you a tale or three about 'The Country'. After eight years of involvement with *Coronation Street* as a writer, he became the show's producer and one of the first moves he made was to dream up a treat for the cast. After all, he thought, didn't they turn up, rain or shine, at the Granada back-lot for rehearsals and taping days, with tedious and unfailing monotony? Their professionalism was legendary. They made their journeys from Altrincham and Settle and Wythenshawe and Lytham St Anne's week in week out, and in hair-nets, macintoshes and their one good suit, propped up the bar of the Rover's Return, the corner shop, the Church Hall. *The Street*. Wouldn't it be *wonderful*, he thought, to get them *out to the country*. To the fresh air, to the birds and the bees. To breathe again. A treat, to say thank-you to a show which had changed the face of television. An OB (Outside Broadcast) would become the Rosenthal equivalent of an OBE. Oh, man of such naïveté.

When the plan was gloriously announced to the cast, old PT Barnum couldn't help but notice a rather muted reaction, ranging from the instant rolling upwards of Thespian eyes, through to heavy sighs and frantic searches for train timetables and ominous mutters of previous arrangements.

Of course it had never occurred to Jack how well the tedious monotony of 'The Street' routine suited 'The Street''s protagonists. It fitted neatly in with lives they had previously organised to fit neatly in with 'Street' life. The last thing any of them wanted was a change in that tried and trusted tradition. There were cats and dependent relatives to be rearranged and personal appearances in enterprising handbag shops to cancel. The original idea of staying overnight in a lakeside hotel was scrapped in favour of a spot within commuting distance of Piccadilly station, and the script compromised by having the residents of 'The Street' club together to visit a nearby stately home. Permission and extra budget were sought out and, with a fair amount of grumbling from them-on-high, granted.

The day of the OB dawned as days do, and the cast and crew convened in a field bordering on to the stately home location. As the first shots were being set up, a crisis revealed itself in the shape of actress Sandra Gough (Irma Ogden), who was moving rapidly from one foot to the other, lifting her knees. When asked what was wrong she revealed that she had a worm phobia. 'I can't act where there's worms,' she cried, tempting the only possible reply that she'd better get out of show business fast, then. Instead, Jack calmed her and cajoled her and diverted her gaze and probably did an ancient Hebraic worm-rebutting dance to boot, and the scene was finally in the can.

A whole new can of worms was ahead. For in the following scene the glorious Jean Alexander (Hilda Ogden) began to duck and weave in a manner reminiscent of Sugar Ray Robinson. 'Cut! What's the problem, Jean!' 'Butterflies,' moaned the actress. 'I can't stand butterflies – oh my

God, there's another one . . .' This on the move as she dashed back to hide behind a van.

Jack was mortified. His generous gesture had backfired horribly. People were grumbling and moaning all around him, checking their watches and their timetables. Nobody wanted to be there – including him by now. 'Telephone for you, Jack, in the production office,' called a PA and off he stalked, angry and hurt, to answer it, muttering all the while to himself, 'Fine, just fine. Be like that. See if I care. You do your best. Who wants thanks? My God, I'm a city boy if ever there was one. But you'd think they could appreciate a bit of bloody nature. Nothing's gonna wound anyone or maim anyone.' So saying, he reached out for the phone and put his hand on a wasp which stung him so badly that First Aid had to be called from Manchester.

In future they filmed in the studios be it hot, cold or indifferent. After all, if it was change they wanted they'd hardly have been in *Coronation Street* for ten years.

'Uneasy lies the head . . .'

My trip to the Palace had its moments. Here's the full run-down, with pre-match special and action replays. First thing was the Commander of the Queen's Household ringing whilst I was out and Jack was in the middle of writing Act 1 Scene III.

'This is the Commander of the Queen's Household' is not a sentence Jack is used to hearing on an ordinary damp Thursday in north London, and it prompted the reply 'Yes and I'm Dick Turpin. Gerroff the phone, Denis.' A little convincing dialogue later, and Jack was the recipient of the news that his wife had been invited up Buck House for a little light luncheon.

When I phoned in later from rehearsals in the Elephant & Castle, he received the same line in disbelief from me. 'Geroff, will you?' I hooted. 'It's Denis pulling your *good* leg.' Finally I was convinced and immediately lapsed into reverse paranoia of the 'Why me? What have I done to deserve this?' variety. I then began to await every postal delivery with the enthusiasm of a postman-hating dog. Alas, contrary to expectations, no gold-rimmed invitation arrived, and after a few weeks I *knew* it was Denis. Just to check, however, Jack phoned the Palace. It's easy – you just look up Buckingham Palace in the phone book and a rather suburban-sounding voice replies, 'Hello, Buckingham Palace. Can I 'elp you?' It transpired that my invitation had indeed got lost in the post, and the next day it arrived, as gold rimmed as a spectacle and twice as easy to read through.

How to prepare for such an event? It appeared there would only be seven other people there besides me. 'There's no way I can help but screw this up,' I wailed, having imagined it to be more like the Royal Garden Party I'd once attended, which was memorable for the large numbers of delightful ladies from the WVs, vicars and Lyons Cup Cakes. I phoned Barbara Dickson, who'd once attended such a lunch, and asked her the format. She told me in her soft Scots brogue what she'd worn, how 'She' had behaved and the overall thrill of it all. She advised me to buy *Debrett's Guide to Etiquette* if I was worried about that side of things, although she said the whole thing was so well stage-managed that I shouldn't really bother myself.

The night before the day after, I played *Wonderful Town* somewhat distractedly, like someone with matters of state on her mind, and a great deal of ironic bowing and scraping went on in the wings.

Ben Frow had brought round 'the dress' at the weekend. It was the old Fifties design I love to live in, made up in gent's suiting material in tiny rust and cream check with rust trim, with a circular skirt sweeping the ankles. At 7.05 I shot up in bed, peered through the blind at the cold day, and realised that none of my coats came near to the length of the dress. I could either freeze or look like a bag lady. At 8 o'clock I was rifling through Jack's wardrobe, searching for and finding a jacket in almost exactly the same check, with half its lining ripped out and a rather tweedy smell.

My mother's help took out her nimble needlework kit and did us both proud, then, whilst I popped into Goldilocks to have the last remnants of perm removed, she 'Palace-dropped' down at the cleaner's to persuade them to replace the nice macho pong with the heady smell of dry cleaning fluid. And there I was, booted and bespoke, man's jacket, brown leather purse – sort of Vesta Tilley crossed with Kay Kendall.

At least a week before I'd alerted the mini-cab company that I should need to be at Buckingham Palace at ten to twelve, preferably in a nice clean *posh* car – howzabout a Merc, I implied? The company assured me that they had a swanky line in Ford Granadas and the odd Jag. 'Fine,' I said. 'And a nice shiny driver to go with it, please.' At eleven o'clock I looked out of the window and saw IT arrive. It was a Jag all right. But shiny it wasn't, and the lanky, long-haired, blow-dried gent in a Guiness sweatshirt and jeans was not exactly what I'd had in mind either. There was no time to trade him in and I'm no snob. So I got somewhat sniffily into the rear seat and kept my mouth pursed on the subject of shirts, ties and peaked caps.

'Where to?' enquired my sartorial escort.

I gawped. This had to be the best-kept secret in North London. 'Buckingham Palace. Didn't they tell you?'

'No, I only got this job twenty minutes ago. I was on my way here. Going to 'ave a look at it, are you? You from overseas then?'

'No. I live here. And I'm going for lunch. As I informed your controller several times.'

'Blimey,' he roared with appreciation. 'If I'd known that I'd have given the vehicle a rub-over.'

I could feel my jaws rippling – I'd have to pull myself together or Her Majesty might think I was Clint Eastwood. The journey passed quite affably, actually, and the jaw didn't seize up until we drove through those oh, so familiar gates and the Palace Guards gave us those oh, so unfamiliar salute arms. Then through into the inner courtyard. More guards, more salutes. Suddenly we were at the red-carpeted steps and I watched painfully as my fellow guests dismounted from their gleaming black limos and Rolls, doors carefully closed behind them by their flawless chauffeurs. Only me, *only me*, I muttered, could be propelled out of such a banger by such an escort, straight into the waiting arms of The Keeper of the Queen's Household and at least a dozen designer flunkies.

My worries were, of course, groundless. 'Loved you in *Agony*,' whispered a scarlet-suited footman in coiffed periwig, looking not unlike Maria Charles who played my mother in the same programme. 'Would you like to wash?' The question startled me as I'd spent at least ninety minutes in the bath that morning and had to be the cleanest person in London and the Home Counties. 'Oh. Yes. Please.' My head was spinning on its own axis like the kid's in *The Exorcist*, from trying to take in all the surroundings at one glance. All I now remember is yellow silk wallpaper and bronze statues and the lady in the wash-room saying, 'Why on earth did he send you in here – I've just put flowers in the other one.' I wanted to comb my hair, but on seeing that the comb I'd brought was a joke one with integral tits and bum, I decided to use my hands instead, thus landing myself with moussed hands for the rest of the luncheon hour.

Another beaming footman escorted me into the Reception Room, part of the Royal Guest Suite, he informed me, adding that he'd enjoyed *Wonderful Town* much more than the original version. Why do I never expect people to lead normal lives in public places? I gaze at two floor-length Canalettos and a magnificent portrait of Queen Charlotte, who looks remarkably like the Queen. Whatever else, I suspect that these are not Athena repros. The carpet is embroidered silk in russety shades like the bright autumn light shining through the long windows. The sofas are fat and traditional, the fireplace marble. Glasses? Shall I wear them or not? I decide not and put them in Jack's jacket pocket, which is somehow miraculously made to disappear, so that's more or less the last visual picture I'll be giving you. The rest will be tastes, smells and sounds.

The eight guests had a certain Agatha Christie Chapter 1 feel about them. One judge, two knights, one headmistress, one art curator, one newsreader (Trevor McDonald), one actress and one bishop – well, reverend. All agreed on one thing. Our reaction to the invitation: 'Why me?' According to the Press Secretary, everybody asked that same question. At this point we lined up formally around the room to be introduced to HM, all glancing towards the open doors, anticipating her entrance. Instead, around the corner came two corgis. I held back on my 'bob' fearing it might be misinterpreted by them.

Seconds later around the corner came the Queen, reassuringly familiar and unnervingly different. She spoke first with Mrs Brigstock, the headmistress of St Paul's, whilst I mentally rehearsed my knees into doing what my brain instructed. No fear of repeating what she said to me, as I've blanked it out. The only thing I remember is talking about *Wonderful Town* and bemoaning the thinness of the audience in the pre-Christmas period. Then, for some reason I'll never quite understand – probably my fatal and chronic need to entertain – I told her that the musical *Chess* had been cancelled on Saturday night, giving us rather a decent overflow of Swedes in the house. When asked why it had been cancelled I heard myself say in a somewhat Su Pollardish way, 'Well, the drummer was stuck in traffic in the Finchley Road.' Her Majesty expressed some surprise at there not being another drummer who could have been recruited, at which I chuckled, 'Well, you'd think so, wouldn't you, with Ronnie Scott's just round the corner.' I don't know if she thought I was speaking in code, or whether she had the remotest idea that Ronnie Scott's is a jazz club, but she passed on quite quickly to the next guest, leaving me royally flushed and kicking myself.

It is strange how unnatural one feels in such a situation. I remembered standing next to Wayne Sleep and Su Pollard in the line-up at the Royal Variety Performance earlier that year, awaiting the Royal couple's walkabout round the circle of performers. I'd said jokingly to Su, 'Now, when Her Majesty arrives just move your mouth about and I'll throw my voice, 'cos you're bound to put your foot in it.' When Su was actually confronted by the Queen she immediately burst out with, 'Oooh, Yer Majesty, wharra luvly booquet! Wharrarethey, lilies? Oooh, can I 'ave a sniff?' and so saying stuck her spiky head straight into the Royal posy. I didn't speak at all after that.

Luncheon was served in the 1832 Room (each room in the Palace is dated, so to speak), and was a deliciously light, refreshing menu of watercress soup, salmon en croûte and lemon mousse, served on china I hardly dared touch. The only problem was that each course was offered on a silver salver from which one served oneself with two spoons. Having been brought up in a house where meals were put on the plate in toto, it took me years to get used to taking veg from a casserole dish in front of me, let alone from a silver salver in mid-air somewhere by my left ear.

As it was, I somehow contrived to get the salmon on my plate whilst leaving the croûte hooked over the edge of the serving dish and dangling dangerously from platter to plate. (I had a similar job with the mousse. Thank God it wasn't jelly.) Things were going well as I chatted to Sir Edwin Nixon, head of IBM, on my left, about osteopathy, until the Queen's Press Secretary asked me a question on my right. It so happened that I had a boiled potato on my fork on its way to my mouth, and as I turned my head to speak to him I realised, with a sinking heart, that my potato had left my fork and was in mid-air, sailing neatly across the room to land on the priceless Abyssinian carpet, hand-knotted by four hundred blind, underprivileged monks from a silent order in Nepal. Royal flush No. 2. I sat there willing a comatose corgi to eat it, but no. Far too well trained for that – or on a low carbohydrate diet. Who knows? At the end of the meal we all returned to the Reception Room for coffee. As the Queen rose the two dogs leaped attentively to their feet, causing me to remark how very well trained they were. Her Majesty opened one hand to reveal a couple of crushed biscuits, which was all the explanation needed for their obedience. Nice touch.

Before you could say 'It'll all end in tears' the lunch was over, and we were on our way. Final glances around the décor, thanks and coats from the cloaks, and I was outside pretending the old Jag with the sweatshirted driver belonged to someone else. Everything was so beautifully stage-managed – smooth as soapstone, unobtrusive, efficiency itself.

On the way home I thought, 'Shall I pop in on a friend and let it all hang out a bit?' but decided against it. I felt rather exhausted and fancied half an hour's rest before going on to the theatre. Back home, and having been charged £22 for a £12 return trip for reasons best known to the driver, I found the house for once deserted. Jack at a meeting, mother's help gone for the kids, no builders, no repair men. No one to brag to at all. I tried to ring my friend Lizzie. Out. Julia? Out. Astrid? On an answering machine: 'Hello, it's me. I've been to the Palace for lunch. It was lovely . . . I've just got in . . . everyone's out . . . that's all really . . . Talk to you soon. Bye.'

Beattie-Tude

I suppose the first time I became aware that Beattie was bigger than both of us was one Saturday in February 1989 just after a visit to a Vietnamese acupuncturist. I would put the time at 1.20pm, the location Baker Street and my companion a clone-like version of myself, my daughter Amy, fresh as a daisy after having a needle in her skull. Suddenly Amy stopped dead in her tracks and said 'Mod – what does THAT mean?' 'THAT' turned out to be the headlines in bold black type, of an advertising magazine called *Campaign*, and the headline concerned read:

LIPMAN SET TO TAKE OVER THE WORLD.

It was the turn of my tracks to be stopped dead in. I swallowed, with difficulty. It could mean one of three things:

1) My brother, who is in the airline business, had made a takeover bid for PAN-AM.
2) I had unwittingly lent my name to some obscure army of liberation under the misapprehension that it was a ladies' luncheon club in Brent.
3) I was still fast asleep with a needle in my skull and dreaming of Broadway.

But, two of us had seen the sinister sentence and two of us now approached it with stealth. A short and shifty read explained what had been clear to J Walter Thompson's advertising company and British Telecom for some time. Out of the five advertising agencies covering various aspects of BT's then current campaign, one of them, JWT, had beaten off another to win the International Phone Calls contract for themselves and their creation Mrs Beattie Bellman, née 'Lipman'. The monster was growing two heads.

It was the culmination of two years of mounting media attention for Beattie. Editors instructed their journalists to find out how many telephones I had, how many telephones my mother had, how often we use them, what model? A reporter scurried up to my mother's house in Hull on the pretext of an interview in *Bella*, only to sell it to the *Daily Mail* for

141

a double-page spread on Beattie's real mother, where the real mother in question was quoted as saying she used Mercury because it was cheaper. The real mother then cut the ribbon on a new telephone shop in her native town. For a fee. A magazine showed me on a walkabout phone – clearly not a BT model – also showing my phone number. After some weeks of hilarious phone calls from their deeply witty readership my entire phone system was 'Telecom'd' and I found myself the proud owner of three switch boards, two lines, 13 phones and a 12 ton phone box. All for a five bedroom house! (On behalf of my 15-year-old daughter and the rest of us who occasionally make a call, I'd like to thank Crouch End Customer Service!)

It had taken me twenty-two years to reach Beattie-fication. Quite a long time spent in theatre and TV, rep and national companies, always trying to work new ground and play different characters. Above all, never to be stereotyped. Twenty-two years to be known primarily as a white-haired Jewish GRANDMA with a sharp tongue, a warm heart, and a fatal obsession with food and family. A household name – like Harpic. Twenty-two years to be greeted by one and all with, 'You look so much younger in real life' and to find myself on the financial pages of *The Times* alongside a report of BT's quarterly profits.

Don't get me wrong. I'm not knocking its success. The commercials were funny, well made, and they proved a point. That with all the techn'ology involved in advertisements – all the angles and video cutting – what the public actually want to see, and always remember, is characterisation, plot and relationships – like in a play.

But back to the beginning. It all started with a phone call to my agents. Apparently I was on the wanted list for the part of the as-yet-unnamed Grandmother, so I agreed to meet the people from the advertising agency. Now, I don't know who they'd seen before me, but I gather it was quite a few. I was obviously too young by twenty years, too thin by half and, as they would find out, too opinionated by plenty. On the plus side I knew the character as well as I knew my son's sock drawer – why shouldn't I? I'd lived with her for 18 years and been chained to the phone by her for the other 22 – and I seemed to get on well from an ideas point of view with the prima donnas who would be behind the campaign. At the end of the meeting I felt that *they* felt they had their 'momma'. My agent was in seventh heaven – and on 15% why shouldn't he be. My son began negotiations for a dinghy with outboard motor for the swimming pool he felt we should be adding.

Then, two weeks later, they announced they want to do a 'test'. I said no. Penny Rose, wardrobe, an old friend, said it's only for wig and make-up, so I said yes.

It was a riot. I was dressed in an over-the-top silk blouse, winged spectacles, heavy make-up and a gunmetal bouffant wig. I looked rather like everyone's favourite Auntie Freda, the one who ran a gown shop in Temple Fortune and never asked anyone for a favour. As far as the Beattie we came to know and tremble in front of, she was very much Mark One.

It was clear from the beginning that this was no mere wig and make-up test. It was an audition without a script. I took several deep breaths, contemplated telling them to shove it, then – remembering the school fees – launched into a sort of 'clap hands here comes forty years of showing off in public, at your service with a smile, a song, a joke, some with an ethnic slant – we fill the stage with bagels!' By the time I'd finished, I suppose the camera had been whirring for over an hour, and the over-the-top silk blouse was wet through and sticking to the actress in question like a T shirt to Linda Lusardi.

But they must have liked it. Because the following day 'the deal' was agreed and a short time later I started work at Wembley studios.

Meanwhile, they were still looking for someone to play Harry, the husband – you know the old joke – *Son:* 'Momma, I got the part! I'm playing the husband!' *Mother:* 'You couldn't get a speaking part?' I'd worked with Geoffrey Chiswick in a BBC play called *Shiftwork* and I suggested he might be just the fellow for the mission. This left the youngest grandson, Oliver – 'a voice like an angel' – to cast.

A couple of days before filming began it was Yom Kippur, the Day of Atonement. It's a long and hungry day and it's best spent in the synagogue, participating in the service, in order to forget and forego your longings for braised steak and onions.

During a break I saw a small boy shinning up a pillar. I asked him his name. 'Alastair,' he replied in mid-shin. 'And do you like acting, Alistair?' He picked his lip thoughtfully, 'Well, I was a sheep once in the Christmas play, but I never got any lines.' I wrote a note to his mother and the next day they hired him.

And so to the 'shoot'. The director was Tony Smith, who'd made *Tutti Frutti*. He was an actor's director. Concise and economic, he kept my performance small. The 'Mrs Jones' script went like a dream. The crew, a single personality on a set, quietly came round to his point of view.

We were working flat out. One evening we filmed a commercial at six o'clock, the script for which I'd been handed at five o'clock. It was a monologue called 'Good News'. In it Beattie poured gratitude for some fabulous piece of good news into the ear of a young man called Clive: 'Oh that *is* good news – that's the best thing I've heard all day! What do I mean? It's the best thing I've heard all year! Oh Clive I *am* grateful' etc. etc. The punchline was to Harry: 'It's alright – he's had a cancellation for a tint. He's fitting me in.' Simple enough. But Tony had me pacing back and forth in front of a small mantel mirror and filmed me through the mirror. It was incredibly complicated to say exactly the same word at either side of the mirror each time to enable me to walk back to the mirror for the key words which had to be seen. It was, without question, the hardest and most technical piece of acting I've ever done.

On Thursday, 15th October 1987, in spite of Michael Fish, we had the great hurricane. I, of course, experiencing hurricanes of one kind or another all week, slept right through it. The next morning, George, my driver, called at seven o'clock and we drove in shock across the whole of London from Muswell Hill to Battersea. It looked like World War 3. A huge poplar down in a garden; great shattered monsters lying uprooted all over Hampstead Heath and making the roads impassable. Regent's Park – a cemetery. Hyde Park . . . Battersea Park! We were numb.

As I dressed as Beattie for a Phonecard ad with Zia Mohyeddin, the sun was shining brilliantly. We shot a few seconds then the weather changed dramatically and driving rain and gloom fell. A canopy went over the camera bit in the end and we abandoned work and that particular ad never really recovered.

I got home to see my housekeeper Yvonne's boyfriend had arrived from Wales. Normally, this didn't fill me with delight, but this time he was up on my roof putting back the slates. It's an ill hurricane . . .

One more day and it was over. In a little over two weeks we had shot ten commercials. Then I went home, dropped more flowers at the old people's home and collapsed in a heap. The diary reads: 'I've done it. Badly – but I've done it'. Gradually, the ads were shown and the consensus seemed to prove the diary wrong.

After JWT won the International contract, the next move was to widen Beattie's family. Enter a Canadian brother Lionel and a sister Rose in Australia. It seemed fairly clear that Lionel needed to be played by an actor from across the water, but Rose? Wouldn't it be fun to dress up the same but different and affect an antipodean accent? The agency loved the idea. But guess what? Would I be willing to do a test?

So Penny and I went 'Kanga' and Rose emerged with a red wig, blue contact lenses, and a smart line in three-piece knits and heavy gilt costume jewellery. True to form, Richard Phillips took one look at the test and decided it was all wrong. Only the blue contact lenses survived.

Anyway, one thing led to another and in no time at all, I had the Qantas tickets in my hand and two weeks in the sun were gleefully anticipated.

The diary reads: 'The first day's filming took place in a garden overlooking Sydney Harbour. The bridge was growing out of my shoulders and the Opera House looked like a hair ornament. I was wearing a fetching array of grey wig, blue contact lenses, pink sun visor, a yard of padding in my sun-dress and two wads of sponge in my cheeks to fatten them out. I was sipping a cool guava juice. The only slight drawback was the howling wind and the blinding rain coursing relentlessly down on the heavy plastic sheeting over the camera, and the sizzling of the cue lamps burning down to simulate Australian weather. I gripped the sides of my garden chair to prevent myself being blown onto Bondi Beach, and at 4 o'clock we abandoned all hope and headed back to the hotel, the proud possessors of the long brown Australian mac known as a "Driza-bone". Wistfully I phoned England, to be told the weather was in the 70s and they were out having a "Barbie". Actually, we had a ball. Being together on location has turned a motley crew into a company and the next commercials we do should be a treat.'

Well, the next commercials we did *were* a treat. Albeit a late-night treat. We worked from 7–10 at night, and till 2 in the morning on the night shoot. We reached, I think, a watershed in Beattie-tudes. I got over my paranoia that she was taking over my life – I accepted the fact that if I opened in Lourdes in a play about Sister O'Grady of the Convent of Sacred Hearts the press would ask me how being Jewish affects my daily life.

The fact is, she was funny. Beattie was funny. The story was funny, the awards were funny. You should see them! As I said at the Golden Break awards: 'Awards are like haemorrhoids – sooner or later every bum gets one.'

Extracts from the fateful day when I first tried out for the part . . . not so much improvisation as desperation.

'Are we on the air? 'Cos he said to me: "Come along for a test" and I didn't exactly know what a test was, so I'm here and . . . er . . .' I put down my only prop, a cup of tea, and looked at the ocean of faces looking straight back at me.

'I don't have any lipstick on my teeth do I?' There followed two well-documented Jewish jokes, one concerning a vase and the other a gorilla. The camera operator began to shake and the studio erupted into laughter. I began to enjoy myself. 'So all of a sudden – it's turned into a show!' Then: 'Hello operator? Helloo – is anybody on the job? Operator, I want Greenmans the Kosher Butcher, I want some meat for the weekend. My son's coming and I can't get through. Thank you, dear – Hello? Hello? Hello Clive, how are you? Oh very, thank you dear. I want a nice piece of brisket for a casserole. No fat. How's the baby? Aah! Aah, is she? Aah, already? Bless her! Mine? Very well, thank you, all of them prodigies. I want some liver and I want it thinly sliced. Calves'! What do you mean, what sort? You didn't think I mean pigs' did you, eh? (Laughs) How's your

145

mother since the . . .? Ooh, I *am* sorry. Oh dear – *all* out – oh I am sorry, well, a lot of people manage with just the one . . . and have you got the frying sausages? I'll have 24 in two separate bags for the freezer. The big ones. Listen, I've got to go, there's someone at the door, you'll send that round, will you? If I'm not in you can leave it with her next door – she's not bad . . . Bye bye, Clive, thank you very much, bye bye.'

(Help! There was a silence, I racked my brains for inspiration.) 'Did you hear what happened? Well, you know of course that Percy Wacholder died just as the new rabbi arrived in the town. Well, of course it was difficult for him not knowing Percy personally – listen, it was difficult if you *did* know Percy . . . So he stands up at the house of mourning and he asks for someone to say a few words about the late Percy Wacholder and of course – well, you know what it is – nobody said a word. Well, what could ya say? He was the biggest . . . Well, yes, but the man died and something had to be said, so he asks again: "Will someone, anyone, say a few words – a syllable – about the late Percy Wacholder?" And again, not a murmur – terrible thing. Finally he said, "I appeal to you for the last time. You knew the man – I didn't. I would *like* to say something about him, but I can't. Will someone *please* say something – anything – about the late Percy Wacholder." Finally, at the back of the room, an old man raised himself from his seat, looked around the room, sighed, and said: "His brother was worse." '

And then it was over. And then they changed my wig, changed my wardrobe, changed just about everything. Other than that they liked it.

1. Extend Domestic bit in 'Thank U 4 Having Me'

2. Google search: Where can I buy Vim?

The Door to my House is Always Open

The front door of my house is probably the costliest item in it. It's probably the costliest front door in North London, if not in the northern hemisphere. Yet only a few months ago it was one of the least financially demanding items on which our lives ever hinged. Let me explain.

When my publisher Jeremy Robson made his tri-monthly call to discuss the states of both our lives, he managed to end the conversation with a sentence which chilled my plasma. 'So,' he said, with a cheery mixture of timidity and aggression, 'what's the new book going to be called?'

It was news to me that there was going to BE a book, since writing one is the second hardest thing I've ever been forced to do, and this is not the time to discuss childbirth.

Still, I'm a trained improviser and respond like whatsit's dogs – Anna Pavlova's – you know, she did ballet, desserts and dogs – to a challenge. I just open my mouth and provocation comes out like fumes from a Fiat. The next thing I know about it, somebody is reading me a quote from the *Sun* which came from almost anybody's lips but mine.

'Erm. It's going to be called *Holding Your Own*,' I said.

There was a pause and, I thought, a slightly embarrassed giggle.

'Well, maybe *Holding My Own* then? And on the cover I'll be holding out my arms and all my friends and associates will be standing on them. My arms I mean. Very small.'

I could tell by Jeremy's silence that he was totting up the cost of the trick photography. Another tack was called for.

'How's about you photograph me outside the phone box in the garden and we call it *I'm IN the Book*? Funny, yes?'

'Very funny,' said Jeremy. 'Er – how closely do you want to be associated with BT?'

If I'd had a drawing board I'd have gone straight back to it.

'Got it,' I eureka'd. 'We paint the front door like a *trompe l'oeil* and I wear a party dress and we call it *Thank You For Having Me*.'

'Er . . . yees,' said Jeremy, understanding as much of what I'd just said as you have. I was in my designer's hat and the brim was covering most of my brain.

'I'll ask Chris Clarke to paint marble veins running through the door – he's a brilliant stage painter – and we can subtitle it *Maureen the same vein,*' I yelled. "'More in" gettit? Ben Frow can make me a backless dress from this wonderful piece of mottled pink and blue chiffon he showed me once, and we'll have balloons and streamers and lilac wisteria in the same colours, then on the back we can have the same shot only I'll be leaving drunk as a skunk and –'

'Fine, it sounds – er – great,' said Jeremy.

'Lovely,' said Chris Clarke.

'When do I start?' said Ben Frow.

'Must remember to bring some film,' said Anthony Grant, photographer.

'I'll pick up the wisteria,' said Steve Ridgeway, the jacket designer.

'*WHOSE DOOR ARE YOU USING?*' said Jack Rosenthal, flattening himself protectively against his own.

Well, we talked about doing it in a studio like proper professionals, and I looked out for suitable front doors on my way to the swimming-pool and even contemplated ringing the doorbell of one particularly entrancing portal hung with claret clematis, and offering them a few readies. In my heart, however, I knew whose front door was about to be pillaged – the writing was on the door. After all, *How Was It For You?* featured my bathroom, *Something To Fall Back On*, my dining-room curtains – I was following a tradition as old as Prince Harry.

'It'll just be for a day, love. Then we'll have it painted back. Whatever colour you like.'

'I like it the colour it *is*,' he wailed. He likes a nice brown door, does Jack.

Two days before the shoot we had a dress rehearsal. Chris Clarke, who'd been working on the door for several days, had painted seven or eight hardboard door samples, using all the pinks and blues in the scrap of fabric which Ben had left for him. The door was now sporting a deep blue undercoat and Steve Ridgeway was cutting out cardboard covers for the stained glass panels, which were also to be painted, and Madam was framed against the lintel wearing all she had of the halter neck – a small silk collar and the contents of a pin-cushion. Steve and Ben held up some plastic wisteria, I smiled into the sunshine and Anthony Grant took the polaroids. 'OK. We have a cover.'

The next day, I was working at Elstree on the British Telecom 'Anniversary' advert. My main concern was my hair. Not only was it lying under Beattie's wig all day, but it was generally in revolt against the treatment, or lack of it, meted out to it all year. Carmen-rollered and lacquered for my one-woman show, *Re:Joyce*, every day and twice on Saturdays, brown in some places, grey and coarse in others and burnt brass in the places where the henna misfired, it had all the gloss and consistency of a bag of potting compost.

Robert came to my rescue – Robert being the exquisitely handsome Scots make-up artist who assists Lorna on the BT shoots. He promised to whiz round to me the following morning and reassemble my head. He arrived about midday and we agreed that the cut would be the thing and we'd paint the grey out later. I wonder if the public realises how haphazard and home-spun most personal appearances are? Or is it just me? Do the other lady writers (and presumably Jeffrey Archer) have the services of John Frieda and Barbara Daly for their photographic shoots? Is Joan Collins to be found like me, scrabbling through sticky make-up bags in search of a stick of kohl which turns out to be stuck all over the inside of the bag? Suffice it to say Robert cut my hair beautifully, and with a good haircut everything else just falls into place. Like your face.

It was to be a late afternoon shoot, to give the impression of leaving a party at dusk. Ben arrived at three o'clock with the dress. It was a thing of great loveliness, clingy where it should cling and wide where it should hide. The young genius knows my body better than my osteopath does.

The doorbell – which by now was the only thing left on the door apart from cardboard, veins, stippling, spongeing, marble-ising, three balloons and a colourless glaze – rang. It was John Henderson, director of the television series *About Face*, calling to keep the appointment I'd forgotten to cancel, to discuss Series Two. He admired the new door and my backless dress rather quizzically, and asked who was having the party. Since John never drinks tea, or anything else as far as I can see, I couldn't stall him with a cuppa whilst I slipped into something with a back (and a bit more front), so I pushed him into Jack's study for a chat.

At 4.30 I excused myself again, took off the clothes I'd just put on for modesty's sake, and carefully painted my face to match the rest of me. Ben came back, Steve arrived replete with the plastic wisteria and more balloons, and Anthony Grant zoomed into the driveway with lights and cameras ready for action.

Whereupon the heavens went black. Then they opened up, emptying fourteen thousand litres of baleful, hailful rain on our halter-necked shoot, halting any chances we ever had of shooting anything.

Anthony, undaunted, donned a kagoul and laid his cables through the front living-room window. The rest of us huddled indoors, whilst Amy, clutching a packet of henna, told us the exact shade of red she intended to dye her hair. Many cups of tea later, the skies cleared, we wiped down the door, and I stood shiveringly on the steps, improvising vivacity.

At which point a man arrived in a van carrying a crate of wine. It was my fee for writing an article on My Favourite Tipple. The 'vin driver' surveyed the scene before staggering through the door scattering balloons and streamers in his wake. 'I like your vine,' he said as I signed something.

'Oh, it's not real,' I smiled cheerily, 'it's just plastic. We stuck it on.' He looked at me and left.

'He said, "I like your *wine*", I think,' hissed Ben, as he left. We returned to the shoot. I smiled, I grinned, I looked meaningful, I drank fake champagne, I donned a party hat and blew a party blower. Then the sky blackened and it tossed it down again. Out of the blackness ran a small drenched figure in white carrying a cricket bag.

'We were rained off, Mod,' he mumbled. 'I scored nine. I'm wet – what are you doing?'

'Change your clothes and dry your hair,' I muttered without moving my lips or my vivacious demeanour.

'S'all right, they'll dry on me.'

'Excuse me, Anthony, for a minute – I have to dry my son.'

I came back, wet, and somehow we did it. There were twenty-six mugs in the sink when everyone left, and I felt like one of them.

In the following days everyone who came to the house commented on the loveliness of the front door. Everyone except the door owner. Finally Les came round for his weekly handymanning, sighed, removed the cardboard and sanded all the paint down. 'What colour do you want it?' he asked. 'Same as before or different?'

'Same' – 'Different,' said Jack and I, at the same time.

Les produced a chart.

'French Navy,' I said, 'with cream on the mouldings.' Jack looked mournfully at me. 'You'll love it, darling. It's smart.' I went out.

Les undercoated. ''S'funny,' he said. 'The paint's drying immediately. I don't understand it.'

'It looks a bit bright, Les.'

'Yeah. It's only the undercoat though.'

'Yeah. Bye, Les.'

I was out for most of the following day. When I arrived home it was to find Les putting the finishing touches to a door which was the colour of a packet of cornflour.

'I hate it.'

'I thought you would.'

The cream had run into the blue.

''S'funny,' said Les. 'The paint just sits on the surface like . . .'

'Like paint on a glazed finish?'

'Yeah.'

'Yeah.'

I rang Chris Clarke, who explained that he'd explained to me about the glaze and how the door would need a lot of work on it.

'Oh. Yeah, I remember now.'

Les went home. I said I'd think about it. I thought about it. The next day Layla phoned a French Polisher she knew. Paul. He came over.

'Yeah, I could do it. The door will have to be taken away and dipped in acid. It'll come up very nice.'

I swallowed. 'All right, Jack?'

'Why can't you paint it brown?' said Jack for the seventeenth and final time.

'It's a good old wooden door,' I argued. 'It would look wonderful stripped and stained. It's probably mahogany.'

'The burglar alarm's in the door, you know, you'll have to ring George the burglar.' (He's our Cypriot burglar-alarm man, and not an easy chap to pin down.)

I rang him. 'He can come on Tuesday,' I told Paul. Paul consulted his diary. 'Yeah. Should be all right.'

On Monday Paul rang to say the people with the acid bath could only do it on Friday.

I rang George. He could only do it Tuesday.

I rang Paul. Paul rang another firm. They rang me. They'd pick it up tomorrow.

When I got up in the morning the door had gone. We all wore a lot of woollies through a breezy day.

George arrived back at 3.30 to re-fix the alarm. He waited. By 5.30 the door was still not back. George left for his next appointment.

At 6 o'clock the door came back, looking bleached but far from perfect. The good old wood turned out to be a pine surround, one fruitwood panel, two old planks and a piece of hardboard. Jack did not say 'I told you so'.

Paul arrived Friday and so did the first firm of strippers, whom he'd forgotten to cancel.

'Whoever did this has got no bloody idea,' said the stripper. 'How much did this cowboy charge you, eh?'

Paul stripped the rest of the paint off by hand and started patching up the cracks and holes with filler. It took most of the day. And the next day.

A few days later he came back and started staining the wood. 'These mouldings are in terrible shape,' he said. 'If I were you I'd have new mouldings made.'

We had new mouldings made.

A week later Paul returned with the new mouldings and continued staining. He brought his son Duran, aged seven, with whom I immediately fell in love. He is solemn and his straight blond hair is cut straight round like a pudding basin.

He wandered into the room where I was pretending to write. I work with Radio 2 on. 'Would you like a coke?' I asked.

151

'No, thank you,' he said. 'Do you have any Pavarotti records?' I was hooked. His dad paints and stains. Duran and I talked.

'You will bring him with you next time, won't you?' I asked anxiously.

'Yeah,' says Paul. 'Looking better, isn't it? You know the stained glass is cracked, don't you?'

I look up 'Stained Glass' in the Yellow Pages.

He finished staining and varnishing. The next time he called and replaced the letter box and house numbers. Once they were screwed back the door began to look lovely.

Jack said, 'The brass bits should have been polished before they were screwed back.'

Paul unscrewed them. Jack and Duran polished the door furniture. Paul replaced them. I watched.

Then, out of the blue, a strange red-faced man in a back-pack wandered down the pathway and stood in front of the door. He surveyed it for a while. Jack and I surveyed his surveillance from behind the wooden blinds.

'What's going on with this door, then? Eh? One minute it's brown, the next minute it's mauve, then it's blue, then it's nothing. What is it now, eh?'

Paul continued varnishing and said, 'I'm varnishing it now.'

'Oh yes,' the man droned, 'very nice. Better, much better. I couldn't understand what was going on. One minute it was brown, then it was blue, I thought, whatever next? Eh? But this is it, is it? This is how it's going to be, is it?'

'Er, yes,' Paul reiterated, varnishing away.

'Very nice. Yes.' He stood back. 'I like it. Better, much better.' He paused. 'I couldn't understand it. Brown, then blue, then something else. Whatever next I thought. Eh?'

Jack and I got a serious attack of the giggles. We slid down the study wall and heaved silently. With the occasional squeak. 'Right, then,' said Paul, 'best get on.'

'I'll say,' said our over-interested party. 'Me, too.' He took a step backwards and returned. 'Friend of mine. Now, he's got a door. Now, that's what I call a door. Stained glass! Stained glass! From top to bottom. Top and bottom. All glass. All stained. Beautiful. Mind you, this one looks a lot better now. I thought to myself, "Hello," I thought, "what's it going to be today?"'

I left them to it. I don't know how Paul got rid of him and finished the finish, but he did. All right, so he varnished over the spy-hole. What the hell? You can only see who's out there if they're exactly five foot one anyway.

So folks, we have a nice front door. And a cover. Like I said, it cost a mere arm and a mere leg and several weeks of several people's lives.

P.S. The lower door panel has now cracked straight across in two places. Paul says it's shrinking and we'll have to wait till it stops shrinking before we re-fill and re-stain it. The way I look at it, if the cat diets, in a couple of weeks she'll have a built-in cat-flap. Every cloud . . .

Examination Unnerves

I think we're through the worst of the exams now. One more week and life should be back to normal, and those of you who've read the Lipman Diaries before will know how normal that is.

An excerpt from June 1988 read:

'The pre-match tension has been mounting for weeks, as both children approached their end-of-term exams. Whey-faced, they've haunted their rooms all evening long – emerging only for testing times. Testing for us, I mean.

'"Er, how does the act of fertilisation take place?" I ask.

'"It doesn't start there – you have to start with pollination."

'"Yes, but what if they phrase the question differently – you have to know the whole –" As I'm questioning and she's groping for words like stigma and stalk, I realise that I'm stalking her for what she *doesn't* know, not encouraging what she does.'

'Course, the difference these days is the fact that, as a mother, I'm testing *anything* except the consistency of a sponge cake. Both Jack and I agree that no one at home showed much interest in *our* educational progress, for better or worse. I mean, a good report meant the difference between a pleasant tea with your face in your *Bunty* and the same pleasant tea with the air throbbing with 'Just you wait till your father gets home' and smirks over the spaghetti hoops from the brilliant brother.

Occasionally, my academic prowess got a universal disclaimer as in: 'This is not a good report. Far too much time is being taken up showing-off and trying to create an impression. She has ability but she is wasting it in silliness.' To pre-empt the throbbing on such occasions, I tended to take the law into my own feet and stamp the whole bloody report into the nearest bike track – or worse.

Of course, PTA meetings didn't really exist on account the Ps and the Ts rarely Associated. We had a Founders' Day, but that was more on the lines of flowered hats, resonant versions of 'For Those in Peril on the Sea', and one piece of your neatest work on the Biology Room wall. Teachers tended to vanish into stationery cupboards, or spontaneously implode for all I know, at the approach of a Parent. Nowadays we queue up for hours for a little chat with Rog the Rugby and Del the Classics on the further adventures of Rosenthal Junior on the pitch or in Academia, clutching a reporter's notebook for fear we forget his negative qualities on the way home. I shudder to admit it, but we've even moved his bar mitzvah 'cos it clashed with his Common Entrance. Not perhaps a problem with which Moses' mother had to contend.

I mean, is it because we fear their joblessness that we've become so obsessed with their education? I was a deeply mediocre student. So was Jack, he tells me, though I think the gentleman doth protest too much. It was only when the Sixth Form loomed large and the subjects grew more subjective that the Click happened. You know the Click. The same one that Tennessee Williams tells us you hear when you're good and drunk, or one of the two. The moment when you suddenly realise that it's You against You, not You against Miss Buss, Miss Beale and the Rest of the World.

From that day forth learning becomes a pain-free zone. If I've got a piece to write, a play to learn, I just go into that room with the L plate on it and do the necessaries. Easy. It only took forty-two years to perfect this skill. Unfortunately, nowadays my powers of retention are somewhat limited.

But I digress. The fact that my timing was twenty years off doesn't mean the lesson wasn't valuable. And it shows how easy education should be. All you need to learn is how to learn. Oh – and one inspired, wonderful educator helps. A leader. A Corn-is-Greenius. Personally, I've decided not to hold my breath till He/She comes along. Instead I'll keep saying: 'So how do you say "I will be leaving the table?"' And she will keep saying, 'We haven't done that tense of whatsit – er – thingy – sortir. No, I mean partir. No, don't tell me –' 'But you *must* have done the future!' 'Oh, you always think you know better than – ANYWAY, I KNOW *LA TABLE*!'

Now all we have to do is brace ourselves for the results. These come in dribs and drabs with varying degrees of defensiveness, ranging from one child who yells 'Eighty per cent for Latin! That's appalling! I'm going to bang my head on the door till I'm less of a pranny!' to the other who drawls 'I don't know why you're looking so miserable. Fifty-two per cent is *good* – 's' great. Everyone got about that 'cept the goody-goodies! I thought you'd be *pleased*. Honestly!'

The most humiliating part of the whole business is my sheer ignorance of the subjects on which I'm testing them. Logarithms, fractions, matrices, cross-sections of plant-wort, Homer and his load of old belli – it's all Greek to me. It's like trying to recall the taste of gripe water. Been and gone, mate! And in what stead did it stand me, I wonder, as I skim through the batch of middle-brow sit-coms staring back at me from a bulging in-tray.

And it doesn't get any better. Excerpt from the diary, June 1990:

'Right now in our house, it's GCSEs and Common Entrance. Every night that dawns, as my mother is wont to say, Amy and I sit facing each other across a groaning table whilst she draws endless doodles of herself with a giant nose, and I write letters to almost anyone.

"'What animal reproduces itself asexually?" said today's Biology paper. "A kangaroo," wrote Layla's daughter, Yvette. "What did *you* write, darling?" I ask Amy gingerly. "Nothing, but I was going to write 'lobster'," she mutters, eating hair at a rapid rate and thumbing morosely through Linda Goodman's *Love Signs*. "No point. Nothing I revised came up." "What about Plasma?" "Nope." "Respiration?" "Nope." "The components of soil?" Hadn't we spent most of last night building elaborate words out of the initials of its components, to make it memorable?

'SHE: "It's no good. I'll remember MOASM all right, but I won't know what the hell it stands for . . ."
'ME: "Go to bed, darling. Have a nice hot bath and do the rest in bed and I'll bring you a –"
'SHE: (*tearfully*) "How can I? There's millions of checklists left and I haven't done the pancreas at all and it's History of Art in the morning!"
'ME: "Well, let me test you on it."
'SHE: "There's no point. I hate being tested. Besides, I don't care about Biology – it's History of Art as well and I've got to get an 'A' and I haven't touched Fauvism since Friday. I'm just useless. Why do people have to have exams anyway? I can't remember a thing! Melanie remembers *every single* date and I don't want to let everyone down and I'm so tired."
'ME: (*weakly*) "We've all been through it, darling."
'SHE: "Yes, I know, but it's different for me."

'In the end all I can do is all I can ever do. What I always do. I make her laugh. It's the only thing I'm good at. All through the next day I have a knot in my stomach from morning till the thinnest whitest face in town (other than her mother's) comes through the door.

'At 5.30 she rushes in and dumps herself in front of *Neighbours*.

'ME: "How did they go, darling?"
'SHE: "Shsh! Terrible. Shsh!"'

It'll be alright. It's May now and it's only four months till the results come through – I'll be fine. I mean *we'll* be fine. I'll take up a hobby. I'll volunteer for the peace corps or something. I'll learn to hang-glide. Something peaceful to take my mind off it all.

It doesn't stop does it? For years. Their thin pale faces and hunched shoulders. They'll come back from college or university the same. I know. And I'll be up in arms as usual, threatening to take the Board of Examiners to the International Court of Human Rights. This time one of the questions in her Biology GCSE was: 'What are the symptoms of gonorrhoea and how can the use of a condom help prevent its spread?'

'I don't believe it!' I shrieked from my safe little Nancy Drew world. 'What did you put?'

'Nothing,' she replied airily.

My face changed. 'What do you mean, nothing? You can't put nothing. You have to have a stab at it!'

'No point, I hadn't a clue.'

'Well, you must have known what a condom was.'

'Yes.'

'Well, then?'

'Well, then, what? What *is* gonorrhoea?'

You see what questions like this do to an average North London family? An entire lasagna dinner ruined by a description of gonorrhoea causes and effects. Thank you, GCSE Board, wherever you convene.

This would seem to be the ideal moment to mention the duck joke:

A duck checked into a hotel with his girlfriend. They were about to make love when she asked him if he had a condom.

'Er, no,' said the duck embarrassedly, 'I thought *you* . . . I mean . . .'

'Look here,' quacked the emancipated bird, 'this is 1990 – safe sex, remember? I'm not just any old duck you know . . .'

'No, of course,' said the duck hastily. 'Er, what shall I do?'

The lady duck sighs heavily. 'Phone room service, of course.'

'Just like that? Er, yes, of course . . .' He phones down, covered in all kinds of confusion and says, 'This is Mr Duck, in room 314 . . . Is it possible to have a . . . pot of tea sent up please . . . and – er – a condom?'

'Certainly, Sir.' And in less time than it takes to boil a duck egg, there's a knock on the door and the waiter enters with a pot of tea and a condom on a silver tray.

'Will that be all, Sir?' says the waiter as the duck presses a tip into his hand.

'Yes, thank you,' replies the duck in his most dismissive tones.

'And shall I put it on your bill, Sir?' asks the waiter.

'What do you think I am?' hurls back the duck, 'a flipping pervert?'

Where was I? Oh yes, exams . . .

The most vivid picture I have is of Adam, unable to swallow because of a sore throat, alone in a schoolroom about to commence his Common Entrance Greek exam. Just Adam and the invigilator – for fear he might copy from himself, presumably – an odd little odyssey if ever I saw one. His headmaster had told the boys not to revise over the weekend before Common Entrance, but instead to have lots of physical exercise to tire them out. Adam and his friend Will took the advice to heart and spent Sunday afternoon on a two-hour hike in the pouring rain. 'It was great!' he beamed, hair clinging to his head like Robert Robinson's and wearing Will's mother's clothes. 'We had the BEST time!'

I had the best time, too. Lemsips/Zincolds/hot Ribena and honey were poured down the boy most of the night, and as he staggered off in the morning, looking as though he'd been tumble dried and minus his mislaid glasses, he was decidedly unprepared for a day which would, at least, affect his entire future.

'Don't worry, love,' you lie, 'only another week and it's over and you'll never have to do it again.' No mention here of the inevitable fact that life, the rest of it, is one big exam. Will I get into college? Will I get a job? Will I meet my deadline? Will his parents like me? Will the bank give me a mortgage? Will my kid make the school team? Will I cope with his mother living with us? And that those two great examiners who know it all, who sit in judgement, never quite give us the marks we think we deserve. I mean, of course, ourselves and our Maker.

Towards the end of term, there were a whole bunch of balloon debates in which the speaker is given a famous character from History and must justify his reasons for being the last person in the balloon. Both of the kids seemed to fare less than well in these flights of fantasy, Adam being ditched from his balloon in the last round in favour of Moses and Mr Chips. This would have been totally acceptable had Adam not been debating under the name of God.

'It's a great title for your autobiography, Ad,' I told him, 'The Day God Came Second.'

Meanwhile his sister was faring even worse, under a less auspicious mantle, and hers was part of the GCSE oral exam.

'How did the balloon debate go, love?'

'Oh, it was appalling – I lost by a landslide. Even my best friend didn't vote for me.'

'No! How awful. Who did you choose to be?'

'Well that's the thing,' she somewhat sheepishly replied. 'I was the producer of *Neighbours* and Tasha was Nelson Mandela.'

Last week I stood in the hall of my son's new school with a crowd of other nervous new parents, passing my entrance exam into his next school. Trying to think of the right question to ask the maths master which would make me look like an intelligent, caring parent who wouldn't make too many waves, when all I really wanted to ask was 'Are there any other parents here from Muswell Hill who'd like to share a school run, and does anyone know the score from the England–Ireland quarter final?'

'Education,' said Pete Seeger, 'is when you read the fine print. Experience is what you get when you don't.' Wish *I'd* said that! (You will, Maureen, you will.)

Bar Mitzvah Joy

Well, it's all over now Bar the shouting. The Bar Mitzvah, I mean. It was no trouble. Looking back, it was a breeze, really. Gale force 13. And like every major event in one's life it passed by like a gale leaving nothing in its wake but ruffled hair, a trance-like calm and a lot of bills for the repair work.

The boy himself was a triumph. I suppose the nearest equivalent to a bar mitzvah in terms of emotional build up would probably not even be one's wedding day, but one's coronation. It seems like only yesterday, although he was six at the time, when he crept, white-faced in his red Batman pyjamas, into our bedroom and said in trembling tones, 'It's only seven years to my BAR MITZVAH and I don't know a word of it yet!'

Well, he knew every word *backwards* on Saturday. He could have sung it standing on his head – a feat which was suggested several times during the day in reference to his dad's TV play *Bar Mitzvah Boy*, written, curiously enough, thirteen years ago, and remembered with mixed emotions by most of the people who attended the ceremony.

It was a tough act to follow. Not only for the boy. The year had been spent finding the right location for the party. As Jack said in his speech, 'Welcome to what was booked to be breakfast at Claridges, brunch at the Savoy, lunch at the Grosvenor Rooms, Willesden, but is now, Maureen assured me on the way here, almost certainly dinner at the Arts Club in Dover Street.' I had, in fact, booked four other venues before a friend stumbled upon this lovely old club in Mayfair, with parlour and conservatory, stunning pictures, a cosy dining-room and a familiar air of eccentricity about it. Rather battered and leathery – not unlike your host and hostess – what sold me completely was the bronze rhinoceros in the lobby. My husband is a rhinophile. Another endangered species had found its natural habitat.

Over the months the tension grew. Appearing in *Re:Joyce*, a one-woman show, was time consuming enough. Appearing in a one-woman show whilst choosing tablecloth colourings and checking the consistency of leek tartlets is beyond this particular Thespian. My then secretary Jo had built up an intimate phone relationship with Mr Gomes the – yes, you guessed it – *Irish* manager, and we decided to hammer problems out and prices down over lunch at the club. We'd got about as far as the Campari and soda when fire broke out in the kitchens. The dining-room was evacuated, and we lunched at Wheeler's – which almost became Location Number Five.

'We're having sea bass,' I told my mother back home.

'Sea bass?' she repeated, as though I'd said 'sea horse'. 'You can't give them that, it's not a Jewish fish!'

I pointed out that sea bass don't have trotters, don't crawl on their bellies on the floor of the earth and don't, to my knowledge, suffer from PMT.

Her response was typically predictable. 'Don't put it on the menu. If it's pink they might think it's salmon!'

I was due to close in *Re:Joyce* two weeks before Adam's opening. And it came to pass that both Jo, highly efficient secretary, and Yvonne, long-suffering mother's help, suddenly got offers they couldn't refuse and left two weeks before the event. It was pure coincidence and pure hell. The team was rudderless, the house was in chaos, my parents had been staying for four months. My father was in the house recovering from a stroke, and my mother was in the house giving *me* one.

On the last Monday the doorbell rang and the builders arrived. Irish and disarming, they laid dustsheets up the stairs, and removed the upstairs toilet. The following day, they returned and put in a new one. Then, as they were taking the wallpaper off the walls, Jack said, 'Why did they remove the toilet – it was the best toilet in the house?'

I looked at him askance and said, 'Do you mean *you* didn't ask them to?'

He hadn't. Actually they did a bloody good job. Whoever they were.

The invitations had all returned bringing joy and laughter. On the reply card we put: 'Please answer yes or no if you will be at the Kiddush' – this latter being a celebration with wine and food after the ceremony. One very dear, non-Jewish couple replied in the negative and when we asked if they were sure they didn't want to come, admitted they didn't think they could *do* it.

'Do what?'

'Well, *beat* the Kiddush.'

Poor souls obviously thought they were going to have to club a baby goat to death.

In the last week we did the table plan. Let me rephrase that. On Monday night we did the table plan. On Tuesday we redid the table plan. Then, slowly and inexorably, on the other remaining nights the table plan did for us. One night at 2am we finally pushed the last place-card round the dining-table and said. 'We've done the bastard.' A hundred and forty-four people. A gross of guests. Ten people, all of whom vaguely spoke to one another, at the thirteen tables, and fourteen at the top. We gazed at one another, held hands, smiled a forgotten smile, and I said those three all-important words that mean so much to a married couple in a time of crisis: 'Bessie Edelson's missing.' An hour and a half and five tables reorganised later, we found her place-card underneath Helen Feldman's – almost where she ended up sitting.

The night before – some cancellations, some further reorganization – no word yet from my friends the flamenco dancers, who'd volunteered to liven up the cabaret. Mañana – mañana – worried? Me? Noooo! What's Spanish for panic attack? Hispanic attack?

Meanwhile, the boy who's becoming a man tomorrow practises and practises, with drier and drier mouth, what is already practised till perfect. Underwater eyes, freshly cut hair, pale face grown up with grown-up worry. Only his dad knows how he feels – empathy being his trademark. Together they hear each other's Hebrew speeches and after-dinner speeches. Together they try on their prayer shawls, inquiring Talmudically over each fold and drape, Adam's a brand-new shawl, Jack proudly wearing Adam's old one. That night Adam does the Sabbath blessing and cuts the Chollah loaf. We're all a bit quiet now. The tension and nervous quibbling over – the calm before the dawn.

The day. Perfect. That's all I can tell you. I spent it as glazed as a carrot in a nouvelle cuisine restaurant. According to the *Mail on Sunday* I had 'Four hundred guests and Julia McKenzie'. According to the 144 people who were *really* there, we had a service in the West London Synagogue which took their breaths collectively away. Adam took half the service and sang his portion like the pro he is with fervour and modesty and pure clarity. Rabbi Hugo Gryn beamed with pride. I did my two words of Hebrew with only three mistakes, Jack and Amy were good and glorious, the choir took the roof away and the sharing of joy was everywhere. Relatives and friends convivial, speeches hilarious, and food, they tell me, divine. I choose to believe this in spite of Mother returning from a protracted table hop to say, 'No one's eating the sea bass at the far end.'

All over Bar the thank-you letters. And if anyone didn't like it – listen, we'll do it again next year – at Claridge's or the Savoy or the Grosvenor Rooms, Willesden – or probably the Arts Club. Possibly with salmon.

During the ceremony, like a drowning parent, most of Adam's life flashed before my eyes. I remembered his birth very clearly. It was on the same day that Selfridges delivered £800 worth of green- and white-flowered sofas to the house. I seem to have been present at both occasions. I'd bought the furniture in a pit of freak because the gynaecologist had told me that Adam was upside-down and I would need to have another Caesarian. On reflection I was relieved he was upside down thirteen years ago and not on this day, in a park somewhere in Willesden, like the lad in *Bar Mitzvah Boy*.

As a baby, he looked extraordinarily like Sir John Gielgud. Funny that. His face went sideways, not longways like the rest of us. People would pop into my hospital room and say, 'Gosh, you know who he reminds me of?' and I'd say, 'Yes. Sir John Gielgud' and they'd say, 'That's right. I knew it was one of them.' And I'd think, 'But all we *did* together was recite, "Shall I compare thee to a summer's day . . ."'

He didn't talk much. He didn't need to. His sister was in charge of words. Adam just sat there thinking long and hard. Only his dad knows what he's thinking. To see them together is to be reminded of the two old men in the theatre box in *The Muppet Show*. Cricket and Latin, etymology and philology, Hebrew and cornflakes. They never stop discussing. When Ad showed a keen interest in astronomy his dad sent away for an eight-inch Newtonian reflector and stood with him for hours on frosty February nights in search of the universe through the flora and fauna of Muswell Hill. If the boy had said to *me*, 'Mod, I love the stars,' I'd probably have got him Des O'Connor's autograph. Incidentally, an eight-inch Newtonian reflector is eight inches *wide* not, as I thought, eight inches *long*. It came through the front door at 10am and it was still coming through at noon. It also had to have an observatory built around it. With a sliding roof. It looks very nice in the garden and probably caused more trouble to build than the house did in 1910. In the end, no one was speaking to anyone, but the sight of the moon in the palm of one's hand is almost worth it. He's not in it *quite* as much as we expected, but we're optimistic that he'll take it up again once the cricket season is over and *Blackadder* stops being repeated.

Amy and I rather cherish our roles as the dumb brunettes of the family. On a trip to Brent Cross for THE SUIT, Adam broke the strains of Streisand singing Sondheim with the outcome of his own particular strain of philosophical thought, to say: 'What would you say was a definition of the word courage?'

His sister rolled her eyes roof-wards and groaned. 'Courage is going to Brent Cross on a wet Wednesday for a ruddy bar mitzvah suit.'

It was the same week that their father's new shirt had to be purchased. When I suggested stopping off at the suit shop to buy one he demurred. 'I can't do it *now*.' 'Why not?' I asked him. 'I've got the wrong shoes on,' he replied lamely. Absent-minded professors, the pair of them. Was it not Adam who, when I pointed Dustin Hoffman out to him and told him that Hoffman was in London playing Shylock, said, 'Really? D'you mean Shylock Holmes?'

His sister has a few words for the change in the boy becoming a man. 'One day he was listening to all my doll stories and doing what I told him, then suddenly he got very pale and thin and his legs grew and his pyjamas shrank and he stopped moving his mouth when he spoke, batted the air and made repetitive clicking noises. I sort of carried on talking and he stopped listening . . .'

Mind you, Amy was in a fair state of tension herself. Two weeks before the big day was her biggest day yet. The day she starred as Anne 'with an E' in her school production of *Anne of Green Gables*.

It was the end of a two-year audition period in our house. The play had been on and off more times than Prince's clothes. The saga of whether to have real boys or girl-boys or teachers in short pants or total strangers who happened to be passing the school entrance, had been more tedious than the Channel Tunnel. The auditions were heart-stopping and the tension between them and the announcement of the casting made *A Chorus Line* look like half an hour in the Lisson Grove Job Centre.

Finally she landed the role, and glory be to God, her best friend Melanie landed the role of Anne's best friend. Not one drop of help did she get from her showbiz parents, who were far too preoccupied with the shape of twenty-four table centre-pieces, and 'Do we invite the cousin from Belgium who's never seen Adam and doesn't speak to his parents?'

I only saw the dress rehearsal, as I was Re:Joycing in the evenings. It was more temperamental than any show I've ever been involved with, and had all the hallmarks of success. Which it was. And she was. Was? She's now moved into the attic room, painted it green, dyed her hair red and is working on the freckles, with the aid of a soft brown crayon.

'Don't you miss a play *dreadfully* when it's over Mod?' she cries, and looks disbelieving and disparaging when I say, 'Never: I like the memories, I like to look through the bar mitzvah photos and the *Anne of Green Gables* video and, when pushed, Grandma's scrapbooks, and to think: "Thank God *that's* over – next?"'

Almost a year after, I watch the bar mitzvah boy carving fastidious marks in the ground with his beloved Swiss army knife. The trouser-press was a godsend, particularly for my trousers, and all of the good and generous gifts have evolved into household necessities. Perhaps our favourite memento is the certificate given to him by ex-secretary Jo Kydd and her husband James. It is from the International Star Registry, Toronto, and it certifies the existence of a star in the firmament called 'The Adam Rosenthal Star'. So, aeons after my theatre greasepaint has sunk into the coal seams and Jack's plays have been recycled into kitchen rolls, there will still, thank the Lord, be a star in the family.

Now *that's* immortality.

Me, Myself and Eyes

It seems to me that I wore glasses before I wore zinc-and-castor-oil cream. Let's be honest, I was conceived in glasses. It was spectacular! This may well be a little rose-tinted, but that weighty, bulldog-clip-round-the-nose sensation appears to have been with me, and indeed to have shaped – not only me, but my nose – not only my nose, but my personality – for as long as I can recall.

Neither of my parents wore them. My mother didn't need them and was far too pretty to wear them even if she had needed them. My father preferred to screw up his eyes and lean forward should he need to see whether the pink or blue was about to be potted. His glasses were always 'in me other jacket pocket, behind the clock on the mantelpiece'. (There isn't a clock on the mantelpiece. Come to that, there isn't a bloody mantelpiece.) Elder brother Geoffrey (the Paragon), blond, brainy, sporty, the white sheep of the family, had, of course, the full 20/20. And no buck teeth. How he managed to *live* with all I had going against him was an East Yorkshire miracle.

I suppose I was ten when the school said I couldn't see. I invariably sat at the back of the class for reasons not unconnected with gang warfare, and if I needed to glance at the blackboard there was always someone to show me roughly where it was. But, no. A second opinion was sought and, short-sightedly, my parents agreed to put me in those gorgeous National Health jobs which are now sported by your average Yuppie but which then made you look second only in berkishness to the kid in the owl specs with elastoplast all over one lens. This was to correct a lazy eye. I certainly had one of those. It went with the rest of me. If the treatment really worked I should have been elastoplasted all over.

At first I only wore the bins for homework and blackboard but, as the years rolled myopically by, I came to rely on them more and more, too lazy to take them off. Ultimately I took to wearing them all the time, only whipping them off when approached by a boy I vaguely fancied, or at the door of a friend of my mother's with a boy *she* fancied for me inside.

My first boyfriend seemed to like me, specs and all. I couldn't believe it and, at the pictures, persisted in dragging them surreptitiously on and off whenever he took his eyes off the screen and looked at me. Mind you, he'd come home from university one time to see me in bed with 'flu, glasses and no front teeth, so I guess he was pretty immune to my charmlessness – or was too shortsighted himself to notice. Or maybe love really *is* blind.

During the Seventies, in my Lovin' Spoonful London Hippie period, I favoured tiny, blue-tinted, gold-rimmed Lennon specs like everyone else – and for the first time felt utterly at peace (man) with my bespectacled self. Meeting Jack in his butch horn-rims gave me a feeling of intense familiarity, and the first time we banged glasses together in mid-kiss I knew it was sight at first love.

Since then, whatever the frame, I've rarely had them off – to the extent that I began to hide, defiantly Su Pollard-like, behind them, never fighting being four-eyed except occasionally in the odd incongruous evening dress.

I am a woman who has always been prepared to make a spectacle of herself. Since the days before National Health glasses were associated with lazy eyes, lazy pupils and Elastoplast, rather than young men in baggy linen and floppy quiffs, I have sported maybe thirty or forty assorted pairs of glasses and have a proud and pinkish indentation on my not inconsiderable nose to prove it.

I had three pairs of hideous – by my standards I hasten to add – glasses for Beattie, after the producers realised that they added years to my age, and in the series *About Face*, three out of the six characters I played wore glasses, ranging from half-moon rimless for the batty animal rights liberationist to matching frame to every outfit for Deirdre, the career woman on the up. I love character glasses. I feel safe behind them. In 2007 I used my 1969 Lennonesque blue-tinted specs to play an American talk-show host opposite Joanna Lumley in *Sensitive Skin*. They looked fantastically trendy.

I have a pair that are not that dissimilar from the ones I wore on that fateful evening, gold-rimmed, small, but rounded. They say on them, Paul Stig Design, and they come with a variety of frame covers in different colours, rather like a Swatch. I rarely wear the frame covers but I love having the gimmick. I'm delighted the fashion for huge spectacles has passed on because on a face as small as mine they tended to make me look like a pair of inverted garden shears.

I'm also intrigued by the High Street Opticians turning into the glamour shop of the Nineties, replacing the Moroccan Wall Hanging shops of the Sixties, the Habitats of the Seventies and the Nexts of the Eighties. Opticians' windows used to favour a couple of rows of spectacles, a merry laughing four-eyed family group and a snap-shut glasses case. Nowadays you'll see the head of Zeus in life-size proportions, draped in Thai silk with a picnic hamper from Fortnum's spilling out its classical repertoire of fine goods on to a surface of gleaming perspex. The music of Saint-Saëns will be playing sweetly through the open doors and the only way you'll know it's an opticians is by the number of people walking straight into the clear glass doorposts.

I'm getting long-sighted, of course. Isn't that fun? Bifocals beckon. My eyes feel seriously stuck together in the mornings and I have to swab them down like we used to swab our tortoise, Zuckerman, after a long winter in the bike shed. Almost everything, from a baby in a blue babygro to an old Fred and Ginger film on Saturday afternoon telly makes me cry these days and no mascara invented by man or Maybelline can stop the rivulets. My glasses are my friends, comforting, covering, protective, dirty and dependable – and once I'm done with my current ones I don't put them out to glass, they go in a special drawer with all my old friends to show my huge appreciation for services rendered, over the increasingly bleary years.

Occasionally, it must be admitted, I have begun a sleazy, adulterous relationship with a contact lens container, but, in the end, loyalty has prevailed and I have returned, penitently red-eyed, back to the glasses case sulking in my dressing-table drawer. I'm short-sighted, astigmatic and as daft as a brush, so the lenses always ended up in the wrong eye.

My first venture into contact lenses was a classic. I accustomed my pupils to the tiny hard lenses – building up their resistance fastidiously for an extra hour per day – then lost one down the sink and the other down the Holborn Public Baths. Back came the 'face-furniture' which required no solutions except that of remembering to wear them. But the problem remained of seeing and being seen. On stage, short sight is a positive advantage and many are the flowering eulogies some of our more sensitive critics have launched into in praise of this or that actress's misty gaze into the middle-distance, which could be more truthfully ascribed to her frames being confined to the dressing-room table, having failed to match her period costume.

Many are the TV panel games and Awards Ceremonies where actors are required to open envelopes and read the contents. At such occasions, actors' glasses are on and off more times than a bridegroom's pyjama bottoms – and millions thrill to the sound of '. . . And the winner is Dustman Hoffbin'.

During a run in a Neil Simon play, I struggled with soft lenses but they made me cry constantly – which was unfortunate, as Neil tends to expect laughs. Pink-eyed, I returned to the lens boutique in the Earls Court Road (on the cornea, actually) and complained bitterly that the lenses were a pair of over-priced disasters through which I could neither see nor play Neil Simon. Patiently, the practitioner examined them, me and us, and proclaimed that I would probably be able to see jolly well if I didn't have them inside out and in the wrong eyes.

'You must think I'm a very stupid person!' I said rhetorically.

'We're used to it, madam,' he sighed. 'The gentleman before you complained his lenses gave him double vision and headaches. Which they do if you wear your flatmate's instead of your own.'

Even as we speak, I'm wearing the new, soft 'Torric' lenses. These are specially constructed to cope with astigmatic people such as myself and have two tiny lines on their edges which mean 'This way up'. These lines are only visible if you're already wearing contact lenses! So you have to get a man in to line them up for you before you put them in. Once in, and pain subsiding, they very deliberately move around so that the two lines are elsewhere – and what you are reading looks like basic Sanskrit.

In America recently, I wore the lenses for a ladies' luncheon, then went straight to the theatre for the show, and did make-up, hair and costume in record time. As I took my place in the darkened centre stage for the opening of the first act, and the lights slowly came up, I saw a sight which chilled me to the marrow and froze me to the spot. The audience. By now I was talking and singing on automatic pilot whilst my heart and brain were thudding with a heady mixture of adrenalin. I'll never know how I made it through to the interval, an hour later, but I do know that I wrenched those lenses out with such force that in the second act I was as red-eyed as the Bride of Dracula. It's not that I've anything against audiences, it's just that when they're a blur they're *so* friendly – just one big smiley mess. Sorry, but that's how I like you – warm, faceless, friendly and available – like a mother's breast.

Another innovation of lenses is seeing yourself without the cover of glasses from a three-foot distance for the first time since puberty. You simply freeze with the shock of the new. Or, in my case, the old. Mirrored lifts are the worst. No, I lie. Marks and Spencer's food halls are. Overhead fluorescent lights and mirrored columns prove beyond doubt that M & S have a deal with top Harley Street plastic surgeons – and 'Shall I take your bags, madam?' takes on an entirely different meaning.

Some time later I attempted a new idea in lenses which gives you one lens for short sight and another for long sight. Then the brain, apparently, does the business of adjusting. That's how the blurb goes anyway. In my case, my brain decided it was April Fool's Day all year round. When I tried to read, the print fox-trotted, and when I looked into the middle distance, I fell over. Back to the drawing board, I'm afraid – if I could see it. I'd love to have the laser operation and just wake up with normal sight. As the man said, 'Show me a guy with 20/20 vision and I'll show you a gentile!' It wouldn't work though. Something would slip. The laser wouldn't lase. I'd wake up in the middle and my tears would wash away the surgeon . . .

Listen, I'll just have to improve my groping – why not? I look at my desk and there's a pair for going downstairs in, there's the smart Raybans for venturing out of the door in, there's the very chic, non-prescription sunglasses to go over the corrective lenses which I'd given up on, there's the cheap and not very cheerful prescription sunglasses for quick trips up to the pool when I daren't risk losing my best ones, and there's the querulous gold-rimmed ones, hanging on the end of my nose, for the increasing long sight. Putting one pair of specs on to look for another is no longer amusing to my family as they wait, all dressed up in the hall, while I race around the house barking and swearing. [So far, nobody has patented my design for a tiny beeper attached to the leg of your glasses which is activated by your mobile phone. It could bleep and say 'We're over here, pinhead' or just shout 'Senile!' but it would free up bags of time for us Freedom Pass holders.] The day I give in and allow the word trifocal to enter my vocabulary, is the day I'll also stop dying my roots, having my teeth capped and cantilevering my boobs. It'll be a courageous moment and fortunately I shall be too dead to see it. 'Glasses to glasses and bust to bust . . .'

It is You, isn't it?

I had a holiday recently in the Algarve. It was, in truth, the finest holiday I've ever spent on a building-site and I may never look a sardine in the gill again. But that's not the point.

The point is my face. My familiar, peaky little face. It's now what you might call 'on the circuit'. People see it and they have this immediate compulsion to come close and mull it over. It's too thin, it's too sharp, it's better than it looks on the telly, it reminds them of the wife, it gets right up their nose, etc. etc. Whatever it is, it's not my property any more and I can't put a 'Kindly Keep Off The Grass' notice on it. Sometimes I can handle it very well, other times I feel empathy with the gorilla-house on a wet Thursday in February.

At a one-donkey crossroads deep in the Algarve countryside, we stopped to take photographs. Outside the all-purpose store, bar and scrubbing-brush shop was a line of toothless old men on a bench. Whilst Jack sat with them and had a beer and a photo taken, I wandered into the gloom of the shop and rather studiously examined some Portuguese washing-up bowls. Into the shop came a young and very hot couple, leaving their bicycles outside. We exchanged a smile as they struggled to make their need for agua without gaz understood. 'Are you English?' I heard myself inquire. 'No, we're from New Zealand' came the reply. Then (and without surprise), 'And, you're Maureen Lipman, aren't you?' You could have knocked me down with a kiwi fruit.

It's when you see them coming towards you that your heart sinks. Not the nice ones, the kids or the ones who say 'Sorry to bother you but . . .' After all, it goes with the job, doesn't it? I mean, 'Cripes, dear, if it was anonymity you'd wanted you should have gone into the family tailoring business,' I hear you say, with some justification. And why not? A lifetime of measuring men's inside legs and making weak jokes about dressing on the right side or the left – 'of the bedroom, I mean, sir! Haw, haw!' – would not have differed greatly from an average week in your average sit-com.

No, the ones who get me are the purposeful ones who are out to pull you down a peg or two when you were quite happy with the peg you were on. You can almost hear their conversation when they get back home . . .

'Listen, you know me. I'm not backward in coming forward. I went straight up and I said, "Sign this. It's not for me, I can't stand you, it's for my mother-in-law, she liked your book. I don't know why! She's got no sense of humour!'"

One particular day I had a skinful of them. Amy and I went out for the day. At one point in an art gallery, I turned to see a formidable-looking woman dragging her recalcitrant husband and children in my direction. 'Come on, she won't mind, she's used to it,' she bellowed, blocking my exit. 'Sign this for the kids, will you?' A ticket-stub appeared beneath my chin. 'There, I told you she wouldn't mind!' I signed obediently, asking their names and writing one for each. 'Actually,' boomed their upwardly registered mother, 'I'm always being ACCUSED of looking like you!' Amy and I exchanged speaking eyelids – it was the use of the word 'accused'. It could only mean trouble. 'I suppose it's *this*,' she went relentlessly on, 'I've been lumbered, too!' This was, of course, accompanied by violent jabbing of forefinger on aquiline bridge of nose. I smiled weakly. 'Oh, well, never mind, it hasn't affected your nature,' I said to her departing back. I looked round at Amy. Her eyes were filled with tears. 'Why do they always *say* these things, Mod?' she wailed, 'I think you're beautiful!' It was quite a moment. I hugged her in front of the Matisses. 'Well, that's all that matters, then, kid,' I said, and we went off to Fortnum and Mason for a Peach Melba.

Later that day, and with a good half-inch of our respective hair on the floor of a Soho salon, we hit the black suede pump shop, where I was noiselessly relieved of a week's rehearsal pay on a pair of boots the same as the ones which fell apart in three months last time and a pair of the suede pumps ('EVERYBODY'S wearing them!') which, one week later, were flat and circular like dinghies. A couple of men were trying on shoes. One stood up to walk about in a left brogue and stopped in mid-tread. 'It's you, isn't it?' he beamed, poking an elbow into his companion's anorak. 'Well, bloody hell! You look quite *normal* in real life. No, I didn't mean that, it's just that on the telly you look so . . . so . . .' Obviously, the appropriate adjective failed him because he burst into riotous laughter, abandoned the shoe and left.

Generally speaking, it's the voice. They look me full in the face and say, 'It's the voice I recognised, not you.' I wonder if Samantha Fox has the same problem? Someone once said he'd have known me anywhere by the voice but he'd have passed me by in the street on account I look *much* better in person than I do on the telly. They always mean that as a compliment, but it's a dubious one when you think about it: is it so very satisfactory to look MUCH better to one person than you do to twenty million?

One favourite came after a horrendous week of moonlighting (working during the day on a comedy, *Exclusive Yarns*, in Southampton and whizzing back at night for the musical, *Wonderful Town*). At the end of the second show on the Saturday night, I virtually crawled out of the stage door and into a waiting cab. I collapsed into the front seat – I'm not a good backseat driver – and tried to harness my heartbeat. My eyelids fell. There was a twitch in my left cheek which I couldn't control. My body was leaden. Round about Camden, I was drifting into sleep when the driver slapped his thigh and said 'Well, I don't know, I *do* not know.' I opened one lip and managed to speak. 'Pardon?' I said. 'I'm saying,' said the jaunty fellow, 'my wife is going to be dead disappointed. Oh dear, oh dear, oh dear.' 'Why?' I asked politely, knowing the fault could only be mine. 'Well, when she finds out I had my favourite comedy lady in my cab and she weren't a bit funny – not one bit – well, what a shock she's going to get!' As you might imagine, I ignored him. For a full twelve seconds. Then I launched into the apology, the explanation and finally, by dint of superhuman endeavour, the jokes.

Ever Felt Red?

It was a red, circular skirt. Cut on the bias, my mother pointed out helpfully. In felt. All I knew was that I felt biased towards having it. Mother thought it was a liability, i.e. it would have to be dry-cleaned, but I was twelve years old and had a PhD in Advanced Whingeing. So finally, smugly, snugly it was mine.

Then came the search for the perfect sweater. In my mind's beady eye it was white with just a soupçon (had I known the word soupçon) of scarlet such as I'd once seen June Allyson sport in a skating sequence in some Saturday morning picture. Maybe if I got her outfit I'd get her husky voice to match?

After three successive Saturdays spent hissing in a changing room in C&A, I found it. It was white wool with a band of red figures waltzing round the welt. Gorgeous wasn't in it – but before you can say 'It'll show every mark' – *I* was.

That evening, while the rest of the family watched *Dixon of Dock Green*, I gathered together the total ensemble and placed it upon my person. Red skirt, white sweater, snowy socks, shoes Tuxon'd scufflessly white – not by me, needless to say. To top it all I added a red and white ribbon to the crest of my perm. To do my family credit, no one actually *said* I looked like an animated barber's pole.

The party was at the weekend. Saturday. In school. The teacher had been specific about dress: 'Don't wear your best clothes, girls, there'll be lots of running around and some floor-games!' Sod that for a lark, thought Lipman, who felt anxious to flash her felt at all costs. I climbed into it. Mentally I'd never been out of it. Peered into the mirror, pinched my cheeks, fiddled with my frizz, stuck out what should have been a chest, and, well pleased, sashayed, stiff with petticoats and pride, through the storm porch and out to the bus stop.

Strange to be in school at the weekend. Like some forbidden city. The cloakroom was all of a gossip with the 'ooh's' and 'aah's' of it. I bided my timing till the last, then, Gypsy Rose Lee-like, flung off my good nap coat to reveal all. It was worth it – a gobsmacked silence followed by the 'ooh's' and 'aah's' to end them all.

'What? This?' I demurred. 'Oh, I've had it for aaaages – just never had the opportunity to wear it, so, y'know, I thought I might as well . . . You coming up or what?'

Flanked by friends all a-flutter, we flowed into the Assembly Hall, cleared of chairs for dancing and floor-games purposes. The teacher in mufti (giggle, giggle, point, snigger) called over the rabble: 'Girls, girls, please, now can you all make a circle and – QUIET, PLEASE – settle DOWN!' Here she caught my eye, and then, swiftly, the rest of me. 'Ahem . . . Could you all sit down' – here she definitely shot me a disdainful and slightly triumphant look – on the FLOOR!' I drew myself up to my full 4 feet 8 inches, flared my pupils at the teacher, picked up my scarlet skirt, Vivien Leigh-style, and, with a thud, parquet met felt and felt met parquet. Frankly, my dear, I didn't *give* a damn!

It was halfway through Pass the Parcel that the penny finally dropped. 'Nelly the Elephant' had just been chorus-interruptus as she was saying goodbye to the thingy, and a large girl in her mother's dirndl skirt from IIIB was attacking the string round the paper with her teeth and pretending not to hear that the music had started again, when I felt the red drain out of my skirt and into my face.

'Don't wear your best clothes, there'll be floor-games' doesn't mean don't wear your best clothes, there'll be floor-games, you dull-brained twerp! It means don't wear your best clothes, there'll be some girls who don't *have* best clothes, so we don't want any showing off. Or up.

This thought, followed by an affirming glance round the circle, was enough to ruin not only the rest of the party but also the possibility of ever wearing my outfit carelessly again. It sat in my wardrobe malevolently for a while until, out of sheer defiance, I grew two inches in as many months and in most directions. Dry-eyed, I acquiesced when it finally hit the bag of clothes for 'Poor Peggy, she's you-know-what-again, God help her', and I'm delighted to say I haven't given it a thought since. Not more than once a day, that is. For thirty years.

It was, I think, my first real understanding of what being spoiled meant, in more than one way, and it gave me a lifelong horror of over-dressing which, having just glanced though the photo-albums in search of an illustrative self-portrait, I seem to have conquered only too well.

Love in the Time of Colic

Virginia Woolf was asked once why she stayed married for so many years to Leonard, a man most of her colleagues found to be her intellectual inferior. Her definitive reply was 'Because when he comes into a room I never know what he is going to say.'

I don't know about you, but that comment, which was surely not a carefully considered one, rings truer than any homily on the state of matrimony I've heard on *Oprah* or seen embroidered on a sampler.

When I knew from nothing about affairs of the heart or the mortgage, I played a short season at the Edinburgh Festival. Aged nineteen, never kissed back and greener than Kermit, I was sipping crème de menthe in the basement of a jazz club, when an elderly roué (as in twenty-two) from the Oxford Union made a pronouncement which made my spine stiffen. 'Love,' he pronounced, with the world-weary wisdom of a man who wore dark glasses after sundown and owned at least three psychedelic ties, 'love is farting in bed with someone who doesn't mind.'

I was horrified. Mortified and every other 'fied' including 'petri'. '*How* can you say that?' I piped with all the passion of a Cartland virgin (which indeed I was, mentally if not technically). 'You've obviously NEVER been in love or you'd never think of it so vulgarly! Some love *you're* talking about. I'm sure Elizabeth Taylor and Richard Burton would have a slightly different story to tell – huh! Or Shakespeare – no mention of farting in *Romeo and Juliet* that I noticed. How disgusting. How *pathetic*.' Exit trainee Thespian to toilet for good cry for no obvious reason.

I'm not saying, twenty-five years later, that big Dave's metaphor was quite as incisive as Virginia Woolf's, I'm just saying that I know now why he wasn't entirely wrong.

I guess people fall in love with other people for all sorts of odd reasons, most of which are chronicled once monthly in the glossed-over pages of *Hello!* against a background of stately piles and Smallbone finishes. But no one ever mentions two things which seem to me of prime importance in the whole relationship saga. One is that the process of *falling* in love is as different from the process of *loving* as it is from any other experience in life. And for very good if slightly mean-spirited reasons.

I mean, could one do the Tesco superstore, pick up the bedding begonias and the kids from their respective nurseries, shell peas for the

175

boss's wife and remove the rotary drier from its rotospike so as not to offend the neighbours who've stuck a Sky dish up against your patio view, whilst obsessed by lust? I'm asking . . . could you do any one of those things, as well as eat, sleep, do it a lot, *and* phone your mother, if you were permanently in the chemical state induced by falling in love?

To put it another way: when the cat is on heat (which she hasn't been since the vet gave her the unkindest cut of all), nevertheless when she *was*, she had very little time for chasing moths, hanging unsubtly round the fridge or cuddling up for a neck scratch. She was out cruising for a bruising from morning till night, and when she was apprehended soliciting for trade up the High Street and gated for the evening, she spent it flat up against the back room window, flashing her underparts at any passing Harry, Dick or certainly Tom, and making the most loud and ear-curdling noises by way of enticement.

You take my meaning? Combine this imbalance with a tendency to introduce the loved one's name into every topic of conversation. (They're selling cabbages for £1.25 at Austins' – 'Oh, really? Funny that, when *Jack* was a student in Sheffield he worked in a fruit store and THEY sold cabbages. Gosh! Funny that, Jack was only mentioning . . .') Or the need to race to the phone like a lunatic every time it rings (for someone else) and to blame your mother because you were at the pub when he *did* phone. Add to that a predilection for falling off buses because you think you see Him on every corner, in every crowd, at every window, and the inevitability of actually seeing Him in the off-licence when you weren't expecting to, and feeling your entire stomach lurch forward involuntarily like waking from a dream of falling. All this with a thudding heart, hot flushes and the school run? Please – forget it.

Whatever the rapture of first love and the obsessiveness of courtship (sweet old-fashioned word) and marriage, it is a class act which can retain that rapture through the rigours of parenthood, child care and mortgage repayment. Obsession is easily diverted, and an all-consuming passion for your lover can shift almost transparently to one for your child, making your partner vaguely uneasy and prone to a curious sense of loss.

This is a minefield which few of us admit to being trapped by. Honestly, though, who out there hasn't at several junctions been reduced by sleeplessness, exhaustion and sheer frustration into staring over the heads of your babies at the man who fathered them, and thinking what in hell's name am I doing with this person? And it's no use giving out with the 'Try a little tenderness' technique, you know, 'Let Granny take the little fellow for the afternoon – draw the shades, chill the wine, slip into a backless silk negligee, and remind yourselves how much fun it was making the little fellow in the first place.' Great advice. Particularly when Granny lives in

Nairobi, the shades are spattered with Milpar, you haven't bought a bottle of wine since you opened your Mothercare account, the backless negligee is fine so long as you don't roll over and reveal the stretch marks on what used to be your breasts, and you feel about as compelled to have sex as you feel compelled to have gangrene.

The theory is that it passes. You know, the – er – off-it thing. It certainly does. After – oooh – a mere nine or ten years, when quite suddenly you become consumed with lust and frighten your by now placid partner into a state of wary suspicion. It's at this stage that one or other of the partners may start to get an eye so roving as to become a nose and take up with the first cloth-eared bimbo who gazes up or down and says, 'I can't believe you're over forty – that's sooo sexy.'

Of course, the cloth-eared bimbo sometimes graduates into becoming the Second Mrs Tanqueray and becomes the person about whom your children start saying, 'Sophie makes these *wicked* cakes – they just melt in your mouth and *she* doesn't mind what time we go to bed and she and daddy are always giggling and cuddling up and when can we go there again?' Where does that leave you? It's all very well for our rejuvenated Lothario. For a while. Except, more often than not, the Second Mrs Tanqueray reveals herself to be a carbon-copy of the first one in almost every way but one and *that's* only until the new Tanqueray brood arrives, whereupon Lothario takes to ringing up the first Mrs T to say 'Where did we go wrong?'

Do I sound cynical? If so, I'm sorry. I don't mean to, it's just the way my pen slants. I also don't mean to be sexist because the same scenario works when the sexes are reversed. And I certainly don't mean to be marriage-ist or altar-ist or whatever else the expression isn't. I'm all for it. And even if I wasn't, would that stop lovesick mortals from shelling out for orange-blossom, hiring a vicar and promising to love, honour and mumble at least once in their lives? It's no secret that swans mate for life. It's no secret either that they are one of the most nasty, bad-tempered species on God's earth. Elephants, on the other hand, kick out the boy children as soon as they've started to shave, and live in a contented matriarchal world afraid of no man but the ivory poacher.

Within a week of meeting Jack, I knew I was going to marry him. It only took him another four years to feel the same way. When we met I felt the most enormous sense of 'coming home'. Almost of familiarity. It could have been just relief that someone would have me. Over the years my thoughts as well as my eyes have roved and as Jimmy Carter once said 'Ah have lusted in mah heart,' but as the car leaves the party and we've waved our goodbyes to the other guests, it's a rare night indeed that I haven't looked over and thought 'Thank God I'm going home with *him*.' I like to think Virginia would have approved of that.

Leaving a Vacuum

'Which would you say is the dirtiest room in your house?' said the vacuum salesman to the actress.

'Do you mean in my opinion or in my mother's?' thought the actress grimly, but responded, instead, with 'Well, the kitchen – I expect.'

'Not so,' said Mohammed the salesman, for it was he. 'It is your bedroom. Are you aware that you shed your skin every four months and sweat one pint of liquid a night and all of that is in your bed?'

'As long as it's only in Jack's half,' quipped the actress.

It was a Saturday night and Jack and Adam and I were being entertained by this smart enterprising young man, in our own home, after a string of broken dates had caused me to slam the phone down on the Kirby Company saying, 'I don't care if it picks up more fluff than Rod Stewart, I wouldn't give your bloody vacuum houseroom.'

I say enterprising because pitching up on a Saturday evening with a smart suit and an 'I was just passing and I wondered . . .' smile is just the way to get straight into both my house and my room. We put the kettle on.

'Now what ever you think of it,' hissed my husband, caution being his middle name, 'don't buy it today, tell him you want to think it over.' I concurred in a smirking sort of way. I wasn't *going* to buy it. (I was going to *think* about it. For a year or so. Then I was going to entertain people with the story over dinner and then I was going to write about it. To the accompaniment of Christine wielding the old wheezy Electrolux.)

I should explain the background to this unusual Saturday night beaver. Since, what I can only describe as our nuptials, some seventeen summers ago, we have hoovered our way through three residences and four vacuum cleaners. Each machine from Junior Hoover through Senior Hoovermatic to Elderly Turbo-powered, increased in sleekness and two tone, multi-faceted plasticised glamour. Each machine, according to the weary engineer, majors in 'What we in the trade call "built in obsolescence"', a condition which applies to my son but not my latest Electrolux, which suffers more from premature ejaculation than early redundancy.

Christine (Tuesdays and Thursdays), who is what my mother infuriatingly calls 'my woman', which makes me feel like a cross between Lady Bracknell and Vita Sackville-West, copes with the machine by alternately kicking it, and calling out in a hopeful manner 'Ja – a – a – ck!

'S'not workin' again.' Whereupon we call the engineer, the Christiaan Barnard of the vacuuming world, to transplant yet more new parts into this terminal three-year-old.

'They're not built to last you see,' chortles the engineer as we sign yet another docket. 'Cut your losses and get a new one – they're all the same.' By which he meant they're all lousy.

I vaguely shopped around – vaguely being the only way I know how to shop unless I'm in Joseph's of Knightsbridge. But, oh my! Cylinder or upright? Turbo or not Turbo? Miele or Bosch (could I sleep nights if I bought a German vacuum cleaner?). There are even machines which *tell* you when their bags need changing. 'My bag is full' it whinges. I wondered if it would end up nagging me, like all the other speaking objects in my house, 'Shift your ass' it would snarl, 'just because you're on the telly, don't think you can push *me* around . . .'

So it was with some interest that I heard from my old friend Les (our friendly fireman who not only married our Swiss au pair, Ruth, but also gave Jack the inspiration for *London's Burning*), that he and Ruth had fallen in love with the Kirby cleaner, after an enlightening demo in their own home.

'I mean at *that* price,' laughed Les, 'I had *no* intention of *buying* it, NONE, but – I mean – this machine is unbelievable! It's . . . it's . . . it's phenomenal and they even take your old Hoover in part exchange!' For a moment I thought the normally prosaic Les was going to burst into song and levitate.

Instead, he told the tale of how the salesman had emptied a tin of salt on to the carpet, then swept it up thoroughly with their old Hoover, then put a clean bag into the machine and recovered another sackful of salt left behind by the previous vacuum.

'It sucks up to seven inches deep,' said the salesman.

'There's no answer to that,' said Les.

I booked a demo immediately, of course. Then, an hour before demo time, the firm phoned to say the salesman couldn't make it. Four days later I phoned them and made another appointment.

'Mohammed will call at eight o'clock. Thank you.'

At 8.45 Jack turned to me and said, 'Wasn't the vacuum cleaner salesman supposed to be . . .?'

The following day I phoned them and blew them out in a way I can only do at the end of a telephone, and told them where to stuff their upright . . . after all, if Mohammed won't come to Muswell Hill . . .

So you had to admire him for pitching up on the doorstep of a telephonic virago without an appointment, expecting a meat cleaver through his barnet.

'Oh my Lord, it's you!' gasped Mohammed (I hope I'm allowed to write that without having a death threat put on me!). 'It's The Telephone! Beattie! Oh my heaven! Wait till I tell them at head office.'

So to the demonstration. Well, there is no question this gorgeous Art-Deco, aluminium robot can do everything your average 'woman' can do, and a few not even your lover can. Apart from shampooing, dry-cleaning, fluffing up, removing ceiling cobwebs, dusting, polishing and blow drying, it has attachments for spraying plants, sink plunging, sanding, blowing up *balloons*, massaging your HEAD and spraying sodding paint. I mean it just about stops short of making you a crème brûlée, but only just – and I reckon with the right attachment . . .

While Mohammed drew breath, I caught Jack's eye and launched into the old 'Well, it's very impressive, but my husband and I would like to think it over, it's an *awful* lot of money and . . .'

As I spoke, the old Hoover, in a fit of rivalry, vomited the contents of its stomach all over the patch it was supposed to be showing off on. Whereupon the husband in question – cautious Jack, remember? – interjected, in lordly fashion, to say, 'No, actually I think we should take it,' and produced the right kind of attachment for paying for it. Mohammed went home in prophet.

At the time of writing, Mohammed has been made Salesman of the Year and sent to Marbella as a bonus. We've never used anything but the vacuum head and the bed remains full of termites and sweat but it is a great investment and one day when Zelma gets off the Hull bus, tired and in need of succour, I shall plug in the Kirby, get the balloons blown up and on the door and welcome her into my termite-free house with the offer of a shampoo and a head massage. What I won't do is tell her what it cost.

Sofa so Good

It was a bleak and wintry Thursday when the family chesterfield died. This wasn't entirely unexpected, it had been sickening for some time. (Even so, the suddenness of her demise – not entirely unconnected with my son's congenital need to fling himself horizontally on to it from a distance of eight feet two or three times an hour – was a shock.)

First the castors shot off in a westerly direction, closely followed by two legs, cast and north, north-west. Then the seating cushions spontaneously imploded revealing toys we haven't seen since *Star Wars*, the arms inverted into a sort of shrug, she gave a long, deep sigh and her back buttons popped off. It was clear that this was, at best, a late chesterfield, soon to be despatched to the Great Furniture Repository in the Sky.

The problem is that this was one irreplaceable sofa. It was more than just an obscure object of design. It was . . . well, it was almost part of the furniture. It came with Jack. It was virtually his dowry. It was accompanied by some paintings, a desk, two grey jerseys and a complete set of Peter Sarstedt LPs.

When we moved down South into rented accommodation, it lived patiently in 'kennels' in Blackpool until we became first-time home-owners. (This, you understand, was in the days when 'the chain' was something you locked up your bike with and a recession was the space on either side of your mantelpiece.) In time we sent for the chesterfield and she took her rightful place on the ginger twistpile – our 'Lasting, Casting Couch'.

Over the next seventeen years, out-of-work actresses 'rested' on it, confirmed bachelors 'camped' on it, a baby daughter pee-ed down and a baby son pee-ed up on it and the family feline, practising her famed impersonation of a shredding machine, all around it, gave it the look of one of PJ Proby's discarded waistcoats.

The whole thing came to a head on the night of our 'Come as You Were' party, when I saw Denis Norden, six foot three, and Lesley Joseph, five foot one, at each end of the settee. Lesley was considerably taller than Denis. The sofa, like most of my guests, was legless.

'The Sales are on,' said Mother, the Humberside Oracle. 'Come on, we'll go to John Lewis and you can change that lampshade you've had cluttering up the floor all these months, and then we can do Selfridges, they're bound to have what you want. What *do* you want, actually? A three-seater or two two-seaters? Armchairs are nice, mind you. Have you thought about re-upholstery? There's nothing wrong with that couch really and whatever you get that cat will make "ashenblotty" out of it.'

By the time we reached John Lewis my brain was on circuit jammed. Rain was pouring down in biblical fashion and I parked on Level Three. There was no lift. Words were exchanged. We made it through the deluge and legged it to Lewis's.

'Look at the price of those chandeliers,' said Mother, shaking out her rainhood on to a Donald Duck desk-lamp. '£150. That's what my parents, God rest their souls, paid for their first house.'

I stood in the queue with my lampshade.

'Why are you standing in the queue?' she demanded. 'Why don't you speak to the man walking around? Your Uncle Issy always said, "go to the man at the top".'

'There is no man at the . . .'

'Excuse me. Are you there? My daughter bought this lampshade . . .'

I'm dying. Water is dripping down parts of me that only my acupuncturist knew I had, my skirt is suctioned to my thighs and I'm suffering from terminal embarrassment. The queue has begun to titter. Mrs Jones lives.

She's right, of course. We make the exchange and, leaving the new shade for a later pick-up, we head for the furniture department which instantly yields a rose-pink chesterfield at a 'Have we gone raving mad?' reduction. Mother is horrified and says to a passing assistant, 'Excuse me. Are you there? Would you say this was a serviceable fabric for a family with two teenage children and a cat? I mean, has it been Scotchguarded? There you are – you'd be *much* better off with a patterned Dralon.' It was time to be blown to Selfridges.

'My coat's drenched through,' grumbled Mum. It was my fault and I knew it. 'I'll have a job to dry it before I catch that bus back to Hull tomorrow.'

I put my foot down. (Always a mistake when you're standing in six inches of rain.) 'Come on,' I said, 'we're going home. I can get a couch any time.'

Mother stood stock-still as if she'd been freeze-framed. 'Home?' She gave the word three syllables and several changes of key. '*Go home?*' You'd think I'd suggested a stop off at a Pork Scratchings Shop. 'Whatever for? We're only five minutes from Selfridges. You'll be sorry. You'll kick yourself.' Little did she know as she squelched heroically on her way that I already was.

Finally we slid into the dry warmth of the Handbag and Hosiery

Department and thence into Furniture. 'You look,' moaned Mother as she sank into the first available sofa-bed, 'I've had it.'

I looked. I saw. I sat upon. It was perfect. An Elizabethan-style sofa with brass knobs on. Literally. One small point. It was upholstered in ivory silk moiré. How was I to hide that fact from . . .

'Have you gone mad!' came a voice I knew and often loved. Too late. I'm nabbed. 'You're not thinking of cream, Maureen . . . Excuse me, Miss, are you there? What we need is something to go on a green carpet, have you got such a thing?' Given such a wide brief, the saleslady could only think of one thing to say . . .

'Well, if it's good enough for Mrs Jones, it's good enough for . . .'

Mother caught up with me somewhere in Oxford Street and we grimly monsooned our way back to the car park.

'You get the car, I'll pick up the lampshade,' she said, undaunted by the John Lewis security man locking the last customer out of the store. As I dashed across the square to the car park, I heard, 'Excuse me. You've got to let me in. I'm catching a train to Hull in half an hour and if I don't have that parcel with me I shall lose my job and everything.' He let her in.

'Closed. Please use entrance on other side of Square', said the NCP entrance. I paddled back, cursing pleasantly and finally climbed back into the car, pausing only to lower the brim of my trilby and release a pint and a half of acid rain on to the driver's seat.

Much later, as we sat sniffling in our bath-robes, the chesterfield and the delinquent tabby seemed to be regarding us with mutual smugness: 'Need a psychiatrist, those two,' they seemed to be saying, 'not a ruddy couch!'

It's eighteen months since I went out looking for that sofa. We still don't have a new one. The chair and the existing sofa's been minced into a sort of chilli con carne by the delinquent cat and I've taken to throwing throwovers, American style, over them, which fools no one. Decorating time has rolled round again but I think it would be simpler all round just to move. The kids go apoplectic at the thought, but they'll be off and gone soon. Living in rodent-infested student digs with ovens which open of their own volition on account of the livestock left in them.

So, why am I still here? Erm . . . basically because I like the house and I'm passionate about the garden – I'd have to take it with me. No, really. Some people take light bulbs and fireplaces and fitted shelves and brass doorknobs. Not me. I'd be carrying five tons of earth, two wisterias, one stone urn, one pillar box, fourteen flowering yuccas, three bleeding heart bushes, two chimney pots filled with magenta petunias, a mass of Canterbury bells and a thriving passion flower. And that would be my *first* load. I'm also as indolent as a basking cat, there's an excellent cheese shop, I like the view and tea chests give me hives.

Finally, I made an impulse buy, near Halifax, of a Thirties 'Clouds' suite with inlaid walnut. I bought it in a flash after an embarrassing moment. I was filming a series called *Art Deco with Maureen Lipman* – or something similar – and I was interviewing one of the two owners of the Emporium, whilst sitting on this glorious example of his collection. The suite had two footstools, on one of which perched the firm's director. I meanwhile was assuring Muir, the proprietor, that he had no need to be nervous about the forthcoming interview:

'Just relax,' I told him. 'It will be as easy and informal as the two of us chatting away as we are now.'

At which point, the programme's director said to the cameraman, 'I love the shot as it is now with the two of them side by side on the sofa – but what do we do about the two poufs?'

In the silence that followed I heard myself bid for and buy the entire suite. Back chez Rosenthal, Jack came home from a stay in hospital to find a completely new living-room in soft, restful eau-de-nil, which he adored and was cosy in for the rest of his life. It sits now in my new kitchen-diner surrounded by frosted green glass and dazzling light from six floor-to-ceiling windows, and he would love it still.

It was 2008 when I finally gave up Muswell Hill for the Paddington Basin. 'Always live up in a high place, Maureen,' said a Birmingham fortune-teller, one long-drawn-out afternoon on tour. I took her advice as I always do and bought a lower ground-floor pad in Paddington.

Meanwhile we're sitting on boxes in the sitting room. I'm haunting the sofa websites and stores and swatches are arriving daily to be chewed by Diva the Basenji and I'm no nearer to making a decision than I was all those years ago, only difference being the prices have doubled and the waiting time tripled. I love the look of the leather ones but so will Diva, who already has pulped my new briefcase out of spite at being left at home for half an hour. I am mystified by the sheer scale of some of these corner units which double as king-sized beds and cause your feet to dangle over the edge like a four-year-old and your spine to curve like Richard the Third's – allegedly. I mean, I only go in the sitting-room to – well, sit and watch the TV. And since the TV only yields me David Attenborough and *News at Ten*, I'm not sitting down a lot, to be honest. Perhaps I'll just Scotchguard the rug, put coasters on the coffee table and lie down on the floor with my feet up for another year or so.

In August 2008 I got 'em! Two buttoned back sofas in purple velvet. Purple velvet! Dramatic as a Parisienne boudoir and sheer heaven to crash out on. Never again will you hear me mention the S. word. I may never really veg-out or be a couch potato but a huge amount of celery has gone into my sofas.

Raising Arizona

A SHORT SCREENPLAY

EXTERIOR: Street. Hot day in Muswell Hill. A woman is carefully carrying a plastic bag. She is within twenty yards of her home when footsteps behind her accelerate and a hand touches her arm.

He: 'Excuse me. Sorry to bother y . . .'
She: 'Aaaargh! Christ, you frightened me – don't *do* that!'
He: 'Sorry, sorry, it's just that, I mean, I know who you are . . .'
She: 'Oh, jolly good. So do I, but you really mustn't go touching strange women just because you know who they are.'
He: 'I know. I'm sorry. I . . . Oh God. The thing is, I mean, er – have you got a minute? Can I talk to you?'

He is twenty-five but looks nineteen. Thin, dark, unshaven chin, puppy dog eyes, longish floppy brown hair. The chest hairs which bedraggle out from his sleeveless vest belie his tender years and the brown leather jerkin spell street cred rather than student unrest.

She: (*placing the plastic bag on a low wall.*) 'It's a cheese dish. Old. It's a present from my daughter to her English teacher, what did you want to say to me?'

He shifts his weight. She smiles because he really is ducking and weaving like someone in an early Montgomery Clift movie. She wants to help but not quite as much as she wants to get home and remove whatever it is that is pressing her little toe into a throbbing pulp.

She: 'Are you an actor?'
He: (*astonished*) 'No.'

There is a 'why' in his response. He doesn't realise that eighty per cent of the people who stop her in public places do so because: a) They have a niece who knocks spots off Barbra Streisand and can't get an Equity Card; b) They have just won the Beerbohm Tree Award at the Basingstoke Academy of Performing Arts and they just need a few thousand to see

186

them through the next term; c) They think she was mad to give up those commercials, they haven't seen much of her on TV since, and hasn't she gone thin?

He: 'No, I'm not working at the moment – well, I mean I'm in Sainsbury's Homebase just to make, you know, to live, but the thing is, I know it's ridiculous and why should you be remotely interested – but look. My theory is, that if you don't go for it when you've got the chance then . . .'
She: 'Go on. What's the problem?'

She slips off one shoe and massages the toe tortuously against her other foot.

He: 'Well. The thing is . . .'

His face changes as into shot comes a young girl. She is shorter and sturdier than he, cropped blonde hair, adolescent skin, gamine features and she is looking at him underneath her lashes as a mother would look at a kid who's asked a strange lady why bits of her wobble like that, is it 'cos she's so fat?

He: 'This is Robyn. This is the woman I love.' (*The woman he loves shakes her head in despair.*) 'She has to go back to America on Sunday. Thing is I can't live without her. She's . . . I don't have the money to go back with her. So I thought . . . well . . . what can you lose? That's . . . it.'

Pause.

She: 'You are asking me to give you money so you can follow your girlfriend to America?'
He: 'I just saw you. I'm desperate. Like I said if you don't go for it in life . . .'
She: 'Yeah, yeah – but what are you going to do when you get there? You can't work there. You won't get a permit, unless you get married.'
He: 'We're going to get married. That's the idea. That's it. We can't exist without one another – it's the rightest thing that's ever happ . . .'
She: 'Look, you do understand, I can't just, I mean I'm constantly being asked . . .'
He: 'I *know*.'
She: '. . . for money.'

He: 'Look, I've a letter from her parents saying how much they like me, if that would do any good.'
She: 'How much do you need? A one-way ticket to New York – £179 on Virgin, isn't it?'
He: 'Well, no – you see it's Arizona so it's £409, and you have to get a return or they don't let you . . .'
She: '£409! Hold on, hold on – look. Wait.' (*She turns to the girl, Robin, whose head is down.*) 'What are you going to do with him when you get him to Arizona?'

Pause. *Robyn raises her eyes. Shakes her head again and in a scarcely audible whisper says*:

Robyn: 'Oh, I don't know . . . Jes love him.'

For reasons best known to a Freudian she once visited, tears stream down the cheeks of the total stranger. She walks around in a circle on her good foot and takes pot shots at herself but gravity is inexorable and they trickle beneath her sunglasses. She struggles with her wobbling thorax.

She: 'What's needed here is a second opinion. From a rational person. I'm hopeless. Quick. Give me your name and address, I need to think . . . here . . .'

She replaces the sandal and gives him first her cheque book, then and for fear of giving the wrong impression, a cleaning ticket to write on. Goodbyes are tentative and she finds herself kissing them and wishing them happiness. She limps home blearily, rings the doorbell. A middle-aged man wearing hornrimmed glasses and two warring fabrics opens the door. His face changes from welcoming to concerned in a milli-second.

Husband: 'Hello lu . . . what's happened? Tell me. What's the matter?'

He takes the cheese dish and sits her down. She's still weeping but now with the odd gurgle of laughter because she knows his concern will be temporary. It is. Throughout her dramatised reconstruction we linger on his face, as it turns into the kid and the fat lady expression.

He: (*not unkindly*) 'You're bloody mad.'
She: 'But I should have just given him the money. They were so – beautiful. I mean, it could have been Romeo and Juliet!'

He: 'Or Bonnie and Clyde.'
She: (*sighs*) 'Yeah, well.'

Enter her daughter, eighteen, whey-faced and A-levelled, and her son, fifteen, who has recently learned to whistle tunelessly. They've heard the bare bones of the story from LSF (as in long-suffering father) and want confirmation from the HM (as in horse's mouth).

Daughter: 'But who *were* they? Had you met them before? I mean what did they say to upset you and did you give them anything?'

  The camera stays on the children's faces as their mother ruefully explains.

She: 'It's just that they were so young. And so passionate. I don't know, I just feel as if I should have given them a chance.'
Daughter: 'You should have. Changing someone's life. It's so romantic. Can't you run after them?'
Son: (*glancing up from sponge ball attached to his sock*) 'I think you should have told them to bugger off.'

THE END

The woman with the cheese dish has since a) lost the cleaning ticket; b) worked out that her royalties would easily take the young man to Arizona; and c) awaits his call.

There is a sequel to this story and it's one I love. After writing the story up for *She* magazine a year went past, I'd lost the address and I'd put the whole episode on a back burner. Then, one day, I received a letter postmarked Arizona. It was from Peter.

Dear Mrs Lipman,

Hi, this is a letter from the skinny hippy boy who stopped you in the street and asked you for money. As you see from the postmark, I did make it to Arizona.
  Robyn (my lover) went back to the US, as planned, a few days later and then, I don't know how, but after about two months I managed to get the air fare together and left with the rucksack on my back. It was a very exciting and packed time of experiences. When I landed

189

in the US without any money, the customs officers zeroed in on me and were going to deport me on the next flight which was scary. However, in the end I convinced the head guy to let me stay and on I went to Phoenix.

It was great to be with Robyn and we spent a few weeks getting back together before we married on 2 July 1992. Then we went through another palaver trying to get the paperwork done so I could stay. Of course eventually it was and we could get on with our lives.

Now I work as a clerk in a hospital and Robyn has gone back to University to study and become a psychotherapist. These have been the happiest times of my life and so you could say this is one of those 'and they lived happily ever after' stories. We get along together really well.

I feel there are a few things I should say about me asking you for money. I don't know that it was right or wrong and it's not a thing I've done before or since. It seemed a good idea at the time.

The fact that you didn't feel right about giving money was fine with me and totally understandable. In the same shoes I would probably have done the same. What was really neat for me was that you took the time to listen to my story and had empathy with it. That was really important and gave you a place of fond remembrance with me for ever.

Despite my impositioning you, you listened and offered me this, and that's what's needed in the world.

Well, I don't mean to preach. Apparently you said that this meeting had remained in your conscience, wondering whether you did right or not. I wanted you to know it was right because that was the way you felt at the time.

Well, I guess this is all I have to say.

I hope that you and your family are in good health and wish you luck in whatever you do.

Lots of love,
Peter

Fifteen years after writing 'Raising Arizona' I found myself reliving it. I was rehearsing a new play at the Birmingham rep. It was a play by Charlotte Jones called *Martha, Josie and the Chinese Elvis*, in which I played the eponymous Martha, an Irish cleaner with Obsessive Compulsive Disorder. At some point early in the play a man reaches out to shake my hand and I jump away, saying 'I'm afraid I don't shake hands' whilst silently counting under my breath. It's a very funny play. I've seldom heard such hysteria in a theatre, particularly when the Chinese Elvis, Paul

Courtenay Hu, magnoperatic in white spangled jump-suit and broad Manchester accent, began to strut his gyratory stuff and give of his 'Blue Suede Shoes'.

One matinée-day morning I was sitting in Starbucks, trying to up my caffeine levels, in one of those aimless, character-free, pedestrianised precincts so beloved of the kind of town planner who has no intention of ever visiting one, when I noticed a young man of about twenty in a pull down beanie, carrying a sign which read 'FREE HUGS'. Intrigued, I watched for ten minutes or so whilst people of all class, gender and creed responded in All English fashion. Some went out of their way, literally, to avoid him, skulking in Haagan Daaz until forced to buy a praline and caramel cone in inclement weather. Some went into paroxysms of wheezy laughter and plumply pushed one another into his arms, some walked past with showy ferocity, some tried to look busily into their tote bags and walked straight into lampposts.

On the phone to a gentleman friend at the time, I told him about the purveyor of hugs and he said, 'Tell him you want one,' so I tapped on the window and mouthed through the froth on my lip, 'I'll have one,' and in he came and, as they say, gave me one. Post-prandially, over a latte and a chatte, in his soft American accent he asked me, as casually as he could, if I knew anything about Jesus Christ.

'A bit,' I told him and added, a shade provocatively, 'I mean, I know he was a very gifted and innovative Rabbi.'

His boy's handsome face lit up. 'You know that?' he asked. 'I mean . . . that's true . . . Jesus *was* Jewish.'

'Yeah, I know,' I smiled, 'and if the orthodox clergy had just listened to what he had to say instead of fearing for their authority when he said it, then there would have been no need for a breakaway religion and how much trouble would that have saved the world?'

'Yeah, but what we believe is that all of that was ordained, and that Jesus knew he had to break away to fulfil his Father's plan . . .' and he was off on a faith bender, his bright black eyes illuminated with the desire to proselytise to someone who would give back as good as they got. It turned out that he and his young friends all travelled the world as missionaries for their faith, going wherever the sect told them their love was most needed. His devotion was touching and we both enjoyed the exchange a lot. Outside the coffee shop, as we were parting, I held out my hand to shake his, but he backed away:

'I'm sorry,' he said, 'but I'm afraid I don't shake hands.'

I laughed. 'I'm going to be saying exactly that line on stage in about an hour from now.'

'On stage?' he asked. 'In what way?'

'Oh, well, I'm an actress by profession and my character in the play . . .' I explained the coincidence.

He was dizzy with delight. 'I've never been to the theatre,' he told me. 'None of us has.'

'Never been to the theatre? *In your lives?*' I mean, things were bleak in Hull in the Fifties but we still got to see the panto every year, and David Whitfield, if he was at the Palace and my Dad had made his blazer.

'No. I guess our parents always had other things for us to do. Gee, so do you do the same play every night or will it be a different one tonight?'

There was no way I was not about to corrupt this gentle, woolly hatted boy in his taste-free clothes and his chaste free hugs. I laid on six tickets and that night a bunch of showbiz virgins lost it at the Birmingham Rep. It was only as the play progressed and, backstage, I heard the play through their eyes, that the enormity of what I'd done actually hit me. The play was set in a house of correction – the Josie of the title actually ran a bondage brothel. There would be a discussion of teenage abuse and men would dress up as maids and be spanked and I would end the play in full tango gear promising my body to the transvestite masochist! Oh, my God – no – Oh, *his* God – Rebecca of Sunny Brook Farm this wasn't. I trembled by the stage door, fearing the worst corruption known to man since Julia Andrews bared her breasts in *S.O.B.*

'It was awesome!' said a flush-faced lad. 'A-mazing!' agreed a sweet-faced girl in a plaid skirt and Mary Janes. 'How do you learn all that stuff? Gee, it was, like, unbelievable – we loved it – I wanna see it over!' I breathed out for the first time in an hour. The missionaries had survived to tell the tale. Mission Possible. I stood them half a dozen lemonades and with a free hug and a flurry of swapped email addresses, I moved on to Malvern, Woking, Oxford, Cambridge and Bath, and he moved on to a Romanian orphanage. We're still in touch. His faith in Jesus is intact and my faith in the producers, who failed to bring this lovely play into a West End home, is in crisis for ever.

Innocent Parties

'I think we'll have a New Year's Eve Party this year,' I told my daughter, who'd come to join me on location during her half term.

'Great,' she said absently, 'I'll ask my class.'

'Well actually,' I added hastily, 'I wasn't thinking of your sort of a party – erm – I mean, you know, your friends all want booze and cigarettes and messing about – I'd thought more of a *proper* party . . .'

She was looking at me strangely. I'd certainly got her attention.

'It's going to be an MDL party.'

'You mean people are going to come dressed as your initials?'

'More than that dear. MDL also means "Mutton Dressed as Lamb". A "come as you were" party – you know with jelly and cake and Pass the Parcel and Dead Lions when we're tired, which knowing most of our friends will be around 10.30.' (I didn't add 'Ducking for Apples' because it always reminds me of that wonderful Dorothy Parkerism: 'There but for one small typo goes the story of my life'.)

I could tell by the set of her brains that she was racking them. Finally she said: 'I've got a better idea. Why not have a "Come as your Favourite Noise" party.' This led to some minor hilarity and the confession that in the Sixties I had attended a 'Come As Your Suppressed Desire Party'. It was more than a little embarrassing for me, as I didn't have one. A desire, I mean. Suppressed or otherwise. Unless you counted getting a flat with a bedroom of my own, or never having to go down the Labour Exchange again.

In the end I went as 'The Wicked Lady'. I'd never actually seen the film – I just liked the sound of the words and I happened to have a black lace negligee in which I'd recently died (in more senses than one) in *Wuthering Heights* at the Palace Theatre, Watford. I swanned in, rigid with what I hoped passed for sex appeal, but apart from one brief interval sharing a dodgy stogey with a large American who wore his underpants over his tights and a large Star of David appliquéd to his T-shirt (he'd come as SUPER-JEW), I spent the evening chatting to my former college mates about the state of show-business and eating myself pear shaped.

My friend Sally tells of a mother and daughter who went away on a holiday weekend, one of the attractions of which was a fancy dress dinner and dance. As they emerged from the lift, dressed to slay, the manager rushed over excitedly and said, 'Ooh, thank goodness you've bothered to dress up. We were beginning to think no one would do it!'

So saying he pushed them unceremoniously into a dining-room filled with diners whose main concession to the art of fancy dress was a feather in their hair. Sally's friend's Mum had come as a blackbird. Her march to the table on huge padded yellow feet was something she'll remember, in a flushed fashion, at least once a day for the rest of her natural life.

Similarly or simian-arly, *About Face* costumier Jimmie Dark told me he'd set out in the car for a costume party, discreetly dressed as a gorilla, and found on a foggy night in February that he had to stop the car and ask a passer-by for directions to the house. Another friend went to a costume ball thrown by a frozen chicken firm called Sussex Sovereign Chicken. She decided to take the firm's name literally and went in her wedding dress, a red velvet fur-lined cloak, with an orb made from a plastic Easter egg sprayed gold, a chicken's head fashioned from a Balaclava helmet and yellow felt-covered flippers. She won first prize, but didn't get too many dances. When I last spoke to her she was planning to use the same outfit for a country and western costume ball, substituting a tan catsuit for the wedding dress. Her intention was to go as a barbecued chicken.

Most actors, who spend their lives dressing ridiculously, are more than happy to knock off in real life. (Even as I write this I am wearing a shoulder-length grey wig, broken veins, half glasses on a chain, several layers of ethnic gear and an awful lot of clanking beads, and that's just at 7.15am in the location Winnebago.) But those of you who've chanced upon these odd jottings in dump bins before, will know that as a general rule, my husband and I will leap into fancy dress at the drop of a Fedora.

Indeed we do exactly that for our bi-yearly meetings with our accountant. It began as a joke to enliven his otherwise grey day, and has developed into a tradition as ritualistic as Christmas and almost as expensive. The first time he called we were in ball gown and tuxedo – not both of us, one each – and we've gone steadily down-market ever since. For the last serious discussion of our company earnings, the co-directors wore matching scarlet combinations, topped by Stars and Stripes underpants – well, overpants really – and baseball caps. Our accountant was impressed. He smiled. He even chuckled, called the meeting to order and got down to the important business of the day. Lunch.

My job at these meetings is to take the minutes, which I do with such verisimilitude that when read back they are funny enough to send accountants and pension planners into breath-racking paroxysms. Actually, one meeting was videoed by our then secretary, Layla, as a response to the frequent question: 'What's it like working for the Rosenthals?' At the time we were in full Arab dress, with beards, yashmaks and many Marks and Spencer bags.

As for the 'Come as You Were' party – well, I found it hard to think of an incarnation I hadn't already played. Jacko's was easy. He spent his two years' National Service in the Navy – the only Jewish sailor they seem to have had, and that's another story shortly to be televised. The only other job I'd ever had was a week's work as a waitress in Bridlington. Consequently, we made several visits to our local party hire shop in East Finchley, and emerged as considerably more interesting-looking versions of what we once were. Leading Coder Rosenthal metamorphosed into Cap'n Jack and I was a waitress who wouldn't wait long, in a pink and white thigh length dress. Amy, who has a self-confessed desire to remain six years old and who knows *Peter Pan* by heart, was keener than mustard to get back into a baby bonnet and Adam, who spent at least one of his formative years wearing blue tights, a red cape and a large S on his chest, just raided my tights drawer. My mother refused to do anything but wear her most elegant knitted suit, so Jack wrote a label for her back which said 'I looked like this last week'.

The best thing about a fancy dress party is the entrances. After that, but for the odd shriek as someone who's been eating trifle on the terrace wanders in to meet someone who's been sipping Sangria in the study, the evening becomes a matter of how comfortable you are. Nobody knows more than I do the agonies of spending an evening bopping whilst disguised as a crab or an inflatable hippo. But the standing at the door screaming 'I don't believe it! Jaaaaaack, come and look what Pikka's come as!' is unforgettable. In actuality, Amy's friend Pikka's costume was the wittiest of the evening – she wore a huge cardboard eye over her head through which her face appeared to one side of the pupil. She had come as 'the glint in her father's eye'.

A (shall we say) receding-haired Ivan suddenly had a mass of black, shiny locks and Denis King donned his old 'King Brothers' velvet jacket plus taped-on photo of the gang of three. Astrid wore her college sweater and hot pants which were practically pyromaniac. Lyricist Don Black dressed perfectly normally but for a blue knitted baby hat with earflaps and his wife, Shirley, who is what's known as the salt of the earth but in a very glamorous form, came with no discernible differences from her normal self, which for some reason made me laugh. What reason? Well, it was because Don had made the gesture for both of them and Shirley was there to be just Shirley. Claire Rayner and husband Des were harking back to their flower power years, with Des *very* scenic in some sort of tan suede ensemble which made him look like a refugee from a Sherwood Forest that Calvin Klein used to inhabit. Actress Stella Tanner wore a lurex bodysuit and a hairpiece and eyelashes which looked like twiglets and Louie Ramsay had somehow fished out her somewhat elderly North London Collegiate straw hat. Lizzy and Roger were adorable schoolchildren, very public school, and their kids, Sarah and Mark, were giant nappied babies.

Most priceless award should have gone to two of our eldest friends, Bryan and Edith Butler, who had not only dressed up in full school uniform but had worked superbly hard at accoutrements. Bryan's 1939 satchel contained not only a squashed sandwich but a rubber frog, gobstoppers and stinkbombs and he had an Elastoplast on his knee, and his glasses. Barry Cryer, conversely, had made the minimum of effort. On his besuited back was a placard which read 'I've always looked like this'. We put him with my mother.

The food flowed and the wine did something similar and at midnight the motleyest looking guest list in town gathered around one King Brother at the piano. The kids held up the words:

> 'I saw the old homestead and the places I love
> I saw England's valleys and dells
> And I listened with joy
> As I did when a boy
> To the sound of the old village bells.
> The log was burning brightly,
> 'Twas a night that could banish all sin,
> For the bells were ringing the Old Year out
> And the New Year in.'

The idea is, first, to sing it all together, then again with gestures, some nicely vulgar, on each line, then, finally, with gestures but no words. It's harder than you think and does add mirth to the proceedings. Denis Norden, who like Jacko is a man who'd prefer almost anything to standing up at a New Year's Eve Party with drink in one hand and a neighbour's wife in the other, was definitely having the best of times, I noted whenever I hobbled past, singing all the old songs at the top of his, and Barry Cryer's, voice.

The prize for the most inventive costume went to Pikka and the prize for the most interesting costume went, of course, to Shirley Black for coming as – er – Shirley Black.

At 1.30am, Miriam Margolyes and Susannah York arrived from a more fashionable downtown party and stayed throughout the clearing up and out bits, nibbling things round the kitchen table. I was surprised but not displeased to see Miriam giving my mother a much needed back rub – but not as surprised as my mother was.

At 7.30 I'd been caught muttering 'Whose bloody idea was this anyway?' as I raced around throwing throwovers over bits of the furniture which seemed to have been masticated in the last year. 'Next time you hear me say "Shall we have a party" I want you to remind me how I feel right now! Murderous and hostile to everyone who's coming. *Not* that they will come – and look it's nearly eight and there's not a soul here! *God*, that's the bell and I'm not even dressed – Adam, get off the floor and answer the ruddy door. Who's had my mascara?'

At two o'clock I snuggled up next to the fellow who always seems to be in my bed and said: 'Well it wasn't that bad was it? Everyone seemed to have a really good time, wasn't it nice to see all those old friends again. I really like giving parties, don't you?' The snores confirmed he did. Or didn't. Whatever you like, love. S'fine. G'night.

Reading back on 'The Old Homestead' in the improbable but historically accurate year of 2008, I had to smile. This New Year was spent in Salzburg with long-married friends, Irene and Richard, at the timbered, snow-strewn, picture-postcard chalet house of Fritz and Angela who, second time around, were shortly to be wed. It was perfect. Snow is the piquant accompaniment to a season which, these days, makes me melancholy. Just trudging through it, earning my pub Glühwein, brings a flush to my withered cheek. Also, when I'm with my biddies, as a 'widder woman' I never feel like a spare shepherd's pie at a Jeffery Archer party.

Mostly we ate – Fritz is a great cook – and wandered the historic walled town and munched the odd sausage (Austrians overdose on sausages), then went home for warmth and a snack before dinner. A happy five-some. On the morning Fritz and Angela announced their engagement we all piled into one bed to drink champagne and – well – eat again in a manner reminiscent of The Chalet Girls. (The books, I mean, not the mountain resort where Debs did their work experience.)

On New Year's Eve though, Fritz had invited an Austrian couple, a jolly, retired heart surgeon and his very formal wife. He arrived in a floor-length fur coat and hat – no, the hat wasn't floor length, please don't be so literal – and the wife wore Loden. I tried manfully not to count the years so I could work out what he was doing during the war, and a jolly evening ensued.

Then, after advanced force-feeding, Irene did my late mother's perennial trick of saying: 'Maurr . . . een, now you must do your song.'

'I don't *think* so, Irene . . .'

'But yes . . . YES, MAUREEN – OH, IT IS SO FUNNY. YES, YOU MUST, OH PLEASE . . .'

My eyes were swivelling weirdly as I tried to indicate to her that perhaps what brought the house down in Muswell Hill might fail to shift a roof tile in Salzburg, but no. This is a Belgian/Italian woman who ran a building company and is trained to get what she wants. I sang it. Then I sang it with gestures. Then I mimed it. The English, Belgian and German factions joined in loudly. The Austrian ones struggled to understand why. After about three years or so it stopped and there was merciful applause. Then Hans's wife handed him a bound folder and did an Irene on him.

'Hans writes splendid limericks,' she announced. 'They are very amusing also.'

We all expressed massive enthusiasm/astonishment/admiration, and with unspoken assent avoided each other's eyes for the duration. Hans donned some half-spectacles and, twinkling in a Wogan-like fashion, began to recite his limericks. In German. We all of course recognised the rhythm – as in (off the top of my head):

> There was a young chap from Eilat,
> Who invented a surgical hat.
> With some tape and a crane
> It could access your brain
> And pop in and give it a pat.

Or my favourite anti-limerick:

> There was a young man of Dundee
> Who sat down with a bump on a bee.
> When asked if it hurt,
> He said 'No, not a bit,
> You can do it again if you like.'

Hans's limericks might have been side-splitting – certainly Fritz and Angela laughed . . . now and again. Sadly, the rest of us will never know. When I asked for a translation he merely said, 'No, no. To share the meaning with you is difficult – almost impossible.' Then he read another eleven.

On a scale of ten, how sorry are you that you don't get to come with me on holiday?

Mid Life Cry Sis

'You must be prepared to be very patient, Maureen,' said my drama school principal, wrinkling his already wrinkled face into contours of concern, 'because you won't really come into your own until you're forty.'

It was 1967, my nineteen-year-old eyes filled with badly concealed tears and in spite of every Judy Garland film I'd ever seen, I resolved to give up acting immediately and take up, at best, typing and at worse marriage. Forty! Was there such an age? Forty meant support tights and roller sets and evenings where the men played cards at one end of the room and the women talked of millinery at the other. Blearily I thanked him for his advice, tottered out into the dusty warmth of the Earls Court Road and instantaneously blanked out his prediction for the next twenty-one years.

Five minutes, a few jars of moisturiser and several hundred meatballs later, it was 1986. It was spring. It was the Year of the Dog and I was starring in *Wonderful Town*. My first musical. I embarked on a feverish campaign of vocal and physical exercise that would have put Arnie on amphetamines.

I spent my fortieth birthday doing eight shows a week, twice on Saturdays and Wednesdays, and I can't recommend it strongly enough as a means of ignoring the onset of middle age. Try it. All you need are eight young chorus boys, a revolving staircase, a thirteen piece orchestra, a town full of tourists and an awful lot of chutzpah.

Of course the real revelation of crossing the dateline, is that in your mind's myopic eye you stop ageing at twenty-four, and whatever evidence the overhead lighting on the Marks & Spencer mirror reveals, you remain that slim, earnest, questioning, confident young thing. Witness the phenomenon of bringing home your first baby from the hospital. The sudden hysteria of responsibility for this fragile tyrant, when you've scarcely begun to accept responsibility for yourself. You look down at 6lbs of pink fledgeling and it looks straight back saying 'I've got your number, Matey. Unskilled labour if ever I saw it.' You may bluster your way through but you know as well as baby that you are seriously under-qualified for this post.

When did I last feel mature enough to deal with my son's teacher, my doctor, my hairdresser, my plumber or anyone foolish enough to be in my employ, without tears and abject grovelling to their face and accusations of total mendacity to their backs?

In shorts, the child becomes no further from the man, and we're mostly just actors playing grown-ups in a ludicrous farce, raising our hopes and dropping our trousers with Rix-like regularity.

Recently, Julia McKenzie and I had lunch with our respective spouses to celebrate her birthday. Now, between the four of us we clock up well over 200 years and our sell-by date is perilously close. However, we all confessed to the same feeling of shock when confronted by indisputable proof of our longevity, i.e., our gums, our children applying for a driving licence, or the news that Helen Shapiro is celebrating thirty years in show business.

'I suppose it really hit me,' mused Jack, removing his glasses so that he could see something, 'when I was walking down a corridor in some American hotel, with my young research assistant. Limping towards us was a fat, crumpled and very ethnic looking old man with a young micro-skirted blonde by his side. God, I thought, how ridiculous that man looks – if only he could see himself. It was only after another fifteen feet or so that I realised that we were walking towards a mirror.'

All the same, when I see a marvellous, indomitable old lady like say Dame Freya Stark, or sturdy Joyce Grenfell, or meet a Hannah Hauxwell, I'm aware that what endears and propels me towards them is the child, still so evident in the grown-up. A child-like enthusiasm which I find infectious and reassuring.

When I spoke at the Cambridge Jewish Society this year, I was immediately fazed by the extreme youth of the students. Why I should have expected otherwise may faze *you*. After all, my daughter will be an undergraduate in a few months, though I still have the irrational desire to follow her at a discreet distance every time she goes for a bike ride. It's not easy. On the one hand she tells me she's never going to grow up, and accordingly has willed herself to stay 5′ 3″ and a size four shoe. Her fifteen-year-old brother, who has no such hang-ups, overtook her in height some years ago and his feet are like coracles. On the other hand I'm not to treat her like a child, interfere, make 'chicken's tochas' faces when she's on the phone for 180 minutes or criticise anything about *her* personally or any of her friends.

Also, I must never again embarrass her as I did after Eddie Kulukundis's birthday luncheon by turning up in a black cab at her school with an orange helium balloon tied to my head. This is *not* the way mothers behave, she tells me, maternally.

How would *I* know? I'm so used to being embarrassed by mine that I'm anaesthetised. So used to sentences such as the one she threw me telephonically after she'd travelled to Brussels by overnight ferry to stay with my brother, 'I say, Maureen, you know that girl I slept with on the way over to Brussels – well, she's ever so nice and she's going to show me round NATO.' Once you know and love her it rolls off your back like a duck but, even for me, that one took a couple of minutes to sort out. I'm being utterly patronising, don't tell me, I know. Fortunately, now *I'm* a mother, it cuts both ways. Last week I had tickets for the Shakespeare in Regent's Park.

'Adam,' I said, 'would you like to come out with me tomorrow night?'

'No thanks.'

'Well! That's *very* nice! I've got tickets for A *Midsummer Night's Dream* in the Park.'

'Oh! Sorry. Yes, I'd love to. I thought you meant to go to Pullens.' (Pullens, for the non-initiated, non-north Londoner, is the school uniform shop in Temple Fortune.) The poor child thinks that's the only place I ever *take* him to. He's not far wrong.

Similarly, a conversation with him about a weekend break turned into a music-hall routine.

Me: Adam, I've been talking to Uncle Geoffrey in Brussels – how would you fancy us joining him for a couple of days in the mountains at Abondance?

Him: Er. No thanks.

Me: (*to his father in a hiss*) That child is ruined! I ask him if he'd like to go skiing with Geoff and me and he turns me down flat.

It was only after I returned from work a couple of hours later that his father told me the reason for his son's outright refusal. *He* thought the sentence went 'How would you fancy joining Geoff for a couple of days in the mountains at a barn dance?'

Under the circumstances I guess 'Er. No thanks' was mighty polite, paternal even. Get out the knitted throwover, Maureen, put your teeth in a tumbler and rock on. I've already reached the stage where I've forgotten whom I've rung by the time they pick up the phone: 'Hi – er – it's me, Maureen . . . er – how's things? Good, good, fine – and how's er, how are you, er both . . . still in the show? You're not in a show? Nooo, I didn't say *show*, I said – *so* – so, er who, I mean how *are* you?'

When I visited the Nightingale Home for the Aged, I met a very dear old man who whiled away his time making and painting small Jewish gnomes. Shrugging, tailoring, beaming, bearded gnomes. I ordered *six*. Sometimes I gaze out my window at the five who haven't been decapitated by a football and think – I could do a lot worse than end up at a respectable age, sitting in a favoured chair, surrounded by admiring friends, doing a job there will always be a market for – gnome painting.

In actuality, aside from his timing, my drama school boss wasn't far wrong. At fourteen I looked forty. At forty I felt twenty. At thirty-eight, the *Guardian* congratulated me on my forty-eighth birthday. At forty-four, the *Sun* wrote: 'Lipman, forty-six, was quoted as saying . . .' On top of which the entire British public thinks I'm a sixty-five-year-old telephobic, who's had plastic surgery to appear on chat shows. Maybe maturing is for cheese and wine parties, not for real life.

It was shortly after my forty-fifth, that I stopped in Hampstead to buy, on a whim, a mushroom crêpe from a crêperie stall. (Hampstead specialises in stuff like that. And candle shops and Moroccan wall hangings – but try and find a nice tea-towel!) The crêpe was delicious and I virtually slurped it back all the way to the car. As I revved up, I noticed a vanload of men waiting for my space. I indicated that I was about to leave. To my astonishment the driver leaned forward and somewhat suggestively ran his tongue around his lips. Well! See Mother Maureen bridle and bristle and stiffen imperceptibly or even perceptibly! I shot him one of my most disdainfuls – a 3B as it happens – only to see the passenger seat occupant lean forward and join him mid-lick for more slow tongue turning. I was appalled. Or was I? Secretly, a little voice murmured 'Well, I never did – there's life in the old girl yet' and I stole a coy glance into the driving mirror to check how I looked. Yes, you've guessed it. There was mushroom all round my mouth. It was quite embarrassing actually, although the occupants of the van seemed to find it hilarious. From now on 'crêpe' is relegated to blouses and necks where it belongs.

Trance'd be a Fine Thing

It had to be the coldest, wettest day of the year when my mother and I drove to the hypnotherapist in Hampstead, and the new parking restrictions had to entail a half a mile walk and the kind of pay-and-display techniques which could only be interpreted by a traffic warden with X-ray vision or an ex-member of SMERSH.

Why the hypnotherapist? Well – look at it this way – I have occasional depression, my mother has anxiety attacks which make *me* anxious and the hypnotherapist's PR had written me a charming letter suggesting I might be anxious to try it. Accordingly, I put on my fake fur, grabbed my simulated crocodile bag and set off in search of reality.

Mr Robert Farago of the Farago Clinic is a young Clark Kent-like American with trendy hornrims and a ready smile and, after consultations with my mother, he took the short straw and decided to deal with me first. I filled in a form citing my blocks and before I actually spilled off the form and began writing on his shirtfront, we decided to deal with the sleep problem first.

In reply to his casual question, I gave him a run-down of my bedtime routine. His eyebrows drew together and his voice was quietly incredulous.

'OK, so you're telling me that you give a performance of two and a half hours till 10.30, drive yourself seven or eight miles home till 11.00, eat a full meal with meat and two vegetables whilst entertaining your children, your mother and various houseguests from assorted corners of the globe till 12.30, drink a caffeinated drink, stimulate your brain reading through a script or an article until one o'clock then attempt sleep? Would that be right?'

I made my face suitably rueful as we agreed that as wind-downs go, this was winding strongly upwards. I would, at that point, have been happy to pay my money and relinquish the leather chair a sadder but wiser woman – but the treatment was only just beginning.

Mr Farago wondered if I would like to be taken down to a medium trance, slowly. The fanged face of a traffic warden imploded across my middle eye and I said:

'Er, no. If it's all the same to you, I'd like to go into a deep trance very fast.'

There followed some experiments to see if I was a good subject. He suggested one of my hands became a magnet and the other a metal slab and we both watched them being drawn together. Then there was some light-fingered stuff involving an imaginary helium balloon and it seemed we were off. His voice was authoritative and his manner persuasive as he issued commands to my subconscious. My limbs soon took on an uncharacteristic slump but my brain continued to buzz. I tried to stop myself comparing his American patois to those self-help migraine tapes you inadvertently pick up at the health shop with the Evening Primrose Oil, the tropical pic'n'mix, and the leaflet on do-it-yourself breast examination.

'Your mind is a deep pool within which all human endeavour dwells. Unlock the channels of that innermost cavern and the river of life will pour forth, bringing peace and harmony and a state of undreamed of bliss. Remember your destiny is within your own head.'

'So is my headache,' you growl, struggling with the desire to karate chop the tape recorder.

Right now, however, I was struggling with the concept of visualising a place where I had been supremely happy. It didn't have to be a real place and I was to raise my thumb when I'd thought of somewhere. The first picture which came to mind was a somewhat clichéd desert island, replete with timber shack and palm fronds, and I was just about to raise my thumb when a ruddy great crocodile padded up the sand and forced me to change the visuals to the lyrical calm of the Italian lakes, over which descended the biggest black storm cloud you've never seen. I began to panic. OK, my bedroom. I'm happy in my bedroom. No, he'll think I'm agoraphobic – or nymphomaniac even. Now I was starting to laugh – control yourself – my thumb was twitching . . . Oh God – Cornwall! That's it Cornwall. Lake House. The sloping lawn, the cedar tree, the hammock. Fine. I stuck a triumphant thumb in the air and resumed basic breathing.

Over the next few minutes, his authoritative voice talked me down to a state of complete relaxation. At his suggestion, I left all my cares and woes in a rucksack at the top of a flight of stairs – I felt the sun on my face, the weight of my limbs, the movement of the hammock, the gentle breeze running through the windows of my mind.

'I'm going to talk you down from twenny to zero and each number will take you into a deeper state of relaxation. Whenever you think of this magic place you will feel as peaceful as you do now – twenny, nineteen, eighteen . . .'

I began to feel quite soporific . . .

'Twelve, eleven, ten . . .' I gave myself up to the persuasion in his voice . . .

'Six, five, four . . .' Parts of me which had been tensed since teething, unfolded . . .

'Three, two, one . . .' I was sinking, sinking, sinking, when 'CRASH' into my head, into my hammock, into my Cornish rhapsody came an insistent, familiar, familial sound . . .

'Hellooo. Are you there? I don't mean to suddenly interrupt but how long have you got on that meter, Maureen? . . . I mean, you don't want to unnecessarily get another ticket do you? . . . Hellooo?'

Fixing my practitioner with my most hypnotic gaze, I said, 'And there, in a couple of split infinitives, you have the story of my life.'

It wasn't his fault. It was mine. I'd made the appointment forty-five years too late.

As I beetled back through the biting rain towards my shortly to be hostaged Hondamatic, a police van sounded its alarm, alarmingly, to my left. I swerved and focused my spectacles on the dozen or so traffic wardens seated snugly inside, hands waving wildly, faces all pressed to windows mouthing 'Hello Beattie – how's your Melvyn?' In vain I tried to regain my trance-like calm, but the words 'piss off' seemed to bubble effortlessly to my lips with accompanying gesture.

An hour later I picked up Mother who appeared with rainhood, gloves, umbrella and all the other accessories which manifest themselves from within her handbag, and the broadest smile I'd seen in weeks. My God. It's worked. She looks happy. I mused. Oh ye of fickle faith.

She got in the car and said triumphantly: 'He's very good, isn't he? I enjoyed it. I never went to sleep though. Did you? I kept opening my eyes all the time and saying "I'm not hypnotised you know".'

I'm sorry. There are some challenges that stump even the mastermind. Small wonder then that I picked up my *Independent on Sunday* to find that women are attending this clinic in order to increase their breast size. The *Tatler* journalist reported an increase of half an inch (per breast, I presume) after one session. And if it can do that for WOMEN – then every man in England must be leaping into his car. No wonder the residents of Hampstead are complaining there's nowhere to park.

Easter-Egg'tomy

'The doctor said I might as well have it done,' said I over meatballs and rice around the family dinner table.

'Have what done?' said the child who'd been listening.

'Fibroids, love,' I replied, ever the up-front parent. 'They're sort of fibrous masses which grow inside the womb.' Amy put down her meatball fastidiously.

'So what do they do to them?'

'They take out the womb – no, it's OK. You don't miss it, honestly.' Her face registered pure disbelief.

'But I don't want them to take away your womb! It was my first home.'

It was a good point. I hadn't actually considered it in the light of getting rid of a house without considering a sitting tenant, as it were. Over the coming months my daughter's comment was to be the least confusing of the ones I received.

'Fabulous,' said a dear actress chum. 'I was up and about and back in a musical in six weeks. It's the best thing I ever did. Honestly – your hair gets better, your skin gets better – you'll feel a different woman!'

'Really?' I disputed, purely on the grounds that I felt happy with the one I was. 'Oh. That's good to hear.'

'Oh I *am* sorry,' said another. 'You must give yourself at least three months of absolute total rest – and I mean you don't even pick up a blender! None of that opening Tesco's on Sunday mornings and saving pygmy hippos on Monday lunchtime that you go in for . . . Absolute rest! Go to the Seychelles for a month with Jack.'

'Really?' said I, closing the bulging diary quietly. 'Oh. Well that's good to hear. I'll call the travel company right away . . .'

'Oh it's *nothing* these days,' said Mother dismissively. 'Everyone I know's had one. Dorothy had it when she was twenty-nine. Shall I come down and stay while you're in?'

'But why are you doing zis?' said my French amie, Simone. 'I 'ave 'ad fibroids also and my gynaecologist she just took them out and, *voilà!* I went 'ome the same day!'

'Really?' I went. Again. 'Well, that's good to hear.'

'Ring her. At least get a second opinion. 'Ere is the nombre.'

I rang her. The second opinion was crammed in between *Start the*

Week and a speech at my old Drama College. It was 'in and out' in most senses of the phrase. Fortunately it confirmed the first opinion. I was, and not for the first time in my life, opinion-sated.

'Just remember,' said a woman I hardly knew, but for every detail about her womb. 'Just remember, you're bound to get weepy afterwards – it's only natural – the hormones will be all over the place. Make sure they give you HRT and take a small pillow in to press against the wound.'

I took a positive stance. This was *not* going to apply to me. I was not going to weep on cue on the fifth day, come over all wobbly on the sixth and demand a refund on the seventh. *Au contraire!*

This was going to be my finest performance. That of a brave woman. If necessary I would be doing the crocodile joke under anaesthetic – and I'd be back on stage in eight weeks if it killed me, as fit as a fiddling flea.

Ten minutes later I found myself weeping incoherently as I dismembered an economy sized box of super Tampons. Pathetic. I mean who in their right minds would miss having periods? Me. That's who. Suddenly that small navy blue box with the unbreakable cellophane cover spelled romance, fecundity, mystery, femininity and *youth*. Maybe I'd just put off the whole thing. Jack could drop me at the hospital – I'd wave goodbye, go in, come out again and head for Heathrow for a longish holiday, just me and my adorable little fibroids. Little! What did I mean little? At my first check-up, they were oranges, apparently. Six months later they were grapefruits. If I funked it now, by the time they opened me up there'd be a couple of watermelons, a barrow load of ugli fruit and I'd be shaped like Roseanne Barr.

I thought of that first consultation. My three queries to the gynaecologist had been, 'Look, this won't interfere with my sex life will it?'; 'Had you better just examine my breasts while I'm here?'; and 'Well, can't you just suck 'em out?'

What must he have thought of me? A middle-aged nymphomaniac with an internal fruit stall. No, it was time. I took a positive stance, girded my loins, whilst I still had loins to gird – packed an overnight bag, drove to the clinic and went within to get without.

The anaesthetist, bless him, rang me on the Sunday before to promise me I wouldn't: a) wake up during the goriest bit and be too paralysed to politely point out that I'm in agony; b) never wake up again; or c) lose my immediate memory and keep saying 'Who am I?'.

Then he said: 'Do you have any crowns on your teeth?' I laughed somewhat mirthlessly.

'Almost exclusively,' I replied. 'In fact if you can find a genuine tooth in this mouth, there's a bottle of Asti Spumanti and a Cadbury's Cream Egg in it for you.'

'Well, it might be an idea to ring your dentist and ask him to make you a gumshield because people sometimes crack their crowns by grating their teeth when they come round.'

I could hardly wait to phone the dentist. I could feel the punch-line bubbling to the surface.

'Hello Martyn – It's Maureen Lipman. Sorry this is such short notice. I'm having a hysterectomy on Wednesday – could you possibly make me a gumshield?'

Putty in his hands really. At least I'll be able to get back into the rugby scrum when I come out of hospital.

Amy was decidedly wobbly chinned when I dropped her at school on the morning of the op. Jack had started treating me like a hundred-year-old Chinese egg. My friends all phoned and made moving little speeches about how they'd be thinking of me and Mother was on the bus from Hull, her fish-frying hat in her holdall.

In actual fact, the way I see it, is this. Ten days in a nice hospital room and eight weeks at home with no speeches to make, no grey wigs, no learning, no laundering, no lifting, all the yoghurt balls I can eat and no womb for complaint at all. Oh, and a lifetime of clapped-out stomach muscles, of course.

One of the more extraordinary occurrences of the whole episode was when I sat in bed, post-op, watching the Christmas edition of *Only Fools and Horses*. It concerned the birth of Del Boy's first child whom Nick Lyndhurst's character assumed was Damien the devil baby. It was unbearably funny, even if you hadn't just sacrificed your stomach muscles and been sewn up like a duck's bum. For grim life I held a small pillow against the wound and tried desperately not to disclose the surgeon's work, alien style, to the visiting medics, and in the end, just gave in and accepted the pain with the pleasure. The next day I wrote to John Sullivan, the writer, admonishing him for unleashing such agony on a woman in recovery from a hysterectomy. He replied by return of post. On the same day, he had received a letter from our mutual friend Linda Agran, from a different hospital, which read as follows: 'Last night I watched the Christmas episode of *Only Fools* . . . and I want to ask you how you could do such a thing to a woman lying in hospital recovering from a hysterectomy.' The coincidence was pretty spooky, considering that Linda and I were born on the 9th and 10th of May respectively and often celebrated our birthdays together with our husbands – who were both born on the 8th of September.

A Little Learning

I've discovered after a mere forty-mumble years a propensity for learning. Having wasted the allocated teaching years in search of the perfect imitation of the people teaching me, I have discovered the latent pupil in me is burning with attentive zeal.

One year it was flamenco, which I learned for a TV play and took seriously enough to crack open the cellar ceiling with my persistent stamping on the kitchen floor. (During the TV sequences when I was supposed to be inept I found myself struggling against the desire to do it perfectly, and for months after the show was over I became a flamenco groupie, haunting the tapas houses of Kentish Town in search of Sevillanas.)

A recent foray was into the wonderful world of the auctioneer. Now, I'd frequently wielded the gavel at ladies' luncheons, and it was a cinch. 'So, I've got a lovely voucher here for nail extensions at the "Hard as Nails" salon in Finchley Central – and I'm going to start the bidding at twenty. Do I hear twenty-two? Oh, twenty-five from the lady in the fuchsia jumpsuit – I'm sorry, of course it's cerise. Twenty-seven – this is one you can't afford to miss – you'd be a fool to yourself. YES! Thirty pounds, sold to the lady in the emerald green two-piece. Now ladies, don't fight, it's only a bloody nail voucher. Stop tearing each other's clothes! You'll break your nails!'

Little did I realise as I entered the hallowed doors of Sotheby's, that their auctioneers received a rather more formal training. I was to receive a day's training from top auctioneer Peter Simkin. After one hour's training I was ready to be auctioned off myself.

Readers, you have no idea of the complexity of this business. Peter began by saying 'It's fifty per cent showmanship' at which I beamed 'and fifty per cent mathematics', at which I was beamed up. The thing is that you've got your reserve price, and your commissioned bid price and you've got to work out your starting price and your *increments* on the bases of these bids not arbitrarily, so that you don't end up 'wrong-footed' with the bid resting in the audience and not with the house. Got it? Yeah, me too. I took home my sheaves of notes, phoned up the *Financial Times*, who were fronting the charity, and resigned from the job. Kindness itself, they understood my predicament totally and refused to accept my resignation.

Thus it was that I found myself shaking and quaking with the remnants of a bottle of Rescue Remedy in my stomach, in the Imagination Gallery, auctioning off photos and paintings by the great and the near great to roughly one hundred of the most uninterested people I've yet to hector and fawn upon.

Within seconds of going 'on' I increased the show-business percentage considerably and reduced the maths one by about 100%. Wrong-footed wasn't in it – I was legless. At one point I got so excited at the prospect of *nearly* reaching the reserve price that I threw in my own bid and ended the evening as the owner of a huge panel of engraved glass which I have absolutely no idea what to do with – although I suspect Jack is aching to tell me.

This year's preoccupation, also brought on by a projected TV play, is golf. Now, I'm not one of nature's most natural movers. At school my created position on the hockey field was 'left outside' and my idea of an adventure holiday would be removing a fly from my Tequila Sunrise. However, from the first lesson I felt a smile creep across my face and I realised what the advantages might be of becoming the oldest swinger in town.

Of course I was standing fairly still for my lesson, which is always a big plus. If I could learn a sport lying down, it would be even better (suggestions in a plain brown envelope, if you please). Also, I'm totally in love with the one-to-one system of learning. For a start, you never have to fight for the teacher's attention with the kid in the front row with shiny blonde hair, clean plimsolls and a photographic memory. Furthermore, when you only have an hour, and you know the cost of every minute, you tend not to waste them in gazing out the window at the gardener's pectorals or carving 'Elvis is God' on the leg of your friend's desk.

Anyway here I am on lesson one, bending my knees, keeping my eyes on the ball, extending my wrists and, most complex of all, sticking out my bottom in a fair impersonation of Margaret Thatcher showing concern on a disaster walkabout. My teacher, a man gifted with a perfect swing and the patience of Mother Teresa, keeps replacing ball after ball as I smash 'em wildly and impressively over the green. By the end of half an hour I'm convinced I'm in the presence of a genius, my own I mean, and swagger off the course with the jaunty jowliness of Nick Faldo's Fanny – if you take my meaning. And if you don't you've probably formed your own interpretation which is much more fun.

This burgeoning of confidence lasts roughly till lesson three, when for some reason my nicely co-ordinated limbs go into spastic conflict with my number six iron and my eyes start to work independently of one another.

In short, I'm bloody useless and moderately bad tempered to boot. It can, as a sport, bring out the very worst in your nature.

Apropos of which:

A rabbi, a priest and a vicar were playing golf. (I'm sorry I sound like Bernard Manning at a welders' convention, I can't help the way my mind meanders.)

Anyway, this set of golfing clerics were stuck at the ninth hole behind four of the slowest players ever to wander over a green. Finally, in desperation, they complained to the steward about the appalling lack of courtesy shown by the players ahead of them.

'Aha,' said the steward meaningfully. 'My dear sirs, what you perhaps do not realise is that the gentlemen ahead of you are all blind.'

'Good gracious! Heavens above,' said the vicar. 'How churlish are we to complain, when faced with such a shining example of the indomitable spirit of mankind!'

'By all the saints, my sentiments exactly,' added the priest. 'How very humbled I feel and what a lesson it is in patience and forbearance.'

'My sentiment exactly, and manifold,' says the rabbi. 'But tell me, why can't they play at night?'

(I only gave the punch line to the rabbi to avoid letters from affronted Protestants and Catholics. I'm used to letters from affronted Jews – I've got drawers full.)

Meanwhile back at tee-hee, I slowly and laboriously practised that most unnatural of acts between consenting adults until I achieved the knees bent, bottom out, glassy-eyed look so adored by golf pros and mothers who are trying to potty train their children. 'Relax,' urges the golf pro. It's not easy to relax when you look like Rumpelstiltskin on Entero-Vioform.

After six lessons, and having recovered some of my early promise, I ventured during my summer hols, on to a Cornish golf course. Shock. Horror. My dear, the legs! All that walking! By the third hole I was desperate for one of those little golf carts to come and scoop me up and drop me on the nearest piece of Axminster. By the sixth hole which my friend and fellow holidaymaker Lizzy birdied with ease, and our sons bogied or beagled or some such nonsense, I just picked up my ball more or less manually and lurched on to the seventh with my face to the heavens praying to be hit in the rush by a golf ball and carried off for an early bath. By the ninth I more or less personified the term 'in the rough'.

By the time the play was due to be filmed I was as the saying goes, 'quietly confident, Brian'! On my first day of filming I narrowly missed death by golf ball whilst standing beneath a birch tree minding my own

211

business and eating an Eccles cake. I saw Goliath of Gath's dimpled missive hurtling towards me and threw myself athletically in what, thankfully for the other five plays in the series, turned out to be the right direction. My own fault. Rule thirty-eight of the Golfers' Manual: Never take Eccles cakes on to a fairway.

On my second day I stood in front of the camera in four inches of mud being soaked to the skin by an overhead fire hose, attempting my first shot.

'I did it! I did it!' cries the character, Peggy, 'I got it in the air.' The ball was supposed to travel thirty yards. I gritted my teeth, thought of England and swung like a pendulum do. The ball left the mudbath, soared into the skies, travelled about 200 feet, skimming the top of a catering bus crammed with ducking extras, and landed just north of a Tupperware vat of sauce tartare. My confidence grew noisier. I swaggered past the scores of real golfers flanking the clubhouse, protesting, 'No, honestly. It was nothing – really. Just a fluke. No please – what technique? Gracious me . . .' and swept loftily straight into the loo. The gents' loo.

My finest hour was yet to come. In the play, my character Peggy and her husband were to play a game of life and death golf, winner takes all, sort of thing. I was to swing from a bunker and the ball was to land straight in the hole. Obviously the shot would be faked. My golfing double stood by, ready to oblige. It was obvious she would be sorely needed. After ten minutes thwacking away in the sand, I couldn't shift it an inch. Patiently the prop men built up a little egg of sand and placed the ball on top. Red faced and mindful of the gathering crowd, I thwacked again. Suddenly there was a concerted gasp and the air was filled with rapturous applause. I clambered out of the bunker. 'What happened? Who did what?' I blinked myopically.

Well, gentle reader, disbelieve me if you must, but the ball had flown out of the bunker, shot past the hole, hit the tracks bearing the camera, reversed direction and bounced straight back into the hole. Incredible. Useless, but incredible. Something to tell my grandchildren. Something to tell Tiger Woods' grandchildren even.

Meanwhile, even as we speak – well, *you* read and I brag – my son is erecting, by dint of a crumpled page of Japanese hieroglyphics, a seven foot practice net complete with chipping pocket, in the erstwhile tailored lawn. Spiked shoes, spelling death to Amtico flooring have appeared in my wardrobe. I am the sly possessor of a perspex visor, a set of Wilson Graphite clubs and a pair of trousers of such appalling loudness as to make Rupert Bear look like 'Something in the City'. A packet of tees has taken up residence in my contact lens bag, and I don't mean Lapsang Souchong. I could be considered a lost causeway.

So, anyway, as I was saying, this priest plays a sneaky round of golf, on a

My Great, great grandparents in Kovna, Lithuania. My great grandmother is in the back row, second on the right. I see a lot of myself in the matriarch seated in the second row.

My paternal grandparents and all my aunts and uncles in Hull. My father is the lad in the front row saying: 'Yeah? You and whose army?'

Top
Zelma and Maurice on honeymoon, gazing with trepidation into the future?

Left
Two great aunts and an uncle – part of the Boris Fridkin troupe which toured the US warming up the boards for me.

Right
Mo at Butlins showing something of my great great granny's levity.

Below
On hols with the Bennett family in Scarborough and totally unaware there's a camera in the vicinity.

Left
This is how we dressed for best in Hull.
Aged twelve . . .

Right
. . . and today? Sixty is the new twelve.

Left
Flora, Fauna . . . and Zelma – my favourite photo.

Left
1966, playing hooky from LAMDA at the Edinburgh Festival in a play called *The Burn*. We made the front pages when Tamara Ustinov sat on the lap of critic Harold Hobson. He loved it.

Below
First Cup is the Deepest . . . Hull musical festival, age 14.

Left
Age 26, as Diana Rigg's understudy in Stoppard's *Jumper* at the Old Vic, 1972. I can still hear the audience response to the announcement: 'Oh Noooo!'

Right
What a lovely pair! Old Vic, 1970. Louie Ramsay and I essay the roles of first and second Randy Women, in the little known William Blake musical, *Tyger*.

Left
'One day he came along,
The Man I Loved . . .'
Wedding Belle and Beau Jest.

Right
Film Director Mike Apted said, 'I've never seen
two more legitimate children in my life.'

Left
Bar Mitvah boy and his party planners.

Right
Two English nationals explain our heritage to
our Colonial friend Astrid King.

Left and Below
When Zelma was eighty, with refundablecake in the days before 'bags for life.'

Below
My bride and my boy. Adam and Taina's wedding with brother Geoffrey and sister in law.

Below
Too drunk to slice . . .
Too old to care . . .
My 60th party at the University Women's Club.

Right
An Even Keel. The late, great Howard Keel at special Oh!klahoma! Gala. On left, Josefina Gabrielle; on right, director Trevor Nunn and wife Imogen Stubbs.

Right
Another bag for life. 1991, Jack's play *Bag Lady*
for my series *About Face*.

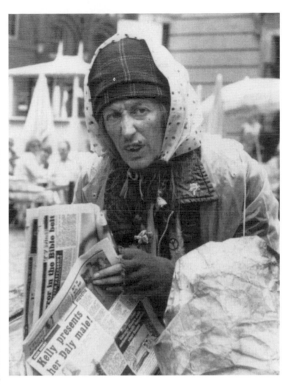

Below
We are absciling
We are abseiling . . .
Skins. 2008

Bottom Left and Above
The Iron Lady and the Iron Butterfly or 'We are a
Grandmother'. As barmy Bella with Rosemary Harris as
scary gran and Janette Legge as sister Gert, in Neil
Simon's *Lost in Yonkers*, 1992, and as PM Tension in
About Face, 'Send Her Victorious.'

Left
The infamous Book Jacket for *You Can Read Me Like A Book* 1995. The caption 'free jacket with every copy' was meant to be ironic. ML with publisher Jeremy Robson at launch party.

Right
BT – A legend speaks. And a career careers.

Left
Linda Bellingham, Janet Suzman and I in *The Sisters Rosensweig*, 1993. One of us played the part of 'Gorgeous.'

Right
Zelma at Buckingham Palace: 'Fancy . . . they don't give you a cup of tea and there's not even handrail on the steps!'

Below
Parting is such neat horror . . .

Left
This is the one I'd like on the Obit, rather than the ethnic owl on the phone (please note kids).

Left
'I say!' Joyce Grenfell and I share a virtual stage, on and off, from 1988 to 1997.

Right
'Murder on the high C's' or 'Something of the Queen of the Night'. As Florence Foster Jenkins in *Glorious* by Peter Quilter, Duchess theatre, 2005.

Left
Richard Wilson and I rehearse ou triumphant 'All of the colours in all o the sizes Madam' routine in err . . Carry on Mugging?

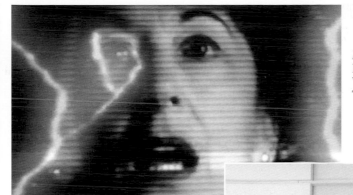

Left
Lipman sucking energy in *Dr Who*, 2007, as a dastardly alien – The Wire.

Right
101 uses for Baby Bel cheese.

Left
Incognito in The Ivy with (sshh . . .) Hugh Jackman.

Right
Wistful Era. Photo by Natalie Percy

Left
Back to my roots.
Courtesty of Fritz von der Schulenberg

Right
The endangered Lip-woman of Ethiopia.
Courtesty of Fritz von der Schulenberg

Above
On our tenth Tamarind Tequilla of the day. Amy and I in Ajihic at Mexican wedding. I think.

Right
In Cafe Mahogany on Greek Isle of Zakynthos. Is this some new form of water cooler, or am I just pleased to see him?

Right
'This'll make your Eye more Private.'
I fit a sun hat on Editor Richard
Ingrams on *Oldie* Cruise.

Left
Our loving last holiday in Megeve.

Above
Eve Pearce and I in Zakynthos Griddle (that's a Greek Idyll).

Left
Roger Allam. 'Oh No It Isn't!' Ian Mckellan. 'Oh Yes It Is!' Joe McFaddon. 'He's Behind You!' In *Aladin* old Vic Panto 2004.

Right
The Szpillman family: Frank Finlay, Adrien Brodie, Jessica Kate Meyer and Julia Rayner and I gaze wistfully out towards an Oscar in Polanski's *The Pianist*.

Left
Jimmy Johnston escorts a Aunt Eller into a reluctant Dozy-Do'nt in *Oklahoma!*

Right
As Mrs Meers in *Thoroughly Modern Millie*. I wonder if anyone got the joke that a Meerskite is Yiddish for an ugly woman?

Right
Mother and son – homicide by side – with Mel Raido
in Adrian Shergold's *He Kills Coppers*.

Left
Out for a duck shoot. Playing the governess,
Charlotta Ivanovna in *The Cherry Orchard* at
Chichester, 2008. I realised I never want to do
anything but Chekhov again.

Above
At Alan and Ann Sugar's Ruby wedding:
ML: 'Nice to see you, Brucie'
B: 'Oh, yes . . . and your name was again?'

Left
The barkless, water-fearing dog of the Congo (born in Ealing) is rescued from the Serpentine by Natalie.

Right
Welcome to my fabulous apartment.

Above
Last year in Muswell Hill. At home in the land of canine.

Above
Three-pronged attack:
Get Fit.
Advertise a product.
Display logo for charity.

Above
Warren auditions for *Britain's Got Talent*.

Sunday. St Peter turns to God in Heaven saying 'Tsk, Tsk. Do you see Father Hannegan playing nine holes on a Sunday?'

'I do indeed,' says the Lord, 'and I plan to teach him a lesson!'

The priest tees off. The ball flies one hundred feet in the air where it is swooped upon by an eagle who carries it a further two hundred feet and drops it into the waiting mouth of a rabbit who carries it on to the green, where a mouse kicks it up against the flagpole and a swarm of gnats push it straight down into the hole.

'I thought you said you were going to teach him a lesson?' gasped St Peter.

'That's right,' says the Lord. 'Who's he going to tell?'

And while we're on the subject:

A golfer hits the ball into the rough and whilst recovering it, fishes out a small leprechaun from the water. The leprechaun is so grateful that he tells him that from now on he will play scratch golf, be successful in business and have a fantastic sex life.

A year later the same golfer hits into the rough again and encounters the same leprechaun, who asks how he is getting on with his golf.

'Incredibly well,' boasts the golfer, 'my handicap is down to three and I never lose a game. Golf pro can't believe it.'

'And the business?' asks the little chap.

'Phenomenal – couldn't be better.'

The leprechaun sidles closer. 'And the sex life? Have you noticed an improvement there?'

'Aaah, well, can't complain. Once or twice a month, you know . . .'

'Once or twice a month!' echoes the leprechaun. 'Sure, that's terrible – not nearly what I had in mind.'

'Ah well, it's not so bad, not so bad at all, you know – for a priest with a small parish and no car . . .'

I promise it won't last. Honestly. After all, I now use my squash racket to strain fettuccine, my castanets to frighten rooks off the bedding begonias and my unicycle is propping the door open. 'It's just,' as my home help is prone to say, 'a phrase she's going through.'

Toujours Provinces

In 1990 I played The Royal Exchange Theatre in Manchester. It wasn't a long run. In fact it started at 11.30am and it finished an hour later. However, it was very well received by the 750 ladies who made up the audience. They were not a tough house. I think if I'd read my way through the Florence Greenberg cookbook they'd have given me as good a reception, but I didn't. Only slightly daunted by the first totally in-the-round theatre I've played, with people sitting all round me at stage level and similarly two levels up, I soon realised that the best way to make a relationship with them was to walk around with my mobile mike, ringmaster style, until I tied myself up in knots. It was all good stuff, and sold a few copies of *Thank You for Having Me*.

The theatre's director, Braham Murray, was away on the day of my talk, so we didn't get the chance to renew an acquaintance which began in the mid-Sixties when he was a hungry young director and I was a drama student and not a bit hungry, thanks to the weekly food parcels from Hull. Braham's rather exotic girlfriend, Jasmina, was in my class at LAMDA, and he took some workshop classes with the students with a view to creating a show. In fact we spent a couple of merry but puzzling weeks putting together a revue about prunes. I'm quite serious. Prunes. The fruit world's visual answer to an excess of eggs.

Anyway, the idea was to re-evaluate the humble prune for an advertising agency. It didn't, on reflection, look like a great idea for a musical, although *See How They Run* might have been a nice alternative title. Then who's to say what a good subject for a musical is? 'Erm, hello Mr Macintosh, I wonder if you'd be at all interested in putting the feline poems of TS Eliot on stage, with all the cats played by ballet dancers and a pile of rubbish centre stage?'

'No I wouldn't. Sod off and don't waste my time again.' Who's to say?

Actually, years later, driving through France with Jack, we happened upon the 'prunier' region of the Dordogne and were startled by the attention the wrinkled fruit was getting. Whole shops were devoted to their versatility. Elegantly wrapped, beribboned boxes, some heartshaped, some velvet, some multi-layered – 'Ooh la la, Simone, regard lui – un autre pruneau'. Sweet prunes, savoury prunes, prunes in brandy, prunes in liqueur, prunes nestling in straw beds, prunes wrapped in candied shells, in coconut caramel . . . your humble Bridlington breakfast prune in every conceivable situ; except sitting, scatalogically, in a bowl with juice round them. Revelation. Only then did I bemoan the loss of that potential megabuck West End hit, *Prunes*, starring Dame Kiwi te Kanawa, Placido Domango and Lycheeano Pavarotti, book by William Shakes-pear, lyrics by Banana Moscouri, music by John Lemon and directed, of course, by Hal Quince!

'In the month of June, I softly croon, our favourite tune, while we kiss and share a prune.' Sheer bloody magic! Is it too late for a revival, I wonder?

But I digress. Flashback twenty years to the production that never was. Braham went on his way to becoming a first-rate director and we LAMDA students went on to finish our drama courses without recourse to any further pruning. Just before the final end of term shows, in which I was to play Lucrece in the famous play, *The Rape of Lucrece* (lorra words, norra lorra laffs), we were all frantically writing letters to agents and casting directors: 'Dear Adsa Vincent, I am a third year student at LAMDA and I was wondering whether you would like tickets for the LAMDA production of *The Rape of Lucrece* in which I have the good fortune to play the Rapee.'

It occurred to me that perhaps I should write to our erstwhile director and invite him along. I wrote the letter, but having never seen his somewhat unusual name actually written down, I wrote 'Dear Bra . . .' and left the rest to be filled in after consultation with his girlfriend at college the next day. Needless to say, I forgot to ask her, forgot what I'd written and posted the letter and, needless to say, a polite refusal note came back, headed 'Dear Mau'.

Twenty-five years went by for both of us and there I was in Manchester, addressing his Ladies Who Lunch, and there he wasn't. He was in London lunching with impresario Duncan Weldon, discussing the possibilities of a new West End production, perhaps a Pinero play. However, letters were exchanged afterwards, with careful spelling of each other's names, and dinner at Odette's in Primrose Hill (Pruniers being all booked-up) was arranged for the next time he was in town.

It was tricky renewing a relationship that had never really been. Almost harder than starting from scratch. We were both a little nervous through the hors-d'oeuvres. Fortunately we soon discovered a mutual love of food, football and family, and after that we cared not a fig. He asked me to consider the title role in Pinero's *The Schoolmistress*. I had a fancy for Pinero because the National Theatre's production of *Trelawney of the Wells* had stayed in my mind so vividly and the finest comic performance I've ever seen was also in a Pinero play. It was Alastair Sim in *The Magistrate*.

anti-Semitic. He replied that, aside from Pinero's stage direction, there was no other reference to the man's ethnicity and that Pinero was himself a Jew, writing from the point of view of an outsider. Since he, Braham, was Jewish and the producer likewise, it seemed unlikely that any of us would wish to do a play which contained even suggested prejudice. To allay any doubts I may have had, he forwarded the national reviews from the production he'd done four years previously with Susan Fleetwood and Frank Thornton. I scoured them for anti-Semitic references. But found none.

Furthermore, Braham then phoned to say Derek Griffiths was interested in the role of Lebanon. After a pause of several seconds, I realised this was probably inspired casting. Griffiths, a superb black actor and comic, would play Lebanon as a Semitic businessman, as described by Pinero, but not specifically a Jewish one.

The choice was made. Kitty Twombley would suit me. She was pretentious, vain, snobbish but also skittish, warm and very entertaining. Her origins were humble and her overwhelming love of her 'precious chicks' (her two children) was her redeeming feature. Her tenacity almost outweighed her mendacity. I could see how I could play her. Also, after three years solo in *Re:Joyce!*, it would be a wonderful change to be surrounded by actors. There was a cast of fourteen, three sets, dazzling costumes and a short tour before London. Added to which, we knew that the majority of the critics felt the play and its production deserved a London revival, so all should be well. And if you believe that then you probably believe carrots make you see in the dark and Guinness is good for you.

Unfortunately, Derek Griffiths decided to do a pantomime instead that year, and it was only a few weeks before we started rehearsals that we finally had our Joseph Lebanon in Teddy Kempner. My old sparring partner, Derek Nimmo, was to play the title role, Gwen Watford was to play his sister, the Dowager Dora, and Sara Kestelman the scheming Mrs Gaylustre, part lady, part dressmaker. I'd never met Gwen before but I'd loved her television work over the years, especially in the Charles Wood series *Don't Forget to Write*, which allowed her to use her exquisitely pained face to great comic effect. I might have known she would be one of the great gigglers of our time, and a rock of sanity and good humour through the good times and bad. Sara I had known socially for years but never worked with. She is a great story-teller. I mean great. With almost perfect recall, she can recount events which make you feel like a fly on the wall in a long-vanished drama. I would sit spellbound through car journeys (we turned out to be neighbours), while she Scheherazaded her way through Hornsey and Holborn, her deep, mellow voice weaving spells which held me all the way to Waterloo, with the epilogue in the Old Vic car park.

Julia McCarthy and Malcolm Rennie were to play the Scots mother and son, Lady McPhail and Sir Colin. They had played the same roles in the last production in Manchester and they were perfect from day one. Hilarious. She, tiny, birdlike and tough as haggis; he, gawky, ginormous and gormless. Wee and Large.

And so to the first day of rehearsals, beginning with the customary read-through of the script. I don't suppose the words 'read-through' hold the same sense of real terror for you as they do for me. For me the words are more or less synonymous with smear-test, root canal work and 'the VAT man will be calling Thursday'.

Actually I haven't had one for ages. A read-through I mean. 1987 *Wonderful Town*, Watford. That's the last time I sat down whey faced and icky with twenty or thirty quivering Thespians and heard the equally icky faced director say, 'well, there's nothing for it but to . . . er, read through it, really – is there?'

And you're always unprepared. No matter how many hours you've spent trying out your most comprehensive range of lilts, limps and lisps, it never quite comes out the way you've heard it in the privacy of your bed, your bathroom, your car and your local Curry Paradise. And if it does come out in the right nasal cockney whine in Act I, then you can rest assured that by Act III it'll come out in a Welsh baritone.

Of course before you begin to actually read, there is the ritual of the greeting of the actors you have known, wished you hadn't known, once met at an audition for the PG Tips chimps' voices or once slept with on an overnight couchette from Perth after a particularly gruelling recording of *Martin Chuzzlewit* for Radio 4.

'Hi, I'm Maureen' (they *know*. They've seen the ads).

'Yes, hello! I'm *Chris* – Jerry and Julian send huge amounts of love – I was with them at Stratford East in . . .'

'Oh great! How *are* they?' (*Who* are they?)

'Fine! Jules is just about to do a thing at the Beeb with Dame Judi and . . .'

'Hi *darling!*' (We all call each other darling *not* because we're pretentious prats, although often we are, but because we're so nervous of making the wrong impression that we can't remember our *own* names let alone anyone else's.)

'Where are you sitting? God, isn't this hell? It doesn't get any easier does it?' By now, coffee in polystyrene cups has wobbled into sight and Thespians are cooing 'Oooh biscuits! Hob-nobs, greattt!' as though they had their last square meal when Gandhi did, instead of twelve minutes ago in Joe Allen's.

everyone cranes to look at everyone else's costumes to show they are interested in the design as a whole not just their own part of it. Invariably, by some sort of theatrical ESP, most of the ladies will be wearing more or less the same colours to the first rehearsal as the fragments of material in their designs. This will be remarked on and taken as a good omen for the production.

The director will then talk a little about the play and the social period in which it is set, and pass around a few books and pictures which each actor will be almost frothing with desire to see, will stare at for twenty seconds, pass on speedily, and never look at again. At this point routes taken from Ealing and Clapham to the rehearsal rooms and car parking facilities will be discussed as a last-minute diversionary tactic. Finally the assembled cast open their scripts. The actors who only say 'Sir Paul and Lady Marjorie are in the conservatory, my Lord' have marked their parts in translucent orange pen, and the ones who've not long been out of RADA have divided their scripts up into Battenberg sections of rulered lines to indicate beats, units, intentions, actions, motivations and fag breaks.

The ones who've been at it for rather longer are, coincidentally, all seated together, slightly apart from the younger ones – not for reasons of superiority, quite the reverse. They're scared that this time they'll be rumbled. This time all will be revealed. They can't act. They never could. The awards on the mantelpiece were a case of mistaken identity. The air is heavy with casual terror. There is a silence you could bite. To flee or not to flee? Quiet, almost self-effacingly, another two hairs on your head turn grey.

Rehearsals were the usual mixture of highs and highers with the odd trough thrown in for ballast. Derek Nimmo, as always, was the people-watchers' favourite viewing. Arriving in his chauffeur-driven Rolls, impeccably garbed in three piece Savile Row suit, Alpaca coat and, on one glorious occasion, bowler hat, he fitted us in between breakfast meetings with the Jakartan Ambassador, lunch with a couple of Sirs and a Viscount at the Garrick and cocktails at the first (invitation only) gallery opening of the evening. The corner of the definitely community-centred rehearsal room was turned into his mini-office and his mobile phone was strategically placed so as not to interfere too much with the denouement scene in Act III. His energy is probably enough to fuel Sellafield and there'd be a lot less falling-out.

Derek's chauffeur, John, is eighty-two and a good deal more titled than many of Derek's lunch dates. He drives the Roller and buttles for Derek and Pat, often it must be said at virtually the same time, because he has a relish for good old-fashioned services and he likes the outfits. He has been known to drive guests to Château Nimmeau in his chauffeuring gear, then nip through the garage, change into butler's gear and welcome the guests into the drawing-room. He has a papery, wafer-thin elegance and I never see him without sinking into a deep and respectful curtsy. Since I only ever see him drawing up in the Roller or leaving in the Roller, I invariably end up curtsying in the street, giving the impression of someone with a deep respect for parking meters. Ideally, John should have been played by the late, great Alastair Sim and I'm not sure that even he, genius though he was, could have fully conveyed the glorious moment when, en route to our first touring date in Bath, John took the turning to Bristol instead and, when Derek called out to tell him he'd done so, hollered back 'Don't *shout* at me, sir. It makes my deaf-aid vibrate!'

Back at rehearsals the blocking – deciding on the actual movement in each scene – took days as we all expressed our insecurities by flexing new muscles, objecting to the directorial suggestions and studying the script intensely with over-furrowed brows. This goes on for a week and the furrowed brows go home with you each evening. Notes like 'No room yet for me to invent' and 'More blocking. I'm unsure. And blocked.' 'I put on a long skirt and prayed for inspiration', 'Gwen and Sara are so good – help!' Then, on Friday the 13th, 'At last, a decent lunch in the Young Vic. We all had a hoot over Malcolm Rennie's working with Hylda Baker stories. She once told him to buy a bottle of wine for the company (fifteen people) and gave him a pound from her stocking-top to pay for it! Derek very excited with a find, in the Garrick Club, of the original Pinero prompt copy of the play. It's full of bits of business and D is determined to get them all in. Braham just as determined to leave 'em out.

'This afternoon I paced like a panther, dropped my inhibitions and let rip. Lots of laughs all round. Relaxed company suddenly as Tim Wallers, lovely funny actor attempts to say the word "Strathspey" at least eight times and Melanie Thaw and I become incapacitated. The spade work is done. Braham's in control. We can afford to laugh. Good.'

One fear hung in the air. Julia McCarthy – normally as strong as a very small ox, unsinkable and unflappable – was not well. The chest infection for which she was receiving antibiotics, wouldn't shift. Everyone suggested everything (actors being what they are, we all had at least six alternative practitioners apiece) but she continued to bark and wheeze and the effort of keeping up a strong front was knocking her back.

The Scottish dance had to be rehearsed as often as possible and, in spite of the added stimulus of Mr Nimmo wearing his own tartan trews for practice cloths, it was hard for Julia to keep up her spirits. Just a week before we were due to leave for Plymouth, she was sent for X-rays and blood tests and, horribly and inevitably, she arrived one day to tell us that she not only had cancer but it was a secondary cancer. They had no idea where the first one was.

Julia was made of strong Scottish stock and she was not going to be beaten at the first hurdle. We had all known her at varying times. I had first trodden the boards with her at the Old Vic in 1971 in *The Captain from Köpenick* with Paul Scofield. I took over the part of 'lady on a bench in park' from someone who'd moved on to bigger things. Julia was another old, black-clad lady. Our nightly contact was brief, but her sweetness, jollity and the formidable strength in her tiny frame made a lasting impression on me. The cast members who'd been in Braham's original Manchester production all adored her and those who had just begun to know her in these rehearsals already felt they'd known her for ever.

Her understudy was also my understudy *and*, would you believe, Gwen's understudy. The understudy rehearsals were absurd, with people dodging around the stage, talking to themselves. Paula Topham was up to the task. A calm, steady, handsome and extremely talented actress in her own right, she prepared herself to rehearse and open the show in Plymouth until Julia felt strong enough to return after her biopsy. We all hugged and kissed Julia and sincerely meant our shouts of 'Now you better bloody well *be* there' when she left rehearsals, but inside we all were terribly aware of her increasing frailty.

Plymouth and the Grand Hotel were breezy and welcoming and there is always a 'ping' of excitement on entering a new theatre in a new town. The Theatre Royal was making our sets and costumes and fittings were required with designer Terry Emery and the Theatre's chief dressmaker, Alex. Gwen and I would breakfast each morning in the narrow veranda which overlooked the Solent, silent, she with the full English and the *Daily Mail*, me with yoghurt and the *Guardian*, perfect compatibility. At rehearsals, Paula was word perfect and, though twenty years too young, giving an excellent version of the Scottish matriarch. Julia was scheduled to arrive in time for the dress rehearsal and first preview. Any crises we had as a company paled into insignificance besides waiting for news on her condition. Nightly telephone calls relayed the news that she was feeling stronger like the true 'pro' she was, raring to go.

My wig arrived from London. My brown wig. The one that was supposed to be blonde. The tight, frizzy schoolmarm's wig that was supposed to be in soft sculptured Victorian loops. Keep calm, Maureen. It really doesn't matter that you look like Miss Beale and the back-end of Miss Buss, so long as you remember your lines and don't fall over the footstool. Mercifully, Danutia, who worked part-time in the wig room, was a trained wig maker and she and Kim, our hairdresser, gritted their tailcombs and washed, bleached and reset the offending and extremely expensive item, and it came out just perfect.

The stage was a wide thrust and the theatre quite modern, but the Act I set, a stunning white wrought-iron and glass conservatory, looked well in the space. The costumes were a glorious froth of apricot and cream organza, lilac satin and pink and russet voile, beneath which the boned and laced corsets creaked and whined maliciously. There were bum rolls and a boned crinoline cage and French knickers and I found myself wondering how on earth the next generation was ever procreated.

The technical rehearsal was inevitably endless and, as usual, the play went out of the window whilst we struggled with doors which mysteriously have real knobs on them, open and close therefore much more slowly than the Marcel Marceau variety we've grown to know and depend upon.

It was hot. My corsets had to be peeled off my skin at the end of the run. My dresser was an angel who anticipated my every need. She became my mother, without the familiar traits, and I'd forgotten that I'm one too, until the evidence arrived in the shape of two beautiful, clean, perfect children and their gloriously weathered father.

On our last free evening, we tried to get in to see the Royal Navy Barracks, HMS *Drake*, where Jack was stationed during his National Service, but in spite of a lot of eyelash fluttering and telephone gestures, they were having none of us, dangerous looking quartet that we were. After the family had gone, however, I was privileged to join Mr Nimmo at a dinner party on HMS *Drake*.

Nimmo was a guest, for the week, of the Captain, David Wixon, and his wife – Poppet. On arrival he was leaning down to bring out his baggage from his Roller when a lady Wren, rather over-enthusiastically, slammed down the boot on his head and he had to be led to a comfortable chair until the stars ceased to shine. I told him she was probably angling for promotion. The party was incredibly glamorous, with much withdrawing and circulating the kind of silver and glassware which make your contact lenses flash semaphore all evening. Striking sub-lieutenants in dashing uniforms stood to and wafted aft, and I kept thinking 'I must remember every detail of this' before I promptly forgot it. It's a disease I suffer from. It's called CRAFT, as in 'Can't Remember a F— —-g Thing'. Would that Sara Kestelman had been there to describe it to you. The only bits I can accurately recall were the main course being pork, and that poor Poppet took to leaping around organizing an omelette, much to my embarrassment, when I would have been quite happy with a couple of potatoes and a mange-tout or two. I also recall an incredible amount of drink being passed around and, after dinner, Poppet rising and mouthing to all the ladies: 'Ladies, shall we withdraw and powder our noses?' I heard myself say, 'Not really? Really? Can't we stay, if we like, to bite the ends of their old cigars off?'

But we really *did* all pop upstairs, with Poppet, to the powder room and we – er, powdered. In the old days, of course, when the ladies withdrew, the fellas would point percy at the porcelain chamber pot in the sideboard, but I guess nowadays it's just cigars, whisky and speculation. I wouldn't begrudge them the cigars and the whisky, or even the percy pointing – but I'd be furious if I missed a good joke. Otherwise, it was a rivetingly good evening out and very jolly–tar.

Came the day of the dress rehearsal and first preview and with it came Julia McCarthy from her biopsy in London. Derek had given up his ground-floor dressing-room for her and we'd filled it with flowers. She was very pale and breathless but quite determined to be up to both shows, and do both shows she did. The boned bodices were hell against her biopsy scar and her voice was little more than a whisper. The effort of giving was so palpable that a less plucky mortal would have given up before the evening show. Pluck, however, was Julia's middle name and on she soldiered.

At the next day's rehearsal, the effort was etched all over her face. During notes there was a fire alarm in the theatre and we all fled outside. By the time we returned, Braham, having come to the inevitable conclusion that Julia was not strong enough to carry on, had told her so as gently as he could. I don't know how relieved or how despairing she was. I only know that suddenly she was in a taxi and gone and that although I spoke to her fairly frequently in the next few weeks, I never saw her again. Within weeks she was in the St John and St Elizabeth Hospice and when Gwen and I tried to visit, we were told she had too many visitors and she was unable to get any rest. Dear lady, she is resting now and we all missed her amazing spirit.

Her part was eventually taken by Ann Way, that quaint and fine actress who has probably graced more films than Michael Caine in her time (and not a lot of people know that). With steely verve she seamlessly slotted into the dowager role. Malcolm Rennie, playing her son, coped very well with playing his scenes with three different mothers in as many weeks, but inevitably Julia's loss hovered over the production throughout its early incarnation and the balance of the comedy was in danger of tipping.

The first night came and went, as all first nights do, and the local reviews were good for us, for the play and, justifiably, for Paula: 'Understudy Paula Topham shines as Lady McPhail'. Of my performance, they said, 'The comedy proper starts when she arrives on stage'; for Derek, 'Plays his role with his customary gentle, bumbling humour'; and for the play, 'Pinero's comedy may have been written in 1890, but the pomposity

and snobbery he punctures are familiar enough in genteel society today.'
It was a review which reflected everything we'd all been striving towards.

That night we were given a celebratory drink by the Friends of the
Theatre Royal and then Derek dropped me off at my hotel and set off in
search of his new lodgings, a stately country hotel, just over the border into
Cornwall. He was more sober than most judges I've had the pleasure of
meeting.

The next morning I met him outside the theatre. He was quite grey,
haggard looking and, uncharacteristically, wearing the same clothes as the
previous night. 'I've spent the evening in a police cell,' he told me, with a
wry smile and an expression of mild crossness.

'Pardon?' I said, and over strong coffee he told me the events of the
previous evening.

He'd been driving slowly, consulting the map as he searched for the
route through the narrow roads, when a car had flashed its headlights close
behind him, forcing him to stop. By the time the police, for it was they,
got to his car they had already radioed Swansea and they knew exactly who
he was. ''Ave you been celebrating then, Mr Nimmo?' they said. He was
breathalysed and taken to Plymouth police station, where he was thrown
into clink, his regular medication taken away and his cufflinks removed.
(This latter as a precaution against suicide. Now I know that there are
many ways of attempting suicide, but death by cufflink?) He was then left,
a man not in the first flush of youth, in October, in a cell, without a
blanket, access to his beloved mobile phone, or food. Inclement treatment
for a serial killer, but for a man who might or might not have been one
over the eight after drinking a couple of glasses of M&S Chardonnay after
a first night, I think erring on the side of over the top.

Apparently at midnight, a square in the cell door was opened a fraction
and a man pushed through a cup of coffee. 'Mr Nimmo,' he said, 'Oi'd
just like to thank you for all the hours of pleasure you've given me and moi
family over the years.'

He was released on bail, having not slept a wink all night and told,
interestingly, that had he been driving a *Lada* he would probably not have
been stopped.

Reminds me of a blackout sketch we used to do in revue:

Copper: ''Scuse me, sir, would you mind blowing into this?'
Man: 'But I haven't been drinking . . .'
Copper: 'Just do as I say, sir. Blow into this.'
Man: 'Oh, very well.' (*He blows*) 'But I assure you . . .'
Copper: 'Thank you. And now, if you wouldn't mind blowing into
         this one.'

Man: 'But, officer, I haven't touched . . .'
Copper: 'Please, sir, just do what I tell you and blow into this.'
Man: 'But – oh, all right.' (*He blows*) 'But I promise you . . .'
Copper: 'Thank you very much, sir. Nothing I hate worse in the morning
          than putting on a pair of cold gloves.' (*Ba-boom*)

By the time he left the station at eight o'clock in the morning, the press
had been tipped-off, and by the evening every paper in the south-west was
carrying a drunken driving rap on its front page. Christmas was coming
and they wanted an example of too much Christmas spirits. They got one.
And so did Derek – one of the prices of fame.

We were due to open in London after the eight-week tour and, during
those eight weeks we played to standing room only, broke several box-
office records and, on the whole, had good press. Some found the play fell
between two shooting sticks, but most described it as 'a comic delight to
the eye' and 'a brilliant poke in the ribs of the English Upper Classes',
which, naïvely or not, is how I had always seen it.

During the days we re-rehearsed, chopped, changed, cut, put back and
generally experimented, during the evenings we tried it out on captive
audiences and during the nights we stomped comically round various
hotel rooms with cramp and indigestion.

On Sundays we fled by train, bus, Hondamatic and hot air to blink at
our loved ones and launder our smalls (getting smaller) for the next week
away. In Guildford you couldn't get a seat if you pawned your mother-in-
law's stockbroker. The play was accelerating in pace, the performances
becoming surer, and on the whole our confidence was growing as the
word of mouth grew more fulsome.

At Bath, I relaxed enough to shop. This is a good sign, though not
necessarily for my accountant. (The boutique in question stocked clothes
called Nipon and for some reason every single item on the rails leapt on
to my body and refused to budge. I managed to stop at six outfits, telling
myself they would be perfect for an upcoming *Jonathan Ross Show*. 'All
SIX?' Accountant)

There are two ghosts in the Theatre Royal. A grey lady who drifts into
Box A and a lucky butterfly which appears only when productions are
going to be *very* successful when they reach London. On the first night I
lost my way back from the dressing-room to the hospitality drink upstairs
and, fearful of the grey lady, went through the first door marked Exit. The
door fell shut, leaving me outside, in the pouring rain locked in a gateless
garden squared in by sharp railings. Upstairs, as people drank champagne
and shrieked 'Darling you were average', the leading lady was damply
banging on the windows shouting 'Let me in! Let me in!' Lights came on

in windows around the square and people watched the floorshow bemusedly. Finally a bicycle-wheeling saviour gate-crashed the party, broke the news of my plight and I was humiliatingly rescued.

On the Thursday evening, in *October* remember, a beautiful winged creature in vivid red, black and white fluttered into the conservatory set and perched on a banquette through Acts I and II. No, it wasn't Julian Clary, it was our lucky post-pupa, signalling success to a cast now quite light-headed with joy.

Then back home for Sunday's piles of old undies, a tentative 'Hi! – Bye!' to the kids and off again, this time to Newcastle. Now *there's* a city built to last. There the audiences didn't clap the sets, or the leading actors. They *listened*, made up their minds and finally rewarded us rapturously. There I walked on the freezing beach at Whitley Bay and learned how to breathe again. Somewhere along the tour I'd dropped a stone – and it wasn't in my shoe.

The publicity machine demanded interviews – London bums must be lured on to seats. In vain I tried to keep the subject on Pinero and off BT. My failure was on a grand scale: 'Lay off the BT stuff, Jonathan,' I begged Mr Ross in the Hostility Room before the show, then froze behind the curtain as his entire introduction revolved round the phone. For twelve dizzy seconds I contemplated sodding off and leaving him to drench his Armani. On the thirteenth I went gloomily on and lacked lustre.

Final week. Brighton on Sea. Sara Kestelman and I shared a flat in the man-made Marina, and, like two kids at summer camp, we lived on puréed food, yoghurt and confessions and occasionally moped round the Asda superstore buying knickers. Our director returned and we re-re-rehearsed, fine tuned, prayed, yawned and rubbed Ralgex into the bits the osteopath couldn't reach.

As we neared London, the headlines developed a familiar 'ring'. I want you to envision the news press montage you've so often seen in Hollywood movies, *Chicago Tribune! Dallas Monitor! LA Times!*, only here the headlines shout 'Beattie goes west', 'Beattie to rescue', 'New lines for Beattie', 'Beattie's curtail CALL' and 'Beattie rings the changes'. It put a slight chill in the air but on we soldiered, foolishly trying to talk about the play, rather than Alexander Graham Bell's little folly.

The two London previews were nightmarish. When you've played your last performance at Brighton to a house filled to bursting point with cheering punters, then opened in London to the public equivalent of Death Valley, you wonder what in hell's name happened between Sussex and Shaftesbury Avenue to cause such hostility. Braham was the height of positiveness, in spite of having to sit it out there amongst it. 'You are all giving marvellously,' he told us, 'and the show is in great shape – you know

227

London preview audiences, they haven't been told what to think yet . . .'
Poor lamb did his best and better, but the chill descended further.

Opening night. London. The Albery Theatre. My dressing-room looked like a Mafia funeral parlour and smelled like Dolly Parton. Cards, telegrams and last minute pep talks allayed the terror, only slightly. (Jack and the kids poked tremulous noses round the door at 6.30 and retreated knowing it was hallowed ground – no place for people whose stomachs lay in the usual place for stomachs.) There was wig glue in my ear and a toad in my throat.

At seven the curtain went up and at 9.30 it came down. The applause was genuine and the performances, said the director, couldn't have been bettered. Judderingly, frailly we ate our post-theatre solids and unwound very slowly like hostages getting re-accustomed to sunlight. Jack was very quiet.

Meanwhile, nine or ten assorted journalists tapped out their icy assessments into Dockland printing presses and returned, untroubled, to their Vodka Sours. A day's work done. And, even if you didn't read 'em, the message of doom got through.

Then, all you have to do is go on. Because the show *must* go on. Or must it? (Answers please on a plain yellow envelope care of the Brazilian departure lounge, Heathrow. And hurry!)

As for the Bath Butterfly . . . where *is* the little swine? Here boy! Here boy! Come and get your nice little drop of formaldehyde . . . here boy!

Good Housekeeping

In 1983 an untried and untested columnist was commissioned to write a thousand words on a subject of her choice for the dashing new magazine, *Options*.

The subject on which the untried columnist decided to test-pilot her writing skills was my kitchen. For yes, gentle Poirot and Morse followers, I *was* that columnist. At the time I was renovating Château Rosenthal in Muswell Hill, gateway to the North Circular, and my handbag, my pockets, my sleeves and my mouth were bursting with fabric samples, offcuts of lino, crumpled brochures for white enamel taps offering 'Swan-Necked Versatility' and white Circotherm ovens offering all-round cookability and self-cleaning sides (would that I could have found such sides for my son!). On the subject of kitchen accoutrements, I was a Mastermind. 'Bong – Lipman, London. And your special subject is . . . Waste Disposal Grinder Noises . . . and you have thirty-seconds starting *now*.'

In short, I had a nouvelle cuisine before that became a meal which only covers one third of your plate. A Smallbone fitted kitchen. One of the early models. Drag-finished in canary yellow with tiled work surfaces in cobalt blue, courtesy of a tile shop you needed a second mortgage just to phone. (I'd never used the words 'epoxy resin' before. Not together at any rate.) I had Amtico flooring in oak-look 'random plank', trendy down lighting, wobbly pine circular table and chairs and blue gingham café curtains and tablecloth. When finished, it looked exactly as I'd dreamed it would. Like a cross between Monet's restored house at Giverny and the set of the old *Mary Tyler Moore Show*. Since then, on birthdays and at Christmas, everyone who knew me added yellow plates, blue china, yellow and blue egg-cups and I even managed to buy, mail order, a free-standing wood carving of Clint Eastwood in denims and yellow shirt, which *really* made my day.

So, fade out and fade paintwork, the years rag-rolled by and the truth and the woodwork began to reveal themselves. I, the kitchen expert, the *maven* even (What! you don't speak Yiddish? Fear not. You will.) was forced to admit, Spock-like, that I hadn't always been right. Let's be honest, I'd been fifty per cent extensively, expensively wrong.

First off, there is no such thing as a fitted kitchen. They don't. On the whole, *you* fit in with *them*. It may be that all you've ever dreamed of is an American fridge large enough to marinate a yak in and a wall oven high enough to avoid traction, but if you've only got one-and-a-half integral walls and a dining area, then you too will end up with a gnomic fridge which spews out family-sized foodstuffs – Mount Etna style – each time you open the door, and an undercounter oven with integral grill, under which you crouch, squint, steam up your glasses and up from which you have to be forcibly winched. Both appliances will, however, fit in to 'housing units'. Boy, if there were as many housing units for humans as there are for dishwashers then the Cardboard City would be as anachronistic as the Forbidden City.

What matters, I now know, is not the streamlined look so beloved of gas commercials and sit-coms. No, what matters is to have a place to store cutlery and crockery, a place to chop very near to a place to tip and wash, a place to serve close to a good-sized double oven, with easy clean – no, *ludicrously* easy clean – hob which I'm afraid means ceramic for hygiene and halogen for speed and a fridge the size of Demis Roussos. Oh. And forget white, for anything. It chips. On *taps* it doesn't chip – it peels, revealing dull, leprous brass beneath. And, while we're at it, if you can stretch the budget, get a water filter because the entomology in the water supply is yet to be revealed, and it's about to be re-overfluorided.

Talking of floor riding, he – lover, househusband, new man, MCP, or hunk who came to read the meter and never left – may worship the ground beneath your feet, but will he sweep and mop it? Mine will – but he's old enough to have done National Service and anything's fun after polishing your kit-buckle for four-and-a-half hours. If he won't, then buy something easy on the feet, and patterned to the point of camouflage so *nothing* shows. Ceramic tiles? You want to run downstairs at 3.00am for a hot milk and a Diazepam only to develop toes like Ranulph Fiennes? I don't care how much you adored their glazed splendour during that week in a villa in Ischia – they don't work in Esher.

So. Painted kitchens? Gorgeous. What fun to change the colour scheme every four years. Oh yes? *And* the plates, and the cloths, and the tea-towels and the little Delft pottery village over the plate rack? Terracotta and slate with distressed stencils, or more likely, water dye all over the washing machine, china all chucked in the skip and a distressed homemaker.

One more word. Sinks. The bigger, the better. One bowl big enough to bath a two-year-old or baste an endangered species in, one small with waste disposal if you're still on speaking terms with your bank manager, and proper draining boards built in. Forget the 'Oh you just drain in the sink and transfer to the dishwasher' routine. It's a fallacy. The dishwasher's always full, the sink's always waiting for the dishwasher to empty and you've got to have somewhere custom built to stock three days' pans, haven't you?

Recently, an age-old grudge against a work surface of stained tile grouting resurfaced. Out went the tiles and in came Corian. Ah. Now you're talking. Slate-blue, speckled man-made stuff, it flows over the work surface and, without a murmur, transmogrifies itself into a white double sink with a blue stripe. I must confess to a sinking feeling when the new draining area held on to quite so much water. The fitter said: 'Yeah – well, they're not really built to drain. As such. It's more an area for definition.'

I gleamed dangerous. 'An "area of definition", eh? Listen, mate. If I'd wanted an area of definition, I'd have put two sodding white *arrows* by the sink! Make it drain!'

Also it's not fantastically good at taking hot things on its gorgeous surface and, furthermore, it's gorgeous surface is already unbelievably scratched, but it does look wonderful against the new butter-cream of the units and blue wash of the walls.

Goodbye Circotherm oven with variable grill element, I want to cook a chicken and have a piece of toast and Vegemite at the same time, thank you very much, and 'Hello, Good Housekeeping Institute? Can you tell me what's the best performing electric double oven on the market today? No, it *doesn't* have to slide into an undercounter hob – if it cooks nicely it can stand in the middle of a two-acre pig farm!'

Finally, and most financially trying, every Sunday night, my son and his father carried ten bags of dripping, dog-chewed garbage, in the dark, round the back of the house, squeezed juicily past the car and wet-footed it down the drive to the road. This placates the dustbinmen into taking them away on the Monday. This is called life in Haringey: highest rates in England, no wheelies. Enter Natasha the trasher, stage left, escorted by Mark the demonstrator. Out comes Natasha's drawer, in go two bags of Rosenthal refuse. 'Prrrrrr' goes Natasha and reduces said refuse to one-third normal size. Whaddya think of it so far . . .? Rubbish, only smaller.

Then it was done. The whole thing took a week and two days. Day one: my mother stood in the midst of workmen, plumbers and piles of used mugs and said, 'Ooh, I love anything like this . . . You know . . . workmen – and a mess.' Days three and four: agreed upon original colours and textures then changed mind in night. Much sighing from daughter Amy. 'It's all horrible – why do you always have to *change* things?' Day seven: son Adam, home from school, blinks myopically and, whilst extracting salt and vinegar crisps from drawer, says, 'There's a big chunk chipped out of the crisp drawer. Wasn't me!'

Me? I feel genuinely ill throughout the whole operation – something to do with the heart of the house developing an irregular beat? Jack, the writer, writes 'Scene 1', then nothing but cheques.

Once it *is* done you never notice it again. As long as you continue to go out to work, that is. It's when you stop and 'stop in' that you start to notice things. My enforced 'noticing came after a spell in hospital when I was forced from a supine position to re-examine the disintegration of my surroundings. Sick woman – sick building syndrome.

Fro years, on every visit, my mother has had to stare into my mystified, uncaring face when she utters, as only she can utter, the inevitable: 'Oooh, that small toilet's in a shocking state, Maureen, why don't you get George to do it with some nice blown vinyl?' and, 'Hasn't your kitchen scuffed, can't believe it can you, all that money, it's not worth doing it again, is it?' and, 'That rug will stop walking if you get some Rug Grip' and, 'I bet you'd never get a green carpet again, would you? They're all the same, they go a horrible shade of grey, don't they? Have you noticed?'

Well. I did. Notice. Everything. She was right. About *everything*. It's just that I'd never focused on it before. Things like 'Rug Grip' never impinged on my day-to-day existence. 'Just say no to rugs' was my maxim. 'Blown Vinyl' was surely a Sunset Boulevard hooker? It's all to do with shovelling your own sh-you-know-what . . . and if you've delegated all the household tasks, then you don't see chipped paint and fulminating Hotpoints. Other people see them, and other people don't give a tossed salad how rundown they are as long as there's a Christmas bonus. Once you're clean out of acting and take over the Marigolds yourself, you become a woman who's cleaned up her act.

Training Cats and Dogs

I've never had a dog. As such. We didn't have any as children because they were not Dralon-friendly. One Saturday night my dad, a tailor, brought home a pup which someone had brought into the shop, probably in lieu of payment for a Prince of Wales check hacking jacket or a bale of Terylene mix. The pup was black and white and had already shown its aversion to Morris Oxfords by sprinkling the passenger seat halfway down the road back from town.

My mother took one look at him and did the only thing a woman of mature sensibilities could do under such circumstances. She had hysterics. Furnishing fabrics, the life expectancy and spiralling costs thereof, were brought into play. Axminster carpets were invoked, mounds of shedding hair touched upon. Mention was made, more than once, of 'Who'd end up feeding it? Who'd have to schlepp it for walks?' and, most pertinent of all, 'Who'd be cleaning up its never-ending lorry load of "you know what"?' This led to finger pointing at certain inhabitants of the house who never lifted them (fingers, that is) or cleaned out *jet black* rings from baths, or even Blanco'd their own plimsolls!

The innocent victims of these slanderous accusations began to bleat their protests. Their protests turned into full-scale demos. Satchels were flung. Doors slammed. Minor bashings ensued. 'S'not fair,' they wailed. 'S'like everything else in this house!' Everybody in their entire classes, their entire school, the whole world and Hessle Foreshore had a dog. Some had five! And terrapins! How could the accused possibly learn a sense of responsibility if they had nothing to be responsible for? *Of course* they'd clean up after it . . . or . . . they'd train it do to it in the garden – o-oh, bad move . . . hadn't the garden just been nicely asphalted over to prevent other dogs from popping in, uninvited, to drop off their calling cards? *Cack On My Asphalt*, a slim volume by a woman never parted from her Domestos bottle, sprang to mind.

It was all over – bar the cowering. The puppy cowered, Dad cowered, we cowered. A coward would've cowered against such determined opposition. The dog dematerialised. Dad sulked for a few days, his tail between his legs. Mother told the same story with magnificent additions over the phone for twenty-four hours. My brother was eventually lured back with egg and chips and red jelly. I stayed in my room, sucking the place where they'd *nearly* hit me until it turned into a truly hideous blood blister which took weeks to heal. That'd show 'em.

Of course I may not have been good dog material. I may never know. I was always scared stiff of Alsatians. There was a short cut through to the back of the houses which entailed passing a fence, behind which prowled next door but two's Alsatian. He had one job in life. To bark. And he was bloody good at it. I can still feel my heart exploding as I tip-toed the first few feet, then, at the first sounds of his jaw opening, ran like a ripcord, making ambulance noises all the way through to the back alley. I probably frightened the poor animal half to death.

Years later, I grew inordinately fond of Suki, a wonderful old boxer belonging to my landlady in Stratford-upon-Avon, Peggy McDonald. Whilst other actors swanned in and out the Dirty Duck and swarmed the noticeboard for possible breakages amongst star limbs, I sat home night after night with Peggy and Suki, and there was never a merrier threesome. In a row, our suppers on our laps – well, Suki's lap left a lot to be desired but she made mincemeat of ours – we watched the box and poured scorn on what we watched from sedentary heights. Suki had character. She was, if anything, rather grandiose with an airy, often slightly pie-eyed look which suggested she might well have been at the cooking sherry whilst we were out. And I tell you, until you've been wakened in the wee small hours by a boxer's tongue all over your bare essentials, you haven't lived – and no, there will be no Mike Tyson jokes at this juncture, thank you.

No, dog-wise, I think I Peked with Emily, the Brontë-named Yorkshire terrier and downstairs inhabitant of our first married flat. It was a lovely, bay-windowed flat in Hampstead and the glass and chrome oval dining table and perspex chairs took pride of place in the bay overlooking the garden.

Emily's owners, Edith and Bryan, became friends and when we moved in Emily decided to make us welcome in her own way. She chose, curiously enough, to do this at meal times. No sooner did the tin opener come out or the gas fail to ignite – ah, those were the days – than Emily would step out and start what we could only describe as her 'Meandering Heights'. She would pad up the steps in a sort of jaunty, jowly way, for all the world as if contemplating a constitutional, glance round casually, sniffing the air and then, as if an interesting new thought had occurred to her, she would stroll, no, I really mean saunter, across the front of the window, pause, yes, it has to be said, nonchalantly, then swiftly mount our kitchen steps virtually whistling with indifference. It was a class act, followed by her look of absolute 'Have you gone raving mad?' shock horror when, inevitably, the contents of our plates found their way on to hers. Chaplin must have based a lot of *The Kid* on Emily.

The only pet to grace 'Schloss Rosenthal' save Zuckerman, the much-chronicled tortoise and escapologist, has been the tabby bought for Child One when Child Two came along to screw up her entire life. Pushkin and the aforementioned assassin are now nineteen-years-old and it's hard to say which of them is more eccentric. Pushkin talks to me, sleeps – disastrously – on my head, wipes her nether regions on my script, waits by the garage for my car to return from the show, tells me when and how to brush her, lies cradled in my arms when I'm on my trampoline and decimates my tights.

She is fed, vetted and nursed by my husband and she only has eyes for me. Which is why I love her. Every fraction of upholstery in the house resembles shredded wheat, the chair legs are grated and I *still* love her. But I do have intensely disloyal thoughts sometimes about, sh! wanting a dog . . .

One of my favourite programmes in the Radio 4 series *The Lipman Test* was concerned with dog shows. I *know* that where our own personal obsessions are concerned we are all quite mad – but these people took the shortcake.

'He's a little Shitsu, aren't you?' yapped one owner. 'You know, a "coming and going" dog. They are actually the reincarnation of the souls of the dead monks of Tibet. That's how we like to think they are, anyway.' Makes you wonder what the poor monks spent all that time meditating for, doesn't it? To end up on the Shitsu-heap.

'I'm just grooming him out for the Show,' said another. 'When I'm finished he's supposed to look like a chrysanthemum.'

'That's what you call fulfilling his potential, then, is it?' I tried not to add.

Another woman was the owner, no, let's not beat about the bush, the *mother*, of a dozen or so Chinese Cresteds – sort of Oriental rats with quiffs. Her house sounded like a budgerigar convention. 'They're my whole life,' she trilled. 'My husband can go tomorrow, but the dogs – they're wonderful – I really love 'em.'

Dog shows are for bitches of all varieties and what goes on during and after them is the stuff of tragedy. Losers have been known to pour paint over the winners' transport home, to loosen their car wheels or worse. There was a famous dog-show winner who was apprehended for tampering with the goods. Every show dog must be the proud possessor of two testicles, both, obviously, descended into the scrotum. It seems that one of the show dogs had the underwhelming disadvantage of having just one. Undaunted, his ingenious and determined owner did a home op with pliers, sutures and a glass marble, or, as we used to call 'em, glass foggies. No judge ever spotted the deliberate mistake (or even suggested a swap) and the little chap went from trophy to trophy until one fateful day, a bemused judge found himself feeling not two testicles, not one testicle, but, clunk, clink, three testicles! Game, set and match and new balls.

One recent weekend when the temperature reached into the 90s, I understood for the first time why people speak the way-ay the-ey do in Tennessee Williams's pla-a-ys, largely because moving your lips is *exhausting*. Pushkin, being totally caparisoned in fur, took to lying flat on her side under the magazine rack, and worried us all by losing her appetite and thus most of her erstwhile haunches.

'What I do with my dog,' said the lady minicab driver as we hit Cricklewood en route to the BBC and air-conditioning, 'is drench tea-towels in cold water and lay them on him. It's a bit of a shock when you first do it, but he feels the benefit.'

I phoned Jack from my dressing-room with the idea. His excitement was palpable. He couldn't get off the phone quickly enough. When I got home he had the air of a trainee conjurer about him. 'Sit down, love, have a drink,' then, 'Pushkin – come and show Maureen . . .' I can't describe what came into the living-room. It was a Garfield produced by Spielberg. Draped wetly in a white linen handkerchief – you know, the crumpled linen look – she looked like the rolled-up napkin you get at the end of a Chinese meal. On legs. Her face said it all. 'I have not spent nineteen years of my life, 133 in your terms, gaining wisdom and maturity to end up in a wet T-shirt competition for amused householders in North London. I'm a cat, for God's sake!' She managed to get all this across to us whilst walking sideways, for some reason not unassociated with desperate embarrassment, across the room. She then finished off a meaningful performance with a haughty and somewhat ghostly leap on to a chair where she lay, tripe-like, maliciously staining the cushion. It was one of the great silent performances of the age. Like a tiny sheikh. Sort of Yasser Arrocat, if you like.

It has to be said that she made no attempt to shrug the whole thing off. Instead she knelt down on the new kitchen cushions and remained there, drying out, kipping and looking like a tiny Pope kissing alien tarmac.

Perish the thought, but one day she'll perish and we'll bury her under the grapevine because all good grapevines should have a dead cat under them. She's slowing down and takes the stairs with stiff back legs. Sometimes she jumps optimistically on to the dressing-table and misses. Sometimes her eyes look cloudy. I'll never tell her I've always wanted a dog, or that one day I may throw catflaps to the wind and buy a pack of beagles. Then at last I'll be able to invite Mum over for Sunday morning beagles and licks.

Suffolk Catered

The BBC *Holiday* programme have this tendency to ring up and say, 'Feel like a weekend away with a camera crew for company?' and I have developed an alarming inability to refuse. It's when they say, 'Where do you fancy going?'; and flutter a map of the world in front of me that I go blank. It's rather like those questions that go, 'What makes you laugh?' or 'What's your most embarrassing moment?' Your mind goes completely blank and, as Joyce Grenfell once said, 'The only thing I can think of is my own rear view, in trousers.'

So, under the aegis of 'better the devil you know', I suggested Southwold.

I'd visited this quaint and low-lying seaside spot in Suffolk twice before, the first time for a weekend break with my husband when the kids were small, and it proved perfect for rock-pooling and wave-chasing and sand-sifting in a way reminiscent more of *Five on Kirrin Island* than the 'Gelati Moi-Tutti-Frutti Lollipop let's all do the Birdie Dance' type Continental holidays we'd previously given them. The second visit was to play *Re:Joyce!* At the tiny Southwold Summer Theatre run so professionally by Jill Freud from a charming Church Hall. It is perfect Grenfell country and one could almost believe, looking down at rows of brightly painted, individually named beach huts, that time had stopped and Joyce might well pop her head around one and hoot, 'I say! What a simply spiffing day!'

It occurred to me then that my ideal travelling companion would be my mother. She would adore the whole business of filming and a nice break away together would be good for us.

I did try to explain to Mum that she would be *on* screen, up there with me, 'fronting' the show, sort of thing, but I could tell in the preceding phone calls that she was persisting in regarding the whole thing merely as three days' unexpected 'skiving off'. Originally, I'd planned to go with my daughter, but Amy grasped the BBC principle immediately and baulked, 'Appear in front of the camera? *Me*? With *you*? I'd never hold my head up in the Union bar again!'

No, fair's fair. I'd rather be told it like it is. I'm not proud. Not these days, anyway.

So, relatively speaking, my mother was next on the list and, bless her sporting heart, she didn't take too long to make up her mind. The conversation went: 'Hi, Mum, I don't suppose you'd like to come with . . .?'

'Yes, I'd love to. Where?'

So, up on the bus from Hull she came with a 'shocking cold' and the worst backache since simians went from four legs to two and somehow, mysteriously, as the chauffeured car drew up and our luggage made its way into the boot, she became as fit as a flea and positively bristling with energy and joie de vivre, unlike her daughter who was characteristically whey-faced and irritable.

On our first venture out of the Swan Hotel, microphoned up and with a cameraman backing down the street before us, we encountered a similar camera team backing towards him. The director was someone I knew and her squad were covering a genius schoolteacher nearby. Small wonder that a formidable tweed-clad lady rounded on me saying, 'I wish to high heaven you people would stop publicising this town by telling the world how *unspoilt* we are! I mean, there's nowhere to *park* on weekends now!' Ah, such is civilisation.

Well, sorry, ma'am, but unspoilt you are, and though we haven't come on a spoiling mission, I have, in my task as a roving recommender, to report that the air was clean (always excepting the Sizewell signs marring one's approach), the natives friendly and the place sedate. The town is lively with binoculared visitors, bustling with bistros and, after twenty-four hours, I felt better than I had in weeks.

I do love Southwold. It's often painted as the town that time forgot but its memory has lingered on with me. An unchanging harbour the colours not of Hockney but of Turner, a proudly named ferry consisting of old Bob in his row boat, a sedate market-place and a Norman church big enough for most of Suffolk to worship in.

'So you like it here?' I prompted Mum as we walked, microphones down our bras and cameramen backing down the street before us, towards the sea front.

'Ooh, it's fabulous,' she beamed. 'What a wonderful spot. Who'd have thought it? I mean, I've never even heard of it before . . . And isn't it *clean!*' (Mum's greatest accolade, a sort of Egon Lipman, highly polished, five stars.) 'You could eat off the streets. And isn't the Swan marvellous! It's like a five-star hotel, there's *nothing* you could want for. I mean, it's so refined and . . . well, I couldn't fault the place really, it's beautiful.'

'It is,' I nodded then, probingly, for the viewers, 'so would you come here with a friend for a weekend?'

She looked at me as though I'd suggested throwing a bar mitzvah in the Vatican. '*Me?* Come here? Nooooo! What would I *do?* I'd be bored stiff!'

My eyes were jitterbugging warnings to her. I felt like a lighthouse. But

Mum was blissfully unaware that this was perhaps not the way to 'present' to camera and, well – who knows? – perhaps her approach was a healthy one. Certainly it might make for funnier viewing. I can't imagine Judith Chalmers, wishing she *wasn't* here in quite Zelma's fashion.

'Cut!' said Jon, the director.

Later, Jon had arranged to shoot the Town Crier welcoming us into Southwold in traditional fashion. In full regalia and Cap'n Birdseye facial fuzz, he rang his bell, 'Oyez'd' thrice, unrolled his scroll and, in a barnstorming baritone which made Brian Blessed sound like Blossom Dearie, boomed, 'We are proud to welcome Miss Maureen Lipman and her mother, *Zemla*, to Southwold.'

Mother and daughter fell off their bench, Jon called 'Cut!' once more and pointed out politely that although Zelma *was* an unusual name, it would probably be better to say it, since Zemla sounded like a tiger cub in Whipsnade or something you rub on your bunions.

Later that day, we took Bob's ferry over to the delightful and slightly rivalrous village of Walberswick and wandered around the tiny village green. Jon suggested we walk down the slope, chatting, and go into the impressive village craft shop. Whilst they were setting up the camera, Zelma and I looked around the shop for possible gifts. When the shot was set up, Gary, the Production Assistant, called us and we set off from the slope to walk back to the shop.

'Shall you *go* to Clement Freud's wife's house for dinner, then?' Mum threw in as a somewhat cryptic opening gambit to those eight million or so viewers who didn't know that Jill Freud lived nearby and I'd stopped by earlier to say hello.

'Oh *look*, Mum!' I said over-emphatically by way of response. 'There's a lovely craft shop here, let's see what's inside.'

Mum stopped in both our tracks and gave me 'the look' again. 'What do you mean?' she challenged, disbelievingly. 'We've just *been* in there – there was nothing you wanted.'

'Cut!'

The three days fled past. We ate well, the sun shone, I bought a watercolour of bluebells in one of the many local galleries, we laughed a lot, no one more than the person who caused the laughter, and we came home refreshed and replete.

On the quayside I bought fresh-today fish from an extraordinarily chic fishmonger, to butter up my husband. I seemed to buy at least forty quids' London's worth of fish for £18. You could've knocked me down with a wet turbot. Perhaps *that's* why they call it the town that time forgot.

It is a perfect base for exploring nature, wonderful birding, exquisite light for painting, frightfully cultural and did you know that *really* fresh fish doesn't smell at all fishy? I even pointed out a windsurfer struggling to maintain his balance on the sea.

'That's not a *man*,' said Mum.

'Yes it is,' I retorted.

'Don't be ridiculous,' she countered. 'What's he hanging on to then?'

I followed her gaze which was firmly fixed on a hovering seagull a hundred feet up. 'Grim death, Mum. With his beak.'

The crew and 'Zemla' said emotional farewells. Gary was off to Greece the next day. 'Oh, are you going cruising?' said Mum blithely and gazed in astonishment when, not for the first time, the lads' beer went all over the table.

Material Girl

We were driving back from a Sunday stopover in Oxfordshire, full of good cheer from my friend Julia's excellent cooking and empty of pocket after a crumpled linen splurge in a Burford boutique. I could hear my mother's voice in my inner ear as I tried on each garment. 'Well, I'm sorry but if you want my opinion . . .' (What do you call a rhetorical question when it's gone five stages beyond rhetoric? Oratorhetoric?) '. . . that looks like an old rag on you. Look how it's crushed! You haven't even sat down in it. Are you mad? Listen, it's your money but honestly . . . it's like . . . like an old sack! You're not thinking of buying it, are you? Oh, my God!' And by now, of course, I'm trying on the next old sack in a slightly different shade of sacking and buying both in some vain attempt, at 54, to be my own man, as opposed to my own mamma.

Sometimes I do, sneakingly, give the odd garment the 'crush test'. In my mother's case this involved grasping a handful of material from the hem of the garment, turning her head away as though to distance herself from the procedure, pulling a face which indicated she was either removing a lid from a jar of pickled gherkins or lifting a van, then squeezing the fabric with enough pressure to strangle a bison. It was the same face she used on my children to potty-train them, only then it was accompanied by a glottal croak which indicated exerted pressure. I always hated both gestures and expression with a passion bordering on the violent.

Now I love and cherish my mother more than Popeye loves spinach or Madonna loves Guy (she may not by this time but, what the hell!). The fact remains, though, that I am from Venus and my Ma is from Mars.

We disagree on most things – that much we agree on. It may be generational, but I don't think so. From the moment man began making man-made fibres, my mother leapt onto the brandwagon. Tricel, Nylon, Bri-Nylon, Banlon, Polypropylene, Fablon, Crimplene, Tencel – anything which sounds like an emetic doubling as an anti-depressant and Mom adored and ordered it. I guess that after years of dolly tubs and twin tubs, flat irons and airing cupboards, anything which fell into its original shape thirty minutes after you hung it over a bath was A-OK with her. And since I work like a drone bee so that someone else can launder my linen for me, it's all too easy to want to put my skin next to it permanently. I feel the same way about pure cotton – and silk, and soft

241

leather and fresh flowers. I'd rather have one of the real thing than six of the rest.

Before you label me as a snob and a fat cat, let me swear to you that I would only wear a designer label on the outside if the designer was advertising my latest TV play on *his* outside; that I'd rather sport a fake Cartier than a real Rolex, and I make my own fish pie! – whatever that means.

Take hotels. Zelma loves hotels. For her, a good evening on holiday in Spain or Israel would be to come downstairs for dinner in a nice hotel, have coffee in the lounge, then perambulate the main street, popping in all the other hotel lounges to take tea and look at the décor and the clientele. This to me is hell. All I ever want on hols is my own little villa or flat, or an eclectic bedroom in a chintzy B & B run by a couple of fabulous gay men who love to cook. Throw in a lurcher cross whippet, a village, town or seashore to walk to and shoes I can walk and walk and walk in, and I'm as near to bliss as a person can be without access to George Clooney.

Mom hates to walk. Particularly in anywhere verdant. Fair's fair; she has wear and tear in her discs and painful court shoes to boot, and, worryingly, the pain seems to manifest itself whenever we're together. One day it got so bad that I was practically holding her up a hundred yards out of Selfridges. To my amazement, she started the next day brightly by stating: 'I think I'll go to Brent Cross Shopping Centre for the day.'

I all but swallowed my organic oatcake – which is more difficult than it sounds. 'But how will you walk? How will you manage? Shall I get you a taxi?'

'Nooooo! I'll be fine. It doesn't hurt when I'm *looking* for something.'

Then there is the subject of weather. Me, if it's cold I wear a jumper, if it rains I wear a hat. Before Mom goes out she searches the skies like a Hubble telescope. 'What do you think it's going to do? They said rain in the news. It was gorgeous when I opened the curtains, look at it now. Should I take an umbrella?' Getting wet seems to have a similar effect on Zelma as it had on the Wicked Witch of the West. Complicated rainhoods are folded and unfolded, macs of different lengths unfurled. Extreme heat is equally the subject of heated debate. 'But Mom,' I cry, 'this is England. In April. It's . . . the weather.'

Then there's Alternative Medicine. As you know, I will try anything. Someone tells me the best cure for migraine is warm camel dung ingested up the nostrils and I'll go for it. I've got a collection of vitamins that could raise hundreds on *The Antiques Road Show*. Zelma on the other hand relies on the doctor. And pills. 'Why not try reflexology for high blood pressure?' I've been known to wail as I see pill after pill go chasing down after her mug of tea. 'What's that?' And I descend into gloom at the thought of even trying to explain that the reflexologist can get to her blood pressure via her *feet*! Meanwhile, she looks 50 and I look 54.

Sigh. Clothes. Mom loves black, black drains me. Mom loves royal blue. I quite like it on a door. Mom loves emerald green – I dislike it even on a shamrock.

Harrumph! TV: Mom loves watching actual operations with real blood, fly-on-the-wall documentaries and *This Is Your Life*. I don't.

Films: Mom loves *Mrs Doubtfire* and *Brassed Off*. Any film I love – and a lot of them sport sub-titles – will be interrupted after five minutes with 'Don't you think this is *slow*?'

Look, the list is endless. You say tamayto and I say tomato, you potato and I say potahto . . . (Does anyone actually say potahto?)

And love? Yes, there we differ again. I love her and she, amazingly enough after reading this, apparently loves me.

Surprise Partly

Mother was going to be seventy. It was inevitable to everyone but mother. The line to Hull crackled with suggestions.

Me: Would you like to go to a health farm?
Mother: Nooooo! What for? I'm alright. I'm not even thinking about it.
Me: Would you like me to send you and Amy to Jersey for a week?
Mother: Nooooo! I don't want you to send me anywhere. Honestly. I mean it. I'm just going to forget it. Why spend all that money for nothing?

Anyone less schooled in the art of the subliminal message could have accepted her emphatic denial as mere emphatic denial. After forty-six years at the Humberside College of Advanced Sub-Text, this cum laude graduate started planning the surprise party immediately.

Invitations were sent out a few weeks before the event: 'It is Zelma's Seventieth Birthday on 15 April. Zelma thinks no one knows this but herself and a man who once worked at Somerset House . . . For once, Zelma is wrong.'

It warned guests to enclose receipts with gifts, because the exchanging of them would be the best birthday present of all, and, when RSVPing, if Zelma, who was now staying with us, were to answer the phone, to please say they have phoned for her recipe for Stuffed Monkeys. No, it's not what you think – Zelma isn't a taxidermist. Heavens, no. She won't even take a mini-cab. No, Stuffed Monkeys are her speciality biscuits which are deliciously chewy, sit just above your windpipe for about a week and have as much resemblance to anything simian as I do. But I digress.

At this point, caterers were consulted, the event priced and the host and hostess given a warm milk and brandy. A hasty phone call secured the support of Judy Bastyra, neighbour and cookery writer. A planning meeting was planned and the codename 'Smiley's People' was agreed upon. The next time Judy rang and said 'Re Smiley's People', I thought she'd gone raving mad and said so.

There is no one on earth more blessed than I with good friends. Lynn is my Californian friend. We go running together of a morning when she

244

hasn't got a bad knee and I haven't got a migraine, which means roughly the Wednesday before St Agnes Eve. This day we ran to The Balloon Shop and, £32 later, we ran out of money and ran home. The Balloon Shop! I ask you! Recession-ridden East Finchley shops opening and closing like a bridegroom's pyjama bottoms (you should pardon my language) and The Balloon Shop is thriving. (Since I wrote this it's gone up, up and away!)

The cake. A three-act drama involving dozens of eggs and a concept. It was to be a large Marks & Spencer's carrier bag with humorous lettering on the theme (Mum's relationship with the Customer Service Department being somewhat closer than Richard's relationship with Judy) of refundable cake. Lynn would make it. I would ice it. Astrid, my artistic American friend, would supervise. (By this time Zelma had arrived in London, so we had to tell her we were going for a run. A five-hour run. With a dozen eggs.) We arrived at Astrid's with no icing sugar and a migraine. Astrid iced. I sipped herbal tea with Nurofen and went off to my evening performance at the theatre, leaving Astrid to clear up a kitchen which looked like William Hill's after Grand National Day. Like I said, I'm blessed with my friends.

By now, the phone was ringing on a regular basis. I'd invited all her Hull friends who I knew would be in London staying with their children, plus old friends of ours, plus the odd friend of hers who didn't mind getting on a dawn bus from Hull on a Sunday morning, plus my globe-trotting brother from Brussels and his five children from the five corners of the world. This, with eight shows a week and one hard-pressed secretary, Jacquie, was faintly more foolish than challenging Anneka to a 'Who's got the tightest bum?' competition. There were seventy acceptances and that was before the 'I've got a guest staying . . . Can I bring . . .?' syndrome raised it to eighty-four.

Tables, chairs and helpers were hired, glasses and crockery borrowed and a speech written in between Acts I and II. Every time the phone rang at home, one of us grabbed it and immediately went into the garden, which was fine in mild weather but insane in the middle of a thunderstorm. The condemned woman appeared not to notice our indifference to inclement climes.

The birthday itself was a couple of days before Party Day. She was thrilled with her presents. She loved her cards and was only temporarily miffed by the lack of her son's presence and presents on the day. How could we tell her that that weekend all seven of them were coming over? And that he and his wife had given up an all-expenses paid trip to Hawaii in order to be with her? Still, by the evening, she was in merry mood as I drove her to see *Crazy For You*, the hottest ticket in town.

'How was it?' I asked later.

'Ye . . . es, it was very good, you know, nice but daft. The scenery was *wonderful*!'

'How about the show itself?'

'Ye . . . es . . . you know . . . it was a musical . . . What can you say? Far-fetched.'

Two days to go and she still hadn't tumbled it. She met her chums for lunch at Selfridges, but the cat was still in the bag. Incredible. Driving her to town with Amy, I heard myself say, 'Jacquie's daughter is coming on Sunday.'

'Coming where?'

The British Museum came into sight. 'To . . . to . . . the exhibition!' I blurted.

'What exhibition?' Mother was on to it like a lurcher.

'The Georgia O'Keefe'/'The Turner' said Amy and I adamantly and simultaneously.

'I thought you had people to brunch,' she accused. I had earlier embarked on a fib that Tom Conti was coming over. This was to ensure that when Lynn took Zelma over to another friend, Lizzy, for Sunday morning coffee, she would dress as a woman of certain years might well dress for scrambled eggs with Shirley Valentine's rejuvenator.

'Yes . . . Well . . . *afterwards*! Oh, I don't know! I'm tired! We'll see!'

One night before the day after, I brought home a card from a friend. After another frantic day and twenty-two phone calls, I wasn't thinking and gave it to her. 'I'm so sorry I can't be with you at your party,' it said.

'What party?' said Zelma.

'*Whatalovelycard!*' I yelled, snatching it, 'I *must* show Jack, *Ja-a-ck* . . .' I ran from the room, stuffed the card behind a radiator and tried to give myself mouth-to-mouth resuscitation.

I slept fitfully and woke up stiff-necked like a meerkat. Mother came down. She wasn't well, she wasn't sure she could go out, she wondered if she should phone Lynn and cancel . . . Poor woman, we had her dressed, made up and out the door before she could blow on her porridge. It was 10.15am. At 10.30am the massed brigade of Mothers in Support of Women with Mothers descended on Muswell Hill.

Salmons with cucumber scales fanned out beside Thai salads, tri-coloured rice and watermelon baskets of fruit salad. 'Groan' said the table. Flower arrangements flowered, three charming Irish girls set up a helium pump in the hall and balloons ballooned, and the cake was smuggled in, Astrid still licking food colorant from her leggings. Ice clattered not a dustbin, wine cooled. The sun came out, outside furniture was hosed down, inside furniture arranged by me and rearranged by Jack . . . A hush fell. One o'clock prompt and the first guests crept stagily in . . . the story of Zelma's whereabouts was told seventy times, Jack positioned himself on the stairs with the video, Adam tried to tell him how to use it. 1.40: no sign of Lynn and Zelma. I rang Lizzy. She said they'd gone to a deli in St John's Wood . . . my heart began to Lambada . . .

'Quick, they're here! Everyone into the two rooms save Geoff's family and ours. She's walking down the road.'

'It won't start! It won't work!' – Jack on the video.

'Turn it on, dad' – Adam on automatic pilot.

'RRRRing!' – the door bell. My heart and I opened the door and Louie Ramsay ducked in hissing 'She's seen me, I'm late, oh shit!' before being yanked into the kitchen.

This time, when the bell rang, it was Zelma. 'Geoffrey! Phillip! Mei-Mei! Joey!' her voice could get no higher, but did. Then out burst the Hull contingent. 'Nora! Ruby! Rae! Helen! Aaaargh!' Jodrell Bank must surely have been on the alert . . . 'David! Kim! Aaagh! Look at the baby!' Lynn and I hugged each other. 'We did it, we did it!'

In my speech I ran through her early life; her first stage role at The College of Commerce School in *The Marvellous History of St Bernards*; her appearance 'Oooh, I was beautiful! I had the most gorgeous curly hair!'; her first boyfriend; her first job at the aircraft factory when all the men would whistle the Laurel and Hardy theme as she walked through their ranks, head down, face purple.

There were tributes, too, for her bravery and care looking after Dad, then her sister-in-law, Rita, till the end, and special greetings, surprisingly enough, from the Customers' Exchange Point at Marks & Spencer's, Debenhams and Binns of Hull, and the makers of Redoxon and Woolworths' 'pic'n'mix'.

A video machine was then brought in, to her patent horror, with a label which read:

No, you won't have to schlepp it back to Hull, it will be driven!
Yes, you will be able to work it.
Yes, it does have a device like Lily's got, for recording
while you are away.
Yes, there *are* tapes included!

Her delight was now transparent, so Jack added, 'and the first instalment's due in July!'

(It worked. Since Zelma moved into her new flat, there isn't a single inhabitant who hasn't been subjected to the twin indoctrination ceremony of the video of *Re:Joyce!*, an interval of tea and cake, and *My Seventieth*

Party, starring Z Lipman. I try not to think about it, as I get a bit hot around the ears.)

The final presentation was six advanced driving lessons to lessen the chance of, once again, backing out of the drive into her own back wall, involving lengthy insurance actions on car and wall. (I remember my mother taking lessons in her forties. She'd had sixty-three lessons to date when my brother took her up the street for a practice. As they reached the end of the street, Geoff said, 'OK, Mother, change down.'

'What?' she exclaimed, 'on my own?'

Geoff expressed some disbelief.

'Oh no,' she rejoined firmly, 'Mr Middleyard always holds my hand!'

Some years later she was fully weaned and passed her test. Alone. She still, however, drives as though waiting for Mr Middleyard to help her change gear.)

The loveliest part of the video is the sight of everyone who knows and loves her, rocking with laughter and clutching at each other with recognition. And no one laughed more than the Golden Girl herself.

My mother and my muse, Zelma, died four years ago, so there will be no scramble to phone Interflora come Mothers' Day to buy her the bouquet of flowers she so hated to receive. 'I'n't it a waste of money?' she'd say crossly whenever flowers arrived for her from a loved one. 'Now I'll have to arrange them. And I've just got all my surfaces clean.' Then she would clamber up a stepladder, fetched from a broom cupboard, lean into a high shelf at a precarious angle, bring down a dimpled glass vase, chunter her way back, one-handed, down the ladder. 'Anyway, they'll be dead in a week.' Then, hiss – the water went into the vase, newspaper was spread out, leaves were grabbed off stalks and flowers were unceremoniously shoved in vase. 'I'm hopeless at doing flowers,' she would say, glumly. 'Now, a planted bowl . . . *sniff* . . . well, that's a different thing altogether.'

It was equally useless sending champagne to her pristine sheltered accommodation flat in Hull. 'Ooh, I hate wine. It makes my eyes go small!' Chocolates were a no-no, too, because I knew from experience that she would keep them 'for best' or, worse, wrap them up and bring them to London over Christmas, in case one of my friends asked her to lunch and she found herself 'empty-handed'.

As for taking her out for a meal – this was a sin more Cardinal than shoe polish. 'Why anybody would want to sit in a restaurant and eat luke-warm food, for all that money, is beyond me. What for? I'm not even hungry. I just fancy that cheese on toast that Jack makes – ooh, I love that, don't you?'

If she was staying with me in London over what I can only describe as

'Hallmark Day', I might well have booked a show for her. If she was here now, then *Cabaret* or *The Sound of Music* would have done the trick. I can hear her so clearly: 'Did you think that girl was the best? Connie? I did. They were all saying she looked like you. I couldn't see it, could you?' Actually, I could, and A A Gill's comment that Ms Fisher looked like a cross between Maureen Lipman and Lassie did not pass without a grin and a bark in our house.

Even then, after seeing the exorbitant show, she would have arrived home looking vaguely aggrieved, flung herself into the nearest chair to the door and said, 'Ooh, somebody make me a cup of tea, will they? My back's like a vice and my feet are frozen into stumps.'

Inevitably, the question would have arisen as to whether she had enjoyed the show and her reply would never cease to bring a purse to my lips and a zip to my purse: 'Yeee . . . s. It was very good. Nice. You know – ever so long and . . . well, I don't know, it was a musical – y'know, far-fetched. There was ever such a nice woman sitting next to me, though. Ooh, she was attractive, auburn hair, curly, and she'd come all the way from Margate with her daughter-in-law. We had a lovely chat. She was a teacher – the daughter-in-law – ever-so well spoken. I treat them to an ice-cream in the Interval.' (Treat. Pronounced *trett*. Instead of 'treated'. The past tense of the verb 'to treat'. It's a word that only Hull people use, alongside *upsetment* and *pikelet* and *tenfoot*. I was well into my fifties before I realised there was anything suspect about any of them.)

My father was thirteen years older than my mother, a fact that she seldom allowed him to forget, and he was famously forgetful. They had only known each other for three weeks before they became engaged. Mom, shy, pretty and just 19, was already engaged to someone else but Dad, with his gents' outfitters shop in the centre of town, was considered more of a catch. She was hugely suggestable and probably not in love with either man but did what she was told. She sent back the first engagement ring in a tin of Stothard's Head and Stomach Powders and the rest was history. My history.

The story goes that shortly after my parents' wedding he took her into town to the Regal Cinema, but grew quickly tired of the movie, which I suppose we would now call a chick's flick – Dad favoured Westerns or something with George Raft in it. So he left her dabbing her nose with a hanky and went across to the Station Hotel for a game of snooker. After the film was over, Mom stood outside for half an hour waiting for her new groom to pick her up. It never happened, so she got on a bus and went home. He wasn't there either and it was only after further footwork that it was discovered that Dad had come out of the hotel having totally forgotten that he was married and gone home to his mother's for his usual dinner.

He was pretty unlikely to have remembered Mother's Day but he always told her that she 'had the rest of 'em knocked into a cocked hat', which I guess was the nearest she was ever going to get to a declaration of love.

The fact that I'm still getting laughs out of my late mother should cause you no concern, by the way. She would be thrilled skinny by it. 'Ooh, tell them what I said about going to Bernard, the hairdresser for a blow-job.' My problem then was how to deliver a story whose punch-line had just been announced to all and sundry. When all and sundry were, of course, doubled up with laughter. 'I didn't think anything of it,' she'd say, wide-eyed and incredulous.

It's a wonderful bonus to me and a comfort too, that both my daughter Amy and I can still reduce a room to helpless mirth by impersonating her voice, her timing and her homely observations. She was the master of the rhetorical question: 'Ooh, doesn't it soon get to ten to ten?' she'd coo. 'Ooh, I say, aren't eggs useful?' 'Doesn't a black skirt cover a multitude of sins?' And then be amazed by our reaction. It's a form of immortality, I tell myself, that we carry Zelma around in minds and hearts and, without pause for thought, on the tips of our tongues. And that's every day, not just on manmade days of remembrance. It is at specific occasions, though, that I feel her spirit in the room. At any kind of present-giving she would stand with a huge black plastic sack and crumple up the wrapping paper into it the second it came off the gift. At parties and celebrations, she wiped surfaces moodily and said, 'Isn't it a load of fuss about nothing, though – go on, admit it – you work and slave your fingers to the bone and then everyone just eats it and all you've got left is the mess to clean up!'

'Oh, I know that I owe what I am today, to that dear little lady, so old and grey . . .' went the song, 'to that dear little Yiddishe Mama . . .'

'Hang on,' she's saying, 'that's not me! Grey? Me? My hair was Golden Chestnut to the very end and I never got old!' She never will. She was the only woman I've ever met who was perfectly satisfied with her looks. 'I love the way I look,' she would say, quite matter-of-factly, 'I wouldn't change a thing if I could.'

I still have some of the cards she sent to me. They featured hearts and flowers and horseshoes and say 'dearest daughter' and some of the daftest verses ever composed: *On this special day, tho' we're far apart/I treasure your presence in my heart/When you're next in town please look me up/And Joy will runneth out of my cup.*

My own kids would always present me with home-made Mothers' Day cards. I may get one still from my daughter and a bunch of garage flowers from the lad. They were always brilliant – witty, topical, artistic and fiercely competitive cards that I accepted as the absolute norm, and I say that with totally partisan bias. Isn't that what every Mod (sic) got on

Mothers' Day? I've kept many of them and all of Jack's, which were both loving and hilarious. Sometimes I've happened on one of his cards on a birthday or near to a special occasion. More precious than diamonds, it will fall out of a jewellery box or an old folder and make my heart plummet.

I think I can say, honestly, that I no longer expect cards or presents from my thirtysomethings. Nor that they will ask me out to an expensive lunch or a far-fetched musical or tell me I'm the best mother this side of Barnstaple. When I mentioned to my son that it was Mothering Sunday his reaction was: 'Oh hell, is it? I still haven't got you your Christmas present.'

So come Mothering Sunday, I shall be mothering my friends Trevor and Donald over scrambled eggs, smoked salmon, grilled haloumi, toasted bagels, and a nice drop of pomegranate juice for their antioxidants. They will bring their dog Piccolo and I will give Warren the rabbit a piece of fresh parsley, clean the beloved Basenji's teeth with chicken-flavoured toothpaste, and watch her with a misty-eyed look as she stands by the door, impatiently waiting for the guests. If either or both my kids and all their friends turn up I shall simply crack more eggs and a few jokes and have the mother of all brunches.

Let It All Hang In

I was sucking the toe of an ex-presidential candidate recently, when the mobile rang. I switched on the descrambler and in a heavy Columbian accent said, 'Jello?'. It was someone asking me to talk about my recent conversion to Islam on a morning television show alongside a heavy metal rock star who'd given up smoking Odor-Eaters, and an international cover girl who recently admitted on national TV that she'd been abused as a toddler by the village nit nurse.

I mean, what in the global village is going on? Is it really better out than in, as the defrocked bishop said to the soft porn actress, or has confession become nothing more than a sound career move?

Let she who is without stones throw the first sin. Well, all right. Some years ago I participated in a programme called *Mothers by Daughters* and to my amazement, whilst talking quite animatedly to a sympathetically inclined Bel Mooney, my eyes filled up to the brim as I touched on something touching and I blubbed all over my lilac mohair sweater, without missing a cue or slipping a syllable. In fairness, I had no idea I was going to do it. I thought it would just be a few affectionate quotes and the odd deadly impersonation. But no. I learned something that day: that nothing makes better television than slow pain on fast exposure.

'Do you want to stop?' asked Bel, sincerely.

'No-o-ooo. I'm OK . . . sniff . . . sorry . . . no, carry on, really, sniff, I'm fine . . .' The show, of course, must go on and even if it doesn't, they can edit round the gap. Let's face it, I must have been aware, even in my lachrymosity, that cracking good TV was being made. I've never had such a mailbag, before or since, and all from people identifying with feelings that I had thought were entirely personal. 'It was so wonderful to hear someone actually saying what I'd only ever *thought*.' 'I couldn't believe what you said about your mother. It could have been me talking!'

Which left me wondering. Should it take a revelation from a total stranger to reveal your own heartache? If so, then, what are best friends for? And priests? And shrinks? And good literature? And *mothers*, for God's sake?

Here we are, the generation who buys our magazines for headlines like 'The great swallowing debate: should we or shouldn't we?' and 'Your orgasm: is it enough?'. Who supply boysenberry-flavoured condoms to our sixteen-year-olds and shout 'Gerremoff' at oiled Chippendales. And really, we are no more able to communicate our deep-seated problems than were our great-grandparents. Or perhaps we just can't distinguish between fact and fiction – truth and *True Confessions*.

I mean, *must* we know what amused Mona Lisa? Whatever happened to imagination, for Heaven's sake? I'd be just as happy to believe that she was suppressing a grin at something her mother-in-law said over the fuselli, or that she'd found a way of clenching her stomach muscles just to give her something to do while Mr da Vinci went on and on telling those terrible old jokes of his than any amount of pedantic speculation on with whom she may or may not have spent the previous night in a cabana on the Lido.

How much more interesting and satisfying to kiss and *not* tell, or even kiss and tell something completely different. What's so appealing about revealing? The child who will loudly and ingenuously inquire, 'Mummy, why has that lady got a beard?' will not necessarily answer as frankly when you ask whether she likes school or not. 'I like jelly!' she may say, and we'll all laugh and ignore the fact that it's a diversionary statement.

Once in the public eye you quickly learn to field the inevitable questions asked by the public at large . . . like 'How do you learn your lines?' (the Thespian equivalent of asking Albert Roux how he turns his oven on), and the inevitable, 'Has anyone ever told you how much younger/prettier/thinner you look in real life?' (Yes. Everyone. And I'd much rather look younger, prettier and thinner to twelve million viewers.) And, 'How do you manage being a wife and mother *and* an actress?' Answer: badly.

Then there are the questions that journalists ask you, to fill a small gap between an article about Regal colonic irrigation and a colour picture of Dawn French on a day bed. They come accompanied by a faxed replica of the same questionnaire as completed by Mariella Frostrup in last week's issue and the Dalai Lama in the week's before, and a fulsome note from the journalist saying, 'I know you must be very busy with requests like these, but . . .' Usually one fills 'em in last thing at night with *Eurotrash* corroding the brain on the cathode ray tube, a plate of banana on toast and the prospect of a day off.

Q: *What word or phrase do you most overuse?*
A: 'Yes.'
Q: *How does a girl know when she's really a woman?*
A: 'When she compares her wage packet with a fellow doing the same job.
Q: *What really bores you?*
A: 'Questionnaires.'

Not too difficult the questions. Not overly interesting the answers. But what would *you* do if you received the *Express* Questionnaire, as I did, a few weeks ago? 'It is lighthearted,' said the letter, 'and in the best possible taste.'

Oh yes? It began with an aphrodisiac question which I could easily have answered by pleas to the poacher to lay off killing the rhino for the lacklustre quality of its horn, but I doubted whether too many poachers read the *Express* and those who did would write me off as a leftie . . . 'my hair extensions are not tested on endangered voles'. Loony. I left a gap in which I doodled a drunken-looking frizzy-haired beast whom I later christened Afro-dizzy Yak, and continued downhill.

The second question was: *Barbara Cartland and Debbie Reynolds waited until their wedding night. Where and when did you lose your virginity?* Now the truth might be interesting since he was the handsomest man I've ever seen, before or since, and I was so flattered and shattered that he chose *me* that to this day I swear I was unconscious throughout, so instead I wrote: 'I was queuing up in Waitrose for a pound and a half of coley for the cat's tea, when I happened to notice it was gone. I rang King's Cross Lost Property only to be told that anything not reported missing for thirty years would probably have been sold.'

The next question was *Do you think sex cures insomnia?* Since the truth is that my old man can fall asleep mid-sentence, mid-flossing – mid-riff even – and I tend to require forty or fifty minutes' good solid mental filing of every worry, panic, deadline or fear of retribution I have in the world before I slip soundlessly into full, threshing about REM, I thought long and hard before writing, 'I find my insomnia is at its peak whilst I'm having sex.'

I was beginning to enjoy this: next please.

How many lovers do you admit to? I took the Bic between my teeth and wrote 'I admit to all my lovers, and so far they've been very understanding about it.' The nice thing about this questionnaire was that patently no one was ever going to use one word of my cocky replies. Onwards.

What is the most flattering thing you've ever been told in bed? I would have loved to give them 'You are the best', but, instead I wrote, 'Darling, he's done a fabulous scar!'

By now I was in great danger of having what can best be described as a good time . . .

'Whoever loved that loved not at first sight' quoth Shakespeare. Do you believe in sex on the first night? Thoughts of this took me back to the handsomest man I ever met, and I had to put my head in the ice-making compartment of the fridge. I wrote, 'Personally, I'm usually so nervous on a first night – what with the critics and the reviews and everything – that I try not to have sex until after the curtain call.'

And now for the next question in this crucial cultural assessment of man's most basic, pre-Sharon-Stone-age, instinct: *If you woke up in the morning to find you had changed sex, what would be the first thing you would do?* Yes, you got it in one: 'Phone my wife.'

So, penultimately, *Where and when was your most memorable sexual experience on holiday?* 'There's no comedic competition here, it was, without question, the breakfast buffet at the King David Hotel in Jerusalem. Don't believe me? Don't knock it till you've tried it . . . and perfectly permissible between consenting adults in the privacy of someone else's dining-room.

And now the end is nigh and as I reach the final question: *When do the partners you have had sex with* (sic) *say they lost their virginity, and . . .* and . . . *do you think they were lying?*

So I'm forced to fabricate again and devil take the hairy palms: 'Mostly they say it was Michaelmas Eve 1964 after a heavy Lamb Pasanda and a crate of Advocaat 'neath an inky sky, in the back seat of a Reliant Robin.' *Do you think they were lying?* 'Partially, and partially squatting.'

I can't help wondering as I post off the coupon, whether *anyone* answered this absurd questionnaire earnestly and, if so, why? Looking back through all of the ones I've kept over the years I came across a slightly more original question than usual. It said 'Can you sum yourself up in not more than fifteen words?' and, underneath, someone, who I can only assume was me, had written: 'She told everything and revealed nothing. With laughs.'

Personally, I think one of the unsung virtues of our times is stoicism. I'm all for a bit of quiet bottling up. It may stall your career, it may even decimate your dreams and eventually come out as a cluster migraine, but it stimulates the creative juices and saves the kids the embarrassment of turning on the telly, opening up the tawdry tabloids or being persecuted in the playground when Mummy's felt the need to tell that nice radio psychiatrist that she used to have afternoon love-ins with Cary Grant dressed as an oven-ready chicken and that she began life as a stevedore called Dwayne in Nantucket.

Cambridge Blues

I found myself in Cambridge – seat of learning, cradle of academia, world centre for spy recruitment and supplier of satirists to the Sixties – filming Jack's BBC play, at that time titled *Eskimo Day*, subject to the author finding something he liked better, which he did roughly twice a day. It was about Cambridge candidates going for their interviews. Actually, it was about parents 'letting go' of their kids. You might say there were parallels in my life.

We'd been filming for a week and the sun was shining down heartlessly on the stone portals of historic Queens' College, the birds were singing on the ancient spires and the punts were punting smoothly along the glassy Cam river . . . This was not good news for the cast and crew of *Nice Here Inuit* or whatever they were calling it that day.

Then it rained. All day long. Great sad, dreary, endless shards of rain fell on filmmakers and actors as we huddled together in damp clumps. Anoraks balanced on the shoulders of our real anoraks, which we couldn't get wet, large umbrellas were held high by weak-wristed wardrobe assistants, and acting shoes were held in hands until the last minute to replace wet loafers. David Ross and I played the working-class parents of Neil (Ben Sandiford) and over and over the three of us walked the 25 yards up to the approach to Queens' College with suitable trepidation on our faces.

Camera operator:	'Sorry, we'll have to go again – water spots on the lens.'
Sound operator:	'One more time, please – there was a plane.'
1st Assistant:	'First positions, please, last time now. Very good, actors! Passers-by, would you *please* not look at the camera!'

'Does anyone want to see anything before we go again?' shouts the 1st Assistant. 'Yes,' chunters one of the largest riggers. 'Me muvver!'

It is very rare for 'one more time' to be called because an *actor* is dissatisfied. We know our place in the pecking order. First in the lunch queue – last in the decision-making process. Rest of the time, keep your head down. That's OK. Gives us more gossiping time.

The prop men hosed down the streets with industrial pipes, to make the ground match up with previously filmed rainsodden ground, and the passers-by looked mystified as gallons of water poured out for reasons to which they were not privy.

The best part of working away from home is *not* working. A day off is a heady mixture of irresponsibility, mischief and idleness. David Ross and I, being inveterate shoppers, ignored the medieval splendours on offer for the entirely evil pleasures of Marks & Spencer. Several shirts and jackets later, guilt entirely assuaged by token socks for our other halves, we shared a plate-sized amaretto cake for brunch and headed off for the cinema. There were only five people watching *While You Were Sleeping* that day and two of them were us. I began to snuffle ten minutes into this Cinderella saga and soaked David's hanky to a pulp. He just sniffed, and pretended not to.

A damp couple of hours later, we left. It was 3.55pm and I couldn't help noticing that *The Bridges of Madison County* was beginning in Cinema B at four o'clock. He bought the tickets, I bought the popcorn and we lurched back in. It would end in tears. It did. I, who had read the book in a two-hour sitting and been appalled by its tacky tricksiness, was enchanted by Eastwood and Streep to the extent that my tears became a medical complaint and my body weight plummeted. I hadn't had such a good time since Bambi's mother popped her clogs.

Cambridge reminds me, subtly, of Stratford-upon-Avon. It has a slight attitude problem. As in, 'What we have here is eternal. Don't like it? Don't come again. Next!' Reasonable enough if you look at it from their point of view. Why would they want 70-odd rogues and vagabonds queuing up for pasta with pesto on plastic plates from a van in the middle of Jesus Green? Take a film crew to a verdant hamlet in Connemara with a post office, a blacksmiths and a pub called The Skillet and Shillelagh and you'll be welcomed with open cash registers. This is not quite so true of historic, international centres of knowledge with one-way traffic systems. Here, mostly you just get right up their patrician noses. A violent little lady in Country Casuals asked me what was going on as we filmed by a churchyard. 'It's a TV play,' I whispered. 'What's it about?' she insisted. 'Erm . . . Cambridge,' I replied. 'Well,' she said huffily, 'I've never seen such a bunch of scruffs in all my life!'

One day I wandered on to the set before my own scenes were due to be shot. It was a breathtaking picture – Tom Wilkinson and David Ross, playing parents of interviewees, crossed the famous Mathematical Bridge into Queens' College, out-vying each other to extol the brilliance of their offspring. Two extras placed in punts on either side of the bridge were to glide past on 'Action'. The day was bright and the air heavy with expectation as the camera prepared to roll towards the bridge on specially laid steel tracks.

It was at this point that a heartfelt cry rent the air, shattering the fragile peace. 'For Christ's sake!' bellowed the director. 'Where's the fucking punt?' It was perfect. I firmly believed we might have finally found our title.

Later on in the day, leaning up against the curved niches in the entrance to Queens', there was a lull in the shooting as we waited for clouds to cover the sun. David and I decided to launch into an improvised busking session, using lips for double bass, blown cheeks for trumpets, sibilant teeth for cymbals. Obviously impressed, the crew chucked a twopence piece at our feet. Mere seconds later, the world's most malicious pigeon crapped on my head. It received a standing ovation from the crew.

Back to the hotel, a large Campari and soda, my one cigarette of the day and Chinese food to follow. There are many reasons why I became an actress. These have been several of them.

Knowing Pains

I love my kids. I always have, but never more than now when they are so very tolerant of me.

I gaze at them with awe when they set off alone for foreign climes. I'm rapturously grateful when they tell me their plans and over the moon if they ask for the money for them, which on the whole they don't.

My gratitude is touching when they announce they will be coming home to eat and can they bring five friends. When they party in the garden, I watch them jealously through the windows and wonder wistfully whether what has just made them fall over with laughter would be even vaguely comprehensible to their mother.

I also love their friends. Nothing thrills me more than the sight of Will's size elevens spanning my hall or Melanie's Fiesta blocking my drive. I like to come into the kitchen when scores of coffee cups and a picked clean fridge herald an all-night, all-girls' sit-up and I cherish the sound of massed baritone mirth from the one hundred and seventy-eighth viewing of A *Life of Brian*.

I don't even mind being turfed out of my living-room because they need it for *Red Dwarf* and I'm tickled pink by the memory of Adam and Will celebrating the end of 'A' Levels with tea and toast and the *Guardian* crossword. Rebellious coves! And I'm reduced to a blubber by the sound of two six-foot lads teaching each other to cook and ride a bicycle respectively.

When I come home from a hard day in the mind-slamming world of sit-com, the sound of an electronic guitar from an upstairs room is music to my years. And the pleasure of one of them perched on our bed at night, tucking us in and kissing us goodnight before settling down to a video or two, is almost unparalleled.

Occasionally we sit, fogey-like, at the table whilst they clear up, appallingly, after dinner, or make us a coffee, and we watch them exchange derisory glances at one of our childish witticisms. At that point the fogeys have been known to get giggles of the 'church' variety and resort to a lot of mouth covering and shoelace tying.

I don't know where the time has gone, forgive the yawning cliché, since they needed us, looked up to us and totally tied us down. When, suddenly, did I become an amusing pet, inevitably putting my foot in it whilst trying too hard to be a cool parent?

'Thanks for doing so much of the clearing up, love,' I said to Adam last night.

'I *have* cleared up!' he countered defensively. 'Look at all the stuff in the draining rack . . .'

'No! I *meant* it!' I cried. 'I meant, "thank you".'

'Oh, sorry,' he grinned. 'I just found it difficult to accept that there wasn't an element of sarcasm in your statement.'

There was a lot of history in that response.

Meanwhile, the University Kid is home and we've managed to overcome the first powerfully charged weeks where we don't mention the state of her room for so long that it is *bursting* out of every sentence we utter.

'Did you sleep OK, darling?' ('In spite of the fourteen black plastic bin-liners full of books surrounding your unmade bed, darling'); and 'Will you be on the phone much longer, darling?' ('Because if you've got time to talk to Emma and Melanie and Emma Jane and Neal and Emma then you've got time to pick five tons of *ironed* clothes off the floor, darling!').

I've managed to learn all the important features like who goes out with whom and who used to go out with whom and who wouldn't be seen dead with whom. Also, I never ask any question concerned with the 'W' word. The four-letter expletive deleted word. I'll say it quietly in case anyone's listening if you *promise* not to repeat it . . . 'work', because that is not what University is about, is it? It's nothing to do with essays and reference books and theses and lectures, it's about getting legless and getting off and getting together and basically learning to live without, well, me, really.

I was watching, as is my wont, a stunning programme on mountain parrots. The mating was spectacular, the brooding and hatching meticulous. Hungry mouths open to be fed, beak to beak, dowdy grey down waiting to be changed into glorious plumage. Such single-minded instinct to raise 'em, rear 'em, make sure they've got all *their* instincts right. Then, whoosh! One day, a gust of wind, a flap of orange-crested wing and, 'Ciao, fogeys, I'm off backpacking across Nepal. No thanks, I *don't* need any seeds, I've got plenty of my own, if you take my meaning, nudge, nudge, wink, wink.' And that's it. That was a late parrot. That parrot had ceased to be.

The strongest note of optimism is that it is only in one's own experience of parenting that one gains knowledge of how difficult we made it for our own parents. This was never more strongly illustrated than last week when Amy sat in the garden reading her father's latest play which revolves around a group of parents accompanying their offspring to their Cambridge interviews. Some time later, she called me over in a rather strained voice. 'Can I borrow you for a moment?' and I found her spilling over with the kind of tears I dimly remember from her twelve-year-old school-days of 'best friend betrayal'.

'Poor Dad,' she sobbed. 'I feel so awful. I didn't know he felt like an old Eskimo – I feel so terrible.'

By now, we were both awash – a not unusual phenomenon chez Rosenthal – the men just stare at us, more in pity than in sorrow. 'But that's how it is, darling. It's supposed to be like that. Dad's fine now, and there's a whole play come out of it and that's wonderful because it makes people think and understand.'

Still, when I think of every stage and its accompanying worry – 'Will they ever walk, will they ever sleep through the night, ever socialise, stop clinging to me, learn to read, learn to share, go to school by bus, ever go out, every stay *in*?' – I have to smile and shake my head in a way only American moms in movies ever seem to do. Everything in its own time, Maureen, the instincts are all there – all that's required of you is to be there and be consistent.

There is a tribe in the Kalahari Desert, I'm told by the fascinating book, *The Language Instinct* by Stephen Pinker, which builds complex sand sculptures to teach their babies to stand, to crawl and, finally, to walk. The children do these things, ultimately, at exactly the same growth stage as do any other babies in the world, but the parents feel as though *they've* done it for them. And the children let them take the credit. For a while anyway.

Good Risibility

The doorbell had just rung. It was a Sunday, our wedding anniversary and, for a treat, we were all watching Manchester United thrash Leeds United to within an inch of its FA Cup life. We were two goals up, so my husband went to the door. There was a slight scuffle, a thump and a half-strangled shout and I heard him moan, 'They've done us again!' Even after this, when he could have been lying in a bleeding heap of mugged citizen, it was hard for my son and I to tear ourselves away from Ryan Giggs's neat corner flicks, but we did. There in the hallway was a helpless Jack. Beside him is a large traffic cone covered in silver and white with the words 'Happy Anniversary' on the rim and an assortment of Jelly Babies and clotted creams stuck around the perimeter. Alongside is a large amber warning lamp. Flashing. And we can't find out how to turn it off.

'How did they get them in?' I asked, knowing immediately the identity of 'they'.

'Left them on the step and scuttled back to the car,' said Jack.

'Now what do we do?' I wiped away a tear. 'Our move, I guess.'

It was the culmination of a continuing saga of mutual harassment between consenting adults which began on a quiet weekend at the glorious culinary retreat of Chewton Glen in the company of two friends, the Morrows. On the drive down to Dorset we became mildly, then wildly, hysterical over the number of traffic cones bordering, abutting, nay, even pie-frilling, the road. I shall become even more of a bore on this subject later.

They were like a bad attack of acne – 'They'll only spread if you pick 'em!' They were single file, double file, rolling about, teetering in circles, copulating, breeding, suppurating . . . Anyway, there were a *lot* of them on the Bournemouth road and we four began to build up the sort of jokey scenario which was very funny in an enclosed space hurtling down the M3, but less so if I were to relay it to you now. Suffice to say it involved Cone'n the Barbarian, Sir Arthur Cone'n Doyle and Mr and Mrs Cohen and their son, Raffik. With a combined age of over 200 years in the car, all we needed, really, was someone to settle us down with a boiled sweet and point out the window cooing 'Look, darlings, gee-gees!'

Once installed in the hotel, Jack and I left the Morrows sleeping next door and went for a sedate swim and a leisurely sauna. We were sitting in the jacuzzi, wondering, as ever after two minutes, what the hell we were supposed to do *now*, when we couldn't help but notice a by now familiar orange and white striped plastic object by the poolside. 'Do you mind if I borrow this for a while?' I asked the poolside receptionist. Sometimes it pays to have a familiar and, let's be honest, mad-as-an-orange face, because she agreed immediately and offered me the loan of a bollard.

We crept past our own room, placed the cone outside the Morrows, rang their bell and, giggling, crouching and tiptoeing more than was strictly necessary, returned to the safety of our room.

Throughout the next twenty-four hours that cone turned up in more obscure places than Judith Chalmers. It was in our bed alongside a chocolate and a rose – what the chambermaid thought I can hardly conjecture – it was under the breakfast table, it accompanied us to a local tea shop and when we waved it goodbye, we all felt withdrawal symptoms.

A week later, when it was little more than an after-dinner story – one which, on the whole, received polite but glassy-eyed smirks as opposed to hallelujah choruses of hilarity and requests for telling the whole thing again from scratch – Jack received a bill. The bill came from the hotel. It was for a missing traffic cone and it was for £18.

Easy to say, after the event, but had *I* been there I *might* have viewed it with a small soupçon of suspicion, but Jack had no such hesitation. He was outraged. A man possessed. A massive injustice had been perpetrated and straightaway he got on the phone to the hotel to rectify it.

'This bill I've received is preposterous! Unbelievable! We asked permission to *borrow* the cone from the pool and we put it back *immediately* after we'd used it! It was a joke. You seriously expect me to pay this ridiculous ...' There was consternation behind the Hotel Reception, as well there might have been, since the bill had been invented and typed on hotel stationery by none other than our friend, Mr Morrow, a fact which was suddenly, and with absolute certainty, comprehended by my husband as he studied the 'bill' he was brandishing.

It took a lot of grovelling *and* forelock tugging to convince the staff not to call a manager, a lawyer – and an ambulance – but in the end he succeeded. It was, we decided, touché.

This part is a confession. Yes, it was me. I took it. The derelict and torn traffic cone I found under my Honda, some weeks later in the Waterloo Road. Under cover of darkness and spurred on by a spirit of revenge, I popped it in the boot and, looking neither left nor right, sped home like a common criminal. Later that day, having first wrapped it in bandages of silver paper and tinsel and superglued Woolworth's 'pic'n'mix' chocolates all over its surface, I left Jack to deliver it to the Morrows' pristine home in Finchley as a house-warming gift. The weather was wet, icy and one might even say inclement if one was the sort of toff who also said 'one'.

It emerged that their new house was situated down a long lane fronted by a barrier, erected specifically to prevent unknown cars driven by lunatics carrying gift-wrapped contraband traffic cones down ice-covered driveways. Braving life, limbs and any sense of dignity he ever had, he placed it in situ, then, mission accomplished, limped, slid, tottered and skeetered back to the car, losing the rest of his will to live on the way.

I might point out to those of you who are not practical jokers that the receiver of the said item *never* mentions to the sender that anything in any way unusual has arrived. The idea is to smile grimly, simmer a while and retaliate, if necessary, after years.

But, it wasn't years. It was the other night. The night we were going out to dinner with our friends, the Morrows. We drove over there to pick them up taking the warning lamp with us. When they walked out to greet us it was on the top of our car, flashing. No one mentioned it and we put it back where it had come from, on the way out. The following day we mailed them a box of forty-eight ice-cream cones from the freezer centre.

I'm not sure what the next move is, but I think, and here Jack's dismay is palpable, that it involves a megaphone, two traffic wardens' outfits, a search warrant and some very, very dirty boots. Suggestions welcome on a plain brown warrant.

I wonder why any pre-planned joke is called a practical joke. I suppose it just means actual, or involving a physical item, as practical props on stage mean using a real object instead of just a mock-up. I shall look it up. I've looked it up. It's a joke with actions . . . or, in my case, libellous actions.

The verbal jokes have been thin on the ground lately. Political correctness has put paid to most minority jokes, and without someone 'inferior' to laugh at there's little chance of laughter at all. Imagine this one and supply the incorrectness yourself. There's an Englishman, a Scotsman and another man eating their sandwiches on the building site. The Englishman complains, 'Bloody beef again! Every day, beef, beef, beef! If I get another beef sandwich tomorrow, I'm going to throw myself off the top of that crane!'

The Scotsman concurs, 'Me too! Ham again! Ham, ham, ham! Everyday the same. One more ham sandwich and, tomorrow, I'm gonna join ye on that crane and jump!'

'Cheese again,' groans the third man. 'Cheese yesterday, cheese the day before. Nothing but sodding cheese. If I get cheese tomorrow in my sandwich – I'm jacking it in as well, off that crane!'

The following day, all three men opened their snap tins, found, respectively, beef, ham and cheese in them and jumped to their deaths from the top of the crane. (Don't you just love the credibility factor here?)

At the funeral the three wives were commiserating with each other. 'I had no idea he didn't want beef in his sandwich,' says the English wife. 'I could have given him salmon or egg mayonnaise if only he'd said . . .'

'I know,' weeps the Scottish widow. 'I only gave him ham because I thought he loved it, I had tuna and tongue and all sorts . '

'The same with me exactly,' moans the third man's widow. 'He could have had anything! And the thing that makes it even worse is that he made his own sandwiches!'

One of the cleverest stories came via George Baker. It concerns a Professor of Logic at Cambridge University on a brief visit to his childhood roots in the East End of London. Walking down a narrow street and peering up at the street signs, he hears a gruff, strangled cockney sound and feels a heavy hand on his shoulders.

'Bowers, innit? Phil Bowers, innit, eh? Ent you Phil Bowers from the Old 'All School in Fry'sgate?'

Professor Bowers, for it was he, took a step back and examined the red, coarsened man before him. 'Yes. That's correct. Professor Bowers, and who might you be?'

'S'me! Jimmy Stover, innit – used to sit behind you in 1946, copy yer 'omework! Gawd strewth, you was an 'ell of a swat! What yer doing wiv y'self now, then?'

'Well, I'm a Professor of Logic at Cambridge University, actually.'

'*Are* yew really? *Are* yew really? Well, stone me, ent that somethin'. Tsk-tsk-tsk. Professor of Logic, eh?' He took off his cap and scratched his head. 'Wass Logic, then?'

The Professor glanced first at his watch and then at the heavens and said, 'Well, er, James, Logic is – well, look here, I'm going to assume that you have a couple of goldfish at home.'

'Yeah, thassright, Flossie and Mossie. Gottem in a bowl on the telly, how d'you know?'

'Very well, James. Then I shall further assume you have a cat who watches these fish.'

'Yeah, thassright, Phil, she can sit there for hours and . . .'

'Very well, and I shall further presume that you have a couple of children who . . .'

'Yeah, thassright, boy 'n a girl, Phoebe an Des . . .'

'So, James. I shall now make the *logical* deduction that you are heterosexual.'

Jimmy was flabbergasted but had no time to comment as Professor Bowers tapped his watch saying 'Must dash, splendid to see you – er, James

– some other time,' and disappeared down the road at a lick.

Jimmy Stover made his way to the pub where his mate, Ron, was already two pints ahead.

''Ere, Ron. You'll never guess who I just saw in the street. Bowers, Phil Bowers, the swatter, 'member 'im from the Old 'All School?'

Ron's face cracked into a wide beam of recognition. 'Yeah, Bowers! Gawd, 'ee was a clever bugger all right – Wass 'ee doin' neow, eh?'

Jimmy assumed his full height. ''E's a Professor of Logic, innee! At Cambridge University.'

Ron shook is head in awe. 'Is 'ee really? Is 'ee *really*?' Then he drained his glass and said, warily, 'Wass Logic, then?'

Jimmy was in his element. He put down his glass, wiped his mouth clean of froth and took a lecturing stand. 'Well, Ron,' he began. 'I am gonna assume that you 'ave a goldfish bowl on your telly wiv two goldfish in it.'

'No,' says Ron.

'Well, you're an 'effing poofter, then ain't yer!'

It ain't practical, but it's practically the funniest joke I know.

Sprung Chicken

In my youth I never understood the joke: 'Why did the chicken cross the road? To get to the other side.' It was far too sophisticated a concept. The one which made me crow was: 'Why did the chicken cross the road? To see the Duchess lay a foundation stone.' Still, you could generally generate a decent laugh or two with a chicken story, a chicken allusion or a chicken imitation.

Chickens are oddballs. It's an accepted fact that if chickens had big brown eyes and long lashes, then Animal Rights Liberators would be placarding battery farms and throwing eggs at Dudley Moore on a regular basis. Chickens somehow don't have the innate appeal of veal calves: they are infinitely more expendable, less individual, more spiky, more scratchy, less characterful – look, let's face it, as far as good PR goes, they are in need of an image consultant. 'Mum, can I have a hen for my birthday?' is not the cry of your normal primary school kid and 'Let's go and feed the fowl' is pretty low down the pecking order on your average outing in the park.

So it was with some surprise that I surveyed the title of one of the children's books I was to read on tape: *Hilda, The Hen Who Wouldn't Give Up* by Jill Tomlinson. I know Jill as a good children's writer responsible for one of my finest hours as Plop, the Owl, on the cassette version of *The Owl Who Was Afraid of the Dark*. No, I'm not being arrogant, nor facetious. As Plop, I peaked. Simple as that. Everything since has been steadily downhill. Owls were familiar territory to me and baby owls with husky voices, a hoot.

But a hen. A stubborn hen, who sought various means to travel five miles to another farm to view her auntie's new chicks, then become broody for chicks of her own. Round the house I wandered, clucking under my breath and trying to feel feathered. Should Hilda be a 'kentry gurl' hen with a soft Gloucestershire burr, or a sturdy northern lass with nice round Yorkshire vowels so similar to my own? My preoccupation did not go unnoticed at home and snide comments began to emanate from him indoors.

'I hope it won't *ruffle your feathers* if I ask you where my green jacket is?' and 'Do you still want to meet at the theatre or does it go *against the grain?*' At one point, a *peck* on the cheek was requested and references made to being no *spring chicken*! But when it was suggested that I remove my glasses to take the weight off my beak, I'm afraid I snapped, and more or less told him to cluck-off!

One lunchtime, I regaled Lynda Bellingham with my dilemma. 'So,' I told her, 'Hilda sits on her eggs to make them hatch into chicks but the farmer's wife keeps taking them away.'

'Where was the cock?' asked Lynda.

I assured her there were no 'cocks' in *Hilda, The Hen Who Wouldn't Give Up*, but she, a farmer's daughter, persisted.

'No cocks, no fertilisation.' I felt as I had felt when I discovered you didn't get babies through eating Stork margarine. 'Well, what do you think God created cocks for?' she said.

It was an interesting question at my time of life. 'To wake you up in the morning?' I ventured.

The next morning in the studio went reasonably well and I didn't fall foul of too many interpretation problems. Hilda emerged as a regular member of the village of Ambridge and the producer seemed chuffed enough. I went to work that evening with my pride intact, feeling I'd managed to pullet out of the bag.

Later that night, on my return home, Jack was in the kitchen. 'How did it go, love? The recording?'

'Oh. OK. I think. Yeah, all right really. I think I managed to be birdlike without being too . . .'

Here I broke off at the sight of my husband, a mature man in the summer wine section of his days, circling the kitchen with a basket under his arm, scattering imaginary grain hither and thither on the kitchen floor. 'Peckish at all, love?'

I'm not one to harbour a grudge. Not for me the long brooding silence, the clipped retort and the crisp closing of partition doors. Certainly not. I'm only too well aware of the value of a sense of humour to a long-standing relationship, the ability to laugh at oneself, yes, to see the yolk, if you like in a mature marriage. 'Never go to sleep on a quarrel' said someone – Louisa May Alcott? Claire Rayner? Idi Amin? Whoever. And we didn't. No fear.

But the following day I phoned the East Finchley Party and Fancy Dress Shop to inquire after the cost of hiring a complete hen's costume. Gravely, the assistant informed me that it would be £18 but unfortunately they had no hens in stock. My disappointment must have been palpable because just as I was about to hang up, she called out, 'I don't suppose by any chance you'd be interested in a chicken?'

It was a yellow-feathered balaclava with blue eyes, an orange beak and a voluminous yellow fluffy body with cosy mittens and black tights. I was somewhat surprised that *feet* were not included at that price, but a new pair of yellow rubber gloves seemed to do the trick nicely. I was stuffing cushions down the body when my son arrived home from school. 'Hi Mod,' he intoned, deadpan. 'I see you're dressed up as a hen. What's for dinner?'

Dave, the gardener, was hoeing round the stone urn in the front garden. I hopped up on to a small brick wall by the porch and waited for him to hoe in my direction. He was listening raptly to Cloria Hunniford and didn't turn round until my feet, in their rubber fingers, were iced to the brickwork. Finally, he looked round and said, 'Oh yeah?' a whisper of a smile forcing his roll-up to one side. 'What's this then, Maureen? You goin' to a fancy dress party or what?'

I considered telling him what I was doing and why, but by now I was a frozen chicken. 'Yeah, that's right, David. It's a hen party.' He went ho-ho-ho-ing back to his hoeing.

Jacquie, my secretary, was helpless with laughter by now as I sat down in the living-room to await Jack's return. I was rather affronted by her amusement. It has always been the way that once I put on a costume, however, ridiculous, I feel completely and utterly at home. I spread myself out on the sofa, my colourful rubber feet akimbo up on the coffee table, my chin on my chest and two hardboiled eggs and a small dish of pumpkin seeds by my side.

The door slammed and his hello sounded cheery enough. 'Everyone all right?' he called. Stifled noises from the study and the kitchen were the only response he got. 'Where's Mum?' he asked Adam, who obviously swerved into another room muttering 'Living-room' in strangled tones. 'Why is everyone smirking? What's happened? Why is the . . .' he entered the room and the rest I leave to your fertile imagination. Suffice to say that his glasses went AWOL, his body collapsed, his knees jack-knifed to his chin, his breath came in hoarse rasps followed by violent, painful brays. Finally, painfully, he put up both hands and said 'Alright. You win.'

If I'd had fluffy ears, it would have been music to them.

'Maureen – don't do that'

When I was in Scarborough, *Re:Joycing!*, I had a request from my primary school in Hull to open their new library and read to the children from some of my favourite books. It was irresistible.

I had not been inside Wheeler Street School for thirty-eight years. It was, of course, smaller than I remembered and the years had freshened and jollied up the dark tiled walls of my memories. I imagined the tiny toilets had gone too. The ones down which I was convinced the spiders lived and whose cubicle doors burst open the minute you'd started an undeflectable pee.

Visiting schools is always joyful and invariably exhausting. After a mere half hour of the children I was flailing around – and teachers have a seven-hour day. Plus all the wretched administrative work so generously thrust upon them by the National Curriculum. They are, give or take a few miscreants, heroes to a man or woman, and their status, salary and the respect due to them cannot be elevated high enough. There now. It needs to be said and I've said it.

Moreover, when successful people revisit their old school to talk about their lives since school, I don't suppose there's one who wasn't inspired to succeed by some unknown, unsung (Emlyn Williams aside) educator. Someone who suddenly reached through all the sham and the rebellion and the gauche poses to the still, receiving centre of that child and opened a door to a way of life with possibilities.

So here I am, in my nice dress, standing on the stage which looked so huge and imposing to me when I was under three foot and I realise it's about a foot high and maybe ten feet wide by seven across, and I'm gazing out at a funfair of faces.

It is Comic Relief Day and every chid is in fancy dress sitting cross-legged on the floor. They look magnificent. There are Blobbys and Batmen and clowns and nurses and shiny-headed robots and huge-headed dinosaurs who wished to heck they'd come as cowboys, and I start to talk about reading after the first tumult has died down. For a while they listen because that's what they've been told to do. Then I ask a question and everyone answers at once, and I ask another and a chorus breaks out, and I panic for a moment because how will I ever retain order, and the teachers down the sides in their chairs are wondering whether to help me out or not . . . And, suddenly, as has happened so often and in such timely fashion over the last six years, Joyce Grenfell comes to my rescue.

'Children! Children!' I call in that pitch so known and so attended to by those of a certain age – and I clap my hands together. 'Children! Gather round now, because we are going to do our lovely *moving to music now*. And Miss Boulting is going to play her piano,' and I gesture towards the wall of the Assembly Hall where there is no piano and they all look left to where I'm pointing and accept there is one. 'And we are all going to be lovely flowers, growing and dancing in the grass.' There is a puzzled silence . . . 'Now isn't that nice?' They are not sure that it is. 'Yes, it *is*, Sidney. It's *very* nice!' And they start to laugh, and we're away.

It really is magic. Thirty-five years after she conceived the slightly out-of-control teacher, Joyce's creation is as fresh as the daisy in the circle suggested by Peggy, the invisible pupil.

You should have *seen* those kids. How they looked around at George every time he did whatever it is that he does and I tell him not to. How their eyes followed Sidney out of the room in disgrace and back in again when he refused to give me whatever he'd had in his mouth. 'A big button, Sidney? Well. I'm ashamed of you. Yes I am. A big boy of four, eating a button off the back of little girls' dresses! Well, I'm very glad you spat it out. You didn't? Oh. I see – you've, yes, well . . . Do you *feel* all right, Sidney?'

And when Jemima came back into the circle and I said, 'Oh, Jemima dear, what do we do when we come back from the littlest room? We pull our knickers *up* again, do we?' I thought the roof would fly off. Knickers of every hue were revealed as they rocked backwards and screeched out their pleasure. It was a triumph that the lady herself would not have been able to resist. Later, I received a letter from the head teacher thanking me for entertaining the school. 'One of the girls laughed so much, she wet herself,' he wrote. 'And that was the geography teacher.'

Joyce once asked a roomful of children to tell her what the word frugal meant. One little chap said it meant 'to save', and she congratulated him on his knowledge and suggested the class might all write her little stories that contained the word frugal. The prize-winning story went as follows:

The princess was inprisoned in the tower and she shouted Frugal me, Frugal me, and the hansom prince came and he frugalled her and they lived happily ever after!

I think even Miss Blyton might have flashed a knicker at that one.

Memories Are Made of – Er –

Well. They are going. The cells. The little irreplaceable ones that perish in the brain, never to be replenished. Going. Going . . . With a rapidity that had me devouring with indecent haste an interesting article on memory then, four minutes later, forgetting what it had advised . . . Gone.

I work in chaos. My desk, as I survey it from my vantage point, looks like a sock drawer in *Men Behaving Badly*. Telephone wedged on unread comedy script from anxious writer. Radio lying on three unused glass paperweights, empty cassette case, empty tea mug, small wooden doll's house chair, cylindrical rape alarm reading 'Emits 30+ shrills' in five languages (which foreigner, I ask you, is going to assault me in my own study?). Ahead of me, there's an oblong maroon box which reads 'More Balls Than Most' and contains implements to teach me 'The Joy of Juggling'. It's been there for a year. Have I juggled? Have I bollocks!

All of which serendipity, plus two-dozen assorted Christmas cards, a half-consumed packet of Lockets, a foot-high pile of scripts and a video tape inexplicably labelled Richard Stilgoe, inspire me to the task of creativity which lies before me.

My husband, the proper writer, has a clean desk. Just a silver blotter, a fountain pen and eight assorted chewing gums. Of course, his word processor is on my dining table but my point remains the same. *Real* writers have tidy minds. We 'dabblers' live like pigs, which is why we are so often *sty*mied for words.

Words which keep vanishing. Like serendipity for example. Complete short-circuit on that one. Had to stop, go downstairs, eat huge quantities of rice and make a phone call, before 'serendipity' popped into the mind. And it's not even the word I want. The word I want is long and begins with M*, but every time I get close to it, I can only think of Mesopotamia. If I'd had a thesaurus to hand, of course, I could have looked it up under 'serendipity' and saved myself the indigestion.

Then there are the books I find I've read before, but not until I'm one hundred and eighty pages in. The countries I claim never to have visited until the man with whom I co-habit reminds me of the week we spent there. On honeymoon. The faces at parties who lunge towards me saying 'Great to see you again, how are Amy and Adam? Gosh, they must be twenty-one and nineteen by now and how's the cat's diabetes?' when I've never clapped eyes on them in my entire life and don't even know what *sex* they are. It's a bit of a joke really.

Which leads me, pedantically, to the memory joke told to me by Barry Cryer. A man rings his friend to enthuse wildly about a restaurant he'd visited the previous night.

'It was fabulous,' he exclaims. 'The food, the ambience, the service – faultless . . . the best . . .'

'Really?' says his friend. 'And what was it called?'

'It was called . . .' he hesitates, 'the . . . er, the . . . er . . . Hang on a tick . . . the, oh, God . . . the . . . er. Wait a minute! What's the name of that long green thing with thorns on the sides and a pink flower?'

'Rose?' suggests the friend.

'That's it!' he shouts. 'Rose! That's it.' He cups his head over the receiver and shouts, 'Rose! What was the name of that restaurant we went to last night?'

My phone just rang actually. It was my friend, Jennifer, the reflexologist. From Manchester. I told her I was musing on memory and she said 'Ginkgo'.

'Ginkgo,' I repeated, largely because I've never said it before and may never say it again. 'What's Ginkgo?'

'The new miracle memory elixir,' she informed me.

'Does it really work?' I asked her.

'I don't know,' she replied. 'I've got a book all about it but I keep forgetting to read it.' Then she added, 'I *must* buy a bookmark.' Oh yes. *That'll* help. We're only in our forties for Pete's sake. What's it going to be like when we qualify for our bus passes? I'll have forgotten what a bus *is*.

Somehow I manage to remember my lines though, said she hastily, remembering that producers' wives have been known to read the odd book. Different parts of the brain, I suppose. The part which isn't irreparably losing thousands of brain cells per minute. And jokes. I remember jokes. In batches. M for memory.

'There's just one thing I can't stand,' I said recently at a gathering. Every eye in the room swivelled towards me, reflecting interest, concern, curiosity and more than a touch of anticipation – except that by now I had no idea why they were looking at me, what had been the first part of the sentence or who was the current President of the United States of America. Mind you, the last one is excusable since most Americans have no idea either. I love the story of Clinton, in despair, seeking advice at the statue of Thomas Jefferson. 'Ahm in a hole, suh, an ah cain't get myself out of it. No one lahks me, or mah wife or mah policies, suh, und ah don't know what to do for the best, suh.'

A low voice from the statue rumbles, 'Go to the Constitution!' But Bill figures it's too darn late for that, so he goes and puts his problem to the statue of Theodore Roosevelt, and a mighty voice rumbles, 'Go to the people!'

But, once more, Bill feels he needs some miracle that will transform his luck, so he goes to the statue of Abraham Lincoln and he bows his head and mumbles the same liturgy of despair and hopelessness. 'What can ah do, suh?' he cries. The statue of Abe Lincoln rumbles, 'Go to the theatre!'

And finally, a little something for the weekend – old ones, new ones, sad ones, blue ones, remembered ones, forgotten ones . . . Here is a forgotten one . . . Er . . . Um . . . hang on a sec . . . it's on the tip of my whatsit . . .

A couple consult their doctor about their failing memories. He advises them to repeat the cogent word in each sentence over and over to re-pattern the brain. That evening she asks what he wants for dinner and he replies, 'I'll have some steak.'

'Steak,' she mutters on her way to the kitchen. 'Steak, steak, steak.'

'And what sort of potatoes?' she throws back at him.

'Er, I'd like some chips, please.'

'Chips,' she reiterates. 'Chips, chips, chips.'

'And for vegetables?' she asks.

'I think I'd like peas.'

'Peas, peas, peas, peas, peas,' she says.

Half an hour later she calls him to the table and puts his dinner down in front of him. 'There you are,' she says. 'Just what you wanted. Eggs, bacon and tomatoes.'

He stares at her. Puts down his knife and fork and says, 'Where's the *toast*?'

Spine-tingling Success

Doctor: I have some bad news and some worse news.
Patient: Give me the bad news first.
Doctor: You have 24 hours to live.
Patient: And the worse news?
Doctor: I forgot to ring you yesterday.

In this chapter I intend to cover Recovery and Recuperation and, for want of another alliterative topic, I shall begin with *Re:Joyce!* which I performed for the Manchester City of Drama to 2000 people in the Royal Opera House in March 1994. It could have been, I believed, my last performance and I gave it 'my all, and then some'. Short of clinging to the curtains at the finale, blowing kisses to the usherettes and gracefully expiring on the apron, I don't think I could have done more.

Afterwards, somewhat flushed with success and suppressed tidings, I had the unenviable task of telling my student daughter that her performing seal of a mother was about to be clubbed. More precisely, operated on for the removal of a neurofibroma deeply embedded in her spine. My daughter took it, as I knew she would, on the chin. The said chin was loose and wobbly, but otherwise she accepted it like a man, which is more than the man sitting on my bed did. He had a look in his eyes like a two-times loser at Crufts.

The alternative, I explained to Amy, would be paralysis. The 'nodule', which was spotted by my neurologist (or, St Jeffrey, as I now think of him), quickly became a 'tumour' in the mouth of his brilliant but brisk colleague, the neurosurgeon, Mr Afshar.

I had been at the BBC reading a prize-winning short story for radio and afterwards drove straight to Dr Jeffrey Gawler for neck X-rays and consultation. He told me the nodule was in my spinal cord. A neurofibroma. It was wrapped around all sorts of things and it had to be removed right away. Depending on how attached it was to nerve endings, my right arm could be affected. He was 99 per cent sure it was not malignant. He couldn't believe I did not show any side-effects like pins and needles or loss of feeling in any of my limbs.

Mr Afshar came in. He called the neurofibroma a tumour and reiterated that it would be unusual for it to be malignant. I was worried about whether to have it done immediately or after the upcoming Manchester *Re:Joyce!*. Dr Gawler said it should be immediate. Mr Afshar said ten days wouldn't make any difference. He was going away for a few days the following week. So it was then or never. I walked back to the car and rang Jack, just as I'd meant not to, and blurted it all out and wept. The radio played Beethoven's Violin Concerto all the way home. It was a comfort. Jack made me tea and sympathy and we cancelled many of the next week's engagements. In the loo the *American Bath Book* opened to, 'The time to repair the roof is when the sun is shining'.

Re:Joyce! was poignant for those of us in the know, which amounted to five out of 2000, and for others, I guess it was one of our best ever. Sometimes Joyce just flies in, Poppins-like, and does the show for me.

The next day an operation relieved me of most of the deeply attached 'todule', which had probably been with me for twenty years, distorting my spinal cord and pressing on an artery to the brain. I wondered how far I could have gone *without* it. How gorgeous I could have *looked* without it. What a great scuba diver I would have been without it.

Seriously, it was a lesson in how easily a chronic complaint like migraine can be fobbed off for years. Even *I* didn't really believe me. It's the old triple bluff. You're a working mother, you're an actress – listen, you've a headache! Take a pill, take therapy, take a break, take my bill. So in all these years of consultations and their alternatives, I've had my feet kneaded, my torso needled, my cranium manipulated, my mind hypnotised, my eyeballs drugged up to – all I hadn't had was a common or garden X-ray.

So on the same day that the London *Evening Standard* chose to print 'Me and My Health' (in which I'm quoted as saying 'I'm probably the healthiest person you've ever interviewed'), my intrepid neurosurgeon was slicing and digging and sucking and stitching for the best part of six hours. Doesn't time fly when you're anaesthetised?

I shall skip over the intensive care bit because you may be eating your muesli. We are, it is written, a stiff-necked people and, boy, am I stereotypical.

For the next ten days I watched the Thames flow oh-so-sweetly past my window, wept copiously for no apparent reason, and thanked my Maker for making Dolores, the sort of Irish nurse you could lay on an open wound. Sloping-bosomed and apple-cheeked, she came into her own on finding me mid-blub after learning the 'todule' really was benign. 'There now,' she murmured soothingly. 'Don't you feel a whole lot better when you hear it straight from the doctor's ears?'

My husband slept the whole night after the operation in a chair and opened his eyes each hour when they came to shine a light in mine, my kids were impeccable and my mother perched on the bed and told me excitedly that 'a tall tin of red salmon in Sainsbury's is now £1.59'. I felt twice blessed. 'That's amazing,' I replied. There was a lot of love in the exchange.

During my hospitalisation, one visitor was Michael Codron, who was to produce *The Sisters Rosensweig*. It had been a full day if I'm to believe my journal:

> Monday today so a lot has happened and I'm tireder and lower, without knowing why.
>
> Sunday was too many visitors, I think. Sandra and Buddy, then Mom, Jack bearing deli stuff from Hampstead, Christine Goldshmidt looking wonderful and bearing a translucent blue fossil, then Valerie and Ruby, then Bryan and Edith and finally Michael Codron and Mark Raiment.

I mean, can you believe this? Tuesday I have the archaeological dig into the central nervous system; Tuesday night they shine a miner's lamp into my eyes every hour; Wednesday I throw up; Thursday I swallow pain killers and hospital food; Friday I learn the news that the tumour, if left, would have led to a tetraplegic future, and see first visitors, Lizzy and Lynn, who call with gifts and date cookies and I doze through their love and friendship till the physio arrives; Saturday Denis and Astrid and then Julia McKenzie and I sleep a lot.

Then Sunday I entertain twelve visitors in shifts and write 'I feel tired for no apparent reason'!

> Michael suggested I would be happier if I played Gorgeous, not Sara, in *The Sisters Rosensweig*. At this point his optimism is staggering. He only has to *look* at me to realise that 'Gorgon' would be better casting but he's absolutely serious. 'You won't have to carry the show in the same way, shoulder as much responsibility, and it's a far less emotional stretch – think about it.'

It wasn't easy to think about anything. The nadir came when a nurse came to take my stitches out. After a short bout of clipping, she said in clipped tones, 'Oh dear . . . there's a bit of spinal fluid leaking out . . . hold on, I'll be right back . . .' and she disappeared for fifteen minutes.

Now I don't know what the term 'leaking spinal fluid' means to you but to me it meant a few many syllabled words like meningitis, haemorrhage and, ultimately, rigor mortis. That fifteen minutes was the longest waiting period in my life. When she returned with Mr Afshar to stitch me up again, I was rigid with fear and shivering uncontrollably. 'C-c-c-can you pass me some Kleenex?' I managed to stutter . . . and her next sentence should be engraved on her heart: 'One moment please. I'm helping doctor at present. When I've finished, I'll pass you what you want.'

I would march from London to Mississippi in support of higher pay for nurses. I would picket Stephen Dorrell's picket fence with a placard of the chaos his predecessor caused Casualty in London. I would give every nurse in the country a bonus, a rise and, if possible, the Freedom of the City and a flock of black-faced sheep to drive over Tower Bridge – but I wouldn't cross the road to save this particular 'angel' from a colony of fire ants. There you are. It's out. Malevolence. Childish, but I feel better for it.

In the same mischievous mode, I answered a 'How are you?' call from Julia with the sentence, 'I'm fine, love, really . . . pain down to a minimum, just had a decent piece of salmon trout, weather's looking up, I'm gazing out on the Thames flowing sweetly past, the doctor says I can go home on Wednesday and "So-and-So's" just got *terrible* notices – I'm fine.' It was exceedingly un-Christian and I thought McKenzie would never stop laughing.

Once home I set about recuperating, which basically meant trying to find a decent chair to support my back in a house which was a haven for furniture with sick building syndrome. What hadn't been hand-minced by the cat had collapsed under its own aegis and I was reduced to sitting on a straight-backed kitchen chair propped up with duvets. It was strangely comfortable and seemed to cry out for soft-boiled eggs, soldiers and sago pudding.

All was right with the world. So long as you didn't turn on the news. Or the TV. At all. God bless Dennis Potter for saying everything I've thought, but thought incoherently, about what's happened on our screens. One more gross sit-com, peopled by casts of grotesque morons, one more testicular- and menstrually obsessed comic, one more formula-ridden and written corpse and robbers show, and I'm going to have my licence revoked. Thank God for Classic FM, Home Videos, and the best 'best friends' a whinging woman with more rings round her neck than a Masai tribeswoman could wish for, to cling on to and make sodden.

As patients go, I had none. Patience that is. I wanted to be not only up and about but *higher* up and more *visibly* about than before. And I couldn't. It just took one well-meaning stranger to come up to me in the street and tell me how thin I looked for the dam to break all over again. 'Look, you don't even know me,' I bleated. 'I wouldn't dream of commenting on *your* personal appearance. Sod off.' Four weeks after the op and still in my styrofoam collar, I had to meet an American agent who was only here for one day. I spent hours on my face and my hair, but kept ducking out of her eyeline, feeling ugly and unemployable. 'I felt so awful,' I said to my mother afterwards in the kitchen. 'I didn't want her to see me.'

'Don't be so silly,' she reassured me. 'You won't *always* look like that.' Life has a way of going on, hasn't it?

The one day I *had* to pull myself together was the day Jack went up to Buck House to get his New Year's CBE. We discovered his distinct lack of morning suit and top hat a few days before and since I buy his clothes for him, or at best, with him, I had to be slowly perambulated and driven to Golders Green in my collar, like one of those nodding dogs in the back of an old Morris Oxford. It was exhausting but triumphant and I had to be put to bed for the rest of the day. Two days later my friend Lizzy slid a pale blue Ronit Zilkha suit over my wobbly head. 'I'll take it!' I burbled as the skirt slithered over my hips (all shopping should be accomplished this way) and the following day combined spinal monitoring at Bart's with a lightning limp to Selfridges with Julia for the hat. This took twelve minutes flat and was perfect.

All we needed now was two inches and some binding on Adam's trouser (he'd obliged us by lying down growing whilst I was lying down shrinking), a job lot of crumpled linen for Amy and a pot of mortician's wax for me, and we were all set.

I could hear a band playing in the Minstrels' Gallery behind me but I couldn't turn my head to see it. Too vain to wear the neck collar, I sat tremulously in the ballroom whilst four Beefeaters marched solemnly on to the podium to the accompaniment of 'Strangers in the Night'. Then, after six or seven men and women, whose names began with O, P or Q, in walked our Mr R, jauntily out of step, to the tune of 'I'm in Love With a Wonderful Guy'. The whole thing was fabulous and unforgettable and our stiff necks were entirely to do with pride.

No matter that the *Daily Mail* called me Beattie nor that the *Jewish Chronicle* gave Jack an MBE and a daughter called Lucy, we were still ecstatic. I could have complained but, hell, who needs the headache? It's called prioritising and maybe, after forty-seven years, I'm finally getting it right.

Then, quite suddenly, I remembered one migraineous day, when Zelma and I drove to Shepherd's Bush to drop our close relative, Ms Amy, at the medium's. The medium was a New Zealand lady, over for the odd consultation, and Amy was anxious to know how she would best cope with being torn from her home and family and banished to the frozen wastes of a Lancashire campus. When I say anxious, I mean anxious in the sense of 'I'm going to chain myself to the cat and sing protest songs, rather than leave home'. I was driving her to the medium in Shepherd's Bush because it was obviously my fault she felt this way. I'd either made it too pleasant here, so there was nothing to rebel against, or I'd made her too dependent on us to feel anything but fear at the thought of going. Either way, I was a miserable failure and boring.

An hour or so later we called back for her. She answered the door herself, looking rather chipper, I thought. 'She wants you to come in, Mod. There's a spirit guide and he thinks your migraines are to do with your teeth!'

'Me?' I hissed. 'What's all this got to do with *me*?' Nevertheless, I sat down and had my head felt and in due course spent £500 at the orthodontist on a dental bite plate in which I occasionally sleep to render myself *totally* irresistible. 'I cah – I go' dith thig id by gnowth', being the standard reply to 'Give us a kiss then, love'. Well, 'Not tonight, darling, I've got a headache' would hardly be unusual in our house, would it?

On the journey home, Amy clutched the tape she had recorded of her 'reading' and told us as much as she could remember of what was said.

'She said Daddy's going to get a tremendous honour soon,' she remembered. 'But I told her he'd already had one, from the Royal Television Society, but she said, no, it hadn't happened yet. Then she wrote down the letters CBE, on a piece of paper.'

We all sat thinking of reasons why the coal board should wish to honour Jack for a while, then we forgot it. This was in November. In January he was awarded the CBE. Makes you think, doesn't it? I reckon she was an above average medium.

We came back from a lovely holiday in Marbella later that year, as we always come back, with Jack – who hovers in the shade – a deep mahogany brown, and me – who lies motionless on a lounger doused in oil – a brightish beige but for a beaky scarlet protuberance and quietly prepared myself for rehearsals of *The Sisters Rosensweig* to begin in July. I still felt as though I was carrying a small Barbary ape on my shoulders and my energy swayed erratically from up to under, but with the help of Tony Porter's magic reflexology on my feet, every day, in every way, I got better and better.

I wonder if you are wondering about the migraines? Have they gone for ever, you are asking? If only life were like *Dr Finlay's Casebook*. All Tannachbrae, tea cosy and miracles. 'Fraid not. Still, are we downhearted? Er – well, once or twice a month we are, but we cope. We cope and take all the drugs we can and avoid all the dodgy foods and try to lead a stress-free life and if you believe that, you'll believe Persil washes whiter and Bill Clinton didn't inhale. Meanwhile, if anyone has a new miracle cure involving Jeff Bridges and a desert island, I'm aching to hear it.

Doctor: I have some bad news and some good news.
Patient: Tell me the bad news.
Doctor: You have two weeks to live.
Patient: What's the good news?
Doctor: See the man in the bed opposite?
Patient: Yes.
Doctor: He wants to buy your slippers?

You know how it is – well, I hope you don't know how it is, but if you've had a serious medical condition then for the next few years you are monitored to make sure the 'thing' hasn't recurred. Well, that's how it was with me. Every year I'd slide into a steel spaceship called a scanner on the fifth floor of a hospital with the slowest elevator I've ever encountered. (I mean, you could conceive before ringing for that lift and deliver a healthy bawling full-term infant by the time you reached the fifth floor.)

I've often raised money for MR scanners in the past and I thank God that I did because they have one job in life and that is to save seven or eight lives a day. A couple of weeks before my half-century birthday, the scanner revealed that my neurofibroma was back. And he was ugly. It wasn't that the tumour was growing but that it was filling up with fluid and pressing up against things inside my spine which might well start reporting it for harassment.

So I did what any mature woman with a devoted husband, caring kids, a hyperventilating mother and a simmering career on the front burner would do. I ignored it. By that I mean I ignored it in a Jewish kind of way and sought a second, third and ultimately fifth opinion whilst auditioning surgeons on all sides of the Atlantic. (Did I dream I saw a card on a surgeon's door which read 'Please get your second opinion before consulting me'?) One was against the op as I had no actual symptoms. Some were optimistic but gloomy about the prospect of having to sever the nerve to my right hand (the writing, lacquer spraying and pansy-potting one). Others, like the glorious Fred Epstein in New York, six foot three and stunning in snakeskin boots and bleached blond hair, chuckled, 'Come ON, Marine – get without! So you lose a little feeling in your pinkie – I mean, what the heck?' (He made the operation sound as dangerous as having your eyebrows plucked.)

The heck was that, instead, I saw gifted faith healers from the great Matthew Manning who laid on hands to Charlie the veterinary healer in Potters Bar who normally does horses but took stock of my long face and my whinnying and felt at home. And for fifteen months things stayed stable.

Until the last few days of filming the sequel to Jack's *Eskimo Day* before beginning rehearsals for Noël Coward's *Blithe Spirit* in Chichester, when I casually rang the neurologist's office for my latest scan results and got them. Right between the shoulder blades.

Fellow actors Tom Wilkinson and David Ross caught me weeping in my Winnebago and it all came out. Tom immediately recommended a neurosurgeon friend who lived in Muswell Hill nearby. I told him I'd got five surgeons on the go already and needed another like Bill Gates needs a benefit – but I ended up dropping my X-rays in to Mr Bradford on my way home. His words were Balm of Gilead. 'If it were my wife, you'd have had it done yesterday.' (On reflection, of course, any actual doctor's wife must snort with scorn at that particular expression as 'For God's sake, woman, take an aspirin' seems to be the general prescription for members of doctors' families.) He went on to assure me that Alan Crockard, my second, second opinion had taught him all he knew and if it made me feel better he would assist him. I relaxed. My neck and hand were in safe hands – four of them. I had the dream ticket.

Meanwhile, rehearsals for *Blithe Spirit* were proceeding to their second week with me sitting on this bombshell. Madame Arcati was springing on to tables, falling backwards off stools and dancing eccentric tangos. The usual laughing, lunching and luvvying sessions were all happening between Twiggy, Belinda Lang, Stephen Pacey and the rest of the small cast. In short, we were bonding. Part of me, though, was drifting above it all, and on the morning of my withdrawal I'm afraid I withdrew to the toilet and just hid there whilst the cast were told.

I read somewhere that Harry Enfield doesn't believe that actors are brave. I can only assume that Mr Enfield has never been in a stage play. With two weeks to go before opening night and no replacement for Madame Arcati, the cast was only concerned that I got better. Septuagenarian star Dora Bryan had ten days to learn a huge part and complicated illusions. The management wouldn't delay the opening by a day. One night she rushed off stage, leant panting in the wings and said, 'Well, I think they got the gist of it.'

Harry – you're right. Actors aren't brave. They're heroic.

The operation was booked for Monday week. Meanwhile, things were coming to a head and not just figuratively. I had a throbbing abscess under a large section of bridgework and root canal work was the next day's projected treat. Walking away from the endodontist with a lip like a buttock, I bumped into the first surgeon who didn't think I should have the operation. Confused? Who, me? Where was my passport and those South African rands Lord Lucan sent me?

The decision made itself. A date was fixed. The week went fast. 'When shall I come?' said my mother on the Hull extension. 'I'll cancel that appointment I've got on the Monday. I'm only going to Bernard's for a blow-job.' There was no answer to that.

'Come Tuesday,' I said. 'It's not going to be much fun here.'

'Don't be silly,' she said. 'I'm not expecting FUN!'

'For me, Mum, for me . . .' All the medics talked about trying to save the nerve to my right hand, until one night my doctor read out a letter which more or less admitted that the nerve to my hand would have to be severed during the op. For the first time I freaked. I threw the phone across the room and started shaking. Once I started I couldn't stop. My teeth began playing ragtime, my knees a sort of counterpoint.

Now here's the spooky bit. Two days earlier I'd cancelled an appointment with a psychic healer, thinking perhaps I should leave well enough alone. At the start of *Blithe Spirit* I'd visited Belgrave Square Centre for Psychic Studies as research for the part of Madame Arcati, the medium. Rather alarmingly, a message came across, for me, from the psychic in charge of the demonstration. 'You have had some bad health problems and it's not over yet. But it will be OK.' Right now my surgeons were saying the same thing. I felt secure with them. A second psychic opinion I didn't need. I thought.

My teeth were still chattering when the phone rang. It was my friend, Layla. It was she who had recommended the psychic healer. She didn't like the sound of me and phoned again the next day to say she'd reinstated my appointment and if we could get to Twickenham – twelve miles away – in 50 minutes, he would see me. I was dressed, out of the house and picking her up in six minutes.

People will always be sceptical about faith healing. How could they not be? There is no scientific proof, it works for some people and not others, the methodology is often suspect, the practitioner often bizarre. All I know is that for two hours I was manipulated physically and cajoled mentally. There was a strong sense of my late father in the room. I became quite disturbed and at the end Graham told me casually that he'd drained the tumour and moved it slightly so it could be removed more easily from the nerve. Layla and I went to a tea room afterwards and just sat there stunned for an hour until I could face the drive back. She had prayed for two hours. She was more bushed than I was.

Something must have worked. The first thing I did on waking up, post op, was to wave my right hand at the family. Truly, madly, deeply, they waved back. Mr Crockard was delightfully open-minded. 'Whatever it was,' he said smiling, 'the forces were with us.' Someone who'd been present during the surgery told me the surgeon had, actually, consulted a third surgeon when they realised the tumour was in a slightly different place. It was felt that, because of this, they could scrape it away instead of cutting the nerve. I had had so much support. Groups of nuns had prayed for me. People sent tapes and cards and even a slip of paper which had been blessed and which 'you must wear in your bra during the operation'. I felt twice, thrice, a hundred times blessed.

Lying in Intensive Care, my throat like a felt duster, I watched the cup of tea I'd begged for grow cold in the corner whilst I made feeble mewing sounds to attract the attention of the nurse in charge. Later, she astounded me by confiding, 'I'm not often in Intensive Care – I'm usually in Admin, but I like to keep my hand in.' Gulp.

My first meal was days later because, as ever, the migraine kicked in after the anaesthetic. In my mind's pink and bleary eye, I could see crisp lettuce, fresh, barely ripe tomatoes, translucent cucumber and fresh, salty cottage cheese. The reality when it came was limp and over-ripe, and the cheese was rancid.

I called the general manager, who came bustling and beaming round the door.

'Hello, Mrs Rosenmumble . . . Are you enjoying your lunch?' 'Mr Hassid, this is my first food in a week. The cottage cheese is rancid. This is a hospital – I'm a patient. What are you thinking about . . .?'

To my amazement, his grin only widened. 'Oh, yes – you are she, all right. Ha! Ha! You are just the same as you are on TV. You are Beattie, right? Very similar – very funny – I will tell my wife.'

I looked at my right hand. Was it strong enough to squeeze a throat with? I wondered.

Whilst I was recuperating, every live, dead, fanciful, exotic, quixotic form of flora to ever grace the borders of Kew or the display brochures of Interflora came my way. Like Patsy Kensit, I was up to my neck in oasis.

Don't misunderstand me. I was wildly, pathetically grateful to the myriad friends, relatives and relative strangers who were generous enough to cough up everything from Phalaenopsis orchids to whole magnolia plants for little old wobbly necked me. My hospital room looked like a float in the Jersey Festival. I could hear people getting out of the third floor lift and going, 'My God! It smells like a tart's boudoir up here!'

Inevitably, there was one hugely gorgeous all-white arrangement which arrived without its card – so whenever the phone went I said, 'Thank you so much for the gorgeous flowers,' just on the off-chance. This of course embarrassed anyone who didn't send flowers into frantic florist phoning and the whole thing started over again.

Somehow, my friends the Morrows managed to smuggle a traffic cone complete with floral centrepiece and a 'No Loitering' sign into my hospital room.

On Sunday, a couple of days later, I took myself out of the place and started for home. There my mum watched me, marvelling, as I chopped up veg for a casserole.

Another friend, Tom Conti, phoned me at home just as I was frantically trying to find a chair – any chair – that was high enough to support my post-operative neck. For weeks I wore the deepest neck collar the hospital had had in stock – one usually reserved for Zulu tribeswomen and contortionists. 'I feel like one of those wobbly headed beagles which hang in the back windows of Volvos,' I told him. Twenty minutes later Mr Conti was to be seen shlepping a large wing chair up my front drive. My mother almost passed out. For a moment she thought she was headed for a Greek island . . .

I was even sent a tape from a complete stranger who sang me, unaccompanied, Gershwin in Greek for 45 minutes. Extraordinary.

Looking around, I felt absurdly grateful. So, my surfaces were never going to be pristine nor my ambience minimalistic. I was never going to drag-finish my dado or stencil my own parquet and I'd still have to ring Carmela in Marbella when she took her summer hols to ask how to open the tumble dryer door and where the piccalilli's kept these days.

There were, however, compensations. I could still make an excellent chicken and barley pot roast. I was a brilliant doodler. I could make a surgeon laugh immediately after anaesthetic and remember a colour in my head three weeks later in a hat shop. I was married to the finest, funniest and most relieved man in the history of men being relieved. I was alive, I was kidding, and the luckiest, lousy housewife in the whole wide world and Wigan pier.

The Book of Nemesis

'Raindrops on roses and whiskers on kittens, bright copper kettles and warm woollen mittens', these were a few of the wayward nun Maria's favourite things and, with nothing more exciting to do of a morning than shin up a hill and be late for vespers, she was rather easily pleased. What would her *bêtes noires* have been, I wonder, and would Rodgers and Hammerstein have found a rhyme for *bêtes noires*?

There is a joke about the Pope visiting California where he is interviewed by Barbara Walters. 'Tell me, Your Eminence,' she gushes, 'is there anything in life which really gets up your nose?'

'I am sorry?' says the Pope.

She rephrases it. 'Is there anything which drives you crazy, irritates you beyond . . .'

'Oh, yes, sortainly,' breaks in the Pope. 'Zere are two zings vich I hate and despise. Von of zem is Polish jokes. Zay are racist, unfunny, insulting to a fine people and not based on any truth vatsoever.'

'I understand that, sir, and what is the second thing?'

'Smarties,' replies his Eminence.

'Smarties!?' exclaims his interviewer. 'You mean the little colour-covered chocolates?'

'Oh, yes,' insists the Primate. 'I hate and despise zem because zey are *zooo* difficult to peel.'

Affronted Catholics and chocolate makers, please don't write in and abuse me – I do Jewish jokes all the time, I know it's not PC, but it's MA – as in mildly amusing – and I'm willing for my Hull/Lithuanian roots to be dug up and derided, whenever.

Personally, there are so many zings which get up my nose that I'm thinking of having an extension built on. Let me cite, for starters, 'childprufe' medicine bottles which are also grown-up-prufe, arthritic hand-prufe, profanity-inducing and leave depressions on the skin of your hand which refuse, after forty, to bounce back. Many is the middle-of-the-night pain left unrelieved whilst its recipient leaps up and down on top of a small, brown plastic container screaming, 'Open, you pernicious bastard, or I'll break every bone in your body!' It goes without saying that the only people with patience and ingenuity to open the ruddy things are children, particularly those educated at Montessori schools with access to Fisher Price toys.

I reserve the same blind fury for packaging in general. Moulded plastic packaging in particular. It takes two minutes to buy a new toothbrush and two days to remove the sodding thing from the packet. Most of my new toothbrushes are bought en route to somewhere at which I realise, too late, I will need to smile. 'A packet of "Superfreshliplickinstalebreath-devouringwaterfallminty" mints, please. Oh, and a medium toothbrush with narrow, adjustable head for those awkward places which show the spinach.'

Quick dive into the toilets at the appointed place, then attempt to wrench, wriggle, slide, tear and finally bludgeon toothbrush out of moulded plastic. Eventually, mouth foaming, but not with toothpaste, attack the packaging with teeth and remove not, alas, the toothbrush, but £400 worth of bridgework.

Incidentally, this lunacy also applies to most household gadgets which are packaged by sadists to alienate the infirm, the aged, and the pusher of this pen. Hang on, I'm just getting going.

Industrial toilet rolls now come in hand applicators the size of Pavarotti. Ever tried to find the end of one? Whilst on the loo? Hand curved back on itself like a Balinese temple dancer, flailing uselessly at a sealed perforation that you can neither see nor reach. Bumper fun for all the family and not an adorable puppy in sight to help you out, which is just as well, because if there were, you'd probably kick it.

And you've just recovered from this in time to fasten your *snap crotch body* (so called because anybody trying to achieve this will become so crotchety that they will eventually snap), the effort of which causes physical distress in the loo and mental humiliation when you return to the crowded party with an attractive black tail hanging out over your cream linen trousers. For the myopic, now becoming longsighted person, the joys of being unable to see the *self-coloured* poppers which bind the snap crotch together are never ending. Why don't they use Velcro, or brightly coloured presstuds? Or U-Hu, for heaven's sake? Then I wouldn't have to stick my head between my legs like an orang-utang on heat and forever be fishing my glasses out of the toilet.

And why can nobody see it but me? The hand-drying machine in the toilets – I mean, it just doesn't work. It is to the world of drying what Liz Hurley is to the world of tree pollarding. You can stand there for minutes on end wafting your hands left and right, north and south, and all that happens is the bloody thing bakes the soap you thought you'd rinsed off into a sort of meringue. At this point you lose patience and leave the loo. Whereupon, almost without fail, someone of enormous importance and/or good looks steps forward to shake you by the hand. The words freeze in your throat.

I realise a towel is an old-fashioned concept which requires laundering and replacing. I find it equally inappropriate when I visit posh hotel loos and there's a pile of miniature towels of elaborately fluffy texture which you use once and throw into a large receptacle. 'What a waste,' I want to say to my fellow toiletees. 'Shall we share one? I'll take this corner and you take that.'

The other day I was recording a radio comedy before a live audience in the Vanbrugh Theatre. After a couple of run-throughs, I retired to the ladies' room to freshen up the old armpits before the live broadcast. It was only after I'd soaped and rinsed them that I realised the only means of drying them was under the blithering hot air machine. My dears, you had to be there! I looked like a crouching gorilla leaping for a branch.

Do you remember those towels you used to get in old station hotels? They were the total opposite of what is regarded as desirable in today's towel. Like everything else, they've been Americanised. Extra soft, extra deep, extra fluffy – they rise to twice their own width like a soufflé. They come in twelve sizes: bath size, sheet size, elbow size, ankle size, picnic size, Schwarzenegger size – and roughly 900 colours, ranging from chartreuse with olive monogram to wallaby with nectarine overstitch. The one thing you can count on is that not one of the buggers will actually dry a wet person. You can rub yourself, hug yourself, wrap yourself and roll yourself but all you'll have at the end is a wet towel and a slightly wetter body.

Just give me one thin, quite hard (so there's a bit of friction), decent-sized white towel and I'll give you a dry, glowing, enervated and slightly pink person. I did actually fork out a preposterous amount of money for what's called a waffle towel – just for the gym, you understand – which claims to absorb half its weight in water and then some. I'm not actually able to commit myself as to its efficiency since I haven't been to the gym since the last liberal government but it certainly looks nice and flat and hard – which is more than I do.

What else? Light-coloured towels in guest rooms, says my friend Astrid. No matter how many times you wet-wipe your make-up off and follow up with cleansing milk, toner, moisturiser and 'night repair' (in your dreams!), you can be sure of one thing: in the morning the cream guest towel will be tan. You won't remember using fake bronzer, you'll swear on a stack of *Vanity Fairs* you only wiped the towel round your mouth to remove the toothpaste. You'll view your husband with suspicion and start checking his toilet bag for man-tan, but you'll never find the answer. And what is the etiquette here? Do you wet the towel and rub it vigorously to remove the muck? Do you roll it up and take it home to be washed and returned pristine, with a note about how it accidentally fell into your bag? Or do you just get the hell out before breakfast? Whatever you decide, don't under any circumstances glance at the pillowcase and clock the clumps of black mascara clinging to the off-white hand-embroidered pillowcase (which has, notwithstanding, left a hand-embroidered indentation all over one side of your cheek), because the only way out of that one is to announce your partner has decided to come out as a cross-dresser, say 'Thank you for having me' and head for the station.

How long can it be before we can do without towels altogether because the shower dries you with hot air after it wets you and soaps you? My shower gel now says: for bodywash, shampoo and conditioner. What the hell else can it do? Make soup?

My final memory is of my children running from the bathroom after their evening baths, wearing their Mothercare towels with integral hoods, hers blue, his yellow, flying like little exotic birds across the landing to be dried, powdered and read to. I can still feel the damp warmth of them as I speak to one in Bucharest and one going off in search of a flat of her own. Anyone got a muslin hankie?

Onwards. In one sentence, the Americanisation of our high streets, our television system, our language, and, like, our eating habits, man. I may not be a cool dude but I like to see *through* things, not thru' them, I like to *be* a parent (well, not always, but occasionally) not 'to parent' and the double 'll' sound in surveillance is not music to my years. As for sounding the 'h' in aitch and saying 'we was' and 'I aren't' and 'I'm like' well, I could go on – and I do.

As for Cable Television, quite seriously, if *I* wanted to dig up the pavement outside my house and replace it with a load of lumpy tar in a winding and treacherous strip, then replace the tar with paving stones in a different style and hue from the remaining stones, all the whilst diverting and endangering traffic and pedestrians alike for several months of the year, do you think *they'd* let me do it? No, they bloody wouldn't. It was hard enough getting *them* to grant me a new soil stack so I could fumble with my snap crotch in the privacy of my own privy. It took weeks of negotiations. But along comes Mr Cable, or Glark, as I like to call him, wafting zillions of dollars around and the promise of acreage of dreary, violent videos and *What I Keep in my Inglenook* by Michael Winner and – Hey Presto! – pounding drills, juddering flesh and tottering grannies with broken wheelies all over the high street. Bah! Humbug! Speaking of which, why don't *they* taste like they used to?

Leaflets which fall out of fat Sunday papers,
Burgers and Doners and nowhere a draper's,

Monstrous white sneakers with gas in their springs,
These represent my unfavourite things.

Twenty-inch pepper pots, twenty-pound phone books,
Too many satellites, traffic cones, Sloane cooks,
A mobile in a theatre which suddenly rings,
These are some more truly horrible things.

When the cat purrs, when the kids ring,
When I'm feeling glad,
I simply recall these unspeakable things
To *drive myself barking mad!*

PS: sleeping policemen (may the force *not* be with us); baseball caps worn backwards (they weren't dumb enough worn forwards?); cricketers in red and green stripe with Harpic emblazoned across the front; cheapo TV with the public as stars; politicians making 'one thing perfectly clear' . . .

It's no good. I must stop . . . there's no end to it once I get started.

Last Year's Model

I keep seeing them. Everywhere. Nubile, powerful, skinny, feline-featured women with jutting jawlines, disproportionate breasts and lips like scatter cushions. And they're not just striding ferociously up the catwalks or bestriding the pages of the kind of magazines which require a second mortgage or frolicking across the bits you flick through rapidly at the back of *Hello!*. Oh no. Dear me no. *Pas du tout*.

They are everywhere else as well. They fill the pages of the tabloid press, they cause paparazzi riots at Heathrow Airport and paperback panic in Selfridges' basement, they flit through the movie colony and the international jet set, they take tea with Dalai Lamas and Des O'Connor, they pose in Calvin Klein leggings amongst the starving in Somalia and in the ravished rain forests. They are the darlings of the gossip columns and we are on first-name terms with them all. We know Cindy and Claudia and Cheryl and Carla and Christie, as well as we know Diana and Hillary. As well as we *knew* Fergie and Glenys. We know where to buy their videos, their calendars and their swimsuits. We know all their consorts too . . . who dated De Niro, who mated Gere, who Iman-cipated Bowie and Infant-icipated Rod. We know that Gianni's Evangelical for Linda and Armani's Emporical for Naomi. We saw Yasmin's bijou le Bonbon before her gynaecologist did. We're very familiar with Jerry's precious Stone. These girls are not just social, they're sociological. They are superwomen.

OK. No sour grapes around this particular fruit dish. Good luck to 'em. Distorted limbs and distorted salaries are nothing new. I love Wimbledon as much as the next man. But hang on a sec. The skill, training and commitment of a tennis ace is beyond dispute. Likewise your average round-the-globe female aviator, engineer, sculptress, dancer, equestrian eventist, culinary guru, spacewoman, scientist, picket-crossing protester, midwife, *housewife*, for God's sake. I don't begrudge them an inch of print, a handful of dollars, or all the romance in the *Tales from the Arabian Nights*.

But modelling? *This* is what the Pankhursts chained and Gloria and Germaine burned for? *This* should be the height of female wish fulfilment? Women gifted with bodies which resemble less than two per cent of the bodies of the average women, with legs longer than the length of the average woman. With knockers firmer than the average woman's –

firmer than the average *man's*, to be honest. Women to whom God handed out facial bones which leap out and embrace the merest hint of an arc lamp and teeth which are handpicked and matched like pearls from the sea bed. Women who, for sensational salaries, do one thing brilliantly. *They walk*. Up and down a couple of trestle tables. Don't get me wrong. Sometimes they turn around too. Or shed a garment. Or change expressions. But mostly they walk. Fast. Slow. Seductive. Aggressive. It's tough, I grant you. They also walk tall.

And, while they're doing it, they wear clothes. For the most part, unwearable clothes. Clothes which designers would love to see on beautiful boys. Clothes conceived by, designed by, cut out by, sewn together by and placed upon their bodies by other people. Ordinary looking, fat, slouched, balding, scraggy, paunchy, creative, skilled and talented human beings. Then make-up artists paint, hairdressers primp and the supermodel sends forward her perfectly narrowed hips through the curtains and a couple of minutes later, the rest of her follows. 'Oooh, aaah, oooh, la-la!'

Oh I know. They do photographic shoots and commercials too. In studios and exotic locations, as often as not accompanied by an endangered species or a primitive tribesman and a deal of ethnic jewellery. Here the creative team involves a gifted and self-important photographer to whom our superchick is often married, if not before the exotic location, then after, the equally exotic advertising team, copy-writers, clients, and desert-catering crew. Our girl's job is to snarl, sneer, straddle and smoulder, not necessarily in that order, and elongate her already elongated limbs into positions heretofore only ever attempted by teams of Chinese acrobats and the odd lady of the night in Phuket.

Meanwhile, back in the bedsits and offices and tube compartments and high rises and dentists' waiting-rooms of home, others can peruse these pages sitting on their sofa beds in their Next copies of Janet Reger lounging pyjamas, eating their Marks & Spencer's cottage cheese and pineapple chunks and wondering idly if last year's Lycra mini skirt could be stretched into this year's split-thigh midi skirt with the inventive use of a spanner and a course of liposuction and whether anyone will come along to lick the Häagen-Dazs off their knee or should they use a J-cloth.

We'll never get into those high-thigh swimsuits of Jerry Hall's. Not without emerging doubled over from the changing room clutching a towelling robe round our hips and hitting the water at seventy miles an hour still clutching the robe. We'll never wear the slit-to-the-waist, transparent black chiffon body with nothing underneath, without recourse to several rolls of double-sided Elastoplast and an animated but somewhat sheepish discussion about which stretch mark was from which child. And we'll never wear the floor-length, stretch-velour evening dress with the shoestring back because the only time we put it on, our partner fell off the bed laughing and said we looked like a roll of boned and stuffed brisket.

Surely the Trade Descriptions Act can be evoked in situations like this? These girls are making fools out of us women. With our scholarships and our degrees and our careers and our memberships of women's groups and gyms that worked the arses off us and then bored them back on again three weeks after paying the premiums. They are giving us an image to live up to that we can't afford, don't want and couldn't walk in. These are our sisters, sister? Role models? I think not.

Dandy Lying and Murdoch

Sometimes a single sentence can make you hug yourself with joy. I was flying to Edinburgh when I heard the announcement: 'Sir Jeffrey Archer will be signing copies of his new book in W H Smiths on the second floor.' That was all.

It's not that I've got anything against book signings. Many's the time I've sat, solitary, before a cardboard cut-out of myself, willing the floor to open and drop me into the Home Brewing and Dead Languages Department. No, what brought a bark to my lips was the concept that Sir Jeffrey may have been flying off somewhere for the annual summer sojourn with the scented spouse, when the thought struck him: 'I say! There's a bloody bookshop at Heathrow, isn't there? Check-in's at 10.00. Flight's at 11.30. Mmmm . . . seems a shame to waste the hour . . .'

This is pure supposition, I hasten to add, and unfair on the grounds that Jeffrey is such an easy target and is therefore unworthy of attack. As is Jason. And Esther. And Claire. And Cliff. And Grossman. For are they not honourable men? Albeit with one common trait. The desire to be liked. A desire which shows.

But wait. Is this a crime? Don't performers perform in order to be appreciated? Didn't Beethoven and Olivier and Callas and Bernstein? Didn't Van Gogh and Schumann want appreciation *during* their lifetime? Didn't Veronese hope the Doge would pay for his 'Last Supper' and didn't Noël Coward wait up for early morning reviews?

I pose the question, dear reader, because I am troubled by the current fad for character assassination with pen *and* sword, which is engulfing popular and grown-up periodicals alike. Death by tape recorder, I call it. In my *Independent on Sunday*, I see Jason Donovan being pinned to a board by William Reith. In my *Guardian*, Emma Thompson is quietly shredded by Catherine Bennett. Elsewhere Sir Andrew is decimated in an article which suggests that even his mother may not like him. Since when did talent and likeability have to go hand in hand?

Should one expect an artist to be a great human being? Would anyone really expect Mozart's company, on a week's chalet holiday in Leipzig, to be as entertaining as the same chalet with thirty of his best CDs, a red setter and a good bottle of cognac? There is scarcely a poet, composer, playwright or painter whose life is not a compendium of broken love affairs, madness, cruelty, drug dependence, poverty or profligacy. We want it that way. How else would Ken Russell earn a living? Perhaps the talent itself is a compensation for some lack of quality of soul. Perhaps artistic creation is part of a fretful search for happiness which others find quite naturally in living. 'I am not interested in the pursuit of happiness,' said Joyce Grenfell, 'but only in the discovery of joy.'

I first noticed this abusive trend in the photographers who gather at charity premières. 'Over here, Beattie!' they'd yell at me, not unkindly, and the cross-eyed grimace which ensued captured eighteen months' dental work, last night's vegetable biryani and a close-up of my uvula for the Sunday colour mag with the caption: 'Do us a favour, Mo . . . termouth. Keep it closed.' This intellectual exercise alerted me to a spate of 'Twenty Naff Things You Never Knew About Hugh' and 'Anneka – the Dodgy Bits', all of them compiled by a disgruntled office-boy with an aegrotat degree in humour from Uppsala Poly.

Could Ghengis Khan (no relation, Jemima, worry not) have survived Jeremy Paxman? Can we take anything seriously enough, or concentrate on it for long enough, to wish to fight for it? Occasionally, I long for an alien invasion. By gum, we'd soon forget border skirmishes and petty religious differences if something huge, green and knobbly hovered over St Paul's or St Petersburg for an hour or two – 'Invasion of the Killer Gherkins'.

I feel more and more like my late father, God rest his soul, who, suffering from memory loss, would turn over the pages of the *Express* or watch the TV news with the same expression of beaten disbelief and, clucking his tongue, would murmur, 'You can't bloody believe it, can you?'

'Who or what is God to you?' said a *Guardian* reporter to me last week after the obligatory apologies for bothering one in one's own home of a weekend. I was uncharacteristically serious as I strove to describe a feeling of peace, a freedom from worry, a sense of well-being and security . . . when the reporter continued: 'I mean, some people have said Jurgen Klinsmann and others have said Sting.' I felt unaccountably depressed and asked the young lady, rather acidly, if she was happy in her work.

I'm trying to understand whether the rot set in before the Rotweillers got out. Are the press giving the public what it wants? Or are the public being pressured by the press? Does the appetite for junk food increase on a junk food diet? The Sid Vicious school of writers prepare their angle before they reach their subject's door chimes. Happy marriage? Humbug! Normal childhood? Bo-o-o-o-oring. Politics? Bad copy! They reveal the skeleton in the dressing-room and wait for promotion, reputation and, probably, their own alternative underwater quiz show on GMTV.

Julia McKenzie told a reporter recently that her friend Maureen had suggested she should begin an interview by confessing a nineteen-year-old passionate affair with Frank Bruno. Anything to avoid the face as flat as a fish's which asks, 'So, Julia, same marriage, same suburban life, do you ever long for excitement?'

And the *hatred*, oh, the hatred. Give a reporter their own column and call it 'Lynn on the Line' and you can be sure of only one thing: you will learn, in the next one thousand words, a great deal more about the interviewer than about his or her subject. The interview will begin with a couple of paragraphs relating to the difficulties of setting up the meeting, a description of the restaurant and its pretentious/folksy clientele. Then we are treated to a description of the victim (with or without surgical history) and their class-revealing choice of food. By now, we know that the celebrity has an attitude problem, although it never occurs to the writer that this could, in any way, relate to their *own* proximity. From here it's a short jump to regaling the reader with the star's obvious attempts to plug their own book or film which is why both people are there. Ultimately, this leads to the angle on which the writer has been waiting to pounce since grabbing the brief – the celebrity's dependence on cyanide, fratricide, suicide or, if necessary, insecticide.

There was a time when *Private Eye* was the only harbinger of gossip, tittle-tattle and cynicism. The bloodshed's now so widespread that Lord Gnome may have to retitle his worthy tome *Public Knowledge*.

I'm not advocating the *Hello!* school of writing: 'We get to peek behind the magical scenes at her Hacienda-and-Fontainebleau-style mansion where Jane, "This time it's for ever" Seymour, weds her fourth husband.' In fact, this cock-eyed optimism may have spawned the '*Hair* actress Weds Fourth Victim' alternative style. As ballast. Maybe writers are tired of famous personalities using *their* byline to plug anything from Passion Plays to perfumed Y-fronts. 'Oh, Jeez, I've got whatsisname from *Brooksidenders* at 2.00. He's written, directed and starred in his first movie. He's fifteen! I'll give him 200 words on that crap, then I'll hit him with the troilism, the transvestism and the gerbil!'

Often celebrities don't help themselves. Take the trend for expensive public confessionals: child abuse, alcoholism, adultery, near fatal illness, obsessive attachment to *Cell Block H*. Recently, Anthony Clare, interviewing Esther Rantzen, asked her if she didn't feel she had a predilection for airing her personal problems in public. A strange question for a radio psychiatrist to ask a woman who was airing them for eight million listeners . . . and *him* . . .

Unfortunately there's no Youth Training Scheme for handling success. Or failure. It's a surer test of character if you survive the latter than the former, but Kipling was right when he suggested that one should treat 'those two impostors' the same way.

In my experience, one minute you're dancing on a table top with a champagne cork in each ear, celebrating your first speaking role in an undiscovered Belgian farce for STV and the next minute you're marching arm in arm with Glenys Kinnock and Liza Minelli down Whitehall, demanding shorter working hours for Latvian seamstresses. It happens seamlessly and it's hard to handle.

My final word comes hotfoot from the kitchen. It is VE Day and I'm planting fuchsia 'Winston Churchill' in my window-boxes. Jack comes out and says, wearily, 'It's the *News of the World.* They want to know what you think of the sacking of Will Carling as England's captain.'

I put down a handful of organic peat and wiped my brow, channelling soil into my new disposable lenses. 'Oh, for heaven's sake,' I groaned. 'Tell them I know nothing at all about rugby, but I like the cleft in his chin and I admire him for speaking out.'

Jack returned a moment later. 'You won't believe this. I told him what you said and when I got to the cleft in his chin, he said, "The what?" so I said, "The cleft" and he said, "Er, what is that? I mean, what does that actually mean? The *what* in his chin . . .?"'

What can you say? We are cleft apart, the *News of the World* and I, by more than just a five-letter word . . . We are cleft apart by ignorance. Of Cary Grant and Bob Mitchum and . . . Oh, what the hell . . . he probably thought it was a baked lamb dish in a Greek restaurant and wondered what it was doing in Will Carling's chin.

Having said that, I'm oddly fond of journalists. I'm even quite proud when someone calls me one. I like their company and feel at ease with most of them. I just wish that when the wit hits the fan it wasn't 'them v us', because we plainly don't exist without each other. Times are hard for both professions. There are eleven national daily newspapers in a country which more and more relies on Ceefax and radio for its news. Perhaps the new killer journalism is merely a career move.

There is a story about President De Klerk and Archbishop Tutu having discussions about ending apartheid on a boat in the middle of a lake, with the world's press camped around the lake perimeter with zoom lenses trained on the couple. De Klerk's hat blows off on to the lake and Tutu calmly leaves the boat, walks across the water, retrieves the hat and brings it back to De Klerk. The next day, the newspaper headlines scream: 'Desmond Tutu Cannot Swim'.

Still, I'm alright, Jack. Just dashing to Tesco's for some late-night shopping, and whilst I'm there I might as well sign a few of my books for the dumpbin . . .

Wonder-Barbra

The circus left town long ago, leaving nothing behind it but a string of disgruntled critics, a million out-of-pocket but delirious fans, several thousand metres of white satin and a carpet custom-cut to fill Wembley Arena.

I'm referring, of course, to the State Visit of Barbra Streisand (equal emphasis, Strei and sand, soft s) legend, super-star, icon and musical phenomenon. She of the voice which flowed through my adolescence like hormones in honey and gave me the only intimations since Alma Cogan that there was hope and maybe even glory for other 'funny girls' with, let's say, irregular features.

My one previous, and much-chronicled, encounter with my heroine was when, during the time my husband was writing *Yentl*, our six-year-old son informed her that her voice was too loud. 'It really hurts my ears, your voice,' he bleated pleasantly. His star-struck mother then added injury to insult by trying to point out a mistake in the orchestration in 'Memory'. The star's baby blue eyes gazed at the writer's wife for a *very* long time and the rest is silence, of the black hole variety.

It was in the mid-Sixties when I read in *Time* magazine about her 'Miss Marmelstein' in the show *I Can Get It For You Wholesale*. Instant identification. Later, 'People' from *Funny Girl* became my mantra for months before it acquired a tune (Broadway soundtracks were not easy to track down in downtown Hull in '63). By the time I'd acquired *My Name is Barbra* and *Colour Me Barbra* in vinyl, most of the world knew not only that this girl could snake her way into your soul with one note of that most beautiful of instruments, her voice, but also that she had an even more formidable talent for alienating 'People' who needed her.

The story goes that when she was a struggling actress, she was in the apartment of her friend then, and still today, Cis Corman, and began to sing to herself in the kitchen. Corman came in and commented on the brilliance of her voice. Barbra immediately stopped singing. The only way she would ever sing again for Cis and her husband was to stand at the other end of the kitchen and turn her back on them. Pardon my psychobabble but I don't think that phobia has ever really left her. She just finds subtler ways of turning her back.

After *Funny Girl*, director William Wyler, when asked what it was like working with Barbra Streisand, replied that she was quite brilliant considering it was the first film she'd ever *directed*. A cynical comment, perhaps justified, but in the light of *Prince of Tides* and *Yentl* it was an early indication of a real director's eye. Maybe even two.

There were other films where this theory falls apart and perhaps her desire for total control is perfectionism gone AWOL. But consider. To be a superstar in the US for three decades takes more than talent. It takes fortitude, stamina, the skin of an armadillo and a kind of madness to want it. Who else is still there? Shirley MacLaine? Liz? Liza? Not in movies, records, TV *and* stage. No one. And she's done it by demanding the best, moving one step ahead of every trend, fast, and taking no prisoners. In so doing she's got right up the nasal passages of a great many people who would otherwise have nothing up there but very finely cut white powder.

So, if I were to state my bias in the she's a genius/she's a monster debate, I would certainly come out in the same camp as most of the 12,000 loving fans who gave their diva a standing, stomping, salaaming reception, which made my last trip to Wembley, to see a cup final, sound like a day spent in the Fossil Department of the British Museum.

The tabloid press sounded off differently. For weeks before she arrived, the speculation grew increasingly strident. Hysteria greeted the news that top ticket prices would be £250 (normal price for Pavarotti or Glyndebourne) and – shock-horror-have-they-gone-raving-mad? – barmaids from Bootle were willing to pay bootleg prices for a mere two hours of their heroine's time. Full typographical Tourette's syndrome, however, was reserved for the news of her autocue. 'Every line a prompt!' they screamed. 'News At Ten comes to Wembley at £250 a ticket.' The fear and loathing factor was at fever pitch. She was, uncharacteristically, granting no interviews, so each headline was accompanied by snatched street snaps of uniform unkindness.

Her fans knew about the autocue. She'd already used it in Las Vegas. After the press attacks here, she told her audience that twenty-eight years ago, singing to 125,000 people in Central Park, she'd 'dried' as dead as Daedalus and could think of nothing witty to excuse it. As a result of that, she'd stayed off stage for twenty-eight years. We could take her, security blanket and all, or we could leave her. Instant standing ovation, then she caressed her way through classics and songs she had made into classics and I swear, hand on fan club badge, she never looked at her security blanket once.

Afterwards, in the dressing-room, she talked of her fear of performing live. 'But you must feel better now you've done these concerts?' someone ventured. The baby blue eyes hardened momentarily. 'Not a bit. It gets harder.' She's right. It does.

'What I say to myself is . . .' I heard myself burble, '"Maureen, in three hours' time you'll be in bed."'

She considered it for a millisecond. 'No. Wouldn't work for me.'

I toyed with adding 'and home by five', but I didn't.

Afterwards, my Hull chum, Valerie, and I were like the couple of schoolkids who'd just swapped one 'Best Wishes, Helen Shapiro' for two barbershop snippings of Cliff Richard's quiff. It was, in truth, Val's fault I was there at all. We'd considered buying tickets but, to be honest, decided they were a tidge on the expensive side. 'If it was for a charity . . .' I mumbled, parsimoniously.

'Wembley?' said Jack, who reads only the political and sports pages. 'No. Every time I go, they lose.'

'For God's sake,' shrieked Val. 'You *know* her. Ring somebody up! Gedda discount! Whatsa matter with you?' He wouldn't-couldn't, so I rang my agent, they rang someone, someone rang me, and I managed – Eureka! – to get two seats for – yes, you've guessed it – exactly the same price as advertised. Maureen 'I can get it for you retail' Lipman.

So Val and I were all set for Wednesday night. Tuesday evening, I'm in bed resting my neck for the occasion, when the phone announces, 'Hi, this is Kim, Barbra Streisand's assistant. Ms Streisand wondered if Mr Rosenthal and yourself would like to be her guests for the last concert.'

My mind is going like an Apple Mac on print-out. 'Ooooo-er-gosh, thank you, but I'm already coming tomorrow night.'

'Oh, is Jack going to be with you?'

'Er – yes,' I lied. 'But we'd love to see it twice. *Thank* you.'

Phone down. Address book up. Who do I know who'd pay £500 for two seats in eighteen hours' time? No one. What do I do? I cajole Jack into buying another seat for the last night for Val. So, by now, we're up to £750 for three seats and I'm envisaging myself touting Wednesday's seats outside Wembley in a flasher's mac and beard. Six hours before curtain up, we sell at a philanthropic loss.

I wish I could report that the loss was deadly. I wish I could send up the set, the clothes, the fans, the car parking arrangements. It would make funnier reading.

In fact, it was worth twice the price. It was priceless. I could carp about her philosophical patter, perhaps wish her freer, wilder and more spontaneous. But you don't hire Nigel Kennedy for his table manners, you hire him for his talent. Perfect pitch, modulation, phrasing – the voice pours out like mozzarella. She is fascinating and fine like porcelain. What do the critics want – a drama queen? Liza, Judy, Shirley spilling out their guts, sleeves dripping heart, equally for 'Rain Or Shine' or 'Thumbelina'. Instead they got a reluctant diva, not working the house, but working through her angst. Not drowning but wavering. On this night, we were seeing a reflected image of a past. Ours and hers. Not quite the real thing but, in the time it took to get here, an image of the real thing. Astronomically speaking, A Star.

On the drive home, I looked at my programme. It said 'For Maureen. In three hours' time, I'll be in bed.' I hope she had a great supper. She sang for it, beautifully

The Parting of Names

As we speak, someone tired, sweaty and fulfilled, let's say an Emma, is naming her 45-minute-old baby, Jack. 'It's a real man's name,' she is saying mistily, and, 'I don't know why we thought of it – it just was always going to be Jack if it was a boy.'

'They're calling him Jack,' her mother, Heather, is saying down the phone to her friend, Bernice. 'Jack Albert . . . Yes, well, it's modern. You know, the young people nowadays, they like all the old-fangled names . . . Well, of course – I know – but that was five years ago! Five years ago *everyone* was calling them Dominic!'

And so it goes on. A generation of Maisies and Alfreds, rejecting the names of peers and parents, spawn a generation of Brendas and Bobs from whom issue a plethora of Sheilas and Geoffreys, who in turn beget Samanthas and Tristrams, whose trousers are bursting to produce Maisies and Alfreds.

Each of us believes we are being utterly original. Each of us is wrong, a fact only proven on day one at school when, child so carefully named after Louisa May Alcott's most precious of characters, shares her coat hooks with Amy D, Amy S, Amy H-G and Amy Polyandropulous.

Which is not to say that I would extol the originality of the ex-Mrs Geldof. Peaches Fifi Trixibelle Rosenthal would never have been high on my list, nor would I have embarrassed by progeny any more than I already have by labelling her 'Rose' 'China' or 'Second-Hand'. I mean, the child wants to be identifiable but not so's the entire class keels over every time the register is read out. They want to know the derivation of their name, but not if it's a hallucinogenic drug their parents were on or a high-pitched sound their father always made during foreplay.

As always, fashion has a great deal to answer for in that, on the whole, fashion suits the original wearer, and by the time it has filtered down to bargain basement, it fits and suits no one, least of all the buyer.

Fashion also dictates linguistics and you'd be hard pressed to find anyone answering to the name of the nineteenth century's most popular nomenclature. Oh, no. Very few Fannys at your modern comprehensives these days. That ended for ever, I suppose, the day Johnny Craddock, husband of the famous TV chef Fanny said, live on camera, '. . . and I hope all your tarts come up like Fanny's.'

302

People don't change their names as much as they did earlier in the century to avoid being classified. Mind you Meryl Streep hasn't been held back by a name which, according to Barry Humphries, sounds like a gynaecological complaint, nor Uma Thurman by one which sounds like a storage heater.

Just think of the explanation required one day for all those Kylies and Stings and Hayleys, for heaven's sake! 'Well, it doesn't mean anything, darling – it's from Hayley Mills. Well, she's an actress and her mother named her after her own maiden name. No, she was a writer, actually . . . Oh, shut up and be thankful I didn't call you Sigourney like your father wanted . . .'

I am Maureen because my Uncle Louis liked the film star Maureen O'Hara. Fine. The fact that a small sallow baby born in Hull was unlikely to grow up into a flame-haired temptress with flashing green eyes and a cleavage the size of Galway was neither here nor there. Maureen I became. Or *Marine* on the other side of the Atlantic. Also no one in our house could foresee that since my father's name was Maurice. I would be constantly called, with mounting frustration, 'Mauri-Morry-Maureen!'

I longed for a heroine's name. With a 'y' on the end. 'Vicky at St Clair's', 'Nicky, New Girl', 'Ginny Saves St Kilda's'. Somehow, 'Maureen Pulls It Off' sounds more like I got a great bargain in the sales.

My class of '65 was full of Paulines and Valeries and Marilyns and Janets and Susans and Lindas. These post-war names gave us a sell-by date as clear as the one on a Sainsbury's corner yoghurt. And they are just about to make a comeback, it seems to me, in my role as Witch of the North, so watch this space. Or better still, the birth lists at the back of *The Times* and the *Telegraph*. The circle perpetuates.

When my friend Sally became pregnant, her partner Manuel declared, 'If it is a man baby, we call him Manuel, and if it is a woman baby, we call him Manuela,' which certainly solves the *Pan Book of Boys' Names* and the *Pan Book of Girls' Names* nightly saga.

God, if I had a 5p and a marzipan fruit-cake for every thumb mark on those two tattered paperbacks, I'd be a richer and fatter woman.

It seems to me that Henrietta, Geraldine, Edwina and, unkindest of all, Nigella, emerged in direct response to parental expectation of a MALE child. Never mind thinking of something suitable for a small bundle of femininity – just stick an 'ella' on the end. Or an 'ina' or an 'etta'. You don't agree? Then why doesn't it work the other way round? Show me a Fionaron or an Emmatom for every Samantha and Georgina and I'll show you a chauvinistic society in no hurry to advance. Then there are the mysterious 'unisex' ones, rather like the hairdressers which call themselves by that term, but are clearly barber shops with a Wella concession. These include Evelyn, Sydney, Hilary, Jocelyn and, in the US, Marion, the original first name of the aggressively macho John Wayne. I guess it toughened you up, rather like the message in that great song, 'A Boy Named Sue'.

The big trick is to call your baby by a proper name, either biblical, Shakespearean or of historical origin. It may look momentarily dull on a plastic wristband next to cots of squalling Amber Jades but they won't half thank you for it when they are Uncle David and Auntie Rachel instead of Auntie Kimberley and Uncle Keanu.

Having said this, of course, I should steer clear of Romeo, Bottom or Shylock, because it's awfully hard to be identified with a lover, an ass or a money-lender when you weigh six pounds and the only thing you've ever seen is a nipple.

Likewise, diminutives. You can rant on all you like about how your child is going to be Richard not Dick and Alexander not Alex and Beverley not Bev, but when the little guy with the big name gets to big school, his larger mates will call him what they jolly well please, and frankly you should thank your lucky stars it's Dick and not Dick'ead.

As I write, there are hundreds of tiny continents packing their tuck-boxes into their satchels as I write. Little India's mum is picking up little China and little Savanna in the Cherokee, then later it all gets a bit more suburban back at little Chelsea's birthday sleep over, with Paris, Florence and Roma hurrying to the same destination. No sign of a truculent Grimsby or a pugnacious Pontefract yet, but I wouldn't hold your breath. Spicing up the trend for naming by atlas are baby Brooklyn Beckham and Phoenix Chi – it's lucky the girls weren't touring in Middle Wallop when the earth moved with such consequence.

'What's the most famous fact about Winston Churchill?' goes the joke. Answer: 'He was the last white man to be called Winston.' Interesting, though, isn't it? After the war the British threw out the man and his name, wanting no reminders of the years of deprivation, in spite of the victory. But to those coming into the country, the new life and the victory were personified by the man. Not too many Maggies and Johns around but watch out for a millennium crop of seven-pound unisex Blairs.

Finally, here's something which has always puzzled me about calendar names. They only apply to the summer months. I know that most conception is done in the winter months when the night draws in and expectations rise, but is that the only reason why April, May, June, Julie and Augusta book their places in the school register and October, December and February don't? And wherefore Dawn and not Dusk?

As a kid I often amused myself by drawing cartoons of girls called Marian Haste, Jacqueline Hyde, Edna Clouds and, favourite of all, Sheila

Blige. Recently, on Radio 4's *Home Truths*, I heard the story of a 21st son, desperately named Finisher Coronation Kingshill. Apparently, though, there was a 22nd child. For those of you old enough to remember the term, wouldn't Johnny have been appropriate?

Hot Flush Blues

I just passed fifty, 'n' I'm givin' in to gravity,
Got my tongue in a real deep cavity,
Still looking round for signs of depravity –
I'm long in the tooth, short on lust.

Wanna make love when I'm not tired,
Wanna wear a bra that ain't underwired,
Wanna watch Tina Turner and get inspired,
Long in the tooth, short on lust.

I could paint my own pottery – bake my own bread.
I say 'The day I do that's the day I'm dead.'
Don't want cameo brooches, organised coaches,
Wanna smoke roaches and get outa my head.

Won't see a shrink, got no neuroses,
Won't watch the soaps, 'n' get my kicks by osmosis,
Won't read pamphlets on osteoporosis,
'Cos I'm long in the tooth, short on lust.

Don't give me lavender and lace, unless the lace is black,
Wanna face-lift not a stair-lift, and I ain't comin' back.
Wanna sit down and overdose on aphrodisiac,
'Cos I'm long in the tooth, short on lust.

Time to Make Up

My daughter forswears make-up. At 21, and with a naturally fresh skin, it couldn't matter less really, which is not to say I wouldn't give a flagon of aloe vera and a groat of rolled oats to get my hands, brushes and Buf-Pufs on the unchartered territory of her face. Just to delineate, you understand – to give more balance to eye and lip . . . and perhaps to pluck . . . but no, she'd never let me near her, although she purports to admire the reconstruction work I do on my own unaligned visage.

'I hate my jaw! It's repellent,' she moans. 'Why can't I have your jaw? I love your jaw!'

'What's to love?' I splutter. 'It's a jaw. It opens, it closes. It chomps, it grinds. It's a working jaw, for God's sake!'

'Yeah, but you know what I mean – yours squares off! Mine just meanders around then slopes off. I HATE IT!'

I'd like to laugh but I daren't. Besides, I know only too well the pain of comparison, being the daughter of an alarmingly pretty woman who, in her seventies, is still taken for my sister. For years I tried to rub away my nose to make it the same shape as my mother's. To suggest to my daughter a touch of underjaw shading would be to agree with her self-assessment – and would it be my fault if it resembled designer stubble?

'You look so much *older* on stage,' marvelled Jo Public, as I entered the bar each night after performing in *The Rivals*. 'How long does it take you to put on all those lines?'

It pained me to tell them that I didn't apply ANY lines – the ones they saw were my own, breaking through the make-up. Long ago, on the BT ads, we discovered that painting wrinkles on my skinny face made me look not older but merely extra-terrestrial. A pair of glasses, a grey wig and a permanently pressed expression was all that was needed, depressingly enough, and in those days I was a mere stripling of 40, not the woman recently asked by the *Mail on Sunday* to contribute to an article called 'Fab at Fifty'. (On reflection, it may well have been 'Flab at Fifty', in which case I would have had much to contribute.)

Each month, magazines aimed at the 'fairer sex' (a 'darkist' label if ever there was one) extol the virtues of this season's 'new, improved maquillage'. 'Forget last season's insipid beiges and tepid taupes,' they scream, 'and step into spring with lacerating lime, pizzazzing pistachio and orange with oomph!' Orange and lime. Two colours so acidic and draining that only Peter Snow's tie drawer can survive them. So out go the insipid beiges and in come the sizzling hot pinks, peachy whites and fluorescent fuchsias. Theoretically, that is. In reality, most of us approach the 'shock of the new' with scepticism.

My mother's generation, with their Ponds Cold Cream, spit-on mascara and Max Factor pancake, seem to have emerged with skin like a baby's, which is more than can be said for most of my fellow exfoliators racing off for their electrodes and fruit acid peels. They emerge taut as a yacht sail for two hours and then subside like the skin of a kiwi after the fruit's been removed.

Aged ten, I remember applying pancake to our live-in help's arms and back before she put on her evening dress. It seemed to me an entirely exotic exercise to buff her body parts into a smooth matt surface sans freckles, spots, scratches or vaccination marks. Above it perched her face, Max Factor panstick, powder, silvery blue eye-shadow and 'Tangee' lipstick.

Of course, no-one thought, least of all me, that under the heat of a mirror ball and the influence of Ronnie Hilton and too many crème de menthes, the inside of her black crêpe frock would turn a dark orange as would her boyfriend's shirt, tie, lapels and, with a bit of cheek and the opportunity, his trouser turn-ups.

My son, when aged thirteen, once informed me that the word 'gullible' had been removed from the English dictionary, then sat back to watch my blue touch-paper explode. As my 'How dare they do thats!' rose to a crescendo, I realised, from his face how neatly I'd fallen into his trap. Nowadays, I often feel as though I have a PhD in gullibility in the face of the cosmetic industry's extensive, expensive snares.

How did we face life before we had liposomes and antioxidants and exfoliators and light-reflecting pigments and sebum regulators and cell reconstructors and mini-lifts in a jar? I'll tell you how. By being young and not needing 'em, that's how!

Eyeliner goes out of fashion. Kohl pencil comes in at roughly three times the price it was in its previous incarnation as an eyeliner. Our hair requires vegetable-laden shampoos and massive doses of avocado and jojoba conditioner – with panthenol! Invest in them and voilà! – on to the market comes Wash & Go, because which Nineties juggling woman would admit to having time for two separate washing regimes? Meanwhile, rouge is replaced by blusher (same thing – squarer box) which is in turn ousted by sun bronzer which bites the dust when pastel blush pebbles come along.

Powder, always intended to matt down the sheen of foundation cream,

comes 'luminescent' with reflective sheen, basically to make foundation
... er, shiny. Lipsticks come with moisturisers which make them disappear
roughly one cappuccino after application, and gel – guaranteed to reduce
under-eye puffiness – will cost roughly £19.90 more than the most
effective cure, a slice of cucumber.

Not too long ago, I found myself walking late at night down the Champs
Elysées. There, at 11.45pm, was a state-of-the-art make-up shop, open in
all its minimalistic glory. We strolled around as though we were in an art
gallery. Everything was black, save the make-up, which was displayed in
individual items. Rows of lip colours faced front by the hundred in every
shade of the palette. Counters of barely graduating blushers – it was
dazzling. Long black leather chairs invited you to lay back, headphones
on, and just jig about to music of your choice. Internet computers lovingly
awaited your email. The smell of good coffee abounded. It was so
seductive that I lost all judgement, flailed about like a goodtime girl and
came out clutching a pewter-coloured lipstick which makes me look like
I've got mercury poisoning.

When Lancôme rejected Isabella Rossellini, arguably the most
beautiful woman I've ever seen, from their advertising and Max Factor
took on Madonna and Estée took on Liz Hurley, one had to face facts. It's
style over content out there. Kiss reality goodbye and say hello to hype. I
doubt whether Audrey Hepburn would have got past the advertisers'
scrutiny. What's hip is a canvas, a blank one preferably, and a very young
one with not a trace of life's experience on it – why bother, when it can be
painted on and 'Eraced' at will? There are botulism injections available
now to paralyse the frowning lines and the smiling ones too. Collagen will
give you African lips (without the possible inconvenience of Africa
colouring) and your teeth can be whitened over in your lunchbreak.
Listen, if you don't want the *Baywatch* contract, just keep drinking loads
of water and eat fruit. It works for bats.

Underwired

The Queen's corsetière and I once appeared on the same afternoon TV show ('Hi and welcome to *Burbling in the Afternoon* and I'm Fifi, your ditsy blonde lightweight, and today we'll be hearing from Ainsley – how to do 101 unheard-of things to a venison escalope – and from Maureen Lipman about her one-man show, *Live and Ticking*, but first the tragic story of a woman whose face was bitten off by a rabid au pair girl with multiple personality disorder'). The corsetière was a sound, smart-looking lady called June who runs Rigby & Peller, Corsetière by Appointment. It's an uplifting tradition.

Before the camera lit up she whispered to me, 'Now, you are *not* to send me up!' I opened my eyes to their full width – about two millimetres these days – and mouthed back, 'Would I?' I didn't and was duly impressed by the array of basques separating the breasts of the surprisingly well-endowed models who paraded through the tiny studio.

Afterwards, June told me I ought to pop into their salon. She'd already correctly guessed my bra size and, it seemed to me, also deduced that what was nestling under my sweater was threadbare and mangy – not to mention the state of my bra! 'Yes . . . well . . . I will,' I mumbled. 'I ought to pop in . . .' I paused, hoping to curtail the inevitable, but failed . . . 'Before I pop out, as t'were.' Her smile was the epitome of patience.

'Mind you,' I careered on, 'I don't want anyone handling the goods. You know, schlepping them up and under and all around the cubicle. I had enough of that when I was a fledgling.'

'No, of course,' she said smoothly, 'but if you want a bra that fits then you must be properly measured.'

'Yeah, with my clothes on. Then shove the bras through a hole in the curtain and leave me to my own devices, OK?'

She concurred with mild amusement, so I resolved to go in the shop. But childhood trauma was stronger than the resolve. Lingering memories of Hull lingerie departments, me beige-faced and sullen behind the candlewick, my mother boldly going where no man dares and, to my ears, hollering in parade-ground fashion, 'She's very small backed but VERY FULL IN THE CUP.' Then, as every eye swivelled towards me, 'She needs a lot of SUPPORT.' I did and I wasn't getting it. The purchase of firm crossover fronts, adjustable triple-strength straps, long-line all-in-ones

310

with comfigrip suspenders and other such Humberside contraceptive devices rendered me as impregnable as a concrete fortress presided over by Darth Vader.

Remission only came during the Sixties when, braless and corsetless, we grew accustomed to occasionally bopping ourselves in the eye with our own or someone else's renegade boob. Any shape was acceptable. High slung, low slung, wobbly, pointy, pert, pigeon or pachyderm. We let it all hang out. I was a 36C cup and proud of it. I was famed in the Manchester theatre in which I worked for being able to lace myself for period plays into corsets which made me resemble a golf bag with a bum sticking out the top. Two children and two decades later, with the whole thing resembling a well-used candle in a Portuguese bistro, I was poised to re-examine the reinforcements.

The old Warner underwired front-fastening 34C see-through saw me through the grown-up years of smooth lines under fake Jean Muir silks. Then one day in Frank's of Golders Green – one of the last blessed outposts of what used to be called a draper's, where you can buy a pair of gloves, knickers or slippers without having to negotiate an escalator or a food department – one of their wonderfully peremptory assistants told me that my bra size was, in fact, not 36B or 34C but 32DD. My face fell in line with everything else.

'Thirty-two double-D!' I hollered. 'Impossible! I must be a freak. How can any woman who's five foot seven inches be a double D?'

'No, dear. You're a perfectly normal shape.' (For an emu!) 'You just have a narrow frame and large bosoms, that's all.' She moved towards the till, which still looked like it was suffering withdrawal symptoms from the loss of those aerial tubes which used to whizz overhead, ferrying bills from nighties to naughties, and relieved me of the price of three double-D hammocks in black, white and beige. I've been wearing them ever since and washing them together long enough for them to become a uniform shade of pewter.

Imagine my discombobulation, empathic reader – nay, bosom friend – when I finally made it to Rigby & Peller in search of strapless support for under my off-the-shoulder *Live and Kidding* stretch satin, only to be told, quite pleasantly, that they were low in stock in my size – which was a 30E cup. 'Thirty-E!' I gasped. 'For God's sake, I must look like a bloody bus stop!'

So there you have it. Going down, as they say in the talking lift. The world is divided into two sorts of women. Those, often boarding-school educated or elderly, who swim outdoors all year round and shed their clothes in the changing-rooms with the abandon of a two-year-old, and those, like your correspondent, who wear a bathing costume in the sauna and put their underwear on tortuously under a towel with their head in the locker.

'What are the measurements of a mermaid?' goes the old fishwives' tale. And the answer? 'Thirty-eight, twenty-four – and eighty pence a pound.'

Perhaps one shouldn't joke about breasts. The important part is that they work. If they are remodelled into perfect scimitars it means relocating the nipples, and that's curtains for foreplay, which in itself is a marvellous title for a slim but racy detective novel.

When Jordan and the like, with their super-attenuated boobs, are 'on top', it's probably devastating – but lying on their stomachs having a snooze must be like levitating. Thanks for the mammaries.

Silver Salver

It was my Silver Wedding. Twenty-five years since we tied that reef knot –
well, twenty-nine years if you count the four years I spent pretending that
marriage was not on my prioritised list.

Then you blink, put a few thousand meatballs in the oven, appear on
too many touchlines, parent-teacher lines and headlines, then you
stop being able to learn your lines, then to conceal your lines! And the
next thing you know some of your contemporaries are showing you
mugshots of their little Jacks and Chloes – their grandchildren, for
God's sake!

And hey presto – it's time to consider how to celebrate 25 years of
conjugal bliss. And, actually, it was no time at all. It was all very clever,
really, because all the wedding presents had just more or less run out. I
wouldn't have a wedding list in 1973 because it was 'boring and
bourgeois'. I didn't realise then that lists occur to prevent couples
receiving 23 stainless steel dishes as gifts. Which is, in essence, exactly
what we received. Mind you, as I say that, they've been carted off to various
universities as ashtrays, or just disappeared into a tea chest as a dish and
come out as a twisted piece of modern sculpture worthy of a place in the
Royal Academy's 'Sensations' exhibition.

Except I didn't want any. Presents, I mean. I didn't need anything, and
if I did I would have absolutely nowhere to put it. In fact, what I needed
were things to house the things I'm overrun by. I'd like to trundle every old
object off every surface of every mahogany 'what-not' down to the hospice
shop and start all over again. New Millennium, New Minimalism. The
only comfortable old knick-knack I'd keep would be the comfortable old
knick-knack I married all those years ago. And even he could do with a
quick squirt with a can of Shake 'n' Jack.

As for me . . . as for me. Well, after seeing myself on TV over the
Christmas period, I wanted a new attitude, a new hobby and a new nose.
Honestly, I think I've hung on to this one for a heroically long period of
time. I understand that your nose is the one part of your body that keeps
growing *for life* and, frankly, the prospect is not appealing. So, if I show up
in the late summer suddenly looking amazingly like one of those aliens at
the end of *Close Encounters*, well, you read it here first.

I thought about having an anniversary list at our local chemist. Imagine the phone call after a friend receives my invitation to our Silver Wedding party:

'Hello, the pharmacy? Yes, I'd like to enquire about the present list for Mr and Mrs Rosenthal . . .'

'Certainly, madam. What price range?'

'Oh, in the £25 margin.'

'Yes, indeed, madam. The bumper economy Nurofen pack? Ah no, sorry, that's already been reserved by Lynda Bellingham. What about the fourteen-pack flu powders or the elastic freeze-and-heat elbow support – or did Miss Joseph reserve that? No, that's still available, or the hot water bottle with vibrating cover . . .?

'Yes, I had wanted something a little more *personal*, actually –'

'Personal, yes, madam, quite understandably so, madam. Well, there's a year's supply of Oil of Evening Primrose capsules for those violent shouting fits she gets every month, with integral his 'n' hers monogrammed earplug . . .'

Click. Friend replaces receiver. 'Can you drive me to John Lewis? They've got a bargain offer on stainless steel dishes.'

My mother had promised me a knife sharpener, which I really did need, although there was something distinctly ominous about the offer. I put in for a bird table, to pass the lonely empty hours – and what Mr Rosenthal was getting was between me and my mind. But it would be musical. There was no better sight for me than that of Jack torturing his violin, with my singing teacher Jane Edwards in full flow on the piano. His face was glowing, his eyes were shining, his heart was thudding, you couldn't hear a single note he was playing, and it mattered not a jot.

One thing I wouldn't be giving him was a party seating plan, because never again in my life was I going to face such a thing. People could sit on top of each other for all I cared – they could superglue themselves to the person they'd least like to share a desert island disco with, they could make vertical columns like a tired old Halifax commercial, but never, never again would I mix and match my guests into formal choreography. Why?

'Hello, Maureen, we *are* going to be there tonight but is it all right if my Auntie Gloria from Estonia comes with her guide dog? I promise she won't eat much and we won't stay for the dancing . . .'

'But, of *course* – it will be a pleasure to *see* her again after thirty-five years. No trouble at all . . . Lovely . . .' Click.

'Hello! Franco, can you get a large woman and a St Bernard on to Table 14? Well, I know, but Mr and Mrs Shaw won't mind going on the Biggins table. They *are* in amateur dramatics in Slough . . .'

Never mind. This time we would crush up with elbows in our kidneys and red wine and salt all over the floor. Just the sort of party which makes my partner head for the one chair in the room and not get up again for the duration.

Funnily enough, whenever he does this all the really interesting people in the room seem to gravitate to his chair. Of course, his small talk is bigger than most people's.

Evenin' All

I find I increasingly miss the community life at which I used to sneer. The sense of a group of people, meeting and re-meeting for reasons of contentment. It's not that I don't have a social life – oh, good Lord, I'm here, there and everywhere. Phew! I mean, the wear and tear on opaque brownish-black tummy-control tights is unbelievable and my evening gowns are in and out of the closet more often than Michael Barrymore!

It's just that I seem to spend a great deal of time exchanging witty badinage with people I will never see again, or eating suppers I can't taste because afterwards I'm going to have to sing for them.

Returning home from one such expedition, I couldn't help remembering how my parents entertained their circle in Hull. They had 'Evenings'. I know we all have evenings – it's the bit between *The Bill* and bed, isn't it? – but theirs weren't just evenings, they were 'Evenings'.

We kids were scared or bribed off for an early bath after a leanish tea of spaghetti on toast while the house was perfected and bridge rolls covered with greaseproof. Dad's job was to make himself smart with Brilliantine and change one pristine shirt and tie for another and to lay out small glasses for the Scotch or cherry brandy that was to be offered on arrival to the guests according to gender.

Around 8.30 the doorbell heralded the first '*Hellooo!*', always delivered in a tone of intense surprise and delight as if the participants hadn't seen each other only the previous day in town, but rather had just returned from a four-year sojourn in Botswana teaching native children how to make potato *latkes*.

Soon the 'How ARE you?'s began to harmonise with the '*Hellooo!*'s. One always knew that Jean and Leslie would arrive first because Leslie was obsessed with punctuality and that Freda and David would arrive last because Freda wasn't. The murmur changed consistency as the men drifted to one side of the room where politics, religion and racy dialogue held sway, and the women drifted to the other to gently trash their men, their kids and whoever hadn't arrived.

Our one appearance downstairs was the occasion for more shrieks of '*Hellooo!*' and much cheek pinching and height admiration. 'How are you getting on at school?' was asked ritually and rhetorically as we set out 'occasional tables' – this almost certainly qualifying as an 'occasion' – and

316

passed around pots of tea and bridge rolls with chopped egg, chopped herring and cream cheese fillings on doilied plates. All the crockery matched and all the spoons shone. Finally, the home-baked biscuits went the rounds on a three-tiered plate also boasting Madeira cake from the Be-Ro recipe book.

'I don't know why, but it just didn't rise this time . . .'

'Well, it tastes marvel . . .'

'No, the last one I made was like this [gesture]. I mean, really . . . this thick – I don't know what I did differently. I used the BeRo.'

'Oh, I always use the Florence Greenberg for sponge.'

'Really? Oh. Well, I think I will next time. Mind you, the last one I made was like this –' [gesture]

'Listen. They're all knocking it back, aren't they?'

Laughter all round.

During food the sexes mixed. Sometimes the 'Evening' mysteriously involved cards – 'Hearts' for the men in one half of the interconnecting living-room, 'Kalooki' for the women in the other. The laughter linked the whole concept.

Later on, around midnight, the whole thing went into reversal as Jean and Leslie left first and Freda and David lingered last.

'It's been a *lovely* evening.'

'Have you enjoyed it?'

'Oh, it's been *really* lovely.'

'Drive carefully!' (Home was all of two streets away.)

'We've *thoroughly* enjoyed it – haven't we, Mike?'

'Marvellous. G'night.'

'Thanks for coming. God bless.'

And that was that. Fourteen plates, cups and saucers and spoons to be washed up and replaced in the cupboard for 'best'. A quick go-over with the Ewbank, an enthusiastic post-mortem on the proceedings from the washer-up and mumbled replies, too late, from the one shifting the furniture back. Then Dad went to bed and Mum shifted the furniture to where it should have been.

'I don't know why that cake didn't rise – I did exactly what I did for that last Evening . . .'

'Oh, give over, will you? They ate it, didn't they?'

'Still.' Lights went off. 'I think on the whole it went well. Don't you?'

Silence.

'Yes. I think it did. Everyone seemed to think so . . . Anyway. I won't have to do another one for seven weeks, thank God.'

After surviving 'the dinner party years', where I flailed about hopelessly in a sea of salsify, salt cod, salt tears and 'never agains', and the 'Let's try that new Etruscan/Macedonian minimalistic brasserie on the Holborn Viaduct' years, where I paid off a dinner guest list as long as Jeffrey Archer's 'Must dos' at a squillion quid a night, I'm all for reverting to type. As they used to say in Dock Green, 'Evenin' all.'

Bosom Buddies

I'm really not too bothered by the age thing but while I don't much like the sinking physiognomy and the simmering root canals, the thing I'd never bargained for is a sort of general non-reversible 'thickening'. I know I look thin to you but that's because I've got a thin *head* and thin ankles. It's the bits in between that are bearing the brunt of age and my love of the farinaceous. (Once, after examining my breasts for lumps, the doctor said 'You should have a mammogram really because breasts like yours are a nightmare for a doctor.' Quick as a flash, Jack said 'Really? What would they be for an accountant?')

Some time ago it was the mammography. A card came asking me and my breasts to put in an appearance at the car park of my local hospital for a breast X-ray, which seemed to give a whole new meaning to the term 'Pay and Display'. Sure enough, tucked into the side of the hospital parking area was a mobile home with a receptionist, fourteen assorted breasts in a kiosk-sized waiting-room and one copy of *Hello!* I tried to disappear behind *The Queen of Whale Cay*, which just happened to be my current book, about a flamboyant cross-dressing lesbian, but to no avail.

'You are Beattie still?' my neighbour opposite said. 'Er . . . yes,' I admitted.

'I knew that I knew her,' crowed the lady.

'I knew too,' retorted the lady on my right in unison with her neighbour. 'I already told my cousin you was Beattie.'

I held my breath and counted to five. It usually takes about five. 'So why don't we ever see you on the telly any more?' They had much to discuss after my departure into the X-ray room.

'Take off your clothes to the waist,' said the radiologist. I did, and looked around for a gown, a towel or two saucepans. Having never been to ballet or boarding school, I'm a bit shy about letting it all hang out before strangers, so I crossed my arms over my bosoms, which had the effect of hoisting the whole caboodle on to a sort of ledge. It was anything but casual and the radiologist and I both knew it. 'When did you last have a mammogram?' 'Have you noticed any unusual puckering?' 'Have you felt any changes in consistency?' Even if I had I would have answered, 'No', just so I wouldn't have to expand on my answer whilst standing there looking like a naked woman selling rugby balls.

Out of the corner of my eye I caught sight of a notice warning you that 'the breast has to be compressed to see inside it and that any pain or bruising is uncomfortable, but temporary'.

It was then that I remembered why my last mammography was years ago. It's a bit like childbirth. You know, when you think, Well, thank God that's over with because I'm sure as hell never going through that again. Then you completely forget about the pain until *just* after the gynaecologist has confirmed your second pregnancy.

Actually, the X-ray is really not that bad at all. I mean, if you like having your breast picked up by a stranger like a pound and a half of sourdough and flattened, you'll love it! I have this inability to enjoy my pear-shaped bits being made into perfect rhomboids – it's a weakness, I know.

Still, it only lasted a few minutes and I scampered back into my bra and baggy clothing before you could say 'sex goddess'. As I passed through the waiting-room I gave what I hoped was the sort of grin which said, 'Well, that was nothing to get ruffed up about', but they were all too busy discussing the Bob Hoskins campaign compared to mine to notice. Literally, metaphorically flattened, I agreed to sign the prosthesis box she held out for me – and left.

Since my trip to Florida where liver spots are proud to call themselves freckles and osteoporosis makes everyone appear to be permanently shrugging, I have come back feeling like a spring chicken, albeit a slightly spatchcock one.

Yesterday I bought a gorgeous trouser suit. It looks adorable but for two small 'crinkles' between the lapels and the shoulder pads, which somehow made me think of Florida and shrugging.

I called over the smart and snooty shop assistant to ask why such a pricey outfit sported such 'crinkles'. She faffed around a bit, reminding me of mammaries and car parks, then said, 'It could be taken in but, frankly, it would hang much better if your breasts were higher up.'

Remember the recent news story about the man in Houston, Texas, who'd had a remote control device fitted to his penis to deal with his impotence, then found that he had an erection every time his neighbour opened or closed the garage doors? Well, this has nothing to do with the story I've just told you except that I think I know how he felt.

Vanity Box

The world has gone Appearance Mad. Hillary Clinton has gone Appearance Mad. My mother was *always* Appearance Mad. Given a newscast about a typhoon killing twelve hundred innocent citizens, she will always innocently but inevitably make a comment about the neckline on Moira Stuart's blouse.

Which is to confess that I've joined the gym again. Sigh. Yes, after seven painless months of paying £58 per month for the privilege of *not* going to the gym – and I mean not even for two lengths of the jacuzzi and a slice of carrot cake – I have not only crept back in there, leg-warmers aloft, but I've actually hired a whatsit . . . (You see, I can't even be brave enough to say the word.) A personal trainer!

I know, I know. I've mocked from afar the developing biceps of my female friends, I've made snide remarks about Born Again Pilates Proselytisers and I've visibly smirked at the sight of chunky chums puffing past my car in pursuit of less of themselves. Now here I am with them again. Me and young Adam the instructor, filling in charts and lifting weights and treading treads and generally giving all the appearance of one who actually *gives* a damn.

Mark you, I've only done it twice so far and on each occasion I've left my sense of irony firmly in the locker room. And I don't look in any mirrors, either. This is gym technique for me. The first time I clocked myself lifting weights in the gym mirror, I almost dropped them and gave myself a foot-ectomy. I couldn't believe how *short* my forearms were. I mean, here was a pair of perfectly normal-sized hands, the statutory length of my face as taught by my school art teacher, squarish shoulders, decent length upper arms, and two pointy and somewhat dehydrated elbows. But beneath them were missing links. Those weren't forearms – they were elongated wrists. Skinny, white, shapeless things. Root vegetables in soup.

'Look, Adam!' I shrieked, holding my two parsnips aloft. 'Look at my arms! They're disgusting!'

'What's wrong with 'em?' he enquired with the smugness of one whose biceps and triceps have the proportions of a Corinthian column. 'They're alright, aren't they?'

'Alright?' I gasped. 'No, they're not alright – they're all wrong. They're a child's arms on a grown-up body – everything's developed except my ears and my arms.' (It's true, I have very small ears, too.)

'Well, I can't see anything wrong.'

'But you must be able to – get a tape measure – get an arm chart – get a life . . .' I gazed at him. 'Are you telling me there's *nothing* that a fitness instructor can do to lengthen a human arm?'

He did finally prise me away from the arms struggle and into some legwork. He made me do ten minutes of walking up a hill at a ridiculously fast rate and ten minutes rowing and skiing and other things meant for high achievers, not low skivers like myself.

Before I knew it, I'd booked in for eighteen sessions. I've had to cancel two already due to a heady mixture of migraine and appearing on David Mellor's Classic FM programme. (Well, you'd want to look your best for that, wouldn't you?) At this rate it may take me eleven or twelve years to complete the course, but I was back in there today for a Sunday swim. I did three and a half lengths and finished up with a twenty-minute daydream in the steam room, interrupted only by a slight shift of my body on the wet slab causing a noise which sounded like a buffalo fart. Everyone but me left the room quite soon afterwards.

In the changing-room I watched a well-honed woman of about my age leaning over the wash basins, stark naked, to apply fresh lipstick. There was a metaphor in there somewhere. There is, unquestionably, an air of desperation in gyms the world over, or am I mistaking intensity for moroseness?

[My latest craze is the Power Plate. It looks like a weighing machine with a larger platform. It vibrates and after half an hour your whole body is pinging. The first time I went on it I couldn't walk up the steps afterwards to get home, my legs were so weak. It works, I think. The best part of it is that my friend Heidi and I are in there at 9.30am and stuffing our mouths with croissants at Gusto's café next door at ten. After playing *The Cherry Orchard* in Chichester I gained the weight equivalent of an iced cupcake a day for five weeks. In two weeks of shaking I'm back in my pencil skirt. With the help of long-line beige Lycra passion killers.]

The thing is, all the women whose appearance really appeals to me have aged seamlessly from interesting young women into drop-dead gorgeous older ones. They have done it without recourse to silicone, sutures or staple gun. Joan Bakewell – *Dame* Joan Bakewell – looks pretty good in her own skin, and is fighting parking madness and chairing the National Campaign for the Arts with equal feistiness. And I rather preferred Germaine Greer in her Wild Woman of Wiltshire mode, hair cut by Flymow, clothes by Femail order, boots by gum, to her recent incarnation as eyelash-batting, lurex-draped, leg-flashing senior siren. They look good because their thinking is good. Madonna looks astonishing, every muscle individually defined, cheek-bones akimbo, but allegedly on the film she directed she asked to be addressed as 'The Presence'. So the brain's gone AWOL. As for Faye Dunaway – well, she has done away with everything gorgeous that she had in favour of a look which owes a lot to *The Mummy*.

My 'quality paper' ran a photo-spread about women who are ageing seamlessly and their miracle tips to help us to do the same. Some of them, like Yasmin Le Bon and Shakira Caine, I exempt from the mirth which sprang to my puckered and clearly uncollagened lips because these girls were/are/always will be beautiful whether they're six or sixty, but my dears, some of the women on the list were – well, pardon me while I snort, chortle, snigger and possibly, 'pish pish p'shaw'!

Obviously I can't name names because this time next week I could be playing a withered old crone to their Cleopatra. The secret tips generally centred on regular exercise, regular facials, regular Kundalini yoga and, if possible, unusually regular sex. Oh, and lots of freshly squeezed veg, antioxidants and detox or rehab – I forget now because I have to go and sit in a warm living-room and eat Turkish delight to counter the stress.

It's a conspiracy to undermine us, girls! I personally counted up, amongst the photographed elderly primates, three nose jobs, two eye jobs, one permanent wig, four surgically augmented breasts (not on the same person), airbrushing on a monumental scale and several yards of gauze and a vat of Vaseline over the lens.

Which is fine in itself. I'm the last person to knock self-improvement. If it bothers you and you can afford it, fix it – always remembering the advice given by a neatly retrousséed actress: 'Just as long as it's your nose you're trying to fix, not your life.'

Lunch Box

There were about ten of them, although numbers changed depending on the affair – which could be anything from an evening of cards and bridge rolls to a meeting to devise ways of raising money for a small corner of Israel most of them would never see. The one thing the affair never was, was an affair. They all had names which dated them as specifically and nostalgically as a tin of Ostermilk dates a Baby Boomer. There was a Freda and a Nora, two Lillys and a Helen and a Jean, a Miriam and a Minnie and a Rita and also, it really goes without saying, a Zelma. They were 'The Women'. The women of my childhood. The indomitable, never-changing, constant Women. The mothers of all those Susans and Janets and Maureens and the wives of all those Harrys and Maxes and Moishes.

And they were smart as paint. Each woman had lived her twenties through a long and bloody war, which hit them personally in a way which made them shudder at the near-miss of it all. They married in utility suits and borrowed hats, and the men they married donned uniforms and left within weeks or months of their ration-book weddings. In their quiet moments all of them feared that the uniformed strangers who might return would do so with new manners and new mores to which they might not know how to rise. Some of them worked in factories and shops and aerodromes during this time, and all of them loved the work they were doing. The companionable vivacity, the shared jokes and the pooled fears. They were good at their jobs. They were proud of their ability to contribute. They glowed with the pride that only a wage-packet with your name on it can bring.

They were even secretly wistful when the war was over and their contribution was no longer deemed necessary. But there was no question of not returning to the world of housewifery. They knew that their places were in the home and they went along with the Americanised adventurousness which showed them what a fun place the home could be when stocked with labour-saving devices and Persil's New Blue White. And they all had their babies and learned to bake from the BeRo cookbook whilst listening to *Music While You Work*, and swapped one workplace for another. And they were happy comparing their kids and watching their husbands make a living and shopping daily on what they gave them weekly, and socialising with each other at synagogue functions and bar mitzvahs and silver weddings. And still when we came home from school, clutching our 'Could do better if she stopped trying to entertain the class' report, they gave you beans on toast and a homemade macaroon. Year in, year out, putting pancake mixture in the pan and pancake make-up on their arms to finish off their beaded evening-gowns and bouffant once-a-week hair setting. And so it was until the kids left home and the nest sparkled just a little less though the polish now came in spray-cans.

So you asked me, Committee Members of The Women of the Year, high-achievers to a man, what in my role has inspired me, and I think of my heroines from childhood upwards: Enid Blyton's George, and *Lorna at the Wells*, and Pauline, Petrova and Posy in *Ballet Shoes*, and a keen and sensitive English teacher, and Alma Cogan because she was a star *and* 'one of us', and Joyce Grenfell and Elizabeth Taylor and Maggie Smith, and Odette Hallowes and Hillary and Aung San Suu Kyi on a daily level. And in the end I go back to the question: 'What in your role has inspired you?' and instead I see etched on my retina those women in their navy or black pleated skirts with beautifully laundered, brightly patterned blouses and court shoes. Nylon stockings and firm foundations. Max Factor lipstick and shiny blue eyeshadow and carefully co-ordinated costume jewellery. The women who would never achieve what we here today have achieved: the right and the talent to succeed in what we love to do. In a month of Sunday roasts they were never going to make this Lunch, but by hell they were going to make sure that their Janets and Susans and Maureens did.

I'll tell you what inspires people to succeed the world over. Encouragement and love. 'Yes, you can do it and you'll be the best', not 'She'll never come to anything, it's the lad that's got the brains'. When 'The Women' sat round with their china cups and their slices of Madeira cake and Zelma said, 'Sing *Dreamboat* for them, Maureen, or tell them that joke about *Moon River*' (when *Moon River* was the punchline of the joke), the fact that not one of those strong, powdery faces registered disapproval of me and my tiny talent, gave me the go-ahead to perform. And when I'd finished, their hands came together and they shouted for more. It was the warmest and most secure sound I ever knew.

Forty-six years later I take that feeling on stage with me every night. And without it I could never love my audience and expect them to reciprocate. Joyce Grenfell said there is no performance which is not a circle. I put out my hand to give but if you are not there to receive then the circle is not complete. Putting that hand out requires skill and courage and vast vats of vitality, but most of all it requires confidence. And the inspiration for that confidence came from a group of very ordinary, unshowy, provincial, sparky, altruistic and very inspirational ladies who didn't have the time to lunch, except very rarely for a buck rarebit at the Kardomah.

In Praise of Bolder Women

Glory be to God for dazzling things of four score or more. I'm referring to those feisty elderly women of 80-plus who, though revered by friends from six to sixty, get about as much attention from the media and the politicians as a polling station in Penge on European election day.

A few friends of mine spring like chickens to mind. Ruby Bernstein, who lives in Jersey, was born in Hull some 85 years ago. She's the most stylish and sophisticated friend I have, every hair in place, beautifully made up, wildly and often kookily fashionable and, best of all, completely 'up for it'. When Ruby and I are together we never draw breath, swords or conclusions and we rarely stop giggling. Her mind is as open as a university and she thinks nothing of jumping on a plane to Bilbao at the drop of a suggestion because 'I'm just dying to see the Guggenheim, darling'.

Ruby is high camp in the warmest, most life-enhancing, outrageous sense of the word and at any party I've ever given or attended, she's at the kitchen table surrounded by adoring and slightly flimsy young men hanging on her every gorgeously articulated anecdote. 'I've no idea why it is, dear, I attract gay men like nylon attracts static!'

'Don't touch that electric fire, dear,' she once told a guest. 'It's my signal to Albert [her husband] that I'm "interested".'

She and I will be travelling back up North together soon, where I shall be unveiling a 265-ton sewage device that has been named Maureen in my honour. We'll be laughing like drains.

It was only a few years ago that I met the redoubtable Elsbeth Juda. That she was 91 years old, a formidable artist, swims every day and looks stunning in layered linen and ethnic jewellery, is secondary to the fact that on her birthday she had enough friends of all ages and walks of life to fill a theatre. Everyone seems to know and love Elsbeth, and vice versa. Her hair is wiry, short and white, her skin soft and free of lines. From the age of five in Germany her father insisted that she create something every day of the week, whether a poem or a painting, and though arthritis has finally prevented her from creating her incredible collages, she assures me that there is still life in creative leisure. Trained as a photographer in the Bauhaus movement, Elsbeth remembers photographing knitting patterns thirty-five years ago for *Good Housekeeping*. I have only to see a collagened lip on a Hollywood 'beauty' or a French poodle's nose on an English setter face to think: 'Oh, please let me have the grace to grow old like Elsbeth.'

Ruby and I were like mother and daughter, with none of the angst. She died just before Zelma and one was a preparation for the other. Now Elsbeth is 96 and until recently left her flat in Fulham every day and caught whichever bus came first. If it was the 14 she went to the British Museum and if it was the 19 she went to the Royal Academy. Most weeks she visits the Wigmore Hall for concerts and entertains frequently. Every so often she asks me to 'do her in' as a favour and I politely decline – but age cannot wither her, try though it might.

My friend Eve Pearce is in her seventh decade. She is an inspiration to her friends and family in how to live life with a funky spirit, whatever age you are. Until a recent felling by colon cancer, she fitted yoga, dance for the over-sixties, Pilates and a poetry workshop into a constant schedule of theatre and TV work and improbable holidays as the oldest climber on a Himalayan trek, or searching out her sponsored orphan in West Bengal, 'just to see how she was doing'.

Eve has one of those faces which grows more beautiful as her eye sockets deepen and her bones grow become prominent and she dresses in soft floaty pastels and twinkling, twisted jewellery. I've never told her this, but when I used to watch her in the golden years of television, I found her a touch worrying. She and the late Gwen Watford had annexed anxious, hooded-eyed, very sad first wife roles and shared out the worry between them. In fact, when John Doyle cast Eve in my daughter Amy's first play, *Sitting Pretty* for an eight-week tour in 2000, I was – well, a bit worried. Did she do comedy?

She did – with a lightness of touch and deft running gags. We would share digs together and whilst I prepared my 'from-fridge-to-table-via-leftovers' in the shortest time known to man, Eve would tell me stories of her youth in Aberdeen. I love being told stories. It's about my favourite thing after watching tango and eating the crispy bits from under the roast potatoes.

Eve's father, Jack, was one of the last well-to-do young men on The Grand Tour. During his sojourn in the South of France, he fell in love with the manageress of the Scottish Tea Rooms in Nice. After the marriage in 1926, Jack's father married again, and the new stepmother insisted the young wastrel's allowance be cut off. In 1929, with Eve on the way, Jack's wife returned to Scotland, wanting to give her child a Scottish nationality. Seventy years later, in her book of poems, *Woman in Winter*, Eve wrote, movingly:

Her legacy's been worth the telling, worth the pain,
For I have seen sunlight strike Dunottar's ruins
Through curtains of rain, and wild sea-sprayed branches
Cliff-high, glimpsed from a train have enlaced me
With ancient magic.
We are the things we love.

Jack and the family returned to Aberdeen, where, penniless, they lived and slept in one room – indeed, in one brass bed. War was declared on a Sunday in 1939 and Jack was the first in the queue to enlist on the Monday. 'Daddy has to go and fight Hitler,' he told the bairn.

From the age of seven, after her beloved mother died of cancer, Eve lived with her two maiden aunts, May and Elsie. It was the chagrin of 'wee' Eve's life to have to accompany Aunt May on shopping trips as she suffered from a mysterious disease of the lower legs, never diagnosed as anything other than 'a mysterious disease of the lower legs', which caused her to subside at intervals, very, very slowly to the ground, moaning 'Oh, dearie dearie me, oh, dearie dearie me'. Her niece, standing beside her, mortified, would be willing the ground to open and swallow her until such time as Aunt May recovered her equilibrium enough to pick up her shopping and continue up the steep street.

Her father, desperate to get away, sought out his late wife's friend, Pat, in London. Enquiring after Pat Wright in a random Maida Vale newsagent, he was told she lived upstairs. Comically, Pat had been the manageress in the *Irish* Tea Rooms in Nice. They married, and Pat, belying the stereotype, became a beloved stepmother devoted to this – by her own account – odd looking, overly dramatic child. When Pat bought the child a satchel and took her to get it engraved, Eva Elsie Ethel Pearce asked if she could please be Eve. 'Why, yes,' replied Pat, 'you can be anything you want.' Eve never forgot those words.

At sixteen she applied for RADA, dressed in her uncle's McDonald kilt and a white Tyrolean blouse, and miraculously, out of 89 applicants, got down to the last two. The other contestant was a raven-haired beauty and it was to no one's surprise except Eve's when she was called in to be told she should reapply the following year. 'Shan't!' cried the wee lass passionately. 'You've only chosen her because she's nineteen! It's not fair and I shan't come back!'

The next three years were Eve's rite of passage. Pat sent her to the local junior employment office where she told the clerk her ambition to be an actress.

'Well, we don't seem to have any jobs for actors – I'm afraid – but would you like to be a lab assistant in a psychology department?'

Unsure what a lab was, let alone psychology, Eve went along to Bedford College and into her life came Professor D W Harding, who was the first person to apply psychological motivation to literature. Tall and avuncular, he bent down almost double to hear Eve say she was going to be an actress.

He didn't flinch. 'And might I ask what plays you've read?'

'Well . . . er . . . well, I was in . . . *Twelfth Night* . . .' she struggled.

'Yes, yes, yes,' muttered the professor, 'but to be an actress you must *read* plays – *know* plays – Shakespeare, Sheridan, Shaw, Molière . . .' Sixteen-year-old Eve seemed about to lose a job for not having read enough plays. 'Tell you what, Miss Pearce,' smiled the professor, 'how about this as a plan? I'll give you this job, £2 10 shillings a week, and with it a library card, on your solemn promise that you will read one play every week, which you and I will discuss every week.'

By the time she was accepted at RADA in 1948, Eve possessed a cogent knowledge of most of the canon of English and European drama.

I found that story profoundly moving when she told it and I still do. Is there, I wonder, a single youth out there who wouldn't benefit from the one-to-one attention of a patient mentor?

'How are you, Evie?' I ask when calling to check a fact.

'Oh, fine, darling,' she says in her husky voice with its 'received pronunciation' (no trace of the native burr unless called for and then it's as rich as shortbread), 'I'm just off to RADA to watch my "buddy"' (part of the mentoring scheme the Academy runs for their students) or 'Can't talk, Mo, I'm reading to stroke victims at the Whittington Hospital'.

Eve-angelical. Like I said, an inspiration to us all.

They should *all* be Dames, or at least have an entire South Bank Show devoted to them. Alas, 'It' girls and rock chicks will always look sexier to those who are paid to know what the public wants. Still, age shall not wither them nor collagen stale their infinite variety . . .

In Fitness and in Health

Finding myself with a three-day week, I went with a girlfriend to Henlow Grange for a pick-me-up. It's one of the oldest health farms and I first went there in the Sixties when it was very chic, full of clapped-out Thespians and macro-operatic singers in tent-sized bathrobes, and the regime was awfully strict. You were medically examined on arrival and expected to starve on lemon juice for days, after which a shocking headache was de rigueur. Bowel movements were the topic of the day. By the end of the week you'd graduated to a light diet, as in yoghurt and Ryvita, your complexion was on the turn from spotty to clear and you'd lost 10lbs.

Over the years these places have become less strictured, but often they retain a kind of hushed, hothouse atmosphere which, if one isn't entirely balanced, can make one burst into tears at the sound of Nat King Cole or the sight of a crocus.

Still, three days with a chum – Astrid, writer, foodie and super-slim American – looked promising. We started laughing at Hendon when I pointed out a passing German shepherd and she asked how I could tell he was a German and I knew we were in for a laugh. Henlow was warm, welcoming and girding its loins for a massive renovation, which is just about how I'd describe the pair of us.

We signed up for everything – yoga, massage, Pilates, step, reflexology – I haven't been that busy since 'O' levels, legging it from double science in the lab to life and literature in the library. Astrid threw in manicure and pedicure stuff, but I maintain that what my eye doesn't see ain't worth paying for. The treatment girls were wonderfully larky creatures whose romantic predilections I got treated to within seconds.

It seems to go with the territory. In New York recently a lovely Asian American assistant in a tiny boutique in Greenwich Village confessed to a passionate email romance with an artist from Newcastle. I ended up writing him a note to say we'd met and he had to be sure to look after this lovely creature. Next time I went in she told me, 'He was so pleased that our relationship has been blessed by a celebrity.' I didn't know quite how to react to that one. It's so American. Back in Henlow I'm giving careers advice, public speaking tips and migraine relief. All I've really done is shifted my office.

One evening we attended a lecture on facial exercises to keep the muscles of the face taut. There can be no funnier sight than a room full of middle-aged women attempting to frighten away age. 'Ooooh,' we went, narrowing our eyes and pouting ferociously. 'Aaaargh,' we went, inverting our lips and popping our eyes before subsiding into whooping.

'Excellent,' said the male practitioner. 'Now, let's see you pull up your chins into a Bruce Forsyth whilst holding down the skin on your throat, to keep those chicken necks at bay.' (I've been keeping the chicken neck at bay ever since. In the kitchen. In my bed. In New York. Worryingly, I think my neck is losing weight. It's such a short step from swan to buzzard, isn't it?)

In the classes we shone – like a brick shines. In the 'Sinatra Swings' class we were spectacularly uncoordinated. Eyes shut and waving an imaginary top hat, I felt pure Cyd Charisse. Eyes open, looking in the mirror, pure Sid James. One day I wandered into the enormous pool area to hear a boot camp commander bellowing instructions to a ring of startled women: 'TOTHELEFTTOTHERIGHTTOTHECENTRE – MOVE IT! STARTRUNNINGONTHESPOTNOW!!'

He saw me watching and, in the same decibel, yelled 'ARE YOU JOINING US?' I didn't even draw breath – just yelled back, using all my 55-year-old projection skills, 'I MIGHT, I MIGHT NOT, AWRIGHT!?!' The ring of women gave me a floating ovation.

I'll never know whether it was the exercise, the good food, the facial, the massage or just the unending laughter, but it was the best three days I've had in years. 'You look wonderful,' said Jack, when I returned. 'Go back for another three.'

Queue-Tips

Q. What did the inflatable teacher in the inflatable school say to the inflatable boy when he came in with a drawing pin?
A. 'You've let me down, you've let the school down and, worst of all, you've let yourself down!'

All right please yourselves, but we laughed a lot. It was back in April 2002 and we needed a cheer-up after the dear Queen Mother fulfilled her last engagement.

I queued up to see her Lying-in-State. I felt compelled to. My daughter came with me and would probably say it was the most mortifying day of her life. We drove to Waterloo the day before the funeral and the radio told us the waiting time was up to eight hours. 'Why exactly do you want to do this?' she asked.

'Cos it's history. 'Cos we live in London. 'Cos I'll kick myself for years if I don't. 'Cos I want to be able to tell my grandchildren, if I ever have any ruddy grandchildren . . .' I tailed off, pointedly. 'Besides, we'll have a nice day together and we'll meet all sorts of people . . .'

'I know, you're going to embarrass me for eight hours, aren't you?' she said darkly.

'Not for *eight*!' I grinned. 'It'll be much less than that.'

She pulled her polo-neck over her chin. 'Oh, my God.'

I'd detected a sharp wind and dressed up warm as though for the retreat from Stalingrad. Long woollen skirt, vest, sheepskin boots, fake fur and matching hat. I looked like Dr Zhivago's aunt from Omsk. So, there I was, an embarrassment of stitches, on the South Bank where the line stretched back to Blackfriars Bridge. I started walking to the front of the queue.

'Why are you walking *that* way?' asked Amy suspiciously.

'Er . . . I just want to see if I know anybody,' I muttered.

'Know anybody? How would you know anybody?'

'I might.'

'Who else but you would *do* this? Mod, why are you turning your head? Why are you smiling at people? Oh God – *I* get it . . .'

Avoiding her beady glance I started signing autographs for little girls who'd been sent over by a mother who was old enough to remember me.

By now I'd gathered a small crowd and Amy had withdrawn to a discreet distance.

'How're yer doing, Maureen?' called a friendly Midland voice from the queue. 'Maureen – can we have your autograph?'

'You can if you let me in the queue,' I replied, 'I haven't got that long.'

''Course you can – come on in,' chorused the five jolly Birmingham belles. I was in. Sandwiches and coffee were mentioned. Names were swapped and we all cosied up. Amy stood to one side, her face vermilion, her expression long-suffering.

The ladies, all up at the crack of dawn, down to earth and the salt of the earth, were right up my queue. There was a softly spoken black girl, Sarah, in a lavender scarf, who'd been up since 5.30am and was now quietly worried that she'd have to leave before the line reached Westminster Hall.

'Why don't we go down to the other side of Lambeth Bridge and see if I can push in there – then Amy can come back for Sarah?' I suggested. Amy apologised more than I thought was strictly necessary, then off we tottered.

It didn't take long. A jolly Welsh contingent agreed to let us in if I phoned Janet's mother in Llandudno and said, 'Hello, I'm in the queue with Janet.' ''Ere, Dad,' chirped her mum, 'we've got that Maureen Lipton on the phone.'

Amy went back to get Sarah and I waited at the narrow iron gate for fear the police wouldn't let them through if I proceeded with the rest of the line. They returned and once we were inside the hall everything fell silent.

The mood was of fond reverence. The coffin looked far too small to house that immense spirit. The bells of Westminster chimed five as we moved through and the guard silently changed. It was memorable.

Outside a young reporter from *The Sun* asked me if I'd met the Queen Mum. I told her my stories but I was dying to tell my friend Geoff Morrow's. He had met her after a charity do and told her that he was a composer. When she asked, 'Anything I'd know?' he replied, 'Can't Smile without You', (the Barry Manilow hit). 'Oh, I like that one,' she said. Two and a half years later he was standing in the crowd at Ascot as the royal party walked down the track before the race. Her Majesty left the royal party, walked over to the ropes, caught his eye and sang, 'I can't smile without you . . .'

That's worth queuing for, isn't it?

The Female Enoch

Dear Germaine. She never disappoints. Just when you thought it was safe to consign her to a watery bus pass, she reinvents herself. She is the Madonna of Redbrick Academia. She's been in my life for longer than Ken Barlow, and this week she recognised the relationship by haranguing my erstwhile doppelganger, Beattie, as an appalling image of older women.

She's always been a tease. Just when I'd agreed to hate men and embrace women power, she did a Stalinesque realignment and told me it's women who are to blame for submitting to men's penetrative brutality.

After years of extolling sexual promiscuity, she rounded on me to tell me I should be celibate.

Just when I'd submitted to Feminism, she denounced the intent of the sisters on to whose bandwagon she first climbed.

Just when my contemporaries were celebrating being recycled in their middle years by a surge of oestrogen, she chose to tell me that HRT was a denial of nature.

She walked out on Australia and embraced the Old World, and just as suddenly walked away from the glittering fray with only a newspaper column to keep the country chill off her unbrittle bones. For that period the word according to GG came down the line from High Chittering on Turbot. It would seem that I was a fool to live in Samuel Johnson's and Peter Ackroyd's London when I could live miles from anywhere or anyone I know, with geese . . . and you know, when a man is tired of geese . . .

Germaine informed me that reality television was distorting my mind and manipulating my children (she has lots of godchildren). She knew this because, on my behalf, she entered and failed to endure the House of Celebrity, Big Brother.

Germaine believes an extension at Stanstead airport is a good thing and that female circumcision, if done in a humane way, is cultural and not to be discouraged. Germaine also believes that women carry heavy handbags because they are outer extensions of our uteruses.

Yesterday's revelations came in a speech delivered to mark her tenth reincarnation as doctor-diva. It concerned the stereotyping of older women and the axe came down on Julie Walters as Mrs Overall, Prunella Scales for her Tesco ads, and me for those eleven-year-old BT ads.

Now, I am aware that every volte-face and fresh outburst of temper is well timed to precede the publication of a new book, and also that screaming sound bites are often taken out of context and magnified. But in ten years' time will she be telling me the correct way to die? Or has she already covered that one in the book?

The trouble is that I remember her in the babe days, at Granada TV in the Sixties, all legs and lashes, doing a paltry sketch show, lost in the archives of time, called *Nice Time*. Her co-star was one Mr John Birt and I believe there were portrayals of stereotypical dimwits of all kinds, creeds and ages – mostly anyone over twenty-five. Anything for a laugh, for such were the times. We all snatched whatever opportunities there were to 'get on'. Moreover we did it just to get laughs.

For the same reason, Noël Coward gave us Madame Arcati and Shakespeare and Aeschylus gave us wrinkled tights and Jeffrey Bernard gave us . . . Jeffrey Bernard. And Victor Meldrew is also Victoria Meldrew and that is how we restore sanity to a very old and very Nora Batty world. Because that's what comedy is, proving that nobody is a hero to his valet, via the dottiness, eccentricity and clichés of age, class and creed. It's appropriate, or one might even say, germane.

I wonder what she'd make of these stereotypes:

A farmer stopped by the local mechanic shop to have his truck fixed. They couldn't do it while he waited, so he said he didn't live far and would just walk home. On the way home he stopped at the hardware store and bought a bucket and a gallon of paint. He then stopped by the feed store and picked up a couple of chickens and a goose. However, struggling outside the store he now had a problem – how to carry his entire purchases home.

Whilst he was scratching his head he was approached by a little old lady who told him she was lost. She asked, 'Can you tell me how to get to 1603 Mockingbird Lane?' The farmer said, 'Well, as a matter of fact, my farm is very close to that house. I would walk you there but I can't carry this lot.' The old lady suggested, 'Why don't you put the can of paint in the bucket. Carry the bucket in one hand, put a chicken under each arm and carry the goose in your other hand?' 'Why thank you very much,' he said and proceeded to walk the old girl home.

On the way he says, 'Let's take my short cut and go down this alley. We'll be there in no time.' The little old lady looked him over cautiously then said, 'I am a lonely widow without a husband to defend me. How do I know that when we get in the alley you won't hold me up against the wall, pull up my skirt, and have your way with me?'

The farmer said, 'Holy smokes, lady! I'm carrying a bucket, a gallon of paint, two chickens and a goose. How in the world could I possibly hold you up against the wall and do that?' The old lady replied, 'Set the goose down, cover him with the bucket, put the paint on top of the bucket, and I'll hold the chickens.'

Yes of course its politically incorrect and if I correct it it won't have a laugh in it. Lighten up Prof. Lighten up.

Retro-inspective

In the beginning was the end of the Millennium. I only know that because in late 1998, as I drove over Blackfriars Bridge to the National Theatre, the electronic countdown on the bridge said 465 days to the year 2000, and when I last drove over the same bridge, it said only 27 days left.

There was talk of a Masked Ball at Cambridge. 'We won't know anyone,' said Jack.

'It doesn't matter,' said I. 'You'll be masked. Everyone will think they know you, that's the whole point.'

'Alright. If you want to go, love,' he said, sealing with a line the inescapable fact that we'd never go.

'Let's have a dinner party,' I said to nice friends. 'We'll do a course each.'

'We haven't got a dinner table,' said Jack.

It was true. I'd sold the billiard/dinner table for half what we paid for it, in the belief that we could make a sitting-room out of the dining-room if we bought a collapsible dining table. We found one in Burford for roughly eight times the price we had in mind. It was fantastic! It seated fourteen, had five removable leaves and concertina'd into an elegant writing desk. It was gorgeous, it was witty, it was a triumph of a table. It was sixteen and a half grand.

'It's a talking point,' I breathed, getting an instant hot flush. 'Every time we sit down to dinner, we'll have to get up again and show everybody what it does. It'll be like having a precocious child.' I was plucking at my outer garments now and puffing upwards over my top lip. I was about to start bargaining. It's what I'm worst at in the world, including the decathlon and soufflés.

'It's got some flaws,' said Jack hopefully. 'It's a bit warped where the leaves go in.'

'It's nearly two hundred years old,' I said, stoutly defending it, 'you'd be warped at that age.'

The shop owner started the bidding by dropping a thousand pounds. I countered by suggesting a further drop of a few hundred. (About twelve grand was what I actually had in mind.)

Jack looked like he was in a scene from *The Shining*. He couldn't believe I was doing this in earnest.

'Look,' I hissed, 'if this was a second-hand convertible BMW with only 23,000 on the clock you'd think you'd got a bargain.'

'But . . .'

'I know and this will appreciate,' I said with a flourish. In my heart I meant it would appreciate a good home.

'But . . .'

I should point out now that there was another perfectly nice dining table in the shop for a quarter of the price of the expensive one. It had all the qualities we'd been looking for in a table and was only twice what we'd put down as our top whack. Unfortunately, having seen the origami table – the veritable Houdini of tables – doing its stuff, the perfect one seemed incredibly unversatile.

Imagine you're trying to cast *Raging Bull* and Frank Bruno seems like a good idea, then Robert De Niro just happens to walk past the office.

In the end I had to be taken outside and hosed down.

'We'll think about it,' said Jack.

'I hate that.'

'What?'

'We'll think about it. It's what my mother used to say when I'd found the perfect dress and she didn't want me to have it 'cos it was a) pencil slim ('and you're not'); b) too short ('it's not nice on you, love. You've got my knees'); c) not the Crimplene one in C & A which she'd adored and which made me look like Viv in *I Love Lucy*.'

We went for a cooling-off period, during which I bought an old leather football on a silver stand, a long beige linen dress with asymmetrical hems, and a cheese dish. Together they came to one leg of one fabulous table.

On the way home we passed a pub on a roundabout and I saw something which made me forget I was sulking. I saw owls. At 4.30 in the afternoon. Many owls. Standing on pub tables, the tops of cars, the open trunks of estate cars. And – on the top of a van – a vulture. This was just off the North Circular Road. They were a troupe of travelling owls with their incredibly owl-like owner and they came from a nearby sanctuary. I'd never been that close to one before without bars between us. Their plumage put the mahogany table in the shade. Every tone of beige and brown and gold and russet. And the superiority of the look away! I suppose it helps when you can totally rotate your head to denote the end of the interview.

Then there were four tiny snowy owls with carved fur round the eyes. One was a budding escapologist who worked away assiduously at his moorings. Two babies wandered blindly around the beermats looking as if they'd been tarred and feathered. There were two kestrels in the trunk of an estate car, drumming their talons. The vulture surveyed all. There was no other word for the vulture but plain. Awfully plain. You hoped to God she had money.

By the time I got home I'd forgotten the table, but it came back to haunt me during the New Year when I had to hire two trestle tables at £13 each to feed my vulture friends. I feel quite good about it now. When they ask me what I was doing when the year 2000 came in I'll say I was awfully busy saving £16,484.

I Don't Know How You Remember Them ...

There's this Australian living in the outback, miles from anywhere, and he is desperate for a woman. Restless, frustrated and simmering like a pressure cooker, he's pacing his verandah one day when a distant dustcloud on the horizon turns into first a moving dot and then a truck.

Shading his eyes, he moves forward to greet the large stocky, bearded stranger who pads towards him, hand outstretched in greeting.

'G'day, man. My man's Russ. I'm your neighbour from 250 miles due south, by Red Ridge. Come to invite you to a party, Sat'day night, my place. Can you make it?'

Bruce is thrilled skinny. 'Bonza, mate!' he beams. 'I'll be there – can't wait.'

'Great,' says Russ. 'Oh, one thing though I should mention, they'll be loads of booze, a lot of drinkin', is that alright with you, mate?'

'Sure thing,' says Bruce. 'I'll bring some Four X.'

'Yeah, and . . .' Russ pauses. 'There's likely to be a bit of violence . . .' he grins sheepishly, 'you know what I mean . . .?'

'Oh . . . er . . . yeah, sure thing,' murmurs Bruce, slightly wrong-footed now. 'No problem, I can handle myself.'

'Great, man. Oh and . . .' Russ claps him on the shoulder. 'I should point out something else, there'll be *loads* of sex, and I mean LOADS. Doesn't bother you at all?'

'Bother me! Hardly, mate!' says Bruce, now beside himself with delight. Then, as Russ turns to go, he calls: 'What's the dress code, mate? Should I wear something smart?'

'Just come as you are,' yells Russ over his shoulder. 'There'll only be the two of us there!'

I tell you that well-honed joke as a foreword to a slightly more meaningful discussion on humour. Was that, I ask you, a racist joke? Did it demean our antipodean cousins by stereotyping them into big, dumb, beer-swilling woofters? I hope not because I think that joke has much more to do with wide open spaces than cultural clichés. It would work almost as well set in Russia or Iceland. Almost as well, not *as* well, because there is also something terribly open about the antipodean face and the

340

questioning, rising inflection of the accent which suits the story perfectly. I always felt the BT Jewish momma ads would work equally well with an Italian or Asian momma. After all, show me a son who phones his mother often enough and I'll show you William Hague.

It makes me uncomfortable to hear non-Jews telling Jewish jokes, particularly when they are jokes about money. There are parts of the cultural clichés which we buy into, and parts we don't. Smother-love jokes are affectionate, money jokes are not. The drunk Scotsman, the dumb Irishman and the tight Jewish businessman all fulfil a human need to be superior. Sociologically there are reasons for these stereotypes which are probably to do with poverty and exclusion, but the fact remains that we seem to need them. Americans make Canadian jokes, Canadians make Newfoundlander jokes, the Irish make Kerryman jokes and everybody makes Polish jokes. And let's hear it for the poor light bulbs whilst we're at it.

Should there be no good news/bad news jokes because there are sick people in hospitals who might be offended by 'There is good news and bad news. The bad news is you have only 24 hours to live, the good news is you see that nurse over there with the enormous breasts? Well I had sex with her in my lunch break.'

Or the one about the man who is told he has hepatitis, E. coli and Aids and must be put in a secure room and fed nothing but pancakes. 'Will that cure me?' he asks. 'No,' they reply. 'It's the only thing we can get under the door.'

Sadly, painfully, it is the sad and the painful which is at the root of most comedy. And the prejudices and, yes, the cultural stereotypes.

Take Ali G, arguably – no, not arguably, certainly – the funniest man on TV at present, admonished for impersonating a wannabe black rapper when he's actually a Jewish boy from North London. The dissenters miss the point that what Sacha Baron Cohen, via Ali G, is satirising is our incredible gullibility and our universal desperation to be 'on the telly'.

Whenever I see him I have this secret desire to dress up as Beattie, the phone-aholic, for just one final appearance. To don grey wig, glasses, padding and 30-denier stockings and gatecrash Ali's show, simply to pinch his cheek and say 'You can't fool me, you little lobos, I was at your bar mitzvah. I ironed your tie. I bought you a fountain pen! *Ali G*, my tochas!' Then I'd clip him round the ear and exit stage left, but not before I made him sit down and listen to a few perfect Jewish jokes . . .

A couple are locking up the shop one evening and the husband prepares to take the money from the safe to the bank deposit.

'Give it to me,' says his wife, 'I'll put it in my knickers till tomorrow, then we can get to the cinema on time.'

'In your knickers?' repeats the husband, dumbfounded.

'Yes! It's safe as houses – come and get your coat.'

Later that night, back at home after the restaurant and the cinema, she is undressing for bed when she suddenly screams 'Aargh – the money – it's gone!'

'How can it have gone – you said it was safe as houses – retrace your steps – where have we been . . .?'

'Henry, calm down, we had the meal and we went to the cinema and we came home – oh, wait a minute, now I remember.'

'What? What?'

'There was a man sitting next to me in the cinema and he had his hand in my knickers.'

Her husband is aghast. He sits down heavily. 'You are telling me – I can't believe what I'm hearing – you are telling me that a man, a stranger, a strange man, that you sat through the whole film and let a man put his hand in your knickers!'

The wife looks at him in amazement.

'Well, did *I* know he was a thief?!'

Solly and Ruby go to their doctor for a complete check up. After examining Solly the doctor proclaims him to be in excellent shape for a man in his eighties and asks if he has any queries before he takes a look at Ruby.

Solly leans forward conspiratorially and says, 'There is one thing, Doctor . . . erm . . . you see, when I make love to my wife the first time I get all hot and sweaty, but the second time I get all cold and shivery. Why is that?'

The doctor is impressed. 'Well, Solly, I don't know the reason for that but if you would send in your wife, perhaps she can help.'

After examining Ruby he says, 'Well, you're in very good shape Ruby and I'm not suprised after what Solly tells me.'

Ruby looks puzzled so the doctor continues, 'Your husband asked me why he gets hot and sweaty the first time he makes love to you and cold and shivery the second. I've no idea why that might be, do you?'

She shakes her head in despair. 'Silly sod,' she says. 'The first time he makes love to me it's July and the second time it's February!'

We take the same couple back to the doctor a year later and Solly is in bad shape. The doctor examines him and then asks him to go out and send in his wife. He comes around the desk, takes her hand and speaks with great seriousness.

'Ruby, your husband is going to die. It's not a question of *if* . . . it's *when*. Now, only you can prolong his life. It will take great patience, and here's

I Don't Know How You Remember Them . . .

what you have to do. When he wakes you should bring him tea and toast and a lightly scrambled egg and speak very softly to him, and should he wish to make love then get back into bed and do that. At mid morning give him a light broth and a cuddle and if he wants more, I suggest you allow him to have it. Let him sleep till lunch time and give him steamed fish or meat and a home-cooked dessert and then if he wants to lie down for a while after a short walk, then do lie down with him, and if he wants to make love then do so. He should have afternoon tea with a home-made teacake and perhaps you might play a little sudoko or bridge or have a kiss and cuddle, then leave him while you make his dinner – three courses and a cup of real coffee won't hurt – then a little supper in front of the television before an early night, and remember, if he wants to make love then allow him to do that.'

Ruby goes back to the car where Solly is waiting.

'What did he say?' he asks anxiously.

'He said you're going to die.'

So, Ruby has a heart attack and before she dies, she has a near-death experience where she sees the Lord and he tells her, 'Go back – you still have another twenty-three years, eight months and six days to live.'

She wakes up in hospital so exhilarated by the experience that she books herself a face-lift, a nose job, an eye-lift, a chin-tuck, a breast augmentation and liposuction. She leaves the hospital and is knocked down and killed by an ambulance. Furious, she turns on the Lord and says:

'You lied to me, Lord! You told me I was going to live for another twenty-three years! Why didn't you stop the ambulance from knocking me down?'

The Lord replies, 'I didn't bloody recognise you!'

There are more. There are so many more . . . but where do they come from? One day I would like to take a small camera crew, as they do into the wild rain forests of Guyana, and track down the rarely sighted, reclusive, baggy-eyed Scriptor Comicus to the fag-ashed, coffee-laced, crumpled-up A4-strewn cabin whence pours this endless stream of insane, often crudite, bigoted, racy – sometimes racist – but somehow acceptable vignettes, ranging in hue from white collar to blue to black.

I would watch him in High Definition Close-up as he paced and practised, gesticulating wildly, and although he might occasionally bark out short peals of laughter, he would be the most miserable-looking man on the planet. The camera would then follow selected jokes to the equally miserable-looking recipients – the comedians – and thence to the night clubs, comedy clubs, studios, provincial stages and political podiums where these overtly relaxed performers would attempt to make the joke

343

sound newly minted that morning. The programme would end with our hero, 'Poeta Satirica', trying to get a cheque out of an agent for the use of his joke:

'He said it! I heard him say it: "Why is a banjo solo like premature ejaculation? 'Cos you can see it coming but there's not a damn thing you can do about it." One of mine. Wrote it in '62 for Bob Monkhouse . . . I don't care if he says he thought of it while he was shaving, I bloody thought of it first! Yeah? Well, he can shove his Universal Consciousness up where the sun don't shine – I want 150 quid in readies Monday morning or I know where he lives! You get me, blood?'

I can already hear the nominations . . .

Deep Drawers

Last year, about this time, waiting for the turkey to overcook, my husband began idly poking through the contents of the kitchen drawer we never open.

'What's this?' he said, holding up two steel circles on a handle.

'It's an egg separator,' I said. I was tired and grumpy and I knew what was coming next.

'What does it separate the egg from?'

Sigh. 'It separates the yolk (*sigh*) from the white,' I said, in a tone that I hoped would imply that if the next question was 'Why would you want to separate . . . etc.' I would separate his caps from his knees. Instead he said brightly, 'What's this, then?' and held up something similar in cream-coloured plastic.

'It's another one and I don't know why I've got two – it was when we were on that diet and we could only eat the yolk. His and Her Egg Separators, nice, trendy – every couple should have a couple.'

He blinked, thought about it, went back to the drawer and held up something small, brown and plastic. He refrained from using my mother's line: 'I say, Maureen. Is this anything?' and we both just stared at it. Then he passed it over. I examined it. Part of it went up and down.

'No idea,' I said. 'Chuck it.'

He went back to the drawer and held up a thin basketwork sheath with two chopsticks in it and raised his brows.

'Chopsticks in a basket,' I said, then, 'more chopsticks in more baskets.' Then 'Chopsticks, brass ends, one pair minus basket.'

He began to count. There were 49 chopsticks. 'How can there be 49? Where's the 50th?' He gave me a look. I was beginning to enjoy this. Then he held up an unopened box.

'Ice tongs.'

'Ice tongs?'

'For tonging your ice.'

There was a pause. 'Oh. Right.'

Next was a piece of metal shaped like a fish on a long red stick. He turned it round and about like Hugh Scully on *The Antiques Road Show*, this week coming from a kitchen in Muswell Hill.

'Fish thermometer,' I said, intercepting his raised eyebrows. 'Very useful if the fish feel a bit feverish . . . and before you ask, that blue thing's an icing dispenser for cakes, which in my case I haven't iced since the old King died . . . Aaaah – that'll be a honey stirrer bought at a country fête, one owner, me, usage, never.' (I find I prefer to let the honey drip down the side of the jar and coagulate on the melamine shelf. Keeps it firmly stuck.)

He was making a little pile out of three lousy tin openers and the spare corkscrew – the one that becomes invisible at party time. I added a pastry cutter (hah!) and a double-ended butter curler, for curling two tubs of butter at a time at opposite ends of the same area, I suppose. Mostly I tend to eat my butter uncurled these days. How about you?

My standards are slipping, I know.

There was also a closed-in tea strainer of the kind that makes a cup of real tea for one – ideal for herbal teas, which I drink all the time in spite of their tasting uniformly like boiled slug and underpants. It was nestled tenderly in the crook of a defunct asthma spray once dispensed to Jack when his throat mysteriously closed up after a fish supper.

That was about it, really. Aside from the egg slicer which is too big to fit in the drawers we use and the devilishly sharp knife in its own sheath which none of us has ever dared touch. Dental sticks – three packets, and a shiny, state-of-the-art garlic press which couldn't press froth and was the cheapest buy I could make to get myself out of a Conran Shop without embarrassment.

The thing is, that's just one drawer. I shudder to think what the rest of this house is housing. We are, at present, looking around for a smaller house or flat, now that half of the children have left. It's called Half Empty Nest Syndrome. We keep going to look at places which are twice as expensive and half as nice as ours. There just isn't a house in the world as nice as ours. I think that every time I come home to it. We just want to be nearer to town, that's all, and cut out the long distance worry-driving. I thought of putting an advert in *The Times* saying: 'How would you like to bring up your kids in the happiest house in Muswell Hill? If so, and you're ready to leave ditto but smaller around central London, write PO Box whatever and neither of us need ever set eyes on an estate agent again.'

It's the thought of the drawers, though, as much as not seeing a property we like. That, and leaving the shed – sorry, summerhouse – and the postbox and the observatory with electric roof and the wrought-iron swing that took two men to carry, with me at the kitchen window shouting 'No, not there – it looks too big there – try the other side . . .' and the phone box which eight stout-hearted men ferried across the lawn on tracks and the monkey puzzle tree and the plum tree and the blue hydrangeas that always come up pink 'cos the soil's too alkaline. And, oh, be still my aching heart, the spot we buried Pushkin, the family mog . . . How will I ever, ever, every go? They'll have to bubblewrap me and post me on.

Needless to say, I kept everything in the drawer – chopsticks and all. Well, you never know, do you? Just suppose twins with an egg white allergy came to the house for tea – then where would I be without my two egg separators? Exactly.

So, here I am again, a year later, same house, different turkey. Is it cooked? Where's that fish thermometer?

All in all I've been very happy keeping my private diary public and fortunately my life has been eccentric enough to supply one-thousand word adventures without too much difficulty. Often in the fourteen column-writing years of our marriage, I would come home from whatever show I was in, eat a hasty supper – for acting makes me ravenous – and sit down with Biro and vellum to write a fast monthly column. It didn't take long, after so many years of practice, to adapt the thoughts I'd had on the drive home into a thousand words and a smart ending, after which I'd gingerly thread my way around creaking stair boards to bed.

As I tiptoed to my side in the dark, a sleepy voice would murmur, 'Did you finish it?'

'I did, love – after a fashion – go back to sleep.'

There would follow a teeth-cleaning, make-up removing pause, then, as I lumbered into bed he'd say: 'Read it to me, then', and after a few feeble protests I always did.

Afterwards he'd sigh and say, 'I don't know how you do it, love', turn over and go back to sleep. The man whose imagination had created 250 screenplays – three Baftas and an Emmy and the rest – didn't know how I did it.

I have to confess, however, there are times when I mewl and whine like a child with an overdue essay: 'S'not fair. I don't know what to put!' Casting around for inspiration, I suddenly realise that though I buy new clothes for each season and fresh vegetables for each day, it never occurs to me to replace my kitchenware until it develops fissures from which sprout new and possibly life-saving cultures. I mean, I cooked spinach tonight in the same pan in which I cooked Amy's first solids. And she's 28, for heaven's sake! My plates are the ones I bought off the pavement on my way to rehearsals at the Old Vic in 1983. They're chipped, of course, but surely that means I can find them when they're lost?

The only constantly changing items are the glasses. The drinking ones, I mean, although the seeing ones have gone through quite a few variations, and indeed variegations, over the years. They've gone full circle – wire rimmed in 1968 and, as I type these words today – wire rimmed.

They're pounds lighter in weight and pounds dearer in dosh, but still leave the same red canoe shapes on either side of my nose and leave me looking just as pig-eyed when I take 'em off.

The drinking glasses are all new – as in 'new this year'. When the wedding goblets got shattered, I replaced them with boxed sets from John Lewis, and when the kids got their hands, or possibly feet, on them I settled for Woolworths six packs, and nowadays I just grab tumblers whenever I see them, which is mostly when I'm buying petrol and a couple get mysteriously thrown in, presumably in lieu of service with a smile.

So the glassware cupboard looks like an orphanage. Long ones, short ones, sad ones, blue ones – and still there's only ever one I actually like to drink out of. And that's the one that's in my son's bedroom with a five-day old cola in it.

Which brings me to mugs. The kitchen item which saved us feminists from ever having to wash another saucer. Brilliant, egalitarian, classless mugs. Designed to tone in with your hand-dragged kitchen. 'Put the kettle on, love, will you? Tea or instant? You don't mind a mug, do you?'

Well, between you and me, yes I do. They're too thick for tea and too tall for coffee – no, come on, admit it. And they grow inner rings like trees and they bung up the dishwasher and breed in there like wire coat hangers and lordy lord, doesn't a proper cuppa taste a 103 times better in a nice thin china cup with a beautifully angled handle? Besides which, with a cup you don't have to down so much liquid. You just swill down the perfect amount, so you don't get bloated or acquire leather-coloured teeth.

What I need is a street-sized skip. I also want my own life guru with big heavy muscles and a heart of lead to go with it. 'Bin it, Maureen!' he'd holler. 'If you don't use it, lose it!'

Slow cooker? Gone. Waffle/toasted sandwich-maker? Gone. Eighty-six containers from 86-year-old Chinese food containers? Gone. Mini blender with flying-off-lid in middle of fast spin of hot soup? Gone. Cookery books from car boot sales in the days when you didn't just cook chicken on a Friday night and M&S lean cuisine every other night? Going, going, gone!

Should I keep the oven at all, I'm wondering? My friend Judy Price tells me she's sent off for an electric cooker thing that sits on your counter and cooks everything, cleans like a dream and probably froths you a cappuccino and puts you to bed with a story for all I know. If I buy it, what will happen? Will it roast a mean chicken and two maris pipers, then sit staring malevolently at me for five years until I send it a-hop and a-jumping to the next skip? Or will it release me to spend hours thinking of intelligent, meaningful topics for the next occasion when I can't remotely think what to write?

Oyklahoma!

I met Trevor Nunn one evening in The Ivy. We hadn't met for years but it must have sparked off an idea in his head because he asked me to meet him to talk about Aunt Eller in *Oklahoma!*. We had a good, friendly, funny chat for half an hour at the National, then I read the book and felt the buzz of curiosity. He told me how Eller was central to his vision of the show – 'the matriarch, tough, fair-minded and a character the community looked up to'.

'If you don't have a song in a musical,' I told him wryly, quoting my friend, Julia, 'you ain't in the musical.' He promised me a couple of extra verses and I trusted him. Rightly, as it happened.

I took some singing lessons from Janet Edwards. I can sing like I can play tennis. I know the rules and if I forget trying to be good and enjoy the game, I can get away with murder. If I watch myself you can hear the catgut snap.

The read-through was tentative. Curly was a tall, beautifully proportioned, bright, sweet-faced Australian, Hugh Jackman. Laurey was a pale, black-haired, former ballerina, Josefina Gabrielle. Jud, the villain, was Shuler Hensley, a mad, massive, mop-haired baritone from Atlanta, Ado Annie was a slight, just-out-of-RADA, raven-haired orthodox Jewish biologist from New Jersey, Vicki Simon. Will Parker was Jimmy Johnston, a sandy, pugnacious Welshman, and the pedlar from Persia was black-eyed Anglo-Cypriot, Peter Polycarpou. Old pro Tony Selby was a smokey-voiced cockney Pop Carnes.

In short, not one of us was typecast. Not one of us fitted the bill as posted on the front of the hustings in any production of this oft-performed classic, including the Broadway production in 1943. We all sat down in a circle, coffee cups in hand, large floppy bags constantly dived into, pencils sharpened, throats cleared.

First off, Trevor asked us to go around the circle, saying who we were and giving one fact about ourselves. When it came to my turn I said, 'My name is Maureen Lipman and I told my friend Pam that Trevor had cast me as Eller because he was calling the show "Oyklahoma" and it was all set in a kosher prairie. She completely believed me and immediately arranged for two coachloads of elderly Jewish people from day centres in North London to attend the opening.'

349

When we could put it off no more we read the text. When Hugh's glorious tenor rang out the first notes of 'Oh, What A Beautiful Morning' ('And he can sing too,' was Trevor's comment), my heart started to do double time. Each new voice was revelatory but right. The chorus was rich and deep. Oy! We were on to something.

For one day Trevor talked and we listened. He covered landrushes, pioneers and the hardship of survival. The second day we improvised. There is nothing more embarrassing for an older actor than pretending to be a wristwatch or a horse trough in front of 25 twentysomethings. Tony Selby and I put our heads down, smothered our smirks and got on with it. At one point we were kneeling on the floor facing each other, telling and listening to stories simultaneously. I can't remember a word of his, but mine concerned a red fluffy pencil case named Biscuit.

Later we became our favourite cartoon characters. I Olive Oyled myself into a knot of legs and arms, loping across the room squealing, 'Oh, oh, oh, Popeye!', double-taking and doubling back on myself as one-dimensionally as I could. We were not, fortunately, asked to watch each other but only to get involved in our own scenario. At the end of the session I got the famous Trevor hug. I was, rather pathetically, thrilled by this.

Three weeks into rehearsal I tried to resign, feeling thoroughly inadequate. Trevor, thankfully, ignored my plea. I gamely exercised, warmed up, stretched and kicked with the kids, but asked to count eight beats before executing a four-beat shuffle and my eyes would fill up and I'd convince myself that Susan Stroman, the choreographer, wanted my knees in a viola case at the bottom of the Thames. Somehow I managed to busk it by a mixture of bravado and eccentricity. Only weeks after opening could I suddenly hear the prescribed beats and know when to start. It was as though my ears had relaxed. And still, whenever Stro was out front, I'd lose it again. I'd know I was going to lose it, then I'd lose it – then I'd look sheepish, as if to say, 'I told you I'd lose it!'

Don't misunderstand me, these were all tiny moments which an audience would hardly notice, but to me they were the equivalent of saying, 'Now is the winter of our incontinence . . . er . . . made glorious . . . – ooops – I've dried.' Eight weeks' rehearsal was a luxury I'd never even contemplated before. I needed every minute of it.

Because of the scale of the venture, there would be much waiting around. Shuler Hensley would sit on the floor, behind some makeshift prop, like a marooned giant. We'd all forget about him until he'd suddenly appear over the top of a cupboard and slither down the front of it in vest and sweatpants and along the floor brandishing his prop knife like a malevolent six-and-a-half-foot toddler.

Peter Polycarpou would fret and worry away at his lines, doubting himself, his ability, his received place in the company. Often we would prop each other up on a bench outside on the Embankment.

'Pete, you're getting it – honestly. The accent's there, it's truthful – just believe it will be funny with an audience, 'cos it will . . .'

'You really think so? I dunno . . . He never seems to like my suggestions.'

'Well, I know. It's the same with me – I'm so used to chipping in and suggesting stuff and . . .'

'Yeah, well – you should – Who knows more than you about comedy?'

'But this is musical comedy. Who knows less than me about musicals?'

Tony Selby, playing Ado Annie's father, was as enervated as me by the hours of waiting, followed by sudden intensive action. One day his car exploded on him, showering boiling water over his arm, and for weeks he painfully danced and sang sporting a large sling. A couple of weeks later the male chorus danced straight into him, elbows akimbo, and cracked his ribs.

He made a valiant attempt to return but the pain overwhelmed him. After three weeks he'd missed so much new choreography that it was impossible. Annie was right – it's a hard-knock life. Sid Livingstone appeared one day, word perfect, and took his place, temporarily, and then permanently. Poor Tony missed an incredible year.

The technical week was desperate. The actors were in full costume, wigs and make-up for eleven hours a day, Monday to Friday. Most productions have one day of technical rehearsals and the actors are in street clothes and save corsets and make-up for the dress rehearsal. On the Friday night the call went out for the cast to be back in costume ready to go again at 11.00pm.

As the technical rehearsals reached a climax I found myself shop-stewarding the cast against the management. 'My cast are going home,' I told deputy stage manager Barry Bryant. 'They are going home now before they fall over.' I'm not sure this was appreciated. Susan Stroman came to my dressing room:

'We have to go on,' she told me. 'This isn't for the actors, it's for the crew. It's a technical. You know what a technical is?'

I stared at her.

'Stro,' I said, 'I've been doing techs since you got your first pair of block shoes. I know what a tech is. There are no corsets in a tech. These actors have to open the show and it's best if they do that alive.'

We went home at eleven. Couldn't sleep. Wouldn't sleep. Would I be branded unprofessional? I went back the next day clapped out and panicky. No-one mentioned my rebellion. The tech went on. Trevor inexhaustible, living on Ryvita and coffee, never lost it, never raised his voice, and was always reasonable.

We opened calmly and confidently. I sat 60 feet under the stage, rooting my feet into the wooden earth, smelling the butter in the churn. Squinting into the scorching sun. The floor came up and revolved into place, and the audience applauded the whole opening sequence of sunrise, overture, dustbowl, flying clouds, birds and tiny wooden houses in perspective against the sun. We were off. Curly came on, singing, and the bantering began. Two months later, the laughs peppered every quip we made. That night, though, our sincerity was our trump card. We were not expecting any reaction, so any laugh we got was a wonderful bonus. (You know what they say, 80% of acting is sincerity. And once you've learned to fake that . . .) I believe Trevor preferred the show when it was in this tentative stage. Once the seasoned pros had nailed their laughs, it became harder for him to watch it.

My experienced dresser, Elise, led me like a child from one side of the enormous stage to the other, from exit to entrance. Seldom has a cast been so cosseted. The canteen fed us, the car park coddled our cars, costume and wig department dressed and fitted us, the publicity was made painless. The voice coach, Patsy Rodenberg, warmed us up, the dialect coach checked our accents: 'Emphasise by lengthening and hitting the volume, not by inflection.' It was a working community and it worked. No one was ill. No one was off.

I remember, back in 1971, riding my bike ecstatically over Waterloo Bridge on my way to work at the Old Vic theatre. I was a junior member of Sir Laurence Olivier's National Theatre Company. I worked eleven hours a day, rehearsing, playing and understudying. I was very happy. We all hoped that when the new National Theatre opened on the South Bank, we would all transfer with it. I could think of no more inspirational sight for creativity than the sweet Thames flowing past my dressing-room window.

Cue sound of Gods laughing at best-laid plans. Not only did *I* not transfer, but Sir Laurence – architect behind the architect – Olivier didn't transfer. Sir Peter Hall got the job. Furthermore, the dressing-rooms, uniform concrete cells, were all built around a square and empty atrium. Our inspirational view was to be of each other.

Still, gazing out of my cubicle, some 28 years later, it could be that they were right. There was a corseted and bewigged Caroline Quentin feeding her dog whilst the rest of *The London Cuckolds* cast dropped fag ash on their white tights and jabots. To the left Samantha Spiro and Geoffrey Hutchins turned themselves miraculously into Barbara Windsor and Sid James for *Cleo Camping Emmanuelle and Dick*. Up and right rollicking Irishmen chased kids from Tarry Flynn and down centre Sinead Cusack warmed up melodically for her solo *Our Lady of Sligo*. All human life was strutting its stuff, to full houses in three auditoria. The concrete external hid an internal foundry of creativity.

Aside from some carping about why the National would want to spend 'our' money on a musical like *Oklahoma!*, the reviews were marvellous: classic book, score, lyrics, choreography, original play. Why would anybody want *not* to stage it?

For four months we enjoyed being on the Hit List. There were endless rumours of transfers to the West End. Most people wanted this. They needed the money and the exposure. I wanted it because I couldn't bear to think of them doing it without me. Trevor had a plan to make a video of the show in the months of September to November. The Lyceum, which was the only theatre big enough to house us, had a six-month gap before *The Lion King* arrived. TV producer Richard Price had three months to put the project together. It would take at least six. He did it in eleven weeks.

Every Friday we would have a company meeting with Richard and Trevor. Every Friday there would be optimism but no news. It became a company giggle. 'Was that a definite maybe?' someone was heard to say on their way to slap on a false hairpiece and a prairie pinny . . . and that was just the menfolk. The day before the last National Theatre performance, the news came through. Richard Price had pulled off the impossible. Money was in place from Australia, from Japan, from Sky, Italy, Germany, Sweden, Norway, Denmark, Finland and probably a damp briefcase under a Sicilian bridge for all we knew. Or cared. Yecchay! We were on.

Everyone scattered to the five corners of the earth. Jack and I had a huge, fat, glorious week at Ballymaloe in the south of Ireland, forcefeeding ourselves on inimitable food and knocking back the Guinness at all the unsociable hours under Cork skies, and two weeks later the company reassembled for the video, quivering like greyhounds and utterly 'up for it'.

Just as well we were prepared. I think we stopped once a day for lunch from a standing trolley. The rest of the hours that God made we danced inches off our frames. The video crew were knocked senseless by our stamina and we by their fortitude. Every shot had a deadline. Every deadline had a sell-by date. If it couldn't be got into the day, then the day had to have a hairline extension. Some of the dancers were rising at 4.30am to catch trains and lifts to Shepperton, then leaving for home at 11.30pm, dragging their make-up and wigs off in the car park. This job required a designated dormitory on the studio floor. We shot nine minutes a day. Most TV dramas shoot three. But still we cut no corners.

Trevor and Stro and video director Chris Hunt were not compromisers by nature. It was done and we all went home with racoon eyes and a Christmas bonus. The bonus was that the transfer from stage to screen looked honest. True to what it was. What it was, was a stage show on film. The first shot is an aerial pan down the Thames, past St Paul's, into the crowded foyers of the National Theatre. Shots then zoom in on the audience – we did an extra Sunday matinée to achieve these shots. Naturally they were mostly of friends, nurses, off-duty stage-door keepers and mothers.

My mother adored it. After the screening I heard her raving over the phone to Hull: '. . . and it starts with this wonderful view of the *whole* of Oklahoma all seen from above.' Yes, siree! Oklahoma alrightee! St Paul's, Waterloo Bridge, Sweet-Thames-run-sweet ol' Oklahoma. Indian territory.

Another closing. Another show. Christmas came and went, and then, ultra-violet rayed, we reopened the whole caboodle at the newly refurbished Lyceum and ran for six heady months. I won't chronicle the joy of it because it was a once-in-a-lifetime thrill. We got used to people telling us how they first saw the show on honeymoon in bleak 1947 war-ravaged London and how it was an unimaginable oasis of colour and optimism in their lives. We got used to the letters which wrung out the hearts of seasoned troupers because they came from folk who'd felt blue or depressed or bereaved or just plain didn't wanna go out that night. 'Thanks,' they wrote. 'For three hours I forgot myself totally,' or, 'I haven't stopped singing for days,' or 'That's the best tonic I ever had'.

Two, though, stand out in my mind. One because of the guilt I still feel. The other because the letter writer was an agoraphobic who found it well nigh impossible to sit in a theatre surrounded by strangers, a condition which had been worsening for years and had effectively put a stop to her nursing career.

Friends bought her the ticket as a birthday treat. Yeah, OK, some friends, I know, but listen. She tried to get out of it, she finally agreed, she shook all the way in on the bus, her heart pounded, she sweated. In her aisle seat, she experienced panic symptoms and almost bolted, but from the moment the curtain rose, she lost herself, lost her fears, lost her proximity to others and became part of the whole experience. 'I sang the songs all the way home,' she wrote, 'and never noticed that I was on the dreaded tube.' She was promising herself, by the end of the letter, to look into returning to nursing. The letter was eloquent and moving and sat on the noticeboard, melting the mascara of whoever passed.

The second letter was from a man whose name, I think, was David, who'd seen the show, loved it and talked about it on his weekly visit to his father, an Alzheimer's sufferer, in a Birmingham home. His father, who showed little or no interest in any conversation or any recognition of who was talking, suddenly became animated and said, 'I'd love to see that.' By a remarkable series of permissions and complicated arrangements, he transported his father to a special aisle seat, alerting the theatre staff that he might wander off somewhere. As with our nurse, his father sat for three and a quarter hours in rapt attention, barely moving but to laugh or applaud.

All the way home he clutched his programme to his chest, saying, 'I've got to remember this. I've got to remember this.' David wrote to the cast: 'I just want to thank you for giving me my father back for one evening.'

So why the guilt? I put the letter on the board. It disappeared. I was never able to write back. I tried writing to *Home Truths* and a Birmingham paper to no avail. It's on my conscience, so David whoever you are, if you ever read this please believe that the letter meant a helluva lot to us too.

The Lyceum run differed from the National one in one other way. It was five weeks before we played one night with the full cast. My notepad reads: Monday: Jimmy off – groin strain/Peter off throat/Amanda migraine/Mark back but hoarse/David off/Ben off. Tuesday: Hugh off/Phil off/Vicki bad throat – and on it went . . . Every time Jools Gardener, the company manager, arrived in my dressing room it was to tell me of new missing persons. And, of course, when the guy playing Slim was off (six line scattered throughout the show) then Chris moved into his part and Ben moved into Chris's part and suddenly you were playing an auction scene with no idea who the hell Slim was and from under which Stetson the next voice was coming.

Maybe we were tired, maybe we were less well cared for than at the National. Certainly my migraines were on the march. I missed two shows in the six-month run. I sat at home one Friday night, rigid with nerves, as 7.30 came and went without me at my churn. The pain of the loss was almost worse than the pain of the migraine. I knew my cover, Marilyn Cutts, was a brilliant singer and played the part marvellously. Still, I had several letters: 'I had brought my mother, who is, or *used* to be, a fan of yours, all the way from Cheshire – I had checked with the theatre, who assured me you would be appearing. I hope you realise the disappointment and misery you caused to people who were unable to get their money back' etc.

Sometimes on a Wednesday afternoon I'd be carrying my carrot juice into the stage door when groups of Welsh people would howl at me from a coach, 'Oh, you *are* going to be on – there you are, Hew, I told you she wouldn't take the matinée off!' Chance'd be a fine thing!

The last few weeks became corpse-ridden – giggly – as last weeks do when actors are 'all tuckered out', as Aunt Eller might say. One night I laughed so long and loud in the crucial trial scene that I couldn't do anything but squeak and wave my arms around like a beached bream. It was tragic. Most of the cast joined me. Afterwards, on my way home, I was congratulated by a group of theatregoers. I apologised profusely. They had neither seen nor heard anything unusual.

Curly's horse tended to change names. 'Don't sell Dun, Curly,' became considerably funnier when the horse's name was 'Hurly Burly' and a complex and highspeed auction became a bowel churner when the starting price was eleven dollars instead of ten. A scene where Eller and four or five farm workers ran into the smokehouse after a gunshot was fired was even more dramatic when the gun failed to go off . . . 'Pant, pant – who fired off that . . . er . . . who made that loud thudding noise?' And the presence in the smokehouse of one cowboy onlooker in full drag – with cherries on his hat – worked wonders for the progress of the plot.

The wings were crammed with wit during the romantic duo 'People Will Say We're In Love'. Fergus Logan and Nicola Keene were masterly in their attempts to corpse Curly on his line delivered into the wings, 'Anybody out there? I want you all to know that Laurey Williams is my girl!' After the Kama Sutra repertoire had been trudged through, they stood Nicola on Fergus's shoulders with a skirt made from a roll of fabric down to his boots. The next night she was two foot one with shoes on her knees and another night found her topless with vast plastic breasts. Hugh Jackman had a way of incorporating open-mouthed laughter into Curly's sheer pleasure in the actual moment as envisaged by Rodgers & Hammerstein.

I, of course, took no part in this revelry. Except to drag a huge cardboard cow into the wings and spend every interval planning worse and worse tricks. On the last matinée I dressed Hugh's real-life wife, Deb, in my first-act costume and as he sang 'Don't Throw Bouquets At Me', she stood in the wings brandishing a rolling pin. Hugh was captivated. Just clapped his hands and laughed out loud. As we all piled on stage to congratulate him and Laurey, there was one tall, statuesque blonde in a lace 'fascinator' who got more than the average hug and kiss.

It always seemed to land on Hugh. We knew he could handle it. How he kept straight-faced and sang 'And a little brown maverick is winkin' its eye' when faced with twelve mooning cowboys in the wings with dropped trousers and G-strings I don't know. Pop Carnes, actor Sid Livingstone, was stony-faced throughout. We couldn't get him. God knows we tried. In the trial scene he stonewalled a fluffy glove puppet, a left breast, a hairy claw hand, a false eye and, painfully, a long grey retracting tongue. The only thing which finally wiped him was when they cut the legs off his stool, so that his head barely came above the courtroom table. Fortunately, he quickly regained control, whereas the rest of us lost it big time.

The last week was perfectly wonderful and the last Friday, Howard Keel, the original London Curly (in those days, Harold Keel) now almost eighty, was brought round after the show to see us. Stately, urbane and silvery handsome, he twisted his programme around in his hand and spoke with care: 'I don't know if I'm gonna be able to say this – 'cos I'm an emotional old fart – and 'course I didn't see the production I was in . . . but that was the finest *Oklahoma!* I've ever seen or will ever see in my life.' He was enchanting. And enchanted by Josefina, the first Laurey ever to act, sing *and* dance the complex ballet.

The only sadness between the opening and the last performance was the attitude of American Equity to our show. They refused us permission to take the show over. Broadway was swamped with English actors, Kevin Spacey had begged and bargained for five from the cast of *The Iceman Cometh*, Dame Judi and Samantha Bond were being *Amy's View*'ed, Zoë Wannamaker was *Electra*-frying Times Square. There were more. Alan Cummings, Corin Redgrave – it was time to stop Brit-picking and send 'em Brit-packing.

Oklahoma! An American show – a pedigree! Composer through to librettist. Hammerstein, Rodgers, De Mille (middle European immigrants but let's not carp). How bloody dare we? The arrogance of it. I could understand their proprietorial feelings, but in giving way to them, they lost American actors two years' work. Trevor's schedule had no hole other than immediately after we ended. Our company could have gone for three months then left it to them to play on for however long it lasted.

It seemed to me that they refused us, as much as anything, because of the Tony Awards. The Tonys run what runs. 'We don't want trophies,' I wanted to tell someone. 'Just let us show you the show we've created then you can give us tea in Boston and we'll go home.' When the ma who ran us out of town, Equity boss Alan Aisenberg, came to see the show, he visited our dressing-rooms. Too late to admit us, he stood, chastened, and confessed he'd been knocked out. By a real community of players in a landmark production.

I waxed empirically my theory about the melting pot casting being just what the actual Indian territories would have been. I didn't have to tell him the detailed work which had gone into that easy grouping. He could see that. A subdued man said bye and thanks to a wry cast. What the hell? When David Hockney or Lucien Freud exhibit their work in the States, nobody suggests it should be repainted or remodelled by Edward Hopper or Andrew Wyatt. The same applies to musicians from Menuhin to Vanessa Mae. Nobody suggests replacing Charlotte Church with a twelve-year-old soprano from Poughkeepsie. There are enough indigenous borders in our own country, religious or class or kind. To have them in art, especially in international art, to have a 'special relationship' which includes weapons but fails to include art, is a shame and a waste.

357

The last week began with a normal Monday. We tried hard not to think, Well, that's the seventh but last time I'm ever going to hear that song, because frankly it gets you no place but down.

Tuesday was a special lunch given by the Variety Club for American actor Richard Dreyfuss. I had met Richard and his co-star in *Prisoner of 2nd Avenue*, Marsha Mason, over dinner and bemoaned the fact that neither of us could see the other's show, as we played the same matinées. This Tuesday I was to make a toast to him at the lunch.

I thanked the Variety Club for giving me the opportunity to welcome Richard to this small, sceptred, newly devolved island, ruled, quaintly, by Scotland, Bill Clinton and Rupert Murdoch. 'With our customary native charm we offer you tube strikes, anarchist riots, a soaring pound, inner-city riots, a Balkan War, Man Utd supporters in Trafalgar Square fountains and, soon to come, after the torrential spring rains, the summer drought and the hosepipe ban.'

The last joke of the day concerned the agent who went round to congratulate the director after a show and said, 'The show's great, the music's great, the sets are fabulous but where did you get that awful leading lady? She can't sing, she can't act, she looks like a dog . . .' The director says, 'I'll have you know that leading lady is my daughter!' 'Let me finish!' says the agent.

The laughter floated me back to the Lyceum Theatre where a tea party was being prepared for an American family who had bid several hundred pounds on the night of Comic Relief to have tea with the cast. We had all worn red noses for the walk down that night and I'd sent Hugh out into the audience to auction his body (I was prepared to go up to seven million myself) and Shuler to wrestle anyone to the ground for a given sum. We collected £2,000. Now it was pay-up time and we took the kids backstage and beneath the stage and answered their questions and generally shmoozed and kibitzed until it was show time again.

On the Wednesday, we had two shows and a farewell party on a boat until 2.00am. On Thursday night after the show, I drove to a Cambridge hotel to meet Jack and Amy, for Friday was Adam's graduation ceremony from King's College, Cambridge at 9.00am. It was a beautiful Cambridge day. The service was, mercifully, imposing but brief and salmon and strawberries on the lawns was gloriously surreal. We stood with groups of warm, relieved parents whilst our offspring hugged each other, wrote down numbers and mopped each other's tears. It felt so like Jack's play, *Cold Enough for Snow*. So momentous, so fragile, so transient. I was so proud of Adam. Afterwards, we all went up to his room. When I saw the state of it, I had to be forcibly restrained from throttling the life blood out of him.

Back in London, Friday night's show was the best show ever. Ever. It could not have been bettered. It was light; it was easy; it required no effort. I wished I could have seen it.

Saturday's matinée was traditionally a disgrace and I'd like to apologise publicly for having the most outrageously wonderful time. News filtered through that Trevor Nunn was in, but the die was cast (which was probably more than any of us would be in future productions).

At one point Aunt Eller presented dungaree-clad Laurey with an organza dress, wrapped in a box, for the party that night, on account, 'You ain't got nothin' to wear 'cept yer mother's ol' weddin' dress.' She opened the box and it contained another pair of dungarees.

There was a moment in 'The Farmer And The Cowman . . .' when Eller takes the hands of the little children and softly sings the verse:

> I'd like to teach y'all a little saying
> And learn these words by heart the way ye should,
> I don't say I'm no better than anybody else
> But I'll be damned if I ain't just as good.

This day there were no children. Actors Jimmy Johnstone and Kevin Wainwright took my hands and led me forward and the whole cast did a barber shop chorus around me while I tried, red-faced and shiny-eyed, to get through the words.

This was the show where Nicola wore a false ear on her upstage side, the one where dancer Shaun Henson offered young Ben Garner a sweet which turned his mouth blue just before the auction scene where he had his one line – 'I'll give you ten dollars.' It never got a better reaction than when said by a man who had no idea he had cornflower-blue teeth. I can't remember much else, except that there were two rabbits in the trial scene and a woman seemingly levitating in the prompt side of the wings – but I'm sure you get the general picture of a highly professional woman with 32 years in the theatre behind her. And I mean *behind* her.

It was a triumph of smile over content and it left us exhausted. The Saturday night audience seemed to be made up of 2,000 people who'd been before and loved what they'd seen. Hugh had built up a following of excitable groupies and the ovations throughout were like the last night of *Seinfeld*. There was a tiny scene after the death of Jud when Eller warns Laurey that she mustn't give in to self-pity.

'All sorts of things happen to folk – sickness and bein' poor and hungry and bein' old and afraid to die. Thas the way it is. Cradle to grave and you can stand it. They's just one way. Ye got to be hearty. You gotta be. You cain't deserve the sweet 'n' tender in life unless yer tough.'

It was never said more severely than the night of 26th June. Josefina and I were plumb about to lose it. Her eyes were so full of liquid she looked like she needed turning down to simmer. My voice was wobbling up and down like Sally Field accepting an award. It was snarl or die. I snarled, Josefina added terror to her tears and somehow we got through. The curtain calls went on for days. We brought on Trevor. I meant to thank him but words were out of the question. On this day we so missed being able to thank the dynamic 'Stro', stuck in the US, for making us so much more than we were. I clung on to Hugh, the best on-stage partner I'd known. I looked down into Row E on the best off-stage one, banging his hands together for the fifth time and the beam on the upturned mush of his daughter, and we just let the tears come. It would salt the stage for *The Lion King*. The familiar orchestra, the friendly stage crew, stage-door keepers, Wendy wigs, Anne Marie costume – we needed Sally Field after all, to do the honours.

Pack up six months into the car boot, fall into the last supper at Joe Allen's and sleep the sleep of the just, and if you think *that*, you haven't been paying attention. The next day the migraine just stood there in my brain saying, 'You asked for this,' and it was right. I was due at my friendly reflexologist Tony Porter's to cut a cake for the ten-year anniversary of his A.R.T. seminars in a London hotel. Amy and my niece Anastasia, who was acting as my dresser, held me up. Tony took one look at me and got his keynote speaker, a Dutch reflexologist and migraine specialist, down from the podium to the conference lobby where my shoes and socks were removed and my feet seriously pummelled. Waiters came in. The taxi driver brought back my mac. I didn't notice. A Chinese scientist emerged beaming and before you could say 'holistic' I was out there doing my third speech in seven days.

Just an average week at the end of an average year. By the law of averages, I'll never see its like again.

Royal Flush

It was a three Queen day. The first of its kind to my knowledge. Rumour ran rife round the company (i.e. company manager, Jools, tells me, 'On no account mention this to anyone else but . . .') Her Majesty and the Duke of Edinburgh had decided to have a whole day of theatre. This may not seem to be enough for one who is patently happier out in a high wind in a headscarf than stuck in a side box with a perfect view of the wings, but it's a start.

The Duke would visit *Chicago* first thing in the morning (chorus girls, black basques, chair straddling) and we *Oklahomans* should all be ready in full costume and make-up at 10.30am, with orchestra, for the 'scheduled rehearsal' of 'The Farmer and The Cowman . . .' – you know, as you do after playing it eight times a week for six months.

Still. No one minded really. Certainly no one in the orchestra minded (because orchestras are paid by the nanosecond) and the rest of us just buckled down because it was a royal appointment and we wanted to keep it. *Oklahoma!*, the original 1947 production, was reputed to have been a favourite show of the then newly married royal couple and 'People Will Say We're In Love' was their song. When the company manager gingerly asked if this was the case, the Duke, true to form, retorted, 'Not as far as I know!'

So, after the theatre had been Mr Sheened from circle to pit and the minders had swept through doing what minders do, largely glancing from right to left rather rapidly, we got the word 'They're here!', the flymen raised the rudimentary barn, the orchestra struck up and we all went into overdrive. I separated battling factions, parted pounding fists and, finally, exasperatedly fired Curly's pistol in the air, pointed it at Pop Carnes and growled 'Sing it, Andrew!' to start the wildest, most athletic, muscle-demanding seven-minute barn dance you've ever seen.

At the end, instead of the ovation which at night sometimes seemed impossible to bring to an end, there was a smattering of polite applause as we held our final positions on taut, aching muscles. It had been a long time since the silence of a rehearsal room at the National and it was nostalgic to hear, once again, the sounds of collective heart attacks as 25 people under 30 and two codgers over 50 (myself and Sid Livingstone) fought to restart our breathing mechanisms. We could feel the vibrating hairs in our lungs.

As the royal party was brought round backstage, my thirst got the better of me. My tongue was stuck to the roof of my mouth . . . it had to be released before I faced a royal question, or she might take me for a red-neck. I raced toward the water dispenser in the anteroom to the wings, only to find Sir Cameron leading the royal party towards us. 'I need a – water – Sorry, Ma'am, is that OK?' was my somewhat cryptic remark. Bless her, she looked at me more in pity than in sorrow. 'It does look terribly energetic,' she said to the first sweating hand she shook. 'Yesheur esh, Ma'am,' wheezed the first recipient. People always ask what the royals actually say to you and of course you can never answer because your mind turns to polenta as soon as they speak to you. Which is why they have to endure such boring conversations. Actually, Americans and Australians with none of our rigid class distinctions tend to cut a swathe through aristocratic society. 'G'day, Yer Madge, yer lookin' bonsa today,' would be quite refreshing, I guess, after a line-up of, 'Yes, Ma'am, it is . . . very energetic,' and, 'Oh . . . you know . . . er . . . it's not so bad really . . . Keeps the physiotherapist employed . . . heh, heh, heh!'

Afterwards, everybody peeled off their 'slap' and the dancers slipped back into their skinny bootlegs and cropped tops and contemplated which cappuccino bar to conglomerate in and which jazz dance class to attend.

As for me, it was corsets off, broken veins cleaned off, flat hair under wig pleaded with to rise and into my smartest suit for the next gig. One o'clock lunch at The Ivy with the monarch and other members of the theatre world.

The other members chosen amounted to about 50-odd producers, directors and actors assembled in an upstairs room with one question on their lips: 'Why me?' Jonathan Miller was ASTOUNDED to be included. Braham Murray of the Manchester Royal Exchange Theatre 'had no idea' and Thelma Holt, a republican in wolf's clothing if ever I saw one, just grinned and dismissed the whole thing as spin for the people's monarchy.

The actors were there because our shows were the ones visited: Maria Friedman represented *Chicago* and David Suchet *Amadeus*. Before 'their' arrival, David and I compared fatigues. 'Eight a week, though,' he moaned. 'It's a killer, isn't it?' I rolled my tiny eyes.

'What are you on?' I asked him.

He stared. 'Pardon?'

'What are you on?' Still no reply. 'I mean, what are you taking?'

He was clearly flustered. I couldn't understand why. David and I went all the way back to LAMDA – he was a year younger than me . . . Probably still is.

'I can't believe you're asking me that . . .' he stammered.

'Well, why?' I insisted.

'Well, it's not something I tend to . . .'

'I mean, what? Ginseng? Royal jelly? Guerana? What are you laughing at? . . . What? Whaaat?'

It was suddenly clear that he'd thought I was asking how much money he was making – a thing actors never do. Writers, probably, but actors, never. All through lunch – we were at separate tables – David kept catching my eye and dissolving again. My table consisted of the Queen, flanked on either side by producer Michael Codron and director Jonathan Miller, Michael Frayn, me, Braham and then Sir Andrew Lloyd Webber and Genista McIntosh of the National Theatre.

It was a lovely lunch. Dr Miller took up all Her Majesty's time, arms flailing, words bouncing around the roulade, and very occasionally she would turn to Michael for a few words. (I couldn't help but notice the next time I was in his office the placecard 'HM The Queen' sitting on his desk.) Apparently when Dinzey, the rastafarian-locked waiter, tried to offer Her Majesty milk for her coffee, Dr Miller engaged her attention again. Hindered in his ability to pour, the waiter said to Michael, 'Does she take milk?'

'How the fuck do I know?' said Michael's entire expression.

Her Majesty is very dry. She has a sharp sense of humour and although I couldn't say I felt relaxed, the atmosphere was very easy. At one point she mentioned that she understood I would be coming to the palace shortly (to pick up my New Year's Honour).

'If I can possibly find anything to wear, Ma'am,' I replied.

Several weeks after, as I was curtseying and she was pinning a medal to my grey and white coatdress, she twinkled up at me and said, 'I see you managed to find an outfit, then.'

I think that was flaming bonsa, don't you?

After lunch I went back to my dressing-room at the Lyceum to sleep it off on the rickety put-u-up. It seemed like minutes before they were calling us down for the vocal warm-up and the minders and entourage were back sniffing out the areas around which the royals would sit that evening, for tonight they were to see the whole show and afterwards we would all line up again for polenta-brain. I don't know for whom *Groundhog Day* would be more appropriate.

'Y'd shore feel like a queen sittin' up on that carriage' brought the house down, but otherwise the show was as good as ever. And I finally had something to say when I shook her hand for the third time that day: 'I'm so glad you saw us from the front circle instead of your usual place, Ma'am. It must be so much easier on the neck.'

Funnily enough, when my mother saw the show from the box (her eighth visit), she pronounced it the best seat she'd ever had. 'It's fabulous,' she declared. 'You can see the whole audience all the way through.' I've tried every which way to make that into a compliment . . .

There is nothing like being in a hit. It's the headiest feeling, more so because of its rarity. I suppose this was the third time it had happened to me. The first time was in 1973 in a National Theatre production at the Old Vic called *The Front Page*. Written in the Forties by Hecht and McArthur and directed by Michael Blakemore, it starred and made stars of Denis Quilley, Anna Carteret, Alan McNaughton, Clive Merrison, Benjamin Whitrow and David Bauer and gave great lines to every good character actor in the building – including me as Molly Molloy, the tart with the heart. It was always Full House, the laughs were like cannon shots and I never met a soul who didn't love it, punter or pro. A cast of twenty-odd people and never a cross word.

The second was *Re:Joyce!* in 1980. Also a happy company. Just my accompanist, Denis King, and me. And now *Oklahoma!* 1998–99. Three in a 32-year span. I reckon that's a pretty good average.

The difference touches everything. So often the dressing-room door opens on an anxious face, split by an even more anxious smile, announcing, 'Hey! Wow! It's us. We said we'd come . . . Hey! Wow! You old fox . . . you look great . . . Love a drink, yeah. So . . . Gosh, nice dressing-room – wow! Got your own sink and everything . . . Kids all right?' Then finally, 'What an interesting play . . . What do *you* think it's about?'

They love you, hate the play or they love the play but can't stand the leading man – or they hate the play and can't help thinking it would have been better without you. Or, best and most common of all, they never mention the last two and a half hours they've spent in your company, not once. Not during dinner or the drive home – not ever again for the rest of your acquaintance.

So when the hit hits it's above the belt and the newsagent, the chiropodist and the rabbi's wife all tell you they loved it. And the letters come and the TV clips are shot and the Royal Variety Show want an excerpt and the rumours fly about Robin Williams being in tonight and you're tired and exhilarated at the same time and your bones ache but your heart sings. Every night you take a curtain call to cheers and wreathed faces beam up at you and strangers hang about outside the stage door and ask you to sign their collection of heel grips, and it's incredible!

Actually it was HM The Queen Mother's 98th birthday treat to see our show. We were still at the National Theatre and after the curtain call we told the audience we had another song to sing, 'and it's not by Rodgers and Hammerstein' – and the whole audience joined in. I'm not actually sure who wrote 'Happy Birthday To You' but the back royalties must be phenomenal. We presented present-day royalty with an *Oklahoma!* Cake, made by my friends, Judy Bastyra and Charles Bradley, which matched the T-shirt design Amy had done for our first night – an elephant, a large ear of corn and a measuring stick. The corn *was* as high as an elephant's eye that night. Rumour has it that staff whipped her cake away back at the party in favour of the one they'd made earlier, but she insisted it was brought back and that she had a slice. It may not be true but it's a good thought.

Listen, while I'm Queen-dropping, how could I forbear to mention the night of the Home Farm Trust After-Dinner Speech, when Zelma gave me the best one-liner the Princess Royal could have heard that day?

It was during dinner that the build-up began. I'd done my speech and my stomach had undone enough to tackle some food. Princess Anne was on my right, host Richard Price on my left and on his left was my mother. At some point during the main course, she leaned across Richard and hissed, 'MAUreen . . . Maureen.' I excused myself and leaned into her. 'What is it?'

'My bridgework's come out in the lamb chop.'

It sounded like an end-of-the-pier song by Max Miller. I had to ask her to repeat it. Sure enough, 'My bridgework. The three teeth on a bridge. They're on the plate.'

I took a deep breath, turned back to the Princess and said, 'Would you excuse us a moment, Ma'am?' Smiling, I turned regally to Zelma and said, 'Get the teeth.' We headed off for the cloakroom. There, by climbing underneath her jaw, I located the hole in the bridge and, glasses and reading glasses both perched on nose, screwed the appliance back in. Let's face it, I was never going to have my own surgery in Knightsbridge specialising in orthodontics and labial collagen injections – but my mother would be saved from having a mouth like a desecrated village. It wasn't perfect but it would save further embarrassment.

'Now, don't eat and don't talk,' I told her, knowing as I spoke that this was like saying 'Don't burble' to John Prescott.

'Sorry about that,' I told producer and Princess, and we picked up what was left of the conversation. Five minutes later the dreaded hiss came again. 'MAUreen . . . Maureen.' This time I looked at the plate before I looked at my mum.

'Would you excuse me again, Ma'am. I'm awfully sorry . . . but it's a bit of an emerg . . .' This time I had an easier time getting it back in but my warning to avoid the chop was veering on the ferocious.

'I won't. I'm not even hungry any more.'

We both adjusted our lipstick. As we returned to the room I swear she said, 'I'll just have my dessert, that's all.'

This time when I took my seat, I felt some sort of explanation was due.

The Princess was smiling at me whimsically. 'Ma'am,' I said as I sat down wearily beside her. 'I bet you I've just done something for my mother that you've never done for yours.'

The grey and white coatdress I wore at the Palace was by Tomasz Starzewski. I bought it to be CBE'd in March 1999. White crêpe blouse, knee-length grey skirt and slim coat with white piqué collar and white track stitches down the sleeves. I saw a picture of Jane Asher in the same suit at a romantic fiction judging evening. She hadn't stretched to the white-lined grey picture hat and kid gloves but she didn't have Zelma for a mother, so she probably has less need to accessorise. I dropped her a note enclosing a picture of Jack and me at the palace: 'If I ever see Gerald Scarfe wearing this red tie, you will be hearing from my solicitors.' Little bobby dazzler that she is, she wrote back:

Dear Ms Lippmmann
I was very distressed to receive your note of May 4th. As I opened it I was in the process of changing into my elegant, recently purchased Tomasz Starzewski grey suit to attend a Brighton Literary Luncheon where I was to be the keynote speaker to an extremely important group of elderly ladies.

The threatening tone of your letter caused me extreme distress and quite threw my concentration and confidence, resulting in my speech being very lightweight and full of anecdotes about cakes – far removed from the thought-proving, politically astute lecture I had planned on the way forward for the Conservative Party.

I am surprised that a performer such as yourself lacks the kind of sensitivity that so many members of the artistic community pride themselves on possessing, and I trust you will ensure that more tact is employed in future should you wish to criticise my wardrobe.

Never let it be said, however, that I have no sense of humour, and I did much enjoy the picture of you in the funny hat that you had put on to amuse your husband.

Yours sincerely,
Jane Scarfe

The equerry's address to the honour recipients is a collector's piece. He gave a great, sweeping theatrical and hugely patronising performance and one day I shall steal it and use it shamelessly. Her Majesty was friendly, and as I've commented earlier, brilliant at remembering our last conversation, and before you could say 'Why me?' again, it was over and we were being seamlessly transported back to where we came from.

'I hate stairs with no banisters,' said Zelma as she came down the majestic front steps, and, 'Fancy – they don't even give you a cup of tea . . . My mouth's as dry as a bone.'

We had the jolliest of lunches at The Ivy, where dryness was relieved and appetites whetted with dear friends and family, then I set off to walk to the theatre to lay my head down before the evening show. I cut a bit of a swathe in Covent Garden, I can tell you, with my huge picture hat and my gloves and pearls and my bargain shoes, but I was beginning to feel my years.

Just before I turned into the stage door, I passed Charles Fox, the theatre make-up shop. It hit me that I'd promised Amy a week ago that I'd go in there to buy her some fake blood for a production of *Zoo Story* being done by her student friends at Birmingham University. As I hovered, undeterminedly, priorities battling with self-pity, I felt a hand on Mr Starzewski's beautifully cut, fine wool shoulder. I turned round to face two of the most inebriated Scots dossers I've ever seen outside *The Stanley Baxter Show*. They were regulars in the area and they smelled like Yates's Wine Lodge opposite Blackpool Pier.

'Aww, Morreen, yer lookin' grand. 'Ave yew bint' Ascot now, Morreen? Does she not look a cracker?' He turned to his friend, who put a finger through his balaclava to poke his ear out. 'Grand, she looks grand. Can yer give us a little something now, Morreen. We're near starving and . . .'

'Look, fellas,' I groaned, 'we've been through this. If I give you money you'll drink it and . . .'

'NOOOO! Noooo! We won't, we won't, I promise – look, just give us the price of an egg,' he breathed, 'and we'll get outya hair.'

It was an inventive one . . . I was kiboshed by it. I needed to think. I blurted and babbled something and neatly slipped into the make-up shop.

They followed me in. It was quiet in there and the sight of an actress dressed up so high she could only come down with a bump, accompanied by two steaming derelicts in stained trousers, string round their shoes, clinking bottles of ginger wine and swaying, was one for the bar after work.

The assistants stared. The Holy Triumvirate stared back. Finally I spoke. 'Er . . . do you, by any chance, have such a thing as a bottle of blood?' I petered out. 'It's for my daughter . . .'

That night I wore my tracksuit with my CBE medal for the warm-up. Just as it should be, no one noticed.

Rhubarb and Flustered

It was a Saturday night and I was going out. As I left – late as ever – I called out to Jack: 'The duck just needs heating, the instructions are on the pack. Then there's apple and rhubarb in the pan for afters. All right?'

It was. I hurtled out (I can't seem to get out of the hurtling habit) to my two-function stint – first to a memorial service for the late, great Cyril Shaps and then to the National Theatre for artistic director Trevor Nunn's leaving party. Getting dressed for both was a bit stretching, which explained the lateness. I kept putting on and taking off lipstick and climbing in and out of blackish clothes. Finally I settled on a black and white concoction with removable bits for matters of taste.

The National had asked me to walk across the stage to represent *Oklahoma!* in a line-up of all of Trevor Nunn's twenty-five past productions, and present him with a rose. I took it literally and therefore was clutching, as I left the house, a ten-gallon hat and an enormous revolving sunflower as well as some aides-mémoire for the first and more sombre engagement. In other words, I had my hands full. As I turned to wave to Jack and said the historic words, 'The custard's in the utility room cupboard', I tripped over the step, took an arc through the air and landed, all ten stone five pounds of me, bang on my kneecaps.

God, it hurt. It sent shock waves right through me which came out of my mouth in fantastic scatological invective. Jack flapped around offering me hoisting help but he just copped more of the outburst. Amazingly, my cut-off trousers dusted off and the tights I'd thoughtfully worn underneath had soaked up the blood, so I just raised myself from the concrete, hobbled to the car and, leaving Jack looking like a startled meerkat, drove slowly and miserably to West Hampstead and the memorial celebration.

It was lovely. A picture emerged via friends, colleagues and family of an erudite, sweet, funny, devoted and devout man. I managed to hog one of the few chairs until my turn came to eulogise, after which I grabbed my faux fur coat and limped off into the frozen night, stopping only to limp back to return the faux fur coat and hunt for my own. When I arrived at the National, my legs were stiff as a board. I didn't want Trevor to think from my walk either that I had piles or was auditioning for Richard III.

The National Theatre foyer was packed with every actor who'd ever walked, skipped or minced through the last ten years of its history. All my

368

young *Oklahoma!* chums greeted me with hugs and kisses and hot gossip and you could scarcely move an inch for cries of 'Darling, why are you walking like that?' Outside, there were massive slide projections of Trevor's shows, including one of Hugh Jackman and me sitting in a surrey with a fringe on top. I felt very emotional all round. Then tributes poured in from Trevor's fellow workers, then a last-minute, end of term-ish cabaret and loving tributes from the stage ensued. Not knowing quite when the line-up of shows would happen and desperate for a drink, I painstakingly made my way through the crowds to the bar at the far end. I'd just got my mitt around a large glass of Evian when I heard my name being called from the stage: '. . . And representing *Oklahoma!* – Maureen Lipman!'

Rushing or pushing were out of the question. I made a sort of bleating noise and, holding my glass aloft, began the excruciating business of 'excuse-me-ing' my way from back to front, realising as I arrived that a) they'd moved on to the next-but-one show and b) I hadn't picked up the rose I was due to have presented him, many minutes earlier. What a shambles. I gave him a limp hug and waddled back to the underground car park and thence home.

When I finally got into my dear old kitchen, I felt as if I'd run the marathon. I bathed my sad old knees and started to tell Jack the story while decanting some pumpkin soup I'd left in a pan to cool for the freezer. As I spooned away he asked me why I was putting the rhubarb into a freezer bag.

'This isn't rhubarb,' I told him, 'it's pumpkin soup.'

We exchanged wary glances.

'Well, where's the rhubarb, then?' he asked.

'In the other pan,' I told him.

'Well, where's the apple then?'

'The apple and rhubarb are in the same pan. Why?'

'Oh,' he said flatly.

It still hadn't dawned on me, but it had on him. 'I thought the apple was in one pan and the rhubarb in . . .' he tailed off.

While I was out not enjoying myself, my poor benighted old man had finished off his duck dinner with a tasty bowl of rhubarb and cold pumpkin soup.

Square Peg

After a tough rehearsal day, I drove my car slowly and frustratedly through the bottleneck that is Hampstead at school-leaving time. Parents and progeny spilled out onto streets narrowed to closure by carelessly abandoned cars. Names were called, dates and catering arrangements confirmed, still damp paintings dropped and tearfully reclaimed. Teachers looking years younger than my *kids* stood despairingly on school steps praying for the miracle of dispersion. And the weekend.

And still I waited, gridlocked, feeling more and more like Michael Douglas in the film *Falling Down* – the one where a traffic jam drives him, as it were, to incandescent rage, loss of all sense of morality and, ultimately, murder.

The tape was playing my lines from *Peggy For You*, the new play I'd spent the day rehearsing in the tatty, tottering rehearsal room behind Hampstead Theatre Club, where the play eventually ran. In order to get there by 10 o'clock in the morning, I had to leave my house at 8.50am. I live three miles from the theatre. It was the nearest rehearsal room to my home I'd had in thirty-odd years, but at that time of the morning the same kids were being unceremoniously deposited with clean fingers, as were now, inkily, preventing my getting home.

'Take the tube, Maureen,' I hear you cry. 'Commute, dear, like the rest of us. It'll give you something to write about other than the difficulties of pursuing your art in a capital city with a traffic flow designed by the makers of Jenga.' Well, you are right, except there is no tube in Muswell Hill and to get to Swiss Cottage I would have to go all the way down to King's Cross, change, and come back again on a different line – at rush hour. Don't even mention the two – no, three – buses I would have to wait for, be allowed to get on, and run the gamut of 'Don't see much of you on the telly these days' – in triplicate.

So, I drove. And whilst I drove I went over my *Peggy* lines again and again: 'Sorry, darling, have I stopped you working? What? I've stopped you sleeping? I've woken you up? My God, what time is it?' Etc . . . Except I missed out the 'What?' So I went back. Then I said: 'Have I stopped you *sleeping*?' instead of saying 'Have I stopped you *working*?' So I went back again. I never really got past the first two pages because clearly my mind was on the Cherokee in front of me as much as it was on Alan Plater's precise and delicate script.

Peggy Ramsay was a legendary literary agent, who more or less transformed what played in the West End in the three decades from 1960–90. She was a powerful figure in finding new young writers and high-powered producers trembled in her fragrant but salty wake. She found Joe Orton when he was a struggling young writer and she found his battered, pulverised body when he was a renowned and controversial playwright. She was my husband's agent for years and his stories of her eccentricities were legion. How she flung her stockingless legs up on the desk, rearranged her breasts and weaved her way round her Dickensian office, floating words of wisdom and insanity in equal portions over the chaise longue where she famously claimed to have made passionate love to the playwright, Eugene Ionesco.

My only encounter with her was on the phone when I once rang to ask why she had not commented on Jack's new play, *Smash*, when he was waiting desperately to hear from her. Given that Peggy thought the last thing any man, and certainly any writer, needed was a *wife* and that she loathed actresses in spite of – or perhaps because of – having been one herself, she was not best pleased and referred to me ever after as 'Jack Rosenthal's *impossibly* ambitious wife'.

She was, however, quite wonderful with our then three-year-old daughter, Amy, a verbally precocious mite if ever there was one. She and Peggy discussed cats, Barbar, Queen Victoria and Marlon Brando and if anyone was patronising, it was probably the tiny opinionated doyenne rather than the elderly, wafting one.

I did finally get home the night of the great gridlock. It took me an hour and a half and I needed to pee like no one's *ever* needed to pee in the history of bloated bladders – but I didn't actually blow anyone's brains out with a Kalashnikov.

Once home I lay on the couch like one who'd just given birth to sextuplets, gawping at a TV gardening programme. Some men in wellies and a woman whose nipples had a life of their own were transforming a grotty garden whilst its owner was on holiday. They laid strips of planking everywhere and painted them a vicious blue. I realised with some sense of irony that I was literally, and voluntarily, watching paint dry.

We were playing *Peggy For You* at The Comedy Theatre. (After several of his plays were performed there, Harold Pinter once suggested to producer Michael Codron that it should be renamed 'The Pinter Theatre'. Reporting this exchange to playwright Tom Stoppard, Michael was amused by Tom's suggestion that it would be easier if Harold changed his name to Harold Comedy.) The theatre is very small, with a capacity of one hundred and fifty, and the audience for *Peggy* was quite elderly, so there was a tendency for them to pass out now and again. In The Lyceum, where *Oklahoma!* was performed, you could transport eight or nine prone bodies from their seats without much more noise than the steady bump of skull on velvet pile, but in this theatre it made a hell of a commotion.

'Get a doctor! Get a doctor!' the victim's companion hollered, not unnaturally.

'What's happening? Who? Where? Is he alright?' cried everyone else.

'Quick – help – he's fainted!' yelled the original voice.

'Who's fainted?' said a male voice blearily. It was, we later heard, the faintee himself. The situation was explained to him and an excruciatingly careful exit followed.

Then there was a low buzz of 'Fancy that!' and 'Dearie, dearie me' and 'It is awfully hot in here – are you hot, Marcia? Well, take your pashmina off, dear' and then they all returned their attention to what was happening on stage.

What was happening was a pivotal scene in which I explain to a very young writer why the play he's written is not actually a play. The young writer, as played by Tom Espener, had the eyes of a startled marsupial. 'What's going to happen?' was the beseeching subtext behind his frozen smile.

It did occur to me to walk over to the office window and say, in character, 'There seems to be a bit of a commotion in the street – come and have a look', but I rejected that idea on the grounds that Tom might just join the man in the audience in a total faint and then we'd have two of them to haul out.

What actually happened was that the scene went into a sort of underwater state, whereby my speech slowed down to accommodate the 'accompaniment' and everything became very quiet, very concentrated, and rather dangerous. It was great! There's nothing like the feeling that we're all in this together, mate, so hang on in there and we may just pull through.

It may well have added an extra slipper to the crow's-feet round the eyes (which I read are essential for a sincere smile) and the armpit glands were particularly over-active later when I peeled off my blouse. Still, the following day a letter came to the theatre congratulating us on the way we handled the situation and ending: 'It was lovely to actually see you in the flesh. You really photograph badly, don't you?' No chance of making next year's list of seamlessly ageing women, then.

It's the absolute opposite of the compliment they think they're paying me. High Definition television has put paid to looking like you look.

Make-up is sprayed on with an airgun and even that doesn't cover the craters. Presenters get younger and younger. Very soon Miss Marple will have to be played by Hermione from the Harry Potter films.

The morning after *Peggy For You* finished I had twelve artists in steel-toed boots river-dancing inside my brain. This is called an 'it serves you right' headache. I simply cannot drink and repeatedly refuse to believe it.

Still, it *was* worth it. The last night was exceptional, emotional and unforgettable. The next day I'd forgotten it. All I remembered was dancing my fabric mules off in a piano bar. Once back home, at 3.00am, there were stories to tell, flowers to be drowned and boxes and bags to be shifted into the room in which, three weeks later, I'm now sitting surrounded by the same bags, boxes and dead flowers.

The next morning I took two Solpadine tablets before I left my bed, and another two at noon. Then I phoned Ben Glastone, the drummer. Yes, the drummer. For I knew that on the Sunday after we closed I was performing in a concert for the Freedom for Burma campaign and the poem needed a percussionist. Frankly, I could have just let my blood vessels do the job but I felt the audience might hear it less clearly than I would.

Ben arrived at 2pm. He folded himself into a sitting position on the floor and tried out several drums.

'That one's fine – no, really, that'll do fine,' I murmured feebly. We arranged to meet again at 6.30pm at the Royal Court Theatre.

Later that day I wearily dressed up to the nines – when the eights would have done – bid my house-mates an acrimonious adieu and drove ten or so miles across Shopping City – as London on a Sunday has become – to the theatre. It was a balmy day (which I felt was appropriate) and, mumbling my lines over and over, I got a parking space and hobbled on unfamiliar heels across the road to the theatre: the locked, chained and unquestionably closed theatre.

Where was everybody? Where were the car parkers and stage hands? Where was Glenys Kinnock – the autograph seekers – the director, Philip Hedley? Where the hell was *anybody*?

The answer, as I later found out, was they were sitting at home watching *The Antiques Road Show* a week to the minute before the Free Burma Gala was to take place on the 18th, not the 11th. Meanwhile, I was still busy asking the question.

I rushed back to the car where I had my notes from the Free Burma Campaign and managed to ascertain two things. One was that I was one week and fifty minutes early and the other that I'd lost my handbag. I recommenced my wobbling routine across the road, by now close to frothing with anxiety. My bag was sitting on the front steps of the theatre where I'd plonked it down.

Slowly I trudged – all the wobble gone out of me – into the next-door pub. There was a jug of water on the bar. I got out my headache pills and asked the barman if he could possibly let me have a glass. He ignored me. I waited till he'd served the next customer and asked again. 'Can't you wait? I'm serving a customer?' he snarled. 'Please give me a glass,' I said evenly. 'I need to take some pills.' As he began a conversation with a man by the bar about European football I felt myself grow into The Incredible Hulk. I felt the demon burst out of my chest, a distant roaring came out of my mouth and I let him have it for the end of *Peggy For You*, for the five months of tiredness, the lack of advertising and the price of petrol, for God, Harry and the Burmese generals, for the European Cup and the weather at Wimbledon.

My language was unbelievable. And so was his as I reached behind the bar, seized a glass, swilled down the tablets and left what was now a totally silent bar. At the door, I turned back and rasped, 'Consider yourself lucky I didn't break the glass on your — —ing throat' and swept out. I was thirty yards down the road when I realised I'd left my mobile phone on the bar.

I mean, picture the scene: 'Er, excuse me, has anybody picked up a phone? I was in here earlier . . . I don't know if you remember but . . .' Slowly the barman handed me my phone and I left without a shred of dignity to my name. Peggy would have loved it.

Into Africa

There were just ten days between finishing Alan Plater's play *Peggy For You* at the Hampstead Theatre Club and transferring it to the West End. If I played my cards right I could be airborne Sunday, lightly tanned by the following Sunday, home Tuesday and full of vim and vineyard at my own opening night, Thursday. Why are you smiling in that knowing way and why didn't you remind me earlier that the best-laid plans of mice and Maureen . . .?

Since it was winter, the obvious places to head for would be Israel, Tunisia or some small Balearic island. Short flight, sun, sea, sand and a fat foot-thick paperback or three. That's what everyone told me. So I nodded obediently and booked for South Africa.

We arrived in Cape Town in the early hours of Monday morning after the best night's sleep I'd had in ages. I must remember that sleeping upright and belted in is refreshing as hell when next I contemplate spending arms, legs and bumpsadaisies on handcrafted, super-sprung beds! Our bijou hotel of character and charm was called The Uitsig. This is pronounced Aitz-ech and every time I said it someone said 'Bless you'.

It was a terrific find. Bungalows nestling round velvet lawns, two uninhabited pools bordered by fragrant lavender bushes, and a couple of renowned restaurants on the premises. Oh, and a cricket pitch, which I strolled around, straw hat in hand, in the pathetic belief that I was Karen Blixen and that Denys Finch Hatton in the shape of Robert Redford might appear and whisper 'Don't move' in that devastatingly sexy way. I mean, where's my head? And will it ever achieve maturity? And if it does what will I do for aggravation?

So, surrounded by the smoky mountains and acres of vineyards, I unwound my weary muscles over a glass or two of 'Uitsig' wine and gazed into the middle distance. Suddenly I realised why the mountains were so smoky. They were on fire. The whole bloody mountain range was belching smoke and by the time evening fell it was a scarlet inferno. Every time the wind changed direction I packed my case. Every night I slept with my jeans, knickers and glasses in a pile by the bed. And every morning I'd scrape the ashes off our bathing suits.

Coming back from a trip to Cape Point, we were diverted off the road by another fire, and ended up driving across a sand dune and – memorably for the players on the 18th – on to a golf course. The apocryphal story doing the rounds was that one of the helicopters involved in sweeping up balloons full of water from the sea to douse the fire had inadvertently scooped up a German scuba diver from the water, winched him thousands of feet up in the air with the water and dropped him on the flames.

I feel bad that I'm telling you the awful bits when the Cape is truly the most beautiful place I've ever seen. When a party of baboons cross the road in single file in front of your car, or a beach beneath your feet is awash with Jackass penguins, or a mountain rabbit pops its head out at the top of a 260-million-year-old table top mountain, you know that paradise can't be that far away. If only the big mammals could just play nicely with one another.

During the flight home, we woke to hear the captain tell us not to panic – always my favourite mode of wakening. We were landing in Lagos (ooh! yippee! Nigeria!) for technical reasons. I glanced round to an adjacent seat where the Chief Rabbi was snoozing. Surely nothing could go seriously wrong with one of the Lord's Department Heads up here with us, could it? Suffice to say we had a drugged loony on board. Air rage is the official term. He was running around the plane trying to open doors thousands of feet up in the air. We landed, he stepped outside for a fag, got clapped in irons and is probably festering to this very day in some dank Nigerian lock-up.

It took two hours for the rest of us to leave Lagos – the man in charge of the fuel tank had gone home and was in a Bacardi bar somewhere. Next, the tube on wheels used to take us from plane to airport went AWOL. I suggested Jack made a human bridge of himself, but he demurred. Now only the train strike and the opening night loomed. I might just put my next holiday on ice.

Fanny by Spotlight

I've been reading through *The Vagina Monologues*. It's a spectacular series compiled by Eve Ensler and written by women of all ages and creeds in response to her questioning the nature of our innermost and largely secret core. They're quite revolutionary in thought and, of course, they set me thinking.

Recently I had lunch with a stranger whose husband had bid for 'Lunch with Maureen Lipman' in an auction. We had many areas in common, thank the Lord, or it could have been purgatory at noon. But she strongly disapproved of the *Good Housekeeping* article I'd written earlier in the year where I recounted my mother's curious request for 'the fellatio and chips' in a Greek restaurant. This bold, bright, intelligent woman was intensely shocked that I would write such copy in a respectable magazine. I was intensely shocked at her intense shock. Quite pleasantly, we agreed to differ.

So here I go again. I believe I'm backed up by Ms Ensler's fine monologues that women are still embarrassed by any serious analysis of their own bodies. And I think they are even further embarrassed on behalf of men. I remember seeing a photo in my mother's house of my late father holding up my then two-year-old daughter in such a way that her tiny dress had ridden up her body, revealing tiny black knickers. Peering closer I realised that the black knickers had been added in biro. To cover her two-year-old fanny. I was, as my lunch-date might have said, 'intensely shocked'. Still there's embarrassed and there's *embarrassed*.

This may be an apocryphal story, as it came via the net, but it convulsed me when I heard it and continues to do so. A woman was late for a gynaecological appointment and, after dropping the kids at school, rushed around the house, getting herself into a muck sweat. Before leaving, she dashed into the bathroom, gave herself an intimate wipe with the washcloth and hit the road running.

As she lay exposed on the doctor's table, she was surprised to hear the gynaecologist say, 'My, someone's certainly made an effort today,' but dismissed it out of hand as a mishearing.

Later that day, hearing her six-year-old call out, 'Mummy, where's the washcloth?' she replied, 'Oh, Mummy put it in the laundry – go and get a nice clean one.' To which her daughter replied with a whine, 'Oooaw –

that's not fair – I had all my sparklies wrapped up in that!' Puts a gleam into 'My, someone's made an effort this morning', doesn't it?

More fun still comes from the difference between the word 'fanny' in England, where it means vagina, and America, where it means posterior. A friend tells of deep embarrassment incurred while spending six months at an American university where she chose gymnastics as one of her modules. 'Have you done this before?' asked her lissom instructor in front of the class and when assured she had, requested that she mount the parallel bars, do a slow somersault and land on her fanny. My friend couldn't believe her ears and asked the teacher to repeat the instructions, but on hearing the same bizarre request and with twenty-four pairs of eyes on her, decided to do her best, landing in the splits and total agony.

'What on earth did you do *that* for?' shrieked the teacher.

'I thought you said land on your fa . . .'

'Your fanny! Your fanny!' she yelled, slapping her own backside. 'Don't tell me you English don't know where your ass is.'

Poor girl, she spent the next few days in physical pain and the next few months in mental anguish caused by repeated catcalls across the canteen of: 'Hey, English – landed on your fanny recently?'

It's only one painful step from there to the American woman in Aquascutum recently who, rejecting the cut of a pair of their trousers, explained, 'They won't fit me – I have an enormous fanny' only to hear the salesman mutter, 'I'm not entirely sure I need to know that, madam.'

Finally, I must tell you the last 'overheard on a train story'. Two elderly Lancastrian gentlemen were returning from a trip to Manchester. A student, attempting to read in the seat opposite, was regaled with the things they'd seen and done.

'Then he dragged me round t'shops, lookin' at fancy clothes – din't yer, Tom?'

'Ay. It were lovely and all, weren't it?'

'Ay, it were. Best 'uns we saw were in that posh 'un, wern't it – what did yer call it? They was lovely. It was in that there Aquascrotum.'

There. I've shocked my lunch-date again. It's becoming a compulsion. Incidentally, I told my mother I was doing *The Geneva Monologues* and that it was all about a group of Swiss women in banking – a load of bankers, since you ask.

The week we opened in *The Vagina Monologues*, Edie (*The Sopranos*) Falco, Sophie Okonedo and I sweated through temperatures in the mid thirties in a theatre with no air conditioning. 'We're having a heat wave', went the song through Marilyn's bee-stung lips, 'a tropical heat wave.' This week the whole neighbourhood was complaining collectively throughout.

Traffic had ground to a standstill, tarmac spontaneously melted, there was a world shortage of table fans and the hosepipe had gone underground for fear of the annual fatwah.

In short, we were having our week of summer and, as usual, it had taken us completely by surprise. The New Ambassador's Theatre was a Louisiana flophouse backstage and hell's kitchen on stage. The set of *The Vagina Monologues* consisted of pink fake fur walls and floor and we perched on black leather stools (for 'perched' read 'slithered') while the audience waved programmes, ticket stubs, sun hats and nail extensions all night long – it looked like washday in a row of Barnsley back-to-backs.

We three actresses were larky with the text that night, including my doing a spirited rendition of an orgasmic monologue delivered in the voice of Baroness Thatcher. Sophie reproached me with the words, 'My grandma's in today!' to which I was able to reply, 'That's nothing – my rabbi's in the fifth row', which he was, bless his heart, and savouring every word. He's from Texas – he's so from Texas his wife's called Suellen and no one relished more than he the insert in the show stating: 'It's illegal to sell a vibrator in Ohio, Georgia, Arkansas, Alabama or Texas. If you're caught with intent to sell you're liable to a fine of $10,000 or one year's hard labour. It is, however, totally legal to buy a gun in any of those states.' The piece continues, 'We have yet to hear of a mass murder being committed with a vibrator.' It was the last night for me, Sophie and Edie, and I think we all felt a good deal more grown up after our three West End weeks. On the last Sunday of the run I invited Sophie, Edie and a friend of hers from New York over and cooked my format brunch of scrambled eggs, smoked salmon, bagels and all the trimmings. Edie's friend had been at college with her and over brunch we talked about our love of New York.

'Where do you stay when you come over?' he asked me.

'Oh, in Greenwich Village,' I responded. 'I have two friends there who have the oldest wooden house in New York and I stay in their guest cottage in the yard. It's a perfect replica of their house, in miniature.'

He looked at me in some amazement. 'Don and Eleanor's house?' he asked.

I nodded. 'Do you know them?'

'Sure I know them, I live next door.'

Ships that pass in the night. When I look at Edie Falco in *The Sopranos* or watch Sophie in *Hotel Rwanda* or read Eve Ensler's articles, I have little sense of actually having known them, but for three short weeks my world revolved around them.

Three times a year, a new family to say goodbye to – shared jokes, disasters, anecdotes – a microcosm of family life. If and when we meet again, will we talk abut our days in *Vagina*? No, it'll be our kids, our losses, who's doing what and with whom – just a chorus of monologues from three loose women.

PS Vagina Day. It was at the Albert Hall and many of the actresses who'd appeared in *The Vagina Monologues* were up on stage reprising their own particular favourites to raise thousands for International Women's Aid. We all wore red or black, the auditorium was full to bursting, the music loud and raunchy and the atmosphere as hot as a Kew orchid house. Looking around me at the stageful of feisty ladies in their push-up bras and platform soles, feathers, tassels, sequins and spray, I was riveted to find myself sitting next to Isabella Rosselini.

Friends, she is quite the most beautiful woman I've ever seen. True beauty is a mixture of grace, proportion and what's inside. (I saw it in my co-star, Hugh Jackman, during *Oklahoma!* I'll never forget the day he took his shirt off for the wrestling scene – 25 women had a monologue with their vaginas.) Isabella was wearing a plain, long, beautifully cut dark red crêpe dress, little or no make-up, and had clean, cropped hair. She laughed from her eyes downwards and when she did she looked so like her mother, Ingrid Bergman, that your heart turned over. She read out a piece she'd written about the day she was fired by Lancôme. It was her 40th birthday and Lancôme had filled her house with flowers. She said she knew then that they were going to fire her. Her beauty, she said, had always been her curse. It had allowed people to abuse her and it had stunted her growth. In her thirties, though, she suddenly realised her own worth and the day she was fired by Lancôme was the day she knew that she had 'grown stronger than the creams'. The company had, she said, asked her not to talk about her dismissal. At this point she looked up shyly at the thousands of people in the Hall and said: 'Well, I'm talking tonight.' The Hall rose to its collective feet and roared its approval. 'And,' she continued, smiling her Helen of Troy smile, 'I shall go on talking.'

Me too, Isabella, me too.

Polish Rap

The great actor Frank Finlay and I go back a long way – to the Old Vic. I was in the National Theatre Company there from 1971 to 1973. So was he. We don't think we ever met. It was a big company of about fifty players and we played in repertoire. But I saw him. His Iago was said to have outstripped Olivier's Othello. It didn't. It's a better part and he filled it magnificently. In Zeffirelli's production of the Italian farce, *Saturday Sunday Monday*, he and Joan Plowright were totally convincing Italians, touching, memorably deadpan and hilarious. I've never seen him give a bad performance, and I've worked with him three times in the last few years.

. In 2000, we screen tested together for the roles of mother and father of Adrien Brody, the actor playing the pianist in the film of that name. The test took place in the absence of the director, Roman Polanski, who is unable to set foot on English soil due to an extradition treaty with our 'Special Arrangement' chums across the pond. He's wanted there on charges of sex with a minor, even though the minor – now a mother – and *her* mother have officially asked for the charges to be repealed.

During the screen test, which took place in the casting director's semi in Clapham, Frank and I were requested not to look at each other in the scene we'd learned, but to perform straight to a small video camera. It's harder than it sounds. We are both naturalistic actors who like to bounce off one another. Frank, though, has the noble head of a lion, presidential bones and is considerably stiller than I am, which explains why he's done so many feature films and I've done two. Well, two which will have a shelf life: *Up The Junction* (1967) and *The Pianist* (2000).

In the interim, I coughed in *Educating Rita*, spat in *Gumshoe*, and tried to disappear in many undistributable British efforts which bulked up the celluloid mountain in the great Artificial Eye in the Sky. *Solomon and Gaenor* in the Nineties was an Oscar-nominated outsider on account of being filmed entirely in Welsh and in Yiddish. It's good. You may not have caught it. There's time . . .

Still, every dog has her daydream and Frank and I were cast as the ill-fated parents in what turned out to be a great European movie. In 2001, *The Pianist* swept Oscar's board clean. Our job description started with a week's rehearsal in Paris where we quickly realised that every movement we made would be prescribed, noted, and from then on would never change. We were to speak in a low and level European/trans-Atlantic non-accent. Yes, it baffled me for a while as well. Adrien and Katie Meyer, playing our son and daughter, are Americans so they had to curb their American vowels. Ed Stoppard and Julia Rayner, playing our other son and daughter, are also English so we agreed to remove our received pronunciation 'o' sounds and never finish a sentence on an upward inflection. That way, Roman told us, we would all sound the same. So far so Polish. In the end we all did a personalised impersonation of Polanski and it worked out fine.

Five weeks in Warsaw, then. What's second prize, you might ask? The city, on first impression, is like a sleeping adolescent emerging from under a utilitarian blanket. Vestiges of reverent Eastern Bloc architecture gaze loftily down on McDonald's and up on the Marriott Hotel. The locals are charming and, according to the ex-pats I met in the hotel bar, Warsaw is swinging. I suppose it matters where you are located on a film. It's probably great to travel the world via a well-paid job. I tend not to get Bali, Mauritius or Rio during Carnival Week. I'm more Whitby, Woking and Warsaw during the first overseas trip of President George W Bush. His secret service guys really had the place sewn up. One floor of the hotel was removed from public use and the café was crawling with Secret Service men with strange lumpy jackets. What George Dubya made of his first trip into the rest of the world one can only conjecture. If you've only ever seen a ranch in Texas, a college campus, a drying-out clinic and the White House, then Warsaw could feel a bit down-market.

On one sightseeing trip I went to the Chopin museum, staffed on the day I visited it by Lotte Lenya's more ferocious sister and the entire staff of *Prisoner: Cell Block H*. As I walked in, heavy street rap music was playing at the ticket office. 'Chopin?' I enquired with a smile, taking out my purse. The look she gave me said it all. How dare I ruin her day by being a customer? If you could cross a sneer and a snarl and insert two glowers into the phrase 'Seven zloty' – what do I mean, *could*? – she did!

My coat was abruptly confiscated by a barking corporal of an attendant and my one query was met with such piercing anger by a thin grey column of a woman that I took out my phrasebook in a vain attempt to find a simultaneous translation for 'You are a thoroughly alarming person and I hope you develop threadworms'.

Actually, it wasn't in your actual useful phrasebook. I'd picked it up in the hotel foyer. It was called *The Red Book* and it was a compendium of so-called social sayings. I just wanted 'Hello' and 'Please will someone turn down the heating in my room as, at present, I'm forced to sit naked in the minibar'. What I discovered between its covers put a whole new spin on the words 'social' and 'guide'. The first page I turned to — I kid you not — said, '*Zaydj na zyemye*', which translates roughly as 'Get your head out of your ass'. There's posh, I thought. I turned the page hurriedly in the hope of stumbling upon 'May I take the bill, please?' only to find on page 40 both a picture of a snarling bulldog (not, incidentally, unlike the cloakroom attendant at Chopin's gaff) and a list of expletives beginning with 'You bitch' and ending with 'You aint got no balls' and encompassing on the way 'Playboy!', 'Dirtbag!', 'Shorty!', 'I don't want to have a baby' and, sublimely 'Your tool is small'. I felt confident this would cover me for the next few weeks.

The week before I'd visited Auschwitz. There are no words to describe it. It was the nearest feeling I've ever had to total depression. I couldn't move my lips to talk, or my arms to wipe away the tears. I could only look. The place is a black hole, sucking all the energy out of you. The grief is in the fabric of the walls. The brutality in the air you breathe. You can't believe the amount of registration: of details of the hundreds of thousands of victims. Measurements of head, feet, details of every heart-breaking possession, extent of punishment, length of nose, length of life. As though the perpetrators were truly engaged in a great universal quest to rid the world of a deadly virus and here were the figures to ensure them the Nobel Peace Prize. I gazed down numbly on a room filled with brushes, clothes brushes, wooden, silver, ebony and monogrammed. Thousand upon thousand of them. Meaningless mementoes of the dehumanised and the dispossessed. The saddest sight I've ever seen. My teeth began to ache – an inflamed root canal requiring a rapid route to a Polish endodontist.

Auschwitz and Birkenau are on the very edge of a small town. You couldn't live there and not know, feel and smell exactly what was happening. Yet, what would I have done? Do I know what's happening behind all the closed gates in my city, my borough, my street? Do I stand up and object when a director bullies a prop girl or a husband humiliates a wife? On the whole, no I don't. I just look at my shoes and thank God it's not me. I don't know where courage comes from.

It's pretty hard to cross Warsaw city centre without going down a concrete underpass. I did this one day and passed several stallholders down there selling their wares. One of them was selling old film posters so I stopped to glance through them. In all there were maybe fifteen on the table. One of them was Roman Polanski's first feature, *Knife in the Water*, not surprising perhaps. More surprising was the discovery of a large pink and blue poster showing a Sixties cartoon dolly-bird, all eyelashes and pout, above the title *Zycie w Battersea*. Apparently, the *rezyseria* was Peter Collinson and *w rolach gtowynch* were Suzy Kendall, Dennis Waterman and Maureen Lipman. It was the Polish version of *Up The Junction*, and as it sits sunnily on my apartment wall I reckon it could be one of the best ten zlotys I've ever spent.

My first day on the film had been marred by Roman being angry with me. It's not something you'd want. It was all to do with my hair/wig. He wanted no wigs in the show, which is why he'd insisted I have all the pigment removed from my hair in a seven-hour marathon at his Parisian hairdresser's. It went pewter green, and as it was February and filming wasn't till April, I made him put a rinse over it. Roman didn't buy my story that the rinse would wear off by the time of the main bulk of filming, and brought the producer with him to my trailer for a shout. I held my own, just – he is formidable – but the Lipman lower lip was trembling as he left.

Day one of the filming was three weeks ahead of the main five-week stint. I wore a scarf over my head for the rounding-up scene as the Nazi guards, aka Polish extras, marched me, my film 'family' and five hundred Jewish prisoners in drab clothes marked by yellow stars (aka other Polish extras, gentiles to a man) out of the Umschlagplatz, over a bridge and into the distance. (Incidentally, nothing can prepare you for the feeling you experience when you are loaded with your 'children' into a windowless cattle train compartment with 60 or 70 other human beings, destination unknown. When that door slammed shut, my heart began to bang against my chest and I screamed a silent scream from somewhere inside me I didn't know existed. Of course, I knew the German soldiers were only jobbing actors in ridiculous jodhpurs, but somehow my heart didn't. We none of us could stop shaking.)

Every time the director shouted 'Cut!' the entire cast of extras applauded him. Afterwards, Frank turned to me and said, 'I looked at your face as we crossed the bridge and you looked terrible – really distraught. What were you thinking of?'

I gave him a rueful grin, and confessed, 'My hair.'

It was all solved amicably by the acquisition of a perfectly fitting wig from Richard Mawbrey at Wig Creations. As I sat in the make-up trailer on the first morning of its appearance, Roman appeared at the door. There was a very noisy silence. Then he said, 'Good. It looks good,' and left as sharply as he'd arrived, only pausing to throw back over his shoulder, 'I don't know why she didn't want a wig in the first place.' Quite. I knew my place. In the wrong.

I have an instinct that the great but tyrannical *resyseria* wanted Mother deflated and slightly cowed for the start of the picture, rather than the jokey personality who'd arrived for the meet-and-greet dinner three weeks earlier. If this sounds paranoid, then read on. One of the daughters, Katya, got tongue-lashed before her first entrance and made to repeat and repeat the scene, of course becoming more and more emotional. He wanted her dour, frightened and in no way 'preppy'.

But the real *mise en scène* was still to come. It took place in the studios on the set of the Szpillman dining-room, with the family gathered around the table, knowing that they were in imminent danger of arrest. I was hovering behind the kitchen door, preparing to take in (at a rough estimate) my twenty-eighth pan of chicken soup in my thirty-seven year career. The atmosphere on the set was reverent. Hushed with concentration. The gist of the scene was Mother asking the family to please, for once, not argue over dinner but just to enjoy what they still had. There is tension between the two sons and some oil-pouring from the oldest daughter. Father has little dialogue but for a terse comment towards the end of the scene.

'Quiet for rehearsals!' shouted the assistant director. Pause, then 'Action,' hissed Roman, and I brought in my soup.

'And please, tonight, can we not have any arguments . . .' I said in the prescribed low, level tone we'd rehearsed so often, and we continued seamlessly through to the end of the scene. Throughout, Frank – slightly removed, his face closed off like a statue on Mount Rushmore – silently spooned his soup into his mouth until he sombrely said his lines.

'Cut,' said Roman. We all held our collective breath. He went over to Frank and knelt conspiratorially by his side at the end of the table. From the low murmurs I picked up that he was asking Frank if he felt he should take more part in the proceedings. Frank held his ground. He felt that Father was probably cut off in his own world. Roman respected and admired Frank – when he saw him in his period clothes for the first time his comment was 'You look like my father.'

Roman returned to his position by the camera. 'We go again.' I returned my soup to the kitchen where it was replaced by a hot counterpart and I prepared to start the scene again. 'Quiet on set. Absolute silence. Going for a take,' called the assistant director.

And 'Action!' said Roman. I picked up my soup and entered the room, set it down and began ladling it out.

'And please for once,' I pleaded, 'could we not have any arg – ' I stopped abruptly as a howl pierced the dialogue. To a man we flinched and a fair amount of good soup hit the velour tablecloth.

'CUT!' shrieked Roman, peering through his view-finder. 'What the fuck – that suit! He look like he comes from fucking Savile Row!'

'That jacket!' He pointed to Frank. 'That jacket! It looks too smart, too good. Wardrobe! Where is Anna? Get her on set! Now!'

Headless chickens began to bump into each other as assistants ran for the door. The message came back that the costumes had all been approved and left for her assistant, but the actual – Oscar winning – designer, the same one who had dressed *Schindler's List,* was away buying costumes that day. Oh, my Lord. The silence vibrated in the room. This was not going to go down well.

It didn't. Head down, the expletives simmered and popped.

'Not here! Not in the studio! Why? Where the f—? Jesus! Do I do everything!' He sucked in his breath and added, mystifyingly, 'Bring me sandpaper! Now! Bring me a large piece of sandpaper! Quick!'

Frank's face was a picture of stolid lack of expression. His Yorkshire granite was about to be tested. Roman took the sandpaper from the selection of grades proffered like gold, frankincense and myrrh by the tremulous props person, bent it round his hand and proceeded to rub down the suit with Frank in it. The studio of several hundred people was silent but for the sound of a veteran and distinguished CBE actor being thoroughly sandpapered by a small, angry, kneeling, Polish genius. It was totally hilarious, the more so because laughter was verboten and even more so because Frank's expression never changed. Not a flicker throughout what must have been five minutes of pretty solid sanding. I was beside myself and had to retire to the kitchen to seriously check my soup.

Finally the pile rose on the barathea and we studiously went back to work, never catching one another's eye for a second. Back went I to my kitchen and the third pan of steamy soup, out came Mother on the call of 'Action!', and once again in a low trans-Atlantic tone I implored my sons not to argue. Once again the air was rent with Polish prima donna-dom.

'Cut!' quoth he, hurling the view-finder away from him. 'Still he look too refined, still the lapels – why are they not shiny and worn? What the f—' He stopped, the air quivered. My soup quivered. A quiver would have quivered. Then, unbelievably, 'Go bring me the German sausage we had for lunch! Bring it! The whole thing. Quick! Do it now!'

Well, you could have cut the atmosphere with a fish-slice. Nobody moved. No one laughed. No one thought the unthinkable, as in 'Where is he going to *put* that sausage?' I mean, the catering on this film left much to be desired. Pork in pork sauce with a garlic and lard sauce was much the order of the day. Meals tended to be very white. That sausage could have practically walked in on its own, it was so robust. As it was, it came in on a plate in the hands of a bemused member of the art department. It was about twelve inches long, three inches thick, orangey-brown and horseshoe-shaped. Be scared, Frank, I thought. Be very, very scared.

But Frank didn't look scared. He looked even more solid and deadpan than before. Who could tear themselves away from such a denouement? Certainly not me. I could dine out on this one for years. And have. And shall continue to. In several countries. To howling gales of laughter. Oh, shut up and get back to the story.

Gentle readers, Mr Polanski tore the sausage in half, took a half in each hand, broken side facing away, knelt down again beside Frank and – yes, picture the scene – thoroughly sausaged Frank from nape to turn-up. I looked down – up – round – but always in my peripheral vision I saw Frank's impassive face and it convulsed me. Finally I headed back to the kitchen, buried my face in soup steam and silently roared. It took about five or six minutes, I suppose, and we were told to stand by. When I entered the room with my fourth or fifth pan of soup, Father was tattier and shinier than I'd ever seen him, and almost certainly smellier. I said my lines, the boys said their lines. The girls poured oil, and as Frank lifted his spoon to his lips, I saw that his hand was trembling.

'Cut! Print it! And one more!' A couple of takes later it was over. In the can. See the film – it looks convincing. It looks authentic. Did Roman go through all that just to make Frank more unsettled in the scene? I wouldn't stand up in court to claim that, but one day I'll ask him. After all, with a great actor, all you need do is whisper the slightest suggestion, convince him or her to try it just for one take. Great direction is the result you get, not the way it was achieved. And the result was perfect.

On only one occasion during the filming was I able to slip in something spontaneous. There was a memorable scene where the Nazis threw an old man in a wheelchair out of the window. It was shocking. It took place in the apartment across from the Szpillman's house and of course when our reaction to it was filmed there was nothing actually happening so we had to imagine the horror. When a loud bang happened we were all told to react. It was towards the end of the shoot and, emboldened by not having been in any trouble for a while, I planned a little physical routine. I piled up some books on the counter by my elbow, and when the bang happened, unlike what we'd originally rehearsed, I spun around, knocking the books to the floor, stumbled slightly into a chair, sat down and forcibly stopped myself from retching. The director yelled 'Cut!' There was a moment of silence during which I braced myself for a blast from the expletives department, and a return to start position. Instead he said quietly, 'Cut – and print it. Next scene.' It was never discussed but it stayed in the film. I owe Mr P a lot. He made me be still and unsentimental. The kitchen scene was my little concession.

A few days later when the screenwriter Ronald Harwood and his wife Natasha came to visit the set, I was invited to join the party for dinner and Roman and I swapped our joke collections like the oldest of friends.

As *The Pianist* started to win awards at Cannes and in the US people began to ask if I was going to the occasions. It never occurred to me or to any of us to ask. The family was murdered twenty minutes into the film and only Adrien Brody and Roman were the stars. I did go to BAFTA, though, and felt a surge of company pride when it won the best film category. It felt like being back in the happiest years of my life at The Old Vic, when a company of souls survives the highs and lows of getting a show launched and pulls off a great first night. The only downside – or maybe upside, depending whether you are me or Tony Hopkins – is that if it's a movie, you can't do it again the next night.

Soap Box

I was cruising into Civitavecchia on the SS *Caronia*, or *Catatonia* as we'd affectionately named our ship after viewing our fellow passengers, when the fax from my agent came stuttering onto the purser's desk. 'Julie Goodyear – total collapse,' it said. 'Coronation Street request you to manage Rovers for two weeks. Interested?' Interested? Was Joan of Arc single-minded? Was Mozart musical? Of course I was interested! Thirty-three years in the business, man and boy, and I'd never been roped into a soap.

My husband Jack, however, had written 130 episodes of the Street years ago. When the watch was stopped after his first-ever read-through and the PA announced it was a bit too long, Albert Tatlock, the great Jack Haworth, had said, 'Ay – about 29 minutes too long.'

(The previous day, outside the Pantheon in Rome, we'd bumped into Sir Denis Foreman, the ex-managing director of Granada and Jack's erstwhile boss. Over pasta in the piazza they'd got misty-eyed over the good old days when intelligent TV wasn't an oxymoron. It seemed like an omen when the call came to troubleshoot in Wetherfield.)

We arrived on dry land. ('Nice to get your feet back on terra cotta,' as a friend's mum once said) on Friday, and I shopped for clothes with 'Corrie's wardrobe supervisor, Janet, in the two hours I had free on Saturday. We had to dress eight episodes – minus shoes and jewels. Janet read me out a description of Lillian Spencer – I had read no scripts yet (I doubted that *anyone* had, the speed of rewriting after Julie's shock departure was so fast that even the writer couldn't have read them). 'Though Lillian hails from Manchester, she has spent much of her life in Cheshire, where she managed a golf club bar.' Say no more, I thought, mutton dressed up as venison. We pounced on a blue Chanel-style tweed suit with ruffled neckline. Tweed *or* ruffles, yes – but tweed *and* ruffles – ah! Perfect. The deal was clinched by lime green and shocking pink mix (and match followed, and spangled aqua twinset). The rest would be from the Lipman waddle-in wardrobe and Granada props.

I learned lines like a dervish on Sunday, travelled surreally down The Mall on a Jubilee float on Monday with the other two Windsors, Babs and Frank, then I got on a train to the city where, 34 years ago, I lost my heart and gained a sweetheart. Seven am the next morning I was in make-up, by

8.30 I'd done my first scene. (It was beautifully written by veteran John Stephenson. Phew!) This looked like a job for Super Luvvie!

One move I made may have been old-fashioned. I insisted on the young producer coming down to meet me before I started filming. With their insane schedule, I suppose face-to-face greetings with every new artist are no longer obligatory. I felt I had to put a face to the glass-box voice above the studio. I'm not convinced the producer agreed, but a brief handshake ensued, albeit below a rather baffled face.

The cast enveloped me in a blanket of care, warmth and just a little relief. After the first scene where John Savident (a real life neighbour in Muswell Hill) introduced me to The Rover's, the nervous tension ended and the jokes and send-ups started. I'd heard Jack's stories of how newcomers to the Street were sometimes made to feel like outsiders. Times must have changed. We were all in this one together. Bill Roache explained the green-room coffee machine, Anne Kirkbride gave me a guided tour of the smokers' green-room, which she'd hand-decorated into a House & Garden salon, and Eileen Derbyshire offered to vacate her dressing-room since there was no room at the inn for the new girl.

I didn't mind being in the nurse's station, though. It was roomy and there were plenty of aspirins. ('They're carpeting the Quick Change Room for you, love,' said the floor manager.) Scene followed scene. Rehearse, record, rehearse, record. I hadn't filmed at this rate since *Thriller*, live, in 1971, at the old Rediffusion Studios when *Dads' Army* regular, John Le Mesurier, tried to murder me in a library.

Lillian came equipped with a mynah bird. The only respite we got that first day was when the bird had to be removed from its cage for drowning out the dialogue. The director, Di Patrick, was a first-timer too. We'd swapped paranoias over the phone and were very gentle with one another. At the end of day one we'd recorded eight scenes and I lay in my hotel bath feeling as though I'd been kicked by Shrek's mule. Next day more of the same. (I had to get accustomed to the emptiness of the Granada studios. When I last worked there, many years ago, it was a throbbing, bustling, teeming joint. Drama seeped out of its floors. Michael Apted and Mike Newell cut their motion picture molars there. Mike Parkinson hosted *People and Places*. Now I 'swiped' myself into each deserted corridor, hoping I wouldn't get trapped between two doors and starve until Matthew Kelly came to rescue me on his way to *Stars in their Sodding Eyes*. At the end of the day John Savident 'lifted' me to the hotel in his black open-top Morgan. Very Lillian!)

The feisty twosome behind the bar, Jenny and Sally, had asked me out clubbing on Thursday to watch Curly (one of the characters played by actor Kevin Kennedy) rock with his group. What's more, I nearly went. (I'd corpsed Sally rigid in a background scene in The Rover's by demanding condiments for my son's dinner. She came back and banged them on the table. 'Ketchup. He likes ketchup,' I rasped, adding, 'And wipe the bottom and I don't mean your own.' Pulling her hair over her grinning chin she crabwalked back to the bar.)

On Sunday I filmed in the Street itself. Like The Rover's, it was smaller, more colourful and less detailed than TV would suggest. I drove, badly (I haven't driven manually since you last saw a blue and white striped baby buggy) down the cobbled Street for my first-ever appearance, greeted Fred Elliot, and on seeing the pub for the first time, gave a physical lurch. Rumour had it that a car had been requested to run a certain actress from the studio to the Street. It was all of fifty yards from Deirdre's smoking salon. The story couldn't be true. As ever, the make-up room is a hotbed of good sense and gossip. Helen King applied just enough make-up to make me luminous on a dark night and I was very happy not to alter a thing.

It was World Cup week and I watched every 7.30am game and chunks of the midday ones in the green-room, hurling abuse with the rest of the cast. It's like living in a bubble. The cast have their own food in their own section of the canteen. They are cheerful, amiable and, from an outsider's point of view, genuinely fond of each other. Like a good repertory company – and like actors the world over, the talk is of gardens mown, building work not done, movies seen, and very little about the business there is no business like.

By Tuesday I was back in London for a charity engagement in Stanmore. I pulverised my lines all the way up and slept all the way back. By now Lillian had barred Norris from The Rover's for appearing in a Commonwealth Games shell suit. The scripted line was 'You come in here dressed like a punk rocker!' On the rehearsal, feet under the table now, I changed it to 'You come in here . . . dressed like a tropical fish!' and brought the pub down. Word came down that they'd like me to say what was written. I didn't argue – but ooh, it hurt to give up that laugh.

By Friday it was over. My demise was sudden. There were storylines to return to. I hugged Betty Driver who had so affectionately welcomed me on day one and promised a carpenter's phone number to Sue Nichols, who made me bark with laughter at her scattiness. The team upstairs gave me champagne and flowers and as I staggered off, I had a real lump in my throat at the thought of them all going on living there without me. That's the thing about two-week vacations, isn't it? You almost forget the street where you live.

Music Box

I'm in Birmingham, rehearsing a new play. It's called *Glorious* and as yet it isn't quite. Birmingham, however, is. I'll run that one past you again, because you might have thought it was a misprint. It's glorious here. The city centre has been completely renovated in the sort of flagstone and decking, hanging basket, towpath-y canal sort of fashion, so loved by town planners of today. It's terribly attractive in the sunshine of a September morn as I walk through fountained piazzas, past latte-sipping tourists under pastel sunshades. Melting pot kids leapfrog bubbling water features, and there is an actual ice cream cart manned by a boy in a straw boater. There is also an old fashioned carousel making its revolutions to slightly sinister fairground music. I feel weird, as though I've wandered onto the set of *The Prisoner* and Patrick McGoohan is waiting to twist a balloon for me.

Fortunately, to restore the balance, there are gathering swarms of strappy/stroppy cigarette refugees huddled together in mismatched groups outside the bold glass architectural edifices which house their PCs and their prospects. At night, the city throbs, the sirens howl and stragglers hoot and shriek. It's New York sans delis and attitude.

'I *told* you Birmingham was nice,' says my daughter on the mobile (she took her MA here). 'Have you been on the Eye yet?' I hadn't, and to my myopic one, neither had anyone else. It spins round at considerably more of a lick than its London counterpart, every capsule entirely devoid of punters, including the one with the tinted windows marked VIPs. It occurred to me that the *Glorious* cast of five might get into a capsule one evening and remain there until we knew all of our lines backwards. Even *forwards* would be good. Members of the public always want to know just *how* we learn our lines, as though there was some mystery attached to the process. There isn't. You just slog through it exactly as you did with the dates of the English kings, covering up your cues with a shopping list. I put my entire part on specially bought tapes and took it on holiday to the island of Zakyntos, where I swam up and down the swimming pool so excruciatingly that every Brit expat on the island came to see the wreckage! Back home I gazed hopelessly into my co-star Barrie Ingham's face, praying that his mouth won't stop moving and reveal that it's *my* turn to speak. Only Peter, our patient author, silently mouthing the correct lines at the front knows what they might be, and in what order.

Today, through the rehearsal room windows, I watched a different scene taking place in the park opposite. Wedding photos were being taken. The bride was in traditional white and her groom in tails but one bridesmaid, as far as I could see, was in blue jeans and a spangly top, with a smouldering fag behind her back. Later, in an art gallery café I saw three girls on their way to a hen night wearing sashes proclaiming: 'Bride to be' and 'Bridesmaid to be'. Love was in the air. You could tell that from the fact that all three were carrying dainty pink plastic penises and testicles on sticks. I suppose it makes a change from your traditional corsage.

Glorious is about Florence Foster Jenkins, a woman who insisted on singing in public although her voice sounded like a trapped bat. It's also about some kind of artistic freedom. Should we be free to ban what we don't approve of? Not long ago, at the Birmingham Rep, Sikh extremists demonstrated against a play which they felt insulted their scriptures. The play was withdrawn from the repertoire.

I remember, almost thirty years ago, when my late husband Jack Rosenthal's play *Bar Mitzvah Boy* was screened by the BBC, there were furious protests in the Jewish press. Affronted butchers in Temple Fortune waved cleavers and talked about thin edges of wedges and bearded people discussed lapsed faith on *Late Night Line Up*. How quaint all that seems today, moreover how quaint it *seemed* only months after the showing.

There is a strange quality attached to playing a real person. It makes one very anxious about their feelings. Which is why you often hear actors waxing lyrical about their life-long special bond with Joan of Arc, or Fatty Arbuckle. It's a bit of transference at work. When biographers say goodbye, after years of research, to Joe Orton or Winston Churchill and find they can't quite shake them out of their system, it's accepted, but I suspect with actors, rather like expressions of their politics, it's perceived more as 'anything to pad out their chat show repertoire'.

Today, the day of the first preview, is unkindly hot in the city which only recently survived a tornado. I'm wearing a padded body suit, corset, suspenders and stockings, a wig, a halo, an evening dress and large feathered wings. I'm gulping litres of water every time I leave the stage to change costume and sucking lozenges with my lunch. Next year I'll be eligible for my bus pass. How could Rodgers and Hammerstein have known so much about me when they wrote the song 'Cockeyed Optimist'?

Back in London for a week after rockin' em in the aisles in Newcastle and Malvern. I loved Newcastle, although the theatre is the best kept secret in town. The building is majestic, with massive pillars outside which give it pomp, circumstance and no front of house display at all. It looks like a bank. The only way you could have known we were on was if you fell into the stage door after a few Newcastle Browns and encountered a woman in body padding and a grey wig . . . and I would have mentioned it. We opened on Tuesday, the raves came out on Wednesday and by the time we were full up, we'd gone.

I stayed in a posh service flat opposite the theatre with fire doors so heavy that I used to ask strangers for help to get in and out of it. Outside on the pedestrianised street was a vast screen which, from eleven o'clock at night onwards, showed the artists Gilbert and George, in bank teller suits, intoning the Ten Commandments. The flat was all fur coat and no knickers. Lots of blond wood floors, spiral staircase, glass tables and the obligatory rustic pottery bowl filled with coloured bark and balls of dyed twine. Fantastically useful though they were, I'd rather have had a telephone which worked without opening an account, soap and some milk. You haven't lived until you've tried to drag a full suitcase and a computer through two clamped fire doors and down a spiral staircase.

My childhood friend Bernice picked me up from the theatre and took me home to Gosforth where she showed me her late father's cine films of both our families on a beach holiday in Fifties Scarborough. I know that the amount of time we *actually* spend on a beach is disproportionate to the amount of photographs showing us doing so, but these transferred-to-video films were a revelation. Why does one remember the sad times, the conflicts and frustrations of childhood, when there is the proof of the happiness and sheer compatibility of our family? Dad, rolling up his trousers to reveal his shapely, fridge-white legs, was only topped by my absolute knowledge, at seven, of where the camera would be at any given time.

After two shows on Saturday, where I mangled Strauss and Mozart so badly that a man fell out of his seat laughing and rolled dangerously near the orchestra pit, our director Alan Strachan heard a woman say: 'I don't understand it, she was here with that Joyce Grenfell show and she sang perfectly well.'

I took the crazed decision not to travel back to London the next day but to take the train to Hull to visit my parents' graves before the Jewish New Year. I could hear my mother's unique voice, ringing in my ears: 'Maureen, 'ave you gone stark raving mad? What are you doing it for? I'm dead, you silly sod. Go home and sort out your washing for God's sake!'

As of old, I ignored her and headed for the station at 9am, expecting nothing but buffet-less carriages and a four-hour delay due to a panini on the track. Then they confounded me by giving us both punctuality and a flapjack. My cup of Typhoo ranneth over. Admittedly, dragging the suitcase up and over an iron bridge whilst changing at York was second only to schlepping the Antler up the Geordie spiral, but arrive precisely on time I did and as always the sight of the thin brown river Humber, spanned by its exquisite suspension bridge, filled my heart with pride. I left Hull in 1965 and it has taken a lot less than forty years to realise that it never left me. The day before, I'd heard Hull-born playwright, Alan Plater, on *Loose Ends* telling how he'd driven past a shoe shop there which sported a sign saying 'Buy One Get One Free'.

I took a short taxi drive to the house of Rita Charna and her sister Eva, friends of my parents who have known me since I was the precocious star of my own backyard. They gave me, in no particular order, the local gossip, baked cheesecake and the key to the cemetery. Most of our cemeteries have to be kept under lock and key because of constant vandalism. Rita and Eva are of the generation where the energy fizzes out of their elbows. Nothing fazes them, they are smart and beautifully groomed, full of humour and intelligence and it breaks my heart that every time I see them could be the last. We bathed in nostalgia for far too short a time, until Amy arrived by car to pick me up.

On the drive home to London, we decided to eat at a hotel by the Humber bridge in honour of Mum, who always loved seeing it from the window of her beloved flat. It was a mistake. The place was amok with running kids with running noses and as we left, a gaggle of rough lads at a table near the window seemed to be discussing us.

'Yeah, they're Jews, aren't they?' one of them said.

I stopped at their table. My daughter's grip on my arm tightened. Like her Dad before her she would have walked on and, equally like her Dad, knew that I couldn't. She feared for my as yet unbroken nose.

'Yes?' I asked him. 'Is that the end of the sentence, or do you have anything to add?'

He shuffled about a bit and said, 'Yer what?'

I said, 'Do you have anything to add to your assessment? And would you like to say it to my face?'

'No . . . I was just sayin' you're . . . Jews . . . that's all . . .'

His mate stepped in: 'He's drunk . . .'

'No I aren't!' protested his ungrammatical mate.

'Well,' I said, 'since he's got nothing more to add, I'll just take it as a compliment, shall I?'

And we swep' out, as they say up here.

My daughter was at once relieved and impressed. 'Well done, Mod,' she breathed, 'you did that with a lot of dignity.'

Sadly the saying of the line coincided with my giving the young man a hearty finger as we passed the window.

'Ah,' said Amy, 'yes, well *that* certainly blew the dignity side of things.'

Like Liam, the young Billy Elliot, who wrote of his experiences at the Olivier Awards, I attended the bash at the London Hilton. As I read his excited prose I found myself wondering in what part of the house I'd mislaid my rose-tinted spectacles. Although *Glorious* was nominated as Best New Comedy, I wasn't planning to go this year, largely on the grounds that no one had asked me.

I caved in when they offered me a presentation spot and a car back and forth. In my wardrobe I had a perfectly wonderful olive silk dress and jacket, unseen by anyone who hasn't been at Adam's wedding, but I happily threw my wages at a new gown to boost my morale and some fake fur to fool the animal rights lobby. The dress, which required under-pinned lingerie, was cut on the cross, which for the uninitiated means it hugs the waist and clings to the hips, so I kept the fur on for most of the steamy evening to prevent my lower body looking like a bag of bugles, and received several compliments on my embonpoint. Sadly, though, every time I visited the loo, I had to take everything off. *Everything.* It took seven or eight minutes and most of that saw me upended against the cubicle wall, scarlet-faced, with my reading glasses on, trying to fasten the gusset poppers on my strapless basque . . . and as I write this I still wonder why I never hear from George Clooney!

Actually, another great American actor, who shall be nameless because I respect him so much, did make my evening by telling me that he was a great fan of mine and had followed my work for years. I blushed charmingly and was still thanking him as he told me that he first saw me in *A Midsummer Night's Dream* and that what I'd done in *The History Boys* was superb, by which time it was far too late to disappoint him by telling I was not Frances de la Tour.

I took the whole *Glorious* cast along with me. They brushed up beautifully and had a ball. Whilst I was standing in the draughty two-foot wide corridor behind the stage, waiting to go on to announce the winner of Best Costume, I sneakily opened the envelope to make sure the name was pronounceable. A fellow presenter did the same to hers, revealing in one fell swoop that *Glorious* had failed to win Best Comedy. The award was won by an adaptation, *Heroes*, which closed some weeks ago.

Was I bitter? Just because I changed my name to Angostura? *Pas de tout.* We then had a song from *The Big Life*, two Billy Elliot songs, awkward out of context, and, again, 'The Guy's Only Doing it for Some Gal' from *Guys and Dolls*. Later, well into my cups, I asked the show's producer why he'd not asked me to murder 'The Queen of the Night' aria, as I do nightly. He looked at me despairingly, and the words 'pushy bloody woman', only just failed to tumble from his lips. I suddenly realised how much I wished I *was* Frankie de la Tour.

All the American actors spoke of their love for London and how proud they were to be working in the West End. All the English ones got up and took pot-shots at the length of the ceremony or the appetite-defying food. I do love the English, though, as we say in the play, I couldn't eat a whole one.

I was home, far from sober, by 12.30am and into the tiny arms of a warm puppy. It's almost impossible to be cynical with a puppy in the house. Diva is her name and she is, of course, unparallelled the world over in looks, temperament and cleverness – and that's not just me but Mr Paradise, the vet, who says so. She can sit for a treat, her deposits are regular, if peripatetic, and she can pee on newspaper, which would have been a handy trick for me earlier that evening, if I'd thought to take some.

That night, her first away from her natural mother, she slept on the top floor with Nats, who lodges up there, and they slept like a log and a dog whilst I lay tossing and turning downstairs, mentally composing several hundred letters of apology for all the faux pas I'd made, not just in that evening, but in my entire life so far.

Travel Section
* add packing tip

No shame in
wearing the same
shoes 2 nights!

Edinburgh Rocked

It was a family wedding. In Edinburgh. My cousin's daughter was marrying her boyfriend of ten years and Jack was to speak a Hebrew prayer. Of course, when we accepted the invitation it was 1999 and the wedding was to be in mid 2000 and in my business one could be in the People's Republic of Burkina Faso filming a Lillet's commercial a year after you've said 'Yes, of course I'll be there – wild horses wouldn't stop me, etc., etc.' Then the time drew near and I was firmly entrenched in the West End eight times a week. Jack was summoned to Bristol for a read-through and Amy wasn't going on her own because she wouldn't know anybody and she'd feel like a spare whatsit at a wedding.

So I wrote the letter, enclosed the present, explained the cock-up and wished everybody all the happiness in the world. I followed up with a phone call to make sure all was well and realised all wasn't. My cousin came on the line. 'Oh dear,' she chuckled, 'she's not well pleased, she's not well pleased at all.' I fell over myself with apologies and suggestions of hot air balloons from Muswell Hill to Morningside. 'Look, don't worry,' she said, 'she's just a bit . . . you know . . . I think she just wants her relatives to be there around her . . . she'll get over it.'

By now my bottom lip has started wobbling and I'm in danger of seeing this as my own daughter's wedding as opposed to that of an enchanting girl whom I've, shamefully, only met ten or twelve times in her whole life. 'One or more of us will be there,' I promised through a rapidly jamming throat.

I put down the phone, then picked it up again and booked two return tickets to Edinburgh on the day in question. I decided to tell the ticket holders of their surprise trip nearer the event. In my world you get used to upsetting people when you cancel on them. It always amazes me when charity committee members threaten to slay your first-born when you tell them you can't get to Pontefract as promised because you'll be in *Annie Get Your Gun*. I know. It matters. Numbers matter. I guess not so much to me. A friend of mine failed to show at my 50th birthday because she was having a face-lift! I just ate her dinner.

So. On the Saturday before the Sunday of the wedding, Amy and her Dad set off for Heathrow. Amy hates to fly and couldn't understand why I hadn't booked the train. 'It's a treat,' I said. 'You'll be there in no time and it'll be nice for you and Dod to have an outing together.' She has a running gag with Jack that they haven't been out together, alone, since *Pete's Dragon*. It's not entirely factual.

At 12 o'clock, when I had them breezing through Edinburgh airport, the phone rang. 'Hi, Mod,' said a plaintive voice. 'We're at Heathrow.' 'Did you miss it?' I cried. 'No,' she replied, 'we've been bumped off the plane. They'd overbooked.' 'But we confirmed the flight!' I screamed. 'It's no use screaming at me,' she screamed, 'they do this all the time on domestic flights, apparently. We're booked on the one o'clock but we'll miss the start of the ceremony and we'll have to change our clothes in the toilets.' 'It's all my fault for making you go by plane,' I bleated. 'Is Dod breathing or has he started puffing?'

The next time I heard from them was after the wedding. They'd had a *lovely* time. The bride was as late as they were, the setting was divine. They were really glad they'd gone. I breathed properly myself for the rest of the second show.

Sunday to myself – to lie in bed for the omnibus *Archers* and to eat cold chicken for breakfast and onion crisps for lunch. In the afternoon I took a long walk and came back to prepare a proper Sunday lunch for their return around 3.30. At 4 o'clock the phone rang – plaintively. 'Hi Mod,' said the plaintee. 'We're in Manchester.'

Through much swallowing, she told me that mid-flight from Edinburgh the oxygen masks suddenly descended. Everyone had been panic-stricken until the Captain informed them that something had gone very wrong with the air pressure in the cabin so they would have to fly at half the normal height and then land at Manchester. 'The next thing we knew, our ears started killing us and we had the most frightening landing you've ever known. There were fire engines waiting on the tarmac. It was awful.'

My baby. My twenty-six-year-old child, whom I'd spent a lifetime persuading not to be afraid of flying (wasn't it Mel Brooks who said 'If God had meant Jews to fly he'd have given them tickets'?), was now refusing to get back on the plane provided to get home to London. 'You get on the train then, love,' said I, never a believer in the school of getting back on the horse after the fall. Better to get rid of the horse and buy a bike.

I turned off the oven, rearranged the lunch into a dinner, and waited. At 8.30pm the phone rang. 'It's me,' said a hysterical voice. 'The train's been diverted to Northampton. They said "'Cos of danger ahead!" . . . Expect us when you see us.' They had set off from Edinburgh at 1.15pm. They arrived home ten hours later.

If the wedding had been in Mexico they'd have got back sooner.

Ten years later. Actually, I've just flown back from a wedding in Mexico. In Ajijic to be precise. At sunset in a sort of latter day native settlement on a hillside overlooking a lake, Jonathan and Rita Lynn's son Edward was marrying Jenny, who has a Mexican Dad.

Jonathan had appeared in two of Jack's most popular plays, *Bar Mitzvah Boy* and *The Knowledge*, had directed Jack's only stage play, *Smash*, and played my husband – 'my little Kev – look at him, like a whippet in the slips . . . ooh, I'm gonna give him such a seeing to when I get him home' – in Richard Harris's hilarious cricket play *Outside Edge*. Our kids had grown up together in Muswell Hill and Edward was the reluctant stage manager in many of Amy's early cellar, if not stellar, productions.

After writing the inimitable *Yes Minister* with Tony Jay, his success took him to Hollywood and directing fame with *My Cousin Vinnie* and *The Whole Nine Yards*. There may be reasons beyond our ken why Tony Jay, Nigel Hawthorne and Paul Eddington were all rewarded with gongs by the Thatcher government and the fourth member of the creative team wasn't, but these we will never know. There were years when J and R and I and JR didn't see each other, but we always retained the flame of those early days of struggle and achievement and kept feelers out to each other.

On a *Holiday Programme* expedition to Las Vegas I escaped to their house on Rodeo Drive, LA and with inimitable timing, wobbled and whinged my way through the 6.8 earthquake the day after I arrived. After Jack's death, it seemed only natural to retreat to their California sunshine to lick my wounds. Although Rita is a psychotherapist, it was her cooking and her bear hugs I needed rather than her advice.

No one can tell another person how to handle bereavement. You do it as you *are*. One can by all means read other's experiences – there are some wonderful books and poems on loss out there – check out Dannie Abse's *The Presence* or Joan Didion's *The Year of Magical Thinking* – but ignore the self-help sages who say: 'You'll be numb for three months, you'll be angry for six, then you'll feel ready for a latte with female friends, then . . .' Hogwash! If your means of recovery is to weep in company, bawl out Chinese epithets at the bus stop and shoot semolina at crows, then damn well do it.

It felt right for the Rosenthals en famille to travel to this wedding. Then it transpired that Adam's wife, a cinematographer, was to shoot a film in Mexico City the following year. To be together, see the country and pick up the threads of childhood . . . It was a three-day 'do'. The bride's real father was a rangy, olive-skinned, long white pony-tailed and bearded architect rumoured to be on his twelfth marriage. The mother of the bride was tiny and wonderfully well preserved and now married to the judge who'd let her off a parking fine then called her for a date. This was going to be fun.

They had an astonishing hacienda in the centre of the arty, cobbled town and it was filled to the last bougainvillea with Teddy's Winchester friends, Stamford friends, and a quarter of Glasgow, London and California. By the end of the three days we'd heard more mariachi bands than Cantinflas ever did and danced off the two hundred bottles of tequila which had transmogrified into three thousand tamarind tequilas. Two thousand beers had seen us bopping and bingeing and dipping into more turquoise water than we later remembered.

At the ceremony itself all the men wore specially grown or applied Zapata moustaches . . . as, apparently at some point of the evening, did I. We were bussed from Ajijic to a hilltop restaurant overlooking the lake and sipped our tequilas under coloured bunting to the sound of mariachi guitars. Rita, her beautiful mum Ada, Amy and I laid out the table settings and lit the red candles. There were ten bridesmaids in strappy scarlet chiffon and twenty-two moustachioed ushers in open white shirts and red socks. The mothers wore scarlet, russet and vermillion and several fathers matched the groom in white suits, red boutonnières and red shoes. A tiny moppet in a Mexican frilled dress threw red petals on the floor for several minutes until boredom set in.

The mariachi band was supposed to join in the taped music of 'All You Need Is Love', but they were off on one and played what they liked. It didn't matter, we all knew the words, as down a flight of thirty or more steps danced the bride in ballerina white with red lilies in her chignon. As the aisle was narrow, her two fathers walked together and she literally danced down the walkway on six-inch red Manalos, throwing caution and her red roses to the wind. It was very dramatic.

As vows were exchanged, the scarlet rose in the sky plopped noiselessly into the lake and the bride and groom kissed it better. It was a movie, and as such deserved a dissolve. My thoughts drifted back to Adam and Taina's wedding at the English Speaking Union, two years earlier. The couple had been sweethearts since they were nineteen and had spent much of their three years at Cambridge and Oxford sleeping on coaches on their way to see each other. Now they were thirty and the relationship was older than several of their friends' marriages.

My fears that the loss of Ad's Dad would have a sorrowful effect on their wedding day had been unfounded. The sun shone, the venue sparkled and love was everywhere. Amy and Alina, Taina's sister, wore dark turquoise and carried dark red roses. The bride wore pale gold lace with her ravishing corn-coloured curls threaded with red roses. The groom wore a smart dark, dark, brown suit, just as his Dad had done. Me? Olive silk three-piece. Long. Green feathers on the head. Three of Jack's handkerchiefs in my bag. Strangely enough, I didn't need them. It was such a joyous day.

Their friends hoisted them up on bridal chairs and Kletzmer music filled the courtyard. We danced in circles like a travelling troupe from the Old Country. Taina's parents are Romanian so it all melded beautifully. Jack would have loved it. What do I mean? He did love it. His radiant beam was all over us. As I danced wildly with my colourful, *softic Macha tonim* – only Yiddish has a word for the mother of your son's wife – the thought never once passed through my mind that there would ever again be a moment of true love for the mother of the groom. Watch this sorry space . . .

Popping by Cork

I know they exist and I know they're insoluble and I know that most of them are our fault, but as far as I'm concerned, there are no such things as 'Irish Troubles'. On the contrary, there are only Irish Joys. This autumn we had them all.

One week in Ireland – it's all I need to rid me of my neuroses, fill up my stomach and refresh my visual memory. Apart from all that tosh, I just have such a good time.

We started out on Inchydoney Island. It's a Lodge Hotel and Spa balanced on the edge of a promontory, so you have miles of beach on your left and kilometres of it on your right. In the middle was our room, with massive windows on three sides framed by fluttery sea-green and azure voile, and a large brass telescope through which I peered for ages in some confusion before finally realising you had to remove the brass cap from the end. Then, before you could say 'plankton', I was in that sea warming my bones in the gentle Gulf Stream current.

It was a paradise for children of all ages. It boasted a pleasant pub and an awfully good restaurant, specialising in the black and cream stuff in the one and the nouvelle cuisine in the other. The monkfish on peas in the pod and organic wine was just fine. I have to report that Southern Ireland sports the most wonderful food. However, it invariably comes in a tottery pile the way it does in Soho. So if you're into culinary dismantling, Ireland is your island.

One night we asked about Irish food and everybody fell about. 'D'ye mean cabbage and bacon?' snorted one of the charming young hotel staff, and sent us in a car to Dillon's pub in Timoleague where we waited one and a half hours for a choice between those well-loved staples of Celtic cooking, enchiladas with salsa and Thai curry with fragrant coconut rice. You had to laugh. And as we handed over our £40 return cab fare, we did laugh. Quite a lot. Back at the Inchydoney Jack taught me how to play draughts. He gave me so many tips that I hammered him. 'Next time, you're on your own,' he said evenly. 'Oh well, then next time I'm not playing.'

The hotel had a thermal pool of warm silky sea water, into which were set various jets and hoses. You could stand between bars and have your stomach pummelled into your coccyx or stand beneath a curved jet which

403

played percussion on your shoulders. Jack loved it. I left him going round like a kid in an adventure playground, wearing the red and white cotton cap, obligatory in Irish pools, which makes any person, irrespective of age or shape, look like a bandaged finger.

I was having a seaweed wrap. You lie naked on cling film whilst a girl covers you in a bucket of warm mud. It's hilarious. Then she wraps you up and leaves you to nod off and bake. Afterwards you emerge with a very soft skin and you pong of oysters. I also had an ace massage and face mask, while Jack had the 'Brumisation' which is not a course in speaking like Jasper Carrot, but a lie-down in a room full of wet ozone. You reap the benefits via the hairy bits in your lungs. I'm not being too scientific for you here, am I?

I love passing by a sign which says, on the same post, 'Clonakilty 8 miles' with a sign pointing right and 'Clonakilty 5 miles' left. This was on the way to Kilbertain where, in a charming converted cottage restaurant, I had a bowl of cream of mushroom and spring onion soup which, described at length, could make your mouth gush.

Lingeringly, we set off for the Sheen Falls Hotel in Kenmare. It was a perfect Van Gogh-coloured day and we stopped for a cidery salad at Hayes Bar, overlooking the tiny bay of Glendare. We'd just missed the ferry to the popular, unpopulated beaches of Sherkin Island, so we drove on to Lough Hine, where Jack spotted a house I'd once almost rented from a lovely and charismatic lady builder, Irene Beard, whom I'd met at a Women of the Year Lunch. The elegant white house overlooking the glassy water of the lough was surrounded by fir forests and nature parks. We were too shy to knock on the door but later we rang Irene and were straightaway seduced back for lunch, then dinner, then breakfast. Along with her husband, children and five of the smartest, funniest Italian cousins I've ever met, we had what the Irish call a 'craic'. As a consequence of our visit to Irene, we arrived a day late at the Sheen Falls Lodge in Kenmare. The drive took us through spotless Skibbereen, with rows of stucco houses painted aqua, fuchsia and apricot. Past the Skibbereen Acupuncture and Moxibustion Centre and two flame-haired lads in Manchester United away strips of at least five seasons past, and back through the clean clear lines of Bantry Bay. We went back to Skibbereen every year for the next four years and I'll be off there this summer. It's a healing place.

The Lodge was a sumptuous house set in heather-covered hills overlooking the Sheen River. We had a posh tea and a look through the library, where Jack settled his crossword angst by discovering 'qualms' really *could* mean slaughter and murder. Then we murdered a delicious dinner and the kind of Pimms that induces a kind of glacial drunkenness. Our room was comfortable, pretty and you could swing a cheetah or two around in it. Outside the Falls gurgled and cooed like Classic FM without the adverts, as inside I devoured Harry Potter's Third Task in the Triwizard Tournament.

Next day, the man in Creagh Gardens, where we'd gone to see a giant myrtle, said we shouldn't bother with the scenic Ring of Kerry. 'Beara Peninsula's just as gorgeous,' he confided, 'but without the coaches.' He was right. Our massive, kippery breakfast tightened our jeans as we took in the spectacular views. Springy soft valleys flanked our journey through narrow passes from County Cork into County Kerry. Shadows spread over deeply rigid rock running round the mountains like amphitheatres.

Our first call was Glengarriff where the sweep of the scenery suddenly resembled the Yorkshire Moors set against stunning views of peninsulas nosing down into endless bays. Here we picked up a magenta-haired backpacking DJ – you just do in Ireland – it feels right. Only after he departed did he call back, 'I like your work on the telly, by the way.' People know you, recognise you, greet you and leave you in peace. It's unique. 'If you hurry, Maureen,' said a ticket seller with four teeth, 'Billy'll row you to the Italian Gardens on Garinish Island; it's worth a sight.' There were basking seals as we slid past with silent Billy at the oars. He spoke once, to tell us the last boat left Garinish at 6 o'clock, and we clambered out with only fifty minutes to do the Happy Valley *and* the Italianate Gardens. Suddenly there are colonnades and sunken pools and tall, twisting trees from New Zealand.

Looking back, if I hadn't got into conversation with a family of five, if I hadn't decided to climb the hundreds of steps to the Martello tower and if I hadn't come down a different way, I would never have lost Jack and ended up shouting at a boatful of trippers, 'Wait! Help! Don't go! I've lost my husband! Help!' A search party finally found him waiting doggedly where he'd last seen me, whilst I raced round the Happy Valley shouting 'JACK! ANSWER ME! HAVE YOU FALLEN DOWN SOMETHING?' at the top of my lungs.

We lunched in the tiniest village, beyond the Caha pass, consisting of twelve houses and six pubs, choosing one at random and wandering out with our Murphys onto the tiny terrace overlooking hills and dales. There was one other couple out there, from New Zealand it appeared. 'What do you do?' I asked. 'Oh, we take actors from *Coronation Street* out to New Zealand on promotional tours.' We left with much name and card swapping, the air heavy with promise.

We spent our last night in Kenmare in two places at once. Eating a 'to die for' dinner at the Lime Tree Restaurant, where I had a lime cheesecake with lime sorbet which I will never forget, and across the road at Cleo's boutique buying handmade linen and knitwear. Eating my heart out.

Our final three days took us to Dromoland Castle hotel in County Clare, via soft drizzling rain, several converted castles and a stop-off at The Captain's Table pub where our Iranian-born host gave us moussaka and told me he'd lived just down the street from me in Hull for ten years and often visited my dad's shop.

It was very grand, i.e. Jack had to borrow a tie, and the staff raised tureen lids in the air in synchronised fashion, like percussionists in the Philharmonic Orchestra. But they do it with a twinkle, thank the Lord, which takes the curse off it. It was filled to bursting with American golfers, who played on through Wagnerian thunderstorms with a stoicism shared by wedding guests in gauzy hats and morning suits outside in the glorious walled gardens. I counted eleven colours of snapdragon, from sunshine to a bronze like crème brûlée set in autumn leaves.

Dromoland Castle's stately panelled decor belied a warm heart. The restaurant gave us a harpist and a violinist with dinner and a linnet-voice folk singer with Irish coffee in the bar. Show me a happy Irish song and I'll show you a Jewish leprechaun. Next morning, at 3.00am, I finished my Harry Potter, and we pottered contentedly home.

This year, 2008, as usual, I was picked up at Cork airport by John D. Whooley, coin expert and ghost hunter. His card states, decisively, 'I will find them!'. For an hour and a quarter I cajoled this small, bearded and prosaic man to tell me all his encounters in the spirit world.

'Did you actually see him?'

'Well, not exactly see . . . more like I felt him . . .'

'And did he go away when you asked him to?'

'Well now, in the end he did, but not before he threw a brass plate at my head.'

It's a land of stories and the story tellers are the best in the world . . . and I'm the best listener. Besides, where else can I be that silent?

Cool and Hip

Jack's hips always embarrassed us at metal detector points and Toulouse airport was no exception. 'C'est mes hanches,' he explained, in flawless pidgin. 'Ils sont titanium.' Six Gallic eyes stared blankly at him before one Gallic mouth barked a command to wait behind the barrier for 'la police'. Jack looked horror-stricken. Not because he was guilty, naturally. We're not the types to smuggle illegal substances. (I once took prunes to Miami on the advice of a nutritionist and when the customs man rapped 'Any plants, fruits or seeds?' I confessed and he confiscated my prunes!)

No, Jack's concern was missing the plane. He had started to breathe in a shallow fashion, and sweat, which I knew was to do with his horror of foiled travel arrangements, but feared customs would confuse it with guilt, so I yelled across the divide: 'Don't worry, love, we can always get a later plane', which increased his breathing rate to a demi-pant. The police failed to show up and I resorted to outraged Franglais: 'Mais c'est une opération très populaire, ne'est pas? Les hanches?' Le douanier just shrugged. 'En la France aussi?' I continued. They looked at one another and tapped their foreheads. When I think of the anguish I gave Mr Hart, my beleaguered French teacher, it occurs to me he was now getting his own back. Jack was giving me warning looks but I was unstoppable: 'You mean to tell me that chaque personne qui arrive ici avec une replacement, must attendre pour le police?! C'est ridicule! Impossible! Loco!' We were gathering a crowd by now, but the officials were as impassive as ever.

I spotted a policewoman walkie-talking her way past and I started banging on the windows to attract her attention. 'Non!' All three officials were on to me. 'Elle est une femme.' Apparently only a male policeman would do. All at once I realised that Jack was going to be searched. I got both nervous and giggly, which, combined with his temperature change and panting, made us look like an elderly Bonnie and Clyde.

When the young armed policeman finally arrived, he swept Jack off into a little cubicle. I pressed my ear to the wall, holding my breath and standing on the balls of my feet, ready, in the event of the sound of a snapping rubber glove, to spring him. Happily the young policeman merely wanted to see Jack's scar, which Jack was only too happy to show him. 'OK,' said the policeman, and turned to leave.

'Non!' dit Jack assuredly. 'Regarde ici aussi', which sounds funnier than it looks. Then, lowering his trousers to the other side, insisted that the policeman look at 'l'autre' scar. The guy seemed a bit embarrassed. 'OK!' he kept saying whilst sidling out of the cubicle, away from what he no longer took to be a cool smuggler but a hip flasher. No doubt during all of this two or three travellers with packets of white stuff in their bums sauntered blithely past, whistling.

It's not airport security's fault and I don't blame them for protecting passengers from dealers and terrorists, but the whole thing does seem a bit Heath Robinson. If a scanner beeps when held near a human hip, you'd think that would be enough to convince your average official that there is a pin in there somewhere.

Incidentally, are there any sillier questions than 'Did you pack this case yourself?' 'No – actually my case was packed by a swarthy man I'd never met before and this ticking parcel was given to me outside Gate 16 by a nice Celtic man in a black balaclava.'

Now I think about it, given that most of us find packing a suitcase even more wearisome than voting in European elections, how about a packing service at the airport, staffed by retired air stewards? Can't you just see it? 'These shoes with that suit? You must be joking. I'd bin 'em, love, if I were you!' Then you could go off on holiday with nothing more than a jumbo-sized inferiority complex and a voice in your ears calling: 'By the way, ducky, I've separated your gas cylinder from your heated brush – you'll be needing that brush after that local cut they've given you! Still, at least no one'll recognise you where *you're* going. Bon voyage!'

Wife in Bath

I'm back from touring in my daughter Amy's play, *Sitting Pretty*, which means I've seen physiotherapists in six different cities and a reflexologist in Bath. My hair is salt and paprika, I'm fat and I think my teeth have dropped a shade or two down the paint chart. When I woke up this morning in my own dear bed, my first thought was 'Hell, I forgot to tick Continental on the breakfast slip.'

During the final week, in Bath, much as I love the city, I was hallucinating about home. I always stay at the Bath Spa Hotel but this time I was booked into the smaller Dukes Hotel. 'Miss Lipman, checking in,' I informed Toby, the fresh-faced young man on reception. He blinked, excused himself and made computer noises on his computer.

'Sorry – er, but no one of that name is booked in for tonight.' He had an engaging West Country accent, but it was wet and cold and I was in no mood to be engaged.

'Well, OK, then, it's under Rosenthal,' I insisted. He made more technological sounds and came back looking slightly terrified. 'Erm, no, Oi'm afraid we've nothing under thaat name either.'

I studied the carpet. 'Look, I don't care if you've got me down as Osama Bin sodding Laden, can you just show me a room, and I'll not trouble you again until lunchtime?'

'Erm, certainly Oi can allocate you a room, madam, but –'

'Well, allocate it then, love – I booked this six weeks ago and I'm too tired to – oh hell, where's your manager?'

'Oi'm the night manager, madam, so if you would just like to fill in this f—'

'Aaaaargh!!!' I was about to lose it when a thought struck me. 'Wait! Just wait.' It was an inner voice. In a cold sweat. It said, 'Maureen. Before you start the fishwife/virago act, just remember how often you're *wrong* these days. Like, always.'

'May I use your phone, Toby?' I asked.

'Hi Mod,' said Amy, whose fault it was I was in Bath in the first place. 'How did it go?'

'Never mind how it went. Get the diary and tell me where I'm sleeping tonight.'

She sounded my death knell. 'The Bath Spa Hotel.' I put down the phone and said carefully, 'Toby, I would like to apologise unreservedly for everything that has come out my mouth in the past ten minutes and my threatening body language. I am a fool and a menopausal one at that.'

He flushed and mumbled beautifully.

When I reached the Bath Spa I was too tired to take off my greasepaint. When the chambermaid collected my pillowcase the next day, she must have thought I was a hooker.

That was Monday. On Tuesday night I briskly walked the twenty minutes' uphill trek back to the large, stately Bath Spa, had a laugh with Colin, the concierge, over the previous night's antics and retired to Floor 6, looking forward to my one cigarette of the day. No sign of the pack in my bag, so I undressed and began taking off two night's warpaint when I remembered the 'Do Not Disturb' sign. It was, after all, 1.15am and actors sleep in. It's the major perk.

In pyjama top and streaky face, my body well hidden behind the door, I hung out the sign. As I retreated though, I saw a cigarette lying on the hall carpet, where it had obviously fallen from my bag. Unthinkingly I went to retrieve it – and heard the door click shut behind me, leaving me powerless, knickerless and trouserless on the sixth floor without key, glasses, phone or visible means of support.

Loyal reader, only you can understand why I began to laugh. It was so perfect. There was nothing for it but to circumnavigate the stairwell, back pressed to wall, SAS style, praying that no one was coming down or – worse still, horror, coming *up*! – clutching my navy jim-jams (well, just jims really) to cover back and front, all the way down to reception.

Why didn't I use the lift? Please! You've read this far. You must know that a party of Japanese businessmen would have got in on the second floor and bowed. And I'd have had to bow back or they'd have lost face. And God knows what I'd have lost.

'Pssst! Pssst!' I'm stage whispering round the corner of the foyer. 'Help! Pssst! . . .' Oh, what the hell. I appear at the desk, head swivelling left and right and gibbering.

The night manager was unperturbed. Happens all the time, it seems. 'Happens all the time – can't count the number of men I've seen at this time of night, wearing nothing but a Do Not Disturb Sign. Here's your new key, madam. Have a pleasant night's sleep.' I'm off like a whippet in the slips, back up the stairs and into my nice warm room. No matches, of course, but who needs artificial stimulants anyway in my line of work?

Anyhow, *The Wife of Bath* was always my favourite *Canterbury Tale*.

Thoroughly Mod and Millie

A weekend in New York was mentioned by producer Duncan Weldon, to give me a chance to see *Thoroughly Modern Millie*, the musical he'd offered me here in London. Tickets to the American theatre's Tony Awards were hinted at. Hugh Jackman, my old *Oklahoma!* partner, was hosting the Tonys (and here we're talking about the man I love – no, when I say love, I only mean carnally. And cerebrally, of course – and I love his wife, too, but perhaps a tad less carnally). I called my daughter.

'How would you feel if I went to New York this weekend, would –'

'Oh, great,' she retorted, grimly. 'You as well? All my friends will be in New York on my birth–'

'– and you'll come with me, of course, and see your friends for your birthday?' I interrupted, quick as a flash. 'That's what I meant. Obviously.'

Truthfully I'd had no intention of going until Julia got on to me at St James's Palace. We were doing cabaret for the Queen. I'd been summoned to re-create my Joyce Grenfell as part of a jolly entertainment to celebrate the 50th anniversary of her Coronation. Julia sang from *Guys and Dolls*, Jamie Cullum, whom I love second best after Hugh Jackman, sang 'In The Wee Small Hours of the Morning' and 'The Men In Coats' and stole the show. On the way in to the palace a policeman had stopped my car, leaned in and said, 'Are you doing your Maureen Lipman tonight, then?' My eyes misted over. 'I do it most nights, actually.'

Anyway, Julia told me I was going to NY because I deserved a break and Jack would be well looked after because she would be moving into the house with a cooked salmon, a chicken casserole and an apple pie the way he liked it (shortcrust not puff). I knew better than to argue with a red-head, even if a large part of the red came from Pedro of Bond Street.

On Thursday Jack got great results on his blood tests and was happy to let us go and on Friday I packed everything in a small hand case after dinner for eight and the washing up.

It was only after a frantic, asthmatic run to Gate 55, following a *last* call when I hadn't even heard a *first* one, that I realised my dress for the Tony Awards was still hanging on the wardrobe door where I'd left it overnight so it wouldn't crush in the case. I would have to fly in and raid Saks Fifth Avenue or go in a crumpled orange T-shirt and a pair of Sloggies.

The situation was taken in hand immediately by Jeff Thacker, a TV producer sitting in the opposite aisle of the plane and also en route to the Tonys. He made two phone calls that ensured my frock would be picked up and taken to the house of his PA, who was flying out to join him the next day. He would then bring it to my hotel. Howzat for the 'Smile High Club'?

We did Saks anyway and saw a $1,000 figure-hugging possibility but bought only a long-line girdle in case the dress didn't arrive and I had to wear Amy's (it was mine once, in 1983, when I didn't have a bum like a helium balloon). We then went straight on to see *Thoroughly Modern Millie* and due to shop-lag and jet-lag, we slept right through some of the finest tap dancing on Broadway.

Next morning we brunched with friends in the Village – and got back to the hotel in time to pick up an apologetic message telling me that the PA's plane had been delayed and there was no way my dress would arrive before the Tonys. I ran out to try to grab the Saks dress, only to find a massive parade had blocked all my routes. I slunk back to the hotel, covered in ticker-tape, and took out the ironing board.

Amy's dress, ironed, bore no resemblance to the dress beforehand. It fitted like a glove, i.e. it touched me in five places, four of which revealed my girdle. Furthermore it kept crawling up my bum as though my knickers were magnetised. I couldn't fathom it at all. 'It was fine before I ironed it!' I bleated. 'P'raps it's back to front,' said Amy. I tried it. Now it showed my bra and both vaccination marks. Amy gazed at me and spluttered, 'It's alright [*snigger*] – honestly – just wear a cardie.'

I had the most uncomfortable night of my life, outside childbirth. Worst of all, in all the kerfuffle I'd forgotten to ring the Jackmans. As I made it round to the stage door I was just in time to see their quadruple-tinted limo sweep past me. I felt like the Little Match Girl.

We hit the pillow at 2.00am and got up for the plane at 4.00am. Back in London I gave in to back pain and lost the will to smile. But others do when I tell them the story, so, what the heck.

Czech This Out

My feet. I've walked them off. They're pink and puffy and strangely distant. In the mornings they feel arthritic. They need oiling. Truthfully, they need kneading. I blame global warming, summer soles and the great city of Prague, where I was visiting my son and daughter-in-law who have been living there for a year. Wanting to travel with hand luggage only, I took just one spare pair of heels and my trusty espadrilles. (I did once fly to Amsterdam for the premiere of a vanished film called *Supertex*, held in a stunning Art Deco movie house. Unknowingly, I had taken one black shoe of my own, size 6, and one of my daughter's, size 4. I couldn't work out, as I hobbled up to be introduced from the stage, what had given me the fetching limp.)

Prague is a less sturdy Amsterdam crossed with a less sinister Venice. Framed by verdant hills, nothing rises above the magnificent houses save elegant spires. It is lovely. The streets are cobbled, there are towers on bridges and clocks on everything and I wanted to see it all and soak up its atmosphere. I set off on foot around squares and into museums, around the eerily preserved Jewish quarters, back to the hotel to change, then out again for dinner, in the heels. The result was a couple of burning blobs at the far ends of my legs. Most people seemed to be wearing these huge, luminous, man-made fibre creations called Crocs, in lime green and hot pink, which are reputed to be so beyond comfort they spoil you for your Blahniks. They also make you look like Shrek's mother but hey – that may be no bad thing.

I recently invested £125 in a pair of ergonomic trainers which claim to give you balance, weight loss, better posture and a brilliant sex life. (I could be lying about one of those.) I'm supposed to build up an hour a day before I can wear them all the time, but right now they're sitting boxed up in the hall waiting to be exchanged for a pair of pyjamas and a sports-bra.

In Prague, my son and I took a tram and a bus to see the zoo which is particularly human- and animal-friendly. A leisurely breakfast of fried eggs and spinach in his local café meant we arrived in the heat of the midday sun in which only mandrills and Englishmen go out. On that baking day, even the mandrills stayed indoors. Afterwards my son crashed out at his flat but his foolish mother, reluctant to drag her feet, took to the streets in search of culture and dragged them around the Art Nouveau posters of

413

Mucha, the backpack glam-clamour of the Charles Bridge and the Town Square, where she waited, breath bated, for the famous church clock to open its doors on the hour to reveal its gliding apostles. It must have been devilish impressive in the fourteenth century because it still draws a gasp from a generation brought up on *The Matrix*.

The guided tour of the Jewish quarters was two hours of heart-stopping information. In our party was a representative of an 18,000-strong Jehovah's Witness Convention. We knew so little of each other's faith, but he was sympathetic at a distance when I saw the names Rosenthalova and Lippman on the wall list of the 77,000 murder victims. He, like I, had not known that Hitler intended to preserve the synagogues and surrounding ghetto as a proud relic of an extinct species. If things had worked out differently, Mel Gibson and his Daddy would probably have a nice little earner of a film production office there.

We had our last meal at La Perla on the top of a glass and steel building called The Dancing Lady. From a certain angle it resembles Fred and Ginger in mid quick-quick-slow. I had duck liver and artichokes with red snapper to follow and I want to go back there and soon. With very small wheels fitted under my feet.

In hotels I tend to fall asleep with the television on. Only Sky was audible and intelligible in my room and I must have heard their wretched theme music and endless opinions of Jack Straw's outburst over Lebanon. When I awoke about six am it was with a half-finished verse in my head. I wrote it down, as I do with vivid dreams, knocked my sparkling water over it and went back to sleep. When I awoke I read, with difficulty:

> 'So you abhor, oh Man of Straw,
> George and Tony's stance on war.
> "Crikey, this is most unfortunate,
> Israeli strikes are disproportionate."
> Weren't you the chap who, 'ere the sack,
> Blanket-bombed most of Iraq?
> Petrified a civil nation,
> *Without* an act of provocation?
> Gung-ho geezer, Julius Caesar,
> Lenses in, for Condoleeza.
> While Blair's away in the USA
> Contenders all, come out to play . . .'

What does it take to turn off my brain in my sleep? Why would I bother? Hot milk and cinnamon . . . Temazapan . . . *The Terminator* . . . a sledge hammer . . .? I put the scrap of Czech post-it note in the bin. Fifteen minutes later, over The Healthy Breakfast, slyly tinkering, I added:

> 'Your tune's so changed – can I just check it?
> Will no one rid you of this troublesome Becket?'

An hour later my mobile rang somewhere in Mala Strana. 'Hello, it's Allegra from Newsnight.' (Oh, no, please no . . .) 'We're putting together a panel to discuss today's events in Lebanon and we wondered if . . .'

'No, no, I'm on holiday . . . I don't like the loony letters afterwards, I mean, thanks but no thanks, really – try Howard Jacobson.'

The relief when I got off the phone, unemployed, was palpable. Almost immediately it re-rang. 'Sorry, Allegra again, erm, we do have a studio in Prague if you felt like popping . . .'

'I'm sorry, too, but I've booked for a concert in the Dvorzak Hall' (it *was* Vivaldi – yeah – the *Four Seasons* and frankly I can't be doing with it since every corporation this side of Mongolia started using it to fuel BT's Christmas bonuses, but I *was* greatly looking forward to having my eyes closed and my feet up on the chair in front). Oh the relief, the sheer relief, when for once in my life I didn't shake my head and say yes. That night I dreamed of Gerard Depardieu for whom, thankfully, there is no rhyme.

Widow on the World

I'm in my Third Age, like the rest of the free cod-liver oil, orange juice and milk-in-a-crate Maybe Boomers. We are, arguably, the luckiest generation ever to over-populate and over-heat a planet. No major wars on these shores, no student loans, no uncontainable pandemics, no conscription, no authoritarianism, no whalebone corsets. We got rock'n'roll, free grants, free love, the pill, abortion on demand, an NHS which roughly worked, Feminism, Tampax, freedom in the workplace, epidurals, Touche Eclat, underwired bras, IT, Elvis, sushi, The Beatles, Biba, Botox, IVF, launderettes, M & S food and, allegedly, the G spot. What's not to be happy about? Do you hear us whinge and moan? Er – only all the time. With twenty-four-hour-a-day media coverage and the death of the press only a soft disc away, there are acres of space in which to do it. I've always considered myself to be lucky, but the feeling always came with trepidation.

'You're a successful wife, mother, actress . . . How on earth do you manage?' was the most worrying question anyone could ask me. The finger of fate loomed large.

I always knew that everybody gets their share off *tsorres* – pain – and if I didn't imbibe that with the semi-skimmed milk of Zelma then I picked it up from all those fear-based, 'St Peter at the gates of heaven' jokes. There are too many memorials these days and they are all celebrating a life when I want to mourn it. Black-bordered hankies, quivering veils and heaving shoulders, please can you make a comeback?

Above my desk are the faces of Willis Hall, Verity Lambert, Denis Quilley, Ned Sherrin, Alan Coren, Bill Cotton, Dan Crawford, Miles Kington, Nigel Hawthorne, Humphrey Lyttelton, Jonathan James Moore, Carol Shields, Dick Vosborough – just a few of those who once made me rock with laughter, face to face and on the page. Sometimes I think, in the midst of all the jazz and poetry and crackling anecdotes, that if I can't howl like a coyote in the chapel, how will I skip like a lamb into the sitting-room?

I hope I've kept up a whinge-free front. I've worked hard at it. Lines from Jack's last play come to mind. *Ready When You Are, Mr McGill* was a 2002 remake of his play of the same name written twenty-five years earlier, about a TV extra and his one-line part. It was, arguably, the precursor for Ricky Gervais's *Extras* and in its first incarnation had removed the fourth wall in the filming process. It's used for trainee directors, I'm told, by way of showing them what NOT to do:

Director: 'Mr McGill, you'd one important thing to do. And you couldn't.'
Mr McGill (*erupting, exploding*): 'That's not real life, lad! It's pretend. It's all pretend! You're pretending! The damn fool play's pretending!'
Long pause.
Director (*quietly, almost regretfully*): 'Real life is how well you pretend, isn't it, sir? You, me. Everybody in the world.'

I had been in the business of 'pretend' for forty years – with another twenty-two added on if you count (and I do) the rest of my life. The Fifties were all about 'front'. Front gardens, front rooms and, most of all, putting up a good front. I was conditioned to be on the front line.

One day, a few months after Jack's death, at Ray and Linda Cooney's summer party, I found myself telling the story of a recent experience at the Ritz hotel with two friends, Ricci and Rachel. I'd seen a tiny, bejewelled woman in her eighties wearing a pink beaded cocktail dress, platinum wig, tiara, white tights and bedroom slippers, on the arm of a six-foot-four 40-year-old with flowing magenta hair, Zapata moustache, frock coat and steel barred riding boots. As they passed by, I turned to a group of strangers and said, 'If you hadn't seen it with your own eyes, you wouldn't believe it, would you?' It was the sentence my father always muttered when anything remotely modish passed him by.

One of the men in the group nodded and smiled and added, to my amazement, 'I wouldn't have bothered you, Maureen, but since you've broken the ice, I'd just like to tell you that your Dad made my demob suit in Hull in 1945. Lasted me years.'

I didn't get to say much in reply because at that moment my two beautifully attired friends, Ricci and Rachel, were thrown out of the same bar because Ricci wasn't wearing a tie.

As I painted the picture, the table was in hysterics and, quite suddenly, I floated out of my body and saw the scene from the perspective of other guests. What would they think? Shouldn't I be more subdued? Isn't it proper to be reserved, tearful, on the edge of the conversation rather than the life and soul of it? Worse, were people thinking I was *too* OK? That maybe I wasn't even missing him? It was a short trip from there to the realisation that, like most things in life, widowhood must be coped with in your own way – as a reflection of what you *are*.

I hope I'm a shoulder for friends and colleagues, and sometimes I may be too much on hand. I have to take a quick look at the Mother Superior's Prayer:

Keep me from getting talkative, and particularly from the fatal habit of thinking I must say something on every subject and every occasion. Release me from craving to try to straighten out everybody's affairs.

But for my own grief, I just wouldn't know how to share that. It's mine and my family's and the clever aspect of coping with loss is that it lets you down slowly, drip drip drip through a series of firsts. From sheer numbness, through practical dealings, to first dinner party as spare woman to first time in a theatre when something amuses you and you turn to him to share the moment, right through to eventually truly understanding that this is not a rehearsal, it's the end of the run and there will be no future revival.

I am often invited to dinner parties with other widows, as though somehow, magically, we will have so much in common that we will bond not just for the evening but conceivably for all time. I remember how much Zelma used to complain (though not in so few words) about being a victim of bad 'placement' at various functions. 'Oh, it was a nice "do", but they always put me with *the widows* and no one asks you to dance and you feel like a pariah.'

The bereaved meet with the same social awkwardness, feelings of inadequacy and inarticulateness as the terminally ill or anyone in trouble with the law. People don't know what to say so they say nothing.

'Oh, you know so and so,' say friends of a close chum of mine who suffered a prison sentence. 'I've been meaning to get in touch with him for ages . . . how is he?'

'Ring him up and ask him,' is my terse reply.

'Oh, I know, but it's so difficult . . . after all this time . . . I don't know what to say.'

'Say hello! Say how are you? Say how did you cope? Or just say . . . can I bring round a pie?'

I'm aware more and more that we are victims of manners.

Shortly after Jack's death I was at a dinner party where a widower had been invited to make even numbers. His first words to me were: 'You can answer a question for me. It's always bothered me. Now, your late husband wrote *The Evacuees*, am I right?' He knew he was right so I just nodded and he continued, 'Now, I was evacuated at the same time – also from a Jewish School – only from the East End – but it wasn't like that.'

'Pardon?'

'It didn't happen like that.'

'I'm sorry?'

'The scene where the teacher schlepps the kids from house to house – that scene where the boys were following the teacher in a crocodile, and people were rejecting them in all the houses, now I'm sorry, but that never happened.'

I took my time because the temptation to take hold of his nose and push it roughly into the hot bean and barley soup was overwhelming.

'You mean it never happened to *you*?'

He got louder and higher in pitch. 'It never happened to anyone! The Jewish boards had it all worked out – you were billeted! You knew which house you were going to and you went. My brother and I stayed with a very nice couple – not Jewish – but very nice people nonetheless, and we stayed in touch with them for years.'

I smiled tightly. 'What a great story,' I said. 'What a truly great and riveting story. And with a happy end as well. How come you didn't write it?'

It was his turn to look perplexed. 'How do you mean?'

'I mean, what stopped you from turning your nice experience into an Emmy award-winning film?'

'No . . . but I'm just telling you how it was, right?'

'Well, it's not how it was for Jack, RIGHT? Which is why he wrote it the way you saw it, right? 'Cos it happened. To him . . .' and choking with misplaced emotion, I over reacted myself out of the room and out of the house.

No one teaches us how to rear a child or lose a loved one or visit the sick and dying or fall foul of the law or deal with failure or even how to be the 'extra woman'. Sadly it's down to hard experience. How we deal with disaster is a reflection of who we are. Empathy, though, is teachable and it is empathy which is required in these situations. The ability to say, how would I feel if that were me? What would I want? That's all. And if what you say or do is wrong – is it so terrible to say, 'Sorry. I didn't know how to put it and it came out wrong?'

In the valiant or self-pitying or daring or despairing women – and, on rarer occasions, men I meet – I see my own behaviour as though through a prism. There is an episode of *Curb Your Enthusiasm* in which Larry David is impossibly rude about one of his wife's friends whom he calls The Widow. When we meet her, she is in a state of tension, only relieved by the mention of her late husband's name or the out-flowing of tears. She is a self-proclaimed icon of stoicism. It is very funny, but like all David's scripts, it is a harsh assessment of what 'we' do. A brave smile, a lowering of the eyes whilst simultaneously raising the eyebrows, a self-deprecating story or two about coping, and above all a glorification of the deceased, all are evidence of role-playing at worst and attention-seeking at best. I'm aware that I've elevated Jack to a sainthood which he would have hated and that the true story of our 'perfect' marriage is, like all truth and most stories, subjective.

The truth is that I was an ambitious child when I married at twenty-six, and with the passing of Zelma and Jack I finally grew up. Not a lot, but a bit. One of the hardest tasks in the aftermath was to finish his autobiography. The title was *By Jack Rosenthal* – as printed on the covers of all of his 250 screen plays – which was confusing enough, but it also had an unusual format. The autobiography was written as a screenplay, in which Jack was the central character, and it included scenes from his many plays whenever his fiction touched on his real life. After writing six decades of his life in this way, he gave up, saying, 'No one will want to read this.' For once, he was wrong.

'He worked on it feverishly throughout his illness,' Amy wrote in her Foreword to *By Jack Rosenthal*.

'In his first phase of high-dose chemotherapy at the Royal Marsden Hospital, he contracted pneumonia and was moved to the High Risk ward. He was desperately weak and breathless. As we stood at his bedside in the plastic aprons that we had to wear to protect him from infection, he asked me if I had a pen and paper. I did, and he removed his oxygen mask to dictate a passage of prose which you can find verbatim in the book. Later, he described a recurrent nightmare from that time in the Marsden. It was of writing; tiny spidery writing, going on and on, always picking up where it left off, never ending.

'I tell you this to explain that my dad was a consummate writer, a writer to his core; and yet he wrote totally without fanfare, without show. And his writing life was so finely integrated into his *family* life that it took us all a long time to appreciate what he was doing when he sat in his study, deep in thought yet ever poised to leap up and make someone a cuppa, a sandwich or a three-course meal. It is only now, scanning his astounding list of credits, that we see how prolific was his quiet alchemy; with what dedication he spent his time spinning life into stories, spinning stories into glorious life.

'And so it is the kitchen, not his study, where I miss him most. Always conscious of his own impoverished childhood, he took great pleasure in feeding people, especially his family. When we had a Chinese takeaway, he presided over the table like an anxious, loving bird, and although we were more than capable of making our own duck pancakes, he always insisted on making them for us, spreading the "glue" (plum sauce) evenly across the thin rice pancake, adorning it with meat and a sprinkling of spring onions and cucumber, and rolling it up as delicately as if it were a Torah scroll.

'What he didn't realise, as he beamed at the prospect of gluing together another duck pancake for someone who didn't need one, is that he *was* the glue. His sweetness held us together; without him we will have to try harder, we will have to learn patience and care.

'During his all-too-brief remission he kept working on the book, but at the end of 2003, when his illness returned with renewed ferocity and my wonderful grandmother died suddenly of a heart attack, he too lost heart. Perhaps he'd had enough of being haunted by spidery handwriting. Perhaps after over forty years and more than 150 screenplays, in an industry changed beyond recognition from the joyful early days to today's TV drama wasteland where star-billing dictates story and "cutting edge" has the edge on truth, he was ready to lay down his Biro.

'A short time before he died, my mum and I and our great friend Colin Shindler took him out in his wheelchair on Hampstead Heath. He was frail, bundled up in his herringbone coat, a rakish navy-blue sailor's cap protecting what was left of his soft black hair. It was a bright May day and the Heath was thronged with families, children, couples, cyclists, dogs. As I wheeled my dad along the path, he suddenly said:

"This is *wonderful*, you know. All these people. It's the most wonderful thing."

I looked at the people weaving around us.

"You mean, all the different lives . . .?" I asked.

He shook his head, half-smiling, a bit frustrated.

"I can't explain," he said.

'And I believe that he could see something we couldn't. That he had crossed a line, and maybe he could see for real what, as a writer, he had always known was there. A goodness and humanity in people, in spite of ourselves, a fundamental decency that might not be "cutting edge", but which ultimately most of us share. His warm, wry affection for humankind shone through his work, it shone through his life, and as I write these words, it gives me what he always gave me. Hope.'

For me, who'd never written dialogue before, trying to write as he did felt like walking on broken glass:

INT MUSWELL HILL HOUSE – MID-AFTERNOON – AUGUST 2004

Outside the sun shines.

The woman, Maureen, tall, bespectacled, long-necked, chunky-hipped, is standing up from her armchair, tears cursing down her cheeks, fist raised.

MAUREEN
(*shouting*)
Yes!

She is alone in front of the TV. It's 21 August 2004 and the coxless four have just won their gold medal at the Olympics. Maureen couldn't care less about rowing, coxless or – er – coxed, but she is caught up in a rare moment of national pride and empathy with Matthew Pinsett's even rarer moment of tired emotionalism.

It is seven weeks and four days since her husband, Jack Rosenthal, died in the North London Hospice after a two-year battle against multiple myeloma.

MAUREEN
Stoppit. Just stoppit. You've to toughen up. You can't spend the rest of your life crying. You've got to get on.

She makes a funny inward squeak in her throat. She's been doing this a lot lately. It's like a bird asking for food. A phone rings. She answers it.

MAUREEN
Hello. Oh, hi Elaine. Really? It was, wasn't it? It was lovely having both of you. No, actually. It wasn't that hard. I've just finished clearing up and I'm going to start on Jack's book. I know. I keep on talking about it and not doing it and the publisher rang first thing. He just wants me to try to touch on the last decade, you know, the one Jack didn't get to . . . well, he sort of ran out of steam really. I don't know, it could have been the illness – but, I mean, he wrote frantically right through the first year – right through the chemo and the stem-cell transplant. When? Oh God, I think . . . I can't remember when he stopped. Or why. He just sort of lost confidence in it . . . I know, I know. Anyway, listen, I'd best get on. Thanks again for the dessert . . . no, it was a huge pleasure. Talk soon, bye.

She goes back into the kitchen, wipes the surface with a medicated wipe and unstacks the dishwasher of last night's pots. She catches sight of herself in a silver placemat.

MAUREEN (VO)
I look fine. This is a good haircut. Manageable. I don't look old. Fat though. Comfort eating. I should go to the gym each day. I hate it though. The gym is hell; set faces, ugly music. I'll have to go, though. You'd want me to, wouldn't you, darl?

She finishes off last night's aubergine crisps. The phone rings. She hesitates. The machine will answer it. She should pick up Jack's manuscript and get

on with it . . . Endless procrastination. She gives in and answers the phone.
MAUREEN
Hello. Oh, hi love. Yes, it was, wasn't it? Thank you. No, thank *you*.
No, I've nearly got it all cleared away.
Her voice faces out and we pull back to watch her putting the dishes away,
the phone still wedged to her ear.
MAUREEN (VO)
Jack would have unloaded the dishwasher and had the kitchen
shipshape three hours ago. I'd have come down at 10.30 in the
morning, bleary, and he'd have said 'Alright, love. I've made a start
at it. I know it doesn't look like it, but I've shifted a helluva lot.
This is the second load.'

MAUREEN
Yeah, I've got to make a start on Jack's book . . . it's really weighing
on me that I haven't . . .

MAUREEN (VO)
He loved it when we entertained – never much wanted to go out.
'Jack's idea of a good night out is staying in' was my staple phrase.
If I'd depended on him for our social life we'd never have left the
front porch. But he was such good value when we got there. Such
a wonderfully lively guest. Deadpan comments, self-deprecating
stories – I'd interrupt because I'd remember them differently and
wanted them built-up in the way I first heard them. He never
minded my contradictions, like some husbands do – no face-
darkening, wait-till-we-get-home glowering; he was proud of my
vivacity. We were a good couple.

FLASHBACK TO:

INT JACK'S CAR – NIGHT – ANY OLD YEAR
Jack and Maureen are driving home from a party.
JACK
You were on fantastic form tonight.
MAUREEN
Me? What about you?
JACK
Not like you. You lighten the room up. I love it when you do that
'Professor of Logic' joke.
MAUREEN
You don't! Even when you've heard it so many times?
JACK

It doesn't matter. I just love it. Give me your glasses love.
> (*He beams at her*)

I don't know how you can see a thing through them.

At the traffic lights, he takes her rimless specs, breathes on them heavily, buffs the lenses with his pocket hanky and hands them back. It's as natural as changing gear. If he doesn't do it, they stay dirty.

MAUREEN (VO)

The thing is, I don't think I believe he's gone. It's just a part I'm playing. The play will end its run soon.
> (*beat*)

I was good in it. Everyone said so.

Only one section wrote itself. I was trying to describe Jack's patience with his ingenuous mother-in-law:

INT KITCHEN – MUSWELL HILL – DAY – ANY YEAR BETWEEN 1973 AND 2003
Jack is doing letters at table. Zelma, wearing kitchen overalls, pops head round door.

ZELMA

I'm going to make myself that cheese on toast that *you* make. I just fancy some.

JACK
> (*looking up from his work*)

Do you want me to do it for you, Zel?

ZELMA

Nooo. I can do it.

Crash, bang, doors open and close.

Do you want some?

JACK

No thanks, love.

ZELMA

Do you use this grill pan or the one with the grooves in it?

JACK

The one that's in the grill. The grill pan.

ZELMA

Oh, I thought so.
> (*beat*)

Do you use the cheddar cheese or this one in the Tupperware . . .?

JACK

Do you want me to do it, Zel, 'cos . . .?

ZELMA

Nooo. I've told you. I just wanted to know which chee . . .
> JACK

The cheddar. The cheddar.
> ZELMA

One slice or . . .?
> JACK

One. Two. How ever many you w . . .
> ZELMA

I always use the processed at home. That's why I'm asking . . .
She cuts a slice of bread then stands by the butter dish for a very long time.
> JACK

What is it, Zel? Do you want to know if I put butter on first?
> ZELMA

Er – yes, well no, I can't remember – you do, don't you? Or don't you?
> JACK

Zel. Go. And sit down. In front of Richard and Judy. And let me make the cheese on ruddy toast.
> ZELMA

Why? I'm doing it! I only wondered if . . .
Jack gets out of chair, slowly, still looking at his notes.
No . . . you get on. Honestly.
She goes to put the bread under the grill then stands before the admittedly confusing cooker buttons. Pushes one in – it pops out of its socket – she tries to get it back – fiddles about, clicking things until:
I'll swing for this blooming cooker . . .
> JACK

Right. That's it. SIT BLOODY DOWN!
She sits, looking astonished at his attitude. Four minutes alter he presents her with a plate of piping hot ('Oooh, I love food when it burns your mouth!') cheese on toast, two slices, finely sliced tomato, HP Sauce, a cup of tea you could stand a spoon up in – with saucer, utensils and napkin.
> JACK

Nah! Done! Eat!
> ZELMA
> *(rhetorically, with a dewy-eyed look at anyone who'll listen)*

Aaaah! In't he marvellous? I say . . . aah – thank you, you're the best son-in-law anyone ever . . .
The food goes in at a fantastic rate.
Ooh – do you know? – this is fantastic. Ooh – this is my favourite meal. I say. Do you think I could make this in my flat in Hull?
> *(beat)*

425

How did you do it? Just toast? And cheese? Did you just put the cheese straight on the toast? And then what? You put it under the grill – what numero? – Oh, you don't have numeros, do you? 8 or 9? Was it? Oooh, it's just fabulous. The more you have, the more you want. Mmmm.

JACK

(wiping surfaces and cleaning grill pan)

Do you want more?'

ZELMA

More? Me?

Her tone implies was the question would she like to have her head split open with a scythe?

No! I'm full up to bursting. I couldn't eat another thing. Thank you anyway. But no. I couldn't.

Pause, whilst he replaces grill pan and stacks dishwasher.

Why? 'Ave you got more cheese you want rid of? I don't mind if you have. Just one slice though.

(beat)

And a tomato.

Finally, I had to admit defeat and finish the last decade in the only way I could properly express myself: in prose.

Jack's burst of melancholy, after the kids left home, had been easily, if superficially, cleared up. His generation was not one to talk about feelings. He was a 'pull yourself together and get on' sort of chap and it alarmed him when he couldn't do it. It took months of wearing his heaviness lightly for him to come to the realisation that a series of physical symptoms were all related.

He was often incredibly hot. 'Dod's lost his thermostat,' I used to say to the kids when he turned the heating off or threw the bed covers off in the night. He would frequently escape into the street during evenings in restaurants, confounded by the noise and heat. He had skin-rashes and complained that his spectacles no longer corrected his vision. He'd given up smoking twelve years ago, before his first hip operation, in favour of the odd small cigar, but the odd small cigar escalated into an odd small cigar smoking habit. On more than one occasion I caught him skulking by the garage doors with the dog-end of a fag scrunched up painfully in a smouldering hand. He became more set in his ways, his lack of desire to go out became more of a compulsion and his endearing pedantry became more insistent.

I suppose it lasted, in total, about six months and he never, never complained or blamed anyone or anything. Stoically he just stuck it out until it passed.

Had it been me, I would have seen a counsellor, changed my diet, had my feet reflexologised and my chakras checked. Mostly, though, I'd have wept on all my girlfriends and felt unbearably sorry for myself. Come to think of it, that would probably have taken about six months, too, so who's to say whose method was the right one? Horses, of course, for courses.

He handled the multiple myeloma in the same way. 'Tell me what I have to do, I'll do it and I'll get better.' Without bothering anyone. With hindsight, I now realise that the rashes and the over-heating were probably symptoms of the oncoming disease. When the first bone pains in his back started, in 2002, it was diagnosed as arthritis, but it was so excruciating that we were referred to a consultant at University College Hospital and the diagnosis revealed two plasmacytomas on his spine.

Multiple myeloma is a helluva difficult thing to diagnose. It presents itself in so many different ways. In a short film we've recently made for Myeloma UK, the patients filmed had symptoms as differing as wobbly legs, boils, rashes, severe back pain or failure of one or more organs. Jack's plasmacytomas were manifestations of bone marrow cancer on the spine itself, containable through radiotherapy. He had indolent myeloma, the kind that simmers but may not ignite.

In April 2002 he had six radiotherapy sessions, bone-growth hormones and a course of chemotherapy tablets. We believed the treatment had worked. When the pain in his ribs exacerbated we were sent to a rheumatism expert in a north London clinic. She examined him and said he clearly wasn't getting enough exercise. How about enrolling in a gym? Eighty pounds and close the door when you're leaving, please.

There was no treatment. It smouldered. You waited. It could lie dormant for years. He was prescribed morphine patches for the pain and in May we packed, somehow without irritation, for a cruise around the Mediterranean called, rather alarmingly, 'Theatre at Sea'.

It was a group of actors, English and American, among whom were Millicent Martin and the now late, always great, Jerry Orbach (of *LA Law*), Dick Cavett, Patricia Neal and Gena Rowlands. Each of us, along with singers and dancers, were expected to give one night's performance. Spouses were expected to lap up the sun and sparkle over dinner. Over far too much food, fruit machine fixation and high tea on a low deck (where Patricia Neal told her entire life story before daily bingo), we grew to love each other. Jack became healthier than he'd been for months and the passengers, who'd viewed us as father and daughter when first we boarded, were clamouring to sit with him at breakfast and swapping addresses.

Jack boarded that ship a stooped, frail, pallid man and he came off not just rejuvenated but the person everyone wanted to sit next to at breakfast, brunch *and* dinner. When we disembarked we had new friends, new skin tone and a spring in both our steps. Jack went back to a full twelve-hour day on *Ready When You Are Mr McGill* mark II. In at dawn, first at the catering van, last to leave the editing suite at dusk. Sorted.

In the autumn he relapsed. Suddenly it turned into galloping multiple myeloma and it galloped fast. We had changed consultants from University College Hospital to the far-distant Marsden Cancer Hospital in Sutton and we started the weekly trips round the North Circular Road for his first sessions of chemotherapy. It was New Year's Day when we went to the Marsden for a consultation with Professor Powles, a world authority on myeloma. He told Jack that he wanted to start three days of C-VAMP chemo, not just as soon as, but sooner than possible. We'd packed a small overnight bag, but Jack was adamant that he was coming home first. On the way to the car park he stopped, turned round and said 'Come on, let's get the bugger over with'.

He reacted well under the intravenous chemotherapy aegis. Some nurses could find veins in one go, some couldn't find them with X-ray vision. Because they discovered a blood clot on his chest, probably a result of the radiotherapy, he was unable to have a Hickman line inserted, which would have saved him the dread of finding a new vein each time. The hair left behind on the pillow, he lived with. The weakness we fought with fresh vegetable juices, fresh organic food, vitamins, filtered water – we were told, no bottled water – too many bacteria, and no salads. Soft toothbrush and everything double washed with an antibacterial agent. Fine. Let's go.

Colin Shindler was amazing in his absolute devotion to Jack and in the hours he devoted to waiting with us and sharing the prognoses. Adam and I, and sometimes Colin's cousin Ian, shared the driving and we all grew used to the staff, the routine and the other patients, and they to us.

Once home, Jacko rested and slept, took on a frightening regime of seventeen pills a day and gave himself daily Fragmin injections to thin his blood. The days hurried by, as the song says, to a precious few, and it was time to face the worst. High-dose chemotherapy and stem-cell treatment – dangerous at any age but at 71 a gamble. Still, he was Dod, we reasoned, he looked such a youngster, he always had. Besides, the only choice we had was Hobson's. He went in the day after leading the Passover night service in our dining-room with a table full of loved friends around him. 'Why is this night different from all other nights?' was, as it has been for thousands of years, the first question.

He would be in isolation for three weeks. The stem cells would be harvested, cleaned, then fed back into his blood after the high-dose chemo had killed the cancerous cells. That was the plan.

As the high-dose chemo suppressed his immune system, the infections set in. There is no praise high enough for the doctors and nurses in the Royal Marsden's wards and in their Intensive Care Unit. It's the caterers I reserve my distaste for – and of course it's not their fault. They're simply obeying orders. There has to be a point, though, where the vastly expensive drug-therapy and the vastly demanding human resources are backed up by vastly good sodding vegetables. And soups. And protein. All of the highest quality. Next stop Jamie Oliver. If he can do school dinners on a shoestring he should tackle hospitals. It's life and death we're talking here and I've never been more in the presence of both than in that terrible, wonderful week. The sickness, the sound of his laboured breathing, the diarrhoea and the hallucinations were terrible. One long night of the soul, he told us he couldn't take Saddam Hussein's children on the school run the next day. We sponged his brow and wet his parched lips with tiny sponges and told him it was OK, not to worry, one of the other mums would do it. What was wonderful, though, in spite of everything, was the dedication, the overwhelming love and the fact that he lived through it.

To complicate matters, Jack had never told us that he had emphysema. He must have known for ages, but he told us he had something called 'airways disease'. Did he make it up? It sounds like something a writer would invent, not a physician. All the 'puffing Billy' jokes we made, and he never told us the truth. 'Breathe from your diaphragm, darl, not your chest,' I'd tell him from the high realms of my Academy of Dramatic Art training. 'Don't hold onto your breath when you're in the swimming pool, darl – relax into the water.' Well, he couldn't. But he never told us why, so we shouldn't worry. Now, every breath was a struggle and he would have to nebulise through a machine for the rest of his days. It didn't help in the struggle to fight the real villain. Multiple myeloma.

At this point he hadn't eaten for days and everything ran straight through him. We tried to tempt him with build-up drinks but he was having none of it. He couldn't taste anything. Then one night he called out in a surprisingly 'doing us a favour' tone, 'I'll tell you what I'll have.' We all snapped to attention and flexed our fetching muscles. 'I'll have a shandy.'

It was pointed out to him as gently as possible that bowel infections, antibiotics, antiviral pills and steroids probably didn't work with a beer chaser. The craving for beer didn't stop once he was home either. It seemed very out of character. He'd never wanted a beer in the 35 years I'd known him, unless it was the Grand National on a warm day or we'd just shot out of Cork airport in the direction of Skibbereen.

In September 2003, my lad came back from the wars. He was fragile, with that strange, hollow, hospitalised pallor that follows tasteless food, airless rooms and invasion of all your privacies. But we had him back. It had all been worth it, it seemed, and he could be in remission from myeloma for two to five years. His hat was absurdly large and his belts needed new holes. Every step was an effort and every mouthful a major decision. He was pill popping like a rock star and stuff had to be swabbed and injected at all hours. I had to fatten him up, hold him close and wage war on bacteria. The house was industrially clean and became a repository for medicated wipes, zimmer frames, oxygen cylinders, and the odd commode. Jack was exhausted but he was in there somewhere, my heroic boy, dazed and shell-shocked, but he was home and essentially still Jack the Lad.

'When I get home,' he'd whispered, pulling his breathing mask aside at 1.30am in the gloom of Intensive Care, 'I'm going to change a few things.'

I pondered whether, 'I'm going to change a few things' meant I'd wake up one morning next to a fledgling Ricky Tomlinson, sweating and belching on his way down to the Wassailler's Arms to get rat-arsed. 'Where's my piggin' dinner, woman?' he'd bellow as he lurched through the door, 'and get your arse moving 'cos I want me conjugals straight after me rhubarb!' Hmm. Oh, well, 'for better or worse' it said, didn't it? 'Oh, yes, love,' I replied, all scrubbed up and protective-plastic-aproned, from my slumped position at the end of the bed. 'That's nice . . . in what way?'

'Well . . .' Long pause.

'Well . . . I'm going to be smarter for one thing.'

I waited. 'I mean,' he continued, painfully, because his breathing was shallow. 'I mean . . . I'm not going to wear the same shirt for two days running to save on laundry. Bugger that for a lark, eh?'

It wasn't the world's most vaunting ambition. In fact it was so achievable that it made me weep.

'. . . and there's more,' he breathed.

'I know, darling, but perhaps you shouldn't be talking.'

'I'm going to have a mohair suit made. At a proper tailor's.' He lay back and contemplated the wildness of his ways.

'Have six.' I sniffed.

I'd made the house lovely for him. I'd cleared every surface of every 'chatchka' (nick-nack) just as he'd always wanted. Plants were gone, vases were gone, so were ornaments, anthropomorphic objects, Indian stress balls and month-old messages and magazines, and I'd redone the living-room. So when my beloved limped into his sitting-room, it looked wider, greener, comfier and not unlike the furniture of his youth, and there in the corner was a wide-screen television with all the channels Mr Murdoch has to offer. Sometimes you have to sup with the devil you know. Yer man Jack was very happy. His hair and his strength began to come back.

It still wasn't enough. Three months later – three lousy, fucking months later – the remission was over. His blood counts were wrong and we were into the next course of preventative treatment. Thalidomide ('But what will happen to Dod's *arms?*' said Amy). When that failed to stop the infections, we progressed to Velcade, the new wonder drug. It was all too much, too late. Help at home was a nightmare, with no downstairs bathroom and nurses turning up, or not, as the feeling took them.

With the next infection we arranged to take him not to his tried and trusted Parkside, but for ease and convenience to a nearby NHS hospital; good intentions, major mistake. No one knew him, he was just an old man in a bed. Yes, we could visit him three times a day and bring him the food he needed, but there was no individual attention – how could there be? Worse, more fatally, there was no love. None. After they misread all the painstakingly prepared lists of medication I had gone through with the staff, the shift changed and they gave him twice the bowel medicine prescribed, with inevitable results. 'She's not very nice, this one,' he whispered to me, as an officious nurse swept in. 'She's got a very funny attitude.'

I'm afraid I lost it. For the first time, I did. Irrationally, I wanted to kill her there and then . . . on the ward. '*Do you have any idea who this man is?*' I yelled. '*This man is probably – no, not probably – IS, the finest – the most distinguished – y-you will ever meet in all your – years of nursing.*' I was wailing now like a coyote. '*You will n-never, never nurse a better patient . . . or a more wonderful human being! Don't ever, ever, dare to b-be anything other than sweet and courteous to this man. You . . . you should be privileged to – p-p-privileged . . .*' Jack comforting *me* now instead of the other way round. '*Just GO!*' I cried, helplessly out of control now. '*Just bloody GO! And bring me everything I need to make him clean and make him comfy! Go! Do it! Just Go! NOW!*' She went.

The following day we made the decision to take him to the North London Hospice to be made whole again. I'd been doing charity work for them for years and found it the least threatening or doom-laden place in the world. I once witnessed a dear friend's life extend for another year there when he'd practically been given up for dead. We got Jack out of the hospital and into the hospice. I knew it was a place for the living.

He was taken into the warm bosom of the most altruistic people in the land. His room looked out into a pretty courtyard and we stayed with him most of the time. We brought him out of the hospice for Friday-night dinner at home, for trips to the park or to the hospital for blood transfusions and for the Cup Final triumph of Manchester United over valiant little Millwall. '*YES! – The Lads.*' He was surrounded by our most loved friends on Saturday afternoon, all perched on the edge of our new green suite. Man U: 2 – Millwall: Eau de nil.

We experienced first-hand the trials of pushing a man in a wheelchair up and down kerbs that were built for the quick and the able. We watched kids play in the park and saw Denis Potter's blossomest of blossoms from the same viewpoint. We read, we laughed, we stroked and cherished. We said most of what needed to be said. On 28 May, Amy and I slept in an empty bed in an adjacent room and Adam and his fiancée Taina slept, twined around each other, on the window seat in Jack's room. On the morning of 29 May, Colin, Lizzy, Jenny and my cousin Maurice arrived to sit with him as he drifted in and out of sleep.

I had in my wisdom, or not, depending how you view these things, arranged for a healer, Peter, to travel up from Devon to give him some hands-on healing. Five minutes before he arrived at Woodside Park station, Jack sat up, looked at something amazing over all our heads and took his last breath.

When Peter arrived he stood at the door of Jack's room and raised both his hands. 'Ah, he's gone,' he said softly, then he put his hands on those of us who wanted it, then Adam drove him back to the station.

A few days later he rang me. 'It's only happened to me once before,' he said. 'It was a privilege. I saw Jack's soul leave his body. It was surrounded by his guardian angels.' It was a long time before I spoke: 'What did it look like?' I asked him.

'It was golden,' he told me, 'and his angels were blue flames, gathered around it as it rose.' I remembered the first present Jack had ever bought me. It was Blake's *Songs of Innocence and Experience*, with those beautiful illuminated illustrations. A good man, a man to whom good came easily.

A few days before, Colin Shindler had decided to go in to see Jack in the Hospice. He wanted to tell him that he loved him. He told me he was going to do this and I wondered how Jack would react to such a declaration. Afterwards I asked Jack what had happened.

'Colin came in today.'

'I know, love, how was he?'

'Fine. He told me that he loved me.'

'That's nice, darl. What did you say to him?'

'I didn't say anything, really,' said Jack. (*Beat*) 'We had sex and he went home.'

Blessed Beef

This is a story of God and Mammon. Or it may be a story of Mad Gammon. The only reason I'm committing it to hard disc is because it does seem to be a perfect morality story.

It began on the Monday of an even madder-than-most week. Sunday had been my late husband Jack's memorial stone setting a year after his death, and the following Thursday was to be the launch of his auto-biography, *By Jack Rosenthal*, with all the press and public fanfare which that involved. I was emotionally on a taut wire, taking each event as it came with the help of deep breaths and single malt. In between, the book and I had to appear on *Richard and Judy*, travel to Hull, compère some literary events and, more urgently, purchase a dress for my son's wedding.

At eleven, I read the emails. There were two requests from different publications. The first was from Pimms, the people who bring you the drinks which feature umbrellas and cucumbers, offering me £1000 to contribute to a book on barbecues. Since what I know about barbecues could be written on a thumb stall, I passed on to the second request.

The Meat Marketing Board, was offering me – and here my retinas went dry and I had to put my glasses on my head – £5000 (aaaaaargh!) to write a poem of 250 words in praise of meat, to be written in the manner of Robbie Burns's 'Address to a Haggis' and delivered in six days' time for publication. I stared out of the window. The clematis was in bud, a hollyhock had pushed its way through the concrete, a squirrel had freeze-framed on the lawn . . . and the Meat Marketing Board wanted a poem about *beef*. It seemed only natural that their collective mind had turned to me.

What you won't know is that my métier comes in metres. It's what I do when I'm at my lowest. When Jack was hospitalised, I drove the fifty-mile round trip and got myself to sleep back home by composing ludicrous animal poems – dozens of stanzas of nonsense, for a year, until I accepted the inevitable. Then I never again wrote the likes of

> The Lemur Cub was crying.
> 'Why so sad?' I asked her.
> 'I'm a homesick Lemur
> With a broken femur
> And me Mum's in Madagascar.'

433

This led to 54 anthropomorphic verses, published in 2006 by Robson Books under the title, *The Gibbon's in Decline but the Horse is Stable*, all the proceeds of which went to Myeloma UK. Great cartoonists like Mac and Posy Simmonds and Gerald Scarfe illustrated it free and gratis and after that I never composed another stanza. My favourites included:

> My Parrot loved Miss Hepburn,
> Saw all her films twice nightly.
> Found all her epiphanies in *Breakfast at Tiffany's*
> And called herself Polly Golightly.

And:

> 'Take that!' cried the Dodo.
> The scientist just blinked.
> 'Here in Mauritius it isn't propitious
> To call a girl extinct.'

And:

> 'I want to sing Otello'
> Said a classical flamingo.
> 'Haven't you heard.
> You're a fat pink bird
> Not Placido Domingo?'

Or even:

> The Elephant had a make-over.
> The stylist made her punk.
> A pachyderm with a crappy perm
> Singing 'I was born in a trunk'.

Why animal poems? Why cartoons? All I can tell you is that it helped me through a terrible patch and occupied my fevered mind. After Jack died poetry was all I could read, Dannie Abse's breath-taking book of prose and poetry, *The Presence*, written after the tragic death of Joan, his wife of fifty years, was the most comforting of all.

I can't explain it. It's just that the poem, is all-consuming. So now I'm pushing it away because I need it like a hole in a mint and . . . well, on the other hand, mightn't it be interesting just to see 'Address to a Haggis'? Not that I . . . By now I'm on the Internet reading the Burns poem and it's as incomprehensible to me as it probably is to most Scots, let alone a Sassenach with a full diary and a religious problem with offal.

The rhyme scheme is new to me: A,A,A,B,A,B, as in

Fair fa' your honest, sonsie face,
Great chieftain o' the puddin'-race!
Aboon them a' ye tak your place,
Painch, tripe, or thairm:
Weel are ye wordy o' a grace
As lang's my arm.

'Absurd,' I tell myself, and go back to my speech for the book launch. But my brain is dancing. *Beef/relief, boeuf/surf/turf, sirloin/purloin* . . . Will you stop it! And, to divert myself from the beef poem and put off going back to the speech, toss off the 850 words for the barbecue article and send it off. Flippantly I write that, like coffee and bread, the smell is the best thing about 'barbies' and confess that the fancy grill with a lid I bought now has wallflowers growing in it and that my friend Trevor Grove is the only person I know who makes barbecues taste better than what comes out of even an *inferior oven*, and he probably buys his meat in Argentina.

That afternoon my friend Eve Pearce comes round and I tell her my big meat news. She reads the Robbie Burns in her Aberdeen accent with such ferocity that I'm crying with laughter and begging for more. *Now* I understand the sense. Over the next few days – and nights – I torture myself with puns and rhymes and emerge with the requisite eight stanzas. At dinner I tentatively try it on the family, who groan in all the right places. I leave it, and the dinner, on simmer.

The next day I meet my friend Julia in Bond Street, and we hit the Son's wedding dress shops, into which I never venture. McKenzie likes nothing better than watching me spend 'Armani' and a leg on clothes. In Browns she achieves nirvana when I happen upon a rack of separates by an American designer called Zoran, which adore me. I struggle between a yellow trouser suit and a silk three-piece in olive green. I put the green on my body and all three of us are ecstatic. Only problem is the price – over a thousand pounds! More than I've ever spent on anything that I couldn't drive or live in. McKenzie is outraged by my recalcitrance.

'For heaven's sake, girl, it's your son's wedding!' she cries. 'You work like a horse, you've had a terrible year, you deserve it.' My face registered some doubt. 'And you've just earned six grand, for nothing, sitting on your bum!' she added triumphantly.

She was right. I stalked over to the counter, jaw thrust out, and heard someone who I now know was me, say, 'How much would you charge me if I took two?'

Reader, I must inform you that two is what I took. Three thousand English pounds changed hands before you could say chump chop.

Back home I tweaked the poem a little and rang the agent. 'I've done them,' I bragged, 'the beef verses.'

'Oh,' said the agent.

'What do you mean, "Oh"?' I asked nervously.

'Er, they never confirmed.' She did at least have the grace to sound sheepish.

It seemed after further enquiries that the Meat People had put the poem 'out to tender' – if you'll pardon the pun. Probably to Andrew Motion himself, not to mention Pam Ayres, Wendy Cope and probably, for all I know, Jordan. Oh, and the winner, of course: Brian Blessed. For he it was apparently who got his steak stanzas published and copped the five biggies to prove it. Sadly, I never saw his loins – sorry, lines – but I bet they were beefy!

So, I'm just the three grand down – well, two if you add the barbecue money. I reassured myself as the phone rang. It was the agent. 'The Pimms People don't like your barbecue piece. Apparently it's too negative.'

Still, at least I have the two outfits. I wear one of them, the yellow jacket, trousers and camisole on the night of the book launch. It is hugely admired, I feel great and, for once, never think about the expense. Julia's right, you pay for quality. The book sells well. It's a lovely evening.

A week later a friend rings me. 'Have you seen the pictures of your launch in *Hello!* mag?' he asks.

'Nooo, I haven't,' I say, 'are they good?'

'Mmmmmm,' he replies, on a downward inflection.

At the newsagent, I skim through pages of doctored minor royals and enhanced soap stars. On page 37 I found Joanna Lumley looking gorgeous. As did Bill Nighy, Michael Palin, and Lord and Lady Puttnam. There was, however, a strange, heavily pregnant yellow gnome in the midst of the guests, who on closer examination turned out to be me. The combination of shimmery silk and a photographer's flash had turned my middle-aged spread into a custard filled balloon.

I'm not going out any more. Mutton dressed up as beef – not me.

Et maintenant, une bouchée de viande:

> Beef on the barbecue, beef in a roll,
> Surely tastes better than toad in a hole,
> Or spicy fajitas with lime guacamole.
> Besides, it's ancestral –
> Our foremothers knew it was good for the soul
> And low in cholesterol.

Piano Piece

This year – 2008 – Aung Sang Suu Kyi, the sixty-three-year-old leader of the National Democratic League of Burma is in her thirteenth year of house arrest, in a crumbling house partly destroyed by the terrifying cyclone which devastated much of Myanmar, the former Burma. She is refused access to her doctor, her followers and even a radio or telephone. Her piano, her solace, has fallen into disrepair through humidity and she is denied even a piano tuner.

At the 2007 Women of the Year Lunch, Joyce Hytner, a prominent voice in the arts and mother of Nicholas, the Director of the National Theatre, told me about the piano. I asked our president, Joan Armatrading, if we could announce this to the influential women present at the lunch and perhaps, by the dessert, we would be able to fund a new piano for the Lady, so that once more her followers could stand in University Avenue, listen to her playing and know that she was alright. Joan felt it was perhaps not the right moment for the idea and might detract from the amazing women of courage and inspiration we were honouring that day. She was probably right. Undaunted, producers Norma Heyman and Sue Summers, former producer Linda Agran and I went into pow-wow mode and by the next day we had been donated a piano of our choice, freight to Burma, and all the music scores we wanted – done deed. It was what the Women of the Year Lunch is all about.

Within a week, though, *The Sunday Times* had picked up the story and although the journalist promised to hold it back until the idea had a chance to progress, it was printed that weekend and became a political statement instead of an altruistic act. We were warned off by some groups and laughed off by others.

Immediately afterwards the monks staged their demonstrations for freedom and thousands of them were incarcerated. It was no time for an actress and a TV crew to be pushing a piano in Daw Suu's direction. Her answer would be: 'I cannot receive a luxury when my spiritual brothers are in chains.'

Over the course of the next nine months an idea was conceived of mounting a series of piano concerts to raise consciousness about The Lady of Burma. The BBC and Channel Four were interested in the documentary, then ITV. At one point thee was almost a scramble for it.

Lunches with directors ensued. Budgets and planning started. Sue Summers and I planned an itinerary. We went to Suu's former Oxford college, St Hugh's, and heard David Milliband give a half-fervent speech about how best to deal with this most repressive and secretive junta.

Few people know or care about Burmese politics. The savagery, state torture, slave labour, closure of universities, and the oppression of a kind and gentle race with many historical links to England, seldom get beyond page five of even the most socialist newspaper. On the advice of his astrologer, General Shan Win moved the capital from Rangoon to an impenetrable jungle location, requiring massive amounts of forced labour and dragging civil servants away from their families. How astute, and how unconquerable he must feel now that the rages of a cyclone have caused the deaths of thousands and thousands of people in Northern Burma.

In the latest development, Aung San Suu Kyi has been refusing to take in her food packages or see her physicians. This is the third week of her hunger strike. Students in Japan and Thailand are fasting in solidarity with her. My greatest fear is not just that her health will give out, but that she knows, as I do, that the world will only pay attention to her plight and that of her countrymen, when she is a martyr and merely a symbol of Burma's heinous repression.

Yet global interest in the imprisoned democratic leader is a penny whistle in the din of international outrage compared to the trumpets surrounding Mandela's solo, Zimbabwe's drumbeat chaos, and the Wurlitzer organ of the Middle East. Gradually, TV interest is lost. Heads of departments changed more frequently than Peter Snow's ties. With each successive change, ideas that had been hanging fire fell to the bottom of the pile. If I tell you the idea, will you promise to keep it to yourself? Most people love it. So far only I know the dream cast – certainly the dream cast don't. Until they read this, of course.

We start by choosing a wonderful piano but one that requires little tuning, which means it probably has to be digital, and preferably not a grand as her house is small. We take the piano to St Hugh's College where a piece by Bach is played by a young Burmese musician – apparently, Daw Suu loves Bach (and Bob Marley). We then play the Royal Festival Hall – director Jude Kelly kindly offered it to me for free at the Women of the Year Lunch – oh, and I'd want Alfred Brendel *and* Jools Holland, all things considered.

We would transport it to Ireland and ask Damien Rice to play the Song of Freedom he composed for Aung Sang Suu Kyi. Then we go to Paris and ask Jane Birkin, who has spent time with Daw Suu, to sit at or even *on* the piano and sing for her. From there we go to Warsaw to play Chopin where the ghetto stood and Prague for Smetana, then to a former communist state to play Shostakovich and then to the Far East – where I'd like Lang Lang to play, please, and taking in Daniel Barenboim and the West-Eastern Divan Orchestra – if that's not asking too much – and to Ethiopia for a Bob Marley concert on a hill in Addis Ababa, with the great man's son and colleagues, and to New York, and a small cabaret club where Barbara Cook sings and Steve Ross plays . . . How is it sounding so far?

Look, we won't get into Burma – Myanmar   call it what you will. Maybe that's the whole point. I want to take Victoria Wood with me to play on board a ship and Jamie Cullum would play on a train through Canada whilst kd lang sings 'Hallelujah' and we'd finally wash up by a Karen refugee camp on the Thai/Burmese border with the funkiest concert ever, and if that's as far as we can go then hell, I'll leave the piano there as a metaphor for how music can cut through reason to a place we seldom have time to acknowledge. I can dream, can't I? Maybe, by the time I get my wish, Aung Sang will be free to play us out with a little Bach fugue.

Body Double

In the absence of Sir Terence of Maidenform, it has fallen to me to replace the irrepressible Oldie – and I use that term only in the sense of he and I being fellow judges for The Oldie of the Year awards, scheduled for the 11th of March – for today's *Telegraph* Diary piece. I am therefore, ostensibly, his body double. He'd be shocked if he knew that. I don't know where big bird in sky has taken him but I imagine it is some rhapsodic, eight star, golf and gourmet hotel with a native bearer outside each individual bungalow pouring fresh mint tea from an absurd height as he and Lady Wogan are massaged with bougainvillea essence by tiny but exquisite Nubian handmaidens.

I received the call to cover for His Portliness whilst trudging down Westbourne Park Road, fresh from my Friday morning exercise session on the vibrating Power Plate. I fell, wobbly legged and whey-faced, into Gusto's café afterwards for coffee and calorie replacement. My outfit was a fetching conflagration of black cotton pants, sexily elasticated at the knee, black socks, sneakers, and a floor-length faux fur. Mrs Doubtfire meets Jade Goody.

The café filled up with the young and the beautiful.

'Hey you look great – love the hair gel!' 'Yeah,' agreed her male companion, 'you been watching *There's Something about Mary*? Have you come in your hair?'

I had watched that film only the other night and couldn't let the moment pass. 'I'm just having my breakfast,' I told him pleasantly.

He turned his designer scarf towards my sweaty 'Myeloma UK' T-shirt. 'Er – sorry – yeah, I probably shouldn't have . . .'

'It's OK. It's just that I see you're having bottled water – but I am actually having a yoghurt.'

He took my point.

I'm also having a chest bug at present, or rather it's having me. It makes me what my dear old Dad would have called *heiseric*. I cough when I should be sleeping and sniff and wheeze when I should be working. The night-time coughing allows me to listen to all manner of ephemera on the World Service, none of which (though it's riveting at the time) can I remember in the morning, except that Hillary keeps losing primaries and it makes me feel vaguely sick.

I sat up bolt upright though, for Max Pemberton's reading of *Trust Me, I'm a Junior Doctor* during the section when he almost caused a patient's death. He was so focused on the position of the stent in her neck that he failed to notice the classic symptoms of a pulmonary thrombosis. Not for the first time, I thanked my Maker for giving me a vocation which may bore the armpits off you but is unlikely, Abe Lincoln aside, to kill you or even make you write a living will before seeing a play.

This week, I've seen The Jerusalem String Quartet breathe life and lyricism into Beethoven and Ravel at the civilised hour of 11.30am at the Wigmore Hall. Pin drop silence, a dry sherry to follow and home by 1.30pm. Perfect. On Monday, however, I drove round the Ring Road in Watford three times and parked in a scary concrete-and-urine car park, to spend two and a half hours, or was it a couple of years, watching a play, got lost on the fog-bound M1, and finally parked the car outside my flat at 1.20am. The Oberrammegau Passion Play might have been more concise.

So, Tel, wherever you are, I shall be raising a steaming Lem-sip and a vat of Manuka honey to your health and I shall look forward to seeing your mahogany torso and gleaming mandibles at the Oldie Awards on March 11th, where the winners are a riot of wit, colour and withering brain cells. You can pay me there.

As I entered the dim fug that is the Oldie Awards luncheon at Simpsons in the Strand, I became aware of a familiar pink face smiling its way over to me. En route, he had to pass the waxy twinkle of Barry Cryer, the avuncular weskit of Sir Bill Cotton, the lacy steel that is Jilly Cooper, and all the myriad of textures and tangles that make up the colour grey. 'You're looking good . . . how are you?'

'New teeth,' volunteered Sir Terry.

'Lovely,' was my response.

He reached into the pocket of his corduroy uniform and extracted a rolled up, quarter-full tube and added, by way of evidence, 'Polygrip.'

I nodded my empathy and approbation, even though most of mine are screwed in for the duration – although I might not have been so confident had I anticipated the weight of the treacle pudding to come.

'If I were writing an article about this lunch,' I mouthed between hugs from Katherine Whitehorn in a dazzling jacket of embroidered flora and fauna, and Beryl Bainbridge in St Trinian's black looking for an outlet for her fag, 'I would start my piece with what Terry just said.'

It's an annual occasion which no *Oldie* reader would dream of missing. None of us knows why because, under the strict aegis of Lord Gnome, the distrait, distinguished and crumbly Richard Ingrams ('the man for whom the word cute was invented' – Terry Wogan), we know exactly what we are in for. There will be drinks downstairs with shouting, a school dinner upstairs with tables fanned so tightly from the top one that the waitresses have to be issued with rubber suction pads on their shoes so they can collect up the discarded steak and kidney pie plates by abseiling up the walls. There will be ludicrous prizes for the winners and one or two short but hilarious speeches. It is somewhere between *I'm Sorry I Haven't a Clue* on Radio 4, *Blankety-Blank* on BBCTV, and Rag Week. *Oldie* readers fight to get in and, it has to be said, the staff of Simpsons fight to get them out.

This Tuesday's awards were hugely popular and the envelope stuffed with old pound notes and an *Oldie* Annual went to Dame Eileen Atkins, Stanley Baxter, David Hockney, Dr Ros Altmann, Moira Stewart and Sir Ian Paisley (bit of a dark horse, that one), who were cheered by their peers and public alike. Stanley's award was particularly enjoyed not just because of his witty speech but because he went to the lavatory just before Terry started the presentations and had to bang mutely on the glass doors for ages to get back in.

At some point a very infirm but merry as hell Sir John Mortimer will be pushed in a throne on wheels through the throng and his fantastically jolly-hockey sticks wife, Penny, will take up her position nearby and yell at Peter O'Toole, who will do daring shticks of his own with tenor inflections. Mavis Nicholson, our esteemed Agony Aunt and the best interviewer TV ever let go, will be seen nestling up to someone, seamlessly removing from them every shred of discretion, and Clive James and Ian Hislop will giggle pinkly, like the broker's men. Mortality sits in the air and makes us defiantly amusing.

What is a spring boiling fowl like me doing at an *Oldie* lunch? At sixty-one I qualify (thank you, *Times*, for adding ten years to that last birthday – and *Jewish Chronicle* for taking ten off) and it's the best fun a sprightly young 'un will have without wearing hold-ups. On every place-setting was a card saying 'Because You're Worth It'. We are.

Dog Days

I had the most wonderful time playing Chekhov's *The Cherry Orchard* in Chichester. In truth, I enjoyed Chekhov's characters so much that I've decided in future never to play anything but Chekhov again. The production, the set, and – in one review, my dog – were generally derided by the critics but the cast didn't read 'em, the audiences seemed to have a really good time, and we just got on with being in the best play ever written. To a man we felt bereft when it was over.

Frank Finlay was touching as the old retainer, Firs. I was Charlotta, the sad and lonely German governess, complete with magic tricks and dog. I know that for Frank, as well as for me, the high point of the evening was the two-page scene we had together each night on a stone bench. 'I think our scene went OK tonight, don't you?' he'd say as we came off stage. 'I think we were knockout,' I'd tell him. 'We're a dream team, you Hardy, me Laurel.' He'd look at me quizzically to see if I was taking the piss, and say, 'You having a drink in the pub afterwards?' and off we'd go.

An actor through to his bones. And I love actors. They're braver than boxers with three times the longevity.

It was a weird gig, though. We rehearsed for five weeks in a church hall in Southwark, then packed up clothes for all seasons, make-up in vanity bags battered by endeavour, and our household pets – in my case legitimately, because she was to appear as Charlotta's dog – and legged it as cautiously as our clapped-out estates would take us down the M4 to our digs and B&Bs in and around the Chichester basin. Once there we would rehearse technically on the stage for one week, open to the press on a Friday, play for two weeks only and go home. *Go figure . . .*

On arrival in Bosham Ho, I started to cough. I never get colds so I took Manuka honey and willed it away. Then I started to wheeze, so I drank hot lemon. Then I started to sweat, so I opened the windows. Finally, on the first day of the technical rehearsals, in the kitchen of the borrowed house, I started to faint. A friend drove me to the nearest doctor where I found myself unable to speak or even breathe properly. I opened my mouth and a small squeak came out followed by two hiccups and some sobs. It didn't bode well for opening night. Blood pressure dangerously low and a respiratory infection. Complete rest for two weeks. Panic. Antibiotics. Bed.

'Stay in bed,' said our company manager. 'We'll tech without you and

I'll get you an appointment with our theatre doctor.' I did. They did. Two days later, the company doctor declared me a fit woman with a rough chest – yeah, I'd heard that one before – and crackingly good blood pressure, so back I went, wheezing like a VW exhaust, to the theatre where Alice, my dresser, laced me into a boned corset and layers of heavy clothing just in time for the last dress rehearsal before opening night . The only thing I couldn't do was laugh. If I did I went into croup hell and couldn't stop.

The Chichester Festival Theatre is a Sixties construction with one of the most unforgiving stages on earth. Now, I don't mind it personally. I'm of the school which tends not to notice the space. If there's a stage, I'm such a show-off I tend to fill it. The stage thrusts out into the area on three sides and the seats leap up from there and embrace the stage on all three sides. Entrances are made from two steep, narrow flights, or alternatively via the steps up from two vomitoria – yes, the Romans knew all about first night nerves – under the front block of seats. Our costumes were long, layered and heavy. Baffled Basenji on lead, I told her, in the German accent I was using for the part, to vait and I would give her a treat. She looked as doubtful as only a furrowed-browed dog can look as we crouched, leaned or huddled in the dark on the narrow staircase awaiting our cue.

On a green light, six over-dressed actors, two stage managers, several suitcases and a dog all started improvising loudly about trains being late and we walked up our own skirts, bashing the walls as we went and burst forth, naturalistically, onto the brightly lit stage.

'I give my dog nuts. She likes nuts' was my entrance and exit line and with the help of a chicken-and-spinach crunch, dog and mistress managed it fine. At the end of the play we did the same thing again, in reverse, and left the cherry orchard forever. On the opening night my son swore that Diva gave a last lingering look back at the fourth wall which brought a tear to his eye, though obviously not to the eye of the *Express* critic who wrote that I'd brought on my own dog to pull focus from the other actors. Against the rule of a lifetime, I wrote to the critic enquiring whether it would have been less distracting if I'd brought on *Express* owner Richard Desmond's dog.

Sometimes bad reviews can bind a cast together and galvanise the show into improving more and more by the night. Dame Diana Rigg was valiant. The sun shone, the houses were full and we all relaxed and started the serious business of being in a play out of town, i.e. where to eat, who's bringing in the cupcakes and which is the most canine welcoming pub.

Only Diva showed any signs of depression. Her life became weird. She was understandably less affected by reviews and full houses than she was by *Where's me own bed? Where's me Hyde Park? And why do I have to keep going up those effing stairs six nights a week and twice on Wednesdays and Saturdays?*. By the second week she'd developed the hysterical squits, a poorly paw, and the expression 'hang-dog' had been reinvented for her. 'Two weeks' rest,' said the vet. Richard, our company manager, suggested a week in The Priory with Amy Winehouse's lurcher.

The suggestion came down from on high that I should take on a glove puppet in the absence of a dog. I rejected this on the grounds that a psychotic governess wasn't in any of Chekhov's drafts. Instead I seized Jemma Redgrave's large, affable black labrador, Mabel, who had none of Diva's elegant neuroses and, for a handful of 'Good Boy' chip cookies, unquestioningly performed both scenes to perfection. William Gaunt had a spaniel and a Yorkie and I was accepting bribes.

Chichester audiences accepted a black labrador in rural Russia with the same aplomb as they'd accepted the barkless dog of the Congo, and Diva returned for the last few shows looking like Margo Channing at the end of *All About Eve*. I think our favourite comment on the whole production was overheard by our director, as one white-haired, floral-dressed lady said to another as they left the theatre:

'Well, I thought it was very enjoyable, didn't you, Mary? But why on earth they had to set it in *Russia* is utterly beyond me.'

(Incidentally, who was the only actor in the company to have a film job to go straight on to? Stand up Mr Finlay, it's your call.)

Amazon Grace

Sometimes, on a cruise like the one I took up the Amazon with other *Oldie* writers, Rosie Boycott and Mavis Nicholson on the *Spirit of Adventure* (privately known as the *Spirit of Dementia*), I get so involved in shipboard life that I cease to care where I'm going and I come back more geographically ignorant than when I left. It's appalling.

We saw not one creature save a giant moth – dead – and two lumpish manatees in the Caribbean. I think the good Lord was having a bad prayer day when he created manatees. They don't look like anything – fish, fowl or mammal. They look like cigars on growth hormones and their mouths slide open like a cross channel ferry. Once you've popped a few handfuls of grass in there – normal roadside grass, that is – you cease being amused and wonder what on earth they are *for*. On our last day in Manaus as we waited around a miserable hotel for news of our vanished plane, Rosie and I saw a sign reading 'Mini-zoo'.

Ms. Boycott exploded. 'I have not come all the way to the bloody Amazon to see a sodding mini-zoo!' she shrieked.

I want an experience like that of my friend Guido who travelled to Madagascar to see the lemurs. Hearing that they loved custard apples, as he did himself, he bought a few, took them into the forest and sat down on a stump to slice one up. After a few moments he looked up and there in front of him was an orderly queue of ring-tailed lemurs, their tails waving lyrically from side to side. Not one stepped out of line, not one pushed or shoved, they just waited their turn, took a piece of fruit, tugged a virtual forelock and left. I've been to a lot of buffet suppers in very smart hotels where ring-tailed lemur behaviour should have been emulated by jewel-encrusted females.

Towards the end of the cruise we disembarked in a tiny town where a mosque, a church and a synagogue nestled together in harmony in the village square. As we toured the synagogue, the volunteers told me they could not afford a rabbi for high holy days.

'Surely a rabbinical student would be happy to come to this beautiful place?' I said. It was beautiful, with its vaulted, wood beamed ceiling with plaster walls, carved wooden pews and sawdust on the floors.

Her eyes lit up. 'Can you find us one?' she breathed. 'It would be most wonderful if you could.'

I swallowed. 'Erm . . . I . . . er . . . thing is . . .' I under-articulated, 'it's – well, it's not really my field.'

Her face fell a foot.

'No . . . but . . . er . . . I'll certainly do what I can.'

She seemed certain that I could do it. At that moment so did I.

Could I Google for a rabbi? Let my fingers do the walking through Yellow Pages? 'Peripatetic rabbi required, short working week, must love inter-faith work.' When I left they all came to the door to wave me off. I waved tenderly and walked backwards all the way to the rickety pier to await my rickety tender.

Why did I walk backwards? Well, there was a joke I always loved when I was a kid about a duchess visiting a home for the mentally deficient, who encounters one seemingly entirely sane man who tells her his story. It seems that he was sectioned by his evil brother because he was set to inherit all the family money. He explained that his was only a minor depression, he played the piano beautifully for her, talked philosophy with her and generally convinced her to bring his case to the governing body.

'I'll do that,' she cried. 'It is appalling that a man of your intelligence and gentle disposition should be incarcerated here for so long, for no reason. Trust me, I will bring up your case at the governors' meeting on Tuesday and plead with them to release you.'

The man's eyes fill with tears. He kisses her hand and thanks her with all his heart. She turns and walks away, visibly moved. Suddenly, as she reaches the door, a huge brick smashes into her head. She stumbles and as she falls to the ground she sees the patient standing there, his hand still raised from the throw. He grins widely and calls out:

'Don't forget Tuesday!'

I've mentioned the Amazonian vacancy often at various places since, but frankly it produces nothing ecumenical, merely a smile. Please write in if a gig like this has always been your dream and especially if you'll do it for a plane ticket and all the small green bananas you can pack in a canvas rucksack.

Spirit of Dementia

This cruise is not quite what we thought on our flight,
Some details aren't what we supposed,
Some ports don't expect us and promptly reject us
And others are frequently closed.
We've sat on the quay after two days at sea
In Almerein, feeling bereft.
As part of a fun day we went on a Sunday
Where we saw two dogs screwing and left.
We've Imodium potion for fear of the motion
And cameras set up for splendour.
Still we sit in Sirrocca observing the dock and
Bemoaning the lack of a tender.
There's no gambling or bingo, a Portuguese lingo,
No yoga or lap dancing strippers,
Just Clive at the pianner playing 'Hard-hearted Hannah'
In wet suit and snorkel and flippers.
We've seen a lagoon, an impossible moon,
Frangipani and churches quite holy,
We've sat up late gabbin' and groaned in our cabin
While the captain spoke ever . . . so . . . slowly.
Amazonian sounds and large termite mounds
Have been talked of and couldn't be scarier,
We've had big swirling seas and obese manatees
And stood up to take pills for malaria.
As the Amazon neared, it was just as we feared –
The weather got hotter than Hades.
Hear the art teacher cry, 'Are your cherries all dry?'
To a roomful of middle-aged ladies.
Disembarking at Brevis felt just like Ben Nevis,
It's a place where few folk expect to go.
Banned from bunkering down in the middle of town
We almost got moored up to Texaco.
The Oldies, a menace, play fierce table tennis
No wind surfin', deck quoits or golfin',
But we all crane our necks on the passenger decks

448

Someone shouts 'Look, a pink dolphin!'
The embarrassing deals when no one's got 'Reals',
The sweat running inside your collar,
The breathtaking views and kids in canoes
Calling 'Hey Gringo – gimme a dollar!'

The pool and the sauna, the flora and fauna,
The ingestion of vanishing cultures,
Ornithology talks and the furious squawks
When we see only bloody great vultures.
What a wonderful break – no decisions to make
Save into which bar you'll meander,
You just make up your mind where you'll be wined and dined
In the posh place or up the veranda.
Now we're all so relaxed, like our brains have been waxed,
We'll remember the best of *Adventure*
Whether small ship or boat, or a B&B afloat,
We'll rename it the *Spirit of Dementia*.

Gripes of Wrath

Have you ever been been on the receiving end of someone's anger for reasons you can't quite fathom? I ask because a Pilates teacher once tried to chuck me out of a class of two students. She didn't like my attitude, apparently. It took me right back to Wheeler Street School circa 1956, a tiled Victorian institution in Hull, where my needlework teacher tried to have me ejected for alleged dumb insolence.

It was during a double sewing period. For the entire term I'd been sweating my way towards the completion of a damp, grubby gingham sewing bag. Every time I thought I'd finished it, Miss Petersen made me unpick it and start again. My mates had all hemmed neat piles of dirndl skirts, pinafores and tray cloths with ease, not to mention élan. As the bell sounded for the end of class, I let out, not completely under my breath, a hoarse 'Hooray' for which heinous crime she rewarded me with some deranged vitriol and several slaps on the back of my legs. At that point I gave her what my father would have called 'a mouthful' – I've always had a problem with authority – and she decided she no longer wanted to teach me. To my surprise, my parents were livid – with *me*! Dad dragged me by the ear or some such taut appendage to apologise, which I eventually did between clenched molars.

I still can't stomach a hectoring tone, particularly in an exercise class where I feel it's either fun or hell. Humourless intensity cuts through me like a laser and makes me both tetchy and sardonic. On this occasion I misunderstood an instruction the teacher gave in good but Spanish-accented English. I thought she said the opposite of what *she* thought she said, and our relationship spiralled downhill. At one point in the ensuing discussion I said, 'Look, love,' which is common currency in Hull but in Spain, seemingly, is the equivalent of 'You foul, one-eyed inebriate who eats the leftover giblets of her uncle's proctologist.'

She was not pleased. 'Leave my class,' she yelled. 'Go! Now! You must leave!'

'Oh, have *you* got the wrong woman,' I murmured, instantly transporting myself back to the Sixties, lying on a verge, placard aloft, singing, 'We shall not be moved'. 'If I were you, love, I'd just get on with teaching Lorraine and I'll get on with my single leg stretches.'

Castillian mayhem ensued. Then she left the room clutching her

450

phone and was gone for a very long time. Lorraine and I pulled our purple stretch bands in silence. Then she admitted she'd heard the instructions wrongly, too, and we both got rather giggly. I haven't been back since.

Another place I was ordered to leave was the Peacock Shopping Centre in Woking, a place which contains all the requisite monstrosities of shopping centres everywhere. Hideous lighting in lurid colours, daft fountains, empty chain boutiques sporting everything you don't need and then some. Natalie, Diva and I had left the car in the car park beneath, from which the only way to access the stage door of Woking Theatre was through the Centre. As we walked past Clinton's Cards, a uniformed giblet with epaulettes and a walkie-talkie stopped us and told us in peremptory tones that dogs were not allowed in the Centre. I informed him that we were passing though en route to the stage door, where I was performing in a play. Unimpressed, he ordered us out. I protested. Voices were raised. Nats told him to eff off, and before you could say 'Starbucks' he was on the walkie-talkie, shouting 'Two abusive females and an animal are refusing to obey the established rules of the building.'

We walked on, tails in the air, and heard him scream, 'You are all banned from the Peacock Shopping Centre for one year!'

I fell to my knees and begged, grovelled, cajoled, prayed: 'No! No! Anything but that! Have mercy, I beg of you – how will I live if I'm Wokingless?'

To date I have not tried out the ban. When I want desperately to source pick'n'mix liquorice and dolly mixture selections, or purchase a pair of cerise-coloured crocs or a handbag that looks like a cow's intestines, I might have to throw caution to the wind and head for the M3 and trouble.

Yet I am not a volatile person. You could fuel a small country on what I bottle up. At the Bafta Awards, the French producer of *The Pianist,* an award-winning film in which I appear, sat through the whole meal with his back to me, smoking a fat cigar, and spoke not one word to me. If I ever see him again I'll – I'll – probably say, 'Hello, good to see you.' I once (famously in our family) told the kids that I was going to give Roald Dahl a mouthful the next time I saw him. They were mortified in advance. Some months earlier he had been provocative with me in a borderline racist way on a TV chat show. Because I'd not had the wit to respond at the time, it had simmered in my gut ever since and I longed for the day when I could meet and challenge him to pistols at dawn. The day came when, travelling down in the lift in a small hotel in Sydney, we stopped at the first floor and in walked the great writer himself.

'Hi Roald,' I said. 'How nice to see you again. How are you?'

'By gum,' said my husband to me afterwards, 'that told him.'

The kids were relieved and appalled.

When Amy was a child, weekend after weekend she masterminded plays in the cellar, memorising and extemporising and roping her unwilling but obedient brother and friends – all of whom would have been happier playing footie – into elaborate costume dramas with titles like *The Management Will Decide That*. Echoes of Jack and my disputes with theatre managers and agents imbued the text, alongside snippets from Queen Victoria, as seen on TV, and snatches from *Peter Pan* and *Ballet Shoes*.

Occasionally, after half an hour or so of her inventive stage-hogging, we parents would make a move to leave, saying 'Bravo! But we really must go now', and her fury would have no end. How dare we walk out of her latest play! How dare we leave before she'd decided how or even if it would end? I recognised the 'pro' in her even then, but Sundays were precious to the working Mum and I'm afraid it was the source of some fabulous fights. Neither of us giving in. Identical faces screwed up into identical anger. Adam quietly disappearing and Jack pouring oil.

Now her anger has dissipated and she is so much her father's daughter, it seems strange that she could have been such a ball of spitting flames, and I worry that I didn't let her win enough. Then I console myself that anger has the power to fuel our work, and comedy is anger's child. How Jack, so benign, could turn a phrase or a sentence into bitter irony, and how Amy and Adam now do the same in their writing. Always wrapping their savagery in a carapace of comedy.

> I was angry with my friend
> I told my friend, my wrath did end.
> I was angry with my foe
> I told it not, my wrath did grow.

I used to believe William Blake was right when, pre-empting both Freud and Oprah, he told us that keeping the lid on one's anger leads to all manner of self-imposed ailments both in the heart and in the head. These days, I'm not so sure. These days I'm more in favour of good old polite bottling up, being circumspect, swallowing it, counting to ten, being English, for heaven's sake. How bad for you can it be?

I'm not saying I've mastered this myself, I'm just saying it's sometimes better for the well-being of both protagonists. I once grew a benign tumour in a place which is, allegedly, the Chinese point for anger, SO I KNOW WHAT I'M TALKING ABOUT, RIGHT?

Recently, locking up my car in a side street off the Euston Road prior to going to the theatre, I saw two middle-aged women approaching. One of them, round-faced, bespectacled and faded, was clearly going to say something. I braced myself for 'Don't see much of you on the telly these days.'

Instead, smirking with sarcasm, she said, I suppose you're going to see that pro-Israeli play, are you?'

'Pardon?'

'I said, I expect you're going to see that *pro*-Israeli play like the rest of your friends.'

There was indeed a preponderance of Jewish people piling in to see the dazzling American actress Tovah Feldshu in *Golda's Balcony* in its twenty-only performances at the Shaw Theatre. More's the pity, because the play is written by William Gibson, a non Jew, and it probably gives a better analysis of the foundation of the State of Israel and Golda Meir's attempts to secure peace than you'll see in textbooks, newspapers or BBC news reports.

Anyway, the woman was angry. She was particularly angry with me. Mostly, it seemed, for being me.

'Have you seen the play?' I asked her. 'Do you know me? What is your problem?'

'I don't need to see propaganda! I've read the things you've written about the Palestinians . . .'

Should I argue my case, tell her that I'm in favour of a Palestinian State, that the play deals on a very human level with this very issue? In other words, should I miss curtain-up? My gentleman friend was urging me not to get involved. I walked away leaving her shouting at my retreating back. I ended up – I say this with no pride – giving her the one finger. Nobody won the game – it was over at deuce, but it left a ferrous taste in the mouth. Perhaps I should have congratulated her on her courage in confronting a total stranger whose opinions she happened to refute.

A mere twenty-four hours after that street confrontation I had another. I leapt off a bus crawling down Regent Street, late for the much-praised revival of Enid Bagnold's *The Chalk Garden*, a play I had been forced to abandon a few years earlier when Jack was first ill, and for which I had a fondness. Its theme of 'dryness of the heart' had come back into our own arid and cynical times, and the revival was a triumph for the Donmar Warehouse. I hailed a cab in Soho. It went straight past, then changed its mind and swerved to a halt at the kerb.

'Donmar Theatre – er, Earl Street – Covent Garden,' I said. 'I'm going to be late, so if you could –'

No response. The driver stared ahead stonily. I got in the cab. It remained stationary.

'Can we go?' I asked.

There was a lethal pause, then, without turning round he snarled: 'Earl-

HAM Street! Earl-HAM Street, Maureen. The Donmar is in EARLHAMMM Street.'

'OK, OK,' I said. 'Earl-HAM Street. Can we just go there?'

His response was novel. 'Don't take that tone with me, Maureen!' he shouted, making my name into a comedy expletive.

'Look,' I countered, 'if you don't want to take me there I'll get out –'

'I can't take you anywhere, Maureen, if I DON'T KNOW WHERE IT IS!' He must have been studying Robert De Niro in *Taxi Driver* for years – he was like a pressurised can of simmering rage.

'Let me out of this cab.' I went to open the door, whereupon he drove off.

'Let me out – now!' I shouted.

He stopped. I got out, hailed another taxi and – oh, my temper – yelled at him to 'Eff off'. Boy, was that a mistake.

'Take me to the Donmar, please . . . I've just got away from a madman,' I told the new driver. He turned down a side street and I was just telling him what had happened when suddenly the original taxi appeared bumper to bumper in the narrow street with the barking driver screaming out of his window, 'I wanna witness! You got to be a witness! She told me to eff off!' He was apoplectic, the veins standing out in his neck.

My driver was alarmed. 'I've never seen anything like it in all my life,' he said, ducking into another street. 'I mean, I wasn't in your cab – I don't know even what he's talking about.' He doubled back and we finally shook him off. 'I don't get it,' he said. 'Everyone knows where the Donmar is – what's his problem?'

It was a bizarre one. He had seen me and for whatever reason, real or imagined, had not wanted to pick me up, then decided that he would but only in order to give me a piece of his mind.

Look, there are people one just doesn't like. Even the benign Jack had certain actors or football pundits he simply couldn't look at. The possessed critic, A A Gill, once wrote in his pleasant little column that I was a 'three flush floater', which had a certain visual appeal. I couldn't stand Mrs Thatcher. But our opinions often say as much about us as they do about the object of our dislike. We loathe the things in other people that we hate in ourselves . . .

I am so used to getting into taxis and talking lovingly about Jack's most popular play, *The Knowledge*, which was about the rigorous exams that cabbies must pass to get the green badge which allows them to drive in London. The high point of the play was when, during one test question, the examiner – played by the late, great Nigel Hawthorne – leapt up and down doing jack-knives with two Vic inhalers up his nostrils to demonstrate that a cabbie must keep his cool at all times, no matter how weird the behaviour of his passenger. The difference these days is that if that driver had had a knife, I cannot be certain he wouldn't have used it. Some people – occasionally I am one of them – desperately need some form of anger displacement. Meditation? Boot camp? ASBO? Cognitive therapy? Boxing? Marijuana?

Answers, please, on plain brown paper wrapped round a rock and hurled at the nearest passing B list celebrity.

The Year of Living Dangerously

It was through charity work that I got myself into a year of living dangerously. One November Friday I finished up two weeks of charity events ranging from musical instruments for the Duchess of Kent, through consciousness-raising for Burma, to a small synagogue in Glasgow – all of them interesting and instructive. Then, on the final Saturday, I did a paid appearance for the Scottish Tourism Board at the Hilton Hotel, Glasgow. It was a Brazilian-themed evening so I wore a green and gold raw silk frock coat and dress from the inspirational Beatrice von Treskow and a specially made headdress of fruit and vegetables. Well, wouldn't you?

After my cabaret, I auctioned the headdress, finished off with Derek Nimmo's line, 'Of all the benefits, affairs and charitable events I've ever attended, tonight's has been the most recent', and headed for my room through the bar, where I was stopped and pestered by a sloshed politician who wanted to question my attitude to New Labour in the light of my jokes.

He was boring and I was tired, but he persisted. 'If you are a politician then your first lesson is to learn to listen,' I told him. 'Oh, come on' – his breath was worse than his opinions – 'you can't give up on New Labour – let me tell you why you're wrong.' It was 11.30pm, I'd had a tough couple of weeks, and as I told him quietly but not unpleasantly to f off, I was aware of an amused face and silver hair topping an immaculate tuxedo, and Mr E entered the fray and my life, warding off Labour and offering to escort me to a lift. His name was later linked with mine very publicly. Why Mr E? He was in the field of energy and energy was one of his most attractive attributes.

My impression was that he was attractive in an American detective, Ed Asner or Judd Hirsch fashion, and when he asked me if I'd like a coffee I didn't hesitate. Two and a half hours later I stood up and he said in his Glasgow growl, 'I think some extraordinary contact has been made, don't you?' I answered 'Mmm' then went to my room, sat on my bed and allowed the thought to go through my mind: 'What colour do you wear for a second wedding?'

I had not had thoughts for another man for many years, had not wanted one, and had not felt desire or loneliness. I worked hard, saw friends, kept my kids close and was reasonably contented. I was about to enter Planet Hypertension.

When Nats met me at Stanstead Airport I was six feet in the air. 'I've met a man,' I said, and continued to say it to everyone I spoke to on my return. When there was time to speak, that is, because Mr E was ringing me up to eight times a day, dawn and dusk, and within a week the M-word had been spoken. I felt no guilt or remorse. I felt it was ordained, natural and the next stage of my life.

'Make sure he's not after your money,' said a good girlfriend. I was angered on his behalf. He was a successful businessman. He didn't need my money. It was an irritating dampener which I took for envy. 'Darling, you're very vulnerable,' said another. 'Do be careful.' I was astonished. They'd feel differently when they met him. He was fun and funny and mischievous and he made me feel bold and dark and different.

'I'm coming to London on Sunday to take you to dinner – book somewhere nice,' he told me. I was fairly faint with excitement and quite unable to learn my lines for two episodes of Joanna Lumley's *Sensitive Skin*. Instead I sat texting and day-dreaming. I told my kids and they were tentatively happily bemused by the sight of their mother reduced to a teenage 'pash'.

On Thursday, he called me at home. 'I'm in Berkeley Square. Can you come and meet me?' This was not the arrangement. I had to sit still with my lines until they were automatic. I couldn't go – wasn't ready. I got in the car and drove shakily from Muswell Hill to the West End. I reasoned I'd go to Harry Morgan's in St John's Wood and get salt beef sandwiches and dill pickles. It was a cold, sharp November day and we would go to Regent's Park. I just didn't want to sit in a restaurant when I had to work. Bond Street was closed off – I circled round and round, getting hot under the collar – and then, finally arriving at Berkeley Square, I saw him on the corner, navy blue cashmere coat and briefcase, surprisingly the waxy complexion of Richard Branson and a strangeness in his eyes that I'd completely failed to notice in my one previous encounter. He got in the car. I kept on my sunglasses. We went to the park and ate the succulent salt beef and he talked. And he talked.

He told me his past form. 'Too much information' is the current phrase. I kept on my dark glasses and let him link arms. I couldn't wait to get away – to get home to my house and my dog and my memories.

I dropped him at Baker Street. How was I to get out of Sunday? I bid him goodbye and drove back to my lines. Whenever I made a gaffe on set, Joanna would pat my knee pityingly and say to the director, 'Aaah, don't be mad at her. She's in love'. But I wasn't. Now I could learn the words. At dinner on Friday night I told the kids I'd made a mistake. He was not for me. I didn't even like the look of him – and it wasn't fair to bring him all the way from Scotland on a fool's errand.

As it turned out the fool was me . . . and there's no fool like an old one. My son, who knows a thing or two about love, looked at me with the wisdom of his genes and said: 'Don't cancel. You've changed your mind but he hasn't. You may change it again.'

'I won't,' I said.

'You should go, though, Mod,' agreed Amy. 'You liked him so much – why not give it another chance?'

On Saturday night I went to the theatre with an actor friend, a friend with whom I have a real rapport – no romance, but closeness and empathy. The Mamet play was predictable so we left and went back to his place for scrambled eggs. There I told him about my new amour, about my change of heart. In retrospect, it was a cry for help. 'Save me, friend, from the abyss that's ahead.' He couldn't. OK. I could deal with this myself. I would go to The Ivy. I would have a nice dinner and explain to Mr E that a relationship was out of the question. I would apologise if I had led him on and I would pick up the bill.

On Sunday night I dressed down and drove to The Ivy in West Street – on my patch – greeted the doorman, and glumly put my coat in the cloakroom as I had so often done before with Jack and our kids, with Zelma, with the cast of *Oklahoma!* to celebrate my gong. I felt tearful and lost. Behind me, the door opened and closed. I turned. It was Mr E. I took one look at him and fell madly in love. As they say in New York – Go figure!

From November to November I lived in someone else's body. I lost who I was. He took up 90% of my time, present or absent. Madness! His phone calls last thing at night sent me to sleep smiling. In New York we danced in an empty restaurant and walked over Brooklyn Bridge sharing a glove. His children were adorable. We shared intakes of breath at *The Jersey Boys*. I surprised him by turning up in Venice, and he ate my cold roast potatoes from the dinner he'd missed the night before. How was I to know that it was my second instinct which was right and my third which got it wrong. Regrets? Not really. It was worth the pain for the craic of it all. Everyone raved about my appearance. I think it was their projection of my situation – as when a woman is pregnant she's told she looks glowing. (I never looked glowing when pregnant. I looked like an emu.)

As far as his reputation was concerned, I didn't want to hear it. I felt both protective of him and probably vain enough to believe he'd be fine now because he had me. Wrong. This was a man who needs to make women angry. He got his wish. Not since childhood had I felt so furious with anyone. On our last night together I punched him. Not my usual style. After we split, a friend came over, saw a picture on the mantelpiece and asked, 'Why do you keep his photo up?'

'Why wouldn't I?'

'Well, why would you want to look at him?'

'Well – because he's my Dad.'

'Oh my God – sorry – I thought it was Mr E.'

I'd never seen the likeness before. Now, I did. And it wasn't just a physical one.

I always knew that in Jacko I had married a man who was the absolute opposite of my father. Non-confrontational, gentle, domestic, cerebral. Irreplaceable, obviously, so I had fallen for the original man in my life – difficult, vain, narcissistic and fucking impossible. A fortune-teller told me that this man was my destiny and I'm programmed to learn from the whole experience that I can't always have what I want.

'It's so easy to make me happy,' I had told him after a fight. 'Just do what you say you are going to do.' It was one of the things he couldn't do. 'I'll arrive at 7.00pm' meant he'd arrive the next day. 'We'll have a holiday' meant he'd be in the hotel bedroom for two days on the phone. 'We'll have a quiet weekend at home' meant we'd head for another city as soon as I arrived. It was exciting – for a minute. We'd walk back home to my flat, I'd go through the door expecting him to follow, only to find he'd disappeared. There were a thousand clues to why he always moved the goalposts but I was too myopic to see them. His generosity was overwhelming and he cared for me. He drove miles to see my opening nights. In public he was fun, warm and gregarious. He just couldn't do intimacy.

It was a shake-up call and with the loss of him came the loss of Jack all over again. I've scarcely ever felt lower than I did in those weeks. I don't do crying on shoulders. I am the shoulder. It had been a year, that's all. Just a blip. From floating to flatlining in less time than it takes to grow back a fingernail.

On Xmas day, bird in the oven, rain pounding the pavements, I took the dog into Regent's Park. Basenjis hate rain. She was reluctant to go and uneasy in her little corduroy coat. I had just got into the park and was walking in the long grass when the phone rang. It was him. Diva had never warmed to him although it wasn't his fault – he trod on her a few times and he wasn't keen on her being on the bed. As I answered Mr E's call, Diva went into a crouch and delivered a particularly disarrayed poo – a metaphor if ever there was one. Attempting to sound civilised while scooping up dreck, I realised that Diva was haring off towards the Italian ponds.

My neck is too long to hold a phone under my chin. The phone fell. The poo bag fell. The lead fell. Then I heard the most unearthly shrieks coming from the pond two hundred yards away. The barkless dog of the

Congo was screaming like a child in peril. The weight of her coat was dragging her down into the water. As she struggled and howled two swans circled her, watching her intently. I dropped everything and took off as fast as my legs had ever taken off. Before I could reach her, a good Samaritan had hauled her out by her coat and she stood shaking and retching in a miserable heap. Lord, how I empathised.

Our last call ever was on New Year's Eve. I was in Salzburg with friends. 'I wish you all you wish yourself,' he said.

'If I'd wanted a Hallmark Greeting,' I responded, 'I'd have bought a card.'

There are the men you marry, the men you have love affairs with, then there are the men for whom the deal is everything. The real aphrodisiac. These are the unobtainable men, the ones who 'do love' only when you have their full attention. These are the men who are utterly yours on a long-haul flight but think nothing of popping a BlackBerry into a pyjama pocket or arranging a conference call at precisely the moment you meet for a reconciliatory lunch.

I regret any embarrassment I caused his family when our names were linked in the paper. I think in retrospect I fell in love with his energy, which could stop a train or power a turbine. The infusion was exhilarating but I'm much happier at my own velocity. I wished I could have been a sophisticated French woman. 'Maybe he comes this weekend . . . maybe not . . . I have my social arrangements – *cela ne fait rien*.' No. I wanted to look after him, get him to eat properly, be the little woman as I should have been with Jack. I picked my nemesis.

There is no closure on such a heightened affair, just the draining stent of a bereavement and the sweet-sour knowledge that today at least, when you find yourself alone in a car or sitting on the edge of your bed, the first thought that came into your mind was not him.

What did I end up with? Some lovely, thought-free jewellery I would never have bought myself. I lost some weight. I wrote a lot of poetry. I learned a decent Scots accent. A wariness of anyone who encounters the public figure before the private one. In spite of that, I'm 'walking out' now with a man who first saw me as I was giving a speech. A gentle man, though. A cultured man. A Jack. We'll see. I'm in no hurry. In Hamlet's words: 'I say, we will have no more marriages.'

End of Tome Assembly

The other night, I had an impromptu dinner in the flat. My guests were Simon Jones, his wife Nancy and their son Tim, and a long-time friend, Millicent Martin. Simon is the actor who played Arthur Dent in *The Hitch-hiker's Guide to the Galaxy* and he'd just flown in from New York where he has lived for the last fifteen years. Millie flew in from Los Angeles where she lives blissfully with her husband Mark, to appear alongside Topol in *Gigi* in the Open Air Theatre in Regent's Park.

I rustled up some chicken soup – no surprises there. Roast chicken and rice and a pineapple for pud, seared by Nats's blowtorch – a Jamie school dinner really. The dog did her tricks for a Babybel cheese and the rabbit came in and selected cards from a pack. We laughed a lot at everything from our young pretensions to our old knees. Tim showed us some hilarious Bush malapropisms on YouTube and a disturbing Australian chat show interview in which Miriam Margolyes discussed her PhD skills in oral sex. It was a lovely evening.

It was also a circle completed. Simon and I had played lovers in a 1981 production of *Design for Living* at the Watford Palace. I can still feel the exploding bubble in my diaphragm when Simon took a leap onto the sofa, as directed, and disappeared completely over the top. It seemed like ages before he hit the ground with a thud and yes, I did laugh a lot. I'd watched him go down even harder in 1976, when, fraught with home life, with two babies under two, I disappeared into a black hole, forgetting every line of the expository scene of Act I in Shaw's *Candida*, and left him panting and clinging to the set saying, 'I suppose you're going to tell me now that . . . er Mr Morrel and his wife have . . . er . . . *have* . . . er . . .' whilst I just stared at him. I calmly poked the fire and tidied the desk while he burbled, alone, for the bulk of a six-minute scene. Afterwards, Deborah Kerr gave me tea and sympathy in her dressing-room and Simon quietly stood in the wings contemplating how much weight he'd lost.

I was at his wedding in Worcester to Nancy the Nice and I've watched baby Tim grow from a great placid infant crawling around an eclectically decorated Central Park apartment, to a six-foot-two, long-haired babe magnet. They all loved Jack and though when I last visited New York with Mr E, they were doubtful about the romance, they were kind enough not to say so.

461

As for my thoroughly modish friend Millie, we go back to 1976 and Coward's *Tonight at Eight-Thirty*. I was her understudy. The producer promised me that when Millie left I would take over her roles in the three plays. To that end, Millie came in early to teach me to tap dance. Never was a teacher more in need of patience and Millie had it in spades, but by the time I'd mastered a triple time step, she was on to her next gig and the producer closed the show. I can still do a triple time step but, sadly, in the intervening thirty-two years, I've never had cause to.

When Jack died and it was to Los Angeles that I fled, Millie and the rest of the 'Theatre at Sea' troupe put their great loving paws around me and whisked me off for borsht and blintzes to the dairy restaurant of their chum, Leah Spielberg, mother of Stephen, a tiny vivacious little lady wearing denim dungarees over a pink gingham blouse with a Peter Pan collar. She has a little apartment in a hotel on the beach for weekends and runs the restaurant every other day of the week. Nothing her son has achieved has gone to her pretty white head. Most Brits who visit LaLa land for work stay friendless and catch the first shuttle back, gasping for Birds Eye custard, and Pears soap, but Millie, along with Jonathan Lynn and Alfred Molina and Jill Gascoigne, live and prosper there and absolutely adore it. The joy of being in the centre of London is that it gives me a chance to repay all that hospitality.

This same week my daughter's new play about friendship opened at the Hampstead Theatre to generally the most glowing three- and four-star reviews. It's about D H Lawrence and Frieda sharing a couple of Cornish cottages with Katherine Mansfield and John Middleton Murry. She has been cogitating it in her little Rosenthal head for sixteen years – she attended the same school as Mansfield, Queen's College in Harley Street. Her Dad encouraged, cajoled and even begged her to write it, and now there it is, giving stellar roles to Ed Stoppard (my son in *The Pianist*), Tracy Ann Oberman (my daughter-in-law in a so-far undistributed Dutch film, *Supertex*) and two other fine actors and friends, Nick Caldecott and Charlotte Emerson. The 'family' evolves, the circle revolves . . . (*close-up*) a mother dissolves.

Adam is writing a film script and working on a translation of *Agamemnon* into hip hop and blues for theatre, and a sit-com about . . . *ahem* . . . aquatic apes for radio. I'm glad they are successfully following in their Dad's footsteps, but more than that I'm overwhelmed with pride that they've inherited his innate good nature. Leaving aside the world population problem, I wish I'd had scores more of them because they and my friends have held me through the difficult times with loyalty, tenderness and the occasional verbal clout.

So last night felt like another circle completing. I had returned from

Bristol, where I was filming for two days on a TV series called *Skins* in which I played a batty aunt who grows marijuana in her greenhouse. My first shot was abseiling in a harness down the side of a twenty-foot tree carrying a chainsaw; the second was stepping out of brown overalls to reveal a tea-dress and pearls with the words, 'Tea and scones, I think?' I got a round of applause from the crew when I did it on the third take. There are not many sixty-two-year-olds who can experience such a ridiculous rush of blood to the head – and get lightly paid for it. All is well and all will be well.

This business is 80% unemployed and there are no repertory companies left for us to learn our craft. Instant fame comes via TV on cop/medic shows and five-times-a-week soaps where there is no time to do anything but learn the lines and stand on the luminous tape provided. Naturalistic though young actors are, without proper training they tend to say the lines and make no attempt to use their surroundings, the props or even each other. It takes courage to use technique when time is money and picking up a mirror or a handful of books and using them may bring the wrath of the busy director down on you. Kids always look good in movies. Sometimes they are amazing, but in my experience their performances are often created in the cutting room. There are too many media courses, far too many drama schools making fist-loads of money out of people who are too young to specialise, and thanks to reality TV and the 'I'm gonna live my dream' mentality it has spawned, when you ask a kid what he or she wants to be, the most likely answer is 'Famous'.

If there has been one piece of advice which has affected the way I think, it was that of Martha Graham, the great American choreographer, to her protégée, Agnes de Mille. Agnes, a member of the famed Cecil B de Mille family, was plump and plain and desperate to dance. She succeeded by sheer tenacity, stamina and grit and became the choreographer of numerous Broadway hits, the dance extravaganza *Rodeo*, and the trail-blazing ballet in the musical *Oklahoma!*.

Agnes was the typical artistic paradox of desperate self-doubt and lack of confidence and stubborn self-belief. Here is the last page of her excellent autobiography, *Who Pays the Piper?*. I think of it every day in almost every situation I come up against and before every entrance I make on stage or set. In reproducing it here I hope maybe to pass on her hard-won wisdom to tomorrow's over-ambitious, plain, opinionated, undisciplined kid with a shed-load of talent and absolutely no idea what to do with it:

I saw Rodeo *again. Due to lack of rehearsals and replacements, it was unrecognisable. I had succeeded all right. Now I did the cold reckoning without the hysteria of failure to underscore my concern. The work wasn't good enough. All changed, all passed. There was no way of ensuring lasting beauty. Verily, I wrote in water and judging my work with a dreadful dispassionate vision, perhaps it was as well. I spoke to Martha Graham on the pavement outside of Schrafft's restaurant. She bowed her head and looked burningly into my face. She spoke from a life's effort. I went home and wrote down what she said:*

'There is a vitality, a life-force, an energy, a quickening that is translated through you into action and because there is only one of you in all of time, this expression is unique. And if you block it, it will never exist through any other medium and be lost. The world will not have it. It is not your business to determine how good it is nor how valuable nor how it compares with other expressions. It is your business to keep it yours clearly and directly, to keep the channel open. You do not even have to believe in yourself or your work. You have to keep open and aware directly to the urges that motivate you. Keep the channel open. As for you, Agnes, you have a peculiar and unusual gift and you have so far used about one third of your talent.'

'But,' I said, 'when I see my work I take for granted what other people value in it. I see only its ineptitude, inorganic flaws, and crudities. I am not pleased or satisfied.'

'No artist is pleased.'

'But then there is no satisfaction?'

'No satisfaction whatever at any time,' she cried passionately. 'There is only a queer divine dissatisfaction, a blessed unrest that keeps us marching and makes us more alive than the others. And at times I think I could kick you until you can't stand.'

I kissed her and went west to my bridegroom.

This has been a hard-working, challenging, maddening, lucky and ultimately fulfilling business for me and I'd really like it to be the same for everyone who can't wait to take wings and fly onto a stage. The future, if I keep those channels open, professionally and personally, looks very alive. In two weeks I start on a sit-com with the remarkable Anne Reid, and am considering another musical – only this time the character's in a wheelchair, so that time step remains to be seen another time. In every other way I'm stepping out.

NB. I was fifty-four, wrote in longhand only and was totally innumerate when the *Daily Express* sent Roy, their IT guru, to my house with the intention of teaching the unteachable. I was to take computer-phobic wrinklies through a journey in print from dinosaur to dab hand. The column was called 'First Net Nerves'. Roy's depression on seeing I couldn't type, even with one finger, and didn't know the difference between the web and the net was palpable. I tried to divert him with offers of soup and a tour of the garden. I told him the then timely joke about Bill Gates picking up Hugh Grant's old squeeze, Divine Brown, on Hollywood Boulevard and spending a few hours with her. Afterwards he says, 'Well, Miss Brown, thank you, I now see why you are called Divine.'

To which she replies: 'And I now see why you are the President of Microsoft.'

I had written six books with a succession of Bic rollerballs on feint and margin pads. I was stupider than my stupidest *Express* reader! . . . If I could learn IT, anybody could. Eight years later, thanks to Roy, Sony and those wonderful folk at Microsoft, although I still shout 'ROSIE!' every time I need to copy and paste and only use one-tenth of the facilities I've got, I actually managed to write this enitre book on a computer. Halle-bloody-luja!

My eyes are pink and sticky, my shoulders are rigid, my posture stinks, my dog doesn't speak to me, my editor's on life-support and my desk looks like the FBI and Stasi have turned it over. But I did it. And re-did it. And then some. Not only that but I found my Annie Phillips batik rug ON-LINE, sold the old sofa on E-BAY and haven't called in a 'little man' for months.

'Past it?' I'm not sure I've even *got* to it yet.